AMSCO'S

AP Statistics
Preparing for the Advanced Placement Examination

James F. Bohan

K–12 Mathematics Program Coordinator
Manheim Township School District
Lancaster, Pennsylvania

with
Beth Chance

Assistant Professor of Statistics
California Polytechnic State University
San Luis Obispo, California

AMSCO SCHOOL PUBLICATIONS, INC.
315 Hudson Street, New York, NY 10013

Author:

James F. Bohan James Bohan is a veteran of more than 30 years of high school and college teaching. He received a BS and MA in Mathematics from Loyola University of Chicago and is completing an MS in Applied Statistics at Villanova University in Philadelphia.

The author serves as a consultant to the College Board for both AP Calculus and AP Statistics and is a member of the Test Development Committee for AP Statistics. Mr. Bohan has also served on the Board of Directors of the National Council of Supervisors of Mathematics and presently directs NCSM's Leadership Academies. He is a member of the Regional Services Committee of the National Council of Teachers of Mathematics.

Mr. Bohan has published many articles and is a frequent presenter at regional and national conferences. In addition, he is on the faculty of several funded projects dealing with statistics and other mathematics content areas.

Collaborator:

Beth Chance Beth Chance received her Bachelor's degree from Harvey Mudd College and her Ph.D. from Cornell University in 1994. She is a faculty consultant and table leader for Advanced Placement Statistics, and has conducted workshops and given presentations on various aspects of statistics education for over 30 groups around the world. After teaching at the University of the Pacific for five years, Dr. Chance moved to Cal Poly, San Luis Obispo in 1999. She is co-author of *Workshop Statistics: Discovery with Data*, 2nd edition, and *Workshop Statistics: Discovery with Data and Minitab*. She is also a member of the editorial boards of the Journal of Statistics Education, JASA Book Reviews, and STATS magazine for students.

Reviewers:

Acknowledgments appear on page 400.

When ordering this book please specify:
either **R 686 W** *or* AP STATISTICS: PREPARING FOR THE ADVANCED PLACEMENT EXAM

ISBN: 1-56765-527-0

To all the courageous high school teachers who accepted the challenge to teach AP Statistics, and to the university statisticians who have supported our growth as statistics educators. And to my wife, Janie, and my four children, John, Jane Ellen, Julie, and Jamie, who are the reasons and the support for all of my efforts and accomplishments.

Contents

Chapter 1: Introduction

Overview 2
How to Use This Review 2
About the Exam 3
Important Features of AP Statistics 4
Conclusion 5

Chapter 2: Exploring Univariate Data

2.1 Basic Definitions 8
2.2 Constructing Graphical Displays of Univariate Data 10
2.3 Interpreting Graphical Displays of Univariate Data 16
2.4 Summarizing Distributions Numerically: Center and Spread 18
2.5 Summarizing Distributions: Relative Location and Position 26
2.6 Comparing Distributions 31
    Chapter 2 Assessment 33

Chapter 3: Exploring Bivariate Data

3.1 Patterns in Scatterplots 38
3.2 Means and Standard Deviations 41
3.3 Correlation and Linearity 42
3.4 Least Squares Regression Line 48
3.5 Residual Plots, Outliers, and Influential Points 54
3.6 Transformations to Achieve Linearity 60
3.7 Exploring Categorical Data 66
    Chapter 3 Assessment 70

Chapter 4: Planning a Study: Deciding What and How to Measure

4.1 Basic Terminology and Census 74
4.2 Sampling 76
4.3 Controlled Experiments 84
4.4 Observational Studies 92
    Chapter 4 Assessment 93

Chapter 5: Anticipating Patterns: Producing Models Using Probability and Simulation

5.1 Basic Concepts 98
5.2 Calculating Probabilities for Combinations of Events 104
5.3 Counting Techniques (Optional) 109
5.4 Binomial and Geometric Probability 113
5.5 Probability Distributions of Discrete Random Variables 119

5.6   Probability Distributions of Continuous Random Variables 124

5.7   Normal Approximation of the Binomial Distribution 129

5.8   The Sum and Difference of Random Variables 134

5.9   Overview of Theoretical Probability Functions 139

5.10   Simulating Events With Random Digits Tables and the TI-83 144

        Chapter 5 Assessment 146

Chapter 6: Sampling Distributions

6.1   Introduction 150

6.2   The Concept of a Sampling Distribution 151

6.3   The Sampling Distribution of a Sample Proportion 156

6.4   The Sampling Distribution of a Difference of Two Proportions 160

6.5   The Sampling Distribution of a Sample Mean (σ known) 165

6.6   The Sampling Distribution of a Sample Mean (σ unknown) 168

6.7   The Distributions Associated With a Difference of Sample Means 174

6.8   Summary of Distributions and Their Assumptions 178

        Chapter 6 Assessment 180

Chapter 7: Statistical Inference

7.1   The Concept of Confidence 184

7.2   Calculation of Confidence Intervals 188

7.3   Properties of Confidence Intervals 192

7.4   The Concept of Significance 199

7.5   Tests of Significance 202

7.6   Type I and Type II Errors and the Concept of Power 223

7.7   Inference for the Slope of a Regression Line 230

7.8   Inference for Categorical Data 237

        Chapter 7 Assessment 244

Chapter 8: Interpreting Computer and Calculator Printouts

8.1   Introduction 250

8.2   Regression Analysis 250

8.3   Confidence Interval for a Mean 255

8.4   Hypothesis Test: One-Sample t-Test 256

8.5   Hypothesis Test: Two-Sample t-Test of Means 257

8.6   Contingency Tables: Test of Independence 259

Five Model Examinations

Model Examination 1 264

Model Examination 2 274

Model Examination 3 284

Model Examination 4 294

Model Examination 5 304

Appendix

Formulas and Tables 316
Technology Resources 322
AP Statistics Resources 323
Recommended Reading and References 323

Answer Key

Answer Key 325

Index

Index 395

Chapter 1   Introduction

Overview

How to Use This Review

About the Exam

Important Features of AP Statistics

Conclusion

Chapter 1 Introduction

Overview

Welcome to the world of Advanced Placement Statistics! This book was written to assist you in preparing for the AP Statistics Examination conducted each May and to supplement your course in AP Statistics. It includes chapters that review and clarify all of the topics of the AP Statistics curriculum. Each chapter focuses on a critical component of the curriculum and includes explanations of the concepts and examples of procedures of AP Statistics.

This review text features a variety of exercises to help you prepare for the examination.

1. At the end of each section, Review Exercises have been included to assess your understanding of the concepts and procedures of that section. These exercises consist of Checklists, Multiple-Choice items, and Free-Response items. Some of them are in the same style as AP questions, while others focus on specific aspects of a concept or procedure.
2. At the end of each chapter, a Chapter Assessment is presented in the same format as the AP examination: there are Multiple-Choice Questions, Open-Ended Questions, and Investigative Task items in the style of AP questions. While most exercises focus on the topics of the chapter, knowledge of topics of earlier chapters is also reinforced.
3. At the end of the review are five complete simulated AP Statistics Examinations. These tests are designed with Multiple-Choice, Open-Ended, and Investigative Task items in the style of actual AP questions.

Answers to all review exercises are included in the answer key at the end of the book.

How to Use This Review

For the Student   This review is not intended to replace any of the approved statistics textbooks available today. Rather, it is intended as a supplement to your text. We suggest that this review be studied along with your current text and that exercises from this review be considered routinely in the normal conduct of your class. Answers with explanations are provided for every exercise. These explanations should be quite useful to you in your preparation for the AP examination.

When the curriculum has been completed in class, you and your classmates should take the model AP Examinations that are included in this review. Be sure to allot the appropriate amount of time for each section as described below. Again, consideration of the answers and their explanations should be very useful in your efforts.

For the Teacher This review provides you with very valuable resources:

- explanations of all of the concepts and procedures covered in AP Statistics;
- a substantial number of exercises with answers and explanations;
- specific instructions on the use of technology, including both the TI-83 graphing calculator and popular statistical software packages such as Minitab.
- examples of computer printouts and calculator displays of typical statistical procedures including lists of important information.

Text and exercises from this review should be spiraled throughout your development of the course using whatever primary resources you choose.

About the Exam

Structure of the Exam At the time of this publication, the examination consists of three parts:

1. **40 Multiple-Choice items.** These items are scored by subtracting $\frac{1}{4}$ of a point for every wrong answer from the total number of correct answers. Blank responses do not penalize the student. This section contributes 50% of the composite raw score grade of the examination.
2. **6 Free-Response items.** These include 5 Open-Ended Questions and 1 multi-step Investigative Task. These items are scored holistically using a rubric that specifies the criteria for placement of an answer in one of six categories:
   (1) Complete answer — Category 4
   (2) Substantial answer — Category 3
   (3) Developing answer — Category 2
   (4) Minimal answer — Category 1
   (5) Unacceptable answer — Category 0
   (6) Blank or off-task answer — Category "–"

The Free Response items contribute 50% of the composite raw score of the exam. Of that 50%, the Open-Ended Questions are worth $\frac{3}{4}$ and the Investigative Task is worth $\frac{1}{4}$. Therefore, the Open-Ended Questions account for 37.5% of the overall grade and the Investigative Task accounts for 12.5% of the test.

The exam takes three hours. Ninety minutes are allowed for Part 1, Multiple-Choice, with another 90 minutes for Part 2, Free-Response, which consists of the Open-Ended Questions and the Investigative Task. It is suggested that 65 of the 90 minutes for Part 2 be dedicated to answering the Free-Response items while the remaining 25 minutes be allocated to the completion of the Investigative Task. Please be aware that time constraints have been found to be challenging for some students.

Grading Criteria Built into the grading rubrics is a dual basis of grading the Open-Ended Questions and Investigative Task. Both statistical content and communication of processes and student thinking are simultaneously evaluated during the grading of each exam. Consequently, teachers are strongly urged to encourage and assist students to communicate their thinking and the reasons for the choices they make in the solution of problems throughout the course. In addition, conclusions should always be communicated in the context of the question.

Important Features of AP Statistics

The Course Description booklet published by the College Board includes detailed information concerning the following areas of importance to students and teachers of AP Statistics.

Themes and Outline of the Course An outline of the course, including the major themes covered, is contained in the Course Description booklet. In addition, the College Board publishes up-to-date information about the content of the course on the Internet. You can visit the AP Statistics website at <http://www.collegeboard.org/ap/statistics/index.html> to find the most current information about the themes and outline of the course.

Instructional Emphasis It is expected that the student of AP Statistics be actively engaged in the construction of his or her own understanding. Active participation in the educational process requires opportunities for exploration of data, projects, laboratories, and cooperative learning activities. Students should routinely use appropriate technology in a variety of applications and environments. This emphasis supports the development of inter-disciplinary studies and activities.

Technology Use of appropriate computer and calculator technology is a major component of the AP Statistics course. Consistent with current philosophy and procedures of current data analysis, students of AP Statistics are expected to be able to read and interpret printouts from statistical software packages as well as to use sophisticated graphing calculators in the acquisition and application of the concepts and procedures of AP Statistics. While pencil and paper calculations are certainly acceptable, using appropriate technology may increase efficiency in calculation. In all cases, however, the emphasis is on interpretation of the data and communication of methods and conclusions.

Calculators Students are expected to take a graphing calculator with statistical capabilities to the exam. Computers and calculators with QWERTY keyboards are not allowed. Memories will not be cleared prior to the exam; however, text should not be entered into memory prior to the exam. This is considered cheating and will be dealt with accordingly.

Tables and Formulas These should be readily available to students at all times. Time and energy should not be devoted to rote memorization; rather, development of conceptual understanding supported by both printed and technological resources is the goal of AP Statistics. Tables of several probability distributions and a list of useful formulas are included in the Appendix and will be provided for the AP examination.

We suggest that teachers and students consult the publications from the College Board and Educational Testing Service that focus on AP Statistics. In addition, a list of resources that we have found particularly useful is included in the Appendix to this review.

Conclusion

AP Statistics provides an opportunity for students to pursue significant and important mathematics that is meaningful, powerful, and interesting to them. We hope that this review will assist in this adventure and will provide greater support for this pursuit.

Chapter 2   Exploring Univariate Data

2.1   Basic Definitions

2.2.   Constructing Graphical Displays of Univariate Data

2.3   Interpreting Graphical Displays of Univariate Data

2.4   Summarizing Distributions Numerically: Center and Spread

2.5   Summarizing Distributions: Relative Location and Position

2.6   Comparing Distributions

Chapter 2 Assessment

Chapter 2 Exploring Univariate Data

2.1 Basic Definitions

The purpose of **statistics** is to gather data, organize them, display them graphically, and analyze them visually and numerically, to observe patterns, determine relationships, and draw conclusions about the data.

We will treat the exploration of univariate data in this chapter and bivariate and categorical data in the next chapter.

A **variable** is any measurable or observable characteristic of a group of objects or people. **Data** are the actual observations or measurements of a variable. Data can be classified by the type of value that they may represent. For example, the variable "ages of my children" has data values in the set {17, 21, 24, 26}.

Quantitative Data

Quantitative data are data that take on numerical values, as in a count or a measurement. For example, consider the set of students in the class of 2003 in your high school. Quantitative data from this population could include the number of males or the number of females, the heights of the students, the number of pets that each student has, the shoe size of each student, or the lengths of the hand spans of each student.

Quantitative data also have the important characteristic that one can describe the data values using numerical measures such as average, range, and so on. Quantitative data can be further classified:

Discrete quantitative data consist of data that are a listable set of values. When data represent counts, they are discrete. The number of males or females, the number of pets that each student has, and the shoe size of each student are all discrete data items. *Note:* Since shoe size can only take on specific values of whole numbers and half sizes, shoe size is considered an example of discrete data.

Continuous quantitative data consist of data that can take on any values in the domain of the variable. The heights of students and the lengths of their hand spans are considered examples of continuous data.

Qualitative Data

Qualitative or **categorical** data are data whose values describe some characteristic of the population. For example, for the set of seniors in your high school, qualitative data could include eye color, gender, race, hair color, and favorite flavor of ice cream. Note that each has values that are verbal descriptors.

The following graphic summarizes the relationships of the types of data:

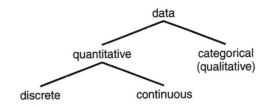

We can also classify data by the number of variables represented.

Univariate data (one-variable data) are data that describe a single characteristic of a population. The data generated by observing the value of one variable for each subject or event is univariate. Each data set from the senior class mentioned above contains univariate data.

Bivariate data (two-variable data) are data that describe two characteristics for each subject. For the example of our seniors, if the information on the number of phones and the variable of the number of pets is collected for each senior, the resulting data set is bivariate.

Multivariate data (many-variable data) are data that describe many characteristics of each subject in a population. These data values can be triples, quadruples, . . ., n-tuples of numbers for each subject.

At this time, the AP Statistics Course and Examination are restricted to the study of only univariate and bivariate data.

Review Exercises

CHECKLIST

Identify the type of data in each case.

Description	Categorical	Quantitative	
		Discrete	Continuous
1. The types of cars in the parking lot.			
2. The heights of students in our class.			
3. The ages in years of current racecar drivers.			
4. Number of teachers whose ages fall in the age categories of 22–30; 31–40; 41–50; over 50.			
5. Percent of students passing all math classes in your school during 1999–2000.			
6. The heights of a falling object at specified moments in time.			
7. The final scores of every game the NY Yankees' baseball team played in 1998.			

8. Give one example each of quantitative data and categorical data.

9. Give one example each of discrete data and continuous data.

2.2 Constructing Graphical Displays of Univariate Data

When we begin to study a set of data, it is useful to create a visual representation or graph of the data to help us interpret it. There are five graphical representations that we will consider for univariate data: *dot plot, histogram, stem and leaf plot, cumulative frequency plot,* and *box plot.* We will illustrate each using the following data set, along with "How-To Tips" for each. In the case of graphs, it is essential that all axes be *titled* and *scaled* so that the context and units of the graph are clear.

This data set lists the number of books that are on the desks of 50 college students at 8:00 A.M. on Monday morning:

3 5 10 4 6 7 2 12 11 9 7 5 3 4 8 5 10 9 14 7 2 1 0 5 7
8 9 14 18 10 1 6 7 8 5 3 10 12 3 4 2 2 6 4 3 5 10 9 9 6

It will be easier to construct each type of graphical display, if we first make a *frequency table* for the data.

EXAMPLE 1

Frequency Table

Value	Tally	Frequency	Cumulative Frequency
0	I	1	1
1	II	2	3
2	IIII	4	7
3	IIII	5	12
4	IIII	4	16
5	IIII I	6	22
6	IIII	4	26
7	IIII	5	31
8	III	3	34
9	IIII	5	39
10	IIII	5	44
11	I	1	45
12	II	2	47
13		0	47
14	II	2	49
15		0	49
16		0	49
17		0	49
18	I	1	50

How-To Tips:

1. List all data values in order under the value column.
2. Make a tally mark in the appropriate row for each data value in the data set.
3. Total the number of tally marks and enter that total in the frequency column.
4. Add the frequencies and enter the cumulative total in the cumulative frequency column. That is, add the frequency of each value to the frequencies of all values less than it.

Note: For very large sets of data, we can group data into intervals or classes first and then count the frequencies in each class. For example,

Number of Books on Desk	Tally	Frequency	Cumulative Frequency
0–5			
6–10			
11–15			
16–20			

EXAMPLE 2

Dot Plot

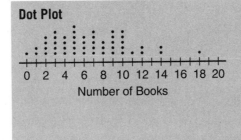

Number of Books

How-To Tips:
1. Construct and label a horizontal number line that is scaled to contain all of the values of the variable of interest.
2. Place a column of dots above each data value, one dot for each occurrence of the data value. For cases when there is a large number of occurrences of the data values, it is customary to have each dot represent more than one occurrence; e.g., 1 dot = 5 occurrences.

EXAMPLE 3

Histogram

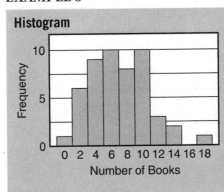

Number of Books

How-To Tips:
1. Construct and label a horizontal number line that is scaled to contain all of the values of the variable of interest.
2. Construct and label a vertical axis so that the greatest frequency can be represented.
3. Construct bars of equal width that are centered above each value. The heights of the bars represent the frequencies of the values.

Note: If data are grouped into classes or intervals, the horizontal axis can be scaled either by listing the *endpoints,* called **cutpoints,** of each interval, or the *midpoint* of each interval. In addition, the bar for each class should have its width equal to the width of the class and its height equal to the frequency of all values in the interval. If a data value equals one of the endpoints of the interval, a decision must be made as to the placement of the value. For example, the TI calculators put data values equaling an endpoint in the interval to the right of the endpoint. Consistency in applying the decision is the key.

Technology Note: Most computer statistical packages allow the user to specify the interval width and style (endpoints or midpoints) in the construction of histograms. Graphing calculators generally allow only for intervals specified by their endpoints; the size of the interval can be controlled by the user. Given the available technology, the ease of changing the widths of the intervals should encourage you to experiment with different interval sizes. Often when you are studying a particular variable you can discover interesting features of the data when you change the interval size. ■

EXAMPLE 4

Stem and Leaf Plots

Stem	Leaves
0	0 1 1 2 2 2 2 3 3 3 3 4 4 4 4 5 5 5 5 5 5 6 6 6 6 7 7 7 7 7 8 8 8 9 9 9 9
1	0 0 0 0 0 1 2 2 4 4 8

Leaf = 1.0 book

How-To Tips:

1. Split each data value into a stem part and a leaf part. Select the digits to be used for stems so that there are between five and fifteen stems.
2. List the next digit as a leaf of the appropriate stem for each data value. Many software packages list the next digit and truncate any remaining digits, that is, chop off the rest.
3. If the original data is not ordered, reconstruct the plot putting all of the leaves in numerical order.
4. Specify the leaf unit.

Note: In this case, we do not have an appropriate number of data points for each stem. Therefore, we redraw the stem and leaf plot by splitting the stems. The plot below shows the same data set with each stem split into two sub-stems:

Stem and Leaf Plot With 2 Sub-Stems

Stem	Leaves
0	0 1 1 2 2 2 2 3 3 3 3 4 4 4 4
•	5 5 5 5 5 5 6 6 6 6 7 7 7 7 8 8 8 9 9 9 9
1	0 0 0 0 0 1 2 2 4 4
•	8

Leaf = 1.0 book

How-To Tips:

1. Show each stem element as an integer and as a dot, or give each stem value twice.
2. Place leaves in the appropriate row using the following rule: if the leaf digit is 0–4, place it in the integer row; if the leaf digit is 5–9, place it in the second (dot) row for that stem value.
3. If the original data is not ordered, reconstruct the plot putting all of the leaves in numerical order.
4. Specify the leaf unit.

Note: For a split into five sub-stems, partition the stem into sub-stems that will hold leaves {0, 1} {2, 3}, {4, 5}, {6, 7}, {8, 9}.

Stem and Leaf Plot With 5 Sub-Stems

Stem	Leaves
0	0 1 1
•	2 2 2 2 3 3 3 3
•	4 4 4 4 5 5 5 5 5
•	6 6 6 6 7 7 7 7
•	8 8 8 9 9 9 9 9
1	0 0 0 0 0 1
•	2 2
•	4 4
•	
•	8

Leaf = 1.0 book

How-To Tips:

1. Show each stem element as an integer and as four dots, or as five repetitions of the stem value.
2. Place leaves in the appropriate row using the five-way split.
3. If the original data is not ordered, reconstruct the plot putting all of the leaves in numerical order.
4. Specify the leaf unit.

Technology Note: Most computer statistical packages have the capability of creating stem and leaf plots. Graphing calculators generally do not have this capability. ∎

EXAMPLE 5

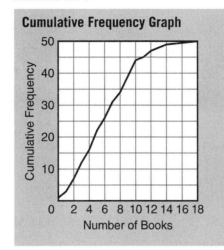

Cumulative Frequency Graph

How-To Tips:

1. Construct and label a horizontal number line that is scaled to contain all of the values of the variable of interest.
2. Construct and label the vertical axis from 0 to n, the total number of data values.
3. Using the frequency table you constructed, plot the value of the cumulative frequency for each data value.
4. Connect the points to display a line graph of the cumulative frequencies.

Note: Another form of this plot graphs the data values against the **cumulative relative frequencies** of each value. The cumulative relative frequencies are computed by dividing each cumulative frequency by the total number of data values. In the cumulative relative frequency graph, the vertical axis is scaled from 0 to 1.

EXAMPLE 6

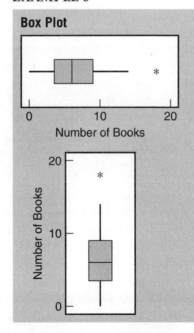

Box Plot

How-To Tips:

1. Calculate the five-number summary of the data: minimum, first quartile, median, third quartile, and maximum. (See Section 2.4 for calculation details.)
2. Draw and label a number line appropriate for the data.
3. Construct a box above the number line bounded by the first and third quartile values.
4. Draw a vertical line in the box at the position of the median.
5. Construct horizontal lines, the whiskers, from the bounds of the box to the maximum and minimum values of the data.

Note: If you create a *modified* box plot, then *outliers* are indicated by asterisks (*) on the plot. In this case, the whiskers extend from the box to the maximum and minimum *non-outlier* values. (Outliers will be discussed in Section 2.4.) Also, box plots can be displayed both horizontally and vertically.

A special caution: Box plots can be very deceptive as a tool for determining the shape of a distribution. For example, the data sets

A = {10, 10, 20, 20, 20, 30, 30, 30, 30, 40, 40, 40, 40, 40, 50, 50, 50, 60, 60, 70, 70, 80, 90}

and

B = {10, 10, 10, 30, 30, 30, 30, 40, 40, 60, 60, 60, 60, 60, 60, 90}

have the same box plots but rather different histograms.

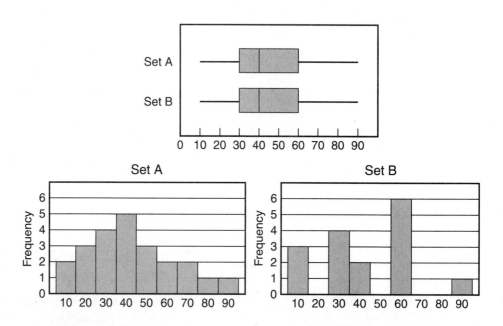

 Technology Note: Both computer statistical packages and graphing calculators will produce box plots. The software packages allow for a great deal of variety of orientation (horizontal or vertical) and fill characteristics not available on graphing calculators. ■

Advantages of Different Plots

While there are no hard fixed rules about the choice of plot, the following rules of thumb can be considered:

1. The *dot plot, histogram,* and *stem and leaf plot* all display the general shape of the distribution including gaps and clusters. The *stem and leaf plot* has the advantage of actually displaying the values of the data as well.
2. The *dot plot* and *stem and leaf plot* are best used for discrete data; the *histogram* can be used for both discrete and continuous data but is generally used for continuous data.
3. The *box plot* displays the center and spread of the data in a very meaningful way that will be described in Section 2.4.
4. The *cumulative frequency plot* is best used when we are considering the proportion of data within specified intervals. For example, the data value below which 50% of the data falls is easily read from the *cumulative relative frequency* plot.

Best advice: If you have the capability of creating all of the plots, do so and choose the one(s) that best convey the important features of the distribution.

Review Exercises

MULTIPLE-CHOICE QUESTIONS

1. Which one of the following is true about a histogram?
   (A) It is exactly the same as a bar graph.
   (B) The number of intervals depends on the range of data.
   (C) Accurate histograms can display either cutpoints or midpoints of the interval.
   (D) The area under a histogram is 1.
   (E) All of the above are false.

2. Dot plots
   (A) can be used for either discrete or continuous data.
   (B) do not indicate spread of data as well as histograms.
   (C) are the same as stem and leaf plots but do not give as much detail.
   (D) are excellent plots for discrete data sets.
   (E) are not as immediately informative as cumulative relative frequency plots.

3. It is easiest to determine quartiles of a data set when viewing
   (A) the histogram.
   (B) the dot plot.
   (C) the stem and leaf plot.
   (D) the cumulative relative frequency plot.
   (E) Quartiles cannot be determined using any of these plots.

4. Given the first type of plot indicated in each pair, which of the second plots could *not* always be generated from it?
   (A) dot plot → histogram
   (B) stem and leaf → dot plot
   (C) dot plot → box plot
   (D) histogram → stem and leaf plot
   (E) All of these can always be generated.

5. Which is true of a box plot?
   (A) One must have a box but may be missing one or both whiskers.
   (B) It is possible to have a box plot with no box or whiskers.
   (C) It is possible to determine the data values if you only have a box plot.
   (D) If there is one outlier, then there are at least two whiskers.
   (E) All of these are true for *all* box plots.

SHORT ANSWER

For the following set of heights of a sample of 91 high school boys at a suburban public school, construct each of the plots indicated.

Heights (inches)	Tally	Heights (inches)	Tally
62	1	69	10
63	3	70	10
64	6	71	9
65	7	72	6
66	9	73	3
67	12	74	1
68	13	75	1

1. Dot Plot

2. Histogram (You may wish to draw more than one.)

3. Stem and Leaf (You may wish to draw more than one.)

4. Cumulative Relative Frequency

5. Which of the plots that you constructed above best describes each of the following characteristics?
   a. *center* of the data values
   b. *spread* of the data values
   c. *clusters* in the data values
   d. *gaps* in the data values
   e. *outliers* in the data set
   f. *shape* of the distribution

6. Use the cumulative relative frequency plot from Exercise 4 to estimate the answer to each. Give your answers correct to one decimal point.
   a. The value below which 50% of the data lies.
   b. The value below which 75% of the data lies.
   c. The values which bound the middle 20% of the data; that is, 40% of the data below the lower bound and 40% of the data above the upper bound.

7. Given the following set of heights (in inches) of 8th grade students at the local middle school this year, determine the number and value of stem elements for an appropriate stem and leaf plot.

   52, 54, 54, 55, 55, 55, 56, 56, 56, 56, 58, 58, 59, 59, 59, 60, 60, 60, 61, 61, 63, 63, 63, 63, 64, 64, 65, 65, 65, 66, 67, 67, 67, 67, 68, 68, 69, 69, 70, 71, 71, 72

2.3 Interpreting Graphical Displays of Univariate Data

Once you have represented data by a graphical display, the next step is to inspect the display for certain characteristics. At this point in the exploration, a visual and intuitive interpretation of the graph is acceptable since a more numerical analysis will follow in the next section.

Characteristics to Look for in Graphical Displays

1. *Center:* Where is the location of the center value of the data set? Graphically, the center can be viewed as the "balance point" of the display.
2. *Spread:* How far apart are the data values?
3. *Clusters:* Are the data clustered around a specific value?
4. *Gaps:* Are there intervals for which there are no data?
5. *Outliers:* Are there data values that are substantially different from the rest of the data?
6. *Shape of the distribution:* Would you describe the distribution as symmetrical (two halves are mirror images); skewed right (long tail to the right); or skewed left (long tail to the left); having one, two, or more peaks; and so on?

Consider the following examples.

EXAMPLE 1

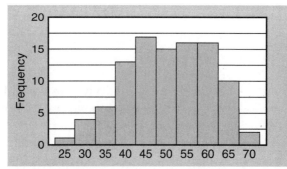

Interpretation:
1. *Center:* Approximately 48
2. *Spread:* Approximately from 20 to 75
3. *Clusters:* None
4. *Gaps:* None
5. *Outliers:* None
6. *Shape:* Roughly symmetric or slightly skewed left

EXAMPLE 2

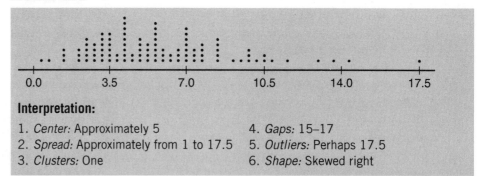

Interpretation:
1. *Center:* Approximately 5
2. *Spread:* Approximately from 1 to 17.5
3. *Clusters:* One
4. *Gaps:* 15–17
5. *Outliers:* Perhaps 17.5
6. *Shape:* Skewed right

EXAMPLE 3

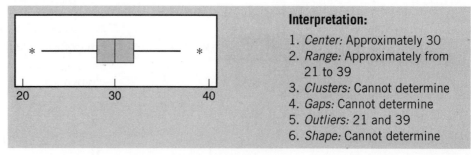

Interpretation:
1. *Center:* Approximately 30
2. *Range:* Approximately from 21 to 39
3. *Clusters:* Cannot determine
4. *Gaps:* Cannot determine
5. *Outliers:* 21 and 39
6. *Shape:* Cannot determine

EXAMPLE 4

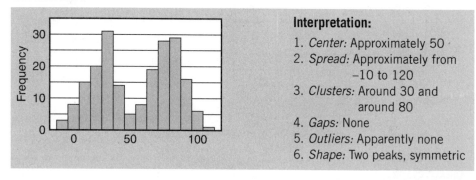

Stem	Leaves
2	1
2	2
2	4 4 4 4 5 5 5 5 5
2	6 6 7 7 7 7 7 7 7 7 7
2	8 8 8 8 8 8 8 8 8 8 8 8 8 9 9 9 9 9 9 9 9 9 9 9
3	0 0 0 0 0 0 0 0 0 0 0 0 0 0 0 0 1 1 1 1 1 1
3	2 2 2 2 2 2 2 2 2 2 2 2 2 2 2 3 3 3 3
3	4 4 5 5 5 5 5 5 5
3	6 7

Leaf = 1.0

Interpretation:
1. *Center:* Approximately 29
2. *Spread:* From 21 to 37
3. *Clusters:* None
4. *Gaps:* None
5. *Outliers:* Apparently none
6. *Shape:* Slightly skewed left

EXAMPLE 5

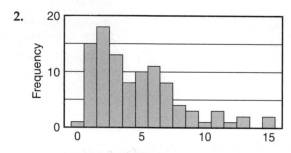

Interpretation:
1. *Center:* Approximately 50
2. *Spread:* Approximately from −10 to 120
3. *Clusters:* Around 30 and around 80
4. *Gaps:* None
5. *Outliers:* Apparently none
6. *Shape:* Two peaks, symmetric

Experience will help you become skillful in the visual recognition of characteristics of data distributions. This is essential to your understanding of statistical concepts.

Review Exercises

FREE-RESPONSE QUESTIONS

Open-Ended Questions

Describe each distribution.

1.

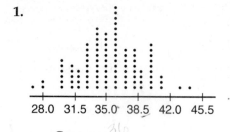

a. Center
b. Spread
c. Clusters
d. Gaps
e. Outliers
f. Shape

2.

a. Center
b. Spread
c. Clusters
d. Gaps
e. Outliers
f. Shape

3.

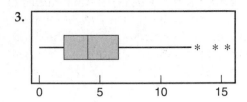

a. Center
b. Spread
c. Clusters
d. Gaps
e. Outliers
f. Shape

4.

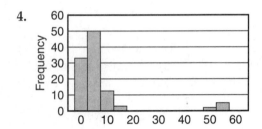

a. Center
b. Spread
c. Clusters
d. Gaps
e. Outliers
f. Shape

5. Stem | Leaves

Stem	Leaves
0	2 2 2 2 2 3 3 3
0	4 4 4 4 4 4 4 5 5
0	6 6 6 6 6 6 6 6 6 6 6 6 6 7 7 7 7 7 7 7 7
0	8 8 8 8 8 8 8 8 8 8 9 9 9 9 9 9 9 9 9 9
1	0 0 0 0 0 0 1 1 1 1
1	2 2 2 2 2 2 2 2 2 2 2 2 2 3 3 3 3
1	4 4 4 4 5 5 5
1	6 6 7 7
1	9 9 9
2	0
2	2

Leaf = 1.0

a. Center
b. Spread
c. Clusters
d. Gaps
e. Outliers
f. Shape

2.4 Summarizing Distributions Numerically: Center and Spread

In order to compare distributions, statisticians have developed some special measures. A numerical summary of univariate data will answer the following four questions:

- What is the center?
- How are the data spread out?
- What is the relative location or position of the data?
- How would a change in units of a given set of data affect the summary statistics?

Measuring the Center

A number that represents the center of a distribution is called a **measure of center** or **measure of central tendency**. The measures of center for univariate data are the **mean** and the **median**. Some texts also include the **mode**, the most frequent data value, as a measure of center.

The **mean** is the numerical average of the data values. The formula for the sample mean is:

$$\text{Mean} = \bar{x} = \frac{x_1 + x_2 + \dots + x_n}{n}$$

$$= \frac{\sum\limits_{i=1}^{n} x_i}{n}$$

where x_i represents the ith data value and n is the number of [...] the sample. Note that the Greek letter μ is used to denote the p[...]

Graphically, the mean can be interpreted as the balance po[...] bution. Consider this dot plot. If we think of the data as weigh[...] tal number line, the *mean* can be considered a fulcrum u[...] distribution balances.

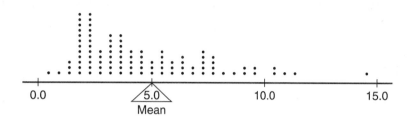

A **weighted sample average** is the mean of two or more data sets calculated by weighting the means of each data set by the number of values in the data set. For example, the weighted mean of two data sets with n_1 and $\bar{x}_1$ and n_2 and $\bar{x}_2$, respectively is given by $\dfrac{n_1 \cdot \bar{x}_1 + n_2 \cdot \bar{x}_2}{n_1 + n_2}$ where $\bar{x}_1$ is the sample mean of the first set and $\bar{x}_2$ is the sample mean of the second set.

EXAMPLE 1

The average weekly earnings of a group of 125 high school juniors were \$45. The average weekly earnings of a group of 110 high school seniors were \$63. What were the average weekly earnings of the combined group?

Solution

$\dfrac{125 \cdot 45 + 110 \cdot 63}{125 + 110} = 53.43$ (rounded to the nearest cent)

The **median** of a set of data is the middle value when the data are listed in *numerical order*. It is a value such that there are as many data values below the median as there are above it. The calculation of the median of a data set depends on the number of elements in the set.

EXAMPLE 2

a. If the number of elements, n, is odd, then the median value is the $\left(\dfrac{n+1}{2}\right)^{\text{th}}$ value:

Consider data set with $n=9$: 1, 2, 2, 5, 8, 12, 12, 15, 16

The median is the 5th value, 8.

b. If the number of elements, n, is even, then the median value is the mean of the $\left(\dfrac{n}{2}\right)^{\text{th}}$ and the $\left(\dfrac{n+2}{2}\right)^{\text{th}}$ values:

Consider the case when $n=8$: 1, 2, 2, 5, 8, 12, 12, 15

The median is the 4.5th value, which is the mean of the 4th and 5th values: $\dfrac{5+8}{2} = 6.5$

The measures of central tendency, the mean and the median, have different levels of *sensitivity* to extreme values.

EXAMPLE 3

Consider the effect of changing one value in the data set below.

{1, 2, 3, 4, 5, 6, 7}; mean = 4; median = 4

{1, 2, 3, 4, 5, 6, 100}; mean = 17.28; median = 4

We say that the median is *resistant* to extreme values, while the mean is *sensitive* to extreme values.

The shape of a distribution, as seen by its histogram, may provide some indication of the relative sizes of the median and mean. One rule of thumb is that if the distribution is:

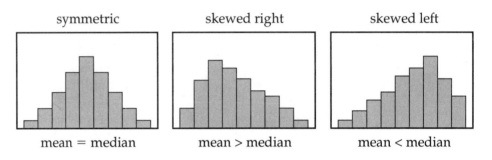

| symmetric | skewed right | skewed left |
| mean = median | mean > median | mean < median |

Caution: The shape of the data set tends to imply these relationships between the mean and the median. The converse is not true. If a distribution has the mean greater than the median, then the graph of the distribution is not necessarily skewed right. For example, the distribution in this table is clearly skewed left, but the mean (53.97) is greater than the median (50).

Values	10	20	30	40	50	60	70
Frequency	1	5	10	15	30	50	30

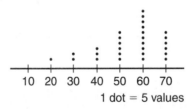

1 dot = 5 values

Measuring the Spread Numbers that indicate how data are distributed or spread out are called **measures of spread or dispersion**. The measures of spread for univariate data are the **range**, the **interquartile range**, the **variance**, and the **standard deviation**.

The **range** is the difference between the greatest value and the smallest value in a data set.

EXAMPLE 4

The range of {2, 8, 10, 16, 25, 32} is 32 − 2 = 30.

The range of {−8, −6, −4.5, 0, 1.8, 3, 9, 14} is 14 − (−8) = 22.

The range specifies the width of the interval that contains all of the data. The range gives little information about the distribution of data, since it is based only on the extremes and does not account for intermediate values.

The **interquartile range** is the difference between the third quartile value, Q_3, and the first quartile value, Q_1; that is, IQR $= Q_3 - Q_1$. These quartile values are found by determining the medians of the lower half of the data and of the upper half of the data when the data are listed in numerical order.

EXAMPLE 5

In the set {1, 2, 2, 5, 8, 12, 12, 15, 16}

$Q_1 = 2$ median $= 8$ $Q_3 = 13.5$

Therefore, the interquartile range, IQR, $= 13.5 - 2 = 11.5$

EXAMPLE 6

In the set {1, 2, 2, 3, 8, 12, 12, 15}

$Q_1 = 2$ median $= 5.5$ $Q_3 = 12$

Therefore, the interquartile range, IQR, $= 12 - 2 = 10$

The interquartile range specifies the length of the interval that contains the middle 50% of the data and corresponds to the "box" of the box plot discussed in Section 2.2. Similarly, each "whisker" of a box plot represents about 25% of the data.

Note: The calculation of Q_1 and Q_3 involves the same process of finding "middle" values of the upper and lower subsets of the data. If the data set contains an odd number of values, then the median is the middle data value and is *not* included in the calculation of either Q_1 or Q_3. If, on the other hand, the number of data values is even, then the median is the average of the two middle values and *all* data values are used in the calculation of Q_1 and Q_3.

The interquartile range, IQR, also provides a criterion for identifying **outliers** in the data. If a data value is greater than 1.5 IQRs *above* Q_3 or is less than 1.5 IQRs *below* Q_1, then it is considered an outlier.

EXAMPLE 7

In the set {1, 2, 2, 3, 8, 12, 12, 30}, IQR $= 10$, so $1.5 \cdot$ IQR $= 15$. Therefore, to be an outlier, a value would have to be less than -13 (calculated from $Q_1 - 15$, where $Q_1 = 2$), or greater than 27 (calculated from $Q_3 + 15$, where $Q_3 = 12$). In this set, the value of 30 is an outlier. This fact is shown by a modified box plot of the data:

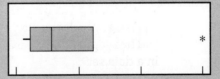

Note that when an outlier is present, the whiskers extend to the most extreme non-outlier value on either side of the box as appropriate.

Technology Note: Computer software usually has a default setting to indicate outliers in box plots. Some graphing calculators allow the option of a box plot identifying no outliers or a modified box plot indicating outliers. ■

The **variance** measures the deviation of each data value from the mean. The variance is the adjusted mean of the squares of the differences of each value from the mean. The formula is:

$$\text{Sample Variance} = s^2 = \frac{\sum_{i=1}^{n}(x_i - \overline{x})^2}{n-1}$$

where x_i = ith data value
$\overline{x}$ = the mean of the data values
n = the number of data values

Notes on the formula:

1. We square each difference so that positive and negative differences do not cancel each other out.
2. The calculation of the mean of the squares of the deviation would suggest division of the sum by n. We actually divide by $n-1$ since this provides a better estimator of the spread of the data.

The **standard deviation** is the square root of the variance. The formula is:

$$\text{Sample Standard Deviation} = s = \sqrt{\frac{\sum_{i=1}^{n}(x_i - \overline{x})^2}{n-1}}$$

There are two variances and standard deviations available for any data set. If the data set represents a population, then the exact values of the variance and standard deviation of the population can be calculated. However, if the data set represents a sample drawn from a larger population, then the variance and standard deviations are estimates of some measures for the population. It has been found that these *estimates* are better when the formulas use division by $n-1$ as opposed to n. This fact will be explained further in Chapter 6.

Measures of Spread

For populations,

$$\text{Variance} = \sigma^2 = \frac{\sum_{i=1}^{n}(x_i - \mu)^2}{n}$$

$$\text{Standard Deviation} = \sigma = \sqrt{\frac{\sum_{i=1}^{n}(x_i - \mu)^2}{n}}$$

For samples,

$$\text{Variance} = s^2 = \frac{\sum_{i=1}^{n}(x_i - \overline{x})^2}{n-1}$$

$$\text{Standard Deviation} = s = \sqrt{\frac{\sum_{i=1}^{n}(x_i - \overline{x})^2}{n-1}}$$

Note: $s = 0$ only when all data values are the same; otherwise; $s > 0$. In addition, s, like $\overline{x}$, is strongly affected by extreme values.

Notice that Greek letters are generally used to denote population measures, while English letters are generally used to denote sample measures.

EXAMPLE 8

Calculate the mean and standard deviation of the data listed in the table below. The data represent the answers of a class of college students regarding the number of different cars that each had driven in the last six months.

x	$(x - \bar{x})^2$	Solution
1	64	mean $= \dfrac{1}{n}\displaystyle\sum_{i=1}^{n} x_i$
1	64	
2	49	$= \dfrac{1}{14}(135)$
3	36	$= 9.643$
5	16	
6	9	variance $= \dfrac{1}{n-1}\left(\displaystyle\sum_{i=1}^{n}(x_i - \bar{x})^2\right)$
7	4	
8	1	$= \dfrac{1}{13}(783)$
11	4	$= 60.231$
12	9	
15	36	standard deviation $= \sqrt{60.231}$
18	81	$= 7.761$
20	121	
26	289	
Total: 135	Total: 783	

The Empirical Rule

Distributions of physical measurements (such as heights and weights) or test scores for very large sets of data often have symmetric, mound-shaped graphs. The mean and median have approximately equal values and the highest point of the graph is above that value. For symmetric, mound-shaped distributions, the standard deviation is a very useful number to know, because the following "empirical rule" is true:

Approximately 68% of the data lies within ±1 standard deviation of the mean.

Approximately 95% of the data lies within ±2 standard deviations of the mean.

Approximately 99.7% of the data lies within ±3 standard deviations of the mean.

Graphically,

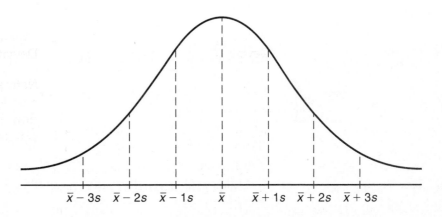

$$\bar{x} - 3s \quad \bar{x} - 2s \quad \bar{x} - 1s \quad \bar{x} \quad \bar{x} + 1s \quad \bar{x} + 2s \quad \bar{x} + 3s$$

While the standard deviation can be calculated for any distribution, the above "rule of thumb" is reliable only in the case of approximately *symmetric* and *mound-shaped distributions*.

The rule also leads to the following percentages of data in the "standard deviation regions":

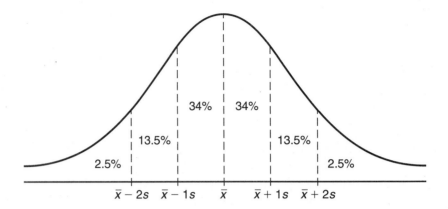

The "peak" of the curve is always directly above the mean since for approximately symmetric and mound-shaped distributions, the mean is approximately equal to the median. The standard deviation determines the shape as follows: the greater the standard deviation, the less steep the sides of the curve are.

Note also that at the location of one standard deviation from the mean, the curve changes from falling "steeply" to falling "slowly." In calculus, we identify such a location as a "point of inflection."

MEASURES OF DISPERSION

Measure	Interpretation	Sensitivity to extreme values
Range	Length of interval that contains all data	Very sensitive
Interquartile Range	Length of interval that contains the middle 50% of the data	Very resistant
Variance/Standard Deviation	Focus on the average deviation of data values from the mean	Sensitive

In practice, the measures of center and spread are jointly used to summarize distributions:

For symmetric distributions: **mean and standard deviation**

For all distributions: **minimum, first quartile, median, third quartile, maximum**

This last set of descriptors is often called the **five-number summary.**

Technology Note: Statistical computer programs and most graphing calculators will produce all of the measures listed above. The Interquartile Range may have to be calculated from the values of the first and third quartiles. In addition, many graphing calculators will return two standard deviations: one with division by n and the other with division by $n - 1$, allowing the user to choose the appropriate measure either for populations or for samples. ■

Review Exercises

MULTIPLE-CHOICE QUESTIONS

1. A distribution that has the box plot shown could be described as

   (A) skewed left
   (B) skewed right
   (C) roughly symmetric but with outliers
   (D) not possible
   (E) inconclusive

2. Which of the following is a reasonable conclusion about a distribution of the distances that employees drive to work when the mean is 13.1 miles and the standard deviation is 8.2 miles? Assume the distribution is symmetric and mound-shaped.
   (A) Approximately 95% of the employee drives are within 16.4 miles of the mean value.
   (B) The minimum and the first quartile are the same value.
   (C) The distribution is skewed right.
   (D) The standard deviation is too large.
   (E) The distribution possesses outliers.

3. If the largest value of a data set is doubled, which of the following is *not* true?
   (A) The mean increases.
   (B) The standard deviation increases.
   (C) The interquartile range increases.
   (D) The range increases.
   (E) The median remains unchanged.

4. The five-number summary (min, Q_1, median, Q_3, max) for the set {16, 42, 95, 3, 6, 10, 17, 14, 18, 37, 92, 19, 20, 20, 25} is
   (A) {3, 3, 15.5, 92, 95}
   (B) {3, 14, 19, 19, 95}
   (C) {3, 14, 37, 37, 95}
   (D) {3, 14, 20.5, 37, 95}
   (E) {3, 14, 19, 37, 95}

5. If the test scores of a class of 30 students have a mean of 75.6 and the test scores of another class of 24 students have a mean of 68.4, then the mean of the combined group is
   (A) 72
   (B) 72.4
   (C) 72.8
   (D) 74.2
   (E) none of these.

6. If the range of a set of data is 36, then a reasonable estimate of the standard deviation is
   (A) 6
   (B) 18
   (C) 72
   (D) 108
   (E) 216

FREE-RESPONSE QUESTIONS

Open-Ended Questions

Use the given data set of test grades from a college statistics class for questions 1–3.

85 72 64 65 98 78 75 76 82 80 61 92 72 58 65 74 92 85 74 76 77 77 62 68 68 54 62 76 73 85 88 91 99 82 80 74 76 77 70 60

1. Construct two different graphs of these data.

2. Calculate the five-number summary and the mean and standard deviation of the data.

3. Describe the distribution of the data, citing both the plots and the summary statistics found in questions 1 and 2.

4. A set of 1,000 test scores has a symmetric, mound-shaped distribution. The mean is 175 and the standard deviation is 10. Approximate
   a. the number of scores between 175 and 195.
   b. the number of scores between 155 and 165.
   c. the number of scores between 170 and 175.

5. A set of 2,000 measurements has a symmetric, mound-shaped distribution. The mean is 5.3 and the standard deviation is 0.7. Determine an interval that contains approximately 1,360 data values.

6. If you were given a graph that was skewed right severely, which summary statistics would you recommend? Explain your reasoning.

7. The mean height of the 24 students in your AP Statistics class is 68.3 inches. A transfer student whose height is 65 inches is placed in your class. What is the new mean height of the students in your class?

8. The mean grade on the 1998 AP Statistics exam of school A was 3.45 with a standard deviation of .3. The mean grade on the same test at school B was 3.45 with a standard deviation of .8. Assuming that the numbers of students are approximately the same and that both distributions are symmetric and mound-shaped, describe any differences you would expect to see in the graphs of the distributions.

2.5 Summarizing Distributions: Relative Location and Position

Statisticians have developed methods for making comparisons within a data set and among several data sets. Measuring position involves locating data values in relation to the rest of the data. We will discuss quartiles, percentiles, and standardized scores.

Quartiles and Percentiles

Quartiles divide the data set into four subsets, each of which contains 25% of the data. For example, if a test score falls in the first quartile, then we know that its location is in the lowest 25% of the data.

Quartile location is useful in comparing data values from more than one set of data. For example, if student A in one class scores 80 on a test and student B in another class scores 75 on the same test, it is clear that student A has performed better than student B in an *absolute* sense. However, suppose we are informed that student A's 80 places the score in the second quartile of her class while student B's 75 places the score in the first quartile in his class. Then we see that B has outperformed A when considering their positions in their respective classes.

We can extend this idea to the concept of *percentiles*. Percentiles provide information about the position of a data value in a data set. A **percentile** is the data value below which the specified percent of data values occurs. For example, if a score falls in the 40th percentile, we know that 40% of the data values lie below the score and 60% of the data lie above the score.

Percentiles are very useful in providing positional information in large data sets. For example, a score of 503 on a standardized test does not tell us the position of the score relative to the entire set of scores. If we are informed that the score of 503 is in the 75th percentile, we know the position of a score of 503 relative to the entire set of scores. Calculation of percentiles requires determining the percent of the data below the data value of interest.

EXAMPLE 1

From the frequency table below, the percentile score of a value of 20 is found by dividing the number of data values below 20 by the total number of data values, to get $\frac{16}{70} \approx 22.9$. Therefore, we say that a value of 20 is in the 23rd percentile.

Value	0	10	20	30	40	50
Frequency	6	10	15	20	14	5

Standardized Scores

The *standardized* or *z-score* allows us to identify the position of a data value relative to the mean and standard deviation of its set of data values. The z-score is calculated using the formula

$$z\text{-score} = \frac{x - \bar{x}}{s}$$

where x = the data value

$\bar{x}$ = the mean of the data values

s = the standard deviation of the data values

The z-score measures the number of standard deviations between the data value and the mean. Note the following properties of the z-score:

1. The mean has a z-score of 0.
2. A data value less than the mean has a negative z-score.
3. A data value greater than the mean has a positive z-score.

EXAMPLE 2

If $x = 25$, $\bar{x} = 20$ and $s = 2$, then the z-score $= \dfrac{25 - 20}{2} = 2.5$. This z-score indicates that 25 is 2.5 standard deviations above the mean of 20.

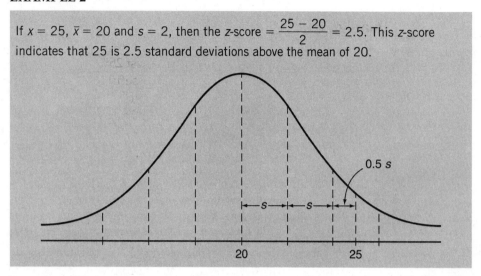

EXAMPLE 3

If $x = 100$, $\bar{x} = 120$ and $s = 15$, then the z-score $= \dfrac{100 - 120}{15} = -1.333$. This z-score indicates that 100 is 1.333 standard deviations below the mean of 120.

If the distribution is relatively symmetric and mound-shaped, we can locate the position of any data value on the *"standard z-histogram"* by its z-score:

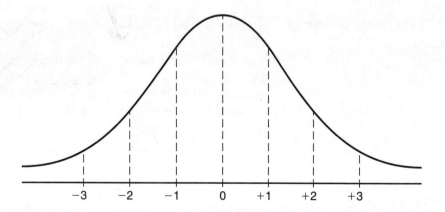

The conversion of data to respective z-scores is a transformation of the data to values with a uniform scale with a mean of 0 and standard deviation of 1. Using this conversion, we can make meaningful comparisons of relatively symmetric and mound-shaped distributions with different means and standard deviations.

EXAMPLE 4

Class	Score	$\bar{x}$	s
A	100	80	10
B	120	105	20

Which score is higher relative to the mean of the respective class?

Solution

Find the z-scores to answer the question.

For class A: $z = \dfrac{100 - 80}{10} = \dfrac{20}{10} = 2$

For class B: $z = \dfrac{120 - 105}{20} = \dfrac{15}{20} = 0.75$

Therefore, the score of 100 is farther above the mean of class A than the score of 120 is above the mean of Class B.

EXAMPLE 5

A student scores 625 on the mathematics section of the SAT and a 28 on the mathematics section of the ACT. She can report only one score to her college. If the SAT summary statistics include, $\bar{x} = 490$ and $s = 100$ and the ACT summary statistics include, $\bar{x} = 21$ and $s = 6$, which score should she report?

Solution

Determine the z-scores:

$$Z_{SAT} = \frac{625 - 490}{100} = 1.35 \qquad Z_{ACT} = \frac{28 - 21}{6} = 1.17$$

Therefore, assuming she wishes to report the more impressive score, she should report the SAT score.

Effects of Change At times it is advisable to be able to change the units of measure of the summaries of the data of interest. For example, if you have completed a science lab report and calculated all of the measures in inches only to find that the science teacher requires all values in centimeters, you might wish to convert the measures rather than recalculating all of them.

Consider a data set $\{x_i \mid i = 1, 2, \ldots, n\}$ with summary statistics $\{\bar{x}, s, \text{min}, Q_1, \text{median}, Q_3, \text{max}\}$.

Change	Summary Statistics
Add or subtract the same number to each data value: $\{x_i + c \mid i = 1, 2, \ldots, n\}$	$\{\bar{x} + c, s, \text{min} + c, Q_1 + c, \text{median} + c, Q_3 + c, \text{max} + c\}$.
Multiply or divide each data value by the same number c: $\{cx_i \mid i = 1, 2, \ldots, n\}$	$\{c\bar{x}, \lvert c \rvert s, c\text{min}, cQ_1, c\text{median}, cQ_3, c\text{max}\}$.

These facts are useful when changing units in a distribution. For example, using the scheme $\{\bar{x}, s, \text{min}, Q_1, \text{median}, Q_3, \text{max}\}$, suppose a set of values

{1, 2, 3, 4, 5, 6, 7, 8} in *feet* has statistics {4.5, 2.449, 1, 2.5, 4.5, 6.5, 8}. Then the set of values of the same set of values in *inches* is {12, 24, 36, 48, 60, 72, 84, 96} and has statistics {54, 29.394, 12, 30, 54, 78, 96}.

Note that the summary statistics of the transformed data could have been calculated by multiplying each of the former values by 12, the conversion factor used to change feet to inches.

Conversion to z-scores is a combination of both transformations:
a. by subtracting $\bar{x}$ from each x, we transform the mean, $\bar{x}$, to $x - \bar{x} = 0$ and the standard deviation is unchanged.
b. by dividing each difference $(x - \bar{x})$ by s, we transform the standard deviation from s to 1.

The set of z-scores for the set of values {1, 2, 3, 4, 5, 6, 7, 8} is {−1.429, −1.021, −0.612, −0.204, 0.204, 0.612, 1.021, 1.429}. The remarkable feature of this transformation is the fact that the mean of the transformed data is 0 and the standard deviation is 1. In addition, note that each data value has the same relative position.

Review Exercises

MULTIPLE-CHOICE QUESTIONS

1. Which observation has the higher z-score?
   I: $x = 25.4$; $\bar{x} = 12.9$; $s = 3.7$
   II: $x = 137.5$; $\bar{x} = 73.7$; $s = 17.1$
   (A) I
   (B) II
   (C) z-scores are equal
   (D) cannot be determined since we don't know the standard deviations of the populations
   (E) cannot be determined since we don't know if the populations are normal

2. The quartile and percentile positions of the value 10 in the set {10, 6, 8, 9, 12, 17, 32, 16} are: (The answers list the quartile followed by the percentile.)
   (A) Q_3; 38
   (B) Q_2; 38
   (C) Q_2; 26
   (D) Q_3; 26
   (E) none of these

3. If $n = 150$ and a score of 75 is in the 30th percentile, what is the percentile position of a score of 100?
   (A) 45th
   (B) 50th
   (C) 63rd
   (D) 75th
   (E) cannot be determined

4. A student is deciding whether to take the SAT exam a second time. He received a 540 on the verbal section on his first attempt. The mean score on the verbal section was 478 with a standard deviation of 92. It is expected that the mean of the next test will be a 485 with a standard deviation of 95. What is the minimum number of points that he would have to improve his score on his second attempt in order to better his performance on the first test?
   (A) 3 points
   (B) 9 points
   (C) 15 points
   (D) 20 points
   (E) cannot be determined

5. If a distribution is relatively symmetric and mound-shaped, order (from least to greatest) the following positions:
   1. a z-score of 1
   2. the value of Q_3
   3. a value in the 70th percentile
   (A) 1, 2, 3
   (B) 1, 3, 2
   (C) 3, 2, 1
   (D) 3, 1, 2
   (E) 2, 3, 1

6. If each value of a data set is increased by 10%, the effects on the mean and standard deviation can be summarized as
   (A) mean increases by 10%; standard deviation remains unchanged.
   (B) mean remains unchanged; standard deviation increases by 10%.
   (C) mean increases by 10%; standard deviation increases by 10%.
   (D) mean remains unchanged; standard deviation remains unchanged.
   (E) the effect depends on the type of distribution.

7. The standard deviation of the set $\{5, 7, 7, 8, 10, 11\}$ is 2. Which of the following sets also has a standard deviation equal to 2? (This exercise should be completed without calculations.)
   (A) $\{4, 5, 5, 8, 12, 14\}$
   (B) $\{2, 4, 6, 8, 10, 12\}$
   (C) $\{3, 5, 5, 6, 8, 9\}$
   (D) $\{10, 14, 14, 16, 20, 22\}$
   (E) none of the above

8. If 12% of the values of a data set lie between a and b and d is added to each value, then which of the following is true?
   (A) 12% still lies between a and b.
   (B) 12% lies between $a + d$ and $b + d$.
   (C) $(12 + d)\%$ lies between a and b.
   (D) $(12 + d)\%$ lies between $a + d$ and $b + d$.
   (E) There is no way to tell how much data is between a and b.

9. If all values in a data set are converted into standard scores (z-scores) then which of the following statements is *not* true?
   (A) Conversion to standard scores is not possible for some data sets.
   (B) The mean and standard deviation of the transformed data are 0 and 1 respectively only for symmetric and mound-shaped distributions.
   (C) The empirical (68–95–99.7) rule applies consistently to both the original and transformed data sets.
   (D) The z-scores represent how many standard deviations each value is from the mean.
   (E) All of these are true statements.

FREE-RESPONSE QUESTIONS

Open-Ended Questions

Use the following frequency table for questions 1–4:

Value	Frequency
10	1
17	3
23	8
42	12
50	10
60	4
65	5
72	10
81	5
95	6

1. Find the quartile position of a value of 65.

2. Find the percentile position of a value of 65.

3. Find the z-score of a value of 65.

4. Which of the three measures (quartile, percentile, z-score) is most meaningful to you? Explain the reasons for your choice.

5. For the data value of 65, determine the least amount of increase to this value that would raise it
   a. to the next highest quartile position.
   b. to a percentile position 5% higher than the present position.
   c. to a z-score .5 higher than the present z-score.

6. If a set of values in meters has summary statistics {mean, standard deviation, minimum, Q_1, median, Q_3, maximum} = {9, 4.898, 2, 5, 9, 13, 16}, what would the summary be for the same set of values in
   a. centimeters?
   b. kilometers?

7. For any distribution, determine the percentile value for each number in the five-number summary.

2.6 Comparing Distributions

Different sets of univariate data can be compared both graphically and in terms of summary statistics. The following two sets of data will be used for this section. The values represent the scores of Class A and Class B on the same 100-point test:

A {70, 65, 66, 60, 80, 90, 95, 50, 65, 75, 65, 60, 80, 85, 60, 70, 75, 60, 55, 99}
B {70, 85, 80, 80, 60, 65, 75, 80, 90, 95, 85, 80, 70, 60, 65, 75, 80, 80, 75, 80, 70, 50, 85, 90}

Graphical Displays:
Back-to-Back

Stem and Leaf Plots

Leaves	Stem	Leaves
0	5	0 5
5 5 0 0	6	0 0 0 1 5 5 5 6
5 5 5 0 0 0	7	0 0 5 5
5 5 5 0 0 0 0 0 0	8	0 0 5
5 0 0	9	0 5 9

Leaf = 1.0

Graphical Displays:
Parallel

Histograms

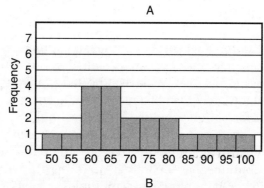

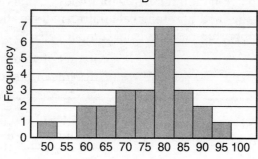

Box Plots

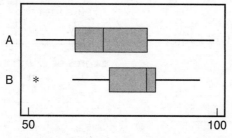

Note: Parallel box plots may be displayed either horizontally or vertically.

Dot Plots

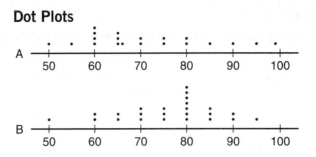

A

50 60 70 80 90 100

B

50 60 70 80 90 100

Summary Statistics

Similarly, comparison of summary statistics can be quite revealing:

	n	$\bar{x}$	s	min	Q_1	median	Q_3	max
Class A	20	71.25	13.43	50	60	68	80	99
Class B	24	76.04	10.73	50	70	80	82.5	95

You should always inspect the summary statistics along with your inspection of the graphical displays. For example, Class B has an outlier that is clearly shown on the modified box plot. This value may exert substantial influence on the value of the mean for Class B. Note that the same value, 50, is *not* an outlier for Class A. Class A has a wider range of scores, as shown by its higher standard deviation.

Technology Note: While most computer programs will produce all of the displays and sets of summary statistics, very few provide displays in the back-to-back format that we have indicated as advantageous for comparison of data sets. However, it is not a major task to create the back-to-back displays using the information provided by the technology. When displaying parallel displays, many computer programs and graphing calculators will produce overlapping histograms; this overlapping may actually hide differences in the distributions that separate histograms, drawn on the same scale, may make obvious. On the other hand, multiple box plots are produced by both computer packages and graphing calculators in a parallel fashion that provides excellent opportunities for visual comparisons. ■

Review Exercises

FREE-RESPONSE QUESTIONS

Open-Ended Questions

Using plots and summary statistics, investigate and report on the comparison of these pairs of data sets. Include a description of the shape of the distributions. Justify your selections.

1. Heights (rounded to the nearest inch) of adults in a random sample:

Men	65	67	69	71	63	62	70	72	66
Women	65	67	67	68	70	64	64	65	65

2. Mileages of sample test cars using the same amount of gasoline in a test:

Vega	Datsun	Vega	Datsun	Vega	Datsun
35	32	32	34	36	32
41	31	24	32	35	30
38	30	27	35	27	32
40	33	35	40	34	31

3. Scores of two classes on the same test:

A	B	A	B	A	B	A	B	A	B
78	78	76	65	83	91	77	77	84	75
83	94	78	76	82	80	86	74		
85	62	77	78	76	84	85	73		

Chapter 2 Assessment

MULTIPLE-CHOICE QUESTIONS

Choose the best answer of those listed.
Use the following data for questions 1–5.
A survey was conducted to gather ratings of the quality of service at local restaurants at a nearby mall. Respondents were to rate overall service using values between 0 (terrible) and 100 (excellent). The data are represented by the following stem plot. (*Note:* A calculator should not be necessary for questions 1–4.)

Stem	Leaves
3	2 4
4	0 3 4 7 8 9 9 9
5	0 1 1 2 3 4 5
6	1 2 5 6 6
7	0 1
8	
9	2

1. What percent of the respondents rated quality as very good or higher (rating of 80 or more on a numerical scale of 0 to 100)?
   (A) 0%
   (B) 4%
   (C) 25%
   (D) 96%
   (E) 100%

2. The median response was
   (A) 49
   (B) 50
   (C) 51
   (D) 62
   (E) cannot be determined.

3. The mean of these data is
   (A) equal to the median.
   (B) less than the median.
   (C) greater than the median.
   (D) an integer.
   (E) cannot be determined.

4. The value of 92 is
   (A) the maximum but not an outlier.
   (B) the maximum and an outlier.
   (C) one of two outliers.
   (D) not a data value.
   (E) none of these.

5. The box plot of the data is

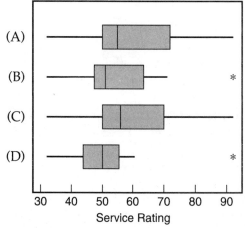

(A)
(B)
(C)
(D)

Service Rating

(E) None of these are box plots of the data.

Use the following data for questions 6–8.
The table below lists the number of applications to a sample of 10 colleges that are located within the same state. The values are in 100's.

Colleges	Numbers (100's)	Colleges	Numbers (100's)
A	72.0	F	26.9
B	63.1	G	25.0
C	54.7	H	23.9
D	54.3	I	23.0
E	29.0	J	20.0

6. What is the sample variance (rounded to two decimal places)?
   (A) 18.54
   (B) 19.54
   (C) 343.75
   (D) 381.94
   (E) None of these.

7. Assuming that the mean and standard deviation are 40 and 19 respectively, what is the z-score for college A?
   (A) .292
   (B) .594
   (C) 1.68
   (D) 2.15
   (E) 32

8. Which display could *not* be used for these data?
   - (A) stem and leaf
   - (B) dot plot
   - (C) histogram
   - (D) pie chart
   - (E) all of these can be used.

9. In skewed-right distributions, what is most frequently the relationship of the mean, median, and mode?
   - (A) mean > median > mode
   - (B) median > mean > mode
   - (C) mode > median > mean
   - (D) mode > mean > median
   - (E) mean > mode > median

Use the following data for questions 10 and 11.
A random survey was conducted to determine the cost of residential gas heat. Analysis of the survey results indicated that the mean monthly cost of gas was $125, with a standard deviation of $10.

10. If the distribution is mound-shaped and symmetric, what percent of homes will have a monthly bill of more than $115?
    - (A) 34%
    - (B) 50%
    - (C) 68%
    - (D) 84%
    - (E) 97.5%

11. The z-score of a house with a gas bill of $150 per month is
    - (A) −2.5
    - (B) .40
    - (C) 1.5
    - (D) 2.5
    - (E) 25

12. The average life expectancy of males in a particular town is 75 years, with a standard deviation of 5 years. Assuming that the distribution is mound-shaped and symmetric, the approximate 15th percentile in the age distribution is
    - (A) 60
    - (B) 65
    - (C) 70
    - (D) 75
    - (E) 80

FREE-RESPONSE QUESTIONS
Open-Ended Questions

1. If the mean of 75 values is 52.6 pounds and the mean of 25 values is 48.4 pounds, find the mean of all 100 values.

2. Of 500 high school students whose mean height is 67.8 inches, 150 were girls. If the mean height of the girls was 63.0 inches, what is the mean height of the boys?

3. Draw a histogram that is symmetric but not mound-shaped.

4. Create a data set of 10 values whose box plot has no whiskers.

5. Which grade is better: A 78 on a test whose mean is 72 and standard deviation is 6.5, or an 83 on a test whose mean is 77 and standard deviation is 8.4? Justify your answer.

Investigative Tasks

1. The following table lists the number of keys that a class of AP Statistics students had in their possession on a certain day:

Number of Keys	Number of Students
0	2
1	5
2	4
3	6
4	10
5	8

   a. Draw a histogram of the data. Describe the nature of the graph.
   b. Draw a box plot of the data. What does the box plot tell you about the distribution?
   c. Describe the benefits of the two graphs. Choose the one that you believe best describes the data. Explain your choice.
   d. Calculate the mean, the standard deviation, and the five-number summary for these data. Which set of summary statistics best describes the data? Explain the reasons for your choice.

2. Use the following table of test grades for two classes, A and B, for this investigative task.

A	B	A	B	A	B	A	B
97	100	75	78	91	74	95	75
86	65	82	98	65	82	45	98
74	75	81	65	62	83		

a. Construct a back-to-back stem and leaf plot and parallel box plots for the data from the two classes.

b. Which plot best describes the distributions of the test scores? Explain the reasons for your answer.

c. Calculate the five-number summary and the mean and standard deviation for each set of grades.

d. Describe the benefits of each set of summary statistics for these data.

e. Which class did better based on your plots and calculations? Defend your opinion.

Chapter 3 Exploring Bivariate Data

3.1   Patterns in Scatterplots
3.2   Means and Standard Deviations
3.3   Correlation and Linearity
3.4   Least Squares Regression Line
3.5   Residual Plots, Outliers, and Influential Points
3.6   Transformations to Achieve Linearity
3.7   Exploring Categorical Data
      Chapter 3 Assessment

Chapter 3 Exploring Bivariate Data

Many of the studies that are conducted involve relationships between two variables. For example, the government might be interested in the association between interest rates and number of new homes built, or broadcasters might be interested in the association between people's ages and the number of hours of television they watch. Such studies involve comparison between two variables (bivariate data). When we explore bivariate data, we focus on:

- determining if an association exists between two variables observed about a particular subject;
- how this association can be measured; and
- how it can be expressed mathematically and used to predict a relationship.

Always keep in mind that association never implies causation. In this chapter, we will review relationships between two quantitative variables and relationships between two categorical variables.

3.1 Patterns in Scatterplots

One technique for visually displaying a relationship between two quantitative variables is to use a **scatterplot.**

Individual observations are written in (x, y) format and plotted. Here are some interesting patterns in scatterplots. Included are brief descriptions of the plots.

EXAMPLE 1

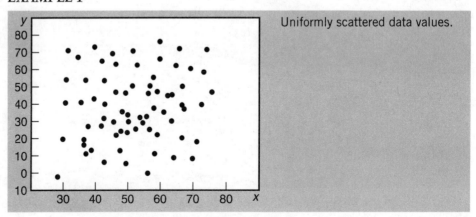

Uniformly scattered data values.

EXAMPLE 2

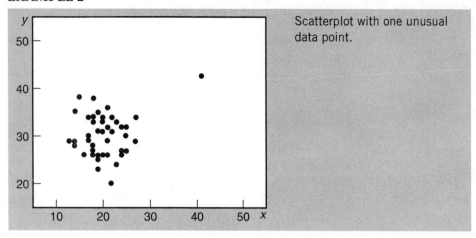

Scatterplot with one unusual data point.

EXAMPLE 3

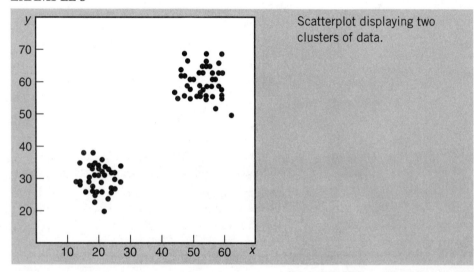

Scatterplot displaying two clusters of data.

EXAMPLE 4

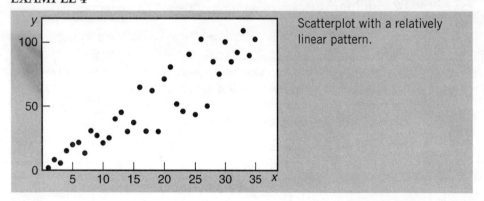

Scatterplot with a relatively linear pattern.

EXAMPLE 5

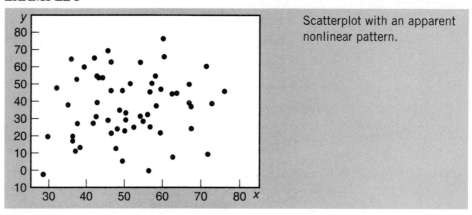

Scatterplot with an apparent nonlinear pattern.

EXAMPLE 6

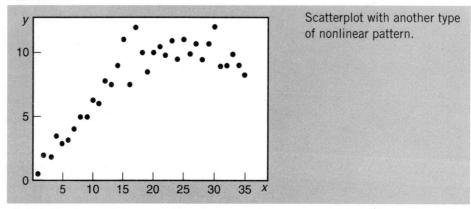

Scatterplot with another type of nonlinear pattern.

Scatterplots will be an important tool in all the sections that follow.

Review Exercises

FREE-RESPONSE QUESTIONS

Open-Ended Questions

Make a scatterplot for each set of data. Include a description of the scatterplot.

1.

Year	Airline Departures (in millions)	Year	Airline Departures (in millions)
1980	5.4	1988	6.7
1981	5.2	1989	6.6
1982	5.0	1990	6.9
1983	5.0	1991	6.8
1984	5.4	1992	7.1
1985	5.8	1993	7.2
1986	6.4	1994	7.5
1987	6.6	1995	8.1

2.

No. of Seats on Aircraft	Airborne Speed (mph)	No. of Seats on Aircraft	Airborne Speed (mph)
396	538	267	468
395	521	261	526
342	535	222	524
291	512	219	496
288	506	186	465
285	490	180	487
283	503	172	498
277	523		

3.

Age	Annual Income (in $1,000)	Age	Annual Income (in $1,000)
18	12.1	35	23.8
20	20.0	37	55.5
21	19.8	40	200.0
25	37.5	44	39.2
28	70.3	49	65.8
30	44.5	53	16.4
33	47.0	60	48.2

3.2 Means and Standard Deviations

All of the measures used in the analysis of univariate data can be extended to apply to the values of each of the variables for bivariate data.

Mean and Standard Deviation of Each Component

Let $A = \{(x_i, y_i) \mid i = 1, 2, 3, \ldots, n\}$; that is, A is a set of n ordered pairs.
$\bar{x}$ = mean of $\{x_i\}$; s_x = standard deviation of $\{x_i\}$
$\bar{y}$ = mean of $\{y_i\}$, s_y = standard deviation of $\{y_i\}$

In this review, we will call the pair $(\bar{x}, \bar{y})$ the **grand mean** of the bivariate data set. In addition, if the distributions of each of the variables are relatively symmetric, then a rule of thumb regarding the percents of data within standard deviation intervals is also true:

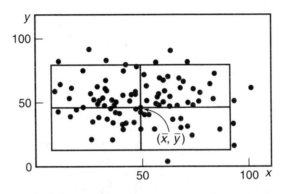

Since approximately 95% of the data lies within two standard deviations of the mean for both $\{x\}$ and $\{y\}$, approximately 90.25% (0.95 × 0.95) of the data of $\{(x, y)\}$ is contained within the two-standard deviation rectangle.

Mean and Standard Deviation of the *y*-values at a Specific *x*-value

The following method of analyzing bivariate data will be very useful in later sections. Consider the distribution of the y-values that occur at a specific value of x. For example, consider the distribution of the y-coordinate for the data values that have an x-coordinate of 40.

Consider the "strip" of *y*-values at *x* = 40.

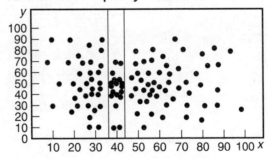

The distribution of *y*-values at *x* = 40.

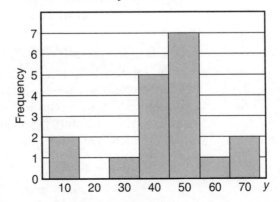

Consider now the set of all means of the sets of $\{y_i\}$ at each of the x_i-values; let us call this set $\{y_i$-means$\}$ or $\{\bar{y}_i\}$. For example, in a finite bivariate set, $\{(x_i, y_j) \mid i = 1, 2, 3, \ldots, m; j = 1, 2, 3, \ldots, n\}$, the set $\{(x_i, \bar{y}_i) \mid i = 1, 2, \ldots, m\}$ represents the means of the m-distributions of the y-values at the m x-values.

EXAMPLE

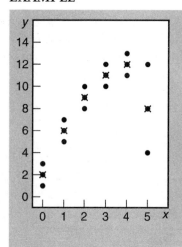

As a very simple example, suppose our data set was

(0, 1) (1, 5) (2, 8) (3, 10) (4, 11) (5, 4)
(0, 2) (1, 6) (2, 9) (3, 11) (4, 12) (5, 8)
(0, 3) (1, 7) (2,10) (3, 12) (4, 13) (5, 12)

The set of *y*-means is

$\{y$-means$\}$ = $\{\bar{y}_i\}$ = {(0, 2), (1, 6), (2, 9), (3, 11), (4, 12), (5, 8)}

in which the second coordinate of each pair is *the mean of the y-values for the particular x-value*.
 If we graph both the set of the data and the set of *y*-means, we see that the graph of $\{(x, y$-means$)\}$ accentuates the pattern in the set of $\{(x_i, y_i)\}$.

Review Exercises

FREE-RESPONSE QUESTIONS

Open-Ended Questions

Use the data set below for questions 1–6.
Forty students were asked to choose a pair of numbers such that the first number was between 0 and 9 inclusive and the second number was between 1 and 10. The results are listed below.

{(0,4) (1,9) (2,5) (3,6) (4,1) (5,2) (6,3) (7,1) (8,6) (9,1)
(0,5) (1,3) (2,1) (3,8) (4,3) (5,9) (6,0) (7,4) (8,6) (9,5)
(0,6) (1,10) (2,5) (3,10) (4,3) (5,6) (6,7) (7,4) (8,4) (9,6)
(0,8) (1,4) (2,4) (3,10) (4,5) (5,7) (6,8) (7,5) (8,0) (9,10)}

1. Draw the scatterplot. Describe the relationship between the variables that you see in the scatterplot.

2. Determine the means and standard deviations for each component of the bivariate data set.

3. Construct the two-standard deviation rectangle about the grand mean and determine the percent of the data within the rectangle.

4. Does the answer to question 3 fit our expectation regarding the two-standard deviation rule of thumb? Explain your answer.

5. Calculate the set of *y*-means and graph them on the scatterplot.

6. Describe the pattern of the $\{(x, \bar{y}_i)\}$.

3.3 Correlation and Linearity

We explore bivariate data to determine if an association exists between the variables. For example, we might explore whether height and shoe size appear to be related. Once the strength and the direction (positive or negative) of the association have been determined, algebraic models can be fit to the data for predictive purposes. In order to quantify both the strength and the direction of the association, we calculate a number called the correlation coefficient.

The **correlation coefficient** is a value that quantifies the strength and direction of *linear* association of the variables in a set of bivariate data. The value of the correlation coefficient, denoted r, is found using the formula:

$$r = \frac{1}{n-1} \sum_{i=1}^{n} \left(\frac{x_i - \bar{x}}{s_x} \right) \left(\frac{y_i - \bar{y}}{s_y} \right)$$

The formula can be considered as the adjusted mean of the products of the z-scores of the corresponding variables.

The value of r ranges from -1 to $+1$. The importance of quantifying both the strength and the direction of the association using the correlation coefficient can be seen graphically.

EXAMPLE 1

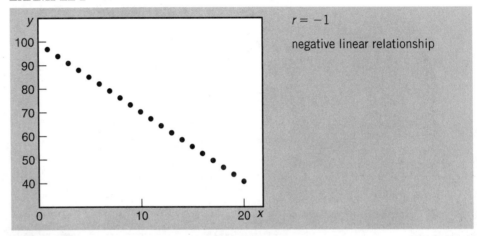

$r = -1$

negative linear relationship

EXAMPLE 2

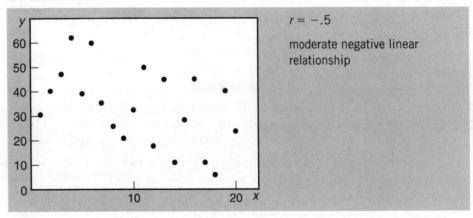

$r = -.5$

moderate negative linear relationship

EXAMPLE 3

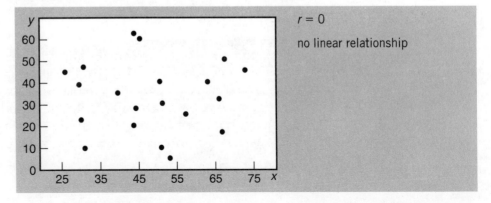

$r = 0$

no linear relationship

EXAMPLE 4

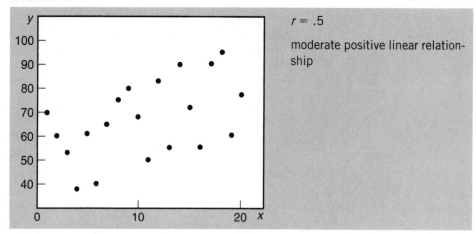

$r = .5$

moderate positive linear relationship

EXAMPLE 5

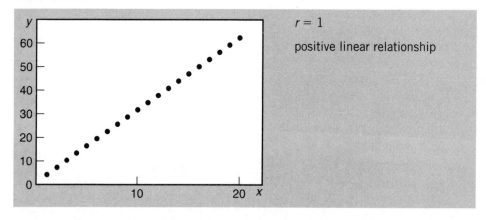

$r = 1$

positive linear relationship

As was stated earlier, the value of the correlation coefficient measures the degree and direction of *linear* association between the variables in a bivariate distribution. A negative r implies an inverse relationship (as one variable increases the other decreases) and a positive r implies direct variation (as one variable increases so does the other). If $|r| = 1$, we can conclude that the variables follow an exact linear relationship. Lower values indicate a weaker relationship. As we have seen above, when $|r| = 1$, the pairs of the data, when plotted on a scatterplot, are *collinear*. In this case, the equation that models the relationship is simple to determine. Similarly, if $r = 0$, then we say that *no* linear relationship exists between the variables.

EXAMPLE 6

Hand calculation of the correlation coefficient can be accomplished with the aid of a table. In the table, x represents the number of attempts at target shooting and y represents the points scored.

x_i	10	14	16	18	20	22	25	26
y_i	5	10	12	18	22	30	28	35

$\bar{x} = \dfrac{151}{8} = 18.875; \ s_x = 5.489$

$\bar{y} = \dfrac{160}{8} = 20; \ s_y = 10.597$

$\frac{x_i - \bar{x}}{s_x}$	−1.617	−.888	−.524	−.159	.205	.569	1.116	1.298	
$\frac{y_i - \bar{y}}{s_y}$	−1.416	−.943	−.755	−.189	.189	.944	.755	1.416	
$\left(\frac{x_i - \bar{x}}{s_x}\right)\left(\frac{y_i - \bar{y}}{s_y}\right)$	2.2889	.8382	.3955	.0301	.0387	.5373	.8425	1.8376	Total 6.8088

$$r = \frac{1}{7}(6.8088) = .9727$$

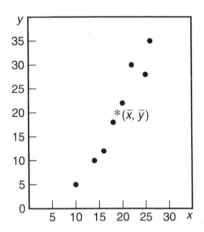
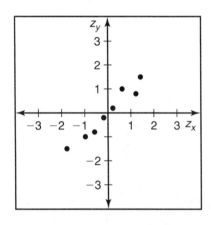

The reasonableness of the formula for the correlation coefficient can be seen by considering a transformation of the coordinate plane of the scatterplot of the original data. In the figures above, we translate the data set for Example 1 into standardized values and in doing so, translate the axes so that the new origin of the coordinate plane is now located at the grand mean.

By standardizing both the x- and y-coordinates, we effectively translate the axes so that the new origin is the grand mean $(z\bar{x}, z\bar{y})$. The quadrants then take on the interpretations listed below.

Quadrant	x-Coordinate	y-Coordinate
First	positive z-score	positive z-score
Second	negative z-score	positive z-score
Third	negative z-score	negative z-score
Fourth	positive z-score	negative z-score

It is clear that the products of the z-scores for each data point correspond to quadrants of the standardized plane in that positive products come from points in the first and third quadrants and negative products come from points in the second and fourth quadrants. When these products are summed in the formula, the accumulation of these positive and negative products is taken into account and the result is a signed number that reflects the positive or negative domination of the standardized data points, not only because of their signs but also because of their magnitudes relative to the grand mean.

One caution: while we can always compute the value of the correlation coefficient, we should also plot the data on a scatterplot in order to determine if it makes sense to look for a linear relationship. If the scatterplot shows the data to be clearly non-linear, calculation of the correlation coefficient becomes an inappropriate data analysis technique. We will include a discussion of non-linear data in Section 3.6.

 Technology Note: Statistical software and graphing calculators have the capability of computing the correlation coefficient for bivariate data. In some cases, the calculation of r occurs when the user requests the calculation of the *regression line* that will be discussed in the next section.

In addition, many statistics packages and graphing calculators provide a value of R^2. The value R^2 is called the *coefficient of determination* and provides information regarding the percent of variation in the dependent variable that the regression line accounts for. For example, if the coefficient of determination between the independent variable, height, and the dependent variable, weight, is 83%, we can conclude that 83% of a change in weight is accounted for by this model. Most importantly, we can also conclude that 17% of the change in weight must be attributable to either chance error (See Chapter 6) or some other variable that is not included in the linear relationship. Therefore, knowing a person's height alone is informative, but does not provide a complete explanation of how people's weights vary. ■

Review Exercises

MULTIPLE-CHOICE QUESTIONS

1. Which of the following would *not* be a correct interpretation of a correlation coefficient of $r = -.30$?
   (A) The variables are inversely related.
   (B) The coefficient of determination is .09.
   (C) 30% of the variation between the variables is linear.
   (D) There exists a weak relationship between the variables.
   (E) All are correct.

2. If the correlation coefficient of a bivariate set of data $\{(x, y)\}$ is r, then which of the following is true?
   (A) The variables x and y are linearly related.
   (B) The correlation coefficient of the set $\{(y, x)\}$ is also r.
   (C) The correlation coefficient of the set $\{(x, ay)\}$ is $a \cdot r$.
   (D) The correlation coefficient of the set $\{(ax, ay)\}$ is $a \cdot r$.
   (E) None of these.

3. Which of the following is *not* true of a correlation coefficient of a set of bivariate data?
   (A) The higher the correlation coefficient, the steeper the line of best fit.
   (B) The absolute value of the correlation coefficient is independent of the slope of the line of best fit.
   (C) A low correlation coefficient does not necessarily indicate a weak relationship between the variables.
   (D) Two sets of bivariate data can have approximately equal correlation coefficients but very different scatterplots.
   (E) All of these are true.

4. A coefficient of determination is found to be .81. Which of the following is true?
   (A) 81% of the variation between the variables is accounted for in the linear relationship.
   (B) 81% of the data points lie on a line.
   (C) The correlation coefficient is approximately ±.9.
   (D) 19% of the variation between the variables is accounted for in the linear relationship.
   (E) All of these are true.

FREE-RESPONSE QUESTIONS

Open-Ended Questions

In questions 1–4, estimate the correlation coefficient for each scatterplot.

1.

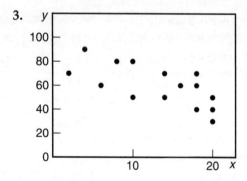

2.

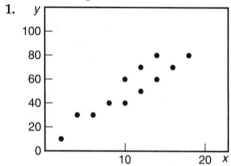

3.

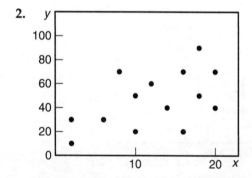

4.

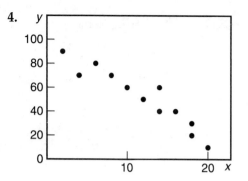

5. Complete the table and calculate the correlation coefficient.

x_i	y_i	$\dfrac{x_i - \bar{x}}{s_x}$	$\dfrac{y_i - \bar{y}}{s_y}$	$\left(\dfrac{x_i - \bar{x}}{s_x}\right)\left(\dfrac{y_i - \bar{y}}{s_y}\right)$
0	4			
2	7			
5	15			
9	21			
13	28			
18	30			
22	43			
27	55			

6. A distribution of {heights, weights} of adult men is analyzed and yields the following statistics: $\bar{h} = 69.2$ in.; $\bar{w} = 172.3$ lbs; $r = .63$. If a particular man has a height that is one standard deviation above the mean height of all men and also has a weight that is one standard deviation above the mean weight of all men, how does this man's weight compare to the mean weight of all men who have the same height? State whether this man's weight would be about the same as, less than, or greater than the weight of all men with the same height. Explain your reasoning.

7. A correlation coefficient $r = 0$ indicates that there is no linear relationship between the variables of the data set. This does not imply that there is no relationship between the variables. Create the graph of a bivariate data set in which the variables are obviously related and the value of r is approximately equal to zero.

3.4 Least Squares Regression Line

Determining the Regression Line

The term **linear regression** refers to the process of finding an equation in the form of $\hat{y} = ax + b$ for a set of bivariate data. In this context, the dependent variable is called the **response variable,** and the independent variable is called the **explanatory variable.** Therefore, the equation supports the prediction of a response variable for a given value of the explanatory variable. Note that this is the same as the "slope-intercept" form $y = mx + b$ from elementary algebra. It is important to note that x and y are variables whose context changes from problem to problem. The a and the b are constants indicating the slope and y-intercept, respectively. From this point on, we will denote these constants by b_0 for the y-intercept and b_1 for the slope, thus presenting the equation as $y = b_1 x + b_0$ or $y = b_0 + b_1 x$. On the TI-83, however, these are shown as $LinReg(ax + b)$ and $LinReg(a + bx)$, respectively.

A **regression line** refers to a linear model that is fit to a set of bivariate data. The primary purpose of this regression equation is to be able to predict a typical value of a response (dependent) variable from a value of the explanatory (independent) variable; that is, an average response based on the value of an explanatory variable.

Assuming that we are working with a set of bivariate data that appears to be linearly related, we will determine the equation of "best fit" for these data. What determines the "line of best fit" determines how we will construct the linear model for bivariate data.

Consider this plot and the line of best fit that is drawn on it:

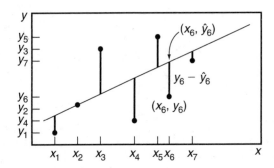

In the diagram, the heavy vertical segments indicate the differences between the actual or observed y-value and the predicted y-value using our line of best fit at each x-value. The length of each segment is called the **residual** at the particular value of x. The formula for the residual is, at each x_i,

$$residual_i = y_i - \hat{y}_i$$

where y_i is the actual or observed value of the dependent variable and $\hat{y}_i$ is the predicted value of the dependent variable at the same value of the independent variable. For example, at x_6, the value of the residual is $y_6 - \hat{y}_6$.

Our definition of "line of best fit" is the line that minimizes the prediction error $(y_i - \hat{y}_i)$ due to the use of the linear equation to predict the response variable from the explanatory variable. In order to accumulate the amount of prediction error because of the use of a particular linear model, there are several options: we could use the sum of the residuals for all x, the mean of the residuals for all x, or the sum of the absolute values of the residuals for all x.

It has been determined that a line of best fit is the **least squares regression line** that is designed to minimize $\sum_{i=1}^{n}(y_i - \hat{y}_i)^2$, that is, the sum of the squares of the residuals. Minimizing this expression will minimize the prediction error. The derivation of this line focuses on minimizing prediction error evidenced by the residuals. The "squares" in the name of this regression line refers to the squares of the residuals. Two key characteristics of the regression line are that it always contains the point $(\bar{x}, \bar{y})$ and the sum of the residuals is zero.

There are two ways to calculate the slope of the least squares regression line. After we calculate the slope, we calculate the y-intercept.

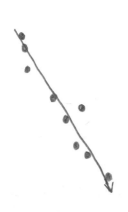

EQUATION OF LEAST SQUARES REGRESSION LINE: $\hat{y} = b_0 + b_1 x$

Slope

From data:

$$b_1 = \frac{\sum (x_i - \bar{x})(y_i - \bar{y})}{\sum (x_i - \bar{x})^2}$$

From summary statistics:

$$b_1 = r \cdot \frac{s_y}{s_x}$$

where r = correlation coefficient
s_y = standard deviation of the y's
s_x = standard deviation of x's

Intercept $b_0 = \bar{y} - b_1\bar{x}$

The formula for b_1 on the left is best used when the raw data values are provided and there is a minimum of technology available. The formula for b_1 on the right is most efficient if the correlation and the standard deviations for both x and y are known. We will provide an example that uses data from the example in Section 3.3.

EXAMPLE 1

x_i	10	14	16	18	20	22	25	26
y_i	5	10	12	18	22	30	28	35

$$\bar{x}_i = \frac{151}{8} = 18.875$$

$$\bar{y}_i = \frac{160}{8} = 20$$

$x_i - \bar{x}$	−8.875	−4.4875	−2.875	−.875	1.125	3.128	6.125	7.125	
$y_i - \bar{y}$	−15	−10	−8	−2	2	10	8	15	**Total**
$(x_i - \bar{x})(y_i - \bar{y})$	133.13	48.75	23.00	1.75	2.25	31.25	49.00	106.88	396.01
$(x_i - \bar{x})^2$	78.766	23.766	8.266	.766	1.266	9.766	37.516	50.766	210.878

$$b_1 = \frac{396.01}{210.878} = 1.878$$

$$b_0 = 20 - 1.878 \times 18.875 = -15.447$$

$$\therefore \hat{y} = -15.447 + 1.878x$$

An important property of linear regression can be seen if we use the regression equation to calculate the "fits," $\hat{y}_i$, and the residuals, $y_i - \hat{y}_i$.

In our example, $\hat{y} = -15.447 + 1.878x$.

x_i	y_i	$\hat{y}_i$	$y_i - \hat{y}_i$
10	5	3.334	1.666
14	10	10.845	−.845
16	12	14.601	−2.601
18	18	18.357	−.357
20	22	22.113	−.113
22	30	25.868	4.131
25	28	31.502	−3.502
26	35	33.380	1.620
Total			0

A linear regression equation created using least squares procedures produces fits such that the sum of the residual values is 0. In symbols, $\sum_{i=1}^{n} (y_i - \hat{y}_i) = 0$.

You should verify the above calculations using a computer program or graphing calculator. At the right, you can study the graph of these data and the least squares regression line.

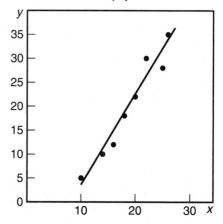

Calculation of the regression coefficients is significantly easier if you are provided with the necessary statistics. In our example,

Given:

$\bar{x} = 18.875$; $s_x = 5.489$

$\bar{y} = 20$; $s_y = 10.596$

$r = .9727$

The calculation becomes:

$b_1 = .9727\left(\dfrac{10.596}{5.489}\right)$

$b_0 = 20 - 1.878 \times 18.875 = -15.447$

$\therefore \hat{y} = -15.447 + 1.878x$

The calculation of the slope of the regression line using the standard deviation and the correlation coefficient also provides some interesting insights into the nature of the regression line. At first it may appear reasonable that the slope of the regression line should be close to the ratio of the standard deviations of the data sets; after all, these standard deviations do quantify the change of each of the variables from their respective means. However it has been found that the ratio of the standard deviations does not fit the data well.

When the correlation coefficient is multiplied by the ratio of the standard deviations, however, the regression line with this slope fits the data more closely using the criterion of minimizing the sum of the squares of the residuals. For our treatment, it is sufficient to understand that the correlation coefficient provides an adjustment to the ratio of the standard deviations to make the regression line fit better.

The regression equation provides a rule for predicting values of the response variable when the variables are linearly related. While it is correct to say that $\hat{y}$ is an estimate of the response variable at a particular value of the explanatory variable, x, it is better to consider $\hat{y}$ as an estimate of the *mean of values* of the response variable for this value of the explanatory variable (refer to Section 3.2). The regression equation is best understood in the context of *being the line of best fit of the set* $\{x_i, \bar{y}_i\}$, the bivariate set of x's and the means of the y-values at each x-value.

Interpreting the Coefficients of a Regression Line

When we write the equation of the line of best fit for a set of bivariate data, we generally use the names of the explanatory and response variables in the statement of the equation itself. In Example 1 above, the regression equation should be written in context:

$$\text{score} = -15.447 + 1.878(\text{number of attempts})$$

Note: In statistics, the y-intercept is generally listed *before* the linear term, that is, $\hat{y} = b_0 + b_1 x$.

It is important to interpret the coefficients (the y-intercept and slope) of the regression line:

- **slope:** The estimated unit rate of change of the response variable per unit change of the explanatory variable.
- **y-intercept:** The estimated value of the response variable when the value of the explanatory variable is zero.

In our example,

- **slope:** The score is predicted to increase 1.878 points on *each* successive attempt.
- **y-intercept:** The score is predicted to be –15.447 *before* any attempts are made.

Great care should be exercised when interpreting the y-intercept in the context of the data set. Sometimes the y-intercept makes no sense, as in our example. It does not make sense that you begin with a negative score before any attempts at shooting at the target.

It is also critical to remember that b_0 and b_1 are *estimates* of the true values of the slope and y-intercept. This fact will be very important in Chapter 7.

Using The Regression Line To Make Predictions

To use the regression line to make predictions, substitute an x-value into the regression equation.

EXAMPLE 2

Suppose x, the number of scoring attempts, is 23. What value for points scored, y, is predicted by the regression equation from Example 1?

$\hat{y} = -15.447 + 1.878x$

$\hat{y} = -15.447 + 1.878(23) = 27.747$

Therefore, when the number of attempts is 23, we predict that approximately 28 points will be scored.

It is important always to reference the value of a $\hat{y}$ as a *predicted* or *expected* value of the response variable.

When we use the equation to predict a y-value for an x-value *within* the x-data set, we are **interpolating.** In Example 2, the x-value 23 is between the data values of 22 and 25. When we use the equation to predict a y-value for an x-value outside of the data, we are **extrapolating.** Extrapolation is generally not used since we must assume that the relationship in the data described by the equation continues unchanged to include the value of x to be used for the prediction.

In our example, if we were to predict a y-value for 100 scoring attempts, that is, $x = 100$, we would find:

$\hat{y} = -15.447 + 1.878(100)$

$\hat{y} = 172.323$

One must question whether such a value (100, 172.323) makes sense in the context of the situation from which the data came.

Review Exercises

MULTIPLE-CHOICE QUESTIONS

1. A simple random sample of 50 families has produced the following statistics:
   Number of children in family: $\bar{x} = 2.1$, $s_x = 1.4$
   Annual Gross Income: $\bar{y} = 34{,}250$, $s_y = 10{,}540$
   $r = .75$
   The linear regression equation relating these variables, based on the data of this study, is
   (A) Income = 5,646(number of children) + 22,392
   (B) Income = 34,250 + .0001(number of children)
   (C) Income = .0001(number of children) − 1.312
   (D) Number of children = 5,646(income) + 22,392
   (E) Equation cannot be determined from given information.

2. You are given the regression equation:
   temperature = 30.4 − .72(*distance*)
   where *temperature* is the temperature displayed on a sensor in °C and *distance* is the distance in centimeters from the sensor to a heat source. Which of the following is *not* a reasonable conclusion?
   (A) The temperature of the heat source is 30.4°C.
   (B) The temperature decreases approximately .72°C for each centimeter the sensor is moved away from the heat source.
   (C) We can predict that the sensor displays a temperature of 21.76°C when the sensor is 12 centimeters away from the heat source.
   (D) The correlation coefficient between temperature and distance indicates a negative relationship.
   (E) All of these are reasonable.

3. A study utilizing a simple random sample of 40 college students studied their hours of part-time work per week and grade point average and found that the correlation coefficient between the variables was $-.43$. If the resulting linear regression equation is

$$\text{GPA} = 3.75 - .05(\text{number of hours})$$

which of the following is *not* a correct statement?

(A) The average GPA of students who don't work is approximately 3.75.

(B) If the correlation coefficient were $-.60$, the slope of the regression equation would be approximately $-.07$.

(C) Students who work 40 hours per week have a mean GPA of approximately 1.75.

(D) The value of the correlation coefficient and steepness of the regression line are not related.

(E) All of these are correct statements.

4. Which of the following could be the equation of the regression line shown on the scatterplot?

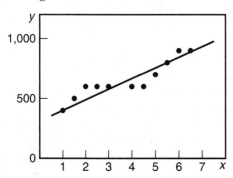

(A) $y = 384.66 - 93.72x$

(B) $y = 93.72 - 384.66x$

(C) $y = -384.66 + 93.72x$

(D) $y = 384.66 + 93.72x$

(E) None of the choices is reasonable.

FREE-RESPONSE QUESTIONS

Open-Ended Questions

Use the height/weight data below for questions 1–6.

Height (inches)	Weight (pounds)
58	95
60	110
62	105
64	120
68	125
68	120
70	135
72	150

1. Construct the scatterplot. Describe the scatterplot in words.

2. Calculate (by formula) the value of r. Interpret the value of r.

3. Calculate (by formula) the coefficients of the regression equation.

4. Plot the regression equation on your scatterplot.

5. Interpret the coefficients of your regression equation in the context of the data.

6. Predict the weight of a person who is 65 inches tall.

7. In each case, provide a verbal interpretation of the slope of the given regression line:

Equation	Units
a. weight = 15.9(length)	weight: grams; length: centimeters
b. length = 90 − 3.2(temperature)	length: centimeters; temperature: °F
c. income = 22.3 + .65(service)	income: $1,000; service: years
d. cost = 5.85 + .35(distance)	cost: dollars; distance: miles
e. score = 40 + 3.24(attempts)	score: %; attempts: integers

8. For each of the equations listed in question 7, give an interpretation of the y-intercept of the equation.

9. Given the following data, answer the questions below.

x	1	2	3	4	5
y	3	4	7	12	20

a. Determine the regression equation. Interpret the slope and y-intercept of the equation.

b. Compute the residual for each value.

c. Find the sum of the residuals. What do you observe?

3.5 Residual Plots, Outliers, and Influential Points

Residual Plots   A very effective tool for testing the goodness of fit of a regression line to a bivariate data set is the **residual plot.** The residual plot displays the scatterplot of the points $(x_i, y_i - \hat{y}_i)$, that is, the set of residuals graphed against their x-values. If the residual plot shows a random dispersion with no apparent pattern, we can be confident that the regression equation does, indeed, fit the data. If, on the other hand, a clear pattern is observed, we can conclude that the regression model does not fit the data.

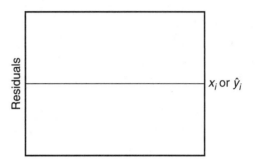

Note: Many books and software tools display residual plots with the "fits" or estimated y-values plotted on the horizontal axis and the residuals plotted on the vertical axis. In multiple linear regression, there may be several independent explanatory variables; therefore a comparison of the residuals to the fits of a linear regression takes into account all of the explanatory variables.

In the case of simple linear regression—a regression with only one explanatory variable—the plot of residuals on x and residuals on fits will display similar shapes depicting similar patterns in the residuals. If the slope of the regression equation is positive, then the two residual plots will be visually the same with only a change on the horizontal scale. If, on the other hand, the slope of the regression equation is negative, then the residual plots will differ only in orientation: the pattern will be the same but it will be reversed. This is true since the fits are a linear transformation (via the regression equation) of the values of x.

EXAMPLE 1

The data shown represent the number of books and the depth of paper (in inches) on ten college students' desks at a randomly chosen time:

Number of books	Inches of paper
1	0.5
3	0
5	3
4	2.5
8	5
5	4.5
5	6
2	3.5
3	5
6	9

We can use the TI-83 to produce the following results.
The scatterplot of the data:

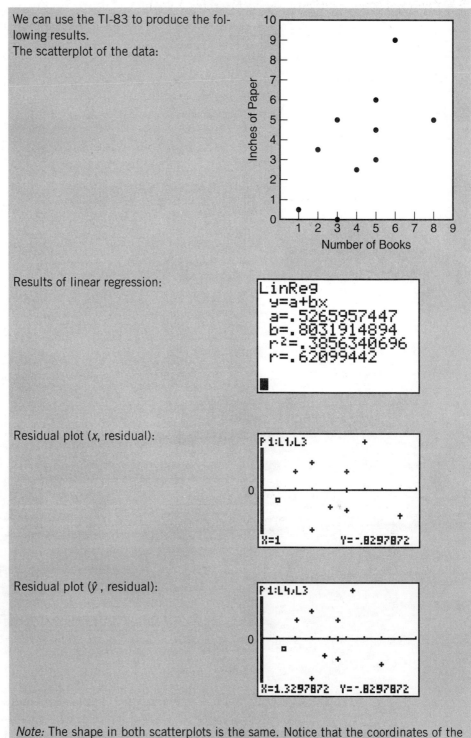

Results of linear regression:

LinReg
y=a+bx
a=.5265957447
b=.8031914894
r²=.3856340696
r=.62099442

Residual plot (*x*, residual):

P1:L1,L3

0

X=1   Y=-.8297872

Residual plot (*ŷ* , residual):

P1:L4,L3

0

X=1.3297872 Y=-.8297872

Note: The shape in both scatterplots is the same. Notice that the coordinates of the highlighted points only differ in their *x*-coordinates.

EXAMPLE 2

Some examples of residual plots with patterns are displayed below:

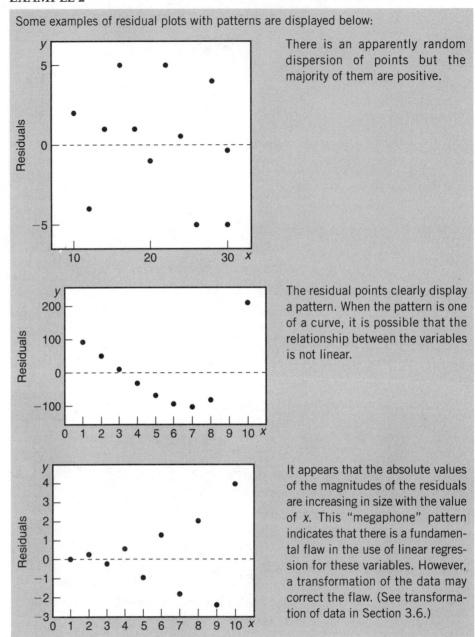

There is an apparently random dispersion of points but the majority of them are positive.

The residual points clearly display a pattern. When the pattern is one of a curve, it is possible that the relationship between the variables is not linear.

It appears that the absolute values of the magnitudes of the residuals are increasing in size with the value of *x*. This "megaphone" pattern indicates that there is a fundamental flaw in the use of linear regression for these variables. However, a transformation of the data may correct the flaw. (See transformation of data in Section 3.6.)

Outliers Recall that in a univariate set, an outlier is defined as a value that is more than 1.5 IQR's above the third quartile or 1.5 IQR's below the first quartile. In bivariate data sets, a data point is considered an outlier only if its residual is an outlier relative to the set of residuals. Consider the data whose scatterplot is shown on the left at the top of the next page. As is displayed in the box plot on the right, both the *x*-coordinate and *y*-coordinate of point A are outliers relative to the set of *x*'s and the set of *y*'s. However, the box plot of the residuals to the displayed regression line reveals that there are no outliers for the residuals from the regression process. As long as the candidate points follow the same pattern as the other points, they may not be outliers.

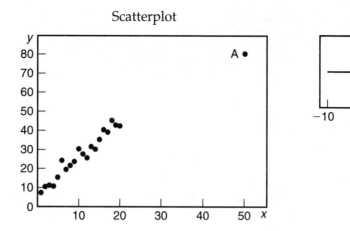

Scatterplot   Box plot

In the figures below, a least squares regression line is fitted to the data in the scatterplot on the left. The sketch on the right is a box plot of the residuals from this regression. Note that there are no outliers for the set of x's nor the set of y's. However, the residual for point A is an outlier in the set of residuals. Consequently, A is considered an outlier for the bivariate set of data.

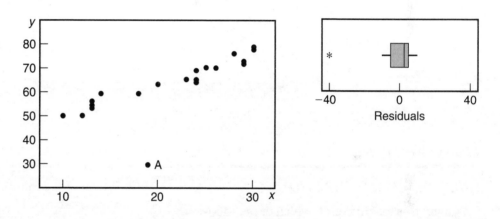

Influential Points   An **influential point** is an observation that has a strong influence on the regression line. Often a point with an x-coordinate that is an extreme value relative to the other x-values turns out to be an influential point.

The existence of an influential point in a regression analysis can be determined by eliminating the candidate point, recalculating the correlation and regression, and comparing the results of the original regression to the regression of the data set with the influential candidate removed.

EXAMPLE 3

In the data set below, point A is an influential point. Consider the scatterplots and the results of the two regressions:

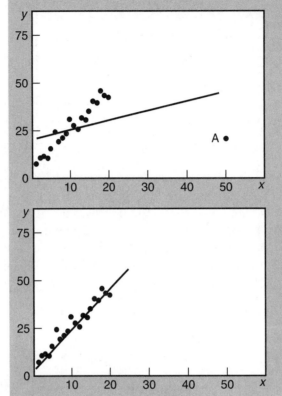

Scatterplot with point A included.

Scatterplot with point A removed.

Based on this analysis, the value (50, 20) is clearly an influential point since its removal changes the regression equation significantly.

Review Exercises

MULTIPLE-CHOICE QUESTIONS

1. Given this residual plot, which of the following is *not* a correct conclusion?

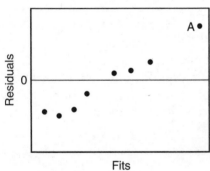

(A) The pattern in the residuals indicates the regression line does not fit the data well.
(B) Point A is a candidate as an outlier.
(C) Point A is a candidate as an influential point.
(D) The relationship between the variables is positive.
(E) All of these are correct.

2. Which of the following residual plots indicates a reasonable fit to a given set of data?

(A)
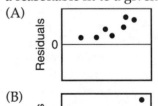

(B)
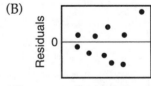

(C)
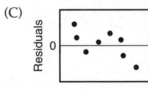

(D)
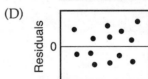

(E) None of these indicates a reasonable fit.

3. Which of the following is a correct conclusion based on the residual plot displayed?

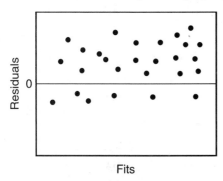

Fits

(A) The line overestimates the data.
(B) The line underestimates the data.
(C) It is not appropriate to fit a line to these data since there is clearly no correlation between the variables.
(D) The data are not related.
(E) None of these choices is correct.

4. Which of the following scatterplots could have this residual plot?

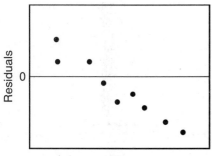

Fits

(A)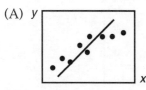

(B)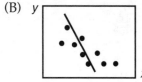

(C)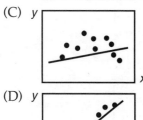

(D)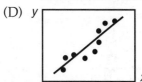

(E) None of these could have a residual plot similar to the given residual plot.

Open-Ended Questions

Use the following data for questions 1–7.

Height	Weight
48	93
50	105
51	102
55	121
60	118
64	135
74	180

1. Construct a scatterplot. Describe its shape.

2. Find the least squares regression line. Interpret its slope.

3. Calculate the residuals and construct the residual plot on the given set of axes.

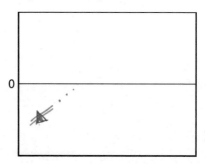

4. Explore the value (74, 180) as a possible outlier.

5. Discuss the goodness of fit of this model.

6. Explore the value (74, 180) as a possible influential point.

7. What does the regression line tell us about the heights and weights in this sample?

8. In a bivariate distribution, must a value that is an outlier also be an influential point? Must an influential point also be an outlier? Explain your answers.

3.6 Transformations to Achieve Linearity

Correlation and least squares linear regression are powerful tools for the analysis and interpretation of bivariate data that are linearly related. In many cases, we can transform nonlinear data and then use our linear regression techniques to develop models and utilize the body of techniques for linear regression. Consider the example below.

The Exponential and Power Models

The table shows the temperature (*Temp*) of an instrument measured as its distance (*Dist*) from a heat source is varied. Although calculation would yield $r = -.894$, the scatterplot shows clearly that the data do not have a linear relationship.

Distance (cm)	Temperature (°F)
1	130
2	105
3	95
4	87
5	83
6	80
7	78
8	77

Scatterplot:

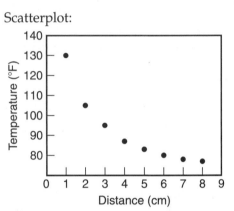

If we perform a linear regression on the set, we produce $\widehat{Temp} = 121.82 - 6.57(Dist)$ with $r = .898$. However, the residual plot displays a clear curved pattern.

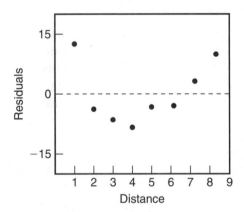

This curved pattern suggests that a transformation may be appropriate.

There are many methods of transforming the data to achieve a more linear relationship. We will describe two methods that lead to either an **exponential model ($y = ab^x$) or a power model ($y = ax^b$).**

EXPONENTIAL $(x_i, y_i) \rightarrow (x_i, \ln y_i)$			POWER $(x_i, y_i) \rightarrow (\ln x_i, \ln y_i)$			
Dist (cm)	Temp (°F)	Ln(Temp)	Dist (cm)	Temp (°F)	Ln (Dist)	Ln (Temp)
1	130	4.86753	1	130	0.00000	4.86753
2	105	4.65396	2	105	0.69315	4.65396
3	95	4.55388	3	95	1.09861	4.55388
4	87	4.46591	4	87	1.38629	4.46591
5	83	4.41884	5	83	1.60944	4.41884
6	80	4.38203	6	80	1.79176	4.38203
7	78	4.35671	7	78	1.94591	4.35671
8	77	4.34381	8	77	2.07944	4.34381

The scatterplots of the transformed data show an improvement in the linearity of the data. Note that the improvement is more substantial for the power transformation. Even so, we will continue both.

Scatterplot (Dist, Ln(Temp))

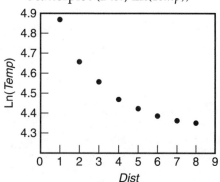

Scatterplot (Ln(Dist), Ln(Temp))

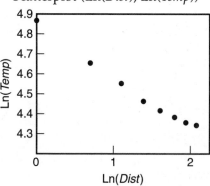

The linear regression analysis for each transformation results in the following equations. Notice how the improved values of r confirm our impression from the scatterplots. *Note:* The calculation of the correlation coefficient uses the *transformed* data that has been "linearized," not the original data. Also, the interpretation of r as a measure of linearity assumes that the variables are linearly related.

Exponential:
$\text{Ln}(Temp) = 4.81 - 0.0680(Dist)$
$(r = -.923; r^2 = .8519$

Calculation of exponential model:
$\text{Ln}(Temp) = 4.81 - 0.0680(Dist)$
$Temp = e^{4.81 - 0680(Dist)}$

$Temp = e^{4.81} \times (e^{-0.0680})^{Dist}$
$Temp = 122.73 \times .9334^{Dist}$

Power:
$\text{Ln}(Temp) = 4.84 - 0.255 \, \text{Ln}(Dist)$
$(r = -.994; r^2 = .9880$

Calculation of the power model:
$\text{Ln}(Temp) = 4.84 - 0.255 \, \text{Ln}(Dist)$
$Temp = e^{4.84 - 0.255 \, \text{Ln}(Dist)}$

$Temp = e^{4.84} \times (e^{\text{Ln}(Dist)})^{-0.255}$
$Temp = 126.47 \times Dist^{-0.255}$

The plots of these models on the scatterplots suggest the goodness of fit of these models. *Note:* The linear regression produces a linear equation relating *Dist* and Ln(*Temp*). This equation needs to be transformed back into a model relating *Dist* and *Temp*.

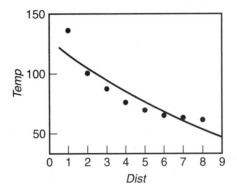
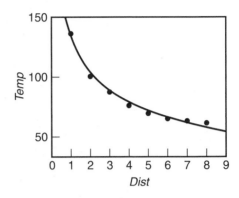

The residual plots must be viewed before we complete the analyses of these models. Remember that residuals are essentially the prediction errors of your fit.

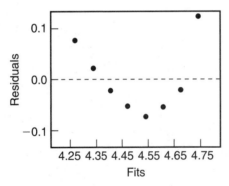
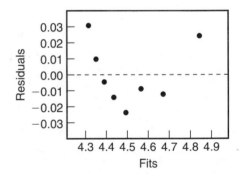

Even though the residual plots have improved, they still display a great deal of pattern. It is worthy of note that the size of the residuals in the power transformation appears to be much less than that of the exponential model.

Technology Note: When exponential and power regressions are performed on the TI-83 calculator, the calculator returns a value for both r^2 and r. This reinforces the fact that the regression is performed by linearizing the data using the techniques listed above. When the TI-83 performs any of the polynomial regressions, it returns only the value R^2. This fact, including the fact that it returns an upper-case R^2, indicates that some strategy other than linearization was employed to complete the regression. In both cases, the coefficient of determination, r^2 or R^2, indicates the percentage of the variation in the response variable that is accounted for by the regression model. For example, if the regression model of height predicting weight has an r^2 value of 84%, we can conclude that 84% of the variation between weight and height is accounted for by the model. In addition, we can conclude that 16% of the variation is not accounted for in the model and is due either to chance variation or some other variable. ■

Other Transformations to Achieve Linearity

There are a great number of other transformations that can be applied to non-linear data. Below are listed some of the more common techniques and the data situations that might suggest them:

Intuitive curve of best fit	Example scatterplot	Suggested transformation
Contains (0, 0) and appears to be a power curve, or a curve asymptotic to both horizontal and vertical axes.		$(x_i, y_i) \rightarrow (\ln x_i, \ln y_i)$ $x_i > 0$ $y_i > 0$
Contains a nonzero y-intercept and appears exponential (either growth or decay).		$(x_i, y_i) \rightarrow (x_i, \ln y_i)$ $y_i > 0$
Contains (0, 0) and appears logarithmic.		$(x_i, y_i) \rightarrow (\sqrt{x_i}, y_i)$ $x_i \geq 0$
Contains a nonzero y-intercept and appears logarithmic.		$(x_i, y_i) \rightarrow (\ln x_i, y_i)$ $x_i > 0$
Has nonzero horizontal and vertical asymptotes.		$(x_i, y_i) \rightarrow \left(\dfrac{1}{x_i}, \dfrac{1}{y_i}\right)$ $x_i \neq 0$ $y_i \neq 0$

The test of the appropriateness of any transformation should include inspection of the scatterplots, the values of r and R^2, and the residual plots of both the original and transformed data.

Other Techniques   You should be aware of other techniques for fitting models to data. While many are not within the AP Statistics syllabus, they are readily available through technology:

Polynomial Regression

1. Quadratic: $\hat{y} = ax^2 + bx + c$
2. Cubic: $\hat{y} = ax^3 + bx^2 + cx + d$
3. Quartic: $\hat{y} = ax^4 + bx^3 + cx^2 + d$

Polynomial regression is not accomplished using a linearizing technique. Choice of a polynomial model should be made via inspection of the scatterplot. Verifying the goodness of fit should be accomplished by considering the R^2 value produced (there is no r value) and the plots of residuals against fits.

Splitting Techniques

Sometimes we can fit a "split" or "piecewise" model to a scatterplot.

EXAMPLE 2

The following data list the temperature readings (in degrees Fahrenheit) at different settings on a thermostat for an experimental cooling container.

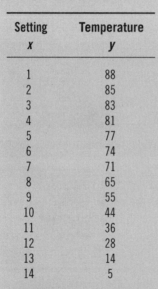

Setting	Temperature
x	y
1	88
2	85
3	83
4	81
5	77
6	74
7	71
8	65
9	55
10	44
11	36
12	28
13	14
14	5

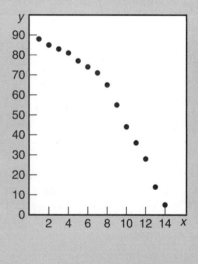

The regression information for the entire set is $\hat{y} = 1.05 - 6.37x$, with $r^2 = .928$. The pattern seems to change at $x = 7$, so consider splitting the data set and performing two regressions.

a.

x	1	2	3	4	5	6	7
y	88	85	83	81	77	74	71

$\hat{y} = 91.14 - 2.82x$ $r = .991$

b.

x	8	9	10	11	12	13	14
y	65	55	44	36	28	14	5

$\hat{y} = 140.5 - 9.60x$ $r = .995$

Therefore, a candidate for a better model is:

$$\hat{y} = \begin{cases} 91.14 - 2.28x & x \le 7 \\ 144.5 - 9.93x & x > 7 \end{cases}$$

Review Exercises

MULTIPLE-CHOICE QUESTIONS

1. A simple random sample of years and earnings was organized into pairs (time in years, earnings in $1,000's). The scatterplot appears exponential and the transformation $(x_i, y_i) \rightarrow (x_i, \ln y_i)$ is applied to the data. A TI calculator yields the linear regression equation $y = a + bx$ where $a = .3079$, $b = .464$, and $r^2 = .922$.
   Which of the following is a valid conclusion?
   (A) The earnings gained after 12 years are approximately 5.8759.
   (B) The earnings gained after 12 years are approximately 356.345.
   (C) The earnings will increase by .464 thousand dollars each year.
   (D) The original investment was $307.90.
   (E) None of these is valid.

2. Which of the following is *not* a reasonable choice of techniques to attempt to achieve linearity for this scatterplot of data?

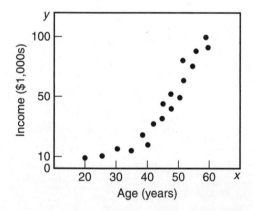

   (A) $(x_i, y_i) \rightarrow (x_i, \ln y_i)$; linear regression
   (B) $(x_i, y_i) \rightarrow (x_i, \sqrt{y_i})$; linear regression
   (C) $(x_i, y_i) \rightarrow (\ln x_i, \ln y_i)$; linear regression
   (D) Perform two linear regressions: (1) domain [20, 40] and (2) domain [40, 60].
   (E) All of these are reasonable techniques.

FREE-RESPONSE QUESTIONS

Open-Ended Questions

Complete a regression analysis for the following age and income data as indicated.

Age (years)	20	25	30	35	40	45	50	55	60
Income ($1,000)	18.5	23.6	29.8	38.5	49.0	64.1	78.5	102.0	130.8

1. Construct and label a scatterplot of the data.

2. Perform a linear regression on the data; plot the regression line on the scatterplot.

3. Discuss the goodness of fit of the linear regression referencing the correlation coefficient and its residual plot.

4. Perform the following transformations: exponential and power.

5. Perform the linear regression on both sets of transformed data.

6. Discuss the goodness of fit of these linear regressions referencing the correlation coefficients and each of their residual plots.

7. Transform the linear models into the exponential and power models and plot each on the original scatterplot.

8. Comment on which of the three regression models fits the data the best. Explain your answer.

3.7 Exploring Categorical Data

Frequency Tables

Categorical data are generally summarized using frequency tables. For univariate data, these tables indicate the names of the categories and the frequency for each category. Graphs of univariate categorical data include bar graphs and circle (pie) graphs. *Note:* A bar graph is not the same as a histogram. In a bar graph, each category of information is separate from the other categories.

EXAMPLE 1

Consider the frequency table of hair color in a high school statistics class and the representative graphs.

Color	Frequency	Percent
Brown	8	38%
Black	2	10%
Blonde	6	29%
Red	2	10%
Other	3	14%
Total	21	101.00%

Note that the sum of the percentages does not equal 100% due to rounding.

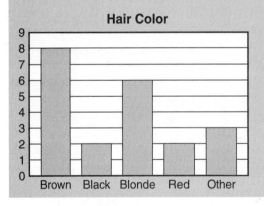

Technology Note: Univariate categorical data can be organized, summarized, and displayed using computer spreadsheets and statistical software packages. In addition, calculation of the percentages of the frequencies in each category is quite simple using a spreadsheet. ∎

Bivariate categorical data can be summarized efficiently using a *two-way frequency table*. Two-way tables are generally described by stating the number of rows "by" the number of columns; for example, a 3 × 2 table has 3 rows and 2 columns. This type of table can then be analyzed to determine if a relationship exists between the variables.

EXAMPLE 2

A study that gathered data about gender and interest in cooking resulted in the following information:

Interest in cooking	Gender	
	Males	Females
High	10	12
Medium	10	8
Low	5	3

In this case, interest in cooking is the *row variable* and gender is the *column variable*. One technique for analyzing this type of table is to include another row and column which contain the *marginal frequencies* of their respective rows and columns:

Interest in cooking	Gender		Totals
	Males	Females	
High	10	12	22
Medium	10	8	18
Low	5	3	8
Totals	25	23	48

In order to measure the relationship between two categorical variables, we calculate *conditional percentages*. For example:

What is the percent of males in the high interest group? $\frac{10}{22}$ = 45.5%

What is the percent of males in the medium interest group? $\frac{10}{18}$ = 55%

What is the percent of females in the medium interest group? $\frac{8}{18}$ = 44.4%

Based on this study, we might predict that in a group of people with a high interest in cooking, about 45.5% would be males. Relationships can be investigated by comparing conditional percentages. For example, the conditional percentage of high interest given males is $\frac{10}{25}$ = 40%, while the conditional percentage of high interest given females is $\frac{12}{23}$ ≈ 52%.

Segmented Bar Graphs   Constructing a **segmented bar graph** allows us to begin the investigation of the existence of a relationship between the two categorical variables. Segmented bar graphs are sometimes called stacked bar graphs.

EXAMPLE 3

The segmented bar graph for the data above is:

This graph is a visual display of the conditional percentages. In our example, it appears that interest in cooking is related to gender. The existence of such a relationship will be discussed in detail later.

Technology Note: Most popular spreadsheet programs such as Microsoft Excel® create excellent segmented bar graphs. ■

Simpson's Paradox You should exercise great care when combining two sets of categorical data into a combined set of categorical data. At times, the direction of relationship between the variables can be reversed in the combination.

EXAMPLE 4

Consider the survival rates for two types of patients at two competing hospitals, as given in the chart below.

| | Good Condition | | Poor Condition | |
	Hospital A	Hospital B	Hospital A	Hospital B
Died	11	12	38	6
Survived	489	488	1,262	194
Totals	500	500	1,300	200

The corresponding percents of each category are:

| | Good Condition | | Poor Condition | |
	Hospital A	Hospital B	Hospital A	Hospital B
Died	2.2%	2.4%	2.9%	3.0%
Survived	97.8%	97.6%	97.1%	97.0%

Hospital A has a lower percent of death for both categories of Good Condition and Poor Condition. However, if we combine the frequencies into an aggregate set of data and calculate the percents, we see

	Hospital A	Hospital B
Died	49 (2.7%)	18 (2.6%)
Survived	1,756	683
Totals	1,800	700

Even though Hospital A has a lower death rate for both categories of patients, the death rate of the combined data for Hospital A is larger than that for Hospital B. The cause of this reversal of relationship is the existence of a **confounding influence**. A confounding influence is a factor that makes the measurement of the effect on the variable of interest very difficult. In this case, the confounding influence is the condition of the patient relative to the hospital that the patient chooses. That is, the majority of patients in poor condition choose Hospital A.

Review Exercises

FREE-RESPONSE QUESTIONS

Open-Ended Questions

Use the following frequency table for questions 1–4.

Income Range	Frequencies
$0 – $15,000	5
$15,000 – $30,000	12
$30,000 – $50,000	26
$50,000 – $100,000	16
over $100,000	2

1. Construct appropriate bar and pie graphs. Comment on the main features of your plots.

2. If middle class is defined as people whose income ranges from $15,000 to $50,000, what percent of the data would be considered middle class?

3. Does the fact that the income ranges do not have the same width cause a problem with either the graphs or the analysis of these data?

4. Is it possible to calculate the average income of the persons represented in this frequency table? Explain your answer.

Use the following two-way frequency table for questions 5–9.

Age Groups	Localities of Residence		
	Urban	Suburban	Rural
under 25	110	150	65
25 – 50	240	220	75
over 50	53	112	58

5. Compute the marginal frequencies.

6. Draw a segmented bar graph.

7. What percent of the urban dwellers are over 50?

8. What percent of the over-50 residents live in rural areas?

9. Based on your analyses, do you believe that these data indicate that there is a relationship between locality of residence and the ages of the residents? Explain your answer.

10. Complete the total and batting average columns for each set of data comparing two baseball hitters who were on the same college team for four years:

FIRST TWO YEARS

Player	Hits	At Bats	Batting Average
A	40	100	
B	120	400	

SECOND TWO YEARS

Player	Hits	At Bats	Batting Average
A	80	400	
B	10	100	

ALL FOUR YEARS

Player	Hits	At Bats	Batting Average
A	120	500	
B	130	500	

Explain the paradox.

Chapter 3 Assessment

MULTIPLE-CHOICE QUESTIONS

1. Which of the following displays is best suited for categorical data?
   (A) box plot
   (B) bar graph
   (C) stem and leaf plot
   (D) dot plot
   (E) scatterplot

2. A bivariate set of data relates the amount of annual salary raise and previous performance rating. The least squares regression equation is

   $$\hat{y} = 1{,}400 + 2{,}000x$$

   where $\hat{y}$ is the estimated raise and x is the performance rating.
   Which of the following statements is *not* correct?
   (A) For each increase of one point in performance rating, the raise will increase on average by $2,000.
   (B) This equation produces predicted raises with an average error of 0.
   (C) A rating of 0 will yield a predicted raise of $1,400.
   (D) The correlation coefficient of the data is positive.
   (E) All of the above are true.

Use the following data for questions 3 and 4.

   A computer printout of a linear regression predicting INCOME based on years of EDUCATION contained

   ```
   β̂₀ = -92040        s = 3213        t = 6.67
   β̂₁ = 228           R² = .66        df = 23
   ```

3. Which of the following is a correct interpretation of $\hat{\beta}_0$?
   (A) We expect to predict INCOME to within 2(92,040) of its true value using the equation.
   (B) We estimate INCOME to decrease $92,040 for every 1 year of increase in EDUCATION.
   (C) We estimate the lowest INCOME of the highest value of EDUCATION of –$92,040.
   (D) The value is highly suspicious depending on whether the years of EDUCATION of 0 is possible and reasonable.
   (E) None of the choices is correct.

4. Which of the following statements is *not* correct?
   (A) The correlation coefficient is approximately .81.
   (B) R^2 is a measure of the direction of the relationship between INCOME and EDUCATION.
   (C) The slope of the regression line is 228.
   (D) It cannot be determined from the information in the printout which quantity is the independent variable.
   (E) All of these are correct.

5. Linear regression usually employs the method of least squares. Which of the following is the quantity that is minimized by the least squares process?
   (A) $\hat{y}_i$
   (B) $x_i - \bar{x}_i$
   (C) $\sum (y_i - \hat{y}_i)^2$
   (D) $(\bar{x}_i, \bar{y}_i)$
   (E) $\sum (\bar{x}_i - \bar{x}_i)^2$

6. Which of the following is *not* true?
   (A) Two sets of data can have the same means but different variances.
   (B) Two sets of data can have the same variances but different means.
   (C) Two different values in a data set can have the same z-score.
   (D) All of the absolute values of z-scores for a data set can be equal.
   (E) All of the above are true.

FREE-RESPONSE QUESTIONS

Open-Ended Questions

Use the following frequency table for questions 1–3.

Score	1	2	3	4	5	6	7	8	9
Frequency	1	11	15	21	35	22	19	10	5

1. Construct a box plot of these data. Comment on the main features of the plot.

2. Calculate the mean and standard deviation of the data.

3. Assuming that all of the values of the scores are integers, what kind of plot would be most appropriate? What kind of plot would be least appropriate? Explain your answers.

4. In a symmetric, mound-shaped distribution, what percentile has a z-score of
   a. 1
   b. −2

5. A symmetric, mound-shaped distribution has a mean of 70 and a standard deviation of 10.
   a. Find the 16th percentile score.
   b. Find the 95th percentile score.

6. The average grade on a math test given to two class sections is 60.98. Section 1 has 27 students with a mean grade of 57.30. If the mean grade of Section 2 is 65.30, how many students are in Section 2?

7. Does the following problem have a unique solution? If so, find it. If not, show how this is possible and find at least two answers.
   A set of five data values has these properties: $Q_1 = 12$, median $= 15$, $Q_3 = 18$. Find the mean of the data set.

Use the following information for questions 8–11.

The average price per dozen received by farmers for eggs has varied as shown:

Year	Cents/Dozen
1985	57.1
1986	61.6
1987	54.9
1988	52.8
1989	68.9
1990	70.9
1991	67.8
1992	57.6
1993	63.4
1994	61.4

8. Find the equation of the best-fitting line. (Use the last two digits of the year as the independent variable.)

9. Do you think this equation will be useful in predicting egg prices for years after 1994? Explain.

10. Use the equation to predict the price for 1995. Compare with the actual price of 64.0 cents/dozen. Discuss the results in relation to your answer to question 9.

11. Including the actual 1995 price, find a new equation of the best fitting line. Comment on how the new data point affects the fit.

12. Lee's z-score on his math test was 1.5. The class average was 62.1 and the variance was 6.76. What was Lee's "raw" score (his score before converting to z-scores)?

13. The following table gives the estimated marginal cost (the cost of producing one additional unit at any level of production) for a piece of furniture.

Units	100	200	300	400	500	600
Marginal Cost	$300	$250	$220	$200	$180	$175

   a. Determine the regression equation that predicts marginal cost from production.
   b. Calculate the marginal cost if 450 units are produced.
   c. Calculate the marginal cost if 800 units are produced.
   d. Discuss the reliability of the predictions in parts b. and c.

14. The following table gives the verbal and math SAT scores for a group of students.

Verbal	Math
565	558
495	511
720	303
498	496
590	600
557	565
410	714
501	491
583	575
526	506
494	594
480	474

a. Construct the scatterplot.

b. Determine the regression equation to predict the math score based on the verbal score.

c. Use the equation to predict the math score of a student with a verbal score of 602.

d. Comment on any outliers or influential points.

e. Discuss the value of the regression equation as a predictor of math scores and any limitations of the model.

Investigative Tasks

1. The table below details the number of units completed in a manufacturing plant over a three-week period (5 working days per week).

Day	1	2	3	4	5	6	7	8	9	10	11	12	13	14	15
Units	10	15	13	10	15	16	18	16	13	20	16	18	18	21	20

a. Construct a scatterplot that displays the number of completed units as a function of time.

b. Draw a histogram of the frequencies of completed units.

c. If you were asked to predict the number of units completed on the 23rd day, which plot would you use to answer the question? Explain the reasons for your choice, detailing why you chose this plot and rejected the other one.

d. Find the equation of the least squares regression line for this data.

e. Draw the residual plot and calculate the value of R^2.

f. Based on your answers to part e., discuss the goodness of fit of your regression line to predict the number of completed units as a function of time.

2. Answer each of the following questions regarding this table of data that details the percentage of rotten apples in a case of fruit based on the number of days of transport to the retail store. These data are from a simple random sample of cases of apples from randomly selected apple farms in Wisconsin.

Days	1	2	3	4	5	6
% rotten	5.1	6.9	7.9	12.3	16.5	21.0

a. Construct a scatterplot of the data. Describe what the plot tells you about the data.

b. Calculate the equation of the least squares regression line.

c. Comment on the goodness of fit of this line referencing both the residual plot and the value of R^2.

d. Choose and execute an appropriate transformation for the data. Show a table of the transformed data clearly indicating the transformation that was applied to the original set.

e. Calculate the least squares regression line for the transformed data.

f. Compare the goodness of fit of this regression line to the original regression line. Make and defend a conclusion as to which regression is more accurate.

Chapter 4 Planning a Study
Deciding What and How to Measure

4.1 Basic Terminology and Census

4.2 Sampling

4.3 Controlled Experiments

4.4 Observational Studies

Chapter 4 Assessment

Chapter 4 Planning a Study
Deciding What and How to Measure

Careful data collection procedures are a very important component of the statistical process. Such procedures are mandatory if the data are to lead the investigator to valid conclusions about the nature of the population from which the data are collected or about the relationships between the variables being examined. In this chapter, we will examine four major types of data collection strategies:

- Census
- Sample Survey
- Controlled Experiment
- Observational Study

4.1 Basic Terminology and Census

The entire collection of objects you are interested in is called a **population.** Statistical measures that are computed regarding the characteristics of a population are called **parameters.** Parameters are often represented by Greek letters, such as μ, σ, θ. A **sample** is a subset of the population; statistical measures calculated about a sample are called **statistics.** Statistics are represented by letters of the English alphabet with some notation added at times, such as $\bar{x}$, s, $\hat{p}$.

A **census** is a method of data collection in which *all* of the members of a population are included in the study. For example, the vote for class officers in a high school constitutes a census if all of the eligible students participate in the election. The U.S. Census Bureau is the office of the federal government that is charged with carrying out a complete census of the entire population of the United States at the beginning of each decade. This mandate is included in the U.S. Constitution since accurate population counts are used for the determination of important issues such as the number of representatives that each district has in the Congress, as well as the amount of federal assistance that localities may receive.

In recent years, the completion of the U.S. Census has become more complicated due to the mobility of the society in which we live and the growing number of citizens for whom the Census Bureau does not have information. Issues of the homeless and other social situations make it extremely difficult for the agents of the Census Bureau to include all members of the population in the study. For this reason, there has been a great deal of debate about using sampling methods instead of a census.

A census is a very complex, time-consuming, and expensive project. These factors have motivated a substantial amount of statistical research regarding the second strategy of data collection: the sample survey.

Review Exercises

MULTIPLE-CHOICE QUESTIONS

1. Which of the following is an example of a census?
   (A) Every fifth person leaving a supermarket is asked to name his or her favorite brand of peanut butter.
   (B) Each employee in a corporation fills out a questionnaire for a management survey.
   (C) All the students who are at a school on a particular day rate the food in the cafeteria.
   (D) A telephone political poll selects ten names from every page of a city directory.
   (E) All the commuters who are dissatisfied with the service of their commuter train company are asked to write a letter of complaint.

2. Which of the following are true statements?
   I.   Data gathered from a census is always reliable.
   II. For many studies, a census is too costly and difficult to implement.
   III. The U. S. Census cannot be considered a complete enumeration of the population.
   (A) I and II
   (B) I and III
   (C) II and III
   (D) All statements are true.
   (E) None of the statements is true.

3. A sample survey of the opinions of the engineers of a small corporation is conducted. The results of the sample indicate that the average salary is $45,987 and 60% have advanced degrees in either business or engineering. Which of the following statements are true?

   I.   The average salary and the proportion of those with advanced degrees are statistics.
   II. The population of interest is all of the engineers in the industry.
   III. The results of the sample should be represented by symbols such as $\bar{x}$ and $\hat{p}$.
   (A) I and II
   (B) I and III
   (C) II and III
   (D) All statements are true.
   (E) None of the statements is true.

4. A census of all doctors who are attending a medical convention indicated that 35% of them employ physician's assistants in their practice. Which of the following statements is *not* true based on this information?
   (A) The population of interest is the doctors who attended the convention.
   (B) 35% is a valid statistic from this study.
   (C) Sample size is not an issue in this study.
   (D) The usefulness of using this proportion to infer information about all doctors is very debatable.
   (E) All of these statements are true.

FREE-RESPONSE QUESTION

Open-Ended Question

Describe how a census of your school's student body could be carried out. Discuss some of the problems that would be encountered in a school setting.

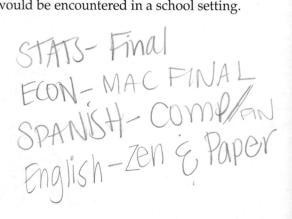

Generally, a statistical study focuses on one or more characteristics of an entire population. When it is not possible to contact the entire population, we can often draw conclusions about the entire population by considering a sample of the population. The process of drawing conclusions about the nature of the entire population based on the data from a sample is called **statistical inference** and is the basis for the usefulness of statistics in the modern world.

Graphically,

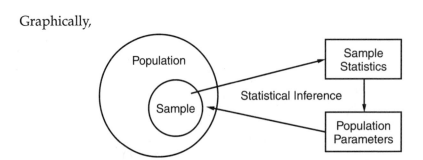

A sample of the population is taken. Statistics are computed from the sample. Population parameters are then *inferred* or *estimated* based on the sample statistics. These parameters are then used to characterize features of the population.

The question of greatest interest is how accurately will the sample statistics estimate the actual population parameters? In many cases, the answer to this question begins with the *design* of the sampling process itself.

Sample Design and Bias

Sample design refers to the technique employed to select a subset of participants from the population and gather the data from the population. This review will consider sample design in the context of surveys. Below are listed four types of sample designs with commentary:

Voluntary Response

This is a very common design employed particularly in opinion surveys. In this design, a general appeal is made for responses to one or more questions. Members of the population decide for themselves whether or not to respond. For example, a radio show might invite listeners to call in their opinions about a controversial issue. It is likely that only very motivated listeners will respond.

Convenience Sampling

In this design, members of the population are chosen based on the convenience of including them. For example, if we were doing a study about the buying habits of suburban food shoppers, we might collect a convenience sample by asking our questions of the first 100 people who come to the store on a chosen Saturday morning.

Quota Sampling

In this procedure, interviewers are assigned to interview a fixed quota of members of the population. The quotas are organized around categories such as race, gender, residence, or economic status; in many cases, the quotas are set to match known or assumed demographic information about the population.

Simple Random Sample (SRS)

There are several important features of a simple random sample:

- In simplest terms, an SRS involves selecting individuals at random from the population *without replacement*.
- In an SRS, a sample of size n is to be chosen from the population, where *every* population subset of size n has an equal chance of being selected.
- In particular, *every* member of the population has an equal chance of being included in the sample.

EXAMPLE 1

The owner of a club with 1,000 members wants to survey 50 members about the friendliness of the staff. What type of sampling does each of the following methods represent?

1. Ask the first 50 members who enter the club one morning.
2. Leave a stack of response cards by the sign-in desk with a sign asking members to participate.
3. Put each name on a single slip of paper. Place all of the slips in a hat and mix well. Draw one slip out and note the name. Continue picking and noting the names until 50 different names are selected.

Solution

Method 1 represents a convenience sample.
Method 2 represents a voluntary response sample.
Method 3 is an example of a simple random sample. The selection process is random and every member (and every sample of size 50) has an equal chance of being chosen.

The first three sampling techniques listed above are flawed because they may be *biased*. **Bias** is a systematic *error* that favors a particular segment of the population or that tends to encourage only certain outcomes in the data. The voluntary response survey above clearly represents the view of only those members of the population who were motivated to respond. Volunteers typically feel more strongly, often negatively, about an issue. Similarly, the convenience sample only includes members of the population that happened to be conveniently available at the time of the survey. It is likely that the first 100 shoppers on a Saturday differ from the rest of the population of shoppers. The major flaw in quota sampling is that the interviewer has the choice of who is interviewed within the constraints of the quotas that have been set. Selection of participants by human choice is always susceptible to bias. A classic episode that demonstrated the problem with this method occurred when three polls using quota sampling wrongly predicted that Thomas Dewey would win the 1948 presidential election against Harry Truman.

The simple random sample, on the other hand, eliminates selection bias since all subsets of a given size have the same chance of being selected from the population.

EXAMPLE 2

Suppose the speaker at a seminar wants to survey 15 of the 100 participants to determine which aspects of the seminar they liked most. What method could be used to pick a sample?

Solution

The participants can be coded by assigning numbers 00, 01, 02, ..., 99. We choose 00 to 99 rather than 1 to 100 so that all random numbers identified will need to be 2-digit numbers.

Using a random number table or technology, the speaker reads two digits at a time, ignoring repeats and stopping when the group of 15 has been selected. For example, the table might show the following numbers:

28817 01368 37811 48461 81231
18420 50809 54298 46634

The participants chosen would be those with numbers 28, 81, 70, 13, 68, 37, 14, 84, 61, 23, 11, 20, 50, 80, and 95 with the duplicate occurrences of 81 and 84 being ignored.

Note that if there were only 80 members, we would code the names from 00 to 79 and ignore any 2-digit number from the table or calculator that is not within this range.

How-To Tips:

An SRS is conducted as follows: Assign each member of the population a code number. Select code numbers using a method that guarantees the randomness of the selection. This goal of randomness can be achieved by several methods:

1. For small sample sizes, you can roll a die, deal cards from a deck of 52, pick numbers out of a hat, etc.
2. Use tables of random digits.
3. Use random numbers generated with technology.

Technology Note: All statistical computer packages and many graphing calculators now include random number generators. Their capabilities range from a simple *rand* command that generates a random number between 0 and 1 through capabilities that generate random numbers that come from specific distributions that will be discussed later. The use of random digit tables has significantly decreased with the advent of technological sources of random numbers.

Using a TI-83, the command RAND INT(0,99,15) will choose 15 random numbers from 0 to 99. However, duplicates may occur in the resulting list. Therefore, if a specific number of distinct random numbers is desired (for example, 15), it may be better to choose more than 15, say 20 values, using RAND INT(0,99,20), and choose the first 15 distinct values. ∎

Alternative Probability Sampling Methods

Simple random samples are generally inconvenient and expensive to conduct, particularly when one is dealing with large populations. Below are listed three other acceptable methods of sampling that use probability in their selection processes:

Stratified Random Sample

If a population has distinct groups, it is possible to divide the population into these groups and to draw SRS's from each of the groups. The groups are called **strata**. Strata are designed so that members in each strata are more homogeneous, that is, more similar to each other. The results of all of the SRS's are then grouped together to form the sample. This technique is particularly useful in populations that can be stratified into groups by gender, race, or geography (such as urban, rural, and suburban) when the researcher wants to ensure representation from each group.

Multi-stage Cluster Sample

This type of sampling is used extensively by companies such as Harris and Gallup to select random samples. The process, as applied to a survey of opinion in the political arena, is to

1. take a random sample of the counties in the United States;
2. from the set of selected counties, take a random sample of the towns within those counties;
3. from the set of selected towns, take a random sample of the neighborhoods in those towns;
4. from the set of selected neighborhoods, take a random sample of the households within those neighborhoods.

At each *stage,* a random sample is conducted within a *cluster.* While this multi-stage technique sounds very complicated, it is actually quite efficient and cost-effective. For example, it is much less expensive and more efficient to interview 20 people on one block than to interview 1 person on each of 20 different blocks throughout the country. We emphasize that the techniques employed to analyze the results of a multi-stage random sample differ substantially from those that are employed for simple random samples. Often we will consider our sample to be approximately equivalent to a simple random sample so that we may use the simple random sample techniques.

Systematic Sample

This method of sampling begins with the listing of the population. Then a decision is made as to a systematic way of choosing members. For example, if it is decided to sample 1 of every 50, the investigator would randomly select one of the first 50 and then continue selecting every 50th member from that point on. In this way, if member #12 was randomly selected first, then members #62, #112, #162, and so on would be selected. For systematic sampling to be valid, the investigator must make sure that the ordering principle is not connected to the nature of the population. For example, if we are studying the use of public transportation, then choosing a 1 in 7 systematic sample from days of the week will guarantee that data from only one day will be collected and will not represent the usage on all days of the week.

Valid probability methods of sampling have two critical characteristics:

1. The interviewers and subjects themselves are not choosing the subject who is interviewed;
2. There is a definite procedure for selecting participants in the sample and that procedure involves the use of probability.

For a method to be valid, it is not necessary that each member of the population have the same chance of being selected, but only that it be possible to calculate the probability that a particular member is selected. For example, if the first stage of a multi-stage cluster sample selects 20 of 50 regions of the country the probability of selection in this stage is $\frac{20}{50}$. However, if a particular member is not selected in the first stage of a multi-stage cluster sample, the probability of that member being in the final stage of the sample is zero. Therefore, the probability of a specific member being selected can be calculated at each stage.

As we stated earlier, one of the requirements of an SRS is that each subset of a given size have the same probability of being chosen from the population. We further stated that this implies that each member has the same probability of being selected.

EXAMPLE 3

Return to the situation in Example 1:

The owner of a club with 1,000 members wants to survey 50 members about the friendliness of the staff. Consider this sampling strategy:

Code every name on the membership list using the numbers 1 to 20 repeatedly. Write the numbers from 1 to 20 on slips of paper, put them in a hat and mix well, and draw out one number. Question each of the 50 members with that number.

This is a systematic sample. Each of the 20 subsets of 50 members created by this method has the same probability of being selected: $\frac{1}{20}$. However, a subset of 50 members containing 2 or more members numbered between 1 and 20 has a probability of selection of 0. For example, two persons numbered 10 and 11 in the first subset of 20 cannot both be in the sample. This fact exemplifies how simple random samples and systematic samples differ, even though both can be valid methods.

EXAMPLE 4

Consider a stratified sampling design in which 10 men and 10 women are to be selected randomly from sets of 100 men and 200 women. The probability that any particular man is selected is $\frac{10}{100}$ while the probability that any particular woman is selected is $\frac{10}{200}$. Again, the probabilities of selection of a man or a woman are not the same but the sampling design is valid.

The use of random sampling, that is, using a probability model in the selection process of sample units, is essential to allow us to generalize the results of the sample to the entire population.

There are many potential sources of bias that should be considered in the design of a survey. Bias can arise in several ways:

Sampling Frame

A **sampling frame** is the list of possible subjects who could be selected in a sample. If the sampling frame is not equal to the population, the sample will be biased in the way the sampling frame is biased. For example, in 1936 the *Literary Digest* magazine conducted a huge sample of voters to determine the outcome of the presidential election between Roosevelt and Landon. The sampling frame for the study included phone books and auto registration records. The results of the sample were completely opposite from the outcome of the actual election since the sampling frame was biased primarily in favor of Republicans, who tended to be wealthier and who were in favor of Landon.

Response Bias

The answers to survey questions can be biased by a variety of influences.

1. The wording of the questions: For example, in a survey of attitudes regarding capital punishment, questions similar to "Agree or disagree: the taking of a human life can never be condoned." may tend to motivate a positive response.
2. The order of choices: It is generally accepted that the option listed first tends to receive a greater number of selections. For example, surveys dealing with preference of candidates should have different forms that incorporate different orders of listing. This concern can also be seen in disagreements as to the

listing of candidates on the ballot for the election itself.

3. The demeanor and/or appearance of the interviewer: In large surveying projects, efforts are made to guarantee that all interviewers are following the same instructions. This can be checked by including similar questions on the survey and analyzing responses for internal consistency. In addition, a small percentage of the survey participants are re-interviewed by administrative staff.

4. Honesty: All surveys are founded on the assumption that the participants will answers the questions truthfully to the best of their abilities. Efforts are made to ensure that the participants feel sufficiently secure during the interview to provide honest answers. For example, guaranteeing confidentiality to respondents may stimulate honest responses. Even if truthfulness could be guaranteed in the interview process, however, people have a tendency to change their minds.

Great care must be exercised to standardize the interviewing process so that it is as consistent and uniform as possible.

Non-response Bias
When members of the population are chosen but cannot be contacted to participate, non-response bias may occur. This is true since non-respondents tend to differ from those who are readily available. Efforts are made to reduce non-response as much as possible. For example, some telephone surveys are programmed to call back as many as 15 times in order to contact a chosen participant and increase response.

Household Bias
Since most professional pollsters only interview one member of each household, there is a possibility that people who live in large households are under-represented in the sample. One device to counteract this possibility is to grant greater weight to the respondent's answers depending on the size of the household.

Sampling errors can be summarized in three categories:

Random Sampling Error
Error that occurs because of chance variation.

Sampling Method Error
Error that occurs because of the choice of sampling method. For example, the choice of a convenience sample would constitute a Sampling Method Error.

Non-sampling Method Error
Error that occurs in the responses by members in the sample. For example, dishonest responses will create error in the sample results even though a probability sample is selected.

Errors that occur due to chance variation can be quantified and accounted for. The others involve bias and therefore cannot readily be taken care of after the sample is selected.

Review Exercises

MULTIPLE-CHOICE QUESTIONS

1. A marketing company offers to pay $25 to the first 100 persons who respond to their advertisement and complete a questionnaire regarding displays of their client's product. This situation is an example of which of the following?
   (A) simple random sample
   (B) convenience sample
   (C) voluntary response sample
   (D) multistage cluster sample
   (E) None of these.

2. A simple random sample was selected of large urban school districts throughout New England. The selected districts were identified as target districts. Within each district, a simple random sample of its high schools was chosen and the principals of those high schools were interviewed. Which of the following statements regarding this design is *not* true?
   (A) This is an example of a multi-stage cluster sample.
   (B) Results from the interviews cannot be used to infer responses of the population of interest.
   (C) The population of interest is the set of all high school principals from large urban school districts in New England.
   (D) Not every subset of principals has the same chance of selection.
   (E) All of these statements are true.

3. The student council of your high school wants to conduct a survey regarding the dress code for school dances. You have advised them that it might be best to conduct a stratified random sample of the student body. Which of the following is not a valid stratified design? Assume the results of the separate samples will be combined into a single sample of the student body.
   (A) Two simple random samples are to be conducted: one of the boys in the student body and the other of the girls in the student body.
   (B) Four simple random samples are conducted: one in each of the four classes.
   (C) Two simple random samples are conducted in randomly selected homerooms: one of the boys in the selected homerooms and the other of the girls in the selected homerooms.
   (D) Two random samples are conducted: one of students whose GPA's are 2.5 or higher and the other of students whose GPA's are less than 2.5.
   (E) All of these statements are valid designs.

Use the following information to answer questions 4 and 5.

In order to assess the membership's attitudes about a new Supreme Court decision, a local bar association selects a simple random sample of 100 lawyers from its membership list. Surveys are delivered to the selected lawyers. Only 63 of the lawyers return their surveys.

4. Which of the following is of great concern in this situation?
   (A) Nothing is known about the parameters of population of interest.
   (B) Nothing is stated regarding the methodology of the simple random sample.
   (C) There may be a problem with the sampling frame.
   (D) There may be a problem with non-response bias.
   (E) None of these statements is of concern.

5. If 43 of the respondents disagree with the new ruling, which of the following statements is true?
   (A) The sample is the membership of the bar association.
   (B) The sample is the 100 selected lawyers.
   (C) The sample is the 63 respondents.
   (D) The sample is the 43 who disagree with the new ruling.
   (E) None of these is true.

Use the following excerpt from a random digit table to answer questions 6–8.

21052 65031 45074 92846 67815 78231
01548 20235 56410 82713

6. Which of the following statements regarding this excerpt of the given random digit table is true?
   (A) This table can only be used for data coded with five-digit numbers.
   (B) In order to use this table for a population of 100 names, the names could be coded 00 to 99; then random two-digit numbers would be selected to identify chosen names.
   (C) It is critical to begin the selection of random digits at the beginning of the list.
   (D) This table can only be used if the data labels include all of the digits in the table.
   (E) None of these statements is true.

7. If data are labeled: 1. Chevy; 2. Plymouth; 3. Lincoln; 4. Volkswagen; 5. Porsche; 6. Ford; and *single-digit* random digit selection begins at the left side of the first row, which cars would be included in a simple random sample of three cars?
    (A) Plymouth, Lincoln, Chevy
    (B) Plymouth, Chevy, Porsche
    (C) Plymouth, Ford, Porsche
    (D) Lincoln, Plymouth, Porsche
    (E) None of these sets would be included.

8. Which of the following statements is true?
    (A) A second sample of three beginning at a different position in the row would always produce the same set of selections.
    (B) A second sample of three beginning at a different position in the row would never include any of the cars selected in question 7.
    (C) Every subset of three cars would have the same chance of selection as the one identified in question 7.
    (D) The sample size is too large relative to the population size to conduct the sample.
    (E) None of these statements is true.

FREE-RESPONSE QUESTIONS

Open-Ended Questions

1. Consider the variable of the heights of male adults in inches. Below are listed 100 heights of male adults. Suppose that these 100 heights are the population of interest. The list is organized in five rows of twenty each.

62 65 65 67 72 74 62 68 65 59 71 70 65 69 68 63 62 65 64 67
68 70 72 65 61 64 64 68 62 72 73 68 64 58 58 74 60 62 64 68
69 72 75 52 54 68 67 64 64 62 60 61 71 75 72 63 63 62 68 64
67 62 58 59 74 76 60 69 70 61 68 68 72 70 59 58 65 54 72 63
66 67 66 62 61 68 69 71 70 75 63 61 69 69 67 72 74 60 61 69

    a. Code each of the 100 heights by its position number using one of the following options:
        (1) If you use a random number generator on a calculator or a computer, code the heights using numbers from 1 to 100, using 1–20 in row 1, 21–40 in row 2, etc.
        (2) If you use a random digits table, code the heights using numbers from 00 to 99, using 00–19 in row 1, 20–39 in row 2, etc.
    b. Select a simple random sample of 10 values from the set of 100. Indicate both the code number and the corresponding height in your sample.

	1	2	3	4	5	6	7	8	9	10
Code										
Value										

    c. Calculate the mean height of the population.
    d. Calculate the mean height of your sample.
    e. Comment on how accurately the mean height of your sample estimates the population mean height.

For each of the sampling procedures listed, comment on the compliance with the two conditions for valid probability-based sampling:

2. Voluntary Response
    a. Interviewer does not choose the subject to be interviewed.
    b. Selection based on probability.

3. Convenience Sampling
    a. Interviewer does not choose the subject to be interviewed.
    b. Selection based on probability.

4. Quota Sampling
    a. Interviewer does not choose the subject to be interviewed.
    b. Selection based on probability.

5. Simple Random Sampling
    a. Interviewer does not choose the subject to be interviewed.
    b. Selection based on probability.

6. Stratified Random Sampling
    a. Interviewer does not choose the subject to be interviewed.
    b. Selection based on probability.

7. Multi-stage Cluster Sampling
    a. Interviewer does not choose the subject to be interviewed.
    b. Selection based on probability.

8. Systematic Sampling
    a. Interviewer does not choose the subject to be interviewed.
    b. Selection based on probability.

In questions 9–12, state the population of interest, the sampling method, whether the sampling method is valid, and the reasons for your answers.

9. Jane wants to investigate what factors lead to success in the fast-food business. She randomly selects 25 establishments from the yellow pages of the local phone book for inclusion in the sample.
   a. Population
   b. Sampling Method
   c. Sampling Valid? Y/N
   d. Reason

10. A late-night news program on TV asks for viewers to register their opinions on a controversial subject by calling one of two 900 numbers: one if in favor, the other if opposed.
    a. Population
    b. Sampling Method
    c. Sampling Valid? Y/N
    d. Reason

11. A sample at a school of 1,000 students is to be selected using an alphabetical list from the office. A number from 1 to 50 is chosen randomly. The sample consists of the student who is in that position on the list and every tenth student from that position.
    a. Population
    b. Sampling Method
    c. Sampling Valid? Y/N
    d. Reason

12. The Student Council wishes to sample its high school. It is determined that 50 freshmen, 40 sophomores, 35 juniors, and 32 seniors are to be included in the sample since these numbers are proportional to the numbers in each class. The specific students are selected randomly within each class.
    a. Population
    b. Sampling Method
    c. Sampling Valid? Y/N
    d. Reason

13. A teacher has the task of choosing five students to display homework problems on the chalkboard at the beginning of class. Describe how the teacher might select the students using each of the following strategies:
    a. voluntary response sampling
    b. convenience sampling
    c. quota sampling
    d. simple random sampling
    e. stratified random sampling
    f. multi-stage cluster sampling
    g. systematic sampling

14. Describe potential *sources* and *directions* of bias in the strategies listed in 13 a., b., and c. Your description should be in the context of the task.

4.3 Controlled Experiments

Terminology   An **experiment** is a study in which the investigator imposes a change or treatment(s) on one or more groups. When the study involves two or more groups, we say that it is a **comparative experiment.** The purpose of an experiment is to determine the effect of the independent **explanatory** variables on a dependent **response** variable.

Experiments are performed on **units.** Human units are called **subjects.** It is important to note that in an experiment, the treatment is imposed on the units in the treatment group(s) by the investigator. As we shall see later, this differs from observational studies where the subjects "choose" the assignment of groups by their behaviors. For example, an experiment to establish the danger of smoking on human subjects would demand that the investigator assign some of the subjects to be smokers. Clearly, this assignment would not be appropriate. When it is not appropriate to carry out an experiment, observational studies must often suffice.

In the simplest version of an experiment, an investigator selects a group and imposes a treatment on the members. In a comparative experiment, on the other hand, the investigator sets up two groups. A **control** group generally consists of the units who are not to receive the **treatment** that is the focus of the experiment. The other group is called the **treatment group** since units in the treatment group receive the treatment. Conditions of the two groups are kept as uniform as possible so that the only difference in the two groups is the treatment itself.

Experiments can be expanded to include several different treatment groups. In some comparative experiments, there may be no control group but rather two or more treatment groups. Again, conditions are designed so that the only difference in the different treatment groups is the treatment imposed by the investigator when the comparison is made.

A major challenge in experimentation is to design the experiment so that the explanatory variables are not **confounded.** Technically, two variables are confounded if the investigator cannot separately identify their effects on the response variable. One potential source of confounding is the effect of **lurking variables.** A lurking variable is a variable that has an effect on the response variable but is not measured as part of the study of interest. It is fair to say that in every experiment, there are lurking variables; in some cases, they may be a source of confounding while in other cases, they may not. An explanatory variable can be confounded with another variable in the study or with a lurking variable that is not included in the study.

For example, consider a test of a new medicine for blood pressure. We wish the explanatory variable to be the dosage of the medicine administered and the response variable to be the effect on the patients' blood pressure. In this context, a change in the stock market can be considered a lurking variable since it has been shown that changes in the stock market can significantly affect the blood pressure of investors.

If the treatment and control groups were set up so that only investors in stocks were placed in the treatment group and only non-investors were placed in the control group, the lurking variable of stock market changes would undoubtedly be confounded with the effect of the medicine on the blood pressure response variable. The investigator would not be able separate the effect of the medicine from the effect of the stock market changes on blood pressure.

If, on the other hand, the treatment and control groups were chosen so that there is a random mix of investors and non-investors in both groups, then the effect on blood pressure can be better identified as being a consequence *only* of the medicine. In this case, we say that the random placement of subjects in the two groups has **controlled** for the changes in the stock market.

The determination of a relationship between the response variable and the explanatory variables, sometimes called **factors,** is the focus of the experimental process. A treatment is a combination of specific values of each of the factors; these values are often called **levels.**

EXAMPLE 1

Consider an experiment dealing with weight loss.

Let weight loss be the *response* variable. Let caloric intake and time per day of rigorous exercise be the *explanatory* variables. Let the levels of each factor be given by this table:

	Factor: Caloric Intake	Factor: Daily Time Spent Exercising
Level 1	800	30 minutes
Level 2	1,200	45 minutes
Level 3	1,600	60 minutes

Since there are two factors with three levels each, the investigator now has the potential to study nine treatments within the experiment. These nine treatments can be summarized by:

		Exercise		
		30 Minutes	45 Minutes	60 Minutes
Caloric Intake	800	1	2	3
	1,200	4	5	6
	1,600	7	8	9

Note: The investigator must assign the subjects to these nine treatments. As we shall see, it is important how the investigator makes this assignment.

Comparison, Randomization, and Replication

There are three major requirements for a controlled experiment:

- comparison
- randomization
- replication

Comparison

Experimental procedures focus on comparison. In the simplest form of an experiment, we make an observation, we apply a treatment, and then we observe the effect of the treatment on the experimental unit.

In comparative experiments that use a control group, units in the control group are given the traditional treatment or a placebo, while units in the treatment groups are given the new treatments under study. A **placebo** is a dummy treatment that should not have a physical effect on the subjects.

The investigator must consider the **placebo effect.** The placebo effect asserts that subjects tend to have a response to *any* treatment, even when the treatment is a placebo; the psychological influence can often lead to a physical change. We counteract the placebo effect by using a placebo in the control group so that we can make the fairest comparison.

Once the experimental treatments have been chosen, the next task is to assign units to the control and treatment groups. However, comparison is only valid when the treatments are applied to groups with similar characteristics. Investigators could attempt to achieve this similarity by a process of **matching** the two groups on the basis of their characteristics. The problem with matching is that it does not address the existence or the effects of lurking variables on the units in each group. In many cases, the investigator cannot anticipate all of the lurking variables in advance. Further, in many cases classification of the characteristics of a specific unit are subject to the judgment of either the investigator or the actual subject.

In order to create control and treatment groups that are as similar as possible, subjects should be assigned randomly, that is, using a process that involves probability.

Randomization

Randomization is the process of assigning units to control and treatment groups using probability. The general design that is displayed below is called a **completely randomized design.**

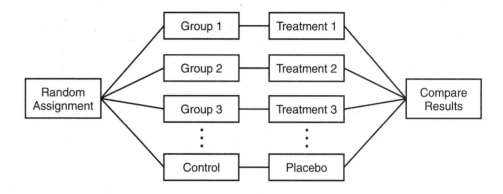

Replication

It is necessary for the experimental results to be replicated or repeated with large numbers of units or subjects so that chance variation can be reduced and the effect of the treatment can be more easily identified.

EXAMPLE 2

The element chromium has long been thought to assist people who struggle to lose weight. Three brands of a FDA-approved chromium compound are available on the market: call the three brands A, B and C. Describe the design of a completely randomized experiment to test the effectiveness of the three brands.

Solution

1. Gather persons who wish to lose weight; weigh each potential subject.
2. Randomly assign each person into one of three experimental groups using A, B, and C respectively.
3. Have the subjects document their adherence to each product's protocol for a period of six weeks.
4. Weigh each subject and compare the weight loss in the three groups.

Graphically,

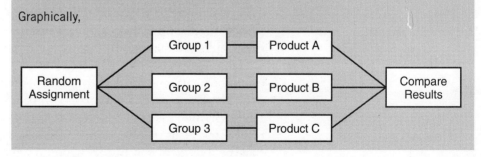

Summary of Important Issues in Experimentation

The experimental design described above makes sense for the following reasons:

1. Randomization should produce groups of units with similar characteristics before the treatment is applied.

2. Using comparative groups should guarantee that any other influences on the results of the experiment are affecting the groups equally, thus isolating the effect of the treatment.
3. Since subjects were divided into treatment and control groups randomly, we can use probability to predict what differences we would expect to observe in the two or more groups due to natural variation alone. If the differences between the groups are greater than what would be expected through chance variation alone, then the results are **statistically significant.**

Remember that the principles of experimental design are:

- **Control:** We control for the effects of lurking variables on the response variable. Comparative techniques are some of the simplest methods to achieve this control.
- **Randomization:** We randomly assign units into control and treatment groups in order to ensure that the groups are as similar as possible before the application of the treatment.
- **Replication:** We repeat the experiment on many units to reduce the amount of chance variation in the results.

If an experiment has these three properties, it is appropriate to conclude **causation** (a cause-and-effect relationship) between the explanatory and response variables.

Note that the word **control** has several meanings in statistics. A *control* is an experimental unit in the *control* group; i. e. the group that does not receive the treatment. A *controlled* experiment is one in which the investigators decide which units will be assigned into the *control* or treatment groups. We *control* for confounding influences, such as lurking variables, by making sure that the treatment and *control* groups are as similar as possible before the treatment is applied.

There are other concerns about experimental processes:

1. The experiment should be conducted in the same way each time. Following a specific experimental protocol (procedure) avoids the introduction of **hidden bias** into the experiment. The only differences that should be present in the experiment are the treatments themselves.
2. The experiment should be **double-blind**, if possible. An experiment is double-blind if neither the units nor those working directly with the units know which units are in the treatment group. This is particularly true in the case of human subjects for whom knowing whether they are being given the treatment or a placebo can affect the experimental results.
3. The experiment should model circumstances that we anticipate will be present in the application of the treatments in the "real world." When an experiment fails this condition, it is said that it **lacks realism.**
4. Due to the expense of conducting a well-designed experiment with randomized treatment and control groups, studies at times utilize **historical controls.** This technique involves comparison of subjects who receive the treatment under study to historical records of subjects who did not receive the treatment of interest. The major concern with this technique is that the treatment and historical control groups may be dissimilar in important ways.

Block Design When an investigator expects that one specific characteristic of the experimental units will likely affect the results of the experiment, a block design is appropriate. For example, in an experiment testing a blood pressure medicine, if the investigator anticipates that gender could be an influential variable, an appropriate design would be:

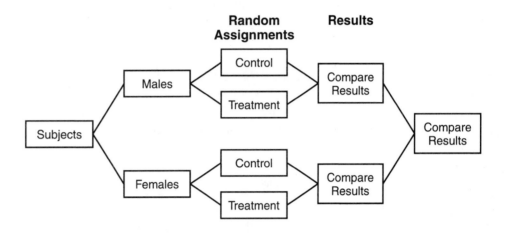

In this design, each of the categories of gender is called a **block.** It is critical that the assignment of subjects into the control and treatment groups *within* the blocks is accomplished randomly and that subjects within each block are assigned randomly to the various treatments.

A block design is similar to the procedure of selecting a stratified sample that we considered in the sample survey section. In both cases, either strata or blocks are created to control for the effects of one or more lurking variables. Then, assignment into groups within the strata or blocks is accomplished randomly using probability. The goal of these techniques is to make the groups being compared as similar as possible apart from the treatment.

A useful blocking strategy is the **matched pairs design.** In this design, data from two variables are paired in order to control for lurking variables.

EXAMPLE 3

An investigator wants to study the effects of two fertilizers on plant growth. How could she design an experiment? The investigator could apply the different fertilizers to randomly selected fields and compare the results of each sample. As we shall see later, one condition for comparing data from two samples is that the samples must be independent. Selection of the test fields can be accomplished so that the samples are independent. However, potential lurking variables of soil composition, amount of sunlight and water, and so on may be present and may make drawing conclusions about the effectiveness of the treatments more difficult.

In order to address this problem, the investigator randomly assigns each fertilizer to half of each of the test fields.

F1	F2		F2	F1		F2	F1
F2	F1		F1	F2		F1	F2
F1	F2		F1	F2		F2	F1

F1 = first fertilizer; F2 = second fertilizer.

The results of the experiment are a set of paired data for each field. Pairing within each field controls differences in plant growth due to variables such as soil composition.

There are different ways that matched pair experiments can be designed. Some studies involve two measurements on individual subjects; for example, before and after a treatment is applied. A pretest and posttest system in schools is an example of a paired design, since the comparison of performances is made within each pair. In other experiments, there exist natural pairings; for example, husbands and wives, twins, etc. Lastly, some experiments are designed using matched pairs in order to eliminate certain effects that might otherwise obscure the differences due to the treatments applied. Our example of testing the fertilizer is in this category.

Sometimes it may be difficult to determine whether a paired design has been employed just by looking at a table of data. The key criterion is whether or not the given samples are independent. That is, do the samples have any association or relationship? Analysis of the context of the problem may indicate that there is an association between the data sets. For example, in a study of weight loss attributable to the effect of taking an herbal supplement for a period of one month, data such as the following indicate a natural pair of weights for each subject before and after the treatment.

Subject	1	2	3	4	5	6	7	8	9
Weight Before	210	155	185	125	145	201	178	192	144
Weight After	198	153	179	122	140	195	175	192	141

EXAMPLE 4

In some cases, the pairing is not so obvious. The following table details the number of males and females determined by a random sample of locations in a college library at the times listed:

Time	9AM	10AM	11AM	12PM	1PM	2PM	3PM	4PM	5PM	6PM	7PM	8PM	9PM
Male	31	36	35	47	45	53	66	63	70	62	44	51	48
Female	32	52	45	52	35	42	60	65	58	62	50	46	35

There are two possible analyses of these data.

1. Compare the mean number of males (50.08) to the mean number of females (48.77).

2. Compare the mean of the differences of the numbers of males and females at each hour (1.31) to a mean difference of 0.

The decision between these two options is based on whether the numbers of males and females are independent or are dependent on the hour that the counts were conducted. One method of attacking this problem is to examine a scatterplot of the pairs of data and consider the correlation coefficient of the pairs. Using the TI-83, we have

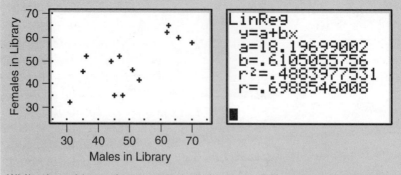

While the evidence is not overwhelming ($r \approx .70$), this analysis does support the conjecture that the numbers of males and females are dependent on the time of the count and therefore, a matched-pair analysis is in order. Technically, you should test the correlation to determine whether it is statistically significant. Techniques to perform this test will be reviewed in Chapter 7.

Review Exercises

MULTIPLE-CHOICE QUESTIONS

1. The three principles of experimental design include:
   - (A) control, randomization, and double blindness
   - (B) control, randomization, and replication
   - (C) control, replication, and simple random sampling
   - (D) randomization, replication, and homogeneity
   - (E) control, randomization, and homogeneity

2. Which one of the following statements about experiments is true?
   - (A) All experiments must have a control group.
   - (B) Blocking is employed to reduce variation.
   - (C) Random assignment is only critical for treatment groups, as opposed to control groups.
   - (D) Matching can be used in any experiment to eliminate lurking variables.
   - (E) None of these is true.

3. In an experiment, if two variables are confounded, which of the following statements is true?
   - (A) One of the variables must be a lurking variable.
   - (B) The variables will have a correlation coefficient greater than $\pm.5$.
   - (C) There is a clear indication that a placebo effect is present in the experiment.
   - (D) The investigator cannot separate the effect of the variables on a response variable.
   - (E) None of these is true.

4. When subjects in both the treatment and control group exhibit favorable responses, the condition is an example of
   - (A) the Hawthorne effect, an improvement merely because of a change from the status quo.
   - (B) the placebo effect.
   - (C) an experiment that is confounded.
   - (D) the regression fallacy.
   - (E) blocking to reduce variation.

5. A randomized block design is similar to which of the following sampling designs?
   - (A) simple random sample
   - (B) multi-stage cluster sample
   - (C) stratified sample
   - (D) convenience sample
   - (E) systematic sample

6. Blocking is utilized to help
   - (A) organize the treatment and control groups.
   - (B) counteract the placebo effect.
   - (C) produce groups that are as similar as possible.
   - (D) replicate the experiment within each block.
   - (E) avoid the need for randomization.

FREE-RESPONSE QUESTIONS
Open-Ended Questions

1. A researcher wishes to determine if there is a difference in the voting patterns of teachers. She wishes to determine whether teachers in rural, suburban, or urban schools tend to vote more often for Democrats, Republicans, or Independents. In addition, she believes that years of graduate education influence voting patterns. However, the effect of years of graduate education is not the primary focus of the study.
   - a. Can her study be considered an experiment? Explain your answer.
   - b. Identify the explanatory and response variables in this study. Indicate the levels of the explanatory variable.
   - c. Describe how the sample can be selected using a simple random sample.
   - d. Describe how the data can be collected in a stratified random sample.

2. A new drug to treat hypertension (high blood pressure) is to be tested. Baseline blood pressures of the subjects are to be taken at the beginning of the study and readings will subsequently be taken once per week for the duration of the study. Preliminary indications suggest that the effectiveness of the drug in reducing high blood pressure may depend on age (young, middle, or elderly).
   - a. Draw a graphic of how you would form the treatment and control groups for this test.
   - b. Draw a graphic of how you would form the treatment and control groups if you wish to control for *both* age and gender.

3. An investigator wants to study the effectiveness of two surgical procedures to correct nearsightedness: procedure A uses cuts from a scalpel and procedure B uses a laser. The data to be collected are the degrees of improvement in vision after the procedure is performed.
   - a. Describe how the investigator can design an experiment using independent samples.
   - b. Describe how the investigator can design an experiment using matched pairs.
   - c. Which technique would provide the most valuable information about the effectiveness of each procedure? Explain your reasoning.
   - d. For this study to be an experiment, the assignment of subjects into treatment and control should be accomplished randomly. Describe the ethical difficulty involved with random assignment in this situation.

4.4 Observational Studies

In an observational study, a researcher collects information about a population by measuring a variable of interest, but does *not* impose a treatment on the subjects. For example, in an observational study of the effects of smoking, the researcher compares the health of two groups: smokers and non-smokers. Similarly, in a study investigating the effects of being an only child on academic performance, the researcher can only compare the academic performance of only children with those who have siblings.

An important difference between observational studies and experiments is the nature of any conclusion. If an experiment is correctly designed and conducted, *causation* between the explanatory and response variables can be concluded. A correctly designed and conducted observational study only provides evidence of an *association* between the explanatory and response variables.

A major concern in all studies is the potential existence of lurking variables. For example, in the case of observational studies of smoking, there is overwhelming evidence that there is an association between smoking and several diseases. However, many in the tobacco industry have claimed that there were lurking variables that were not addressed in these studies. They include such variables as genetic predisposition, air quality of the subjects' environments, eating, sleeping, and exercise habits. Age also can be considered a lurking variable since both smoking habits and susceptibility to illness may depend, at least to some extent, on the age of the subject.

In order to *control* for sources of confounding, such as lurking variables, most studies strive to identify treatment and control groups that are as homogeneous as possible. The similarities of the characteristics of the groups to be compared become critical in the design of the study. For example, a study of the illnesses of smoking and non-smoking men from age 40–50 who all live in similar urban environments with similar prior medical histories has at least the potential of credible results.

Do not be confused about the difference between sample surveys and observational studies. In a sample survey, the subjects are asked for opinions, feelings, and so on; in an observational study, the investigator observes and collects data about the behavior of the subjects.

Review Exercises

MULTIPLE-CHOICE QUESTIONS

1. Which of the following is true regarding the difference between an observational study and an experiment?
   (A) An experiment must have a control group whereas the observational study does not.
   (B) An observational study is used for human subjects whereas an experiment is used for non-human subjects.
   (C) In an experiment, the investigator randomly places subjects into treatment and control groups whereas in an observational study, the subjects are placed into groups based on a characteristic.
   (D) The observational study can produce causal results whereas an experiment can only identify an association.
   (E) None of these is true.

2. At times, medical researchers employ a strategy called a historical study in which current subjects are compared to individuals who are not available for study but whose records are readily available. Which of the following is a valid statement about a historical study?
   (A) A historical study is an experiment in which the current subjects are in the treatment group and the historical records establish the control group.
   (B) A historical study is suspicious since the variable of interest may be confounded with other variables.
   (C) The only consideration in selecting the historical subjects is that they have the same condition or disease of interest as the current subjects.
   (D) A historical study is just as valid as a comparative experiment but is considerably less expensive.
   (E) None of these is valid.

3. Which of the following situations qualifies as an observational study?
   (A) The girls at your high school are surveyed to determine if they believe there is any sexual stereotyping in the school newspaper.
   (B) Two flowerpots are planted with the same type of seed. One is given .2 cups of water each day while the other is given .5 cups of water each day. At the end of one month, the growth of each plant is observed and measured.
   (C) A team of researchers records the number and type of cars that pass a specific intersection.
   (D) A student flips a coin 100 times and records the number of heads.
   (E) None of these are observational studies.

FREE-RESPONSE QUESTIONS

Open-Ended Questions

Each case listed below is an example of a flawed conclusion from an observational study. Comment on each study, focusing particularly on any possible variables that may have been present that may be confounded with the variable of interest. Choose one of the possible confounding variables you have identified and suggest how grouping of subjects may address the confounding.

1. A study determines that deaths due to lung ailments occur more frequently in cities than in rural areas. The study concludes that air pollution in cities is detrimental to one's health.

2. The homicide rates of two states, one with a death penalty option, the other without are compared. It is found that the rates are not significantly different. The conclusion is that implementing a death penalty option is not a deterrent to the occurrence of homicide.

3. A study compared the frequency of riots and the high temperature on the first day that the riot occurred. It was found that the frequency of riots was significantly less on days whose high temperature was greater than 100 degrees. The conclusion was made that high temperatures deter riots.

4. Describe how you would design both an observational study and an experiment for the following question:
   The popping rates of three popular brands of popcorn are to be studied so that a conclusion about the brand with the greatest popping rate can be determined.
   If either design is not possible, explain why.

Chapter 4 Assessment

MULTIPLE-CHOICE QUESTIONS

Use the following information to answer questions 1–3.
A personnel director at a large company studied the eating habits of employees by watching the movement of a selected group of employees at lunchtime. The purpose of the study was to determine the proportion of employees who buy lunch in the cafeteria, bring their own lunches, or go out to lunch.

1. The study would best be categorized as:
   (A) a census.
   (B) a survey sample.
   (C) an observational study.
   (D) a designed experiment.
   (E) none of these.

2. If the director includes only the employees in one department in her study, she is performing a
   (A) simple random sample.
   (B) quota sample.
   (C) convenience sample.
   (D) multi-stage cluster sample.
   (E) census.

3. If the director selects 50 employees at random from throughout the company and categorizes their lunchtime practices by gender, she is:
   (A) blocking for gender.
   (B) testing for a lurking variable.
   (C) promoting sexual harassment.
   (D) testing for bias.
   (E) none of these.

4. Which of the following is *not* a concern in data collection?
   (A) lurking variables
   (B) blocking
   (C) bias
   (D) non-response
   (E) All of these are concerns.

5. You have been given the task of determining if right-handed persons have stronger right hands than left hands. A sample of 10 right-handed persons is selected randomly. Which of the following designs would be most appropriate for this study?
   (A) an observational study.
   (B) a design blocked for gender to determine if right-hand strength differs by gender.
   (C) a matched pair blocked experiment in which each subject represents a block wherein the strength of the right hand and the left hand is measured in random order.
   (D) five of the subjects are randomly placed in the control group and the other in the treatment group. All are tested and the results of each group are compared.
   (E) None of these is appropriate.

Use the following information to answer questions 6–8.
An insurance company conducted a study to determine the percent of cardiologists who had been sued for malpractice during the past five years.

6. The variable of interest is:
   (A) the doctor's specialty, e.g. cardiology, obstetrics, etc.
   (B) the number of doctors who are cardiologists.
   (C) all cardiologists in the American Medical Association directory.
   (D) a random sample of 100 cardiologists.
   (E) none of these.

7. The population of interest is:
   (A) the set of all doctors who were sued for malpractice.
   (B) the set of cardiologists who were sued for malpractice.
   (C) all doctors.
   (D) all cardiologists.
   (E) all doctors who have malpractice insurance.

8. Which of the following could be used to gather the data?
   (A) a designed experiment
   (B) a census of all cardiologists
   (C) an observational study of randomly selected cardiologists
   (D) a survey sent to randomly selected cardiologists
   (E) any answer except (A).

9. Which of the following is *not* a valid sample design?
   (A) Code every member of a population and select 100 randomly chosen members.
   (B) Divide a population by gender and select 50 individuals randomly from each group.
   (C) Select individuals randomly and place into gender groups until you have the same proportion in the groups as in the population.
   (D) Select five homerooms at random from all of the homerooms in a large high school.
   (E) All of these are valid.

10. Which of the following is *not* a source of bias in sample surveys?
    (A) non-response
    (B) wording of questions
    (C) voluntary response
    (D) use of a telephone survey
    (E) All are sources of bias.

11. Which of the following is *not* a requirement of a valid sampling technique?
    (A) All members of the population are coded.
    (B) There is a definite procedure for selecting participants in the sample.
    (C) The interviewer has no choice in the selection of whom they interview.
    (D) The procedure for selection involves the use of probability.
    (E) All of these are required.

12. Which of the following is *not* a requirement of a controlled experiment?
    (A) control
    (B) comparison
    (C) replication
    (D) randomization
    (E) All of these are required.

13. A randomized block design is *not*
    (A) similar to a stratified random sample for surveys.
    (B) a strategy to control for an influence that would affect the outcome of the experiment.
    (C) a strategy that depends on randomization.
    (D) only used for gender comparisons.
    (E) All of these describe a randomized block design.

Use the following information to answer questions 14 and 15.

A research team wished to compare performance in AP Statistics based on whether the students were taught using activity-based or traditional lecture methods. The final grades in AP Statistics for 500 students were collected.

14. The population of interest is:
    (A) the 500 students chosen.
    (B) the students taught by activity-based methods.
    (C) the students taught by traditional lecture methods.
    (D) all students in high school.
    (E) none of these.

15. An appropriate design for the study is:
    (A) a blocked designed experiment.
    (B) a stratified random sample.
    (C) a completely randomized design.
    (D) a simple random sample.
    (E) none of these.

FREE-RESPONSE QUESTIONS

Open-Ended Questions

1. A survey is to be conducted in your high school. There is to be a total of 40 students in the sample. Describe how you would choose the participants if:
   a. there are to be the same number of freshmen, sophomores, juniors, and seniors in the sample.
   b. there are to be the same number of males and females in the sample.
   c. there are no restrictions on the choice of the participants.

2. A hothouse for young plants has immovable planting beds and artificial lights as indicated in the figure below:

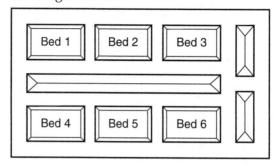

A new quick-grow fertilizer is to be tested in the hothouse. The treatment group is administered the new fertilizer while the control group receives the traditional fertilizer. All other conditions (cultivating, water, and so on) are applied uniformly to both groups of beds. Describe how you would assign the beds to the treatment and control group so that the amount of light does not confound the result. Also discuss the consequences of your design relative to the analysis of data.

Investigative Tasks

1. The following table lists the heights in inches of all 80 of the 8th graders in a suburban middle school:

65	63	58	67	71	56	64	64	63	65
66	70	51	55	57	64	63	69	59	60
62	62	67	66	64	63	72	68	66	63
62	65	56	59	66	68	62	61	58	59
66	67	65	64	66	69	70	70	68	65
63	65	67	68	69	69	71	72	55	58
61	64	68	65	66	69	59	70	70	60
60	65	68	67	63	61	58	68	65	69

Assume that each data value is coded by its position in the list such that the heights in the first row are coded 1 – 10, in the second row 11 – 20, etc.

a. Perform a simple random sample of 10 heights from this population 5 times using a table of random digits or technology. In each case, list the coding number and the value for each element in the sample.

SAMPLE 1

Code	
Value	

SAMPLE 2

Code	
Value	

SAMPLE 3

Code	
Value	

SAMPLE 4

Code	
Value	

SAMPLE 5

Code	
Value	

b. Calculate the mean and standard deviation of the heights in each sample.

Sample	Mean	Standard Deviation
1		
2		
3		
4		
5		

c. Plot the results of part b.

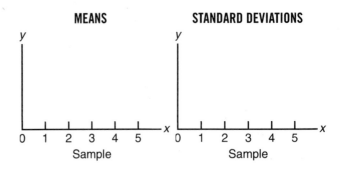

d. What information do your graphs provide regarding the nature of the distribution of means and standard deviations of all possible samples of 10 heights from the population? Explain your answer.

2. A medical researcher is interested in testing a new medicine for migraine headaches. She decides to conduct a clinical trial on 100 randomly selected adults who get migraine headaches at a rate of one per week or more. Although age and gender are not of primary interest in the trials, the researcher is concerned that these factors may impact the effectiveness of the drug.
a. Describe how she should set up her experiment for the 100 subjects without considerations of age and gender. (A graphic is an acceptable answer.)
b. Describe how she should set up her experiment for the 100 subjects if she wishes to control for gender. (A graphic is an acceptable answer.)
c. Describe how she should set up her experiment for the 100 subjects if she wishes to control for age. She decides on age categories of young (21–35), middle (36–55) and elderly (over 55). (A graphic is an acceptable answer.)
d. Describe how she should set up her experiment for the 100 subjects if she wishes to control both for age and gender. (A graphic is an acceptable answer.)

Chapter 5   Anticipating Patterns
Producing Models Using Probability and Simulation

5.1   **Basic Concepts**

5.2   **Calculating Probabilities for Combinations of Events**

5.3   **Counting Techniques (Optional)**

5.4   **Binomial and Geometric Probability**

5.5   **Probability Distributions of Discrete Random Variables**

5.6   **Probability Distributions of Continuous Random Variables**

5.7   **Normal Approximation of the Binomial Distribution**

5.8   **The Sum and Difference of Random Variables**

5.9   **Overview of Theoretical Probability Functions**

5.10   **Simulating Events With Random Digits Tables and the TI-83**

      Chapter 5   Assessment

Chapter 5 Anticipating Patterns
Producing Models Using Probability and Simulation

Probability provides investigators with systematic procedures for predicting the likelihood of uncertain outcomes, and deals with the effects of chance occurrences. In this chapter, we will review the important concepts of probability as they relate to statistical issues. We will further discuss the linking of probability to statistics by considering probability distributions that model real-life situations. We conclude with concepts and techniques of simulation.

5.1 Basic Concepts

Probability   In terms of probability, an **experiment** is any sort of activity whose outcome cannot be predicted with certainty. If we toss a coin, it can land heads or tails; but we cannot be sure before tossing which side will turn up. Rolling a die, performing a test of gas mileage, or testing the effect of different fertilizer mixtures on a particular kind of plant growth all qualify as experiments.

An **outcome** is one of the possible things that can occur as a result of an experiment. The **sample space, *S*,** of an experiment is the set of all possible outcomes.

EXAMPLE 1

The sample space for
a. flipping one coin is {H, T}
b. flipping two coins is {HH, HT, TH, TT}
c. flipping three coins is {HHH, THH, HTH, HHT, TTH, THT, HTT, TTT}
In each case, the elements of the sample space are all of the possible outcomes of an experiment.

The **probability of an outcome** is a number that represents the likelihood of the occurrence of that outcome. Probability can also be interpreted as the long-term relative frequency of an outcome. The probability of an outcome can be expressed as a decimal, percent, or fraction.

Basic Rules of Probability

1. The probability of any outcome is between 0 and 1, inclusive.
2. All possible outcomes must have a combined probability of 1.

In the special case of *equally likely outcomes,* the probability of an outcome in a sample space with n elements is $\frac{1}{n}$.

EXAMPLE 2

a. Consider the experiment of rolling a fair die. The sample space is {1, 2, 3, 4, 5, 6} and since this is a fair die, each outcome is equally likely. Therefore, each outcome is assigned the probability of $\frac{1}{6}$. We write this as:

$$P(1) = \frac{1}{6}; \ P(2) = \frac{1}{6}; \ P(3) = \frac{1}{6}; \ P(4) = \frac{1}{6}; \ P(5) = \frac{1}{6}; \ P(6) = \frac{1}{6}$$

This assignment of probabilities to the outcomes in this sample space does satisfy the Basic Rules of Probability listed above: each probability is between 0 and 1 and the sum of the probabilities of all outcomes equals 1.

b. Consider the experiment of rolling a die that is weighted so that it shows a 6 twice as often as any other outcome. The sample space continues to be the same as in the prior example: {1, 2, 3, 4, 5, 6}. However, the assignment of probabilities to the outcomes must take the form

$$P(1) = \frac{1}{7}; \ P(2) = \frac{1}{7}; \ P(3) = \frac{1}{7}; \ P(4) = \frac{1}{7}; \ P(5) = \frac{1}{7}; \ P(6) = \frac{2}{7}$$

This assignment satisfies both the Basic Probability Rules and the condition that the outcome of a 6 is twice as likely as the other outcomes.

An **event** A is a set of outcomes that is a subset of the sample space of an experiment. An event is said to have occurred if one of its elements has occurred. For example, the experiment of rolling two dice has a sample space of 36 pairs. Below are listed several events and the subsets that correspond to them:

Events	Subsets of the Sample Space
One die shows a 6	{(1,6), (2,6), (3,6), (4,6), (5,6), (6,6), (6,1), (6,2), (6,3), (6,4), 6,5)}
Sum of the dice = 3	{(1,2), (2,1)}
Sum of the dice > 10	{(5,6), (6,5), (6,6)}

The **probability of an event** A, denoted by $P(A)$, is the sum of the probabilities of all outcomes that are elements of the event.

EXAMPLE 3

a. For the fair die mentioned above, let A be the event of rolling a 2 or a 6. Therefore, $A = \{2, 6\}$.

$P(A)$ = sum of the probabilities of rolling a 2 and rolling a 6

$P(A) = P(\text{rolling a 2}) + P(\text{rolling a 6})$

$$P(A) = \frac{1}{6} + \frac{1}{6} = \frac{2}{6} = \frac{1}{3}$$

b. For the weighted die listed above (6 is twice as likely as the other numbers), let A be the same event, i.e. $A = \{2, 6\}$.

$P(A)$ = sum of the probabilities of the outcomes

$$\therefore P(A) = \frac{1}{7} + \frac{2}{7} = \frac{3}{7}$$

In the special case of *equally likely outcomes,* we can simplify the calculation of the probability of an event:

Let S be the sample space of an experiment and let A be an event of equally likely outcomes of that sample space, then

$$P(A) = \frac{\text{number of elements in } A}{\text{number of elements in } S}$$

Note that this simplified statement works well in Example 3a (2 outcomes out of 6 possibilities) since the outcomes are equally likely. However, this statement does not work for Example 3b since a 6 is twice as likely as the other numbers.

Several results follow from the Basic Probability Rules:

1. An event has a probability of 0 if and only if it cannot occur. An event has a probability of 1 if and only if it is certain to occur. Events with a probability of 0 can be labeled as impossible, while events with a probability of 1 can be labeled as inevitable or certain.
2. If the probability that an event A will fail to occur is denoted as $P(\text{not } A)$, then $P(\text{not } A) = 1 - P(A)$. $P(\text{not } A)$ is called the **complement** of $P(A)$.

It is important to understand that these probability calculations provide us with the **theoretical probability** of the event occurring. If we simulate any event or conduct an experiment involving chance, it is unlikely that we would arrive at the exact calculated probability. Probability values that are arrived at through simulation and/or observation are called **empirical probabilities** or **experimental probabilities.** For many real-life situations, such as determining probable life expectancies, the empirical approach is the only way to assign probability.

The Law of Large Numbers

The **Law of Large Numbers** addresses the relationship between theoretical and empirical probabilities: as the number of trials or observations becomes very large, the empirical probability of an event will approach the theoretical probability for the event. For example, if we were to flip a coin a great number of times, the proportion of heads will eventually get close to .5 and will remain close for subsequent trials. This difference between the empirical probability and the calculated theoretical probability is due to chance and is called **chance error.**

Empirical probability is calculated using **relative frequency:**

$$\begin{aligned}
\text{Empirical probability} &= \frac{\text{number of favorable observations}}{\text{total number of observations}} \\
&= \frac{\text{frequency of favorable outcomes}}{\text{total frequencies of sample space}}
\end{aligned}$$

EXAMPLE 4

A coin is tossed 1,000 times with the following results: 676 heads and 324 tails. Based on this experiment, the probability of tossing a tail is estimated:

$$P(\text{a tail}) = \frac{324}{1,000} = .324$$

Note that this value differs from the theoretical probability of .5.

Random Variables When we roll a die, each outcome is a real number (1, 2, 3, 4, 5, 6) with an associated probability. If X represents these potential real-numbered outcomes, then X is a random variable. A **random variable** is a variable whose values are numbers that are determined by the outcome of a random event. Random variables are denoted by capital letters, while values of random variables are denoted with lowercase letters. For example, the symbols $P(X > a)$ represents the probability that a random variable X is greater than some number a.

EXAMPLE 5

a. In the experiment of flipping three coins, define the random variable X as the number of heads that appear. Consequently, X has values in the set {0, 1, 2, 3}.

b. In the experiment of rolling two dice, define the random variable Y as the sum of the dice. Consequently, Y has values in the set {2, 3, 4, 5, 6, 7, 8, 9, 10, 11, 12}.

c. In the experiment of measuring heights of plant shoots, define Z as the height of the shoot. Consequently, the domain of Z is an appropriate subset of the real numbers.

A **discrete random variable** is a variable that can take on a finite or countably infinite sequence of values. One use of discrete variables is in cases of *counts* in which the value must be a non-negative integer. The random variables in Examples 5a and 5b are discrete.

EXAMPLE 6

a. Let X = number of boys in a family of 6 children. This is a finite discrete random variable with a maximum value of 6.

b. Let X = the number of times you must roll a fair die until you get a 6. This is an infinite discrete random variable. Note that there is no guaranteed maximum value.

A **continuous random variable** is a variable that can take on any value of a specified domain; *measurements,* such as in Example 5c, are usually described by continuous variables. Other examples include the heights of students in a high school or the amount of time that students take to complete a 50-minute test. Note that this particular continuous random variable is restricted to any value in the interval [0, 50] minutes.

The set of all outcomes with their corresponding probabilities is called a **probability distribution.** When a random variable X has values that occur based on a particular probability distribution, we symbolize that fact by writing $X \sim Distribution$. We will discuss this topic in great detail later in this review.

Important Random Variables

There are two types of discrete random variable that are worthy of special study. A **binomial variable** is a variable whose domain contains the number of successes observed in repeated trials of a given experiment.

When considered in the context of n trials or observations, it is critical that

1. The n trials or observations are independent of each other;
2. There are only two outcomes on any trial which can be considered *success* or *failure*;
3. The probability of a success is the same for *each* trial or observation;
4. The number of trials, n, is fixed in advance.

Next we consider a related situation. A **geometric variable** is a variable whose domain contains the number of trials that is needed to achieve the first success in a repeated trial experiment. The conditions for a geometric variable are similar to a binomial variable with one major difference:

1. The n trials or observations are independent of each other;
2. There are only two outcomes of each trial: *success* or *failure;*
3. The probability of a success is the same for each trial or observation;
4. The number of trials is *not* fixed.

A binomial random variable counts the *number of successes* in a fixed number of trials; a geometric random variable counts the *number of trials* needed to get the first success.

EXAMPLE 7

Situation: an archer has determined that the probability that she hits a bull's eye is .72 on every shot.

a. Let X = random variable whose values are the number of bull's eyes she could hit on her next 10 shots. X is a **binomial** random variable and we write $X \sim Binomial\,(10, .72)$.

b. Let Y = random variable whose values are the number of shots she must take until she shoots her first bull's eye. Y is a **geometric** random variable and we write $Y \sim Geometric\,(.72)$.

There is also a very important continuous random variable. A random variable, X, the range of whose values occurs with the probability determined by the area under the curve $y = \dfrac{1}{\sigma\sqrt{2\pi}} e^{(-1/2)[(x - \mu)/\sigma]^2}$, where μ is the mean and σ is the standard deviation of the distribution, is called a **normal** random variable and we write $X \sim Normal(\mu, \sigma)$.

We will discuss the binomial and geometric variables in Section 5.4 and the normal variable extensively in Section 5.6.

Review Exercises

MULTIPLE-CHOICE QUESTIONS

1. A die is rolled 60 times with the following results recorded:

Outcome	1	2	3	4	5	6
Frequency	10	6	12	9	8	15

The empirical probability of getting a 3 is

(A) $\dfrac{1}{12}$

(B) $\dfrac{1}{10}$

(C) $\dfrac{1}{6}$

(D) $\dfrac{1}{5}$

(E) $\dfrac{1}{4}$

2. Two dice are rolled and the sum S is recorded. Which of the following events has a probability equal to 1?
(A) $S = 5$ or 9
(B) $S \geq 8$
(C) $S = 13$
(D) $S \leq 13$
(E) None of the above.

3. The probability of spinning red on a particular spinner is $\dfrac{1}{3}$. Then the probability of spinning a color that is not red is
(A) 0

(B) $\dfrac{1}{3}$

(C) $\dfrac{2}{3}$

(D) 1
(E) Cannot be determined from information given.

4. Which of the following could be considered binomial experiments?

I. On each shot, a basketball player's chance of scoring a free throw is estimated to be .38. The player tries 40 shots and the number of baskets is recorded.

II. On a specific island, it has been determined with probability .12 that an inhabitant carries a certain defective gene. Inhabitants are tested until 10 with the defective gene are found.

III. For a certain spinner, $P(\text{red}) = \frac{1}{3}$, $P(\text{green}) = \frac{1}{4}$, and $P(\text{blue}) = \frac{5}{12}$. The spinner is spun 100 times and the number of each color is recorded.

(A) I only
(B) I and II
(C) I and III
(D) II only
(E) None of these gives a complete set of correct responses.

5. In Safeville, the police department has identified four intersections as potentially dangerous. The police collected the following data:

Intersection	W	X	Y	Z
Daily Traffic Flow	1210	210	550	726
Accidents/Year	197	43	78	171

Using the data in the table, list the intersections in order from most to least dangerous.
(A) W, Z, Y, X
(B) Z, W, X, Y
(C) Y, Z, X, W
(D) Z, X, W, Y
(E) X, W, Y, Z

FREE-RESPONSE QUESTIONS

Open-Ended Questions

1. A bag contains 15 cards with the numbers 1–10 printed on them. There is one card for each of the even numbers and two cards for each of the odd numbers. *One* card is to be drawn and the number recorded.
   a. Display the sample space for this experiment.
   b. Assign probabilities to each of the outcomes listed in part a.
   c. Verify that your assignment of probabilities satisfies the two Basic Rules of Probability.
   d. For each of the events listed, display the set of the event's outcomes and state the probability of the event occurring:

Event	Subset	Probability
Number on card chosen is even		
Number on card chosen > 7		
Number on card is prime		
Number on card is a multiple of 3		

2. Consider an experiment of rolling two dice and recording the sum of the numbers on the dice.
   a. Display the sample space for this experiment.
   b. Assign probabilities to each of the outcomes listed in part a.
   c. Verify that your assignment of probabilities satisfies the two Basic Rules of Probability.
   d. For each of the events listed, display the set of the event's outcomes and state the probability of the event occurring:

Event	Subset	Probability
Sum = 7		
Sum is even		
Sum is between 4 and 9, inclusive		
Sum is less than 5		

3. Determine whether each situation involves a binomial random variable, a geometric random variable or neither. Explain the reasons for your choice. Do not attempt to answer the questions.
   a. The probability of scoring between 80 and 100 on an Algebra 1 test has been shown to fluctuate between .4 and .5 depending on what time of the year the test was given. What is the probability that 6 out of 15 students will score in this range on a particular test?
   b. The probability of rolling a sum of 7 on two dice is $\frac{1}{6}$. The probability of rolling a sum of 9 on two dice is $\frac{1}{9}$. What is the probability that you will roll a 9 *before* you roll a 7?
   c. In a production run of 100 parts, what is the probability that a machine will produce 96 or more parts that are within specifications if the probability that each part is within specifications is .90? Assume the production of each part is independent of the production of any other part.
   d. The probability of having a traffic accident while traveling on a particular stretch of highway has been shown to depend on the distance traveled. What is the probability of traveling this 50 miles with no accidents 4 out of 5 times?

5.2 Calculating Probabilities for Combinations of Events

Independent and Dependent Events

Often we are interested in the probability of two (or more) events occurring and whether these events can be classified as independent or dependent. Two events are **independent** if and only if the occurrence of one does not affect the probability of the occurrence of the other. If the occurrence of one event affects the probability of the occurrence of the other, the events are **dependent**.

EXAMPLE 1

Independent events:
a. Flipping a coin repeatedly: the outcome of each flip is independent of the outcomes of previous flips.
b. Drawing two cards from a standard deck of 52 cards, *replacing* the first card and shuffling before drawing the second: the drawing of each card is independent of the drawing of the other. For example, suppose we would like an ace on both draws; the number of aces available in the deck is the same for the second draw as the first.

Dependent events:
a. Rolling a die; then flipping a coin the number of times on the die: let X = the number of heads displayed. The probabilities for X, for example, $P(X = 2)$, depend on the outcome of the roll of the die.
b. Drawing two cards from a standard deck of 52 cards with *no replacement* of the first card before the second is drawn. Again, if we want two aces, the number of aces available in the deck for the second draw depends on whether we drew an ace on the first pick.

Multiplication Rule (Independent Events)

When two events are *independent*, it is simple to find the probability that they both occur.

If two events, A and B, are independent, then

$$P(A \text{ and } B \text{ occurring}) = P(A) \cdot P(B)$$

EXAMPLE 2

Find each probability.
a. P(rolling a 6 on a die and drawing a heart from a deck of 52)

$= P$(rolling a 6 on a die) $\cdot$ P(drawing a heart from a deck of 52)

$= \dfrac{1}{6} \cdot \dfrac{13}{52}$

$= \dfrac{13}{312} = \dfrac{1}{24}$

b. P(2 boys out of 2 children and getting 2 heads when flipping 2 coins)

$= P$(2 boys out of 2 children) $\cdot$ P(getting 2 heads when flipping 2 coins)

$= \dfrac{1}{4} \cdot \dfrac{1}{4}$

$= \dfrac{1}{16}$

Multiplication Rule (Dependent Events)

If two events are *dependent*, then the probability that both will occur is the product of the probability of the first event occurring and the probability that the second occurs *given that the first has occurred*.

$P(A$ and B occurring$) = P(A) \cdot P(B$ given that A has occurred$)$

General Multiplication Rule

The General Multiplication Rule, encompassing both rules, is generally stated as follows: The probability that two events will both occur is the product of the probability of the first event occurring and the probability that the second occurs *given that the first has occurred*.

$P(A$ and B occurring$) = P(A) \cdot P(B$ given that A has occurred$)$

If the events are independent, then the $P(B$ given that A has occurred$) = P(B)$ and this multiplication rule simplifies to the earlier formula.

For example,

P(drawing 7♣, then 4♥ from a standard deck of 52 cards with no replacement)

$= P$(draw 7♣) $\cdot P$(draw 4♥ given that 7♣ was just drawn)

$= \dfrac{1}{52} \cdot \dfrac{1}{51}$

The second denominator is 51 since we have already drawn one card out of the deck, thereby reducing the number of possible cards on the second draw.

Conditional Probability

The Multiplication Rule utilizes the concept of **conditional probability** because it is necessary to calculate the probability that B occurs *given* that A has occurred. Notice that the effect of the conditional probability is that *the number of possible outcomes has been reduced* because of the occurrence of event A. The notation for conditional probability is

$P(B$ given that A has occurred$) = P(B \mid A)$.

The General Multiplication Rule states that

$P(A$ and $B) = P(A) \cdot P(B \mid A)$

Therefore,

$P(B \mid A) = \dfrac{P(A \text{ and } B)}{P(A)}$

If A and B are independent, we know that $P(A$ and $B) = P(A) \cdot P(B)$. Therefore, for independent events A and B, the Multiplication Rule reduces to

$P(B \mid A) = \dfrac{P(A \text{ and } B)}{P(A)} = \dfrac{P(A) \cdot P(B)}{P(A)} = P(B)$

This is a reasonable result because if A and B are independent, the probability of B occurring should not be affected by whether A has occurred or not.

In solving problems involving conditional probability, it is often efficient to use the idea that conditional probability restricts the number of possible outcomes.

EXAMPLE 3

Find the probability of drawing a red ball out of a box containing 3 red, 4 blue, and 1 white ball *given that a blue ball has been drawn previously and not replaced.*

Solution

Let B = event of drawing a red ball and A = event of drawing a blue ball; then

$$P(\text{drawing a red ball} \mid \text{a blue ball has been drawn}) = P(B \mid A) = \frac{3}{7}$$

Note that the denominator has been reduced to reflect that the blue ball has been drawn previously.

Tree Diagrams

In dealing with conditional probability problems that involve multiple events, it is often useful to make a tree diagram.

EXAMPLE 4

The probability of having a certain disease is .05. The probability of testing positive if you have the disease is .98; the probability of testing positive when you do not have the disease is .10. What is the probability that you have the disease if you test positive for it?

Solution

We can represent all of the possible outcomes in a tree in the following way:

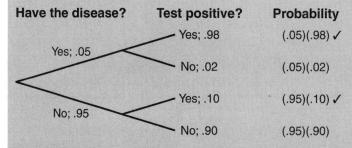

Have the disease?	Test positive?	Probability
Yes; .05	Yes; .98	(.05)(.98) ✓
	No; .02	(.05)(.02)
No; .95	Yes; .10	(.95)(.10) ✓
	No; .90	(.95)(.90)

Therefore,

$$P(\text{have the disease} \mid \text{test positive}) = \frac{P(\text{have the disease and test positive})}{P(\text{test positive})}$$
$$= \frac{(.05)(.98)}{(.05)(.98) + (.95)(.10)} = .34$$

Note that the denominator contains the sum of the probabilities for which the test result was positive. Since you can test positive whether you have the disease *or not*, we add the probabilities of these two situations. Although the problem can also be solved directly from the formula, you may find the tree method less abstract.

Mutually Exclusive Events

The situation in Example 4 gives rise to one more important probability concept. Two events are **mutually exclusive** or **disjoint** if only one of the events can occur at any one time. This means that the occurrence of one event prohibits the occurrence of the other. For example,

- The event of rolling an even and rolling an odd on a die on one throw;
- The event of rolling both a 3 and a 4 on one throw of a die;
- The events of drawing both a red card and a black card from a standard deck of 52 cards on the same draw.

Addition Rule If two events are *mutually exclusive*, then the probability that one *or* the other will occur is the sum of the probability of the first event occurring and the probability of the second occurring. In symbols,

$$P(A \text{ or } B) = P(A) + P(B)$$

If the two events are *not* mutually exclusive, then the formula is adapted by subtracting out the "overlap" between the events:

$$P(A \text{ or } B) = P(A) + P(B) - P(A \text{ and } B)$$

When events are mutually exclusive, $P(A \text{ and } B) = 0$ and the formula reduces to the first one. Note that some books use the notation $P(A \cup B)$ for $P(A \text{ or } B)$, and $P(A \cap B)$ for $P(A \text{ and } B)$.

Venn Diagrams display the two cases:

A and B Mutually Exclusive
$P(A \text{ or } B) = P(A) + P(B)$

A and B Not Mutually Exclusive
$P(A \text{ or } B) = P(A) + P(B) - P(A \text{ and } B)$

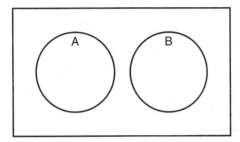
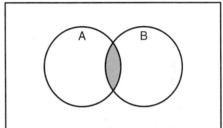

EXAMPLE 5

Find the probability that you will draw either an ace or a red card on one draw from a standard deck of 52 cards.

Solution

Since drawing an ace and a red card are *not* mutually exclusive, we will use the general formula:

$$P(\text{ace or red card}) = P(\text{ace}) + P(\text{red card}) - P(\text{red ace})$$
$$= \frac{4}{52} + \frac{26}{52} - \frac{2}{52}$$
$$= \frac{28}{52} = \frac{7}{13}$$

Review Exercises

MULTIPLE-CHOICE QUESTIONS

1. Suppose a box contains 3 defective light bulbs and 12 good bulbs. Two bulbs are chosen from the box without replacement. To find the probability that one of the bulbs drawn is good and one is defective, which expression would you use?

   (A) $\dfrac{12}{15} + \dfrac{3}{14}$

   (B) $\dfrac{12}{15} \cdot \dfrac{3}{15} + \dfrac{3}{15} \cdot \dfrac{2}{15}$

   (C) $\dfrac{12}{15} \cdot \dfrac{3}{14}$

   (D) $\dfrac{12}{15} \cdot \dfrac{3}{14} + \dfrac{3}{15} \cdot \dfrac{12}{14}$

   (E) $\dfrac{12}{15} \cdot \dfrac{11}{14} \cdot \dfrac{3}{13} \cdot \dfrac{2}{12}$

2. Which of the following is true about dependent events?

   (A) $P(A \mid B) = 0$

   (B) $P(A \mid B) = A$

   (C) $P(A \mid B) = B$

   (D) $P(A \mid B) = 1$

   (E) None of these is true.

3. Identify why this assignment of probabilities cannot be legitimate: $P(A) = .4$, $P(B) = .3$, $P(A \text{ and } B) = .5$.

   (A) A and B are not given as mutually exclusive events.

   (B) A and B are not given as independent events.

   (C) $P(A \mid B)$ is not known.

   (D) $P(A \text{ and } B)$ cannot be greater than either $P(A)$ or $P(B)$.

   (E) The assignment is legitimate.

4. Which of the following events are mutually exclusive?

   I. A = the sum of two dice is 7.

   II. B = the flip of a coin is a head.

   III. C = the sum of two dice is 11.

   (A) A and B

   (B) B and C

   (C) A and C

   (D) A, B, and C

   (E) No pair is mutually exclusive.

Use the following information for questions 5–6.

The probability of any person in your Student Council being selected for the Spring Dance Committee is .3; the probability that a person on the Spring Dance committee is elected Chairperson of this committee is .2.

5. Find the probability that a member of the Student Council, chosen at random, is the Chairperson of the committee.

   (A) .2

   (B) .3

   (C) .5

   (D) .6

   (E) None of these.

6. Find the probability that a member of the Student Council, chosen at random, is *not* the Chairperson of the committee.

   (A) .16

   (B) .85

   (C) .89

   (D) .94

   (E) None of these.

FREE-RESPONSE QUESTIONS

Open-Ended Questions

1. Find the probability of flipping a head on a coin and rolling a sum of 8 on two dice.

2. A box contains 11 nickels, 4 dimes, and 5 quarters. If you draw 3 coins at random from the box without replacement, what is the probability that you will get a nickel, a dime, and a nickel in that order?

3. Find the probability of rolling two dice and getting either a sum of 8 or both dice even.

4. A company estimates that 60% of the adults in the U.S. have seen its TV commercial and that if an adult sees the commercial, there is a 15% chance that the adult will buy its product. What is the probability that an adult chosen at random in the U.S. will have seen the company's commercial and will have bought its product?

5. An analysis of the registered voters in the last primary indicated that 55% of the voters were women. Of the female voters, 35% are registered Democrats, 35% are registered Republicans, and the rest are assumed to be Independents. Of the male voters, the percentages are 30%, 45%, and 25% (D, R, I). Find each probability:
   a. A voter chosen at random is a woman.
   b. A voter chosen at random is a male Republican.
   c. A Democrat chosen at random is male.

6. Find the probability of flipping five heads on five coin tosses.

7. Find the probability of drawing an ace, then a king out of a standard deck of 52 cards, if the first card is *not* replaced before the second draw.

8. One hundred teenage boys and one hundred teenage girls were asked if they had ever made a purchase using the Internet. Thirty of the boys and sixty of the girls said that they had made purchases. If one of these teenagers is selected at random,
   a. what is the probability that he or she has made a purchase using the Internet?
   b. what is the probability that the teenager is a girl, given that the person has made a purchase using the Internet?

9. Donald has ordered a computer and a desk from two different stores. Both items are to be delivered on Tuesday. The probability that the computer will be delivered before noon is .6 and the probability that the desk will be delivered before noon is .8. If the probability that either the computer or the desk will be delivered before noon is .9, what is the probability that both will be delivered before noon?

5.3 Counting Techniques (Optional)

Counting techniques are *not* specifically in the AP Statistics Course Description. However, they are useful in general for determining the number of equally likely outcomes in an event or sample space and to understand concepts related to binomial probability.

Fundamental Counting Principle

For experiments with a large number of outcomes, it is inefficient to use a list or a tree diagram to find the total number of outcomes. The counting principle can be applied to decisions or events that occur in succession.

The **Fundamental Counting Principle** states that if there are m different choices for decision 1, and n different choices for decision 2, then the first and second decisions together can be made in $m \times n$ ways.

This result can be extended to more than two decisions being made in succession, as the next example shows.

EXAMPLE 1

A restaurant offers 5 appetizers, 10 entrees, 6 desserts, and 4 beverages. If a complete dinner consists of an appetizer, an entree, a dessert, and a beverage, how many different dinners are possible?

Solution

$5 \times 10 \times 6 \times 4 = 1,200$

There are 1,200 different dinners that can be ordered.

Permutations A permutation of a set of objects is an **arrangement** of some or all of the objects in a specified order: the arrangements of r objects from a set of n objects are called the **permutations** of n objects taken r at a time.

For permutations, the order of the objects is of critical importance. For example, ABC is a different permutation from BAC.

Permutations can be calculated either by applying the Fundamental Counting Principle or by using a special formula. The formula for the number of permutations of n objects taken r at a time is

$$_nP_r = \frac{n!}{(n-r)!}, \text{ where } n \geq r.$$

Note that for n objects taken n at a time, $_nP_n = \frac{n!}{0!} = n!$ since $0! = 1$.

EXAMPLE 2

How many ways can you arrange 4 out of 7 books on a shelf?

Solution

a. by the Fundamental Counting Principle

Position	1	2	3	4
Number of Choices	7	6	5	4

$7 \times 6 \times 5 \times 4 = 840$

b. by formula

$$_7P_4 = \frac{7!}{(7-4)!} = \frac{7!}{3!} = 840$$

You can see why we don't want to have to list all of these possibilities!

Combinations A combination of a set of objects is a selection of certain of these objects with no regard to order. The sets of r objects from a collection of n objects for which the order of the objects selected is of no importance are called the **combinations** of n objects taken r at a time. The formula for combinations, or "n choose r," is

$$_nC_r = \binom{n}{r} = \frac{n!}{r!(n-r)!}, \text{ where } n \geq r.$$

You should note that this is very similar to the formula for permutations. In fact,

$$_nC_r = \binom{n}{r} = \frac{_nP_r}{r!}$$

Note that $_nC_n = 1$.

By examining the formula above, you can see that the number of combinations is always less than the corresponding number of permutations by a factor of $\frac{1}{r!}$, that is, the reciprocal of the number of arrangements of the r items selected.

EXAMPLE 3

Calculate $_5C_2$ directly and by finding $_5P_2$ first.

Solution

a. directly

$$_5C_2 = \frac{5!}{2!(5-2)!}$$
$$= \frac{5 \cdot 4 \cdot 3 \cdot 2 \cdot 1}{(2 \cdot 1)(3 \cdot 2 \cdot 1)}$$
$$= 10$$

b. by finding $_5P_2$ first

$$_5C_2 = \frac{_5P_2}{2!}$$
$$= \frac{\frac{5!}{(5-2)!}}{2!}$$
$$= \frac{20}{2}$$
$$= 10$$

EXAMPLE 4

How many different possible hands of 5 cards each can be dealt from a standard deck of 52 cards?

Solution

The order of the 5 cards does not matter so we use combinations.

$$_{52}C_5 = \binom{52}{5} = \frac{52 \cdot 51 \cdot 50 \cdot 49 \cdot 48}{5 \cdot 4 \cdot 3 \cdot 2 \cdot 1} = 2{,}598{,}960$$

 Technology Note: Many scientific calculators have the capability of calculating permutations directly. Many graphing calculators have the command *nPr* on the *MATH PRB* menu. Calculation of combinations can be accomplished by formula or by using the calculator: for many graphing calculators, the command *nCr* is found on the *MATH PRB* menu as well. ■

Combinations can be used when dealing with situations that involve more than one choice or event.

EXAMPLE 5

How many ways can a committee of 3 women and 2 men be chosen from an organization comprised of 10 women and 12 men?

Solution

Think of the problem as choosing a committee of 3 women from the 10 women and a committee of 2 men from the 12 men. Therefore, we multiply the number of ways that each can occur:

$$\binom{10}{3}\binom{12}{2} = \left(\frac{10 \cdot 9 \cdot 8}{3 \cdot 2 \cdot 1}\right)\left(\frac{12 \cdot 11}{2 \cdot 1}\right) = 7{,}920$$

Combinations can be used to answer probability questions as long as we remember that for equally likely outcomes, the probability of an event is the ratio of the number of outcomes in the event to the number of outcomes in the sample space.

EXAMPLE 6

Find the probability that a committee of 10 people chosen from an organization consisting of 40 doctors and 35 dentists will include 3 doctors and 7 dentists.

$$P = \frac{\text{number of ways to choose 3 doctors and 7 dentists}}{\text{number of ways to choose 10 people from 75}}$$

$$= \frac{\dbinom{40}{3}\dbinom{35}{7}}{\dbinom{75}{10}}$$

$$\approx .0801$$

Review Exercises

FREE-RESPONSE QUESTIONS

Open-Ended Questions

1. If a young man owns 5 pairs of pants, 7 shirts, and 4 pairs of shoes, how many outfits can he assemble that consist of 1 pair of pants, 1 shirt, and 1 pair of shoes?

2. If an automobile license plate must consist of three letters followed by three single-digit numbers, how many different license plates are possible? Remember that numbers and letters could be duplicated.

3. If a combination lock has a three-digit combination and the wheel on the lock allows any number from 0 to 40, how many different combinations are possible? (Assume that numbers can repeat.)

4. How many four-digit numbers have both the hundreds and units digits even?

5. How many ways can we arrange a row of four girls followed by four boys if the girls must sit together and boys must sit together?

6. Calculate each and verify with your calculator.

   a. $\dbinom{5}{2}$

   b. $\dbinom{5}{3}$

   c. $\dbinom{10}{4}$

   d. $\dbinom{10}{6}$

   e. $\dbinom{52}{5}$

   f. $\dbinom{52}{47}$

7. Do you notice the patterns of the pairs in question 6? Equate each combination listed below to a similar combination form.

   a. $\dbinom{100}{96} =$

   b. $\dbinom{250}{247} =$

   c. $\dbinom{n}{r} =$

8. a. How many ways can a committee of 4 people be chosen from a club of 10 members?
   b. How many ways can a president, vice-president, secretary, and treasurer be chosen from a club of 10 members?

9. The summer reading list for AP English includes 10 non-fiction books, 8 novels, and 5 collections of poems. How many different selections of 3 non-fiction, 2 novels, and 1 collection of poems can be chosen from the list?

10. Find the probability that a jury of 12 randomly selected people contains no Caucasians when the jury pool consisted of 150 Caucasians, 40 African-Americans, 35 Asians, and 20 Hispanics.

11. Find the probability that a hand of 5 cards dealt from a standard deck of 52 cards contains 3 aces and 2 kings.

5.4 Binomial and Geometric Probability

Binomial Probability As defined in Section 5.1, a **binomial** random variable is a variable whose domain contains the number of successes in a fixed number of trials in a repeated experiment.

Recall the conditions for a binomial variable:

1. The n trials or observations are independent of each other;
2. There are only two outcomes on any trial, which can be considered *success* or *failure*;
3. The probability of a success is the same for each trial or observation;
4. The number of trials, n, is fixed in advance.

EXAMPLE 1

a. If we arbitrarily denote the birth of a girl to be a success and the birth of a boy to be a failure, then we can assign a binomial random variable G, to the number of girls in a family with 5 children. We assume that the probability of having a girl is the same for each trial and that the gender of each birth is an independent event. G has values in the set {0, 1, 2, 3, 4, 5}.

b. Assume that the probability of winning any game is .7 for a particular team. Let winning a game be considered a success and losing a game a failure. Then W can be defined as a binomial random variable equal to the number of wins in 10 games. This definition of W as a binomial random variable demands that the probability of a win is the same (.7) in each game and the outcomes of the 10 games are independent of each other. If so, then W has values in the set {0, 1, 2, 3, 4, 5, 6, 7, 8, 9, 10}. Note that $P(\text{lose}) \neq P(\text{win})$ in this case.

c. Let guessing the correct answer on a multiple-choice test be considered a success and guessing the wrong answer be considered a failure; let the number of choices for each question be 5. Then a binomial random variable C can be defined as the number of correct guesses on a test of 10 questions. The identification of C as a binomial random variable demands that the probability of guessing correctly is the same for all questions and the guess on each question is independent of the guesses on other questions. Accordingly, $P(\text{success}) = \frac{1}{5}$ and C has values in the set {0; 1, 2, 3, 4, 5, 6, 7, 8, 9, 10}.

It is important to note that the probability of a success does *not* have to equal the probability of a failure. We introduce some notation to represent all of the necessary information regarding these binomial random variables:

Binomial Random Variable	Probability of each success	Notation
G = number of girls in a family of 5 children	$P(\text{each girl}) = .5$	$G \sim Binomial(5, .5)$
W = number of wins in 10 games	$P(\text{each win}) = .7$	$W \sim Binomial(10, .7)$
C = number of correct guesses	$P(\text{each correct guess}) = .2$	$C \sim Binomial(10, .2)$

This notation can be further abbreviated as $B(5, .5)$, $B(10, .7)$ and $B(10, .2)$. Notice how this notation completely specifies the experiment: $B(n, p)$ represents a binomial experiment in which the number of trials is n and the probability of a success on one trial is p.

All binomial situations need to be reduced to the outcomes of *success* or *failure*, even if we would not apply these terms in many real situations. For example, we can define tossing a head as a success (tail a failure), having a girl as a success (boy a failure), or having a disease as a success (not having the disease a failure). Moreover, we can sometimes impose a binomial context to non-binomial sample spaces. For example, we can define getting a sum of seven on a pair of dice as a success and all other sums as failures. Consequently, by considering the probability of a success, p, and its **complementary probability** of a failure, $1 - p$, we can begin the calculation of a binomial probability.

EXAMPLE 2

Consider the problem of calculating $P(\text{rolling a 6 on one die 3 out of 5 times})$.

$P(\text{rolling a 6 on one die})$ is the probability of a success on one trial, so $p = \dfrac{1}{6}$.

$P(\text{rolling anything but a 6 on one die})$ is the probability of a failure, so $1 - p = \dfrac{5}{6}$

Therefore, $P(\text{rolling a 6 on one die 3 out of 5 times})$ can be analyzed as

$P(\text{rolling three 6's and rolling two of anything except a 6})$

Since each roll of the die is independent,

$P(\text{rolling three 6's}) \cdot P(\text{rolling two of anything except a 6})$

$= \left(\dfrac{1}{6}\right)^3 \cdot \left(\dfrac{5}{6}\right)^2$

The probability statement generalizes to

$P(r \text{ successes out of } n \text{ trials}) = p^r(1 - p)^{n - r}$

There is one problem with the above development. If S represents "rolling a 6" and F represents "rolling anything except a 6", then this expression represents the probability of $\{S, S, S, F, F\}$. However, the original question did not specify the order. Therefore, we must consider other orders that will give us three rolls that are 6 and two that are anything except a 6.

To complete the calculation, we must consider all the ways that the r successes can occur in n trials:

Consider the following cases:

$$P(\text{first 3 out of 5 rolls are 6's}) \qquad = P(SSSFF) = \frac{1}{6} \cdot \frac{1}{6} \cdot \frac{1}{6} \cdot \frac{5}{6} \cdot \frac{5}{6}$$

$$P(\text{last 3 out of 5 rolls are 6's}) \qquad = P(FFSSS) = \frac{5}{6} \cdot \frac{5}{6} \cdot \frac{1}{6} \cdot \frac{1}{6} \cdot \frac{1}{6}$$

$$P(\text{1st, 3rd, and 5th out of 5 rolls are 6's}) = P(SFSFS) = \frac{1}{6} \cdot \frac{5}{6} \cdot \frac{1}{6} \cdot \frac{5}{6} \cdot \frac{1}{6}$$

Note that all three products are equal, and no matter how the 3 out of 5 successful rolls of a 6 are obtained, the product representing the probability will be the same. We can list all of the ways of getting 3 out of 5 successes:

SSSFF	SSFFS	SFFSS	FFSSS	SSFSF
SFSSF	FSSSF	FSSFS	FSFSS	SFSSF

The number of ways we can have 3 successes out of 5 rolls is the number of combinations of 5 objects taken 3 at a time: $_5C_3 = \binom{5}{3} = 10$, which matches the list above. Combining all of the results above,

$$P(\text{rolling a 6 on one die 3 out of 5 times}) = \binom{5}{3}\left(\frac{1}{6}\right)^3\left(\frac{5}{6}\right)^2 = \frac{125}{3{,}883} \approx .032.$$

The situation in Example 2 can be generalized: If the probability of a success on one trial is p and the probability of a failure on one trial is $1 - p$, then the binomial probability

$$P(r \text{ successes out of } n \text{ trials}) = \binom{n}{r}p^r(1 - p)^{n - r}$$

EXAMPLE 3

The probability that a certain (very good) basketball player sinks a free throw is .84 on any one try. Assuming that this probability does not change, find each probability.

a. The player sinks 4 out of his next 6 free throws.

b. The player sinks *at least* 4 out of his next 6 free throws.

Solution

a. Using the binomial probability formula,

$$P(\text{sinks 4 out of 6 free throws}) = \binom{6}{4}(.84)^4(.16)^2 \approx .191$$

b. The words "at least" mean he can sink 4, 5, or 6 out of his next 6 free throws; so we must find $P(4) + P(5) + P(6)$.

$$P(\text{sinks at least 4 out of 6 free throws}) = \binom{6}{4}(.84)^4(.16)^2 + \binom{6}{5}(.84)^5(.16)^1 +$$

$$\binom{6}{6}(.84)^6(.16)^0$$

$$\approx .191 + .401 + .351$$

$$\approx .943$$

Technology Note: Using the TI-83, the calculation of binomial probabilities can be accomplished easily.

On the *DISTR* menu, you will find the command *binompdf(*, item 0 on the menu. This command represents the binomial probability density function (see Chapter 6) and returns the binomial probability of r successes in n trials when the probability of one success is p. The syntax for this command is *binompdf(n, p, [r])*.

The last entry is optional. If it is included, then the command returns the binomial probability of r successes out of n trials. If it is omitted, the command returns the set of all binomial probabilities for n trials with a probability of p on each trial. For example, *binompdf(10, .4)* returns all of the probabilities for $r = 0$ to $r = 10$ successes when the probability of a success on one trial is .4. If the value of r is replaced by a list, then the binomial probabilities for each element of the list are returned. For example, *binompdf(10,.4,{1, 2, 3})* returns the binomial probabilities for $r = 1, 2,$ and 3 successes.

In addition, if we need to calculate binomial probabilities for a range of values, we can use the command *binomcdf(,* item A on the *DISTR* menu. This command returns the *sum* of the binomial probabilities from 0 successes to the specified value of r. For example, *binomcdf(10,.4, 6)* returns the sum of the probabilities for $r = 0, 1, 2, 3, 4, 5,$ and 6 successes when $n = 10$ and the probability of a success on any one trial $= .4$.

Another example: find the probability of between 4 and 8 successes, inclusive, of a binomial event of 10 trials when the probability of success on one trial is .4. The answer can be calculated by *binomcdf(10, .4, 8) − binomcdf(10, .4, 3)*. *binomcdf(* also works with lists. For example, *binomcdf(10, .4, {1, 2, 3})* returns the cumulative binomial probabilities for $r = 1, 2,$ and 3 successes, {.04636, .16729, .38228}. ∎

Geometric Probability

As defined in Section 5.1, a **geometric random variable** is a variable whose domain contains the number of trials that are needed to achieve the first success in a repeated trial experiment. Recall also that the conditions for a geometric variable are similar to those for a binomial variable, with one major difference:

- The n trials or observations are independent of each other;
- The two values can be considered *success* or *failure;*
- The probability of a success is the same for each trial or observation;
- The number of trials is *not* fixed.

EXAMPLE 4

a. Let a success be defined as getting a head on one coin. Let $X =$ the number of tosses necessary to get a success. Then X can take on values from the set {1, 2, 3, 4, . . . }.

b. Let a success be rolling a sum of 7 on two dice. Let $Y =$ the number of rolls necessary to achieve a success. Again, Y can take on values from the set {1, 2, 3, 4, . . . }.

The set of values in the domain of a geometric variable is the set {1, 2, 3, 4, . . . } since the variable represents the number of trials until a success occurs. A geometric random variable depends *only* on the probability of a success on one trial. We could denote this as, for example, *Geom*(.5) or *Geom*$\left(\frac{1}{6}\right)$.

EXAMPLE 5

Let a sum of 7 when two dice are rolled be considered a success. Find the probability that the first sum of 7 occurs on the 3rd roll.

Solution

There are 36 possible outcomes when two dice are rolled, and 6 of these have a sum of 7. So $p = \frac{6}{36}$ and $1 - p = \frac{30}{36}$.

$P(\text{first sum of 7 on the 3rd roll}) = P(\text{not a sum of 7, not a sum of 7, sum of 7})$

$= P(\text{not a sum of 7}) \times P(\text{not a sum of 7}) \times P(\text{sum of 7})$

$= \frac{30}{36} \times \frac{30}{36} \times \frac{6}{36} \times \frac{25}{216}$

The results of Example 5 can be generalized:

$P(\text{first success occurs on the } r\text{th trial}) = (1 - p)^{r - 1} \times p$

that is, $r - 1$ failures followed by one success, where p equals the probability of success on any one trial.

EXAMPLE 6

Suppose a flashlight manufacturer determined that 2 out of every 50 flashlights are defective. What is the probability that an inspector finds that the first defective flashlight is the 5th one tested? the 12th one tested?

Solution

Note that in this situation, a defective item is considered a success. Since 2 out of 50 = .04, $P(\text{defective}) = .04$ and $P(\text{not defective}) = .96$. Therefore,

$P(\text{defective on the 5th test}) = (.96)^4(.04) \approx .034$

$P(\text{defective on the 12th test}) = (.96)^{11}(.04) \approx .026$

It is interesting to note that the probabilities will continue to decrease as the number of trials for r increases. In fact, the greatest probability is that a defective item will be found on the first test!

$P(\text{defective on the 1st test}) = (.96)^0 (.04) \approx .04$

Technology Note: The TI-83 also affords us with the capability to calculate geometric probabilities. Again on the *DISTR* menu, item D is the geometric density function with the syntax, *geometpdf(p, r)* where p is the probability of success on any one trial and r is a positive integer representing the number of the trial for which the first success occurs. For example *geometpdf(.4, 6)* returns the probability that the first success occurs on the sixth trial when the probability of a success on any one trial is .4. *geometpdf(* will also compute geometric probabilities for a list. For example, *geometpdf(.4,{1, 2, 3})* returns the geometric probabilities that the first success occurs on the 1st, 2nd, and 3rd trial. Note that for the *geometpdf(*, the final entry—the trial in which the 1st success occurs—must be included.

Item E on the *DISTR* menu is the cumulative geometric probability function with syntax *geometcdf(p, r)* with the same conditions on p and r as above. *geometcdf(* returns the sum of the probabilities of a success occurring on any trial up to and including the rth trial. This function will also accept lists as one of its arguments. ■

Review Exercises

MULTIPLE-CHOICE QUESTIONS

1. Assume that the probability that a high school basketball player scores a minimum of 10 points in any game is .4. If we are interested in the probability that the player scores a minimum of 10 points in 6 of her next 8 games, we should use which of the following strategies?
   - (A) fundamental counting principle
   - (B) combinations
   - (C) permutations
   - (D) binomial formula
   - (E) geometric formula

2. If we are interested in calculating the probability that 3 boys and 3 girls will sit in a specific order in a row of 6 chairs, we should use which of the following strategies?
   - (A) fundamental counting principle
   - (B) combinations
   - (C) permutations
   - (D) binomial formula
   - (E) geometric formula

3. Assume that the probability that a baseball player will get a hit in any one at-bat is .250. Which expression will yield the probability that his first hit will next occur on his 5th at-bat?
   - (A) $\binom{5}{4}(.250)^4(.750)^1$
   - (B) $(.750)^4(.250)$
   - (C) $(.250)^4(.750)$
   - (D) $\binom{5}{1}(.250)^1(.750)^4$
   - (E) None of these is correct.

4. Binomial and geometric probability situations share all of the following conditions except one. Identify the choice that is not shared.
   - (A) The probability of success on each trial is the same.
   - (B) There are only two outcomes.
   - (C) The focus of the problem is the number of successes in a given number of trials.
   - (D) The probability of a success equals 1 minus the probability of a failure.
   - (E) All of these are shared by binomial and the geometric situations.

5. (Optional) Which of the following is true about the relationship between permutations and combinations? Assume that both n and r are non-negative integers.
   - (A) For all choices of n and r, $_nP_r$ is always greater than $_nC_r$.
   - (B) Neither $_nP_r$ nor $_nC_r$ can equal 1 for any choices of n and r.
   - (C) For all choices of n and r, $_nC_r$ is a factor of $_nP_r$.
   - (D) For all choices of n and r, $_nP_r$ cannot equal $_nC_r$.
   - (E) None of these is true.

FREE-RESPONSE QUESTIONS

Open-Ended Questions

1. Suppose the probability of a particular baseball player hitting a homerun is $\frac{2}{11}$, based on the player's prior history. Assume the probability of the player hitting a homerun is the same for each at-bat and assume that the player has 50 at-bats during her season.
   - a. Is this situation binomial or geometric?
   - b. Define a random variable for this situation.
   - c. Verify that your variable satisfies the conditions for the type you selected.
   - d. Show the set of values that your random variable can equal.

2. A breakfast cereal manufacturer has an incentive program for people to buy its product: in each box of cereal, one picture of a baseball superstar is included. Any one of five different pictures can be enclosed in the boxes and the total number of pictures of each superstar is the same. One of the stars is Babe Ruth. You are really interested in getting a picture of him.
   - a. Define a geometric random variable for this situation.
   - b. Show that your variable satisfies the conditions of a geometric variable.
   - c. Show the set of values that your variable can assume.

In questions 3–8, assume that each variable satisfies the assumptions of a binomial variable and use the binomial probability formula to calculate each probability. Show the formula and evaluate the expression.

3. If the probability that the Cubs will win any game is .6 (very hypothetical!), then find the probability that they will win 7 of their next 10 games.

4. If an NFL quarterback's pass completion percent is 79%, what is the probability that he will only complete 15 of 30 passes in his next game?

5. In question 4, does this situation comply with all the assumptions of a binomial situation? Explain.

6. Find the probability that a family of five children will have exactly three girls.

7. If the probability of a basketball player scoring on any shot is .75, what is the probability that she will score on at *most* 5 of her next 6 shots?

8. A teacher notices that over the past year, all of his students passed his tests 70% of the time. What is the probability that all of his students will pass at *least* 7 of his next 10 tests?

9. A breakfast cereal manufacturer has an incentive program for people to buy its product: in each box of cereal, one picture of a baseball superstar is included. Any one of five different pictures can be enclosed in the boxes and the total number of pictures of each superstar is the same. You are interested only in finding a picture of Babe Ruth. In each case, show the formula you use, the substitution into it, and the answer.

   a. Find the probability that you get your first picture of Babe Ruth in the 2nd box that you buy.

   b. Find the probability that you get your first picture of Babe Ruth in the 10th box that you buy.

   c. Assume that Mickey Mantle's picture is also in the collection. Find the probability that if you continue to buy boxes of the cereal, you will get a picture of Babe Ruth *before* you get a picture of Mickey Mantle.

5.5 Probability Distributions of Discrete Random Variables

A **probability distribution** for an event consists of a list of all outcomes in the event and their probabilities. We will first consider the case of the probability distribution of a discrete random variable with a finite number of outcomes, using the binomial case. We will then treat a probability distribution of a continuous random variable.

The Probability Distribution of a Binomial Variable

The probability distribution of a binomial variable with $n = 4$ and $p = .3$, $X \sim Binomial(4, .3)$ is displayed below:

Successes	Expression	Value	Probability Plot
0	$_4C_0 (.3)^0 (.7)^4$	.2401	
1	$_4C_1 (.3)^1 (.7)^3$	.4116	
2	$_4C_2 (.3)^2 (.7)^2$	.264	
3	$_4C_3 (.3)^3 (.7)^1$	.0756	
4	$_4C_4 (.3)^4 (.7)^0$	.0081	
	Sum	1	

Technology Note: Using a graphing calculator with the distribution (*DISTR*) command provides all of the binomial probabilities with one command. For example, using a TI-83 and the command *binompdf(4, .3)* returns {.2401, .4116, .2646, .0756, .0081} representing, in order, all of the binomial probabilities for successes $r = 0, 1, 2, 3,$ and 4. ■

Technology Note: In order to view the probability plot of a binomial distribution using the TI-83, follow these steps:

Instruction	TI-83 Command
1. Load the possible values of the numbers of successes in L_1.	$seq(x, x, 0, 4, 1) \rightarrow L_1$ [*seq(* is on the *LIST OPS* menu.]
2. Calculate and load the binomial probabilities for each number of successes into L_2.	$L_2 = binompdf(4, .3, L_1)$ [L_2 is in the *STAT EDIT* window]
3. Plot the scatterplot with *X*-list L_1 and *Y*-list L_2	Set *STAT PLOT 1* to scatterplot, L_1, L_2 and press *ZOOM STAT*.

Mean and Standard Deviation of a Binomial Probability Distribution

You will discover in the exercises that binomial distributions, discrete though they are, are somewhat symmetric. Therefore, it is reasonable to consider the mean and standard deviation of a binomial random variable.

Binomial Formulas

The distribution of the outcomes of a binomial random variable with n trials when the probability of a success on one trial is p has

Mean $= np$

Standard Deviation $= \sqrt{np(1 - p)}$

EXAMPLE 1

Determine the mean and standard deviation of a binomial random variable with $n = 4$ and $p = .3$.

Solution

Mean $= np = (4)(.3) = 1.2$

This means that if we have a probability of success of .3 and we make four attempts, we expect to have 1.2 successes.

Standard Deviation $= \sqrt{np(1 - p)} = \sqrt{(1.2)(.7)} \approx .917$

Consider these summary statistics with regard to the distribution considered at the beginning of this section. Even though a binomial distribution is discrete, the mean is still the "balance point" of the distribution.

Technology Note: Graphing calculators can be used to verify these formulas. For the TI-83, load all possible numbers of successes $(0, 1, 2, \ldots, n)$ into L_1. Load the corresponding binomial probabilities into L_2. Executing the command for one-variable statistics, *1-Var Stats* L_1, L_2 will display the summary statistics for the binomial probability distribution requested. (Note that the standard deviation for a binomial distribution is listed as σ_x in the output of the *1-Var Stats* command.) ■

Mean and Standard Deviation of a General Discrete Random Variable

For a general discrete probability distribution, we have the following formulas for the mean and variance of the distribution:

If the sample space of an event contains the values $x_1, x_2, \ldots, x_n$, having probabilities of occurring of $p_1, p_2, \ldots, p_n$, then the mean of the probability distribution is

$$\mu_x = x_1 p_1 + x_2 p_2 + \ldots + x_n p_n$$

$$= \sum_{i=1}^{n} x_i p_i$$

and the variance is

$$\sigma^2 = (x_1 - \mu_x)^2 p_1 + (x_2 - \mu_x)^2 p_2 + \ldots + (x_n - \mu_x)^2 p_n$$

$$= \sum_{i=1}^{n} (x_i - \mu_x)^2 p_i$$

The mean of a probability distribution is denoted by the Greek letter μ (mu), rather than $\bar{x}$ as the mean for sample data. Similarly, the variance of the distribution is denoted by the Greek letter σ^2 (sigma) instead of s^2 for sample data. Consequently, σ is the symbol for the standard deviation of the probability distribution.

Expected Value and Standard Error

In this context, the mean is usually given the name **expected value**; in some books, the standard deviation is called the **standard error**.

EXAMPLE 2

Determine the expected number of heads and the standard error in three coin flips using the definition. Verify by using the binomial formulas.

Solution

Outcome: Number of heads (x_i)	Probability (p_i)	Product, $x_i p_i$	$(x_i - \mu)^2 p_i$
0	$_3C_0 (.5)^0 (.5)^3 = .125$	0	.28125
1	$_3C_1 (.5)^1 (.5)^2 = .375$	.375	.09375
2	$_3C_2 (.5)^2 (.5)^1 = .375$	.750	.09375
3	$_3C_3 (.5)^3 (.5)^0 = .125$	.375	.28125

$$\text{Expected Value} = \mu = \sum_{i=0}^{3} x_i p_i = 0 + .375 + .750 + .375 = 1.5 \text{ heads}$$

$$\text{Standard Error} = \sigma = \sqrt{\sum_{i=0}^{3} (x_i - \mu)^2 p_i}$$

$$= \sqrt{.28125 + .09375 + .09375 + .28125} \approx .866$$

This distribution is binomial with $n = 3$ and $p = .5$. Therefore, by the binomial formulas,

$$\text{Expected Value} = np = 3(.5) = 1.5$$

$$\text{Standard Error} = \sqrt{np(1-p)} = \sqrt{(1.5)(.5)} = .866$$

Expected value is also a useful tool for decision-making in business.

EXAMPLE 3

The Prova Insurance Company offers a homeowner's fire insurance policy. Their records indicate that during a year the company will pay out the following amounts for claims due to fires:

$100,000 with a probability of .0004
$50,000 with a probability of .002
$25,000 with a probability of .008
$10,000 with a probability of .015
$5,000 with a probability of .03
$1,000 with a probability of .07

What should the company charge for each fire policy so that the sum of the premiums will cover the expenses due to claims?

Solution

The expected value of the company's payments is

$$100,000(.0004) + 50,000(.002) + 25,000(.008)$$
$$+ 10,000(.015) + 5,000(.03) + 1,000(.07) = 710$$

This $710 payment is an average over the long run. Remember, the company will not pay exactly this amount on each policy. The standard deviation gives us an idea of the spread of the payments.

To cover its expected payments, the company should charge a minimum of $710 for each policy.

Review Exercises

MULTIPLE-CHOICE QUESTIONS

Use the following distributions to answer questions 1–3.

I		II		III		IV	
X	p	X	p	X	p	X	p
0	.5	10	.2	−2	0	1	−.1
1	.2	12	.2	−5	0	2	.2
2	.2	15	.3	−10	.3	3	.3
3	.1	19	.2	−14	.3	4	.3
4	.1	25	.1	−20	.4	5	.3

1. Which of the tables does not constitute a legitimate discrete probability distribution?
   (A) I only
   (B) I and IV
   (C) I, II, and IV
   (D) III only
   (E) I and III

2. Which of the probability distributions has the greatest mean?
   (A) I
   (B) II
   (C) III
   (D) IV
   (E) There is no maximum.

3. Which of the probability distributions has the smallest standard deviation?
   (A) I
   (B) II
   (C) III
   (D) IV
   (E) There is no minimum.

4. Which of the following is not true of discrete probability distributions?
   (A) The sum of the probabilities is 1.
   (B) The graph of the distribution exhibits symmetry.
   (C) The value of the standard deviation can be less than, equal to, or greater than the value of the mean.
   (D) Each probability in the distribution must be greater than or equal to 0.
   (E) All of these are true statements.

Use the following information for questions 5–6.

A company claims that the number of defective items manufactured during each run of making 100 of their products is independent of the number from other runs and that the proportion of defectives is no more than 4%. Assume that the proportion of defectives for each run is .04.

5. What is the probability that there will be no defectives on the next run?
   (A) .034
   (B) .051
   (C) .017
   (D) .0085
   (E) None of these.

6. The distribution of the number of defectives in each run of the manufacturing process has an expected value of 4 and a standard error of 1.96. Which of the following is a correct interpretation of these values?
   (A) There is a probability of .95 that the number of defectives will be within 3.92 of 4.
   (B) There is a .0196 probability that the number of defectives will equal 4.
   (C) The distribution is symmetric and mound-shaped with the center at 4.
   (D) The rule of thumb dealing with percentages of data with 1, 2, and 3 standard deviations of the mean cannot be applied since this distribution could be severely skewed.
   (E) None of these is a correct interpretation.

FREE-RESPONSE QUESTIONS

Open-Ended Questions

1. Create and display probability plots of each binomial probability distribution specified. The horizontal axis is the number of successes: 0–10.
   a. $n = 10; p = .3$
   b. $n = 10; p = .5$
   c. $n = 10; p = .8$

Compare symmetry versus skewness of your probability plots and discuss how they relate to the value of p.

2. Find the mean and standard deviation of the distributions in questions 1a, 1b, and 1c.

The concept of expected value can be applied to games and the determination of strategies.

3. In the game of roulette, there are 18 black numbers, 18 red numbers, and 2 green numbers. If you bet $1 on a color and win, you receive $1. Consider your "gain" to be +$1 if you win and −$1 if you lose.
   a. How much would you expect to gain on *each* play?
   b. If you were to bet on a color 100 times, how much would you expect to gain?

4. There are two soda machines in your school. A can of soda costs 75 cents from Machine A and Machine A works 100% of the time. A can of soda costs 50 cents from Machine B and Machine B works 60% of the time. When Machine B does not work, it eats your money. You determine to try the following strategy:

   Try machine B. If it does not work, go to Machine A and purchase your soda from it.

   Evaluate this strategy in the long run.

5. If the Cubs are expected to win 70% of their games,
   a. How many games would you expect them to win during a 162-game schedule?
   b. How much error would you expect in this estimate? (Hint: Consider standard error.)

6. In roulette, there are 38 numbers, 00, 0, and 1–36. If you bet $1 on a number and win, you receive an additional $35. How much do you expect to win or lose on each play if you bet on a number?

5.6 Probability Distributions of Continuous Random Variables

The binomial distribution is important, but because it is discrete, it does not apply to an important class of data, namely measurements such as weights, heights, times, and so on. For a continuous variable, probability is calculated and represented as the area under a curve. In Chapter 2 we discussed distributions of continuous variables. Some of these distributions had the property of being mound-shaped and symmetrical. A very special and important type of distribution is the **normal distribution.** Since we have used the concept of area as a measure of the percent of the data within specified ranges, it is most reasonable to use these same concepts and procedures to address the normal probability distribution.

For all continuous random variables, we identify a **probability density function (pdf).** For example, the *pdf* for the normal distribution is the function $f(x) = \dfrac{1}{\sigma\sqrt{2\pi}} e^{(-1/2)[(x - \mu)/\sigma]^2}$. While many continuous random variables have explicit *pdf*'s, we will only display this normal *pdf*. All *pdf*'s have the property that areas under the *pdf* curve will be equal to the probability of the corresponding range of outcomes from the sample space. In these cases, we define a **cumulative density function (cdf)** that calculates the area, and therefore the probability, under the curve from negative infinity to the value of the normal random variable. In symbols, $cdf = P(X \leq a)$ and has domain $(-\infty, a)$, that is, the cumulative density function equals the probability that the random variable X is less than or equal to a number a, and has a domain from negative infinity to the value a.

The following graphs display $P(X < 1)$ for three different probability density functions. In each case, the curve is the graph of the *pdf* and the measure of the shaded area is the value of the *cdf* for the interval $X < 1$.

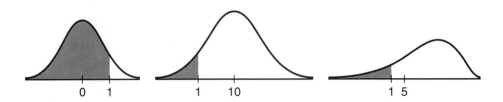

Since a continuous random variable can assume an infinite number of values in its domain, it is impossible to assign a probability to each. Otherwise, we would violate the requirement that $\sum_{domain\ X} p = 1$. Therefore, we only represent probabilities for a range of values of the random variable using areas under probability density functions.

Calculation of Normal Probabilities Using Tables

On the AP Statistics Examination, you will be provided with a table that is like the one in the Appendix, Areas Under the Normal Curve.

The table represents the areas under the standard normal curve, that is, the normal curve for a mean of 0 and a standard deviation of 1. This can be written in statistical notation as

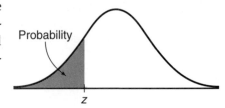

$Z \sim Normal(0, 1).$

This notation indicates that the random variable Z follows a normal distribution with mean 0 and standard deviation 1.

The entries in the table represent the probability of outcomes whose standard score lies below the value of z listed in the columns, that is, $P(Z \leq z)$.

In order to use the table, you must first convert all data values to standard scores or z-scores. Recall that a z-score is the number of standard deviations, σ, between the observation, x, and the mean, μ, that is, $z = \dfrac{x - \mu}{\sigma}$. Appropriate areas corresponding to the probability of the interval of interest are then found on the table and used to determine the desired probability.

EXAMPLE 1

How-To Tip

Steps for using the Normal Probability Table

1. Draw a normal curve, labeling the mean and standard deviation, and indicate the data range of interest; shade the appropriate area of interest.

2. Convert all endpoints of this data range to z-scores.

3. Identify the areas corresponding to those z-scores.

4. If necessary, use numerical operations to isolate the area of interest, and thus the probability for the corresponding data range. For example, since the table returns areas for z-values *less* than a specified number, then to find the area for z-values *above* the specified value, subtract the table value from 1 to determine the area of interest.

It is found that the distribution of salaries in a certain industry is normal with a mean of \$27,000 and a standard deviation of \$3,250. Find the probability that an employee selected at random will have a salary in the indicated range:

a. less than \$30,000

b. between \$20,000 and \$30,000

c. greater than \$28,000

Solution

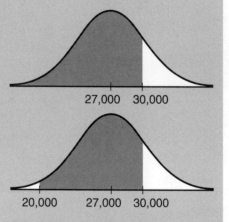

a. z-score: $z = \dfrac{30,000 - 27,000}{3,250} = .92$

We find on the table that $z = .92$ corresponds to an area of .8212. The area below $z = .92$ is .8212 Therefore, $P(X < 30,000) = .8212$

b. z-scores: $z = \dfrac{20,000 - 27,000}{3,250} = -2.15$

$z = \dfrac{30,000 - 27,000}{3,250} = .92$

The area of interest is between the two z-scores. Using the table, we can find the areas for each and then subtract to find the area we desire.

Areas:
Area below $z = -2.15$ is .0158;
Area below $z = .92$ is .8212
Therefore, $P(20,000 < X < 30,000) =$
$.8212 - .0158 = .8054$

c. z-score: $z = \dfrac{28,000 - 27,000}{3,250} = .31$

Area below $z = .31$ is $.6217$
Therefore $P(x > 28,000) = 1 - .6217$
$= .3783$
Remember, the value in the table represents the area *below* that z-score. In this case, we want the area *above* it, so we subtract from 1. (The entire area is 1.)

It is most important that a sketch be drawn for each problem; it will assist you in the calculation of normal probabilities using the tables.

27,000 28,000

Calculation of Normal Probabilities Using Technology

Many graphing calculators have built-in functions for determining areas under continuous probability density functions. In the case of the TI-83, there are two commands on the *DISTR* menu that can be used for the calculation of normal probabilities:

1. *normalcdf(* will return the area under the normal curve for a specified interval using the syntax *normalcdf(lower, upper, mean, standard deviation)*. All four parameters must be included in the command or the calculator will use the default values of $\mu = 0$ and $\sigma = 1$. *Note:* The TI-83 represents positive infinity by 1 E 99, and negative infinity by -1 E 99, both in scientific notation.

EXAMPLE 2

Calculate the probabilities from Example 1 using technology.
Recall the given information. In symbols, $X \sim Normal(27000, 3250)$

Problem	Syntax	Answer
a. *X* is less than $30,000	*Normalcdf(−1 E 99, 30000, 27000, 3250)*	.8220
b. *X* is between $20,000 and $30000	*Normalcdf(20000, 30000, 27000, 3250)*	.8064
c. *X* is greater than $28,000	*Normalcdf(28000,1 E 99, 27000, 3250)*	.3791

Note the discrepancies between the values from the table and from a calculator. This is due to rounding errors in the table.

2. *ShadeNorm(* is a command that will create a sketch of the normal curve with the region of interest shaded. The syntax for this command is *ShadeNorm(lower, upper, mean, standard deviation)*

Note that this command does not reformat the window. Consequently, you must choose an appropriate window before executing the command. To assist you with formatting the window, remember that the total area under a continuous probability density function is 1. Therefore, construct your window so that it is a rectangle whose length includes the data range of interest and whose height is sufficient so that the area of the window is approximately 1.

Finding Missing Values in Normal Curve Problems

To use the normal probability distribution to determine the probability of values being in certain intervals, we determine the z-score, then use either tables or technology (or both as a double check) to determine the appropriate area under the normal curve. The z-score depends on the values of the mean and standard deviation as well as the data value. Consequently, given all but one of the following pieces of information—probability, mean, standard deviation, data value—it is possible to find the missing value.

EXAMPLE 3

The grades on a national test are found to follow a normal curve with a mean of 55 and a standard deviation of 8.2. What score must a student have in order to fall in the 85th percentile?

Solution

We discussed percentiles of data sets in Chapter 2. In this situation, since the scores are normally distributed, we can use the properties and procedures of the normal probability density function to answer the question. Again, we will do the solution first with tables, then with technology.

Tables

85th percentile indicates that 85% of the data is below this score. Let x be the observation such that 85% of the data is less than x. Therefore, using the table we find that the z-score that corresponds most closely to an area of .85 is $z = 1.04$.

$P(X < a) = .85 \rightarrow z = 1.04$

$$z = \frac{a - 55}{8.2} = 1.04$$

Solving this equation for a yields

$$a = 63.528$$

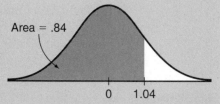
Area = .84

0   1.04

Therefore, the student must score approximately 63.5 on the test to fall in the 85th percentile.

Technology

The TI-83 has a command *invNorm(* that is designed to return the data value given a probability less than the data value, the mean, and the standard deviation. The syntax is

invNorm(probability, mean, standard deviation)

Therefore, in our problem, we execute

invNorm(.85,55,8.2)

The answer is 63.498 which again leads us to the approximate answer of 63.5 on the test to fall in the 85th percentile.

EXAMPLE 4

Earlier studies on the subject have indicated that the standard deviation of study time per week for high school seniors is 2.6 hours. Find the approximate value of the mean of this distribution given that it is approximately normal and that only 10% of the seniors have study times that exceed 20 hours per week.

Solution

Since we are looking for the approximate mean of the distribution, it is not possible to use the *invNorm* capabilities of the TI-83 to find the appropriate z-value that will produce a result of 10% of the seniors. Therefore, using the normal table:

$P(X > 20) = .10 \rightarrow z \approx 1.28$

$$\rightarrow \frac{20 - \mu}{2.6} \approx 1.28$$

$$\mu \approx 16.672$$

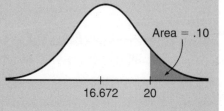
Area = .10

16.672   20

The approximate value of the mean is 16.672.

Check with technology:

ShadeNorm(20, 1EE99, 16.672, 2.6)

Review Exercises

MULTIPLE-CHOICE QUESTIONS

1. For an approximately normal distribution, the 80th percentile is defined as
   (A) The z-score that produces a probability of .80 or more.
   (B) The value whose z-score produces a probability of .80 or more.
   (C) The z-score such that 10% of the area under the normal curve is shaded both at the upper and lower tails of the curve.
   (D) The value whose z-score is such that 10% of the area under the normal curve is shaded both at the upper and lower tails of the curve.
   (E) None of these is the definition of a percentile.

2. The test grades at a large school have an approximately normal distribution with a mean of 50. What is the standard deviation of the data so that 80% of the students are within 12 points (above or below) the mean.
   (A) 5.875
   (B) 9.375
   (C) 10.375
   (D) 14.5
   (E) Cannot be determined from the given information.

3. Which of the following are true regarding means and standard deviations for all distributions?
   I. Approximately 95% of the data will be within 1.96 standard deviations of the mean.
   II. The standard deviation is smaller than the mean.
   III. Calculation of percentages of data will involve a z-score that depends on the mean and standard deviation.
   (A) I only
   (B) II only
   (C) III only
   (D) All are true.
   (E) None is true.

FREE-RESPONSE QUESTIONS

Open-Ended Questions

Use the following information in questions 1 and 2. The heights of adult men in a certain town have been found to follow a normal distribution with a mean of 69.1 inches and a standard deviation of 3.5 inches.

1. Find the probability that an adult man chosen at random will be in the following intervals:
   a. Shorter than 62 inches
   b. Between 62 and 70 inches
   c. Taller than 70 inches
   d. What should the total be of the three probabilities in parts a–c?

2. If you were to order men's pants according to these data, how many of each should you order if the entire order is for 500 pairs of pants?
   a. Short (below 62)
   b. Medium (between 62 and 70, inclusive)
   c. Tall (greater than 70)

3. An individual gathered data from her daily ride to and from school for a long period of time. She found that the times were normally distributed with a mean of 25 minutes and a standard deviation of 12.3 minutes. One day she came home from school at 4:30 p.m. and announced that even though school was dismissed at 3:30 p.m., traffic was such that she was traveling all of the time from dismissal to arrival. Her mother, who knew a great deal about statistics, used her daughter's data from past days' travels to analyze the probability that it would take at least 60 minutes when the mean time was 25 minutes with a standard deviation of 12.3 minutes. Complete the mother's analysis and report your conclusion to her in complete sentences.

4. Assume that the scores on the 2002 Mathematics SAT are normally distributed with a mean of 556 and a standard deviation of 110. What score would put a student in the 95th percentile on this test?

5. Family income in a particular suburb has been found to be approximately normal with a mean of $52,137 and a standard deviation of $19,452. What is the probability that a household chosen at random has an income in the range of $50,000 to $80,000?

6. A set of employee commuting distances from work has a mean of 20 miles and a standard deviation of 15 miles. From this information, what can you conclude about the shape of the distribution of commuting distances?

7. A large study was conducted at a manufacturing plant to determine the average distance employees traveled from home to work every day. The results of the study indicated that the distribution of these distances was symmetric and mound-shaped and had a mean of 9.4 miles with a standard deviation of 4.2 miles. It was also determined, using these values, that the percentage of employees who lived more than 12 miles away from the plant was approximately 27%. A colleague suggested that if the standard deviation of the distribution were smaller, then that percentage would also be smaller. Check your colleague's conjecture by calculating the standard deviation necessary so that the percentage of employees living 12 or more miles from the plant is approximately 5%.

5.7 Normal Approximation of the Binomial Distribution

Traditionally, before the technology became available, a **normal approximation to the binomial** was the preferred technique for calculation of binomial probabilities when n was large or when there were a great number of cases or successes to consider. For example, if we consider the experiment of flipping a coin, to calculate the probability that we would flip *more than* 70 heads out of 100 trials using the binomial formula would be incredibly tedious.

This approximation method works best for binomial situations when n is large and when the value of p, the probability of a success, is not close to either 0 or 1. The rationale for this approximation is that for relatively symmetric binomial probability distributions, the normal curve provides a close fit to the discrete distribution. However, it is critical to understand that by applying the normal curve approximation, we are finding a discrete probability using a continuous random variable. This continuous distribution calculates probabilities by finding the area under the curve.

In this approximation, we use the mean and standard deviation of the binomial distribution as the mean and standard deviation needed for calculations using the normal distribution.

EXAMPLE 1

If $n = 100$ and $p = .45$, then

$$\mu = np = 100(.45) = 45$$
$$\sigma = \sqrt{np(1 - p)} = \sqrt{(45)(.55)} = 4.975$$

Therefore, the normal distribution *Normal(45, 4.975)* will be used to approximate *Binomial(100, .45)*.

Consider the graphs of the two distributions using the same scale:

THE BINOMIAL DISTRIBUTION:
Binomial(100, .45)

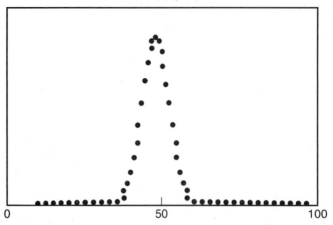

THE NORMAL APPROXIMATION DISTRIBUTION:
Normal (45, 4.975)

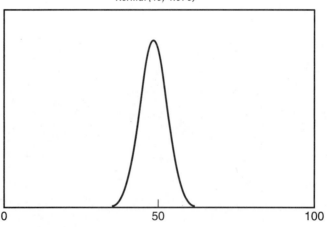

The question arises as to how much skewness must be present before this approximation is invalid. While there is not complete consensus, we recommend the criteria that

$$np \geq 10 \quad \text{and} \quad n(1 - p) \geq 10$$

for the approximation to be valid.

If either of these conditions is not satisfied, then the binomial distribution will be seriously skewed and the approximation by a symmetric normal distribution will not be accurate. Consider the displays described in Example 2 when the criteria are not satisfied.

EXAMPLE 2

Let $p = .1$ and $n = 20$, then

$\mu = np = 20(.1) = 2$

$\sigma = \sqrt{np(1 - p)} = \sqrt{(2)(.9)} = 1.341$

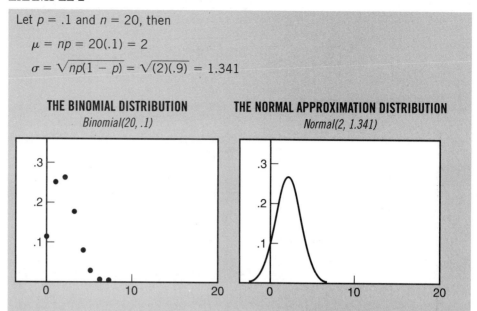

THE BINOMIAL DISTRIBUTION
Binomial(20, .1)

THE NORMAL APPROXIMATION DISTRIBUTION
Normal(2, 1.341)

The normal approximation attempts to fit this highly skewed-right binomial distribution. However, the errors due to the skewness make it inappropriate for these cases.

The conditions $np \geq 10$ and $n(1 - p) \geq 10$ also prevent the application of the normal approximation to the binomial when n is small. For example, it would not be appropriate to use a normal approximation for *Binomial(.5, 6)*.

The procedure to employ the normal approximation involves identifying a region in the domain of the normal distribution that includes the values of the binomial variable of interest.

For example, if $p = .4$ and $n = 50$, the probability of between 10 and 20 successes can be determined by finding the area under the normal curve, with the appropriate mean and standard deviation, from $X = 10$ to $X = 20$ or as $P(10 \leq X \leq 20)$.

If n is comparatively small but still large enough to justify a normal approximation, we should make a **continuity correction** since there will be relatively large "gaps" between the discrete values that are being approximated by a continuous probability density function. This correction is made by adding or subtracting .5 to the endpoints of the region of the domain of interest; the direction of the correction is determined by choosing to include or exclude an endpoint from the interval for which the normal curve technique is to be applied. When n is large, the continuity correction is not as critical but does still provide greater accuracy.

EXAMPLE 3

Let $p = .4$, $n = 50$. Using technology in parts a–c, calculate the probability of between 10 and 20 successes, inclusive, in the ways specified.

a. Binomial probability formula: Note that this exact answer is the sum of 11 binomial probabilities: $\binom{50}{10}(.4)^{10}(.6)^{40} + \cdots + \binom{50}{20}(.4)^{20}(.6)^{30}$. Using the TI-83, this probability, rounded to 4 decimal places, is calculated by

$P(10 \leq X \leq 20) = binomcdf(50,.4,20) - binomialcdf(50,.4,9) = .5603$.

We will use this value as the exact probability.

b. Normal approximation with continuity correction: (.5 is subtracted from 10 and added to 20 so that 10 and 20 will be included in the interval for the normal curve technique.)

$P(10 \leq X \leq 20) \approx P(9.5 \leq X \leq 20.5)$
$= normalcdf(9.5, 20.5, .4 \cdot 50, \sqrt{50 \cdot .4 \cdot .6})$
$= .5562$

This approximates the probability calculated in part a.

c. Normal approximation without continuity correction.

$P(10 \leq X \leq 20) = normalcdf(10, 20, .4 \cdot 50, \sqrt{50 \cdot .4 \cdot .6})$
$= .4981$

Notice how the normal approximation with the continuity correction provides a much better estimate of the binomial probability desired.

d. The normal approximation can also be carried out using tables. Let us rework part b.

$P(10 \leq X \leq 20) \approx P(9.5 \leq X \leq 20.5)$.

Calculate μ and σ:

$\mu = np = 50(.4) = 20$
$\sigma = \sqrt{np(1 - p)} = \sqrt{(20)(.6)} = \sqrt{12} \approx 3.464$

Calculate the z-scores:

$Z(9.5) = \dfrac{9.5 - 20}{3.464} \approx -3.031$

$Z(20.5) = \dfrac{20.5 - 20}{3.464} \approx .144$

Using the table, or *normalcdf* function,

$P(10 \leq X \leq 20) \approx .5557 - .0012 \approx .5545$

EXAMPLE 4

Reconsider the binomial distribution and its normal approximation in Example 2: *Binomial(20, .1)* and *Normal(2, 1.341)*.
Note that *Binomial(20, .1)* does not satisfy the $np \geq 10$ and $n(1 - p) \geq 10$ conditions. Note also that the mean of the binomial distribution is 2 and the standard deviation is 1.341.

a. Calculate $P(X \leq 5)$ using *Binomial(20, .1)*.

$P(X \leq 5) = binomcdf(20, .1, 5) = .9887$

b. Calculate $P(X \leq 5)$ using *Normal(2, 1.341)*

$P(X \leq 5) = P(0 < x < 5) \approx P(-.5 < X < 5.5)$
$= normalcdf(-.5, 5.5, 2, 1.341)$
$= .9643 \qquad$ Not a great approximation!

EXAMPLE 5

Consider the distribution *Binomial(.5, 6)*.
Binomial(.5, 6) also does not satisfy the conditions for a normal approximation, $np \geq 10$ and $n(1 - p) \geq 10$.

a. Calculate $P(X = 1)$ using *Binomial(.5, 6)*.

   $P(X = 1) = binompdf(6, .5, 1)$
   $\qquad\qquad = .09375$

b. Calculate $P(X = 1)$ using $Normal(6 \cdot .5, \sqrt{6 \cdot .5 \cdot .5})$

   $P(X = 1) \approx P(.5 < x < 1.5)$
   $\qquad\qquad = normalcdf(.5, 1.5, 6 \cdot .5, \sqrt{6 \cdot .5 \cdot .5})$
   $\qquad\qquad = .08972 \quad$ Again, not a great approximation!

Important Notes on the Normal Approximation of the Binomial Distribution

1. You should understand that the approximation is based on finding an *area* under the normal curve that approximates the *y*-coordinate of the appropriate binomial probability plot.

2. In order to use the normal approximation to answer binomial questions, you should realize that since the binomial is discrete and the normal is continuous, the value(s) of interest must sometimes be adjusted. For instance, in order to approximate a particular number of successes, it is necessary to adjust the region of interest under the normal curve using the continuity adjustment. For example,

   $P(5 \text{ successes out of 16 trials}) \approx$ Area under normal curve for $4.5 \leq X \leq 5.5$.

3. When n is large, it is unnecessary to apply the continuity correction for an interval of values since the error introduced by not applying it is very small. However, the continuity correction must be applied when approximating the probability of a single value of X.

Review Exercises

MULTIPLE-CHOICE QUESTIONS

1. The reason that we impose the criteria of $np \geq 10$ and $n(1 - p) \geq 10$ is so that
   (A) both p and $1 - p$ will be equally represented.
   (B) application of the binomial probability model is appropriate.
   (C) skewness is eliminated from the solution of the problem.
   (D) the binomial distribution is not severely skewed so that a normal approximation is valid.
   (E) None of these contains the reason.

2. The school library has determined that the probability of any book being returned prior to or on its due date is independent of the probability of other books and is approximately .6. If we were to calculate the probability that more than 70 out of the next 100 books are returned prior to or on their due dates, which of the following expressions would be *incorrect* to use for this calculation?

   I. $\binom{100}{70}(.6)^{70}(.4)^{30} + \binom{100}{71}(.6)^{71}(.4)^{29} + \cdots$
   $\quad + \binom{100}{100}(.6)^{100}(.4)^{0}$

   II. $\binom{100}{71}(.6)^{71}(.4)^{29} + \binom{100}{72}(.6)^{72}(.4)^{28} + \cdots$
   $\quad + \binom{100}{100}(.6)^{100}(.4)^{0}$

   III. $P(X > 70.5)$ using $Normal(60, 4.8990)$

   (A) I only
   (B) II only
   (C) III only
   (D) I and III
   (E) II and III

In each question, indicate the method you choose to use and a reason for your choice. Choices include: Binomial Formula, Binomial Functions (TI-83), and Normal Approximation using either tables or the TI-83.

1. The probability that a bowler will score 200 or more in a given game is .4. What is the probability that the bowler will score 200 or more in at least 3 of 5 games?

2. A gas station has been grossing an average of approximately $1,000 on 8 out of every 10 days over the past several months. Based on this information, what is the probability that the station will gross over $1,000 on at least 5 of the next 6 days?

3. The probability that a doctor will be able to distinguish nervous tension from a brain tumor in a patient who has nervous tension is about 0.95. If 10 different doctors independently examine and diagnose a patient suffering from nervous tension, what is the probability that all 10 will correctly distinguish it from a brain tumor?

4. In a medical school, standard X-rays are kept for use by students. It is hypothesized that second-year students have a probability of $\frac{4}{5}$ of diagnosing the X-ray correctly if there is a pathological condition and only a $\frac{3}{5}$ probability of a correct diagnosis if the X-ray shows normal conditions. Three students examine an X-ray and draw conclusions. What is the probability that exactly one will make the correct diagnosis if
   a. a pathological condition is present?
   b. the X-ray shows normal conditions?

5.8 The Sum and Difference of Random Variables

In Chapter 2 we considered the effect on summary statistics of changing each value of a data set by adding or subtracting a constant or by multiplying or dividing each value by a constant. In the context of random variables, we can state the following results regarding means and variances:

Let X be a random variable with mean μ_x and variance σ^2_x. Then, for any constants a and b, if we multiply X by b and add or subtract this product from a, we create the new random variable $a \pm bX$. The mean and variance of $a \pm bX$ is given by

$$\mu_{(a + bX)} = \text{Expected Value of } a \pm bX = E(a \pm bX) = a \pm b\mu_X$$

$$(\sigma_{a \pm bX})^2 = \text{Variance } (a \pm bX) = b^2\sigma_x^2$$

Note the implication of this variance formula on the formula for standard deviation:

$$\sigma_{a + bX} = \sqrt{(\sigma_{a + bX})^2} = \sqrt{b^2\sigma_x^2} = b\sigma_x.$$

EXAMPLE 1

Let $X = \{1, 2, 3, 4, 5\}$ with each outcome equally likely to occur.

$\mu_X = 3$, $\sigma_x^2 = 2$

Consider the set $2 + 5X = \{7, 12, 17, 22, 27\}$. Again, each outcome is equally likely to occur.

$\mu_{2 + 5x} = 2 + 5\mu_x = 17$
$(\sigma_{2 + 5x})^2 = 5^2 \cdot \sigma_x^2 = 50$

You can verify these numbers by calculating the mean and variance for the new random variable directly.

We now consider a sum or difference of random variables. Let A be a random variable with mean μ_A and standard deviation σ_A and let B be a second random variable with mean μ_B and standard deviation σ_B.
Then $X \pm Y$ is a random variable whose mean is given by

$$\mu_{X \pm Y} = \mu_X \pm \mu_Y$$

The issue with the variance is not so straightforward. In general,

$$\text{variance } (X \pm Y) = (\sigma_{X \pm Y})^2 = \sigma_X^2 + \sigma_Y^2 + 2r \cdot \sigma_X \cdot \sigma_Y$$

where r is the correlation coefficient between X and Y.

If the two random variables are *independent*, that is, there is *no* relationship between variables, then the variance formula reduces to

$$(\sigma_{X \pm Y})^2 = \sigma_X^2 + \sigma_Y^2$$

since $r = 0$ for independent variables.

If, on the other hand, the two random variables are *dependent*, then r does not equal 0 and the sum of the variances cannot be calculated this simply.

EXAMPLE 2

Verify the above formulas for the following situation.
Let X = the random variable of the outcome of rolling one fair die. Therefore,
$X = \{1, 2, 3, 4, 5, 6,\}$, each with probability $\frac{1}{6}$.

The mean of the discrete probability distribution is calculated

$$\text{mean} = \mu_X = \sum_{i=1}^{6} x_i p_i = 1 \cdot \left(\frac{1}{6}\right) + 2 \cdot \left(\frac{1}{6}\right) + 3 \cdot \left(\frac{1}{6}\right) + 4 \cdot \left(\frac{1}{6}\right) + 5 \cdot \left(\frac{1}{6}\right) + 1 \cdot \left(\frac{1}{6}\right)$$
$$= 3.5$$

and the variance of the distribution is calculated

$$\text{variance} = \sigma_X^2 = \sum_{i=1}^{6} (x_i - \mu)^2 p_i$$
$$= (1 - 10.5)^2 \left(\frac{1}{6}\right) + (2 - 10.5)^2 \left(\frac{1}{6}\right) + \cdots + (6 - 10.5)^2 \left(\frac{1}{6}\right) \approx 2.9167$$

Let Y = the discrete random variable of rolling another fair die. Then the mean and variance of its probability distribution should be the same as that of the first die, that is,

$$\mu_Y = 3.5 \text{ and } \sigma_Y^2 = 2.9167$$

Consider the sum of the outcomes on the dice when rolled together; $X + Y = \{2, 3, 4, ...,12\}$. The outcomes and their probabilities are summarized in the table below.

$X + Y$	2	3	4	5	6	7	8	9	10	11	12
p	$\frac{1}{36}$	$\frac{2}{36}$	$\frac{3}{36}$	$\frac{4}{36}$	$\frac{5}{36}$	$\frac{6}{36}$	$\frac{5}{36}$	$\frac{4}{36}$	$\frac{3}{36}$	$\frac{2}{36}$	$\frac{1}{36}$

We calculate the mean and variance of the probability distribution of this distribution:

$$\text{mean} = \mu_{X+Y} = 2 \cdot \left(\frac{1}{36}\right) + 3 \cdot \left(\frac{2}{36}\right) + 4 \cdot \left(\frac{3}{36}\right) + \cdots + 12 \cdot \left(\frac{1}{36}\right) = 7$$
$$\text{variance} = (\sigma_{X+Y})^2$$
$$= (2 - 7)^2 \cdot \left(\frac{1}{36}\right) + (3 - 7)^2 \cdot \left(\frac{2}{36}\right) + \cdots + (12 - 7)^2 \cdot \left(\frac{1}{36}\right) \approx 5.8333$$

These values verify the relationships contained in the formulas:

$$\mu_{X+Y} = \mu_X + \mu_X = 3.5 + 3.5 = 7$$

Since the outcome on each die is independent of the other, we can see that the variance formula is consistent with the above calculations:

$$(\sigma_{X+Y})^2 \approx 2.9167 + 2.9167 = 5.8334$$

These formulas can be applied to data sets as well if we consider the data as values of the random variable with a continuous probability distribution, such as the normal distribution.

For data sets we can state: Let $\overline{X}$ and $\overline{Y}$ be the means of the data sets and let s_X^2 and s_Y^2 be the variances of the sets.

$$\text{mean}(X + Y) = \overline{X} + \overline{Y}$$

However,

$$\text{variance}(X + Y) = s_X^2 + s_Y^2 + 2r \cdot s_X \cdot s_Y$$

where r = correlation coefficient between X and Y.

When X and Y are independent, then $r = 0$. Then the formula reduces to the variance formula:

$$\text{variance}(X \pm Y) = s_X^2 + s_Y^2$$

EXAMPLE 3

True or False: At a particular school, on the SAT Math test, the school mean was 510 with a standard deviation of 102 while on the SAT Verbal test, the school mean was 490 with a standard deviation of 110. Therefore, the school mean composite score was 1,000 with a standard deviation of $\sqrt{102^2 + 110^2}$.

Solution

The answer to this question is *false* since it is not reasonable to believe that the math and verbal performances are independent. Consequently, the school mean composite is 1,000. However, from the given information we can make no statement about the composite standard deviation.

EXAMPLE 4

A candy manufacturer is marketing a gift box containing three nut cluster bars and four pieces of fudge. The manufacturing process for each candy is designed so that the mean weight of the nut cluster bar is 4 ounces with a standard deviation of .2 ounces and the mean weight of the piece of fudge is 6 ounces with a standard deviation of .5 ounces. Assuming that the weights of the nut cluster bar and the fudge are independent, what are the mean and standard deviation of the weight of the contents of the gift box?

Solution

The mean of the gift box contents = 3(4 oz) + 4(6 oz) = 36 oz.
Since the weights of the two candies are assumed to be independent, the variance of the contents of the gift box = $3^2(.2)^2 + 4^2(.5)^2 = 4.36$. Therefore, the standard deviation of the contents of the gift box is $\sqrt{4.36}$ or 2.088 oz.

In order for the variance of a sum or difference of random variables to equal the sum of the variances of each of the random variables, it is necessary that the random variables be independent. Recall from Section 5.2: if two events, A and B, are *independent*, then

$$P(A \text{ and } B \text{ occurring}) = P(A) \cdot P(B)$$

In Example 5, we present two dependent random variables and then show that the variance of the difference is not equal to the sum of the variances of each.

EXAMPLE 5

Let $X = \{4, 5\}$ with probabilities $P(X = 4) = .5$ and $P(X = 5) = .5$.
Let $Y = \{0, 1\}$ with probabilities $P(Y = 0) = .6$ and $P(Y = 1) = .4$.
Also, let the probabilities of $P(X \text{ and } Y)$ be given in the table below. For example,
$P(X = 4 \text{ and } Y = 0) = .2$.

X \ Y	4	5
0	.2	.4
1	.3	.1

X and Y are clearly not independent. Consider the case:

$$P(X = 4 \text{ and } Y = 0) \stackrel{?}{=} P(X = 4) \cdot P(Y = 0)$$
$$.2 \neq .5 \cdot .6$$

Note that $\mu_X = 4.5$ and $\sigma_X^2 = .25$; $\mu_Y = .4$ and $\sigma_Y^2 \approx .24$.

Consider a new random variable $X - Y$. The values and probabilities of $X - Y$ can be calculated.

(X, Y)		(4,0)	(5,0)	(4,1)	(5,1)
X − Y		4	5	3	4
P(X and Y) (from table)		.2	.4	.3	.1

Combining the two ways to get $X - Y = 4$, we can summarize this new probability distribution as

X − Y	3	4	5
P(X − Y)	.3	.3	.4

For this distribution: $\mu_{X-Y} = 4.1$ and $(\sigma_{X-Y})^2 \approx .6901$.
Notice that

$$\mu_{X-Y} = \mu_X - \mu_Y \qquad \text{but} \qquad (\sigma_{X-Y})^2 \neq \sigma_X^2 + \sigma_Y^2$$
$$4.1 = 4.5 - .4 \qquad\qquad\qquad .6901 \neq .2500 + .2401$$

This verifies that the sum of the variances of two random variables does not equal the variance of the combined random variable if the two components of the combined random variable are not independent.

Review Exercises

MULTIPLE-CHOICE QUESTIONS

1. If X and Y are random variables, which of the following must be true?
   (A) $\mu_{X-Y} = \mu_X - \mu_Y - \mu_{XY}$
   (B) $\mu_{3X+2Y} = 3\mu_X + 2\mu_Y$
   (C) $\mu_{X-Y} = \mu_X - \mu_Y$ only if X and Y are independent.
   (D) $X - Y$ is a random variable with a mean equal to the larger of μ_X and μ_Y.
   (E) None of these must be true.

Use this information for questions 2–4.

A new game of dice is being played with two dice on some college campuses. The dice are rolled one after the other. Instead of adding the numbers on each die, each player subtracts the number on the second die from the number on the first die. Let $S =$ this difference. Note that for each die, $\mu = 3.5$ and $\sigma^2 \approx 2.91$

2. Assuming that the dice are fair, which of the following is true about the random variable S?
   (A) $\mu = 0$, $\sigma^2 \approx 0$
   (B) $\mu = 0$, $\sigma^2 \approx 5.82$
   (C) $\mu = 0$, $\sigma^2 \approx 3.41$
   (D) $\mu = 0$, but the variance cannot be determined from this information.
   (E) None of these is true.

3. S consists of the values in which set?
   (A) $\{1, 2, 3, 4, 5, 6\}$
   (B) $\{0, 1, 2, 3, 4, 5\}$
   (C) $\{-5, -4, \ldots, 4, 5\}$
   (D) $\{-6, -5, \ldots, 5, 6\}$
   (E) None of these is the set of values in S.

4. $P(S = -2) =$
   (A) $\dfrac{1}{6}$
   (B) $\dfrac{1}{36}$
   (C) $\dfrac{2}{36}$
   (D) $\dfrac{4}{36}$
   (E) $\dfrac{6}{36}$

5. If A and B are random variables and $A = \{10, 11, 12\}$ and $B = \{1, 2, 3\}$, then a new random variable $3A - 2B$ consists of:
   (A) $\{24, 26, 28, \ldots, 32, 34\}$
   (B) $\{24, 26, 27, 28, 29, 30, 31, 32, 34\}$
   (C) $\{24, 25, 26, \ldots, 32, 33, 34\}$
   (D) $\{24, 25, 27, 28, 29, 30, 31, 33, 34\}$
   (E) The values of $3A - 2B$ cannot be determined from this information.

6. The sales total from the west coast office of a national company for the month of December, 1999 had a mean of \$23,542 with a standard deviation of \$1,257. The figures for the east coast office for the same month had a mean of \$27,735 with a standard deviation of \$1,945. The president wants the values (rounded to the nearest dollar) of the combined data based only on these statistics. Which of the following is the best answer you can give the president?
   (A) The combined mean is \$51,277 and the combined standard deviation is \$3,202.
   (B) The combined mean is \$51,277 and the combined standard deviation is \$2,316.
   (C) The combined mean is \$51,277 but the combined standard deviation cannot be determined since the two offices undoubtedly had two different sales philosophies and therefore are not comparable.
   (D) The combined mean is \$51,277 but the combined standard deviation cannot be determined since the sales undoubtedly reflected national trends and therefore were not independent.
   (E) None of these is an accurate answer for the president.

FREE-RESPONSE QUESTIONS

Open-Ended Questions

1. A class in AP Statistics takes a two-part exam. If the mean for the first part was 42 with a standard deviation of 10 and the mean for the second part was 38 with a standard deviation of 12, find the mean and standard deviation for the entire exam (if possible). Explain your work.

2. In a chemistry experiment, test tubes filled with different concentrations of a substance are heated with a uniform heat source. At a specified time, the heights of the levels of the fluids are measured. Suppose the mean level of the original substances was 65 mm with a standard deviation of 4 mm and the mean level of the heated substances was 72.5 mm with a standard deviation of 6.2 mm. What are the mean and standard deviation of the differences in level caused by the heating of the substances (if possible)?

3. The American Mathematics Contest (AMC-12) (formerly known as the American High School Mathematics Exam (AHSME)) has 100 possible points. The American Invitational Math Exam (AIME) has 15 possible points. Let X be the random variable whose values are the scores on the AMC-12 test and Y be the random variable whose values are the scores on the AIME test. An index score for each student who takes both exams is calculated by the formula (AMC-12 score) + 10(AIME score).

Suppose the mean and standard deviation of the students taking both exams are 113.3 and 3.7 respectively on the AMC-12 and suppose that the same values for the AIME test are 6.2 and 2.7 respectively. Find the mean and standard deviation of the index scores for those that have taken both tests. If this is not possible, explain why it is not.

4. The probability distribution of two independent random variables, L and M, are given by the tables below.

L	$P(L)$		M	$P(M)$
0	.1		5	.1
1	.2		6	.1
2	.3		7	.2
3	.4		8	.6

Calculate:
a. the probability distribution of $2L + M$.
b. the mean and standard deviation of $2L + M$. If this is not possible, explain why it is not.

5.9 Overview of Theoretical Probability Functions

A **theoretical probability function** is a function that provides the scheme by which the probabilities of random variables can be calculated. We will study two major types: discrete mass functions and continuous density functions. Both types of functions must satisfy two major principles:

1. The values of the probability function must be greater than or equal to 0; and
2. The sum of all probabilities generated by the function must equal 1.

There are many theoretical probability functions that have been formulated for different situations in statistics. One of the tasks for the statistical investigator is to find an appropriate model for a given circumstance since real situations can virtually never be fit exactly to theoretical models. There are six theoretical probability functions of interest to us in this course.

Discrete Probability Mass Functions

All discrete probability mass functions give the theoretical probability value for each domain value. The **cumulative density function** calculates the sum of the probabilities for random variables from the lowest value in the domain of the function to the specified value of the random variable.

The Binomial Probability Mass Function
The binomial probability mass function for a discrete random variable yields the probability of obtaining a specified number of successes in an experiment repeated a specified number of times. This probability depends

on the number of repeated trials and the probability of success on any one trial. The formula for the binomial probability density function is

$$P(r \text{ successes out of } n \text{ trials}) = {}_nC_r \cdot p^r(1-p)^{n-r} = \binom{n}{r} p^r(1-p)^{n-r}$$

where p is the probability of a success on any trial and n is the number of trials. This distribution is written in symbols as

Binomial(n, p) or *B(n, p)*

EXAMPLE 1

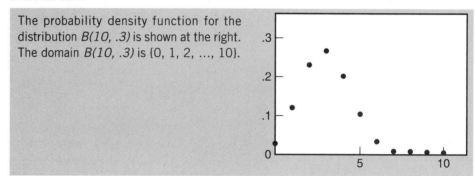

The probability density function for the distribution *B(10, .3)* is shown at the right. The domain *B(10, .3)* is {0, 1, 2, ..., 10}.

The Geometric Probability Mass Function

The geometric probability mass function computes the probability that the first success occurs on a particular trial. The geometric probability mass function is

$$P(\text{1st success occurs on the } r\text{th trial}) = p(1-p)^{r-1}$$

where p is the probability of success on any one trial and r is the number of the trial at which the first success occurs. In symbols, the distribution is written

Geometric(p)

EXAMPLE 2

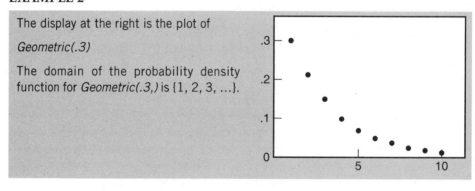

The display at the right is the plot of

Geometric(.3)

The domain of the probability density function for *Geometric(.3,)* is {1, 2, 3, ...}.

Continuous Probability Density Functions   Since probability for continuous variables is calculated using areas, we call their probability functions **probability density functions.** All continuous probability density functions produce curves such that the total area under the curve equals 1. The probability of a value of a random variable occurring in any interval in the domain of the function is equal to the area under the density function within the specified interval.

The Uniform Density Function

In a uniform probability distribution, all intervals of the same length have the same or **uniform** probability. The graph of this function is displayed at the right. Since the probability of the whole region between the values of a and b, inclusive, must equal 1, the height of the rectangle is $\frac{1}{b-a}$. In symbols, the uniform distribution is written as

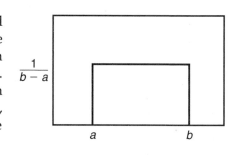

$Uniform(a, b)$

EXAMPLE 3

Let $X \sim Uniform(5, 12)$. Then the $P(X < 8)$ is calculated by computing the shaded area in the graph at the right. Therefore,

$$P(X < 8) = 3\left(\frac{1}{7}\right) = \frac{3}{7}.$$

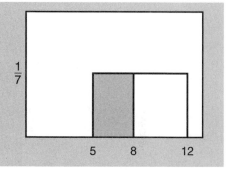

The Normal Density Function

As we have seen before, the normal probability density function is a function whose value depends on the parameters of μ, the mean, and σ, the standard deviation. In symbols, the normal distribution is written

$Normal(\mu, \sigma)$

EXAMPLE 4

The Standard Normal Density Function has distribution $Normal(0, 1)$ and is graphed below.

Note that the area corresponding to $P(-1 < X < 2)$ is shaded in the graph. Consequently, $P(-1 < X < 2) \approx .818595$.

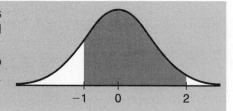

The t Probability Density Function

The t probability density function produces a symmetric distribution similar to the normal distribution. However, the t density function depends on a quantity that will be discussed extensively in Chapters 6 and 7, degrees of freedom. At the right are the graphs of the t probability density functions for degrees of freedom = 1, 2, 5, and 10. It is true that as the number of degrees of freedom increases, the corresponding t density functions approach the normal density function. In symbols, the t distribution is written

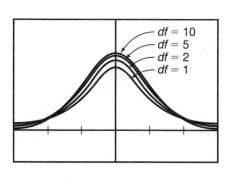

t(degrees of freedom)

The Chi-Square (χ^2) Probability Density Function

The chi-square probability density produces a non-symmetric distribution that depends on the value of degrees of freedom, just like the t density function. At the right is a graph of the chi-square probability density function for degrees of freedom 5 and 10. Again, it is true that as the number of degrees of freedom

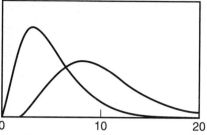

increases, the chi-square distribution approaches a normal distribution. In symbols, chi-square is written using the Greek letter chi (χ)

$$\chi^2(\text{degrees of freedom})$$

The choice of the probability density function and the theoretical probability distribution it produces depends on the situation that you are considering.

Great care must be exercised in checking the assumptions of a given situation that will provide the basis for the choice of density function.

Technology Note: Most statistical software packages include capabilities for the evaluation of these and other probability density functions. In addition, on its *DISTR* menu, the TI-83 graphing calculator provides these functions (and others) and an adaptation of the cumulative probability density functions using the syntax listed in the table below.

Note: A cumulative probability density function is defined as a function that returns $P(X \leq x)$ for some value of x in the domain. The *cdf* functions for continuous distributions on the TI-83 calculator are designed to return $P(a < X < b)$ for each of the distributions. The *cdf* function for discrete distributions mirrors the technical definition of the cumulative density function, i.e., it returns the sum of the probabilities for all X less than or equal to a specified x. In the case of the binomial and geometric, the calculator returns the sum of probabilities from $X = 0$ to $X =$ a specified x.

	Function	Probability Density	Cumulative Density
Discrete	Binomial	*binompdf*(n, p, [x])	*binomcdf*(n, p, [x])
	Geometric	*geometpdf*(p, [x])	*geometcdf*(p, [x])
Continuous	Normal	*normalpdf*(x, mean, st. dev.)	*normalcdf*(lower, upper, mean, st. dev.)
	t	*tpdf*(x, df)	*tcdf*(lower, upper, df)
	Chi-square	χ^2pdf(x, df)	χ^2cdf(lower, upper, df)

df = degrees of freedom
[x] indicates the option of listing a particular number of successes for which to find the binomial probabilities. If this parameter is deleted, the complete set of binomial probabilities (or cumulative probabilities) for all possible numbers of successes is calculated and displayed. ■

In the case of the geometric and binomial probability mass function, we can calculate the probabilities of any set of outcomes of interest. For example: for $x = \{3, 4, 5\}$, *binomialpdf*(20, .4, {3, 4, 5}) $\approx$ {.0123, .0350, .0747} and *geometpdf* (.3, {3, 4, 5}) $\approx$ {.1470, .1029, .0720}.

Review Exercises

MULTIPLE-CHOICE QUESTIONS

1. Which of the following is a geometric probability mass function?
   (A) $P(r) = .3^r(.7)^{n-r}$
   (B) $P(r) = .3(.7)^{n-r}$
   (C) $P(r) = .7(.3)^r$
   (D) $P(r) = .7(.3)^{r-1}$
   (E) None of these is a geometric probability mass function.

2. Which of the following is *not* a legitimate uniform probability density function?

   (A) $f(x) = \begin{cases} .5 & 0 < x < 1 \\ 0 & \text{otherwise} \end{cases}$

   (B) $f(x) = \begin{cases} .5 & 3 < x < 5 \\ 0 & \text{otherwise} \end{cases}$

   (C) $f(x) = \begin{cases} 3 & 1 < x < 1\frac{1}{3} \\ 0 & \text{otherwise} \end{cases}$

   (D) $f(x) = \begin{cases} .25 & -2 < x < 2 \\ 0 & \text{otherwise} \end{cases}$

   (E) All of these are uniform probability density functions.

3. A knife thrower estimates that he can hit his target 95% of the time. Assuming that each of his throws is independent, which of the following probability statements is correct?
   (A) P(4 hits in his next 6 throws) $= \binom{6}{4}(.05)^2(.95)^4$
   (B) P(4 hits in his next 6 throws) $= (.05)^4(.95)^2$
   (C) P(4 hits in his next 6 throws) $= \binom{6}{4}(.05)^4(.95)^2$
   (D) P(4 hits in his next 6 throws) $= (.05)^2(.95)^4$
   (E) None of these is correct.

4. The center of the χ^2 probability density function moves to the right and the shape becomes "flatter" as the number of degrees of freedom increases. Which of the following statements is also true as the number of degrees of freedom increases?
   (A) The graph approaches the graph of a uniform density function.
   (B) The graph approaches the graph of a probability mass function.
   (C) The graph approaches the graph of a normal density function.
   (D) The graph approaches the graph of a geometric probability mass function.
   (E) None of these is true.

5. A store runs a promotion in which each customer is given a token that is redeemable for cash, credit, or merchandise during each visit to the store. One hundred out of the 10,000 tokens are redeemable for a $100 store credit. Assuming that the probability of getting a winning token remains constant and that each visit to the store is independent of other visits, find the approximate probability that a person will receive his first $100 store credit token on either his 6th or 7th visit to the store.
   (A) .002
   (B) .007
   (C) .006
   (D) .019
   (E) This probability cannot be calculated from the information given.

FREE-RESPONSE QUESTIONS

Open-Ended Questions

1. Explain how a probability is determined using a continuous density function.

2. Explain the difference between the situations that should be addressed by either the Binomial or the Geometric mass functions.

3. Choose the appropriate probability function and answer the following question: Suppose the probability of a win for the local minor league baseball team in any game is .6. What is the probability that the first win will occur on the 3rd or 4th game of a 10-game road trip?

4. A student decides not to study. Suppose that the probability of passing any one test without studying is .4. Calculate:
   a. the probability of passing 4 tests out of 10 tests during the semester.
   b. the probability that the first pass will occur on the 4th test.

5. A uniform distribution is defined on the interval $[-1, 1]$.
   a. Sketch a graph of the probability density function.
   b. Define the rule of the probability function; that is, complete $f(x) = \begin{cases} \end{cases}$
   c. Verify that your rule in part b satisfies the conditions for a continuous probability density function.
   d. Calculate the probability $P(0 < X < 1)$. Show a sketch to support your calculation.

5.10 Simulating Events With Random Digits Tables and the TI-83

Simulation can be very productive in helping you to gain insight into the nature of random events. A simulation can be conducted with physical objects, random digit tables, or technology. In this section we will review two simulation techniques using random digits tables and the random number generators of the TI-83.

Standard Simulation *EXAMPLE 1*

It has been published that 40% of mathematics majors in undergraduate school are female. At a local university, only 30% of their 10 math majors are female; the math department suggests that this percentage could have happened by chance. Conduct a simulation to determine how likely it is for only 30% of 10 majors to be female if they are randomly selected from a population of 40% females.

Solution

We will use simulation to approximate the proportion of times we obtain a sample of 10 students in which 3 or fewer are female by taking repeated samples from a population with a true proportion of .4 females.

a. **Random Digits Table:** The published percentage is .4. If we consider the single digits from 0 to 9, we will assign 0, 1, 2, and 3 to indicate females and the balance of the digits to indicate males. This way, P(female) = .4. Consider samples of 10 digits from the random digits table. Record the number of 0's, 1's, 2's, or 3's in each sample. Continue for a specified number of trials (e.g. 50 or 100). In order to answer the question, calculate the percentage of times that the samples of 10 digits contained 3 or fewer females, i.e. contained 3 or fewer of the set {0, 1, 2, 3}.

For example, underlining 0, 1, 2, and 3 in this sample table:

9435974025	9083188611	4668782925	1470195054	0580964187
3381121120	4399198753	3936252594	9546634112	0034026187
9807010099	5189983326	2209784733	3694814382	0078387869
9351587791	1080114624	0062633066	5489861799	8555803142
9770842465	2783088265	2752142947	1217901355	0525898067
2237931570	1256556214	2111829173	0763515019	7220777198
2881701368	3781148461	8123118520	5080954298	4662442672
4532817630	1745017524	9276426494	6183977490	5219829504
2790944111	3850776965	4332199854	0887976326	2867533123
2844570857	3714719971	7769219809	2028398363	8516117032

Out of the 50 blocks (samples of size 10), 17 contain 3 or fewer "females", so the proportion is $\frac{17}{50}$, or .34. Based on this simulation, it seems somewhat, but not highly unlikely that only 30% of the math majors are female. Either repeating the simulation several times or using many more samples would allow us to better approximate the probability.

b. **TI-83:** Using the *randInt* command in the *MATH PRB* menu, we can have the calculator produce sets of 10 random digits using the same scheme used for the random digits chart method. The command *randInt(0,9,10)* returns sets of 10 random integers from 0 through 9. *Note:* This selection is *with* replacement. Consequently, you may get repeats in the sets of ten integers selected.

The command *sum(randInt(0,9,10) ≤ 3)* counts the number of elements in each set that are less than or equal to three. This is accomplished by adding the results of a Boolean test (≤) of the elements of each set. The Boolean operator ≤ returns a 1 if the ≤ statement is true and a 0 if it is false. Therefore, the sentence *sum(randInt(0,9,10) ≤ 3)* adds a 1 for each true occurrence and a 0 for each false occurrence. Thus, the command counts the number of true statements.

Note: sum is on the *LIST MATH* menu; ≤ is on the *TEST* menu. In order to repeat the execution for another sample, press the Enter key for each repetition.

Wait-Time Simulation

A **wait-time simulation** differs from the simulation reviewed above in that we continue the simulation until a condition occurs. This is analogous to a geometric random variable in which we count the number of trials until a success occurs.

Consider the earlier problem of choosing cereal boxes until a box containing a picture of Babe Ruth is selected. He is one of five superstars whose pictures are available for the promotion. Conduct a simulation to determine the "average" number of boxes necessary in order to get a box containing Babe Ruth's picture.

a. **Random Digits Table:** In the standard simulation, each trial was a sample of specified length. In a wait-time simulation, the length of each sample varies depending on when the first success occurs. For this problem, since Babe Ruth's picture occurs 20% of the time, assign the digits 0 and 1 to pictures of Ruth. Begin each trial in the table noting the *number of digits* necessary until a 0 or 1 occurs. Record the number of digits *including* the first success. Repeat the simulation for a specified number of trials. Find the mean number of digits needed in each trial.

For example, using the first two rows of the random digits table above, we put a mark after the "success" digit and note the number of digits necessary to find that success:

94359740|25 90|831|8861|1| 4668782925 1|470|1|950|54 0|580|9641|87
3381|1|21|1|20| 43991|98753 3936252594 95466341|1|2 0|0|340|261|

The numbers of digits in each trial are

8, 4, 3, 4, 1, 11, 3, 1, 3, 3, 3, 3, 6, 3, 1, 2, 5, 22, 1, 2, 1, 3, 3.

The mean of these trials $= \dfrac{96}{23} = 4.1739$. Since the mean number of "boxes" until a picture of Babe Ruth appeared is 4.1739, a minimum of 5 boxes would have to be purchased.

b. **TI-83:** Using the same set-up described above, we can generate sets of random digits using the *randInt* command. However, since this is a wait-time simulation, for each trial, execute the command

$randInt(0, 9)$

repeatedly until a 0 or 1 appears. This command will return only a single digit between 0 and 9 inclusive. The count of the executions of the command (including the success) is then recorded and the next trial begins. Again, repeat the simulation a number of times and find the mean of the number of executions needed to achieve a success.

Review Exercises

FREE-RESPONSE QUESTIONS

Open-Ended Questions

1. Suppose that the probability of finding a special prize in a box of popcorn is .20. Describe how you would set up a simulation to answer each of the following questions:
   a. What is the probability that of 10 boxes randomly selected, only one will contain the special prize?
   b. How many boxes of popcorn would you expect to have to buy in order to get a box with a special prize?

2. It has been determined that a mining company will find gold in 10% of the mines that they dig after they complete their geological research. Describe how you would design a simulation that will address each of the following probabilities.
   a. What is the probability that 2 mines out of the next 20 dug will strike gold?
   b. How many mines would you expect will have to be dug so that the company finds 2 that contain gold?

   (This is a problem whose exact solution is not part of the AP Statistics curriculum. However, the exact solution can be approximated with simulation.)

Use this random digit table to answer questions 3 and 4

9435974025	9083188611	4668782925	1470195054	0580964187
3381121120	4399198753	3936252594	9546634112	0034026187
9807010099	5189983326	2209784733	3694814382	0078387869
9351587791	1080114624	0062633066	5489861799	8555803142
9770842465	2783088265	2752142947	1217901355	0525898067
2237931570	1256556214	2111829173	0763515019	7220777198
2881701368	3781148461	8123118520	5080954298	4662442672
4532817630	1745017524	9276426494	6183977490	5219829504
2790944111	3850776965	4332199854	0887976326	2867533123
2844570857	3714719971	7769219809	2028398363	8516117032

3. Studies indicate that the proportion of women in management positions of companies in a particular industry is .3. A watchdog group has found that the proportion of women at a local company that has 250 employees is only .2. The company claims that this is not an unusual proportion. The watchdog organization decides to run a simulation to determine how likely it is that a company has only 20% female managers when the expectation is 30%.
   a. Would you choose a standard simulation or a wait-time simulation? Explain the reasons for your answer.
   b. Describe the method of assignment of numbers to this situation so that the random digits table given above can be used in the simulation.
   c. Show using only the first four rows of the random digits table above how your simulation operates.
   d. Use the results of your simulation to determine the probability that a company has only 20% female managers when the industry standard is 30%. Explain your calculations.

4. A manufacturer of sound systems claims that their best model will fail during customer events only 15% of the time when installed by the manufacturer's technicians. Your school is thinking about buying the best model but would like you to run a simulation to estimate how many events will occur before the system fails twice.
   a. Would you choose a standard simulation or a wait-time simulation? Explain the reasons for your answer.
   b. Describe the method of assignment of numbers to this situation so that the random digits table given above can be used in the simulation.
   c. Show using only the *last* four rows of the random digits table above how your simulation operates.
   d. Use the results of your simulation to determine the number of events that must occur before the system fails twice. Explain your calculations.

Chapter 5 Assessment

MULTIPLE-CHOICE QUESTIONS

1. If three people, Joe, Betsy, and Sue, play a game in which Joe has a 25% chance of winning and Betsy has a 40% chance of winning, what is the probability that Sue will win?
   (A) 25%
   (B) 35%
   (C) 40%
   (D) 65%
   (E) Cannot be determined.

2. A local law enforcement agency published the following percentages regarding the distribution of altercations that they were called to over the past 3 months:

Altercations Between:	Percentage
Two teens	45%
A teen and an adult	37%
Two adults	18%

Therefore, the percentage of altercations to which the law enforcement agency was called that involved at least one teenager was:
   (A) 8%
   (B) 37%
   (C) 45%
   (D) 55%
   (E) 82%

Use the information below to answer questions 3 and 4.

The primary air exchange system on a proposed spacecraft has four separate components (call them A, B, C, and D) that all must work properly for the system to operate well. Assume that the probability of any one component working is independent of the other components. It has been shown that the probabilities of each component working are $P(A) =$ .95; $P(B) = .90$; $P(C) = .99$; and $P(D) = .90$.

3. Find the probability that the entire system works properly.
   (A) .2382
   (B) .6561
   (C) .7618
   (D) .8145
   (E) None of these.

4. What is the probability that at least one of the four components will work properly?
   (A) .000005
   (B) .238195
   (C) .761805
   (D) .999995
   (E) None of these.

Use the information below to answer questions 5–8.

The following table shows the frequencies of political affiliations in the age ranges listed from a random sample of adult citizens in a particular city:

	Democrats	Republicans	Independents
18–30	25	18	12
31–40	32	21	10
41–50	17	25	17
Over 50	14	32	15

5. What proportion of the Republicans are over 50?
   (A) $\dfrac{61}{238}$
   (B) $\dfrac{32}{96}$
   (C) $\dfrac{96}{238}$
   (D) $\dfrac{32}{61}$
   (E) Cannot be determined.

6. If one adult citizen is chosen at random, what is the probability that this person is a Democrat between the ages of 41 and 50?
   (A) $\dfrac{17}{238}$
   (B) $\dfrac{17}{88}$
   (C) $\dfrac{61}{238}$
   (D) $\dfrac{17}{61}$
   (E) $\dfrac{88}{238}$

7. Given that a person chosen at random is between 31 and 40, what is the probability that this person is an Independent?
   (A) $\dfrac{10}{238}$
   (B) $\dfrac{10}{63}$
   (C) $\dfrac{10}{54}$
   (D) $\dfrac{54}{238}$
   (E) $\dfrac{63}{238}$

8. What proportion of the citizens sampled are over 50 or Independent?
   (A) $\dfrac{54}{238}$
   (B) $\dfrac{61}{238}$
   (C) $\dfrac{100}{238}$
   (D) $\dfrac{115}{238}$
   (E) Cannot be determined.

9. If $P(A) = .4$, $P(B) = .2$, and $P(A \text{ and } B) = .08$, which of the following is true?
   (A) Events A and B are independent and mutually exclusive.
   (B) Events A and B are independent but not mutually exclusive.
   (C) Events A and B are mutually exclusive but not independent.
   (D) Events A and B are neither independent nor mutually exclusive.
   (E) Events A and B are independent but whether A and B are mutually exclusive cannot be determined from the given information.

For questions 10–13, select the most appropriate probability model for the given situation. Use the following answer scheme for each situation. Explain the reasons for your choices. Do not calculate the probabilities.

(A) Binomial model
(B) Geometric model
(C) Uniform model
(D) Normal model
(E) None of these models is appropriate.

10. What is the probability that a family with 6 children will have 3 boys and 3 girls?

11. What is the probability that a person is over 6 feet tall if the mean height of her age group is 5′6″ and the standard deviation is 10″?

12. What is the probability that a shipment of 100 fruit will have no more than 6 rotten fruits if the probability that any one fruit is rotten is .04?

13. What is the probability that the first base hit will occur during the fourth at-bat if the probability that the hitter gets a base hit is .27 for any at-bat?

FREE-RESPONSE QUESTIONS

Open-Ended Questions

Use this information for questions 1 and 2.

Suppose a basketball player scores on 70% of her free throws. Assume each shot is independent and that the probability of scoring is the same for each trial.

1. Find the probability that she scores on 3 of her next 5 attempts.

2. Find the probability that the first time she scores is on her 3rd attempt.

3. A test for a certain disease has the following properties: the test is positive 98% of the time for persons who have the disease. The test is also positive 1% of the time for those who do not have the disease. Studies have established that 7% of the population has the disease.
   a. What is the probability that a person chosen at random will test positive?
   b. What is the probability that a person who tests positive actually has the disease?
   c. Based on your analysis, would you say that this test is reliable for the detection of this disease? Explain your answer.

4. It has been determined that the probability of finding 3 or more rotten oranges in a box of 12 shipped from a southern state is 5%.
   a. Calculate the exact probability that 2 of the next 20 boxes will contain 3 or more rotten oranges.
   b. Does the information in this problem allow the use of the normal approximation to the binomial? Explain your answer.

5. Probability density functions generate the probability that events will occur. Explain briefly the most important difference between the density functions for continuous and discrete variables.

Investigative Tasks

1. Given that the probability that a particular archer will hit the bull's eye at a distance of 50 feet is .6, calculate the probability that she will hit 40 bull's eyes out of her next 70 shots:
   a. by the Binomial formula (show substitution).
   b. by TI-83 functions (show syntax).
   c. Evaluate whether the normal approximation can be employed.
   d. If the result of part c is affirmative, perform the calculation by the normal approximation.
   e. Compare the results of a, b, and d (if applicable).
   f. Describe how you would set up a simulation to answer this problem.
   g. Rewrite the problem so that a wait-time simulation would be an appropriate method for solution of your new problem.

2. As the Vice President of Transportation at a large company, you have been asked by the president to estimate the chance that an important package can be delivered to a remote warehouse within 12 to 15 hours of its pickup. Your Chief Dispatcher responds that, based on the data from a random sample of 15 similar deliveries, the time from pickup to delivery has ranged from 8.5 to 17.25 hours with a mean of 13.65 hours and a standard deviation of 3.75 hours.
   a. Calculate the probability that the delivery time will be in the range of 12 to 15 hours if the variable Time:
      (1) is uniformly distributed on the interval 8.5 hours to 17.25 hours.
      (2) is normally distributed with a mean and standard deviation of 13.65 hours and 3.75 hours respectively.
      (3) follows a Chi-square distribution with 14 degrees of freedom.
   b. Based on these analyses, what would your response to the president be? Explain.

Chapter 6   Sampling Distributions

6.1   Introduction

6.2   The Concept of a Sampling Distribution

6.3   The Sampling Distribution of a Sample Proportion

6.4   The Sampling Distribution of a Difference of Two Proportions

6.5   The Sampling Distribution of a Sample Mean (σ known)

6.6   The Sampling Distribution of a Sample Mean (σ unknown)

6.7   The Distributions Associated With a Difference of Sample Means

6.8   Summary of Distributions and Their Assumptions

Chapter 6   Assessment

Chapter 6 Sampling Distributions

6.1 Introduction

The power and utility of statistics arise from the fact that an investigator can gain insight into the nature of a population by analyzing the results of a sample from that population. As discussed in Chapter 4, the relationship between the sample and its population can be viewed graphically as

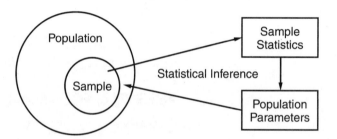

In this chapter, we will explore the variability of sample statistics for a population; this discussion will lead to methods of statistical inference, the focus of Chapter 7.

As indicated in the figure above, there are two distinct descriptors of information related to data. We will define each and then display a chart of common notation for each.

A **statistic** is a numerical value that describes a characteristic of the data contained in a *sample*. This sample may consist of specific values from the population or may consist of the results of a repeated process, such as flipping a coin or rolling a die. Different samples may yield different statistics. Statistics are generally denoted by English letters.

A **parameter** is a numerical value that describes a characteristic in a *population* or a *process*. A population parameter is a unique value. Parameters are generally denoted by Greek letters.

Quantity	Statistic	Parameter
Mean	$\bar{x}$	μ
Standard Deviation	s	σ
Proportion	$\hat{p}$	p

In keeping with the AP program and many other texts, we will use p for the population proportion. Other references may use θ or π for same quantity.

Review Exercise

MULTIPLE-CHOICE QUESTION

Which of the following are true?

    I. The mean of a population depends on the particular sample chosen.

    II. The standard deviations of two different samples from the same population must be the same.

    III. Statistical inference can be used to draw conclusions about populations based on sample data.

(A) I and II

(B) II only

(C) III only

(D) II and III

(E) None of the above gives the complete set of true choices.

6.2 The Concept of a Sampling Distribution

If we were to conduct a census of a population, we could calculate the values of any parameter that we wished. On the other hand, when we rely on a sample, we can only calculate an *estimate* of the population parameter of interest. It is most likely that this estimate, the sample statistic, will differ from the true value of the corresponding population parameter. In addition, the value of the statistic would undoubtedly be different if we were to gather a different sample from the same population. This difference in the values of sample statistics is known as **sampling variability,** and it is the reason that we consider a sample statistic to be a *random variable* whose distribution merits investigation.

EXAMPLE 1

If we roll a die, we expect that each number from one to six will occur approximately $\frac{1}{6}$ of the time. Consequently, we would expect that if we were to roll the die 100 times (i.e., sample size = 100), we should get approximately 17 sixes (or $\frac{100}{6}$ sixes). One method of investigating the event of rolling a die one hundred times is to *simulate* the 100 rolls and calculate the proportion of sixes for each simulation.

For example, if we were to roll a die 100 times and get a total of 12 sixes, then the proportion of sixes will equal .12 (the first entry in the table below). The resulting proportions from 200 simulations of 100 rolls each are shown below:

Simulated $\hat{p}$ Values ($p = .167$)

.12	.18	.17	.16	.12	.23	.24	.24	.17	.14	.13	.13	.12
.19	.14	.18	.12	.15	.14	.14	.22	.17	.15	.22	.12	.19
.11	.20	.16	.21	.16	.18	.15	.12	.19	.15	.14	.22	.18
.21	.18	.16	.21	.14	.21	.10	.17	.16	.14	.13	.13	.21
.15	.19	.19	.18	.20	.26	.18	.11	.27	.14	.18	.15	.20
.17	.19	.15	.18	.18	.21	.20	.12	.15	.18	.16	.14	.12
.13	.20	.19	.19	.14	.25	.19	.18	.16	.14	.21	.22	.17
.19	.19	.18	.23	.14	.15	.16	.22	.21	.14	.14	.19	
.15	.22	.10	.10	.16	.23	.23	.10	.16	.15	.15	.15	
.17	.15	.14	.15	.14	.18	.17	.15	.18	.18	.15	.13	
.18	.16	.14	.14	.15	.19	.16	.11	.17	.16	.11	.16	
.10	.17	.15	.12	.19	.16	.10	.21	.16	.17	.16	.16	
.15	.18	.16	.18	.22	.11	.17	.21	.19	.16	.18	.10	
.18	.21	.22	.20	.13	.21	.17	.16	.17	.17	.15	.12	
.16	.17	.20	.19	.16	.18	.15	.15	.17	.20	.15	.14	
.21	.21	.14	.17	.22	.13	.13	.20	.18	.18	.15	.17	

The summary values for these simulations are:

Number of samples	Number of rolls in each sample (sample size)	Mean of the sample proportions	Standard Deviation of the sample proportions	Minimum of the sample proportions	Maximum of the sample proportions
200	100	.17	.03	.10	.27

A histogram of the simulated values is:

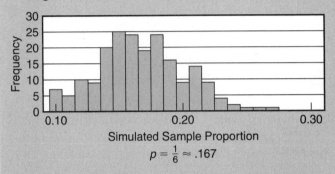

Simulated Sample Proportion
$p = \frac{1}{6} \approx .167$

The existence of sampling variation can be seen clearly in these values. Even though we would expect a proportion of $\frac{1}{6}$, there is a great deal of variation in the values of the proportions from the 200 trials.

Note the following features of the histogram of the 200 sample proportions:

- the population proportion is approximately equal to .167, the expected value of the sample proportion;
- the graph is relatively symmetric;
- the distribution can be approximated with the normal distribution.

Here are the summary statistics and histogram of the simulated values from running the simulations again, this time rolling the die 1,000 times each time.

Number of samples	Number of rolls in each sample (sample size)	Mean of the sample proportions	Standard Deviation of the sample proportions	Minimum of the sample proportions	Maximum of the sample proportions
200	1000	.167	.012	.137	.201

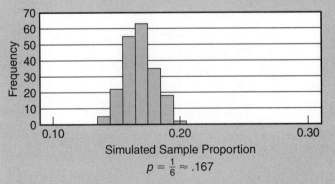

Simulated Sample Proportion
$p = \frac{1}{6} \approx .167$

Note that the distribution appears even more symmetric with approximately the same center. However, the spread of values is considerably smaller. The change in the standard deviations of the two distributions (.03 vs. .012) confirms the graphical evidence regarding the spread of the proportions from the simulations. It is important to realize that these simulations present results which will undoubtedly be slightly different when the process is repeated.

Summary of important information about the concept of a sampling distribution:

- The **sampling distribution** of a statistic is the set of values that the statistic can take on if all possible samples with the same sample size are taken from the population or if all possible repetitions of a process are performed. A sampling distribution is a *probability distribution* showing how the statistic varies. Taking a finite number of samples, as we did above, approximates this sampling distribution.

And, as is exemplified above, many of the sampling distributions that we study have the following characteristics:

- The sampling distribution is symmetric and can be approximated by a normal distribution.
- A statistic, used as an estimator of a parameter, is an **unbiased estimator** of the parameter if the mean of the sampling distribution equals the value of the parameter. That is, if a statistic is unbiased, its expected value is the population parameter. That is, $E(\text{statistic}) = \text{parameter}$, if the statistic is unbiased. For example, if $\hat{p}$ is unbiased, then $E(\hat{p}) = p$; if $\bar{x}$ is unbiased, $E(\bar{x}) = \mu$; if s is unbiased, then $E(s) = \sigma$. If the samples are selected in an appropriate way (such as a simple random sample, stratified random sample, systematic sample, etc.), then the value of the statistic may be an *unbiased estimator* of the population parameter.
- The variability of the statistic is measured by the spread of its sampling distribution. While the amount of the variability depends both on the sampling design and the sample size, it is true that larger samples yield less variability in the sample statistics than smaller samples. It is generally accepted that if the size of the population is very large in relation to the sample size, the variability of the statistic depends *only* on the sample size and *not* on the population size.

Regarding the issue of an *unbiased estimator,* the theoretical process to determine the bias in an estimate is beyond the scope of AP Statistics. However, the concept of unbiased estimators can be investigated if we consider a very small population and all the possible samples of the population. Consider the task of estimating the popularity of a movie recently released at four theaters of approximately the same size. The data on ticket sales for the same showing of the movie are given in the table:

Theater	1	2	3	4
Number of tickets	250	300	400	275

If we consider these theaters as our population, we have the following parameters:

$\mu = 306.25$, total $= 1{,}225$, $\sigma^2 = 4{,}322.92$, and $\sigma = 65.75$.

Now let us take all the possible samples of size 2 and calculate corresponding statistics. There are a total of 6 possible samples:

Theaters in sample	Values in sample	Mean of sample	Total in sample	Estimated total in population	Variance of sample	Standard Deviation of sample
1, 2	250, 300	275	550	1,100	1,250	35.36
1, 3	250, 400	325	650	1,300	11,250	106.07
1, 4	250, 275	262.5	525	1,050	312.5	17.68
2, 3	300, 400	350	700	1,400	5,000	70.71
2, 4	300, 275	287.5	575	1,150	312.5	17.68
3, 4	400, 275	337.5	675	1,350	7,812.5	88.39

Since each sample is equally likely, the probability of each is $\frac{1}{6}$. Therefore,

1. $E(\text{sample mean}) = 275\left(\frac{1}{6}\right) + 325\left(\frac{1}{6}\right) + 262.5\left(\frac{1}{6}\right) + 350\left(\frac{1}{6}\right) + 287.5\left(\frac{1}{6}\right)$
$+ 337.5\left(\frac{1}{6}\right) = 306.25$

2. $E(\text{sample variance}) = 1250\left(\frac{1}{6}\right) + 11250\left(\frac{1}{6}\right) + 312.5\left(\frac{1}{6}\right) + 5000\left(\frac{1}{6}\right)$
$+ 312.5\left(\frac{1}{6}\right) + 7812.5\left(\frac{1}{6}\right) = 4322.92$

3. $E(\text{standard deviation}) = 35.36\left(\frac{1}{6}\right) + 106.07\left(\frac{1}{6}\right) + 17.68\left(\frac{1}{6}\right) + 70.71\left(\frac{1}{6}\right)$
$+ 17.68\left(\frac{1}{6}\right) + 88.39\left(\frac{1}{6}\right) = 55.98$

4. $E(\text{estimated total}) = 1100\left(\frac{1}{6}\right) + 1300\left(\frac{1}{6}\right) + 1050\left(\frac{1}{6}\right) + 1400\left(\frac{1}{6}\right) + 1150\left(\frac{1}{6}\right)$
$+ 1350\left(\frac{1}{6}\right) = 1,225$

Since the results for the sample mean, sample variance, and the estimated total from a sample match the population parameters given above, these statistics are *unbiased estimators* of the corresponding population parameter. Note that the sample standard deviation is *not* an unbiased estimator of the population standard deviation.

Review Exercises

MULTIPLE-CHOICE QUESTIONS

1. Which of the following best describes a sampling distribution of a statistic?
   (A) It is the probability that the sample statistic equals the parameter of interest.
   (B) It is the probability distribution of all the values that are contained in all possible samples of the same size.
   (C) It is the distribution of all of the statistics calculated from all possible samples of the same size.
   (D) It is the histogram of sample statistics from all possible samples of the same size.
   (E) It is none of these.

2. A simple random sample of 50 adults were asked to reveal their gross annual incomes. The variance of this sample:
   (A) is always smaller than the variance of the population.
   (B) cannot be computed since the population size is not given.
   (C) equals the variance of the population.
   (D) is an estimate of the variance in the sampling distribution of the means of the gross annual incomes of all possible samples.
   (E) is an estimate of the variance of the population but may differ from the variance of the population.

3. A simple random sample of 100 high school seniors in a certain suburb reveals that 65% of them have at least part-time jobs in addition to school. If the expected value of this proportion is equal to the proportion of high school seniors who have at least part-time jobs for the entire suburb, then we say that the sample proportion is:
(A) a true value.
(B) an unbiased estimator of the population proportion.
(C) equal to the population proportion.
(D) an estimate whose variance equals the variance of data in the population.
(E) less than the population proportion since only 100 students were sampled.

Use the following information for questions 4 and 5. Suppose you roll a die 10 times and record the proportion of sixes. Suppose you then conduct a simulation of this experiment, first 100 times, then 1,000 times, and draw one histogram of the proportion of sixes found after 100 simulations and a second histogram of the proportions of sixes found after 1,000 simulations.

4. Which of the following is true regarding the mean of the proportions of sixes from each simulation?
(A) The mean of the proportion of sixes for the 100 simulations will equal the mean of the proportion of sixes for the 1,000 simulations.
(B) The mean of the proportion of sixes for the 1,000 simulations will be a better estimator of the theoretical probability of rolling a six than the mean of the proportion of sixes for the 100 simulations.
(C) The mean of the proportion of sixes for the 100 simulations will be less than the mean of the proportion of sixes for the 1,000 simulations.
(D) The mean of the proportions of sixes for both simulations will not estimate the theoretical probability of rolling a six since they are finite samples from a infinite population.
(E) None of these is true.

5. Which of the following statements are true regarding the histograms of the results from the two simulations?
I. The histograms from both simulations will be skewed left since a fair die does not exist in nature.
II. The histograms from both simulations will be mound-shaped and symmetric.
III. The histogram from the experiment that has 1,000 simulations will tend to be more mound-shaped and symmetric than the histogram from the experiment that has 100 simulations.

(A) I only
(B) I and II
(C) II and III
(D) III only
(E) None of these statements is true.

6. Two simple random samples of 50 undergraduates each from two universities are taken to determine the proportion of students who approve of the food service at their respective schools. The first university has an enrollment of 5,000 undergraduates while the second university has an enrollment of 35,000 undergraduates. Which of the following is the most accurate statement regarding these samples?
(A) The variability of the sample from the larger university will be greater than the variability of the sample from the smaller university.
(B) The proportion of students who approve of the food service will be the same since the sample sizes are the same.
(C) The enrollment figures from the two universities are not relevant to whether the sample statistics obtained are unbiased estimates of the parameters of the two populations.
(D) If a university with 100,000 undergraduates conducted a simple random sample of 50 of its students, the results would be less accurate than either sample referenced above.
(E) None of these is an accurate statement.

FREE-RESPONSE QUESTION

Open-Ended Question

Consider the following experiment: Draw a single card out of a box containing 3 red cards and 2 blue cards 10 times with replacement. Calculate the proportion of red cards that are drawn out of the 10 trials. Describe what you would expect regarding center, variability, and the histogram if the experiment is repeated:
a. 20 times.
b. 100 times.
c. for all possible combinations.

6.3 The Sampling Distribution of a Sample Proportion

The focus of many surveys is to determine the proportion of the population that does or does not possess a certain characteristic. For example, what proportion of moviegoers buys refreshments? What proportion of households owns a computer? The question that must then be answered is how well a sample proportion estimates a population proportion.

The Central Limit Theorem for a Proportion

If a sample of size n is taken from a large population with a proportion of success p, the sampling distribution of a sample proportion, $\hat{p}$, is approximately normal with a mean of p and a standard deviation of $\sqrt{\dfrac{p(1-p)}{n}}$.

In symbols,

$$\hat{p} \sim Normal\left(p, \sqrt{\frac{p(1-p)}{n}}\right)$$

Since we are considering the probability that success is equal to p, it is reasonable to compare this distribution to the corresponding binomial distribution. We can then approximate this distribution using the normal approximation to the binomial to arrive at this normal distribution.

Important Notes and Assumptions:

1. A population is considered large relative to sample size n if the population size is greater than $10n$. This allows us to assume the constant probability of success required by the Binomial criterion.
2. $\hat{p}$ is an unbiased estimator of p. This assumption will be satisfied if a simple random sample is conducted.
3. The normal distribution provides an accurate approximation to the sampling distribution when $np > 10$ and $n(1-p) > 10$. If either of these conditions is not true, the normal distribution is not an appropriate choice for the probability distribution for the sample proportion since the distribution of the data exhibits substantial skewness. For example, consider the histogram of a set of sample proportions with an "appropriate" normal curve superimposed on it for $n = 50$ and $p = .2$.

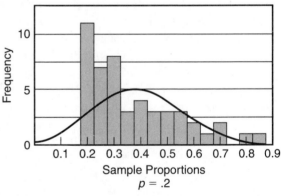

Sample Proportions
p = .2

   Note: Some references use the following phrasing to explain the Central Limit Theorem: "n should be large for the sampling distribution to be approximately normal." Many recommend that students use a "rule of thumb" of $n \geq 30$. The conditions stated above for np and $n(1-p)$ address this need as well as the shape's dependence on p. Consequently, we will include only the np and $n(1-p)$ conditions in this book, as is done in the grading of the AP Statistics exam.
4. The calculation of the standard deviation uses the value of p. We emphasize the need always to use the population proportion in this calculation. When p is known, it is *not* correct to use $\hat{p}$ in the calculation of the standard deviation of the sampling distribution.

When all of the assumptions of the Central Limit Theorem for a proportion are met, the normal distribution can be used to answer probability problems dealing with sample statistics. Remember, it is critical to check that the assumptions are met before you apply the Central Limit Theorem to solve the problem. You should indicate your checks of assumptions *clearly* so that the AP test reader understands that you have verified that the situation in the problem satisfies the assumptions for the sampling distribution.

Technology Note: You can use the TI-83 to calculate the probabilities in several ways.

1. The *normalcdf(* command, found on the *DISTR* menu, returns the area under the normal curve for a specified interval. The syntax to use is *normalcdf(lowerbound, upperbound, μ, σ)*. This command can be used directly from the data using its mean or standard deviation, or can be used with the standard normal variable ($\mu = 0$, $\sigma = 1$) with the bounds specified by z-scores. We will show both formats in the examples. Since the z-score calculation should be shown for all work in AP Statistics, we recommend in all cases that you use the standard normal version in your calculations of areas under the normal curve.

2. The *ShadeNorm(* command, found on the *DISTR DRAW* menu, draws the normal curve specified by the given mean, μ, and standard deviation, σ, and shades the area between the lower and upper bounds specified. The syntax to use is *ShadeNorm(lowerbound, upperbound, μ, σ)*. The display will also show you the area of the shaded portion limited by the lower bound, "*low*," and upper bound, "*up*," that you specified. This area represents the probability you are seeking.

Note that when using the TI-83, the following expressions using scientific notation are used to represent infinity:

positive infinity: 1E99   negative infinity: −1E99 ■

EXAMPLE 1

The Census Bureau reports that 40% of the 50,000 families in a particular region have more than one color TV in their household. What is the probability that a simple random sample of size 100 will indicate 45% or more households with more than one color TV when the population proportion is 40%?

Solution

$p = .4$, $n = 100$, $\hat{p} = .45$

a. Check assumptions.

   ✓ Simple random sample from large $50{,}000 > 10(100)$
       population?

   ✓ $np > 10$ and $n(1 - p) > 10$ $(100)(.4) = 40$; $(100)(.6) = 60$

   Therefore,

$$\hat{p} \sim Normal\left(p, \sqrt{\frac{p(1 - p)}{n}}\right)$$

$$\sim Normal\left(.40, \sqrt{\frac{.40(1 - .40)}{100}}\right)$$

$$\sim Normal(.40, .049)$$

b. Calculate $P(\hat{p} \ge .45)$.

$$z = \frac{\hat{p} - p}{\sqrt{\dfrac{p(1-p)}{n}}}$$

$$= \frac{.45 - .40}{\sqrt{\dfrac{.40(1-.40)}{100}}}$$

$$= 1.02$$

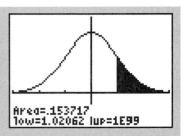

Using a table or technology, probability = .1537
[TI-83 syntax: *ShadeNorm(.45,1,.40,.049)* or *ShadeNorm(1.02,1E99,0,1)* or *normcdf(.45,1,.40,.049)* or *normcdf(1.02,1E99,0,1)*]

Therefore, there is a probability of roughly .15 that a sample of size 100 will have a proportion of .45 or more when the population proportion is .40. A sample proportion of .45 is not necessarily an unexpected event, and could easily occur due simply to sampling variation.

EXAMPLE 2

A large high school has approximately 1,200 seniors. The administration of the school claims that 87% of its graduates are accepted into colleges. If a simple random sample of 80 seniors is taken, what is the probability that at most 64 of them will be accepted into colleges?

Solution

$p = .87, n = 80, \hat{p} = .80$

a. Check assumptions.

✓ Simple random sample from large population?   *1,200 > 10(80)*

✓ $np > 10$ and $n(1 - p) > 10$ *80(.87) = 69.6; 80(.13) = 10.4*

Therefore,
$$\hat{p} \sim Normal\left(p, \sqrt{\frac{p(1-p)}{n}}\right)$$

$$\sim Normal\left(.87, \sqrt{\frac{.87(1-87)}{80}}\right)$$

$$\sim Normal(.87, .038)$$

b. Calculate.
Note that the words "at most" mean 64 or fewer students. Since $\hat{p} = \dfrac{64}{80} = .80$, we calculate $P(\hat{p} \le .8)$.

$$z = \frac{\hat{p} - p}{\sqrt{\dfrac{p(1-p)}{n}}}$$

$$= \frac{.80 - .87}{.038}$$

$$= 1.842$$

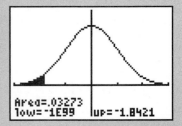

Using a table or technology, probability below = .0327
[TI-83 syntax: *ShadeNorm(0,.8,.87,.038)* or *ShadeNorm(-1E99,-1.842,0,1)* or *normalcdf(0,.8,.87,.038)* or *normalcdf(-1E99,-1.842,0,1)*]

Therefore, there is a probability of .0327 that a sample of 80 students will return a proportion of .80 or less when the population proportion is .87. Such a sample statistic would therefore be somewhat surprising.

Note: Since Example 2 is dealing with a count, it is clear that it involves discrete data. Technically, in order to use the normal curve to approximate its sampling distribution, we should employ a *continuity correction* to the problem (see Section 5.7). This can be accomplished at the time of the calculation of $\hat{p}$. Since we wish to include the value of 64, we add .5 to the 64 and perform the calculation:

$$\hat{p} = \frac{64.5}{80} = .80625$$

From that point the problem proceeds as shown above.

Review Exercises

MULTIPLE-CHOICE QUESTIONS

1. Which of the following is true regarding the variation of a sampling distribution of a sample proportion?
   (A) Variation depends on population size as well as sample size.
   (B) The variance of a sampling distribution of a sample proportion for all samples of size 1 is 0.
   (C) As the size of the sample increases, the variation of the sampling distribution approaches the variation of the population.
   (D) For a given sample size, the maximum variation in the sampling distribution of a sample proportion occurs when the sample proportion is .5.
   (E) None of these is true.

2. The conditions that $np > 10$ and $n(1 - p) > 10$ are imposed on a sampling distribution to protect against
   (A) a sample that is not representative of the population.
   (B) bias in the responses of the sample participants.
   (C) skewness in the distribution.
   (D) a very small population size.
   (E) The conditions are not designed to protect against any of these conditions.

3. Records at a large university indicated that 20% of all freshmen are placed on academic probation at the end of their first semester. A random sample of 100 of this year's freshmen indicated that 25% of them were placed on academic probation at the end of the first semester. The results of this sample:
   (A) are surprising since it indicates that 5% more of these freshmen were placed on academic probation than was expected.
   (B) are surprising since SAT scores have been increasing over the past few years.
   (C) are not surprising since the standard deviation of the sampling distribution is 4%.
   (D) are surprising since the standard deviation of the sampling distribution is .4%.
   (E) are biased since the increase of 5% could not happen without injecting bias into the sample.

4. An investigator anticipates that the proportion of red blossoms in his hybrid plants is .15. A random sample of 50 of his plants indicated that 22% of the blossoms were red. The standard deviation of the sampling distribution of the sample proportion is approximately:
   (A) .051
   (B) .059
   (C) .07
   (D) .116
   (E) Cannot be determined.

Open-Ended Questions

The assumptions of the Central Limit Theorem applied to a proportion are that

1. a simple random sample has been selected from a large population, and
2. $np > 10$ and $n(1 - p) > 10$.

In questions 1–4, check each of the assumptions. If any assumption is not met, write its number, explain why it is not satisfied, and go on to the next problem. If all of the assumptions are satisfied, solve the problem and state a conclusion.

1. A manufacturer of cold medicine claims that 60% of all adults suffer at least one cold during every winter. What is the probability that a simple random sample of 200 adults will report that 65% or more of the subjects had at least one cold last winter? Would you be surprised to find such a sample result? Explain your answer.

2. A company claims that 5% of its products will be shipped in defective condition. A simple random sample of 50 products contained 5 defective products. What is the probability that 5 or more defective products could have happened by random chance?

3. A mathematics department published the claim that a minimum of 70% of students enrolled in their classes receive a final grade of C– or better in any semester. A simple random sample of 50 students from the department's classes indicated that only 65% of the students had a final grade of C– or better last semester. What is the probability that a sample of this size will have a result that differs from the claimed proportion by more than 5% (above or below)? Would such a result surprise you? State a conclusion.

4. A simple random sample of size 200 is taken from a population of 1,000 people in a professional organization regarding preferences on the issue of raising dues. What is the probability that this sample will produce a result of 10% or less favoring the raise when it is known that 3.5% of the population favor the raise?

5. Find the size of a simple random sample needed so that the probability that its proportion differs from the population proportion by more than 2% (above or below) is .1. Assume that the population proportion is .63.

6.4 The Sampling Distribution of a Difference of Two Proportions

It is common for statisticians to compare two population proportions. For example, how does the proportion of teenagers who watch a certain TV show compare with the proportion of adults who watch the same show? The result below is useful for evaluating information provided by two sample proportions.

The Central Limit Theorem for the Difference of Two Proportions

If two simple random samples of sizes n_1 and n_2 are drawn *independently* from large populations whose parameters are p_1 and p_2, the sampling distribution of the difference of the sample proportions is approximately normal with mean equal to $p_1 - p_2$ and standard deviation equal to $\sqrt{\dfrac{p_1(1 - p_1)}{n_1} + \dfrac{p_2(1 - p_2)}{n_2}}$. Notice that this formula for standard deviation is a direct consequence of the formula for the variance of the difference of independent random variables that was reviewed in Section 5.8:

$$(\sigma_{X - Y})^2 = \sigma_X^2 + \sigma_Y^2 \text{ if } X \text{ and } Y \text{ are independent.}$$

The requirement of independence of the samples is necessary so that we can write this standard deviation for the difference of the sample proportions. In symbols,

$$\hat{p}_1 - \hat{p}_2 \sim Normal\left(p_1 - p_2, \sqrt{\dfrac{p_1(1 - p_1)}{n_1} + \dfrac{p_2(1 - p_2)}{n_2}}\right)$$

Important Notes and Assumptions:

1. $\hat{p}_1 - \hat{p}_2$ is an unbiased estimator of $p_1 - p_2$.
2. Each of the samples must be simple random samples.
3. Both sample sizes must satisfy the condition: $np > 5$ and $n(1 - p) > 5$
4. The two samples must be taken *independently*.
5. The calculation of the standard deviation uses the values of p_1 and p_2. We emphasize the need always to use the population proportions in this calculation. It is not correct to use either of the sample proportions in the calculation of the standard deviation of the sampling distribution when the population proportions are known.

Great care should be taken in considering the independence requirement. Sometimes a relationship may be very subtle. For example, consider this situation:

In a large orange grove, a simple random sample of 100 trees is chosen. From each of these trees, one orange is taken for baseline information and categorized as acceptable for shipping or not. After the trees are sprayed with a new treatment, a new collection of oranges is taken from the same trees and evaluated as before. The two proportions are then compared.

Note that these samples are not independent since each utilizes the same trees. Consequently, the Central Limit Theorem does *not* apply. As we will review later, we can use a matched-pairs technique to compare the fruit before and after the treatment.

The Central Limit Theorem applied to the difference in proportions can be used to answer probability questions regarding the difference of sample proportions and to help us decide when a particular difference is significant. In the following examples, the essence of the issue is to find the probability that the two-sample proportions differ by more than some expected amount; consequently, we want to see if this observed difference is surprising. As usual, all of the assumptions need to be checked before the Central Limit Theorem is applied, and the check must be explained clearly.

EXAMPLE 1

In a large urban school district, it has been accepted that the percentages of boys and girls having a 3.0 average or higher are both approximately 10%. A random sample of 80 girls indicated that 15% of the girls fit in this category while a second independent random sample of 100 boys indicated that 12% of the boys performed at this level. If the actual difference of the proportion of boys and girls having 3.0 or higher averages is 0, find the probability that these samples would indicate that the number of girls having at least 3.0 averages is 3% or more above the number of boys with averages in the same range.

Solution

p_1 = proportion of girls = .1; n_1 = 80
p_2 = proportion of boys = .1; n_2 = 100
$\hat{p}_1 - \hat{p}_2$ = .03

a. Check assumptions.

✓ Simple random sample from large population(s)?	*Large urban school district.*
✓ Sample sizes satisfy: $np > 5$ and $n(1 - p) > 5$?	$n_1 p_1 = 12$; $n_1(1 - p_1) = 68$ $n_2 p_2 = 12$; $n_2(1 - p_2) = 88$
✓ Samples are independent?	*Stated in the problem.*

Therefore,

$$\hat{p}_1 - \hat{p}_2 \sim Normal\left(p_1 - p_2, \sqrt{\frac{p_1(1 - p_1)}{n_1} + \frac{p_2(1 - p_2)}{n_2}}\right)$$

$$\sim Normal\left(.10 - .10, \sqrt{\frac{.10(1 - .10)}{80} + \frac{.10(1 - .10)}{100}}\right)$$

$$\sim Normal(0, .045)$$

b. Calculate $P(\hat{p}_1 - \hat{p}_2 \geq .03)$.

$$z = \frac{(\hat{p}_1 - \hat{p}_2) - (p_1 - p_2)}{\sqrt{\frac{p_1(1 - p_1)}{n_1} + \frac{p_2(1 - p_2)}{n_2}}}$$

$$= \frac{.03 - 0}{.045}$$

$$= .666...$$

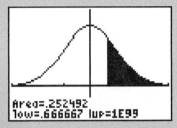

Area=.252492
low=.666667 lup=1E99

Therefore, using tables or technology, we find probability above = .2527
[TI-83 syntax: *ShadeNorm(.03,1,0,.045)* or *ShadeNorm(.666,1E99,0,1)* or *normcdf(.03,1E99,0,.045)* or *normcdf(.666,1E99,0,1)*]

Therefore, there is a probability of .2527 that samples of these sizes will have proportions that differ by .03 or more when the difference in the population proportions is 0. Consequently, having sample results that exhibit a difference in proportions of .03 or more is not very unlikely; an investigator would undoubtedly find this result uninteresting.

EXAMPLE 2

An SAT preparation company claims that students who complete their course score better on the Math SAT test than those who do not. In order to verify this claim, the Math SAT scores of a random sample of 100 students are investigated and it is found that 17% of these students score 600 or more on their Math SAT tests. An independent simple random sample of 60 students who have completed the company's course indicated that 30% of the sample scored 600 or more on their SAT tests. Assuming that the actual percentage of students who score 600 or more after taking the SAT preparation course is 17%, what is the probability that these samples will indicate a difference of 13% or more in favor of those taking the class?

Solution

p_1 = proportion who improved without the course = .17; n_1 = 100
p_2 = proportion who improved afer taking the course = .17; n_2 = 80
$\hat{p}_1$ = .17, $\hat{p}_2$ = .30

a. Check assumptions.

✓ Simple random samples from large population(s)?	*SRS stated; large student population*
✓ Sample sizes satisfy: $np > 5$ and $n(1 - p) > 5$?	$n_1p_1 = 17$; $n_1(1 - p_1) = 83$ $n_2p_2 = 13.6$; $n_2(1 - p_2) = 66.4$
✓ Samples are independent?	*Stated in the problem.*

$$\hat{p}_1 - \hat{p}_2 \sim Normal\left(p_1 - p_2, \sqrt{\frac{p_1(1 - p_1)}{n_1} + \frac{p_2(1 - p_2)}{n_2}}\right)$$

$$\sim Normal\left(.17 - .17, \sqrt{\frac{.17(1 - .17)}{100} + \frac{.17(1 - .17)}{80}}\right)$$

$$\sim Normal(0, .056)$$

b. Calculate $P(\hat{p}_1 - \hat{p}_2 \leq .13)$.

$$z = \frac{(\hat{p}_1 - \hat{p}_2) - (p_1 - p_2)}{\sqrt{\frac{p_1(1 - p_1)}{n_1} + \frac{p_2(1 - p_2)}{n_2}}}$$

$$= \frac{-.13 - 0}{.056}$$

$$= -2.321$$

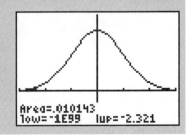

Area=.010143
low=-1E99 lup=-2.321

Therefore, using tables or technology, we find probability = .0101
[TI-83 syntax: *Shadenorm(–1E99,–.13,0,.056)* or
Shadenorm(–1E99,–2.321,0,1) or *normalcdf(–1E99,–.13,0,.056)* or
normalcdf(–1E99,–2.321,0,1)]

Therefore, there is a probability of .0101 that samples of these sizes will indicate a difference of 13% or more in favor of those taking the class when the difference in the population proportions is 0. An investigator would find this a very unlikely situation.

EXAMPLE 3

A well-recognized study has established that 15% of the people in the Midwest dislike winter weather while 19% of the people in New England do not like winter weather. A new study suggests that the gap between the two populations is closing. In independent studies, 15 of 100 randomly selected Midwesterners and 9 of 50 randomly selected New Englanders stated that they disliked winter. Find the probability that samples of these sizes will have a difference this extreme or more extreme (further from .04) when we expect a difference of 4%.

Solution

p_1 = proportions of New Englanders = .19; n_1 = 50
p_2 = proportion of Midwesterners = .15; n_2 = 100
$\hat{p}_1$ = .18, $\hat{p}_2$ = .15
a. Check assumptions.

✓ Simple random samples from large population(s)?	*SRS stated; large populations in Midwest and New England.*
✓ Sample sizes satisfy: $np > 5$ and $n(1 - p) > 5$?	$n_1p_1 = 9.5$; $n_1(1 - p_1) = 40.5$ $n_2p_2 = 15$; $n_2(1 - p_2) = 85$
✓ Samples are independent?	*Stated in the problem.*

Therefore
$$\hat{p}_1 - \hat{p}_2 \sim Normal\left(p_1 - p_2, \sqrt{\frac{p_1(1 - p_1)}{n_1} + \frac{p_2(1 - p_2)}{n_2}}\right)$$

$$\sim Normal\left(.19 - .15, \sqrt{\frac{.19(1 - .19)}{50} + \frac{.15(1 - .15)}{100}}\right)$$

$$\sim Normal(.04, .066)$$

b. Calculate $P(\hat{p}_1 - \hat{p}_2 \leq .03)$.
$$z = \frac{(\hat{p}_1 - \hat{p}_2) - (p_1 - p_2)}{\sqrt{\frac{p_1(1 - p_1)}{n_1} + \frac{p_2(1 - p_2)}{n_2}}}$$

$$= \frac{.03 - .04}{.066}$$

$$= -.1515$$

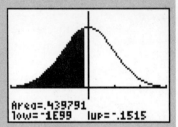

Therefore, using tables or technology, we find probability = .4398
[TI-83 syntax: *Shadenorm(–1E99,.03,.04,.066)* or
Shadenorm(–1E99,–.1515,0,1) or *normalcdf(–1E99,.03,.04,.066)* or
normalcdf(–1E99,–.1515,0,1)]

Therefore, there is a probability of .4398 that samples of these sizes will indicate a difference of 3% or less when the difference in the population proportions is 4%. This result is very likely to be explained by chance.

Review Exercises

MULTIPLE-CHOICE QUESTIONS

1. The sampling distribution of the difference of two sample proportions depends on:
   - (A) p
   - (B) n
   - (C) p and n
   - (D) the proportion in the sample.
   - (E) the proportion in the sample and n.

2. The assumption that the two samples are independent when considering the sampling distribution of a sample proportion is important because:
   - (A) if the samples are not independent, we might choose the same member in both samples.
   - (B) if the samples are not independent, we cannot calculate a combined standard deviation of the distribution.
   - (C) if the samples are not independent, we cannot have confidence in the sample proportions.
   - (D) if the samples are not independent, we cannot have confidence that the values of p_1 and p_2 are accurate.
   - (E) None of these explains the importance of independent samples.

3. In calculating the standard deviation of the sampling distribution of a difference of sample proportions,
   - (A) it is acceptable to use sample proportions since, by the Central Limit Theorem for large samples, the sample proportion is a good estimator of the population proportion.
   - (B) it is safest to use a population proportion of 0.5 since that value will produce the largest standard deviation for the sampling distribution.
   - (C) it is essential to use population proportion so that the Central Limit Theorem applies.
   - (D) it is advisable to use the difference of the sample proportions in the formula since the difference is the focus of the problem.
   - (E) it is a requirement that the two sample sizes be different.

4. A school district had anticipated that the percentages of boys and girls who planned no further education would be the same, approximately 44% for all of the students. Two independent random samples of the seniors at a high school are taken; the first was a sample of 10 boys and the second was a sample of 25 girls. The boys' sample indicated that 50% of them planned no further education after graduation, while the girls' sample indicated that only 40% of them planned no further education after graduation. Which of the following is valid for this information?
   - (A) The sampling distribution is approximately normal with mean 0 and approximate standard deviation .1857.
   - (B) The sampling distribution is approximately normal with mean .1 and approximate standard deviation .0345.
   - (C) No conclusion can be drawn regarding the sampling distribution since the samples are taken from the same population.
   - (D) No conclusion can be drawn regarding the sampling distribution since the sample size of the boys' sample is too small.
   - (E) None of these statements is valid.

FREE-RESPONSE QUESTIONS

Open-Ended Questions

The assumptions of the Central Limit Theorem applied to a difference of two proportions are:

1. two simple random samples from a large population(s);

2. both samples satisfy the condition: $np > 5$ and $n(1 - p) > 5$.

3. the samples are independent

In questions 1–3, check each of the assumptions. If any assumption is not met, write its number, explain why it is not satisfied, and go on to the next problem. If all of the assumptions are satisfied, solve the problem and state a conclusion.

Note: For questions 1–2, even though the data come from a single sample, the performances of males and females can be considered independent. Therefore, the assumption of independent samples is not violated.

1. Studies in a local school district have consistently shown that approximately 90% of high school girls take at least one course from the Department of Family and Consumer Science while only approximately 14% of boys do the same. Two random samples of 100 girls and 75 boys indicated that 87% of the girls and 16% of the boys elected at least one course in Family and Consumer Science. What is the probability that a difference of 71% or less will occur in the results obtained from samples of these sizes if the true difference is the 76% that the studies indicate?

2. A mathematics department at a large university claims that the percent of male math majors that have a 3.0 or higher average is 30% while the percent of female math majors in the same category is 22%. A simple random sample of 100 math majors (56 men and 44 women) indicated that 15 of the males and 17 of the females have averages in this range. Find the probability that the difference in the proportion of male and female math majors with averages of 3.0 or higher is as small or smaller than the sample indicates, assuming that the department's claim is true.

3. Studies have shown that the proportion of rotten fruit delivered to markets from Company A is 4% while the proportion from Company B is 2%. A simple random sample of 50 vegetable markets is chosen: at each of these markets, a simple random sample of 30 pieces of fruit is selected. The results of this sample indicate that 5% of the fruit from Company A and 4% of the fruit from Company B is rotten. Find the probability that this sample would yield a difference of 1% or less assuming the studies are correct.

4. Suppose that the true proportion of insect-damaged plants treated with Insecticide A is .05 while the proportion of insect-damaged plants treated with Insecticide B is also .05. What *equal* sample sizes are necessary to produce a probability of .2 that the difference of the sample proportions between the two insecticides in these samples exceed .03?

6.5 The Sampling Distribution of a Sample Mean (σ known)

As you will see in this section and the next, there are two sampling distributions for a sample mean. The critical distinction in the choice of distribution is whether the *population standard deviation* is known. We will treat each case separately.

The Central Limit Theorem for a Sample Mean When σ is Known

If a simple random sample of size n is taken from a population with mean μ and standard deviation σ, then when n is large, the sampling distribution of $\bar{x}$ is normal or approximately normal with mean μ and standard deviation $\frac{\sigma}{\sqrt{n}}$. In symbols,

$$\bar{x} \sim Normal\left(\mu, \frac{\sigma}{\sqrt{n}}\right)$$

The above result is reasonable because if all samples of size n (with $n > 1$) are taken from a normally distributed population with a mean of μ and a standard deviation of σ, then the distribution of the sample means *is* a normal distribution with mean μ. However, the sample means will not vary from the population mean as much as the individual observations themselves. The standard deviation of the sample means from samples whose size is greater than 1, therefore, is smaller than the standard deviation of all items of the population and is, in fact, $\frac{\sigma}{\sqrt{n}}$, which is less than σ. As the value of n increases, the value of $\frac{\sigma}{\sqrt{n}}$ decreases, which reflects the tighter clustering of the sample means about the population mean.

Important Notes and Assumptions:

1. Since the mean of the sampling distribution of $\bar{x}$ is μ, $\bar{x}$ is an unbiased estimator of μ.

2. If the population distribution is normal, then the $\bar{x}$ sampling distribution is normal ($\bar{x} \sim Normal$). On the other hand, if the population distribution is not normal, then the sampling distribution approaches a normal distribution as n increases. Therefore, if it cannot be determined whether the population is normal, the sample size n should be large. Some references refer to a "rule of thumb" of $n \geq 30$.

3. The Central Limit Theorem focuses on the *shape* of the sampling distribution. That is, it can be shown that the statements regarding the mean and standard deviation of the sampling distribution are true regardless of the shape of the sampling distribution. The Central Limit Theorem adds the fact that the sampling distribution will become "more normal" as the sample size increases.

4. If we consider a great number of samples of size $n = 1$, the shape of the distribution of these sample means will match the shape of the original population distribution.

When all of the assumptions of the Central Limit Theorem for the $\bar{x}$ sampling distribution are met, the normal distribution can be used to answer probability questions dealing with a sample mean. Note that use of the normal distribution for these problems *requires that σ be known*.

EXAMPLE 1

The Census Bureau has established that the mean income of heads of household in a particular city is $41,500 with a standard deviation of $18,700. A simple random sample of 100 heads of households in that city indicates that the mean income of the sample individuals is $45,510 with a standard deviation of $23,156. Find the probability that a sample of this size will indicate a mean of $45,510 or more.

Solution

$\mu = 41,500$, $\sigma = 18,700$, $n = 100$, $\bar{x} = 45510$

a. Check assumptions.

✓ Simple random sample?   *Stated in the problem.*

✓ Population or $n \geq 30$?   *$n = 100$*

✓ σ is known?   *$\sigma = \$18,700$*

Therefore,

$$\bar{x} \sim Normal\left(\mu, \frac{\sigma}{\sqrt{n}}\right)$$

$$\sim Normal\left(41500, \frac{18700}{\sqrt{100}}\right)$$

$$\sim Normal(41500, 1870)$$

b. Calculate $P(\bar{x} \geq 45,510)$.

$$z = \frac{45510 - 41500}{1870}$$

$$= 2.144$$

Therefore, using tables or technology, we find probability = .0160

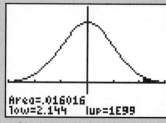

Area=.016016
low=2.144   iup=1E99

[TI-83 syntax: *Shadenorm(45510,1E99,41500,1870)* or *Shadenorm(2.144,1E99,0,1)* or *normcdf(45510,1E99,41500,1870)* or *normcdf(2.144,1E99,0,1)*]

Therefore, there is a probability of .016 that a sample of 100 will yield a sample mean of $45,510 or higher when the population mean is $41,500. Consequently, an investigator would find such a result very surprising. It is a very unlikely result if the mean income in this city is truly $41,500.

Review Exercises

MULTIPLE-CHOICE QUESTIONS

1. A sample of size 49 is drawn from a normal population with a mean of 63 and a standard deviation of 14. What are the mean and standard deviation of the distribution of sample means?
   (A) $\mu = 9$, $\sigma = 2$
   (B) $\mu = 63$, $\sigma = .286$
   (C) $\mu = 63$, $\sigma = 2$
   (D) $\mu = 1.286$, $\sigma = 3.5$
   (E) $\mu = 9$, $\sigma = 14$

2. A sample of size 25 is drawn from a normal population with a mean of 62. If the standard deviation of the distribution of sample means is 3.5, what is the standard deviation of the original population?
   (A) .056
   (B) .408
   (C) 2.48
   (D) 17.5
   (E) 87.5

3. The distribution of SAT Math scores of students taking Calculus I at a large university is skewed left with a mean of 625 and a standard deviation of 44.5. If random samples of 100 students are repeatedly taken, which statement best describes the sampling distribution of sample means?
   (A) Normal with a mean of 625 and standard deviation of 44.5.
   (B) Normal with a mean of 625 and standard deviation of 4.45.
   (C) Shape unknown with a mean of 625 and standard deviation of 44.5.
   (D) Shape unknown with a mean of 625 and standard deviation of 44.5.
   (E) No conclusion can be drawn since the population is not normally distributed.

4. Which of the following statements regarding the sampling distribution of sample means is *incorrect*?
   (A) The sampling distribution is approximately normal when the population is normal or the sample size is sufficiently large.
   (B) The mean of the sampling distribution is the mean of the population.
   (C) The standard deviation of the sampling distribution is the standard deviation of the population.
   (D) The sampling distribution is found by taking repeated samples of the same size from the population of interest and computing the mean of each sample.
   (E) All of these are correct.

5. After repeated observations, it has been determined that the waiting time at the drive-through window of a local bank on Friday afternoons between 12:00 noon and 6:00 pm is skewed left with a mean of 3.5 minutes and a standard deviation of 1.9 minutes. A sample of 100 customers is to be taken next Friday. What is the probability that the mean of the sample will exceed 4 minutes?
   (A) .0042
   (B) .0396
   (C) .042
   (D) .396
   (E) The probability cannot be determined using a normal curve approximation.

FREE-RESPONSE QUESTIONS

Open-Ended Questions

The assumptions of the Central Limit Theorem for a mean using the normal distribution technique are:

1. a simple random sample is chosen from a large population;

2. population is normal or $n \geq 30$;

3. σ is known.

In the following problems, check each of the assumptions. If any assumption is not met, write its number, explain why it is not satisfied, and go on to the next problem. If all of the assumptions are satisfied, solve the problem and state a conclusion.

1. A college bookstore claims that data it has collected for some time indicate that the mean amount of money spent on books by each student per semester is $251.92 with a standard deviation of $58.21. A simple random sample of 40 current students found that they had spent an average of $285.16 with a standard deviation of $63.15. Find the probability that a sample of this size will have an average of $285.16 or more if the average amount spent by the population is $251.92. Do you think the average amount spent has changed? Provide appropriate statistical evidence to support your position.

2. If the mean age of retirees from the teaching profession is 57 years with a standard deviation of 5.6, find the minimum sample size so that the probability that the sample mean exceeds 55 years is .6.

3. Current research indicates that the distribution of the life expectancies of a certain protozoan is normal with a mean of 45.5 days and a standard deviation of 3.4 days.

   a. Find the probability that a protozoan selected at random will live for 49 or more days.

   b. Find the probability that a simple random sample of 50 protozoa will have a mean life expectancy of 49 or more days.

4. At a large bank, account balances are normally distributed with a mean of $1,637.52 and a standard deviation of $623.16. What is the probability that a simple random sample of 400 accounts has a mean that exceeds $1,650?

5. At a large factory, it is found that the mean hourly wage is $16.50 with a standard deviation of $1.50. What is the probability that a random sample of 25 workers will have a mean hourly wage of less than $15.75?

6. SAT Math scores are normally distributed with a mean of 500 and a standard deviation of 100.

   a. What is the probability that a random sample of 100 students has a mean score between 490 and 510?

   b. If a random sample of 100 students had a mean SAT Math score of 525, would you describe these students as exceptional? Explain your answer.

6.6 The Sampling Distribution of a Sample Mean (σ unknown)

As we saw in the last section, the normal distribution is appropriate for the distribution of a sample mean when σ is known. When σ is not known, we estimate σ using s, the standard deviation of the sample. The use of this estimate of σ has a major consequence.

The *t*-distribution

The distribution of a sample mean when σ is not known can be represented by a ***t*-distribution** (sometimes called the **Student's *t*-distribution**) with mean μ, standard deviation $\frac{s}{\sqrt{n}}$, and degrees of freedom $n - 1$ where n equals the sample size. The *t*-statistic is given by:

$$t = \frac{\bar{x} - \mu}{\frac{s}{\sqrt{n}}} \quad (df = n - 1)$$

Important Notes and Assumptions:

1. All *t*-distributions are mound-shaped, symmetric, and centered at 0.
2. The spread of a *t*-distribution is slightly greater than a corresponding normal distribution with greater probability in the tails since the use of s as the estimate of σ introduces greater variability in the distribution. In the picture above, the *t*-function, $t\,(df = 2)$, is flatter and more spread out than the normal distribution.

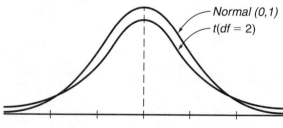

3. The sampling distribution of the test statistic $\dfrac{\bar{x} - \mu}{\frac{s}{\sqrt{n}}}$ will be approximated by a *t-distribution* when both of the following assumptions are satisfied:
   a. The sample is a simple random sample, and
   b. The population from which the sample is taken is normal
      or
      The sample size is large; again the "rule of thumb" of $n \geq 30$ is often employed.

   Note:
   a. If you only have sample information, it is advisable to display the sample data in a box plot. This display can then be used to indicate whether the population is approximately normal. Discussion should involve the shape, existence of outliers, etc. when investigating the normality of the population.
   b. Some texts do not include a consideration of size in the discussion of the use of a *t*-distribution. It can be shown that the approximation to the normal distribution by a *t*-distribution improves as sample size increases. Therefore, it is prudent to consider the sample size in deciding the appropriateness of the approximation. In all the discussions of approximating a sampling distribution by a *t*-distribution in this review, we will include a size recommendation. Thus, we suggest that the *t*-distribution is appropriate for small samples only when the observations are coming from a normal distribution.

4. When $\dfrac{s}{\sqrt{n}}$ is used to estimate $\dfrac{\sigma}{\sqrt{n}}$, we call it the **standard error** of $\bar{x}$ rather than the standard deviation. We will use this term in the balance of this review.

5. When the degrees of freedom are small (n is small), there is more spread in the associated *t*-distribution; when the degrees of freedom are large (n is large), there is less spread and the associated *t*-distributions are closer to the normal. The graph above displays *t*-distributions for degrees of freedom 1, 2, 5, and 10.

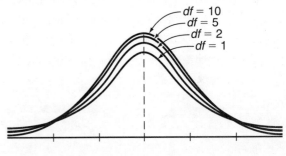

6. The major consideration in the decision whether to use a *t*-distribution or a normal distribution is whether σ is known. In practice, σ is very rarely known so most of the time the *t*-distribution is chosen to approximate the sampling distribution of a sample mean.

Since there are an infinite number of *t*-distributions, the *t*-table in the Appendix is significantly different from the table of normal probabilities. You will note that the columns are headed "Tail probability p" and the rows are headed "*df*." The body of the table contains the critical values of t that produce the tail probability for the degrees of freedom specified.

Use of this table requires you to interpolate between the listed critical values to approximate the tail probability associated with a *t*-statistic of interest.

EXAMPLE 1

Find the probability for $t \geq 2$ with degrees of freedom = 9.

Solution

In the row for $df = 9$, you will note that $t = 2$ falls between $t = 1.833$ and $t = 2.262$ corresponding to tail probabilities of .05 and .025 respectively. To interpolate, complete

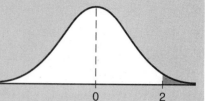

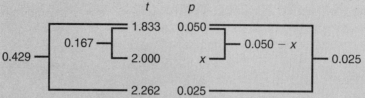

Since 2 is slightly closer to 1.833 than to 2.262, we would anticipate that the probability is slightly closer to .050 than to .025. Using linear interpolation, we can calculate an estimate of the missing value, x:

$$\frac{.050 - x}{.025} = \frac{.167}{.429}$$

$$x = .04027$$

Note: Linear interpolation is not included on the AP Statistics Syllabus. It is sufficient to state that

$.025 \leq$ probability above $\leq .05$.

To solve using the TI-83 *DISTR* command, we execute

tcdf(2, 1E99, 9)

and find that

Probability $\approx .03828$

Note the outcome of the linear interpolation will not match the result of the TI-83 exactly since linear interpolation uses a straight line to approximate the non-linear curve of the *t*-distribution.

Since there are an infinite number of *t*-distributions and tables are necessarily finite, some older textbooks claim that if $n \geq 30$, the normal distribution can be used even when σ is not known. The use of the normal distribution in this situation constitutes an approximation of the appropriate *t*-distribution. Given the accessibility of technology, this approximation is no longer necessary. Therefore, *whenever σ is not known, the sampling distribution of* $\dfrac{\bar{x} - \mu}{\frac{s}{\sqrt{n}}}$ *is a*

t-distribution if the two assumptions listed above (SRS, and normal population or $n > 30$) are satisfied.

In the examples below, where possible, an approximate probability value from the table in the Appendix will be supplied. If this is not possible, the reason will be stated. In all cases, the TI-83 value of the probability will be given with the syntax necessary to calculate it.

EXAMPLE 2

The Census Bureau has found that the distribution of ages of heads of households in a particular city is normal with a mean of 41.3 years. A simple random sample of 20 heads of households indicated a mean of 44.1 years with a standard deviation of 9.6 years. Find the probability that a sample of this size will have a mean of 44.1 years or more if the mean age in this city is 41.3 years.

Solution

$\mu = 41.3$, $n = 20$, $\bar{x} = 44.1$, $s = 9.6$

a. Check assumptions.

  ✓ Simple random sample?   *Given.*

  ✓ Normal population *or* large sample size ($n \geq 30$)?   *Normality is given.*

  Since σ is unknown we have

$$t = \frac{\bar{x} - \mu}{\frac{s}{\sqrt{n}}} \sim t(df)$$

b. Calculate $P(\bar{x} \geq 44.1)$.

$$t = \frac{44.1 - 41.3}{\frac{9.6}{\sqrt{20}}} \text{ with } df = 20 - 1 = 19$$

$$t = 1.3044$$

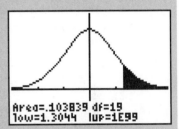

probability = *tcdf(1.3044, 1E99, 19)*

probability = .1038

Therefore, there is a probability of .1038 that a sample of 20 will yield a sample mean of 44.1 or more years when the population mean is 41.3 years. Using tables, the t-value 1.3044 with $df = 19$ falls between 1.066 (p-value .15) and 1.328 (p-value .10). Using linear interpolation we find that the approximate probability is .1046.

EXAMPLE 3

A company plans its expansion based on the belief that the mean monthly sales revenue of its 1,000 offices is $.73 million. A simple random sample of the sales revenue figures from 40 of its offices for last month indicated a mean revenue of $.68 million with a standard deviation of $.02 million. Find the probability that a sample of 40 would indicate revenue of $.68 million or less if the company's belief is true.

Solution

$\mu = .73$, $n = 40$, $\bar{x} = .68$, $s = .02$

a. Check assumptions.

  ✓ Simple random sample?   *Given.*

  ✓ Normal population *or* large sample size ($n \geq 30$)? $n = 40$

  Since σ is unknown we have

$$t = \frac{\bar{x} - \mu}{\frac{s}{\sqrt{n}}} \sim t(df)$$

b. Calculate $P(\bar{x} \leq .68 \text{ million})$.

$$t = \frac{.68 - .73}{\frac{.02}{\sqrt{40}}} \text{ with } df = 39$$

$$t = -15.811$$

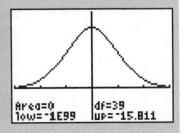

probability = *tcdf(−1E99, −15.811, 39)*

probability ≈ 0

Therefore, there is virtually no chance that a sample of 40 will yield a sample mean of $.68 million or less when the population mean is $.73 million.

Note that the *t*-table in the Appendix does not list *t*-values for areas less than .0005. For degrees of freedom = 40, the critical *t* value for a tail area of .0005 is 3.551. Therefore, it is reasonable to conclude that the probability is less than .0005 for our calculated value of *t*.

Review Exercises

MULTIPLE-CHOICE QUESTIONS

1. Which of the following are true?
   I. Like the standard normal distribution, the *t*-distribution is centered at 0.
   II. The spread of a *t*-distribution is slightly less than the corresponding normal distribution.
   III. A *t*-distribution can be used when σ is unknown and a small sample of a normal population is taken.
   (A) I only
   (B) I and II
   (C) I and III
   (D) II and III
   (E) I, II , and III

2. Which of the following are true?
   I. A *t*-distribution with 6 degrees of freedom will have less spread than a *t*-distribution with 20 degrees of freedom.
   II. A *t*-distribution with 6 degrees of freedom will have a larger critical value than a *t*-distribution with 20 degrees of freedom.
   III. A *t*-distribution with an infinite number of degrees of freedom is a normal distribution.
   (A) I only
   (B) II only
   (C) I and II
   (D) III only
   (E) II and III

3. A manufacturer of power tools claims that based on tests of continuous use, the distribution of the motor lifetimes in its new circular saw is normal and has a mean of 25 hours. A random sample of 6 circular saws indicated the following number of hours of continuous use until motor failure occurred: 21.6, 22.4, 26.1, 23.4, 24.7 and 24.1. Which of the following contains the correct approach to finding the probability that a sample of 6 saws would have a mean lifetime of 25 hours or less if the manufacturer's claim is accurate?

(A) Calculate the sample mean and standard deviation and use the normal distribution to calculate the probability.
(B) Calculate the sample mean and standard deviation and use the *t*-distribution to calculate the probability.
(C) Report that the problem is impossible because there are so few data values.
(D) Report that the problem is impossible because the standard deviation of the population is not known.
(E) Report that the problem is impossible for the reasons listed in both (C) and (D).

Use the following information to answer questions 4–7:

A very selective college claims that the mean GPA of its undergraduates is 3.125. A random sample of 64 of their undergraduates indicates a mean of 2.987 with a standard deviation of .305.

4. The distribution of the *t*-statistic:
   (A) is normal because *s* is a good estimator of σ since *n* is large.
   (B) follows a *t*-distribution since *n* is large and σ is unknown.
   (C) is skewed right since most undergraduates have high GPA's.
   (D) is unknown since we don't know if the population is normal.
   (E) is unknown since we don't know the standard deviation of the population.

In questions 5–7, assume that the distribution of sample means follows a *t*-distribution.

5. The degrees of freedom for this situation are:
   (A) 7
   (B) 8
   (C) 62
   (D) 63
   (E) 64

6. The standard deviation of the distribution of sample means is:
   (A) .0305
   (B) .038
   (C) .305
   (D) .38
   (E) None of these.

7. The value of the t-statistic is:
   (A) -4.52
   (B) -3.63
   (C) $-.45$
   (D) $-.36$
   (E) None of these.

FREE-RESPONSE QUESTIONS

Open-Ended Questions

The assumptions of the use of the t-distribution as the sampling distribution for a mean are:

1. a simple random sample from a large population;

2. normal population *or* large sample size ($n \geq 30$);

3. σ is unknown.

In the following problems, check each of the assumptions. If any assumption is not met, write its number, explain why it is not satisfied, and go on to the next problem. If all of the assumptions are satisfied, solve the problem and state a conclusion.

1. A concerned parents' group publishes the results of a study that claims the average amount of time that high school students watch television per week is 15.6 hours. The Student Council at a large high school conducts a simple random sample of 15 of its students and finds that the mean of the sample is 14.3 hours with a standard deviation of 2.5 hours. Assuming that the population of hours watched is normal, find the probability that a sample of this size will indicate a mean of 14.3 or fewer hours of TV watching per week.

2. The specifications for the length of a part in a manufacturing process call for a mean of 11.25 cm. A simple random sample of 50 parts indicates a mean of 11.56 cm with a standard deviation of .54 cm. Find that probability that a sample of 50 of the parts will have a mean of 11.56 cm or more.

3. If a population is normally distributed with mean 56, which of the following sample outcomes is more likely?
   a. sample size = 25, sample mean > 57.5 with a sample standard deviation of 4.5.
   b. sample size = 60, sample mean > 57.0 with a sample standard deviation of 2.5.

4. A company claims that the life of its batteries when used continuously in flashlights is approximately normally distributed with a mean of 21.5 hours. A laboratory tested 6 randomly chosen batteries and found that their lives were 19, 18, 22, 20, 16, and 25 hours.
   a. Compute the sample mean and standard deviation.
   b. Find the probability that a sample of 6 will have this mean or less if the true mean is 21.5 hours.
   c. Do you believe the company's claim? Explain your answer.

5. A test of 10 randomly selected safety belts indicated a mean breaking strength of 7,910 lbs. with a standard deviation of 90 lbs. The manufacturer claims that the distribution of the breaking strengths of the belts is approximately normal with a mean of 8,000 lbs. What is the probability that a sample of size 10 will have a mean of 7,910 lbs. or less?

6.7 The Distributions Associated With a Difference of Sample Means

To compare, for example, the average annual income of college graduates with the average annual income of high school graduates, statisticians would look at the means obtained from samples of each population.

As in the case of the distribution of a single sample mean, the comparison of two means depends primarily on whether the standard deviations of the populations are known. We will discuss each case separately in this section. In all cases, however, we will include the assumptions that both samples are *simple random samples* and that the two samples are *independent* of each other.

The Sampling Distribution of a Difference of Sample Means (σ_1 and σ_2 known)

If two independent random samples are taken and the sample means of each are calculated, then the following facts are true:

1. $\bar{x}_1 - \bar{x}_2$ is an unbiased estimator of $\mu_1 - \mu_2$, the difference in the means of the populations from which the samples were taken.
2. The standard deviation of the sampling distribution associated with $\bar{x}_1 - \bar{x}_2$ is given by the formula $\sqrt{\dfrac{\sigma_1^2}{n_1} + \dfrac{\sigma_2^2}{n_2}}$. Note that the *variances* add but the standard deviations do not!

3. If the two populations are normal, then the sampling distribution associated with $\bar{x}_1 - \bar{x}_2$ is also normal.

Important Notes and Assumptions:

1. It is most unlikely in a sampling situation that the standard deviations of the populations are known. Consequently, this case is listed for the sake of completeness rather than functionality.
2. Remember the additive nature of the variances that translates into the standard deviation formula is only true when the samples are simple random samples and are independent. This last condition may be quite subtle but is a key condition when dealing with two sample situations.
3. The sampling distribution of $\bar{x}_1 - \bar{x}_2$ is normal *only* when *both* of the populations are known to be normal. Otherwise, we impose the following conditions so that an approximation using the normal distribution is appropriate:

   - the samples should be approximately the same size; and
   - the *sum* of the sample sizes ≥ 40.

   When distribution shapes are quite different, we need larger sample sizes.

The Sampling Distribution of a Difference of Sample Means (σ_1 and σ_2 unknown)

When the standard deviations of the two populations are not known, we can use t-distribution techniques to explore the sampling distribution associated with $\bar{x}_1 - \bar{x}_2$. However, it is important to note that this sampling distribution is *not* exactly a t-distribution. When the populations are normal *or* the sample sizes are balanced and have a sum ≥ 40, the t-distribution provides an excellent approximation to this sampling distribution. Consequently, we can use the t-distribution to answer probability questions about the distribution associated with $\bar{x}_1 - \bar{x}_2$ and calculate approximate probability values for the likelihood of the occurrence of this difference of sample means or a more extreme difference.

If two simple random and independent samples provide statistics $n_1, \bar{x}_1, s_1$ and $n_2, \bar{x}_2, s_2$ then the two-sample t-statistic is

$$t = \frac{(\bar{x}_1 - \bar{x}_2) - (\mu_1 - \mu_2)}{\sqrt{\dfrac{s_1^2}{n_1} + \dfrac{s_2^2}{n_2}}}$$

where $\mu_1 - \mu_2$ is the difference of the population means. Note that the t-statistic satisfies the form $\dfrac{\text{observed} - \text{expected}}{\text{standard error}}$.

The issue of the degrees of freedom of this statistic is a complex one:

- The degrees of freedom can be calculated from the data. The degrees of freedom of this situation are calculated using the formula:

$$df = \frac{\left(\dfrac{s_1^2}{n_1} + \dfrac{s_2^2}{n_2}\right)^2}{\dfrac{1}{n_1 - 1}\left(\dfrac{s_1^2}{n_1}\right)^2 + \dfrac{1}{n_2 - 1}\left(\dfrac{s_2^2}{n_2}\right)^2}$$

Using this formula for the degrees of freedom makes the approximation of the sampling distribution of $\bar{x}_1 - \bar{x}_2$ very close to a t-distribution. The approximation is very accurate when both sample sizes are greater than 5. It should also be noted that this formula for the degrees of freedom does not usually return a whole number.

- The degrees of freedom can be approximated by choosing the *smaller* of $n_1 - 1$ and $n_2 - 1$. If the two populations of interest are normal, this choice provides "conservative" results; that is, it will provide a *slightly higher probability* value than is actually true. Some authors suggest that this is an excellent option when confronted with samples from normal populations, as long as the sample sizes are not both unequal and small.

EXAMPLE 1

Note that the solution will be shown for both calculations of the *df* for the *t*-statistic.
　　It has been accepted for many years that the academic performance of men in technical fields of study, on average, exceeds the performance of women in the same fields of study by a full grade point. A random sample of 40 men and 50 women from a large university is selected. The mean grade point averages by gender are as follows:

Gender	n	Mean	Standard Deviation
Male	40	3.065	.251
Female	50	2.195	.341

Find the probability that the mean GPA, found in samples of these sizes will yield a difference of means of .870 or less if the accepted difference of 1.0 is true.

Solution

a. Check assumptions.

　✓ Simple random sample(s)?　　　　*Given.*
　✓ Independent samples?　　　　　　*Even though one sample was conducted and partitioned, it is apparent that the performances are independent.*

　✓ Normal population(s) or　　　　　$n_1 = 40; n_2 = 50$
　　$n_1 + n_2 \geq 40$ and sample sizes
　　are balanced?

b. Calculate $P(\bar{x}_1 - \bar{x}_2 \leq .87)$.
  Calculation of the t-statistic:

$$t = \frac{(\bar{x}_1 - \bar{x}_2) - (\mu_1 - \mu_2)}{\sqrt{\dfrac{s_1^2}{n_1} + \dfrac{s_2^2}{n_2}}}$$

$$t = \frac{(3.065 - 2.195) - 1}{\sqrt{\dfrac{0.251^2}{40} + \dfrac{0.341^2}{50}}}$$

$$t = -2.081$$

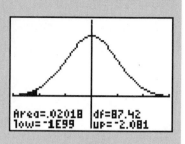

Area=.02018 df=87.42
low=-1E99   up=-2.081

Calculation of degrees of freedom: both the "exact" and "conservative" methods.

Exact: with technology	Conservative: without technology
$$df = \frac{\left(\dfrac{s_1^2}{n_1}\right) + \left(\dfrac{s_2^2}{n_2}\right)}{\dfrac{1}{n_1 - 1}\left(\dfrac{s_1^2}{n_1}\right)^2 + \dfrac{1}{n_2 - 1}\left(\dfrac{s_2^2}{n_2}\right)^2}$$	$df = $ smaller of $\{n_1 - 1, n_2 - 1\}$ $df = 39$
$$df = \frac{\left(\dfrac{0.251^2}{40} + \dfrac{0.341^2}{50}\right)^2}{\dfrac{1}{40 - 1}\left(\dfrac{0.251^2}{40}\right)^2 + \dfrac{1}{50 - 1}\left(\dfrac{0.341^2}{50}\right)^2}$$	
$df = 87.45$	

Calculation of probability.

	Exact	Conservative
Technology	$= tcdf(-1E\,99, -2.081, 87.45)$ probability $= 0.0202$	$= tcdf(-1E\,99, -2.081, 39)$ probability $= 0.0220$
Tables	For $df = 80$, the critical t value for tail probability .02 is 2.088 while t for tail probability .025 is 1.990. Therefore, probability is between .020 and .025.	For $df = 39$, the critical t value for tail probability .02 is 2.123 while t for tail probability .025 is 2.021. Therefore, probability is between .020 and .025.

In both cases, the probability of samples of these sizes exhibiting a difference of .870 or less if the actual difference is 1.0 is approximately 0.02. Notice that there is little difference in the probability value based on the method of calculation of df.

Review Exercises

MULTIPLE-CHOICE QUESTIONS

Use the following information for questions 1–4. Consider two classes in AP Statistics at a large high school in a particular city as independent samples of all AP Statistics students in that area. On their midterm exam, the 25 students in Class A had a mean score of 72.5 with a standard deviation of 10.7. On the same test, the 20 students in Class B had a mean score of 75.3 with a standard deviation of 9.8.

1. The distribution of the t-statistic for the difference of the two sample means:
   (A) is approximately normal because all of the conditions of the Central Limit Theorem are satisfied.
   (B) follows a t-distribution with degrees of freedom = 19 using the conservative approach.
   (C) follows a t-distribution with degrees of freedom = 24 using the conservative approach.
   (D) would follow a t-distribution if the sample sizes had both been greater than 30.
   (E) cannot be determined since the given information does not fit any of our models.

Assume in questions 2–4 that the sampling distribution is a t-distribution.

2. The standard error of the sampling distribution is:
   (A) 2.14
   (B) 2.19
   (C) 3.06
   (D) 4.02
   (E) None of these.

3. If we assume that the true difference between the means is 0 since both samples are taken from the same population, the test statistic is:
   (A) −1.31
   (B) −1.28
   (C) −.92
   (D) −.70
   (E) None of these.

4. The probability that samples of these sizes have a difference in means of 2.8 or more when we expect a difference of 0 is:
   (A) .1029
   (B) .1079
   (C) .1846
   (D) .2462
   (E) None of these.

FREE-RESPONSE QUESTIONS

Open-Ended Questions

The assumptions for the use of the t-distribution as the sampling distribution for the difference of two sample means are:
   1. simple random samples from one or two large populations;

   2. independent samples;

   3. normal population(s) or $n_1 + n_2 \geq 40$

   4. σ_1 and σ_2 are unknown.

In the following problems, check each of the assumptions. If any assumption is not met, write its number, explain why it is not satisfied, and go on to the next problem. If all of the assumptions are satisfied, solve the problem and state a conclusion. In your solution, state the method used to calculate the degrees of freedom.

1. The ages of men and women in a particular city follow a normal distribution. Census data indicate that the mean age of men in this city is 42.3 years and the mean age of women in the same city is 45.2 years. Two random samples of 10 men and 10 women are taken independently from the citizens of the city and it is found that

   • the mean age of the men is 43.5 years with a standard deviation of 8.9 years; and
   • the mean age of the women is 46.7 years with a standard deviation of 12.1 years.

   Find the probability that samples of this size will indicate that the women's mean will exceed the men's mean by 3.2 years or more if the Census Bureau difference of 2.9 is correct.

2. It is assumed that all soft drink companies put the same amount of soda in each of their 12-ounce cans. A simple random sample of 100 of Company A's cans indicated a mean volume of 12.2 ounces with a standard deviation of 0.3 ounce while a simple random sample of 50 of Company B's cans indicated a mean volume of 12.05 ounces with a standard deviation of 0.2 ounce. Find the probability that a difference of 0.15 ounce (in absolute value) or more will occur if the means of the two populations of soft drink cans are the same.

3. A simple random sample of the math and language arts scores of 100 5th grade students was taken in a large school. The mean percentile in math was 78.3 with a standard deviation of 9.8, while the mean percentile in language arts was 75.4 with a standard deviation of 12.9. Find the probability that the mean percentile in math will exceed the mean percentile in language arts by 2.9 or more if, in the student population, there was no difference in their scores.

4. Quality control tests yielded the following ratings on two processes:

Process A: 1.5, 2.5, 3.5, 2.5

Process B: 2.5, 3.0, 3.0, 4.0, 3.5, 2.0

Assume that the samples are from normal populations and are independent.

a. Calculate the mean and standard deviation of each sample. Find the difference of the sample means.

b. What is the probability that two samples of these sizes will produce data that indicate that B's rating exceeds A's rating by this difference or more, if the processes are in reality of equal effectiveness?

6.8 Summary of Distributions and Their Assumptions

The table on the next page summarizes the situations, the statistics, and the assumptions for each of the cases that we have discussed in this chapter. You should learn these facts, with particular attention to the assumptions, since the concepts will be critical for Chapter 7 and for the AP Statistics Examination.

It is important to understand and check assumptions in all work dealing with sampling because if any of the assumptions for a particular distribution are not satisfied then any solution utilizing that distribution is invalid and incorrect. Many students lose credit on the AP Examination because they apply a technique to a problem and either do not verify the assumptions or do not *state* the check of assumptions. A good statistics student must understand that addressing the assumptions for the use of a particular distribution or technique is a mandatory component of any sampling problem.

Note that it is acceptable to show normality of a population by displaying a box plot or dot plot of the sample and writing a clear explanation detailing why the plot supports the claim of normality.

Note too that the sample size consideration is also listed in the assumption column as a reminder that the approximations of sampling distributions by the normal and *t*-distributions improve as sample size increases.

Situation	Distribution	Statistic	Assumption
Sample Proportion	$Normal\left(p, \sqrt{\dfrac{p(1-p)}{n}}\right)$	$z = \dfrac{\hat{p} - p}{\sqrt{\dfrac{p(1-p)}{n}}}$	• simple random sample • large population • $np > 10$ and $n(1-p) > 10$
Difference of Sample Proportions	$Normal\left(p_1 - p_2, \sqrt{\dfrac{p_1(1-p_1)}{n_1} + \dfrac{p_2(1-p_2)}{n_2}}\right)$	$z = \dfrac{(\hat{p}_1 - \hat{p}_2) - (p_1 - p_2)}{\sqrt{\dfrac{p_1(1-p_1)}{n_1} + \dfrac{p_2(1-p_2)}{n_2}}}$	• simple random sample(s) • independent samples • large population(s) • $n_1 p_1 > 5$ and $n_1(1-p_1) > 5$ and $n_2 p_2 > 5$ and $n_2(1-p_2) > 5$
Sample Mean: Case 1	$Normal\left(\mu, \dfrac{\sigma}{\sqrt{n}}\right)$	$z = \dfrac{\bar{x} - \mu}{\dfrac{\sigma}{\sqrt{n}}}$	• simple random sample(s) • population is normal or n is large ($n \geq 30$) • σ is known
Sample Mean: Case 2	$t(df)$	$t = \dfrac{\bar{x} - \mu}{\dfrac{s}{\sqrt{n}}}; df = n - 1$	• simple random sample • population is normal or n is large ($n \geq 30$) • σ is unknown
Difference of Sample Means*	$t(df)$	$t = \dfrac{(\bar{x}_1 - \bar{x}_2) - (\mu_1 - \mu_2)}{\sqrt{\dfrac{s_1^2}{n_1} + \dfrac{s_2^2}{n_2}}}; df^{**}$	• simple random sample(s) • independent samples • normal population(s) or $n_1 + n_2 \geq 40$ and sample sizes are balanced

*We include only the case when the population standard deviations are unknown.

**Two options for degrees of freedom:

a. exact: $df = \dfrac{\left(\dfrac{s_1^2}{n_1} + \dfrac{s_2^2}{n_2}\right)^2}{\dfrac{1}{n_1 - 1}\left(\dfrac{s_1^2}{n_1}\right)^2 + \dfrac{1}{n_2 - 1}\left(\dfrac{s_2^2}{n_2}\right)^2}$

b. approximate: $df =$ minimum of $n_1 - 1$ and $n_2 - 1$

Chapter 6 Assessment

MULTIPLE-CHOICE QUESTIONS

1. The Central Limit Theorem for a sample mean is a critical result because
   - (A) it states that for large sample sizes, the population distribution is approximately normal.
   - (B) it states that for large sample sizes, the sample is approximately normal.
   - (C) it states that for any population, the sampling distribution is normal regardless of sample size.
   - (D) it states that for large sample sizes, the sampling distribution is approximately normal regardless of the population distribution.
   - (E) it states that for any sample size, the sampling distribution is normal.

2. The amount of time it takes a high school class of 1,000 freshmen to swim 10 lengths of the school swimming pool has a distribution that is skewed left due to some excellent swimmers in the class. The mean amount of time needed to complete this task is believed to be 9.2 minutes with a standard deviation of 5.3 minutes. If 64 students were chosen randomly, then the probability that their mean time will exceed 10 minutes is
   - (A) .092
   - (B) .104
   - (C) .113
   - (D) .161
   - (E) None of these.

3. At a university, student records kept over a period of many years indicate that 64% of applicants pass the entrance examination in mathematics. What are the chances that 70% or more of a random sample of 400 will pass the test?
   - (A) 0.6%
   - (B) 1.6%
   - (C) 6%
   - (D) 16%
   - (E) None of these.

4. The heights of adults in a certain town have a mean of 65.42 inches with a standard deviation of 2.32 inches. A random sample of 144 adults living in the center of the town was selected and their mean height was found to be 64.82 inches. Find the probability that a sample of this size would have a mean of 64.82 or less.
   - (A) Probability is very small.
   - (B) .005
   - (C) .025
   - (D) .05
   - (E) None of these.

5. The ages of students in a continuing education class of adults at a local college has a skewed-right distribution with a mean of 31.3 years and a standard deviation of 6.4 years. If we took a random sample of 100 students, we would expect the distribution of the sample means to be
   - (A) approximately normal with a mean of 31.3 years and a standard deviation of 6.4 years.
   - (B) approximately normal with a mean of 31.3 years and a standard deviation of .64 years.
   - (C) skewed right with a mean of 31.3 years and a standard deviation of 6.4 years.
   - (D) skewed right with a mean of 31.3 years and a standard deviation of .64 years.
   - (E) unknown shape with a mean of 31.3 years and a standard deviation of .64 years.

6. It is assumed that 50% of all people catch one or more colds each year. What is the probability that out of 400 randomly selected people, 216 or more will catch one or more colds this year?
   - (A) .0055
   - (B) .0121
   - (C) .055
   - (D) .11
   - (E) .55

7. Under typical conditions, the percent defective contained in shipments of a specific type of ball bearing is 3%. What is the probability that a shipment of 400 contains 4.5% or more defective ball bearings?
   - (A) Virtually no chance.
   - (B) .0039
   - (C) .039
   - (D) .045
   - (E) None of these.

8. The decision whether the distribution of a sample mean follows a normal or *t*-distribution depends on:
   (A) sample size.
   (B) whether you have the actual data or only statistics of the data.
   (C) whether you know the population standard deviation.
   (D) whether $np > 10$ and $n(1 - p) > 10$.
   (E) None of the above.

9. National studies show that 14% of male teenagers and 12% of female teenagers will be involved in a major traffic accident while driving. What is the probability that independent random samples of 100 female teens and 75 male teens will have results that differ by more than 3% in either direction?
   (A) .042
   (B) .085
   (C) .42
   (D) .85
   (E) Cannot be determined.

FREE-RESPONSE QUESTIONS

Open-Ended Questions

1. A multiple-choice exam consists of 100 questions with 4 possible answers. Each is scored in the following way: the student receives one point for each correct answer, loses .25 of a point for each incorrect answer and receives no credit for unanswered questions.
   a. Find the probability that a student who answers all questions by random guessing will pass (60 points or better).
   b. Does the student's chances improve if he or she were to leave 5 questions blank and guess on the rest? Explain your answer.

2. A fair die is one in which each of the six numbers has an equal probability of coming up. You test a die by rolling it 100 times and find that 6 comes up 21 times. What are the chances that a 6 will come up 21 or more times if the die is fair? Does this result cause you to doubt the fairness of this die? Explain your answer.

3. The US Small Business Administration claims that the overhead costs of most small businesses (heat, electricity, water, etc.) are approximately the same. A researcher takes a random sample of 42 small fabric stores and a second random sample of 75 pizza take-out stores. She finds that the fabric stores had a mean overhead cost of $725.60 per month with a standard deviation of $63.50, while the pizza stores had a mean overhead cost of $764.50 per month with a standard deviation of $74.50. Find the probability that samples of these sizes will result in a difference of $38.90 or more in mean overhead cost if the Small Business Administration is correct.

4. A friend of yours calls and claims that the decision whether to use a normal distribution or a *t*-distribution is not really important since each gives you approximately the same answer. Your friend cites the following example to support his claim:

   Studies show that the mean number of times students have cheated on math tests in high school is 5.6. In a random sample of 50 students, it was found that the mean number of times that the students admitted to cheating on a math test in high school was 6.2 with a standard deviation of 2.3. Find the probability that a sample of this size will produce a mean of 6.2 or more if the actual mean is 5.6.

   In order to clarify your friend's thinking:
   a. Solve the problem using a normal distribution;
   b. Solve the problem using a *t*-distribution;
   c. Explain to your friend why the answers are so close; and
   d. Explain why only the *t*-distribution should be used in this case.

Investigative Tasks

1. Your company is about to revise a brochure that is designed to share data about the company with prospective investors. The present brochure states that the mean monthly sales are $3,165,567. You are asked to determine if this value has changed. You choose a simple random sample of 10 of the last 24 monthly means and calculate that the mean of the sample is $3,235,678 with a standard deviation of $125,645.

   a. What is an appropriate sampling distribution to use to investigate the difference between the sales figure contained in the brochure and that obtained from the sample? Explain the reasons for your choice.

   b. Using the distribution identified in part a, calculate the probability that your sample data will have a mean of $3,235,678 or more when the true mean is $3,165,567.

   c. If the population standard deviation was the same as the sample standard deviation, would your answer to part a change? Explain the reasons for your answer.

   d. If your answer to part c is different from that of part a, use the new sampling distribution to calculate the same probability as you did in part b.

   e. Do the results of part b and part d differ? Discuss your findings.

   f. What will you report to your boss regarding the question that motivated your investigation?

2. A colleague has reported that she has taken a number of random samples from a large skewed-left population with mean 41.56 and standard deviation of 5.65. She states that she has taken 10 samples each for sample sizes of 10, 20, 25, 50, 75, and 100 and has calculated the mean and standard deviation of the 10 sample means for the samples sizes indicated in the table below.

Sample Sizes	Mean of 10 sample means	Standard Deviation of 10 sample means
10	38.56	2.02
20	43.21	1.16
25	43.07	1.23
50	40.16	0.83
75	41.23	0.54
100	42.11	0.49

   a. Use the Central Limit Theorem to calculate the theoretical standard deviation of the sample means. Display your answers in the table below.

Sample Sizes	10	20	25	50	75	100
Theoretical Standard Deviations						

   b. Investigate whether the differences between the reported standard deviations and the theoretical standard deviations calculated in part a are extreme. Complete each step:

   (1) Identify an appropriate sampling distribution for this investigation. Explain your choice.

   (2) Calculate the probability of finding these differences or greater if the reported standard deviations are consistent with the theoretical standard deviations found by applying the Central Limit Theorem.

   (3) Based on your answer to part b(2), write a conclusion regarding the reported standard deviations relative to their consistency with the theoretical standard deviations found by applying the Central Limit Theorem.

Chapter 7　Statistical Inference

7.1　The Concept of Confidence
7.2　Calculation of Confidence Intervals
7.3　Properties of Confidence Intervals
7.4　The Concept of Significance
7.5　Tests of Significance
7.6　Type I and Type II Errors and the Concept of Power
7.7　Inference for the Slope of a Regression Line
7.8　Inference for Categorical Data
　　　Chapter 7　Assessment

Chapter 7 Statistical Inference

By using the procedures of statistical inference, an investigator can draw conclusions about a population parameter based on the sample statistic. Methods of inference can be classified into two major categories: confidence intervals and tests of significance. Your knowledge of sampling distributions will be invaluable in understanding and becoming proficient in the calculations of both types of inference techniques. The techniques of statistical inference can be applied to many real-life problems for which it is useful to determine numerically the possible benefits associated with certain decisions.

7.1 The Concept of Confidence

As we discussed in Chapter 6, the existence of sample variation affects the accuracy of a sample statistic as an estimator of a population parameter. The estimators we calculated in Chapter 6 can be described as **point estimators**—specific numbers that are estimates of the parameters. In this section, we will develop the idea of a different type of estimate, an **interval estimate,** which incorporates the sampling variability of the point estimators.

For example, suppose we take a simple random sample of 100 adults and determine that 40% of the sample live in a city. The question that naturally arises is what information this sample statistic provides about the value of the population parameter, the actual proportion of adults who live in a city.

If we consider the sampling distribution of $\hat{p}$, the Central Limit Theorem states that the sampling distribution of $\hat{p}$ is approximately normal with mean p and standard deviation $\sqrt{\dfrac{p(1-p)}{n}}$, where p is the population proportion. Consequently, if we use the 68–95–99.7 rule from Section 2.4, we can expect that 95% of the $\hat{p}$ values fall within two standard deviations of the population proportion, p. Thus, there is approximately a 95% chance that any selected $\hat{p}$ is within two standard deviations of p. The probability of any $\hat{p}$ being within two standard deviations of p can be shown graphically.

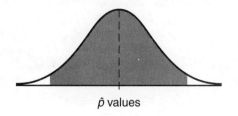

$\hat{p}$ values

The problem is that the value of p is not known. All we know is the value of $\hat{p}$ from the sample. In order to gain some insight into the value of p, we will use $\hat{p}$ to estimate p and the standard deviation using the *standard error*, $\sqrt{\dfrac{\hat{p}(1 - \hat{p})}{n}}$. This standard deviation is an approximation; therefore, we just get an approximate confidence interval. Since the sample information satisfies the requirements for the sampling distribution of $\hat{p}$ to follow a normal distribution, we construct the **confidence interval** by calculating:

estimate of $p \pm z_{(1 - C)/2} \times$ standard error

where $z_{(1 - C)/2}$ represents the *critical value* of the standard normal curve corresponding to the *confidence level* (C) specified. For example,

90% Confidence $\rightarrow z_{(1 - .90)/2} = z_{.05} = 1.645$
95% Confidence $\rightarrow z_{(1 - .95)/2} = z_{.025} = 1.96$
98% Confidence $\rightarrow z_{(1 - .98)/2} = z_{.01} = 2.33$
99% Confidence $\rightarrow z_{(1 - .99)/2} = z_{.005} = 2.58$

Note: Some texts use z^* as the critical value of the normal distribution for the C confidence level.

Consequently, the 95% confidence interval for p in our example is:

$$\hat{p} \pm z_{(1 - C)/2} \times \sqrt{\frac{\hat{p}(1 - \hat{p})}{n}}$$

$$.40 \pm 1.96 \times \sqrt{\frac{.4(1 - .4)}{100}} = .40 \pm .096 = (.304, .496)$$

The meaning of the confidence interval in this example must be understood in the context of the sampling distribution of $\hat{p}$. Since the value of $\hat{p}$ can vary due to random sampling error, there are a large number of 95% confidence intervals that can be constructed for samples of size n using the procedure shown above. The following graphic shows the relationship between some of the confidence intervals and the location of the value of p in the sampling distribution.

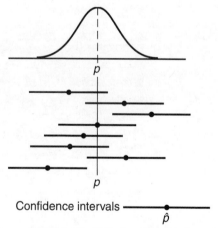

Confidence intervals $\underset{\hat{p}}{\rule{1cm}{0.4pt}\bullet\rule{1cm}{0.4pt}}$

The key to the concept of a 95% confidence interval is that 95% of all possible confidence intervals will *contain* the value p. Statisticians state this fact using these statements:

"95% of all confidence intervals *capture* the value of p." or

"95% of all confidence intervals *cover* the value of p."

Since 95% of all possible confidence intervals contain the value of p, we say we are 95% confident that our sample produces one of the confidence intervals that contains p. This is *not* a probability statement; it is a statement of confidence based on the large number of samples that can be drawn from a population.

EXAMPLE 1

The table below lists the values of a simulation of $\hat{p}$ values, and the lower and upper bounds of the 95% confidence interval for each $\hat{p}$, for 100 samples of size 100 drawn from a population with $p = .40$.

$\hat{p}$	lower	upper	$\hat{p}$	lower	upper
.40	.303980	.496020	.49	.392020	.587980
.33	.237838	.422162	.36	.265920	.454080
.35	.256514	.443486	.41	.313601	.506399
.37	.275370	.464630	.38	.284864	.475136
.40	.303980	.496020	.33	.237838	.422162
.40	.303980	.496020	.34	.247153	.432847
.33	.237838	.422162	.41	.313601	.506399
.46	.362314	.557686	.43	.332965	.527035
.34	.247153	.432847	.43	.332965	.527035
.38	.284864	.475136	.46	.362314	.557686
.35	.256514	.443486	.25	.165130	.334870
.38	.284864	.475136	.43	.332965	.527035
.39	.294401	.485599	.34	.247153	.432847
.43	.332965	.527035	.40	.303980	.496020
.39	.294401	.485599	.38	.284864	.475136
.47	.372177	.567823	.44	.342708	.537292
.37	.275370	.464630	.37	.275370	.464630
.46	.362314	.557686	.42	.323263	.516737
.33	.237838	.422162	.44	.342708	.537292
.38	.284864	.475136	.42	.323263	.516737
.38	.284864	.475136	.42	.323263	.516737
.43	.332965	.527035	.48	.382078	.577922
.40	.303980	.496020	.49	.392020	.587980
.35	.256514	.443486	.39	.294401	.485599
.50	.402000	.598000	.42	.323263	.516737
.39	.294401	.485599	.46	.362314	.557686
.30	.210182	.389818	.40	.303980	.496020
.35	.256514	.443486	.47	.372177	.567823
.44	.342708	.537292	.43	.332965	.527035
.38	.284864	.475136	.34	.247153	.432847
.38	.284864	.475136	.44	.342708	.537292
.40	.303980	.496020	.45	.352491	.547509
.32	.228571	.411429	.43	.332965	.527035
.45	.352491	.547509	.36	.265920	.454080
.35	.256514	.443486	.47	.372177	.567823
.43	.332965	.527035	.35	.256514	.443486
.44	.342708	.537292	.49	.392020	.587980
.41	.313601	.506399	.40	.303980	.496020
.43	.332965	.527035	.39	.294401	.485599
.42	.323263	.516737	.35	.256514	.443486
.32	.228571	.411429	.45	.352491	.547509
.40	.303980	.496020	.42	.323263	.516737
.42	.323263	.516737	.39	.294401	.485599
.42	.323263	.516737	.47	.372177	.567823
.40	.303980	.496020	.38	.284864	.475136
.29	.201063	.378937	.42	.323263	.516737
.40	.303980	.496020	.43	.332965	.527035
.38	.284864	.475136	.51	.412020	.607980
.39	.294401	.485599	.39	.294401	.485599
.38	.284864	.475136	.36	.265920	.454080

The value of p that each of these samples estimates is .40. If you inspect the list, you will note that only 3 of the 100 samples do not include the population parameter, p. Consequently, the confidence level of 95% is somewhat conservative for this simulation. If we took all possible samples, 95% of the confidence intervals would contain p.

To summarize, **the confidence we have that a $C\%$ confidence interval contains the value of a population parameter is derived from the fact that $C\%$ of the confidence intervals constructed around the point estimate calculated from all possible samples will contain the parameter.**

Review Exercises

MULTIPLE-CHOICE QUESTIONS

1. If the 90% confidence interval of the mean of a population is given by 45 ± 3.24, which of the following is correct?
   (A) There is a 90% probability that the true mean is in the interval.
   (B) There is a 90% probability that the sample mean is in the interval
   (C) If 1,000 samples of the same size are taken from the population, then approximately 900 of them will contain the true mean.
   (D) There is a 90% probability that a data value, chosen at random, will fall in this interval.
   (E) None of these is correct.

2. If the 95% confidence interval of the proportion of a population is $.35 \pm .025$, which of the following is *not* correct?
   (A) If the sample size were to increase the width of the interval would decrease.
   (B) An increase in confidence level generally results in an increase in the width of the confidence interval.
   (C) This confidence interval could have been calculated after either a sample or a census was conducted.
   (D) If one would like a smaller confidence interval, one could increase sample size or decrease the confidence level.
   (E) All of these are correct.

3. The critical value for a 99.7% confidence interval for p is:
   (A) 1
   (B) 1.96
   (C) 2
   (D) 2.78
   (E) 3

4. Which of the following is *not* true about constructing confidence intervals?
   (A) The value of the standard error is a function of the sample statistics.
   (B) The center of the confidence interval is the population parameter.
   (C) One of the values that affects the width of a confidence interval is the sample size.
   (D) If the value of the population parameter is known, it is irrelevant to calculate a confidence interval for it.
   (E) The value of the level of confidence will affect the width of a confidence interval.

5. The confidence that we feel about a 90% confidence interval comes from the fact that
   (A) there is a 90% chance that the population parameter is contained in the confidence interval.
   (B) there is a 90% chance that the sample statistic is contained in the confidence interval.
   (C) 90% of confidence intervals constructed around a sample statistic will contain the population parameter.
   (D) the terms of confidence and probability are interchangeable.
   (E) the concepts of confidence and probability are synonymous.

FREE-RESPONSE QUESTIONS

Open-Ended Questions

1. Two simple random samples of registered voters in a large city were taken. The first sample of 100 voters found that 50% of them were in favor of a new bond issue. The second sample of 400 voters also showed 50% in favor of the bond issue. If two 95% confidence intervals were constructed based on these sample statistics, how would the width of the two intervals compare? Justify your answer.

2. A simple random sample of 64 students from a large high school found that 20% of them rode bicycles to school. Construct a 90% confidence interval for the proportion of students who bicycle to school. Interpret this interval in words.

3. An AP Statistics teacher asks her class to construct confidence intervals given a sample proportion of .45 and a variety of sample sizes. Four groups of students are each given a different sample size and the intervals from the groups are displayed on the chalkboard. Which of the following intervals must be incorrect? Explain how you made your decision.

Group A: (.37, .53)
Group B: (.41, .49)
Group C: (.35, .55)
Group D: (.40, .49)

4. A friend who is taking AP Statistics at another school tells you that they did a problem in class whose answer was a 95% confidence interval for a population proportion of $.35 \pm .04$. He says that the class agreed on the following interpretation of this interval:

> "There is a 95% chance that the true value of p is in this interval."

Describe how you would explain to your friend that this interpretation is wrong.

7.2 Calculation of Confidence Intervals

Calculation of confidence intervals is quite straightforward. The basis of this calculation is the sampling distribution that underlies the parameter of interest. Consequently, it is essential to consider the assumptions of the sampling distribution in the calculation. In general, any confidence interval in this course can be calculated using:

sample statistic $\pm$ (distribution critical value) (standard error of the estimate)

This translates into the following procedures:

Confidence Interval For:	Assumptions	Formula
population proportion	• simple random sample • large population • $n\hat{p} > 10$ and $n(1-\hat{p}) > 10$	$\hat{p} \pm z_{(1-C)/2}\left(\sqrt{\dfrac{\hat{p}(1-\hat{p})}{n}}\right)$
population mean	• simple random sample • population is normal or n is large ($n \geq 30$) • σ is known	$\bar{x} \pm z_{(1-C)/2}\left(\dfrac{\sigma}{\sqrt{n}}\right)$
population mean	• simple random sample • population is normal or n is large ($n \geq 30$) • σ is unknown	$\bar{x} \pm t_{(1-C)/2}\left(\dfrac{s}{\sqrt{n}}\right)$ $df = n - 1$
difference of population proportions	• simple random sample(s) • large population(s) • $n_1\hat{p}_1 > 5$ and $n_1(1-\hat{p}_1) > 5$ and • $n_2\hat{p}_2 > 5$ and $n_2(1-\hat{p}_2) > 5$ • independent samples	$(\hat{p}_1 - \hat{p}_2) \pm z_{(1-C)/2}\left(\sqrt{\dfrac{\hat{p}_1(1-\hat{p}_1)}{n_1} + \dfrac{\hat{p}_2(1-\hat{p}_2)}{n_2}}\right)$
difference of population means	• simple random sample(s) • independent samples • normal population(s) or $n_1 + n_2 \geq 40$	$(\bar{x}_1 - \bar{x}_2) \pm t_{(1-C)/2}\left(\sqrt{\dfrac{s_1^2}{n_1} + \dfrac{s_2^2}{n_2}}\right)$ $df = \min\{n_1, n_2\}$

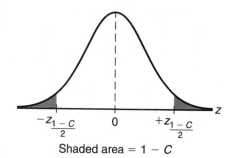

Shaded area $= 1 - C$

The distribution critical value is shown in each formula as either a $z_{(1-C)/2}$ or a $t_{(1-C)/2}$ depending on whether the related sampling distribution is either normal or a t-distribution. Some texts indicate $z_{(1-C)/2}$ as z^* and $t_{(1-C)/2}$ as t^*. In both cases, the choice of the distribution critical value depends on the level of confidence chosen. For example, if we wish to construct a 95% confidence interval, we choose our critical value so that the sum of the *two tails* of area under the distribution curve totals

$1 -$ confidence level, or $1 - C$.

Therefore, in this case, the total area in the two tails is $1 - .95 = .05$. A confidence interval is generally a *two-tailed situation* referring to the fact that the area is split between the two tails; consequently the $\dfrac{1-C}{2}$ notation is used.

In situations whose sampling distributions are modeled by the normal distribution, we can state approximate values of $z_{(1-C)/2}$ for particular confidence levels:

Confidence Level	$z_{(1-C)/2}$
90%	1.645
95%	1.96
98%	2.33
99%	2.576

In situations whose sampling distributions are modeled by a t-distribution, determination of the $t_{(1-C)/2}$ must be made based on both the confidence level chosen and the number of degrees of freedom of the critical value.

EXAMPLE 1

The gas mileage for a certain model of car is known to have a standard deviation of 5 mi/gal. A simple random sample of 64 cars of this model is chosen and found to have a mean gas mileage of 27.5 mi/gal. Construct a 95% confidence interval for the mean gas mileage for this car model. Interpret the interval in words.

Solution

Let μ = mean gas mileage for this car model.
Check assumptions.

✓ Simple random sample?	*Given*
✓ Population is normal or n is large ($n \geq 30$)?	$n = 64$
✓ σ is known?	$\sigma = 5$ *mi/gal*

Therefore, the 95% confidence interval for μ is calculated:

$$\bar{x} \pm z_{(1 - C)/2}\left(\frac{\sigma}{\sqrt{n}}\right)$$
$$27.5 \pm 1.96\left(\frac{5}{\sqrt{64}}\right)$$
$$27.5 \pm 1.225$$
$$(26.775 \text{ mi/gal}, 28.725 \text{ mi/gal})$$

Interpretation: We are 95% confident that the mean gas mileage for this model of car falls between 26.775 and 28.725 miles per gallon since 95% of the confidence intervals constructed from all samples of size 64 selected from this population will contain the population mean gas mileage. Consequently, we are 95% confident that this interval is one of those that contains the true value of μ.

EXAMPLE 2

A simple random sample of 75 male adults living in a particular suburb was taken to study the amount of time they spent per week doing rigorous exercise. It indicated a mean of 73 minutes with a standard deviation of 21 minutes. Find the 95% confidence interval of the mean for all males in the suburb. Interpret this interval in words.

Solution

Let μ = mean rigorous exercise time for all males in the suburb.
Check assumptions.

✓ Simple random sample?	*Given*
✓ Population is normal or n is large ($n \geq 40$)?	$n = 75$

Therefore, the 95% confidence interval for μ is calculated:

$$\bar{x} \pm t_{(1 - C)/2}\left(\frac{s}{\sqrt{n}}\right) \qquad df = 74$$
$$73 \pm 1.990\left(\frac{21}{\sqrt{75}}\right)$$
$$73 \pm 4.83$$
$$(68.17 \text{ min}, 77.83 \text{ min})$$

Note that the df value should be $n - 1 = 74$; the critical t-value of 1.990 corresponds to an area of .025 for $df = 80$ on the t-table.

Interpretation: We are 95% confident that the true mean time of rigorous exercise is in the interval (68.17 min, 77.83 min) since 95% of the confidence intervals of all samples of size 75 from this population will contain the value of the true population mean of rigorous exercise time. Consequently, we are 95% confident that our interval is one of those that contains μ.

EXAMPLE 3

Two independent samples of adults were selected from a large church congregation. Each group was asked their opinion of a proposal to raise funds to build a new teen center. The first sample consisted of 50 members of the church between the ages of 40 and 60 years and the results indicated that 72% were in favor of the proposal. The results of the second survey of 60 church members between the ages of 25 and 40 years indicated that 80% were in favor of the proposal. Find the 90% confidence interval for the difference in proportions between these two age groups. Interpret this interval in words.

Solution

Check assumptions.

✓ Simple random samples?	*Given*
✓ Large population(s) or $n \geq 40$?	*Given*
	$50 + 60 = 110$
✓ Independent samples?	*Given distinct age groups*
✓ $n_1\hat{p}_1 > 5$ and $n_1(1 - \hat{p}_1) > 5$ and	*$50(.72) = 36$; $50(.28) = 14$*
$n_2\hat{p}_2 > 5$ and $n_2(1 - \hat{p}_2) > 5$	*$60(.80) = 48$; $60(.20) = 12$*

Let $p_1 - p_2$ = difference in proportions of the two populations. Therefore, the 90% confidence interval for $p_1 - p_2$ is calculated:

$$(\hat{p}_1 - \hat{p}_2) \pm z_{(1 - C)/2}\left(\sqrt{\frac{\hat{p}_1(1 - \hat{p}_1)}{n_1} + \frac{\hat{p}_2(1 - \hat{p}_2)}{n_2}}\right)$$

$$(.80 - .72) \pm 1.645\left(\sqrt{\frac{.80(1 - .80)}{60} + \frac{.72(1 - .72)}{50}}\right)$$

$$.08 \pm .135$$
$$(-.055, .215)$$

Interpretation: We are 90% confident that the true difference in the proportions of the two age groups is in the interval $(-.055, .215)$ since 90% of the confidence intervals constructed from all samples of these sizes selected from the populations under investigation will contain the true difference between the population proportions. Consequently, we are 90% confident that our interval is one of those intervals.

Review Exercises

FREE-RESPONSE QUESTIONS

Open-Ended Questions

1. A simple random sample of 100 high school seniors in a particular city is taken, and it is found that 15% of the students favor the ban on prayer in public schools.
   a. Define the parameter of interest.
   b. Construct a 95% confidence interval for this parameter. List and verify your assumptions.
   c. Interpret this interval in words.

2. A simple random sample of 40 packages of light bulbs indicated that the mean number of defective bulbs in each package was .79 with a standard deviation of .2. The packages contained 4 bulbs each.
   a. Define the parameter of interest.
   b. Construct a 90% confidence interval based on these data. List and verify your assumptions.
   c. Interpret this interval in words.

3. A simple random sample of 25 new food cans indicated that the mean diameter was 3.13 inches with a standard deviation of .04 inches.
   a. Define the parameter of interest.
   b. Construct a 95% confidence interval based on these data. List and verify your assumptions.
   c. Would the discovery of a 26th measurement of 3.32 inches be surprising? Answer yes or no and explain your answer.
   d. Would the discovery of another sample of 25 cans having a mean of 3.32 inches be surprising? Answer yes or no and explain your answer.

4. There are approximately 30,000 companies that are members of a charitable collaborative across the entire country.
   a. A random sample of 250 of these companies is taken and it is found that 210 of the CEOs hold at least a master's degree. Find the 95% confidence interval of the proportion of the CEOs in all 30,000 companies that hold at least a master's degree. If this is not possible, explain why the confidence interval cannot be calculated.
   b. Interpret this confidence interval in words.
   c. Assume that these 30,000 companies employ approximately 250,000 junior executives. The sample of 250 companies identified above employs 15,000 junior executives, of whom 8,410 hold at least a master's degree. Find the 95% confidence interval for the proportion of the 250,000 junior executives that hold at least a master's degree. If this is not possible, explain why the confidence interval cannot be calculated.

5. Two independent random samples were taken at two neighboring high schools to determine the difference in the proportions of students who had jobs outside of school. The sample of 75 North High students indicated that 60% of them had jobs outside of school while the sample of 40 South High students indicated that 68% of them had jobs outside of school.
   a. Construct a 95% confidence interval for the difference in the proportions of working students at each of these high schools based on these samples.
   b. State the meaning of this confidence interval.

6. Two independent random samples of women's clubs in a particular city are taken in order to determine the average amount of time (in days per month) that club members spend performing volunteer community service. The results of the investigation are listed in the table:

Club	Number in Sample	Mean (days/month)	Standard Deviation (days)
Garden	15	17.25	2.4
Library	12	16.45	3.6

   a. Construct a 90% confidence interval for the difference in the mean service time of the two clubs based on these data.
   b. State the meaning of this confidence interval.

7.3 Properties of Confidence Intervals

Interval Width in Relation to Sample Size The relationship between the width of the confidence interval and sample size can be seen both procedurally by inspecting the formulas and conceptually by considering the idea of a confidence interval.

It is clear from the formulas listed in Section 7.2 that, for a given confidence level, as the sample size, n, increases, the width of the interval:

$$2 \times \text{distribution critical value} \times \text{standard error of the estimate}$$

decreases since $\sqrt{n}$ always appears in the denominator of the standard error.

Conceptually, if the confidence level is fixed and sample size is increased, the width of the interval decreases since including more data will result in a decrease in the sampling variability, thus producing a more precise estimate of the population parameter.

EXAMPLE 1

Look at the 95% confidence interval of a proportion, p, if $\hat{p} = .3$ and
a. $n = 30$

   95% CI = (.13602, .46398)

b. $n = 100$

   95% CI = (.21018, .38982)

Since the width of the interval in this case is $2\left[z_{(1 - C)/2}\left(\sqrt{\dfrac{\hat{p}(1 - \hat{p})}{n}}\right)\right]$, the increase from $n = 30$ to $n = 100$ results in a narrower confidence interval since all other quantities remain the same.

Interval Width in Relation to Confidence Level

The relationship between width of the confidence interval and confidence level can again be seen procedurally or conceptually.

With regard to the formulas, the higher the confidence level, the larger the absolute value of the distribution critical value. For example, for a normal distribution and 90% confidence, we use $z_{(1 - C)/2} = 1.645$, while for 99% confidence, we use $z_{(1 - C)/2} = 2.576$. Assuming that the sample size is fixed, this increase in the distribution critical value will increase the numerator of each formula and thus increase the width of the confidence interval.

Conceptually, if one is to have more confidence that a particular interval captures the true population parameter, it follows that the width of the interval should increase in order to include more values. When a sample is small or we ask for a high degree of confidence, then the price we pay is a wider confidence interval.

Margin of Error

The quantity,

distribution critical value $\times$ standard error of the estimate

is known as the **margin of error** of a sample statistic. The margin of error is also the *half-width* of the confidence interval.

Consequently, the formulas for margin of error are:

Parameter to be Estimated	Margin of Error
population proportion	$z_{(1 - C)/2}\left(\sqrt{\dfrac{\hat{p}(1 - \hat{p})}{n}}\right)$
population mean (σ known)	$z_{(1 - C)/2}\left(\dfrac{\sigma}{\sqrt{n}}\right)$
population mean (σ unknown)	$t_{(1 - C)/2}\left(\dfrac{s}{\sqrt{n}}\right)$ $df = n - 1$
difference of population proportions	$z_{(1 - C)/2}\left(\sqrt{\dfrac{\hat{p}_1(1 - \hat{p}_1)}{n_1} + \dfrac{\hat{p}_2(1 - \hat{p}_2)}{n_2}}\right)$
difference of population means	$t_{(1 - C)/2}\left(\sqrt{\dfrac{s_1^2}{n_1} + \dfrac{s_2^2}{n_2}}\right)$ $df = \min\{n_1, n_2\}$

Note that the selection of the proper formula depends on the parameter to be estimated and the assumptions involved. For example, if the standard deviation of the population is not known, we will use the *t*-distribution to compute the margin of error for a sample mean.

From our discussion above pertaining to the width of a confidence interval, the following points can be made:

1. For a fixed sample size, the margin of error will decrease as the level of confidence decreases.
2. For a fixed confidence level and sample size, the margin of error decreases as the standard error of the estimate decreases. Therefore, less variation implies smaller margin of error.
3. For a fixed confidence level, the margin of error decreases as sample size increases.

EXAMPLE 2

If a sample proportion is given as .35 with a margin of error of ±3%, find the 95% confidence interval for the population proportion.

Solution

.35 ± .03 → 95% confidence interval is (.32, .38)

EXAMPLE 3

A simple random sample of 100 eighth graders at a large suburban middle school indicated that 83% of them are involved with some type of after-school activity. Find the margin of error for this sample result if we are to have 90% confidence in the results.

Solution

Check assumptions.

✓ Simple random sample?	*Given*
✓ Large population?	*Given*
✓ $n\hat{p} > 10$ and $n(1 - \hat{p}) > 10$	*100(.83) = 83; 100(.17) = 17*

Therefore, the margin of error for this sample with 90% confidence is

$$z_{(1 - C)/2}\left(\sqrt{\frac{\hat{p}(1 - \hat{p})}{n}}\right)$$

$$1.645\left(\sqrt{\frac{.83(1 - .83)}{100}}\right) = .062$$

So a 90% confidence interval would be (.768, .892)

EXAMPLE 4

Two independent random samples of registered voters are taken at different times in which the participants were asked to indicate whether they approved of the job that the mayor of their town had done since her last election. In the first sample, comprised of 100 voters, 52% approved of the mayor's performance; in the second sample, comprised of 75 voters, 48% approved of the mayor's performance. Find the margin of error for the difference in these proportions at the 95% confidence level.

Solution

Check assumptions.

✓ Simple random samples?	*Given*
✓ Large population(s)?	*Given*
✓ Independent samples?	*Given*
✓ $n_1\hat{p}_1 > 5$ and $n_1(1 - \hat{p}_1) > 5$ and	*100(.52) = 52, 100(.48) = 48;*
$n_2\hat{p}_2 > 5$ and $n_2(1 - \hat{p}_2) > 5$	*75(.48) = 36, 75(.52) = 39*

Therefore, the margin of error for this sample with 95% confidence is

$$z_{(1-C)/2}\left(\sqrt{\frac{\hat{p}_1(1-\hat{p}_1)}{n_1} + \frac{\hat{p}_2(1-\hat{p}_2)}{n_2}}\right)$$

$$1.96\left(\sqrt{\frac{.52(1-.52)}{100} + \frac{.48(1-.48)}{75}}\right) = .150$$

EXAMPLE 5

A simple random sample of 100 boy scouts is taken at the National Boy Scout Jamboree. The mean grade point average of these scouts (on a 4-point scale) was 3.12 with a standard deviation of .35. Verify the fact that the margin of error increases as confidence increases by finding the margin of error of this sample at both the 90% confidence and 98% confidence levels.

Solution

Check assumptions.

✓ Simple random sample?	*Given*
✓ Population is normal or $n \geq 40$?	*n = 100*
✓ σ is unknown?	*s = .35*

Therefore, the two margins of error are:

For 90% confidence:

$$t_{(1-C)/2}\left(\frac{s}{\sqrt{n}}\right) = 1.290\left(\frac{.35}{\sqrt{100}}\right) = .045$$

For 98% confidence:

$$t_{(1-C)/2}\left(\frac{s}{\sqrt{n}}\right) = 2.081\left(\frac{.35}{\sqrt{100}}\right) = .073$$

These calculations verify the fact that the margin of error increases as the confidence level increases. Note that the degrees of freedom for both calculations should be $df = n - 1 = 99$. The appropriate *t*-values were selected from a *t*-chart using $df = 100$.

Determining Sample Size

It is possible to determine the sample size necessary to achieve a specified margin of error for a given level of confidence. This calculation is only possible in the cases where the distribution critical value is from a normal distribution, that is, a z-distribution. It is difficult to complete a calculation for the sample size in the cases where the sampling distribution is a *t*-distribution; in these cases, the determination of $t_{(1-C)/2}$ also depends on the size of the sample because of the degrees of freedom.

Using *ME* as the Margin of Error, we can derive formulas for sample size:

For proportions:

$$ME = z_{(1 - C)/2} \times \sqrt{\frac{p_0(1 - p_0)}{n}}$$

so $n \geq \left(\dfrac{z_{(1 - C)/2}}{ME}\right)^2 [p_0(1 - p_0)]$

Note: Always round up to the next integer in the calculation of sample size since a size less than the calculated result will not be large enough to produce the specified margin of error.

For means:

$$ME = z_{(1 - C)/2} \times \frac{\sigma}{\sqrt{n}}$$

so $n = \left(\dfrac{z_{(1 - C)/2} \times \sigma}{ME}\right)^2$

Note: Always round up to the next integer in the calculation of sample size.

EXAMPLE 6

It is believed that 35% of all voters favor a particular candidate. How large of a simple random sample is required so that the margin of error of the estimate of the percentage of all voters in favor is 3% at the 95% confidence level?

Solution

$$n = \left(\frac{z_{(1 - C)/2}}{ME}\right)^2 [p_0(1 - p_0)]$$

$$= \left(\frac{1.96}{.03}\right)^2 [.35(1 - .35)]$$

$$= 971.07$$

Therefore, a sample size of 972 is required.

EXAMPLE 7

An investigator wishes to study television viewing habits among teenagers in a particular suburb. She knows that the standard deviation for the number of hours watched per day by all teenagers is 2.9 hours. How large of a simple random sample must be taken to estimate the population mean with a margin of error of 1 hour at the 99% confidence level?

Solution

$$n = \left(\frac{z_{(1 - C)/2} \times \sigma}{ME}\right)^2$$

$$= \left(\frac{2.58 \times 2.9}{1}\right)^2$$

$$= 55.980$$

Therefore, a sample size of 56 is required.

In both cases, the calculation of *n* depends on knowledge from a previous sample: either the sample proportion or the standard deviation.

In the case of the estimate of the population mean, it is appropriate to use a sample standard deviation as an estimate of the population standard deviation as long as the size of the sample is large.

In the case of the estimate of a population proportion, consider the graph of the standard error of the estimate of a proportion for varying values of $\hat{p}$ and for a constant sample size of 100:

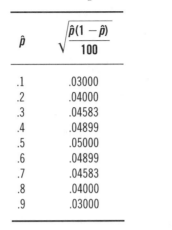

$\hat{p}$	$\sqrt{\dfrac{\hat{p}(1-\hat{p})}{100}}$
.1	.03000
.2	.04000
.3	.04583
.4	.04899
.5	.05000
.6	.04899
.7	.04583
.8	.04000
.9	.03000

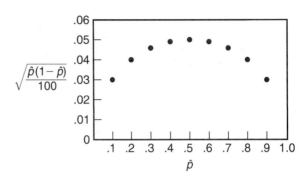

Based on this analysis, it is clear that the standard error of the estimate is *largest* when the sample proportion is .5. Therefore, the most conservative calculation of sample size for a proportion will use $p_0 = .5$.

EXAMPLE 8

A client comes to your company and tells you that she wishes to have a survey conducted to determine the proportion of consumers who regularly use her product. Based on the amount of money allocated to the project, you determine together that a simple random sample of 500 subjects will be adequate to her needs. She believes from earlier studies that her product enjoys a 37% market share. She asks if you can give her some idea of the accuracy of the results of your survey in advance. You recommend that an estimate of the margin of error be calculated and that for the greatest confidence in the results of the survey, a proportion of .50 should be used rather than the .37 market share from the earlier studies. She does not understand; calculate both margins of error (95% confidence) and discuss why the one using a proportion of .50 is more conservative.

Solution

Using a proportion of .37:

$$z_{(1-C)/2}\left(\sqrt{\frac{\hat{p}(1-\hat{p})}{n}}\right) = 1.96\left(\sqrt{\frac{.37(1-.37)}{500}}\right) = .0423$$

Using a proportion of .50:

$$z_{(1-C)/2}\left(\sqrt{\frac{\hat{p}(1-\hat{p})}{n}}\right) = 1.96\left(\sqrt{\frac{.5(1-.5)}{500}}\right) = .0438$$

Therefore, using a proportion of .5 suggests that the 95% confidence interval of the true proportion who favor her product will be the statistics ±4.38%; using .37, the 95% confidence interval will be the statistics ±4.23%. The proportion estimate of .5 produces the wider confidence interval and, therefore, is a more conservative estimate of the level of accuracy of her estimate.

Review Exercises

MULTIPLE-CHOICE QUESTIONS

1. From earlier studies, it is believed that the percentage of students favoring a four-day school week during May and June of every school year is approximately 85%. Which of the following sample sizes will create a margin of error of no more than ±2% with 90% confidence?
   (A) 79
   (B) 93
   (C) 146
   (D) 541
   (E) None of these.

2. Which of the following will reduce the width of a confidence interval?
   (A) Increase the confidence level.
   (B) Decrease the sample size.
   (C) Add .5 to the sample proportion.
   (D) Replace the sample proportion with .5.
   (E) None of these will guarantee a decrease in the width of the confidence interval.

3. A TV news magazine states that the results of their study of the average number of complaints per week about garbage pick-up in the city had a margin of error of ± 2.1 at the 95% confidence level, based on their examination of data from a random sample of a total of 30 weeks over the past 3 years. For this statement to be true, what was the approximate population standard deviation that the organization must have used to compute the margin of error? (Use $n = 30$ weeks as the sample of the population.)
   (A) 4.31
   (B) 5.87
   (C) 8.65
   (D) It cannot be determined from given information.
   (E) None of these.

4. When determining sample size for a study dealing with a proportion, it is most conservative to use .5 as an estimate of the sample proportion. Which of the following is the reason for this fact?
   (A) The study will focus only on two responses: success and failure.
   (B) .5 is the probability of flipping a coin. Since the survey deals only with a yes-no question, this probability is appropriate.

   (C) .5 will produce the greatest standard error. Therefore, the sample size using this value will guarantee that the margin of error for the study is maximized.
   (D) This is a binomial probability situation in which n is sample size, $p = .5$, and r is the number of positive responses.
   (E) None of these explains the use of .5 for the calculation of the most conservative sample size.

5. During an AP Statistics class, the final answer in a "Statistical Jeopardy" game was "… to reduce the width of a confidence interval." Each of the student teams had 15 seconds to write the question for this answer. Their questions were:

   Team A: Why should you increase the sample size?
   Team B: Why should you use a t-statistic instead of a z-statistic?
   Team C: Why should you increase the confidence level?

   Which team(s) were correct?
   (A) A only
   (B) B and C
   (C) A and C
   (D) A, B, and C
   (E) All teams were wrong.

6. Two studies, one conducted by the local newspaper and the other by the humane society, found that the percentage of puppies sold at local pet stores that are returned to the store by dissatisfied customers was approximately 23%. In the study conducted by the local newspaper, the investigators stated that their margin of error was ±2.5% while in the study conducted by the humane society, the published margin of error was ±3.7%. Assuming both used the same level of confidence, what was the approximate ratio of their sample sizes? Answers are in the form of $\dfrac{\text{newspaper}}{\text{humane society}}$.
   (A) $\dfrac{6}{13}$
   (B) $\dfrac{2}{3}$
   (C) $\dfrac{4}{3}$
   (D) $\dfrac{13}{6}$
   (E) The ratio cannot be determined.

1. Verify that the width of the confidence interval decreases as the sample size increases in the following case.
   a. The mean and standard deviation of a sample are determined to be 51.5 and 4.25 respectively. Determine the 95% confidence interval if
      (1) $n = 100$
      (2) $n = 400$
   b. An increase in sample size causes a decrease in the width of the confidence interval. Is there a relationship between the factor of increase of the sample size and the factor of decrease in the width of the confidence interval? That is, if the sample size increases by a factor of a, will the consequent decrease in confidence interval width be a function of a? Justify your position.

2. A preliminary study has indicated that the standard deviation of a population is approximately 7.85 hours. Determine an appropriate sample size if the estimate of the population mean is to have a margin of error of less than 2 hours at the 95% confidence level.

3. What is the smallest sample size needed to guarantee that the results of a survey conducted to find the percentage of voters favoring the incumbent mayor will have a margin of error of no more than 2% at the 99% confidence level?

4. Two statistical consulting companies are competing for the same contract. Company A claims that their results will be within 3% of the true population value given a 95% confidence level. Company B, on the other hand, says that their results will be within 2%, given a 98% confidence level.
   a. What sample size must Company A be planning to use for the study?
   b. What sample size should Company B use to guarantee that they will meet their proposed conditions?

7.4 The Concept of Significance

When a study is undertaken, the investigator anticipates that there will be some variation between the value of the true population parameter and the sample statistic calculated from the data collected. The question of interest is the source of the variation. In this section, we will refer to the sample statistic as the **observed** result and the population parameter as the **expected** result.

EXAMPLE 1

A simple random sample of 50 female adults in a particular suburb of Chicago was taken and the mean height of these subjects was found to be 66.3 inches. Census data indicate that the mean height of adult females in the same region is 65.4 inches. Therefore, we would expect to get a mean of 65.4 inches but we observed a sample mean of 66.3 inches.

We should not be surprised that there is a difference between the expected and the observed values in the example. This difference must come from at least one of three sources:

1. **Bias:** If the sampling procedure allows bias to occur during the data collection, then there will be a difference between the expected and the observed results. Care in the design and implementation of the sampling technique should minimize the effects of bias.

2. **Chance Error:** In a simple random sample, every possible subset of the population has the same probability of being chosen. Consequently, a subset whose measurements deviate from the expected value can occur strictly by chance. Chance error may be restated as "the luck of the draw."

3. **Something Significant:** When the difference between expected and observed results is so great that we can rule out chance error, the observed result is said to cast doubt on the validity of the expected value of the parameter of interest. This idea is the basis for the other method of statistical inference: the test of significance.

A sample statistic is considered **significant** when the probability that the data generated by a simple random sample will yield this statistic or a more extreme statistic is small.

This probability can be characterized in several ways. One way is to consider this value to be the probability that the difference between expected and observed results is due to chance error. Alternatively, this probability indicates how likely it is that a sample would yield the observed value or a more extreme value if the expected value is true. If this probability is small, then we can conclude that the data provide evidence that the result is statistically significant. This probability is generally known as the *P-value* of the test.

EXAMPLE 2

A toothpaste company advertises that a study concluded that 78% of dentists recommend their brand over their closest competitor's brand. The results of a simple random sample of 40 dentists in a particular city indicated that only 72% of dentists recommend this product over the other. To determine whether this sample result provides evidence that the company's claim is too high, the following probability statement must be evaluated:

P(sample of 40 dentists would result in 72% or fewer recommending the toothpaste when we expect that 78% will do so).

The size of the *P*-value determines whether a sample statistic is significant. The criteria for this decision depend on the **level of significance** that the investigator assigns to the study. The level of significance is usually denoted by the Greek letter α (alpha). In general,

If the P-value is less than or equal to α, then the result is considered significant.

If a level of significance is not stated, it is usually assumed to be .05. Some texts also state the following conventions:

If the *P*-value $\leq$ .05, the result is significant.
If the *P*-value $\leq$ .01, the result is highly significant.

The value of α is related to the confidence level C by:

$\alpha = 1 - C$

Therefore, a 5% level of significance corresponds to a 95% confidence level. For significance, we will use α.

Review Exercises

MULTIPLE-CHOICE QUESTIONS

1. Which of the following statements is correct?
   - (A) A sample statistic is significant if its population parameter is significant.
   - (B) A sample statistic is significant if it is very unlikely that such a statistic could come from a sample of this size drawn from the population.
   - (C) A sample statistic is significant if it can be established that it results from bias in the data-gathering process.
   - (D) A sample statistic that is significant is always important.
   - (E) None of these is correct.

2. Which of the following is *not* correct?
   - (A) Significance and confidence are not the same concepts.
   - (B) Significance is a conclusion based only on the calculation of a probability.
   - (C) Significance is a conclusion based only on the comparison of a probability to a specific criterion.
   - (D) Significance depends on the margin of error of the corresponding confidence interval.
   - (E) All of these are correct.

3. Which of the following is true?
   - (A) A highly significant result indicates that the sample result never really happened.
   - (B) If the probability of sample data yielding a statistic as or more extreme than a given value is approximately 0, then we have a good indication that bias must have been involved with the data collection.
   - (C) If the probability of sample data yielding a statistic as or more extreme than a given value is approximately 0, then we have a good indication that the value of the parameter could be significantly different from what is stated.
   - (D) If the probability of sample data yielding a statistic as or more extreme than a given value is approximately 0, then we have a good indication that whoever stated the expected value was lying.
   - (E) None of these is true.

FREE-RESPONSE QUESTIONS

Open-Ended Questions

The concept of significance is based on the following statement:

A sample statistic is considered significant when the probability of data generated by a simple random sample yielding this statistic or a more extreme statistic is small.

In each of the following exercises, write a probability statement (as in Example 2) in the context of the exercise that you would use to determine whether the observed result is statistically significant. Do *not* attempt to find the value.

1. Studies at a local university indicated that approximately 45% of the freshman class is placed on academic probation at the end of their first semester. Data generated by a simple random sample of 50 of this year's freshmen indicated that only 41% were placed on academic probation at the end of the first semester. Do these data indicate that the actual percentage of students placed on academic probation is less than 45%?

2. The U.S. Census Bureau published in 1990 that in a certain city the average number of children under 12 in a household was 2.4 with a standard deviation of .8. A simple random sample of 100 households was taken in 1998 and the average number of children under 12 for the sample households was found to be 2.8 with a standard deviation of 1.2. Do these data indicate that the actual average number of children per household in this city has increased since 1990?

3. The physical education department at a large urban high school has always believed that the percentage of boys who would choose Phys. Ed. as their favorite subject is approximately the same as the percentage for girls. Data from two independent random samples of the boys and girls indicated that 20% of the boys and 17% of the girls chose Phys. Ed. as their favorite subject. Do the results of these samples indicate that the percentage of boys in the population who would choose Phys. Ed. as their favorite subject is significantly greater than the percentage of girls who would do so?

4. Historical league records in the 800-meter track and field event indicate that, on average, boys run the distance 4.3 seconds faster than girls. A random sample of this year's high school track meets taken from the league records indicates that the difference in performance between boys and girls is 4.9 seconds. Does this analysis indicate that the gender gap is getting or has gotten larger than that the historical records indicate?

In statistical testing, we want to show whether a certain claim about the value of a parameter is reasonable or not. For the test, we determine the criteria under which we will conclude the assumption is unreasonable, take an appropriate sample and calculate the relevant statistic from the data, and then compare the results to our criteria.

Test of Significance Template

The procedure for determining the significance of a sample result is straightforward. The following template can be used to organize the numerous tasks that are involved with the complete process. Comments will be made for each section of the template.

TEST OF SIGNIFICANCE TEMPLATE

1. Parameter of Interest	p	
2. Choice of Test		
3. Check of Assumptions	Statement of Assumptions:	Verification of Assumptions: (conditions)
4. Null Hypothesis	H_0: (words) H_0: (symbols)	
5. Alternative Hypothesis	H_a: (words) H_a: (symbols)	
6. Probability Statement	P-value $=$ probability (	
7. Test Statistic	Formula:	Value:
8. Test: Level of Significance $\alpha =$ _____	Sketch of Sampling Distribution assuming H_0 is true: Identify the location of the test statistic in the sketch and shade the region that represents the P-value.	
9. P-value	Reconciliaton of Critical Value with Rejection Region:	Exact P-value:
10. Recommended Decisions	Regarding H_0:	Regarding significance:
11. Interpretation (in the context of the problem)		

Discussion of entries

Note: Although some of the entries may exceed the requirements for full credit on the AP exam, use of this template will foster greater understanding of the concepts and procedures involved in tests of significance.

To acquaint you with the specific entries, we will complete an example and include some discussion about each step.

EXAMPLE 1

A company claims that the mean weight per apple they ship is 120 grams with a standard deviation of 12 grams. Data generated from a sample of 49 apples randomly selected from a shipment indicated a mean weight of 122.5 grams per apple. Is there sufficient evidence to reject the company's claim? ($\alpha = .05$)

Solution

1. Parameter of Interest	We are interested in μ, the mean weight of a shipment of apples.

1. **Parameter of Interest:** It is important that you identify the parameter of interest immediately. Possible choices include a proportion, mean, slope, or any other parameter of the population.

2. Choice of Test	One-sample z-test for a population mean. There was only one sample of apples and we were given $\sigma = 12$ grams.

2. **Choice of Test:** It is recommended that the investigator clearly state the name of the test to be employed. The response indicates the number of samples that are involved and the sampling distribution appropriate for the given situation. Choices include:
   a. one-sample z-test for a mean;
   b. one-sample t-test for a mean;
   c. one-sample t-test for a proportion;
   d. two-sample t-test for the difference of two means;
   e. two-sample t-test for the difference of two proportions;
   f. paired t-test;
   g. chi-squared test for categorical data;
   h. t-test for the slope of a linear regression line.

Note: The last two tests will be reviewed in later sections of this chapter.

3. Check of Assumptions	**Statement of Assumptions:**	**Verification of Assumptions:**
	• simple random sample	• random sample from large population
	• $n \geq 30$	• $n = 49$
	• σ known	• $\sigma = 12$ grams

3. **Check of Assumptions:** This is a very important component in the process. Specific statements of assumptions and verification that these assumptions are satisfied is required on the AP exam and should be part of the process of any test of significance.

4. Null Hypothesis	H_0: (words) company's claim: mean weight per apple is 120 grams
	H_0: (symbols) $\mu = 120$ grams

4. **Null Hypothesis:** The null hypothesis, H_0, is the statement of the expected value of the *parameter.* It is critical that the null hypothesis (as well as the alternative hypothesis) deal with the parameter. In many instances this statement can be expressed in symbols. However, at times, the null hypothesis is clearest when written in words. The template requires that the null hypothesis be written both in words (in the context of the problem that has motivated the test) and in symbols (e.g., H_0: $\mu = 120$).

| 5. Alternative | H_a: (words) company's claim is inaccurate: mean weight per apple is not 120 grams |
| Hypothesis | H_a: (symbols) $\mu \neq 120$ grams |

5. **Alternative Hypothesis:** The alternative hypothesis, H_a, is a statement of negation of the null hypothesis. When the null hypothesis is expressed as an equation, the alternative hypothesis is generally an inequality in the form of $\mu \neq 120$ (two-tailed) or $\mu < 120$ or $\mu > 120$ (one-tailed). The decision about the type of inequality depends on the statement of the problem and the anticipation of the alternative value of the parameter of interest. The implications of this decision will become clearer as we continue through the template. *Note:* Some texts use H_1 as the symbol for the alternative hypothesis.

| 6. Probability Statement | We are interested in the likelihood that a sample of 49 apples will yield a mean weight per apple of 122.5 grams when the true value is 120 grams per apple. Since we have chosen a two-tailed test based on the information in the problem, the probability statement could be P-value = probability (sample of 49 apples will produce a mean weight per apple that differs by 2.5 grams or more in either direction from the company's claim of 120 grams per apple). |

6. **Probability Statement:** The conclusion about the population parameter depends on the P-value of the test. In this section, you are asked to state the meaning of the P-value in the context of the problem. In general, the P-value is the probability that a sample of this size will produce a statistic this or more extreme if the true value of the parameter is the value stated in the null hypothesis. The statement, in words, of this probability is the basis for the test of significance and, therefore, should be written clearly each time a test is conducted.

| 7. Test Statistic | Formula: | Value: |
| | $$z = \frac{\bar{x} - \mu}{\frac{\sigma}{\sqrt{n}}} = \frac{122.5 - 120}{\frac{12}{\sqrt{49}}}$$ | $z = 1.459$ |

7. **Test Statistic:** The test statistic is a numerical quantity that measures, in the cases of proportions, means, differences, and slopes, the quantity:

$$\frac{\text{observed} - \text{expected}}{\text{standard error}}$$

This section requires both the formula and the value of the test statistic. Ideally, you will also show the numbers substituted into the formula. On the exam, this helps the grader identify any calculator keystroke errors.

8. Test: Level of Significance
$\alpha = .05$

Sketch of Sampling Distribution assuming H_0 is true:
Since there is no indication as to whether the claim of a weight per apple of 120 grams is high or low, we use a two-tailed test.

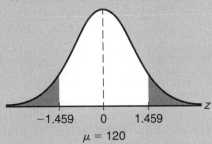

$\mu = 120$

Identify the location of the test statistic in the sketch and shade the region that represents the P-value.

8. **Test:** This section has two components: the statement of the level of significance and the determination of the rejection region including a sketch of the distribution.

a. The level of significance specifies the probability criteria to which the P-value of the test will be compared to determine if the sample statistic is significantly different from the population parameter. The level of significance is generally symbolized using the Greek letter α and, unless otherwise specified, is assumed to be .05. If the P-value of the test is greater than α, then the sample statistic is not significant; if the P-value of the test is less than α, that is, if the probability that the difference between the observed and the expected occurs by chance alone is very small, then the sample statistic is significant.

b. A sketch of the sampling distribution centered at the value of the parameter in the null hypothesis should be drawn. You should also shade the areas that represent the P-value associated with your test statistic, referencing either the one- or two-tailed test. For example, sketches for a two-tailed test with the test statistic $z = \pm 1.459$ at the 5% level of significance could be

(1) referencing P-value

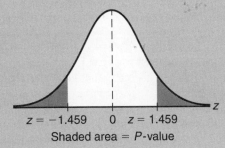

Shaded area $= P$-value

(2) referencing the rejection region

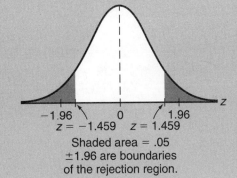

Shaded area $= .05$
± 1.96 are boundaries
of the rejection region.

9. *P*-value	**Reconciliation of Critical Value with Rejection Region:** For a two-tailed *z*-test at the .05 level of significance, each tail has an area equal to .025. The critical values for these areas are ±1.96. The positive critical value is then compared to the absolute value of the test statistic: $$z = 1.459 \text{ vs. } z_{.025} = 1.96$$ The critical value is larger. Therefore, our test statistic is *not* in the rejection region.	**Exact *P*-value:** The probability that the true population parameter has *z*-score greater than 1.459 is .0723. Since this is a two-tailed test, $$P\text{-value} = 2(.0723) = .1446$$ That is, the probability of obtaining this *z*-score assuming that the population parameter is true is .1446.

9. ***P*-value:** The *P*-value is the value of the probability statement in step 5 above. In this step, reconciliation with the critical value, i.e., the boundary of the rejection region or calculation of the *P*-value is made.

a. **Reconciliation of Critical Value with Rejection Region:** The rejection region has been the traditional method of determining significance and corresponds to the region in the tails of the sampling distribution in which the probability is α. In addition, the location of the rejection region depends on whether this is a one- or two-tailed test.

For example, if $\alpha = .05$, the sampling distribution is normal, and

(1) the test is two-tailed   (2) the test is one-tailed

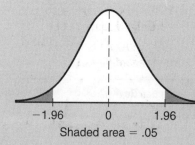

-1.96 0 1.96	0 1.645
Shaded area = .05	Shaded area = .05

then $z_{\alpha/2} = z_{.025} = 1.96$ then $z_\alpha = z_{.05} = 1.645$

Note that the shaded areas in both cases equal the level of significance. However, the absolute value of *z* differs depending on whether a one- or two-tailed test is conducted. *Note:* The sign depends on whether the tail is on the left (negative) or right (positive).

While the use of rejection regions has become less important with the technological advances of recent years, it is useful to include a sketch similar to these in the tests of significance process in order to provide a visual image of the nature of the test. The decision regarding the probability statement of step 5 was based on a comparison of the value of the test statistic to the critical value of the rejection region.

- If the absolute value of the test statistic is less than the absolute value of the critical value of the rejection region, then the result is *not* significant.
- If the absolute value of the test statistic is greater than the absolute value of the critical value of the rejection region, then the result is significant.

Use of the critical value of the rejection region requires tables of critical values for specific sampling distributions.

b. **Exact P-value:** We have always been able to calculate the P-value for a z-statistic, although it is a difficult task by hand. Using modern technology, it is possible to calculate the P-value corresponding to a test statistic for many sampling distributions. Comparison of the P-value to the level of significance, α, is the basis of the decision regarding significance.

- If the P-value is greater than α, then the result is *not* significant.
- If the P-value is less than α, then the result is significant.

Note: The criteria of using rejection regions and of using the P-values are equivalent. For example, if the P-value is less than α, then the test statistic is located in the rejection region.

10. Recommended Decisions	Regarding H_0: Since .1446 > .05, we fail to reject H_0.	Regarding significance: The result of the sample is *not* significant. This probability is not sufficiently low to convince us that the sample result could not have occurred by chance in a shipment with mean weight per apple of 120 grams.

10. **Recommended Decisions:** Decisions focus on two areas:
   a. **Regarding significance:** Based on the analysis in step 9, a statement should be made regarding whether the sample results produce a significant result relative to the level of significance that is the criterion of the test. Step 9 above includes significance statements.
   b. **Regarding H_0:** Again based on the analysis in step 9, a conclusion can be inferred regarding H_0:

Rejection Region	P-value	Decision
$\mid$ Test statistic $\mid$ < $\mid$ Critical value $\mid$	P-value > α	Evidence is not sufficient to reject H_0 (Fail to reject)
$\mid$ Test statistic $\mid$ > $\mid$ Critical value $\mid$	P-value < α	Evidence is sufficient to reject H_0 (Reject)

Note that "failing to reject H_0" is *not* the same as "accepting H_0." It is a substantial error to conclude that we should *accept* H_0. This conclusion can only be made after a Type II error analysis (see the next section of this chapter).

11. Interpretation (in the context of the problem)	There is not sufficient evidence at the 5% level of significance to reject the company's claim that the mean weight per apple in this shipment is 120 grams.

11. **Interpretation (in the context of the problem):** This last step requires that the conclusion of the test be restated in the context of the problem. Consequently, it is also an essential ingredient to the hypothesis testing process.

Summary of Tests and Assumptions

The following table lists common significance tests with their assumptions, null hypotheses, and test statistics. The statement of the test statistic will indicate the nature of the sampling distribution that underlies the test. *Note: All of these assume simple random samples.*

Test	Assumptions	Null Hypothesis	Test Statistic
One-sample z-test	Normal distribution or $n \geq 30$ σ known	$\mu = \mu_0$	$z = \dfrac{\bar{x} - \mu_0}{\dfrac{\sigma}{\sqrt{n}}}$
Two-sample z-test	Normal distributions Independent samples σ_1, σ_2 known	$\mu_1 - \mu_2 = 0$	$z = \dfrac{(\bar{x}_1 - \bar{x}_2) - (\mu_1 - \mu_2)}{\sqrt{\dfrac{\sigma_1^2}{n_1} + \dfrac{\sigma_2^2}{n_2}}}$
One-sample t-test	Normal population or $n \geq 30$ σ unknown	$\mu = \mu_0$	$t = \dfrac{\bar{x} - \mu_0}{\dfrac{s}{\sqrt{n}}}; df = n - 1$
Two-sample t-test (pooled)	Normal populations or $n_1 + n_2 > 40$ Independent samples $\sigma_1 = \sigma_2$ both σ_1 and σ_2 unknown	$\mu_1 - \mu_2 = c_0$ c_0 = constant	$t = \dfrac{(\bar{x}_1 - \bar{x}_2) - (\mu_1 - \mu_2)}{s_p\sqrt{\dfrac{1}{n_1} + \dfrac{1}{n_2}}}$ where $s_p^2 = \dfrac{(n_1 - 1)s_1^2 + (n_2 - 1)s_2^2}{n_1 + n_2 - 2}$ $df = n_1 + n_2 - 2$
Two-sample t-test (unpooled)	Normal populations or $n_1 + n_2 > 40$ Independent samples $\sigma_1 \neq \sigma_2$ both σ_1 and σ_2 unknown	$\mu_1 - \mu_2 = c_0$ c_0 = constant	$t = \dfrac{(\bar{x}_1 - \bar{x}_2) - (\mu_1 - \mu_2)}{\sqrt{\dfrac{s_1^2}{n_1} + \dfrac{s_2^2}{n_2}}}$ $df = \dfrac{(n_1 - 1)(n_2 - 1)}{(n_2 - 1)c^2 + (n_1 - 1)(1 - c^2)}$ where $c = \dfrac{\dfrac{s_1^2}{n_1}}{\dfrac{s_1^2}{n_1} + \dfrac{s_2^2}{n_2}}$ or $df = \min\{n_1, n_2\}$
Paired t-test: one sample t-test on differences	Normal population of differences or $n > 30$ σ unknown	$d = d_0$	$t = \dfrac{\bar{d} - d_0}{s_d}$ $df = n - 1$
One-sample z-test	$np > 10$ and $n(1 - p) > 10$	$p = p_0$	$z = \dfrac{\hat{p} - p}{\sqrt{\dfrac{p(1 - p)}{n}}}$
Two-proportion z-test, equal variances	$n_1 p_1 > 5$ and $n_1(1 - p_1) > 5$ $n_2 p_2 > 5$ and $n_2(1 - p_2) > 5$ independent samples *Note:* Some texts use 10 instead of 5 in this assumption.	$p_1 - p_2 = 0$	$z = \dfrac{(\hat{p}_1 - \hat{p}_2) - (p_1 - p_2)}{\sqrt{\hat{p}(1 - \hat{p})\left(\dfrac{1}{n_1} + \dfrac{1}{n_2}\right)}}$ where $\hat{p} = \dfrac{x_1 + x_2}{n_1 + n_2}$ *Note:* $\hat{p}$ is the combined proportion and is used as an approximation of p, the population proportion.
Two-proportion z-test, unequal variances	$n_1 p_1 > 5$ and $n_1(1 - p_1) > 5$ $n_2 p_2 > 5$ and $n_2(1 - p_2) > 5$ independent samples *Note:* Some texts use 10 instead of 5 in this assumption.	$p_1 - p_2 = c$ c = constant	$z = \dfrac{(\hat{p}_1 - \hat{p}_2) - (p_1 - p_2)}{\sqrt{\dfrac{\hat{p}_1(1 - \hat{p}_1)}{n_1} + \dfrac{\hat{p}_2(1 - \hat{p}_2)}{n_2}}}$

Note that the decision whether to use the equal variance option (*pooled* two-sample *t*-test) or the unequal variance option (*unpooled* two-sample *t*-test) depends on an assumption regarding the variances of the populations. The null hypothesis, $p_1 - p_2 = 0$, implies that all of the data come from the same population, hence the two variances are equal. With this form of the null hypothesis, we use the "pooled" standard deviation in the formula for the test statistic as represented in the chart above. However, when the null hypothesis is that the population proportions are not equal ($p_1 - p_2 = c$, where c is a constant), the variances are not equal and we use the unequal variances version of the formula in the chart above. Notice that the standard deviation in this formula is exactly the standard deviation for the sum of random variables that was discussed in Chapter 5.

In the following examples, we will state a problem and perform a significance test using the template just described.

EXAMPLE 2

The belief is that the mean number of hours per week of part-time work of high school seniors in a city is 10.6 hours. Data from a simple random sample of 50 seniors indicated that their mean number of hours of part-time work was 12.5 with a standard deviation of 1.3. Test whether these data cast doubt on the current belief ($\alpha = .05$).

Solution

The standard deviation of the population is unknown, so we must use a *t*-test for the mean. There is no prior suspicion as to whether the mean is higher or lower, so we use a two-tailed test. For $\alpha = .05$, each tail probability is .025 and, for a *t*-distribution with a *df* of $50 - 1 = 49$, a critical value of ± 2.009 is indicated. The exact *P*-value is found by doubling the *P*-value for one tail.

1. Parameter of Interest	μ, the mean number of hours per week of part-time work of high school seniors in the city of question.	
2. Choice of Test	One-sample *t*-test for a population mean	
3. Check of Assumptions	Statement of Assumptions: • SRS • normal population or *n* is large • σ is unknown	Verification of Assumptions: • Given • No reason to believe that the population (number of hours worked) is not normal, and $n = 50$. • σ is unknown
4. Null Hypothesis	H_0: **(words)** Mean number of hours per week of part-time work is 10.6 H_0: **(symbols)** $\mu = 10.6$	
5. Alternative Hypothesis	H_a: **(words)** Mean number of hours per week of part-time work is not 10.6 H_a: **(symbols)** $\mu \neq 10.6$	
6. Probability Statement	$P =$ **probability** (a sample of 50 students will have a mean that differs by 1.9 (from $12.5 - 10.6$) or more (in either direction) from the population mean.)	
7. Test Statistic	Formula: $$t = \frac{\bar{x} - \mu}{\frac{s}{\sqrt{n}}} = \frac{12.5 - 10.6}{\frac{1.3}{\sqrt{50}}}$$ $df = n - 1 = 50 - 1$	Value: $t = 10.33$ $df = 49$

8. Test: Level of Significance $\alpha = .05$	**Sketch of Sampling Distribution assuming that H_0 is true:** 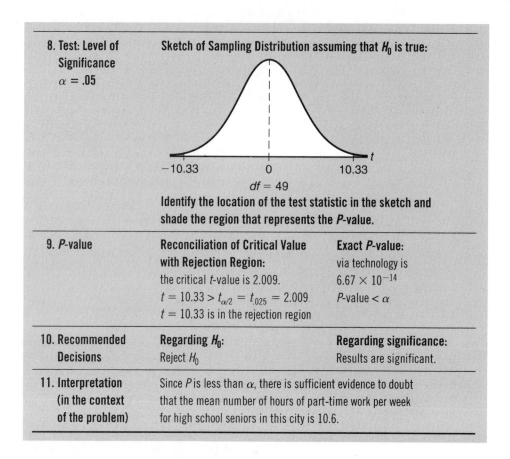	
	Identify the location of the test statistic in the sketch and shade the region that represents the P-value.	
9. P-value	**Reconciliation of Critical Value with Rejection Region:** the critical t-value is 2.009. $t = 10.33 > t_{\alpha/2} = t_{.025} = 2.009$ $t = 10.33$ is in the rejection region	**Exact P-value:** via technology is 6.67×10^{-14} $P\text{-value} < \alpha$
10. Recommended Decisions	**Regarding H_0:** Reject H_0	**Regarding significance:** Results are significant.
11. Interpretation (in the context of the problem)	Since P is less than α, there is sufficient evidence to doubt that the mean number of hours of part-time work per week for high school seniors in this city is 10.6.	

EXAMPLE 3

A company claims that only 3% of its products are defective. A simple random sample of 250 of their products yielded 8 defective items. Do these sample data suggest that the company's claim is too low? ($\alpha = .05$)

Solution

This problem deals with proportions, so we choose a one-sample z-test for a proportion. Since our objective is to test whether the company's claim is too low, a one-tailed test is indicated. The critical value for a one-tailed z-test with $\alpha = .05$ is 1.645.

1. Parameter of Interest	p, the proportion of defective items	
2. Choice of Test	one-sample z-test	
3. Check of Assumptions	**Statement of Assumptions:** • SRS • $np > 10$ and $n(1-p) > 10$? • equally likely event?	**Verification of Assumptions:** • Given • $np = 250(.03) = 7.5$ *does* ***not*** *satisfy this assumption.* Thus, continuation of the test will lead to unreliable results. Therefore, we terminate the test.

When the situation does not satisfy one of the assumptions of the test, the testing process stops. Note that $p = .03$ is used in the check of the assumption since we assume that the company's claim is true.

EXAMPLE 4

The president of an all-female school stated in a interview that she was sure that the students at her school studied more, on average, than the students at a neighboring all-male school. The president of the all-male school responded that he thought the mean study time for each student body was undoubtedly about the same and suggested that a study be undertaken to clear up the controversy. Accordingly, independent samples were taken at the two schools with the following results:

School	Sample Size	Mean Study Time (hours)	Standard Deviation (hours)
All Female	65	18.56	4.35
All Male	75	17.95	4.87

Determine at the 2% level of significance if there is a significant difference between the mean studying times of the students in the two schools based on these samples.

Solution

The standard deviations of the populations are unknown and we have two independent populations (students at each school), so we must use a two-sample t-test. Since the study focuses on whether there is a significant difference in the two means, we will use a two-sided test. We will choose an unpooled two-sample t-test since we have no information regarding the sizes of the standard deviations of the populations. Note that if we were testing the claim of the president of the girls' school (girls study more...), we would use a one-sided test.

1. Parameter of Interest	$\mu_1 - \mu_2$: The difference between the mean study time of the males and females attending these schools.	
2. Choice of Test	Two-sided two-sample t-test	
3. Check of Assumptions	**Statement of Assumptions:** • Normal populations or $\quad n_1 + n_2 > 40$ • Independent samples • σ_1 and σ_2 are unknown	**Verification of Assumptions:** • $n_1 + n_2 = 1{,}0$ • Given • Only the standard deviation of the samples are given.
4. Null Hypothesis	H_0: **(words)** The difference between the mean study times is 0. H_0: **(symbols)** $\mu_1 - \mu_2 = 0$	
5. Alternative Hypothesis	H_a: **(words)** The difference of the means is not 0. H_a: **(symbols)** $\mu_1 - \mu_2 \neq 0$	
6. Probability Statement	*P*-value $=$ probability (samples of these sizes will result in a difference between sample means of .61 hours or more (in either direction) when the true difference is 0.)	
7. Test Statistic	**Formula:** $$t = \frac{(\bar{x}_1 - \bar{x}_2) - (\mu_1 - \mu_2)}{\sqrt{\dfrac{s_1^2}{n_1} + \dfrac{s_2^2}{n_2}}}$$ $$= \frac{.61 - 0}{\sqrt{\dfrac{4.35^2}{65} + \dfrac{4.87^2}{75}}}$$ $df = \min\{n_1, n_2\} - 1 = 65 - 1 \qquad df = 64$	**Value:** $t = .7827$

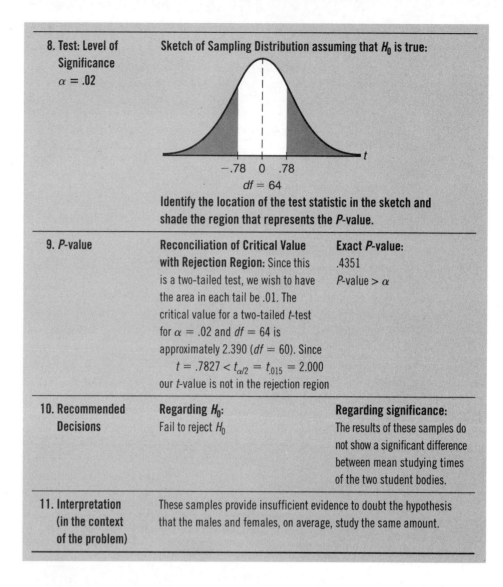

8. Test: Level of Significance $\alpha = .02$	Sketch of Sampling Distribution assuming that H_0 is true:

$-.78 \quad 0 \quad .78$

$df = 64$

Identify the location of the test statistic in the sketch and shade the region that represents the *P*-value.

9. *P*-value	Reconciliation of Critical Value with Rejection Region: Since this is a two-tailed test, we wish to have the area in each tail be .01. The critical value for a two-tailed *t*-test for $\alpha = .02$ and $df = 64$ is approximately 2.390 ($df = 60$). Since $t = .7827 < t_{\alpha/2} = t_{.015} = 2.000$ our *t*-value is not in the rejection region	Exact *P*-value: .4351 $P\text{-value} > \alpha$

10. Recommended Decisions	Regarding H_0: Fail to reject H_0	Regarding significance: The results of these samples do not show a significant difference between mean studying times of the two student bodies.

11. Interpretation (in the context of the problem)	These samples provide insufficient evidence to doubt the hypothesis that the males and females, on average, study the same amount.

EXAMPLE 5

The Guidance Office of a school wants to test the claim of an SAT test preparation company that students who complete their course will improve their SAT Math score by at least 50 points. Ten members of the junior class who have had no SAT preparation but have taken the SAT once were selected at random and agreed to participate in the study. All took the course and re-took the SAT at the next opportunity. The results of the testing indicated:

Student	1	2	3	4	5	6	7	8	9	10
Before	475	512	492	465	523	560	610	477	501	420
After	500	540	512	530	533	603	691	512	489	458

Is there sufficient evidence to support the prep course company's claim that scores will improve by at least 50 points at the 5% level of significance?

Solution

It is clear that these data did not come from two independent samples. Rather, they are a result of a single sample from which two measurements were taken, before and after. Since this study has a matched pairs design, it is necessary to perform a one-sample *t*-test on the difference between the before and after scores for each student. In addition, this test will be one-tailed because we are interested in whether the improvement is less than the company's claim.

Consequently,

Student	1	2	3	4	5	6	7	8	9	10
Before (B)	475	512	492	465	523	560	610	477	501	420
After (A)	500	540	512	530	533	603	691	512	489	458
Difference (A–B)	25	28	20	65	10	43	81	35	−12	38

The mean of the differences is 33.3 with a standard deviation of 26.39.

1. Parameter of Interest	μ, the mean difference between the first SAT test performance and the second after the subjects took the SAT prep course
2. Choice of Test	One-sample t-test (matched pairs)

3. Check of Assumptions

Statement of Assumptions:
- SRS
- Normal distribution of differences or $n > 30$.

- σ of differences unknown.

Verification of Assumptions:
- Given
- Populations of SAT takers are large and approximately normal.
- Only sample statistics are given.

4. Null Hypothesis

H_0: **(words)** After attending this SAT prep course, students will improve their SAT Math scores on average by 50 points.
H_0: **(symbols)** $\mu = 50$

5. Alternative Hypothesis

H_a: **(words)** After attending this SAT prep course, students will improve their SAT Math scores on average by less the 50 points.
H_a: **(symbols)** $\mu < 50$

6. Probability Statement

P-value $=$ probability (a sample of 10 will improve their scores by an average of 33.3 points or less when true mean improvement is 50 points)

7. Test Statistic

Formula:
$$t = \frac{\bar{d} - d_0}{\frac{s}{\sqrt{n}}} = \frac{33.3 - 50}{\frac{26.39}{\sqrt{10}}}$$
$$df = n - 1 = 10 - 1$$

Value:
$t = -2.001$

$df = 9$

8. Test: Level of Significance $\alpha = .05$

Sketch of Sampling Distribution assuming that H_0 is true:

Identify the location of the test statistic in the sketch and shade the region that represents the P-value

9. P-value

Reconciliation of Critical Value with Rejection Region: The critical value for a one-tailed t-test ($\alpha = .05$) with $df = 9$ is 1.833. Since our $t = 2.001 > t_\alpha = t_{.05} = 1.833$, our t-value is in the rejection region.

Exact P-value:
P-value $= .0382$
P-value $< \alpha$

10. Recommended Decisions	Regarding significance: Since our test statistic is in the rejection region and since our P-value is less than .05, these data provide a significant result.	Regarding H_0: Reject H_0.
11. Interpretation (in the context of the problem)	The data provide sufficient evidence that the actual amount of improvement in SAT Math scores after attending this SAT prep course is less, on average, than the 50 points claimed.	

EXAMPLE 6

Data taken from a random sample of 60 students chosen from the student population of a large urban high school indicated that 36 of them planned to pursue post-secondary education. An independent random sample of 50 students taken at a neighboring large suburban high school resulted in data that indicated that 31 of those students planned to pursue post-secondary education. Do these data provide sufficient evidence to reject the hypothesis that these population proportions are equal?

Solution

This question should be answered by a two-sample proportion z-test. Since we are testing the hypotheses that the population proportions are equal, we will assume that the variances of the populations are equal. We will use a two-sided test since we have no indication that the difference is on one side of zero or the other.

1. Parameter of Interest	The difference of the population proportions, $p_1 - p_2$	
2. Choice of Test	Two-sample proportion z-test	
3. Check of Assumptions	**Statement of Assumptions:** • SRS • $n_1 p_1 > 5$ and $n_1(1 - p_1) > 5$ $n_2 p_2 > 5$ and $n_2(1 - p_2) > 5$? • Independent samples? • Equal variances?	**Verification of Assumptions:** • Given • $n_1 p_1 = 60(.60) = 36$ and $n_1(1 - p_1) = 60(.40) = 24$ $n_2 p_2 = 50(.62) = 31$ and $n_2(1 - p_2) = 50(.38) = 19$ • Given • Assumed (see discussion above)
4. Null Hypothesis	H_0: (words) There is no difference in the proportion of urban and suburban students planning to pursue post-secondary education. H_0: (symbols) $p_1 - p_2 = 0$	
5. Alternative Hypothesis	H_a: (words) The difference in the proportions of students planning to pursue post-secondary education is not 0. H_a: (symbols) $p_1 - p_2 \neq 0$	
6. Probability Statement	**P-value = probability** (samples of these sizes will produce proportions that differ by .02 or more (in either direction) when the true difference in the proportions is 0.)	

7. Test Statistic	**Formula:**	**Value:**

$$z = \frac{(\hat{p}_1 - \hat{p}_2) - (p_1 - p_2)}{\sqrt{\hat{p}(1 - \hat{p})\left(\dfrac{1}{n_1} + \dfrac{1}{n_2}\right)}} \qquad z = .2141$$

$$= \frac{(.62 - .60) - 0}{\sqrt{.609(1 - .609)\left(\dfrac{1}{50} + \dfrac{1}{60}\right)}}$$

$$\text{where } \hat{p} = \frac{x_1 + x_2}{n_1 + n_2} = \frac{31 + 36}{50 + 60}$$

8. Test: Level of Significance $\alpha = .05$

Sketch of Sampling Distribution assuming that H_0 is true:

$-.2141 \quad 0 \quad .2141$

Identify the location of the test statistic in the sketch and shade the region that represents the *P*-value.

9. *P*-value

Reconciliation of Critical Value with Rejection Region: The critical value for a two-sided z-test at the .05 level of significance is $z_{.025} = 1.96$.
$z = .214 < z_{\alpha/2} = z_{.025} = 1.96$

Exact *P*-value:
.8305

10. Recommended Decisions

Regarding H_0:
Fail to reject H_0.

Regarding significance:
Since the test statistic is less than the critical z and since the *P*-value $> .05$, these data are not significant.

11. Interpretation (in the context of the problem)

The evidence is not sufficient to indicate a significant difference between the population proportions of students who plan to pursue post-secondary education.

Confidence Intervals and Tests of Significance

An alternative to the significance testing techniques reviewed above can be found in confidence intervals. Once a confidence interval has been calculated, it is sufficient to check and see if the expected value of the population parameter stated in the null hypothesis is contained in the interval. If it is contained in the interval, we can conclude that a *two-tailed* hypothesis test would fail to reject the null hypothesis. On the other hand, if the value of the population parameter in the null hypothesis is not contained in the confidence interval (at the $\alpha = 1 - C$ significance level), then we can conclude that we have sufficient evidence to reject the null hypothesis for the *two-tailed* hypothesis test.

EXAMPLE 7

A company claims that their room deodorizers last an average of 17.3 days with a standard deviation of 2.1 days. A random sample of 20 products yielded a mean lasting time of 15.2 days. Do these results provide sufficient evidence to conclude that the true mean lasting time is different from the claimed 17.3 days at the 5% level of significance?

Solution

Confidence Interval Technique

Since σ is known, we will calculate the 95% confidence interval of the mean:

$$\bar{x} \pm z_{(1-C)/2} \times \frac{\sigma}{\sqrt{n}}$$

$$15.2 \pm 1.96 \times \frac{2.1}{\sqrt{20}}$$

$$(14.28, 16.12)$$

Since the null hypothesis value: $\mu = 17.3$ days is not in the 95% confidence interval, we conclude that we have sufficient evidence to reject H_0 at the 5% level. Therefore, we have sufficient evidence to reject the claim that the mean lasting time is 17.3 days.

Significance Test Technique

(using technology)
Using a two-tailed z-test (since σ is known), we determine that
$H_0: \mu = 17.3$; $H_a: \mu \neq 17.3$ and

$$z = \frac{\bar{x} - \mu}{\frac{\sigma}{\sqrt{n}}} = \frac{15.2 - 17.3}{\frac{2.1}{\sqrt{20}}} = -4.472$$

P-value $= 7.751 \times 10^{-6}$

Since the P-value is less than α, we conclude that this is a highly significant result and we have sufficient evidence to reject the company's claim. We further conclude that the true mean is different from 17.3 days, although we don't know whether it is higher or lower.

Note that the significance test method yields the P-value as well as providing a basis for the decision regarding H_0. This P-value tells us "how significant" the result is in that it answers the question of how likely the sample results are if the null hypothesis is true. Note also that a one-tailed significance test is similarly related to a confidence interval. In the case of a one-tailed test at $\alpha = .05$, we desire to have all 5% of the area in one tail. The related confidence interval (which is always two-tailed) is the 90% confidence interval so that 5% of the area is outside either the upper or lower bound of the interval.

Two-tailed ($\alpha = .05$; 95% confidence)

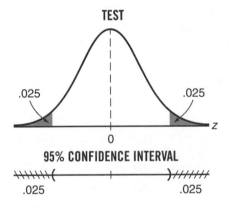

One-tailed ($\alpha = 05$; 90% confidence)

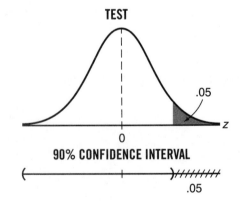

Solving for Missing Information To Achieve a Significant Result

It is possible to use the concepts of significance testing to determine what is required to achieve a significant result.

EXAMPLE 8

A two-tailed significance test for a population proportion indicated that the result of a sample proportion of .47 obtained from data taken from a sample of size 100 was not significant ($\alpha = .05$) when the null hypothesis was $p = .50$. What is the minimum sample size so that a $\hat{p} = .47$ would indicate a significant result for the null hypothesis $p = .50$ at the 5% level of significance?

Solution

At the 5% level of significance, the test statistic for a two-sided one-proportion z-test would have to be more extreme than $z_{\alpha/2} = 1.96$ for the P-value to be less than .05. Therefore,

$$z = \frac{\hat{p} - p}{\sqrt{\frac{p(1-p)}{n}}}$$

$$\frac{.47 - .50}{\sqrt{\frac{.50(1 - .50)}{n}}} > -1.96$$

$$-.03 > -1.96\sqrt{\frac{.25}{n}}$$

$$n > 1,067.11$$

Therefore, the minimum sample size that would produce a significant result is 1,068.

EXAMPLE 9

From earlier records, Company A knows that a small electric motor that it produces has a mean life in continuous use of 28.5 hours with a standard deviation of 2.1 hours. Company B plans to investigate whether its motor exceeds this average life by testing a random sample of 50 motors. What is the minimum mean life that these sample motors must have so that a one-sided z-test will provide evidence at the 5% level of significance that the motors produced by Company B have a longer life than those of Company A?

Solution

At the 5% level of significance, the test statistic for a one-sided z-test of a population mean would have to be greater than $z_\alpha = 1.645$ for the P-value to be less than .05. Therefore,

$$z = \frac{\bar{x} - \mu}{\frac{\sigma}{\sqrt{n}}}$$

$$\frac{\bar{x} - 28.5}{\frac{2.1}{\sqrt{50}}} = 1.645$$

$$\bar{x} > 28.99 \text{ hours}$$

Therefore, it is sufficient that the Company B's sample of 50 have a mean life of at least 28.99 hours for there to be evidence that the motors produced by Company B have a longer life than those of Company A.

Statistical Inference and Technology

The majority of statistical software packages are capable of performing all of the tests discussed in this chapter and others that are not within the scope of the AP Statistics curriculum and most other introductory statistics courses. This section will summarize the contents of the *TESTS* menu on the TI-83 calculator (found by pressing *STAT*). It is *essential* that you understand that technology is a very powerful tool but it does *not* replace the thinking, analysis, and communication of statistical inference. **Remember that full credit for significance tests on the AP Statistics exam requires:**

- statement of parameter of interest,
- statement of null and alternative hypotheses,
- statement and verification of assumptions,
- choice of test and construction and evaluation of a test statistic,
- decisions based on the value of the test statistic, and
- interpretation of test results in the context of the situation.

The TESTS Menu:

Relevant tests for AP Statistics include:

Confidence Intervals and Tests	Input	Output
Z-Test	**Inpt: Data**	**Calculate:** Alt. Hyp., z, p, $\bar{x}$, s_x,
	μ_0, σ, List, Freq, Alt. Hyp.	and n
	Inpt: Stats	**Draw:** density function with
	μ_0, σ, $\bar{x}$, n, Alt. Hyp.	shading, z, p
T-Test	**Inpt: Data**	**Calculate:** Alt. Hyp., t, p, $\bar{x}$, s_x,
	μ_0, List, Freq, Alt. Hyp.	and n
	Inpt: Stats	**Draw:** density function with
	μ_0, σ, $\bar{x}$, s_x, n, Alt. Hyp.	shading, t, p

2-SampZTest	**Inpt: Data** σ_1, σ_2, List 1, List 2, Freq 1 Freq 2, Alt. Hyp. **Inpt: Stats** σ_1, σ_2, $\bar{x}1$, $n1$, $\bar{x}2$, $n2$, Alt. Hyp.	**Calculate:** Alt. Hyp., z, p, $\bar{x}1$, $\bar{x}2$, $n1$, and $n2$, **Draw:** density function with shading, z, p
2-SampTTest	**Inpt: Data** List 1, List 2, Freq 1, Freq 2, Alt. Hyp., Pooled SD? **Inpt: Stats** $\bar{x}1$, s_x1, $n1$, $\bar{x}2$, s_x2, $n2$, Alt. Hyp., Pooled SD?	**Calculate:** Alt. Hyp., t, p, degrees of freedom, x-bar 1, x-bar 2, $s1$, $s2$, $n1$ and $n2$ **Draw:** density function with shading, t, p
1-PropZTest	P_0, x, n, Alt. Hyp.	**Calculate:** Alt. Hyp., z, p, $\hat{p}$ and n **Draw:** density function with shading, z, p
2-PropZTest	$x1$, $n1$, $x2$, $n2$, Alt. Hyp.	**Calculate:** Alt. Hyp., z, p, $\hat{p}1$, $\hat{p}2$, $\hat{p}$, $n1$, and $n2$ **Draw:** density function with shading, z, p
ZInterval	**Inpt: Data** σ, List, Freq, Confidence Level **Inpt: Stats** σ, $\bar{x}$, n, Confidence Level	Zinterval, $\bar{x}$, s_x, n
TInterval	**Inpt: Data** List, Freq, Confidence Level **Inpt: Stats** $\bar{x}$, s_x, n, Confidence Level	Tinterval, x-bar, s_x, and n
2-SampZInt	**Inpt: Data** $\sigma1$, $\sigma2$, List 1, List 2, Freq 1, Freq 2, Confidence Level **Inpt: Stats** $\sigma1$, $\sigma2$, $\bar{x}1$, $n1$, $\bar{x}2$, $n2$, Confidence Level	2-SampZinterval, $\bar{x}1$, $\bar{x}2$, $n1$ and $n2$
2-SampTInt	**Inpt: Data** List 1, List 2, Freq 1, Freq 2, Confidence Level, Pooled SD? **Inpt: Stats** $\bar{x}1$, s_x1, $n1$, $\bar{x}2$, s_x2, $n2$, Confidence Level, Pooled SD?	2-SampTinterval, df, $\bar{x}1$, $\bar{x}2$, s_x1, s_x2, $n1$, and $n2$
1-PropZInt	x, n, Confidence Level	1-PropZinterval, $\hat{p}$, n
2-PropZInt	$x1$, $n1$, $x2$, $n2$, Confidence Level	2-PropZinterval, $\hat{p}1$, $\hat{p}2$, $n1$ and $n2$

Review Exercises

MULTIPLE-CHOICE QUESTIONS

1. In a hypothesis test, the decision between a one-sided and a two-sided alternative hypothesis is based on:
   (A) which one gives you a significant result.
   (B) the alternative hypothesis appropriate for the context of the problem.
   (C) how accurate you wish the results of the test.
   (D) the level of significance of the test.
   (E) the statement of the null hypothesis.

2. The choice of hypothesis test
   (A) should be made after all possible tests are performed using technology.
   (B) is critical only in the case of medical experiments.
   (C) depends only on the parameter of interest.
   (D) depends on the parameter of interest and the sampling situation and the type of variable involved.
   (E) is left to the tester whenever n is greater than or equal to 30.

3. The choice between a z-test and a t-test for a population mean depends primarily on:
   (A) the sample size.
   (B) the level of significance.
   (C) whether a one- or two-tailed test is indicated.
   (D) whether the given standard deviation is from the population or the sample.
   (E) A z-test should never be used.

4. The P-value of a test of significance is the probability that:
   (A) the decision resulting from the test is correct.
   (B) 95% of the confidence intervals will contain the parameter of interest.
   (C) the null hypothesis is true.
   (D) the alternative hypothesis is true.
   (E) None of these describes the P-value.

5. If the P-value of a test of significance is greater than the level of significance, then which of the following conclusions are appropriate?
   I. The test is inconclusive.
   II. Accept the null hypothesis.
   III. The null hypothesis is true.
   (A) II only
   (B) III only
   (C) II and III
   (D) I only
   (E) None of these is appropriate.

6. If the P-value of a test is less than the level of significance, then which of the following is a correct conclusion?
   (A) The value of the test statistic is in the rejection region for this test.
   (B) The sample size should be increased to decrease the margin of error.
   (C) The null hypothesis is true.
   (D) The corresponding confidence interval will contain the hypothesized value of the parameter in the null hypothesis.
   (E) None of these is a valid conclusion.

7. Your company is contracted by a car dealership to do a statistical study. The dealership is interested in testing to see if its percentage of satisfied customers is higher than the industry standard of 67%. The dealership informs your staff that it only can afford a study that surveys a random sample of 100 of their customers. What is the approximate minimum positive difference the sample data must show for a one-tailed test to indicate that the dealership has a higher percentage of satisfied customers, significant at the 5% level?
   (A) 5.1%
   (B) 7.7%
   (C) 9.2%
   (D) 11.2%
   (E) Cannot be determined.

8. A two-sided hypothesis test for a population mean is significant at the 1% level of significance. Which of the following is necessarily true?
   (A) The 99% confidence interval of the mean contains 0.
   (B) The 99% confidence interval of the mean does not contain 0.
   (C) The 99% confidence interval of the mean contains the mean of the null hypothesis.
   (D) The 99% confidence interval of the mean does not contain the population mean.
   (E) The 99% confidence interval of the mean is significant.

FREE-RESPONSE QUESTIONS

Open-Ended Questions

The parameter of interest, choice of test, and null hypothesis all depend on only the population information. From the situations in questions 1–5, identify these components of a hypothesis test.

1. A light bulb company claims that, on average, their new halogen bulb lasts a minimum of 25 hours longer than their former incandescent light bulb.
   Parameter of interest:
   Choice of test:
   Null hypothesis (in words):

2. A bookbag company published a report that in a recent comparison test 55% of middle school children preferred their bookbag to their closest competitor's.
   Parameter of interest:
   Choice of test:
   Null hypothesis (in words):

3. A local newspaper published a report that on the last state math tests, the average performance for a random sample of urban districts was just as high as the average performance for a random sample of suburban districts.
   Parameter of interest:
   Choice of test:
   Null hypothesis (in words):

4. A large county school district proudly announced that data from a sample of 100 of their high school seniors showed that 70% of the boys and 70% of the girls were going on to post-secondary education after graduation.
   Parameter of interest:
   Choice of test:
   Null hypothesis (in words):

5. Reports were circulated that a random sample of average pre-test and post-test scores of third grade students indicated that there were significant gains in average reading level over the course of the third grade.
   Parameter of interest:
   Choice of test:
   Null hypothesis (in words):

In questions 6–10, complete the two requested components of a test of significance.

6. A marketing company claims that 75% of adults prefer a certain toothpaste over all other competitors. A simple random sample of 50 adults indicated only 66% preferred that brand of toothpaste. Do these data indicate that the claim of the marketing company is too high at the 5% level?

Probability Statement	P-value = probability (	
Test Statistics	Formula:	Value:

7. An association of college bookstores reported that the average amount of money spent by students on textbooks for the Fall 1999 semester was $325.16 with a standard deviation of $76.42. A random sample of 75 students at the local campus of the state university indicated an average bill for textbooks for the semester in question to be $312.34. Do these data provide significant evidence ($\alpha = .05$) that the actual average bill is different from the $325.16 that was reported?

Probability Statement	P-value = probability (	
Test Statistics	Formula:	Value:

8. Two manufacturing processes are to be compared on the basis of the proportion of defectives. For process A, a random sample of 100 products indicated that 2.9% were defective. For process B, a random sample of 75 products indicated that 2.5% were defective. Do these data support the claim that process B produces fewer defectives at the 5% significance level?

Probability Statement	P-value = probability (	
Test Statistics	Formula:	Value:

9. A college statistics professor wants to compare the performances of her two large Introduction to Statistics lecture classes. She gave all students taking the course the same final exam worth 100 points. A random sample of 35 students from class A yielded a mean final exam grade of 79 with a standard deviation of 12.7. A random sample of 45 students from class B yielded a mean final exam grade of 81 with a standard deviation of 11.4. Do these results from the tests indicate that there is any difference in the performances at the 10% level?

Probability Statement	P-value = probability (	
Test Statistics	Formula:	Value:

10. The probability that any specific number occurs when rolling a fair die is $\frac{1}{6}$. An experiment consisting of rolling a die 100 times yields 20 sixes. Does this result support the claim that the die is biased, at the 3% level?

Probability Statement	P-value = probability (	
Test Statistics Formula:		Value:

In questions 11–12, complete the tests of significance. In each case, complete the list of components we have given as required for full credit:

- statement of parameter of interest,
- statement of null and alternative hypotheses,
- statement and verification of assumptions,
- choice of test and construction and evaluation of a test statistic,
- decisions based on the value of the test statistic, and
- interpretation of test results in the context of the situation.

Use the template provided in the examples as a guide.

11. A candidate for mayor claims that under the present administration, 45% of complaints about city government are not addressed within two weeks of submission. A watchdog citizens' group conducted a simple random sample of 50 complaints submitted to the city government in the last year and determined that only 40% of the complaints were not addressed within two weeks of submission. Do these data provide sufficient evidence to reject the candidate's claim at the 5% significance level?

12. Experience has shown that male applicants to a small liberal arts college score on average 3.5 points better on the science placement exam than do female applicants. A random sample of the applicants for admission in 1998 resulted in the following data:

Gender	Sample Size	Mean	Standard Deviation
Males	25	71.5	10.3
Females	35	71.2	11.4

Do these data indicate that there is a significant difference in this class of applicants? ($\alpha = .05$)

13. Determine the minimum sample size so that for a presidential preference poll, a difference of 3% from an expected percentage of 50% is considered significant at the 5% level.

14. Public records state that the mean height of eighth graders in a particular state is 62 inches with a standard deviation of 4.2 inches. Data from a simple random sample of 40 eighth graders indicated that the mean height for this group was 65 inches. Do these data differ significantly from the published height at the 5% level of significance? Complete the solution of this problem using (a) the confidence interval technique and (b) the two-sided test of significance.

15. A two-sided t-test of the null hypothesis $\mu = 50$, indicated a non-significant result at the 5% level of significance based on the data from a simple random sample of 50 subjects with a mean of 47 and a standard deviation of 12. Assuming that all other information remains the same, what would be the largest sample mean less than μ that would produce a significant result?

7.6 Type I and Type II Errors and the Concept of Power

Type I and Type II Errors

We are concerned with only two types of possible errors in tests of significance. Let H_0 be the null hypothesis and H_a be the alternative hypothesis. Then,

> **Type I error** occurs when we *reject H_0 when H_0 is true;* and
> **Type II error** occurs when we *fail to reject H_0 when H_a is true.*

In the context of decision making we look for evidence supporting either H_0 or H_a. Consequently,

> **Type I error** occurs when we *reject H_0 when H_0 is true;* and
> **Type II error** occurs when we *fail to reject H_0 when H_0 is false.*

Note: Neither of these errors occurs when we fail to reject the true hypothesis.

In the case of significance testing, we do not make a decision about the truth of the two hypotheses. Rather, we merely make a conclusion as to whether we have sufficient evidence to reject H_0 or insufficient evidence to reject H_0. Consequently, testing for significance focuses solely on H_0.

In the case of testing for a decision, there are three possible outcomes:

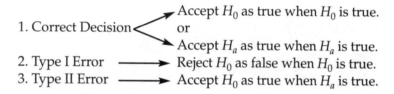

1. Correct Decision — Accept H_0 as true when H_0 is true.
   or
   Accept H_a as true when H_a is true.
2. Type I Error ⟶ Reject H_0 as false when H_0 is true.
3. Type II Error ⟶ Accept H_0 as true when H_a is true.

How well a significance test performs can be estimated by calculating the probabilities of committing Type I or Type II errors.

Type I Error

We have already seen the probability of a Type I error but have not identified it in this context. In the case of a test of significance, the decision whether to reject the null hypothesis or fail to reject the null hypothesis is based on a comparison to α, the significance level. If we consider the rejection region approach to significance testing, we reject H_0 if our test statistic is in the rejection region that is determined by α. Some values of the sampling distribution defined by H_0 will fall in the rejection region by chance. Consequently, we could reject H_0 even though it is true.

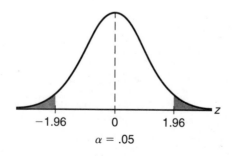

$$-1.96 \qquad 0 \qquad 1.96$$
$$\alpha = .05$$

The area of the rejection region *is* the probability of rejecting H_0 when H_0 is true. Therefore,

P(Type I error) $= \alpha$

This probability can also be written as a conditional probability:

P(Type I error) $= P$(reject H_0 when H_0 is true) $= \alpha$

Type II Error

The identification and calculation of the probability of a Type II error is more complicated. A Type II error occurs when H_0 is false but we fail to reject it. The probability of a Type II error depends on the values of the parameters in H_0 and H_a *and* the value of α.

Consider the case of a z-test for a population mean. Let μ_0 be the mean at which the sampling distribution for H_0 is centered and μ_a be an alternate mean at which the sampling distribution for H_a is centered. Graphically, the value of the probability of a Type II error is *the area under the curve of the sampling distribution for H_a that is also in the fail-to-reject region of the sampling distribution for H_0.*

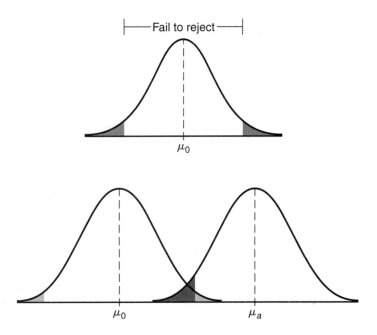

In the second figure above, the dark shaded region is the area for the probability of a Type II error since it encompasses the area under the density curve for the sampling distribution centered at μ_a that lies in the acceptance region for H_0, centered at μ_0. *Note:* Many books use the symbol β for the probability of a Type II error.

$\beta = P$(Type II error)

$= P$(Failing to reject H_0 when μ_a is true)

$= P$(sample mean being in the fail-to-reject region for sampling distribution centered at μ_0 but in the rejection region for μ_a)

Note: The AP Statistics curriculum does not include the *calculation of β*. It is presented here to clarify the *concept* of β.

For another way of looking at Type II error, consider the situation in which an $\bar{x}$ is in the "fail to reject" region for the test of $\mu = \mu_0$.

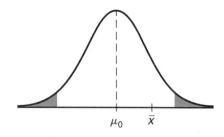

Therefore, we would not reject the hypothesis that the population mean equals μ_0. If this hypothesis is true, then we have made no error. If, on the other hand, an alternative hypothesis, $\mu = \mu_a$, is true, then we have this situation:

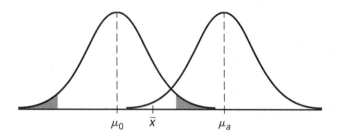

Because $\bar{x}$ is in the "fail to reject" region for $\mu = \mu_0$, we make a Type II error in not rejecting $\mu = \mu_0$ if $\mu = \mu_a$ is true.

EXAMPLE 1

Given $n = 35$; $\sigma = 8.4$; H_0: $\mu = 33$; H_a: $\mu > 33$; test statistic = 1.41. Therefore, at $\alpha = .05$, we fail to reject H_0, since the critical value is 1.645.
Calculate and interpret the value of β for an alternative mean of $\mu_a = 38$.

Solution

a. Calculate the border of the rejection region for H_0.
   We fail to reject H_0 if $z < z_\alpha$. Therefore,

$$z < 1.645$$

$$\frac{\bar{x} - \mu}{\sigma_{\bar{x}}} < 1.645$$

$$\frac{\bar{x} - 33}{\frac{8.4}{\sqrt{35}}} < 1.645$$

$$\bar{x} < 35.336$$

b. Calculate β, that is, calculate how often $\bar{x} < 33.336$ when μ_a is true.

$$\beta = P(\bar{x} < 35.336 \text{ if } \mu = 38, \sigma = 8.4, n = 35)$$

$$= P\left(z < \frac{35.336 - 38}{\frac{8.4}{\sqrt{35}}}\right)$$

$$= 0.031$$

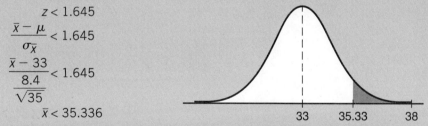

The process indicated above can be shortened somewhat using these formulas:
Calculation of β:

1. One-tailed test:
$$\beta = P\left(z < z_\alpha - \frac{|\mu_0 - \mu_a|}{\sigma_{\overline{x}}}\right)$$

2. Two-tailed test:
$$\beta \approx P\left(z < z_{\alpha/2} - \frac{|\mu_0 - \mu_a|}{\sigma_{\overline{x}}}\right)$$

EXAMPLE 2

Consider Example 1. Using the formula, we have
$$z_\alpha = 1.645; \; \mu_0 = 33; \; \mu_a = 38; \; \sigma_{\overline{x}} = \frac{8.4}{\sqrt{35}} = 1.49$$
$$\beta = P\left(z < 1.645 - \frac{|33 - 38|}{1.49}\right)$$
$$= 0.030$$

Important Properties of Type I and Type II Errors

1. The probabilities of Type I and Type II errors are inversely related. That is, for fixed μ_0 and μ_a, if the probability of Type I error decreases, i.e., the boundary of the rejection region moves farther from the mean, then the probability of a Type II error increases. Graphically,

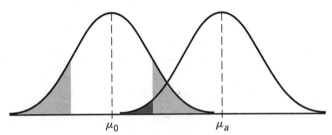

Light shading: Type I error
Dark shading: Type II error

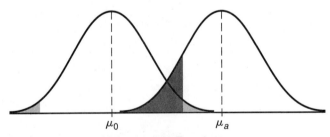

Light shading: Type I error
Dark shading: Type II error

2. The probabilities of Type I and Type II error can *both* be reduced by increasing the sample size, thereby reducing the standard errors of the distributions.

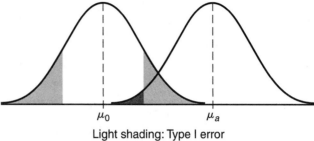

Light shading: Type I error
Dark shading: Type II error

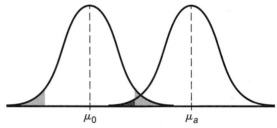

Light shading: Type I error
Dark shading: Type II error

3. The amount of Type II error changes depending on the value of the μ_a from H_a. In the graphic below, let $\mu_1 < \mu_2 < \mu_3$. Using the same μ_0 and α, the area that represents the probability of a Type II error decreases as we consider alternative means farther away from μ_0.

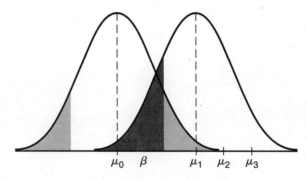

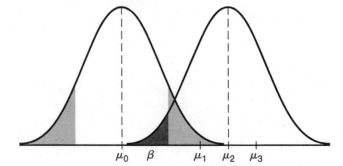

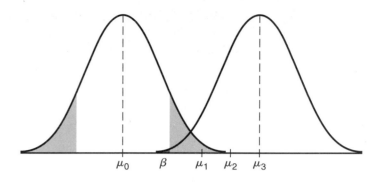

Because of this fact, the probability of a Type II error provides a measure of the sensitivity of a test relative to an alternative value of the mean in H_a.

The probability of a Type II error can indicate whether we should *reject* or *fail to reject* a null hypothesis. For example, if a test indicates that the test statistic is *not* in the rejection region at $\alpha = .05$ and the value of β has been calculated as .11 for an alternative mean, then we can say that we *fail to reject* H_0 being fully aware that there is an 11% chance of an incorrect decision.

The Concept of Power   The **power** of a statistical test is the probability that a test using a fixed value of α will reject H_0 when a particular alternative value of the parameter is true. In symbols,

>   **Power = P(rejecting H_0 when μ_a is true)**

Note: If we consider the graph of the sampling distributions corresponding to parameter μ_0 and μ_a, we see that

>   **Power = $1 - \beta$**

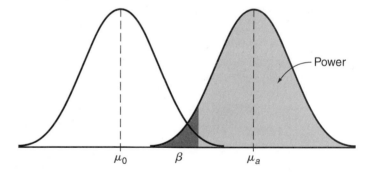

The probability of a Type II error and, therefore, the power of a test can indicate whether we should *accept* or *fail to reject* a null hypothesis. For example, if a significance test indicates that the test statistic is *not* in the rejection region at the $\alpha = .05$ and the value of β has been calculated as .08 (and therefore, a power of .92) for an alternative mean, then we can say that we *accept* H_0 being fully aware that there is only an 8% chance of an incorrect decision. In other words, if the power is .92, we can say that if the samples are coming from the distribution specified by H_a, then 92% of the samples will be in the rejection region of the distribution specified by H_0.

The issue of power of a test should be considered in the early stages of a statistical investigation that will involve a test of significance. The investigator should anticipate the values of the parameter that could be used as alternatives and the power for those alternatives should be checked to determine if the test is sufficiently sensitive relative to these alternative values of the parameter.

The investigator can also use the values of α and β to determine the sample size which will generate a test of sufficient power. The formula is

For a one-tailed test:

$$n = \sigma^2 \frac{(z_\alpha + z_\beta)^2}{\Delta^2}$$

For a two-tailed test:

$$n = \sigma^2 \frac{(z_{\alpha/2} + z_\beta)^2}{\Delta^2}$$

where

σ is the population standard deviation (or an estimate if σ is unknown),
z_α = the z-critical value for α
z_β = the z-critical value for β, and
Δ = the difference between μ_a and μ_0.

EXAMPLE 3

The manager of a hamburger patty company is concerned that a machine designed to make quarter pound (4-ounce) patties may be making patties that are heavier than a quarter pound. She decides to conduct a study and will randomly select a certain number of patties to weigh. From previous studies, she knows that the standard deviation of the weight per patty is approximately .151 ounce. For the test, H_0: $\mu = 4$ and H_a: $\mu > 4$ with $\alpha = .05$. She would like to find the sample size for which the power of the test would equal .99 for alternatives of 4.1 ounces or more.

Solution

From the data presented:
Power = .99 so $\beta = .01$; $\sigma \approx .151$; $z_{.05} = 1.645$; $z_{.01} = 2.33$; $\Delta = 4 - 4.1 = -.1$
therefore,

$$n = (.151)^2 \frac{(1.645 + 2.33)^2}{(-.1)^2}$$

$$= 36.027$$
$$\approx 36$$

If the manager takes a simple random sample of 36 or more patties *and* the one-sided hypothesis test fails to reject H_0: $\mu = 4$ at $\alpha = .05$, she should feel safe in the conclusion to *accept* that the true mean is 4 ounces.

Since the power is .99, she concludes that 99% of samples taken from an alternate sampling distribution for a specific H_a will be in the rejection region for H_0 if H_0 is false. If the test statistic falls in the fail-to-reject region, she will have sufficient evidence to believe that the true value of the mean is 4 ounces and that H_0 should be accepted.

Review Exercises

MULTIPLE-CHOICE QUESTIONS

1. Given $\alpha = .05$, which of the following is true?
(A) $\beta = .95$
(B) The power of the test is .95.
(C) $\alpha = P(\text{rejecting } H_0 \text{ when } H_0 \text{ is true})$
(D) $\alpha = P(\text{accepting } H_0 \text{ when } H_0 \text{ is false})$
(E) The value of β is independent of the value of α.

2. Which of the following is *not* true?
(A) A way to reduce both Type I and Type II errors is to increase sample size.
(B) If sample size remains constant, then reducing α will increase the value of β.
(C) α depends on the null hypothesis; β depends on both the null hypothesis and the value of an alternative hypothesis.
(D) For the hypothesis test of a parameter, α must equal β.
(E) All of these are correct.

3. In the picture below, the value of β is the area of which region?

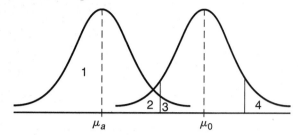

(A) 1
(B) 2
(C) 3
(D) 4
(E) β is not an area shown in this sketch.

4. Which of the following is *not* a valid conclusion of the statement:

"The power of a hypothesis test for H_0: $\mu_0 = 10$ and $\mu_a = 12$ is .91"

(A) $\beta = .09$
(B) The probability of accepting H_0 when the true value is μ_a is .09.
(C) 91% of the time this test will determine a false result with $\alpha = .05$.
(D) 91% of the time this test will be sensitive to any alternative mean as different from μ_0 as μ_a is.
(E) All of these are valid.

FREE-RESPONSE QUESTIONS

Open-Ended Questions

1. An investigator indicates that the power of his test of a sample mean resulting from his research is .87. Interpret this statement in your own words.

2. Draw a relatively accurate sketch of a situation dealing with a μ_0 and a μ_a with $\alpha = .05$ and $\beta = .10$
   a. if $\mu_0 < \mu_a$
   b. if $\mu_0 > \mu_a$

3. Complete each statement:
   a. If the value of α increases and n is fixed, then the value of β _____.
   b. If n increases, then the power of the test _____.
   c. If n increases, then the values of α and β _____.

7.7 Inference for the Slope of a Regression Line

As was discussed in Chapter 3, the least squares regression line is the line that best fits the data using the criteria that the sum of the squares of the residuals is minimized. Recall that we described the line as the best estimate of the "line of averages," that is, the line that fits the mean of the y-coordinates for each x-coordinate.

Consider a bivariate set of explanatory (x) and response (y) variable data. The resulting linear model, $\hat{y} = b_0 + b_1 x$, consists of the values of the explanatory and response variables and the statistics b_0 and b_1. The true regression line, denoted by $\mu_y = \beta_0 + \beta_1 x$, with parameters β_0 and β_1, returns the mean y for each value of x. Since the regression line, $\hat{y} = b_0 + b_1 x$, is an estimate from a sample of bivariate values, it can be shown that b_0 is an unbiased estimator of β_0 and that b_1 is an unbiased estimator of β_1. In addition, the standard error about the regression line is given by

$$s = \sqrt{\frac{1}{n-2}\sum residuals^2} = \sqrt{\frac{1}{n-2}\sum_{i=1}^{n}(\hat{y}_i - y_i)^2}.$$

This standard error provides an estimate of the standard deviation of the response (y) variable at a specific value of the explanatory (x) variable. Note that s^2 can be considered an "adjusted" average of the squares of the residuals or the "pooled" standard deviation of the residuals. This standard deviation is the same for each distribution of the values of the response variable at each value of the explanatory variable.

The assumptions for inference for regression can be summarized as follows:

1. For each value of the x-coordinate, the distribution of y-coordinates is a normal distribution.
2. The standard deviations of all of the distributions of the y-coordinates at a particular value of the x-coordinate are the same. (constant variance of the response)
3. The mean response variable, μ_y, has a linear relationship with the explanatory variable, x.

A typical way to check the second and third assumptions is to view the residual plot. In Chapter 3, we used residual plots as an indication of the goodness of fit and stated that a good model would have a residual plot whose points were randomly distributed equally above and below the horizontal axis and could be contained in a rectangle centered at 0, the mean of the residuals. If, on the other hand, the plot appeared triangular, becoming wider as the value of the explanatory variable increased, we could conclude that the variances of the distributions of y-coordinates are not equal and that perhaps a transformation of the data would be appropriate.

EXAMPLE 1

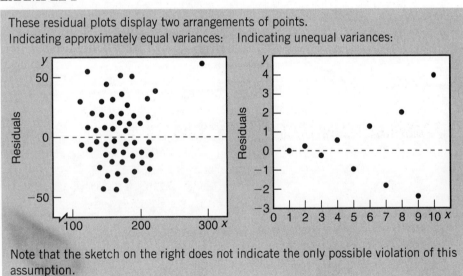

These residual plots display two arrangements of points.
Indicating approximately equal variances: Indicating unequal variances:

Note that the sketch on the right does not indicate the only possible violation of this assumption.

Confidence Intervals for the Slope of the Regression Line, β_1

As we have seen before, confidence intervals, including those for the slope of the regression line, are generally constructed as follows:

point estimate $\pm$ (critical distribution value)(standard error of the slope).

Therefore, the level C confidence interval for a slope β is given by $b \pm t_{(1-C)/2}S_{b_1}$ where

$$S_{b_1} = \frac{s}{\sqrt{\sum(x_i - \bar{x})^2}} = \frac{\sqrt{\dfrac{1}{n-2}\sum(\hat{y}_i - y_i)^2}}{\sqrt{\sum(x_i - \bar{x})^2}}$$

and $t_{(1-C)/2}$ is the critical value of the t-distribution with $df = n - 2$ and $\alpha = 1 - C$.

Technology Note: Most statistical software packages provide both s and S_{b_1}. The TI-83 only displays the value of s. ■

EXAMPLE 2

Information concerning weights (lbs) and neck sizes (inches) is collected from 143 randomly selected subjects. A simple linear regression performed on the data using a statistical software package produced the following printout:

```
The regression equation is
Weight = -173 + 9.26 Neck

Predictor          Coef        StDev         T           P
Constant         -173.20       21.86       -7.92       0.000
Neck               9.2618       0.5767      16.06       0.000

S = 16.98      R-Sq = 64.7%      R-Sq(adj) = 64.4%
```

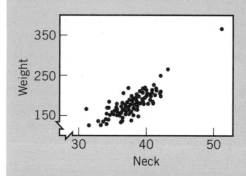

From the printout we see that the standard error about the line is $s = 16.98$ and that the value of S_{b_1} is .5767 since it is the standard error of the slope of this line. Therefore, the 95% confidence interval for the slope is calculated as follows:

$b \pm t_{(1-C)/2}S_{b_1}$ with $df = n - 2 = 143 - 2 = 141$

$9.2618 \pm 1.977(.5767)$ with $df = 141$

9.2618 ± 1.140 with $df = 141$

$\{8.1218, 10.4018\}$

Therefore, since 95% of the confidence intervals for bivariate data drawn from samples of size 143 would contain the slope of the actual regression line of the entire population, we have 95% confidence that our interval is one of those that contains the true slope. Therefore, we are 95% confident that for every inch of increase in neck size, the average increase in weight would be between 8.1 and 10.4 lbs.

Technology Note: Most t-distribution tables will not be detailed enough to provide a t-value such as the one needed to find the above confidence interval with a high degree of precision. The best practice, if using a table, is to approximate the value using an interpolation style of approximation. With the TI-83, one of the ways that you can find a more precise value of t is to use the Equation Solver (Item *0: Solver...* in the *MATH* menu). For the above problem, you would solve

eqn: $0 = tcdf(X, 1E99, 141) - .025$

The solution of this equation will be the t-value that produces an upper tail area of .025 with degrees of freedom equal to 141. ■

EXAMPLE 3

The table below displays the performance of 10 randomly selected students from your school on the SAT Verbal and SAT Math tests taken last September.

Student	1	2	3	4	5	6	7	8	9	10
Math	475	512	492	465	523	560	610	477	501	420
Verbal	500	540	512	530	533	603	691	512	489	458

The linear regression line for these data is *Verbal* = −46.42 + 1.16 *Math* with r^2 = .857. In order to calculate any confidence interval of the slope by hand, it may be helpful to construct a chart such as this:

Math x	Verbal y	$(x - \bar{x})^2$ ($\bar{x} = 503.5$)	$\hat{y}$	$(\hat{y} - y)^2$
475	500	812.25	504.58	20.976
512	540	72.25	547.5	56.25
492	512	132.25	524.3	151.29
465	530	1482.25	492.98	1370.4804
523	533	380.25	560.26	743.1076
560	603	3192.25	603.18	.0324
610	691	11342.25	661.18	889.2324
477	512	702.25	506.9	26.01
501	489	6.25	534.74	2092.1476
420	458	6972.25	440.78	296.5284
	Totals	25094.50	N/A	5646.0552

Therefore,

$$S_{b_1} = \frac{\sqrt{\frac{1}{n-2}\sum(\hat{y} - y)^2}}{\sqrt{\sum(x - \bar{x})^2}} = \frac{\sqrt{\frac{1}{10-2}(5646.0552)}}{\sqrt{25094.50}} = .168$$

We can now complete the calculation of any confidence interval. For example, the 90% confidence interval is calculated:

$b \pm t_{\alpha/2} \, S_{b_1}$ with $df = n - 2 = 10 - 2 = 8$
$1.16 \pm 1.397(.168)$ with $df = 8$
$1.16 \pm .235$ with $df = 8$
$(.925, 1.395)$

Therefore, since 90% of the confidence intervals constructed around the slope of the model which predicts SAT Verbal from SAT Math scores would contain the slope of the actual regression line for this situation, we can say that we are 90% confident that for every 1-point increase in Math SAT score, the average increase in Verbal SAT score is between .9 and 1.4.

Since we have calculated the standard error of the slope of the regression line, we can perform a test of significance for this slope. Many texts suggest that you can only test for a non-zero slope ($\beta_1 \neq 0$) and therefore, for a significant linear relationship between the variables. The formula in the table below allows you to test any hypothesis, H_0: $\beta = \beta_1$.

_t_-TEST

Assumptions	Null Hypothesis	Test Statistic
• Linear regression in the form of $y = b_0 + b_1 x$.	H_0: $\beta = \beta_1$	$t = \dfrac{b - \beta_1}{S_{b_1}}$
• Variables are linearly related.		where $S_{b_1} = \dfrac{\sqrt{\dfrac{1}{n-2}\sum(\hat{y} - y)^2}}{\sqrt{\sum(x - \bar{x})^2}}$
• Distributions of the values of the response variable at a particular value of the explanatory variable have the same variance.		$df = n - 2$
• Normality of response variables at each value of x.		

Since the correlation coefficient and the slope of the regression line are so strongly related (recall $b_1 = r\dfrac{s_y}{s_x}$ from Chapter 3), the outcome of a test of H_0: $\beta_1 = 0$ can be interpreted as a test of the significance of the correlation coefficient of the variables. If we establish that $\beta_1 = 0$, we can conclude that $r = 0$ and that there is no linear relationship between the variables.

EXAMPLE 4

A study is conducted at a small company to determine if there is a linear relationship between the number of miles that each employee drives to work and the model year of the car that employee drives. The data found are given in the table:

	1	2	3	4	5	6	7	8	9	10	11
Miles	20	37	5	10	17	53	2	26	42	57	31
Car Year	96	98	94	95	91	98	91	95	97	92	90

Regression analysis yields:
car year = 92.81 + .053 miles; $r = .3429$

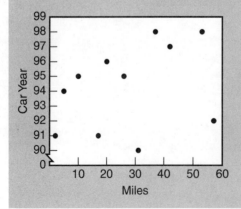

1. Parameter of Interest	β_1: slope of the regression line
2. Choice of Test	t-test for slope

3. Check of Assumptions	**Statement of Assumptions:** • linear relationship between variables • equal variances in y distributions	**Verification of Assumptions:** • yes • residual plot verifies by not exhibiting any curvature of nonconstant variance.

4. Null Hypothesis	H_0: **(words)** the true slope of the regression line is 0: there is no linear relationship between the miles driven to work and the year of the employee's car. H_0: **(symbols)** $\beta_1 = 0$

5. Alternative Hypothesis	H_a: **(words)** the true slope is not 0: there is a linear relationship between the miles driven to work and the year of the employee's car. H_a: **(symbols)** $\beta_1 \neq 0$

6. Probability Statement	P-value = **probability** (data collected from 11 employees regarding miles driven to work and model year of car would show a significant linear relationship between the two assuming there is no relationship)

7. Test Statistic	**Formula:** $$t = \frac{b - \beta_1}{S_{b_1}} = \frac{0.053 - 0}{2.8729}$$ $df = n - 2$	**Value:** $t = 1.095$, $df = 9$

8. Test: Level of Significance $\alpha = .05$	**Sketch of Sampling Distribution assuming that H_0 is true:** $-2.262 \quad\quad 0 \quad\quad 2.262$ **Identify the location of the test statistic in the sketch and shade the region that represents the P-value.**

9. P-value	**Reconciliation of Critical Value with Rejection Region:** $t = 1.095 < t_{\alpha/2} = t_{.025} = 2.262$	**Exact P-value:** P-value $= 0.3092$

10. Recommended Decisions	**Regarding H_0:** fail to reject	**Regarding significance:** not significant.

11. Interpretation (in the context of the problem)	We do not have sufficient evidence to reject the null hypothesis. Consequently, there appears to be some evidence that there is no relationship between miles driven to work and model year of car.

We can also conclude that we do not have sufficient evidence to reject the hypothesis that the correlation coefficient for the entire population equals 0; that is, it appears that there is no linear association between miles driven to work and year of car for the employees of this company.

Test for the Slope of a Regression Line, β_1, and Technology

The TI-83 also contains the command for a test of the slope of a regression line when H_0 states that the true slope is 0. The details are shown in the table:

	Input	Output
LinRegTTest	Xlist, Ylist, Freq, Alt. Hyp. *Note:* All choices for Alt. Hyp. relate β to 0	Alt. Hyp., t, p, degrees of freedom, a, b, s, r^2, r

Review Exercises

MULTIPLE-CHOICE QUESTIONS

In questions 1–4, use the following printout of the linear regression relating the SAT Math scores of 200 randomly chosen college freshmen and their first semester GPA's .

```
The regression equation is
GPA = 1.53 + 0.00170 Math

Predictor      Coef       StDev       T        P
Constant     1.5264      0.3981     3.83    0.000
Math       0.0016990   0.0006098   2.79    0.006

S = 0.5707    R-Sq = 3.8%    R-Sq(adj) = 3.3%
```

1. The value of S_{b_1} for this regression is:
   (A) .0006098
   (B) .0016990
   (C) .006
   (D) .3981
   (E) 1.5264

2. The test statistic for a test of significance for a non-zero slope is:
   (A) .0006098
   (B) .3891
   C) 2.79
   (D) 3.83
   (E) None of these.

3. Which of the following is a valid conclusion that could be drawn from this regression analysis?
   (A) There is sufficient evidence to reject the hypothesis that $\beta_1 = 0$.
   (B) There is not sufficient evidence to reject the hypothesis that $\beta_1 \neq 0$.
   (C) This test is not significant at the 1% level.
   (D) Significance cannot be determined from this printout.
   (E) None of these is a valid conclusion.

4. Which of the following is the 95% confidence interval for the population slope?
   (A) (.0005, .0029)
   (B) (.0129, .0211)
   (C) (−.0170, .0340)
   (D) (.0008, .0026)
   (E) None of these.

5. If the 90% confidence interval for the slope of a regression line does not contain 0, then which of the following is a valid conclusion?
   (A) The confidence interval is not valid.
   (B) A significance test will not be significant at the 10% level.
   (C) There is sufficient evidence to conclude that the slope of the true regression line is 0.
   (D) There is sufficient evidence to conclude that the slope of the true regression line is not 0.
   (E) None of these is valid.

FREE-RESPONSE QUESTIONS

Open-Ended Questions

1. A new process designed to increase the temperature inside steel girders shows great promise. In a test of 90 randomly selected girders, the following regression was performed; a partial computer printout is displayed:

```
Predictor      Coef      StDev      T       P
Constant     0.2074    0.2318    0.89    0.373
Temp 1       1.05651   0.02221    ?       ?

S = 0.6009    R-Sq = 96.3%    R-Sq(adj) = 96.2%
```

Temp 1 is the initial temperature and Temp 2 is the temperature after the process has terminated.
a. State the regression equation.
b. Interpret the slope of the regression in the context of the problem.
c. Interpret the value of R-Sq in words.
d. Find the values of T and P indicated by the question marks in the printout.

2. A midterm exam in Applied Mathematics consists of problems in 8 topical areas. One of the teachers believes that the most important of these, and the best indicator of overall performance, is the section on problem solving. She analyzes the scores of 36 randomly chosen students using computer software and produces the following printout relating the total score to the problem-solving subscore, ProbSolv:

```
Predictor     Coef      StDev       T        P
Constant     12.960     6.228     2.08     0.045
ProbSolv     4.0162     0.5393    7.45     0.000

S = 11.09   R-Sq = 62.0%   R-Sq(adj) = 60.9%
```

Answer the following questions. Show your work.
a. What is the regression equation?
b. Interpret the slope of the regression in the context of the problem.
c. Interpret the value of R-Sq in words.
d. Interpret the value of S in words.
e. Calculate the 95% confidence interval of the slope of the regression line for all Applied Mathematics students.

f. Use the information provided to test whether there is a significant relationship between the problem solving subsection and the total score at the 5% level. Complete the list of components we have given as required for full credit:
  • statement of parameter of interest,
  • statement of null and alternative hypotheses,
  • statement and verification of assumptions,
  • choice of test and construction and evaluation of a test statistic,
  • decisions based on the value of the test statistic, and
  • interpretation of test results in the context of the situation.
  Use the template provided in the examples as a guide.
g. Are the decisions reached through the construction of the confidence interval and through the use of a significance test consistent? Explain the reasons for your answer.

7.8 Inference for Categorical Data

All of the tests of means and proportions that we have discussed deal with a maximum of two quantitative variables. But other questions arise:

1. How do we test for differences in more than two proportions? e.g., proportions of M&M colors.
2. How do we establish the existence of a relationship between two categorical variables?
3. Suppose we make an assumption about the distribution of certain data, such as: the data values are equally likely to occur. Once we actually gather such data, how do we judge if the observed data are consistent with the expected patterns?

Chi-square analysis is used to address such questions.

$$\text{Chi-square statistic: } \chi^2 = \sum_{i=1}^{n} \frac{(\text{observed} - \text{expected})^2}{\text{expected}}$$

The χ^2 statistic is a sum of the weighted differences of observed and expected data values (counts) which takes into account the magnitude of the difference between each observed and expected value relative to the magnitude of the values. So, a difference of 10 is more significant if it comes from 85 and 95 than from 2085 and 2095. The χ^2 probability density function is a function whose domain is $\{x \mid x \geq 0\}$ and depends only on the degrees of freedom. Shown below are three graphs of χ^2 with degrees of freedom 1, 5, and 10. Note that the χ^2-distributions are not symmetric, but skewed to the right. As the degrees of freedom increase, the χ^2-distribution becomes more symmetric and approaches the normal distribution.

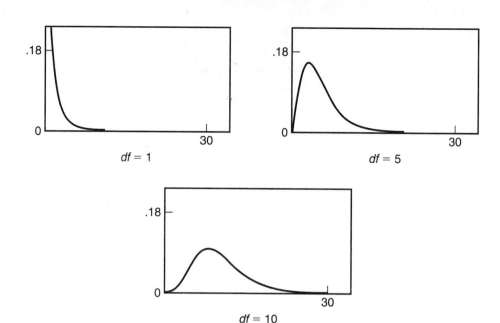

df = 1

df = 5

df = 10

The assumptions for a χ^2 sampling distribution focus on the count of the expected frequencies; there are two criteria currently in use: no expected counts < 5; or no expected counts < 1 and no more than 20% of the expected counts < 5.

χ^2 Test for Goodness of Fit

In the case of a single categorical variable, we are generally testing how well our observations "fit" some expected model. For example, if we roll a die, we expect $p_1 = p_2 = p_3 = p_4 = p_5 = p_6 = \frac{1}{6}$. Note that χ^2 tests are always one-tailed since we only care if the χ^2 value is "too" large. In this case, the degrees of freedom are the number of observations minus 1. To decide if the χ^2 statistic is significant, we compare it to the appropriate critical value for the χ^2-distribution with the df that we are using. For example, at a level of significance of $\alpha = .05$, the critical value for a χ^2 with $df = 10$ is $\chi^2_\alpha = \chi^2_{.05} = 18.31$, but the critical value for a χ^2 with $df = 30$ is 43.77. For a particular χ^2 distribution, the smaller the χ^2 statistic, the better the fit.

EXAMPLE 1

A die is rolled 60 times and the following results are documented:

Face	1	2	3	4	5	6
Frequency	14	15	10	8	7	6

Do these data cast doubt on the fairness of the die at the 5% level?

Solution

If the die is fair, we expect that each outcome will occur approximately one-sixth of the time. We use a table to organize the calculations:

Categories	Observed counts	Expected counts	$\dfrac{(\text{observed} - \text{expected})^2}{\text{expected}}$
1	14	10	1.6
2	15	10	2.5
3	10	10	0
4	8	10	.4
5	7	10	.9
6	6	10	1.6
Total	60	60	7.0

Using the template:

1. Parameter of Interest	p_1, p_2, p_3, p_4, p_5, p_6 (the proportion for each face)
2. Choice of Test	χ^2
3. Check of Assumptions	**Statement of Assumptions:** no expected counts < 5 **Verification of Assumptions:** all expected counts are 10.
4. Null Hypothesis	H_0: **(words)** There is an equal chance of obtaining a 1, 2, 3, 4, 5, or 6 when rolling this die 60 times. H_0: **(symbols)** $p_1 = \dfrac{1}{6}$; $p_2 = \dfrac{1}{6}$; $p_3 = \dfrac{1}{6}$; $p_4 = \dfrac{1}{6}$; $p_5 = \dfrac{1}{6}$; $p_6 = \dfrac{1}{6}$
5. Alternative Hypothesis	H_a: **(words)** There is not an equal chance of obtaining a 1, 2, 3, 4, 5 or 6 when rolling this die 60 times. H_a: **(symbols)** At least one of the p_i differs from the others.
6. Probability Statement	**P-value = probability** (the outcome of 60 rolls of the die will produce these or more extreme values when the expected values for obtaining 1, 2, 3, 4, 5, or 6 are all 10)
7. Test Statistic	**Formula:** $$\chi^2 = \sum_{i=1}^{n} \frac{(\text{observed} - \text{expected})^2}{\text{expected}}$$ **Value:** $\chi^2 = 7.0$; $df = 6 - 1 = 5$
8. Test: Level of Significance $\alpha = .05$	**Sketch of Sampling Distribution assuming that H_0 is true:** 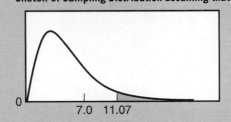 **Identify the location of the test statistic in the sketch and shade the region that represents the P-value**
9. P-value	**Reconciliation of Critical Value with Rejection Region:** $\chi^2 = 7.0 < \chi^2_{.05} = 11.07$ and therefore, our test statistic is not in the rejection region. **Exact P-value:** $P = .2206$ using technology. Using a table, $.20 < $ P-value $ < .25$; P-value $> \alpha$

10. Recommended Decisions	Regarding H_0: fail to reject	Regarding significance: not significant.
11. Interpretation (in the context of the problem)	The evidence is not sufficient to doubt the fairness of the die.	

χ^2 Test of Independence

Earlier (Section 4.7) we reviewed the use of segmented bar graphs to investigate relationships between categorical data summarized in a two-way table. With the aid of the χ^2 distribution, we can perform a significance test to confirm the existence of an association between such categorical variables. This test is called a **test of independence**; the name implies that we are testing to determine whether one variable is independent of the other. Note that even if the test casts doubt on the independence of two variables, we cannot conclude a causal relationship between them. The test utilizes the χ^2 distribution with degrees of freedom $= (r - 1)(c - 1)$ where r is the number of rows and c is the number of columns in the two-way table. The null hypothesis, H_0, is that the variables are independent; that is, there is no association between the two variables.

EXAMPLE 2

An AP Statistics student has compiled the following data from a random sample of seniors at her high school:

POLITICAL PHILOSOPHY vs. GENDER

	Liberal	Moderate	Conservative	Totals
Males	16	10	6	32
Females	20	22	16	58
Totals	36	32	22	90

Do these data provide evidence of an association between political philosophy and gender at the 5% level?

Solution

The first task is to create a table of expected frequencies. We will display a way of determining the expected frequency for three of the cells. The rest are left to the reader.

Liberal males: 32 of the 90 students are male. Therefore, the same proportion of the liberals should be male: $\frac{32}{90} \cdot 36 = 12.8$	Moderate males: 32 of the 90 students are male. Therefore, the same proportion of the moderates should be male: $\frac{32}{90} \cdot 32 = 11.4$	Conservative males: 32 of the 90 students are male. Therefore, the same proportion of conservatives should be male: $\frac{32}{90} \cdot 22 = 7.8$

The expected values for females can be determined similarly, using the proportion $\frac{58}{90}$. In general, the expected counts can be calculated using $\frac{\text{row total} \times \text{column total}}{\text{table total}}$.

Using these results, we can construct the following table of expected counts. (The total of the expected may not equal the total of the observed due to rounding.)

Categories	Observed	Expected	$\frac{(\text{observed} - \text{expected})^2}{\text{expected}}$
Liberal male	16	12.8	.800
Moderate male	10	11.4	.172
Conservative male	6	7.8	.415
Liberal female	20	23.2	.441
Moderate female	22	20.6	.095
Conservative female	16	14.2	.228
Total	90	90	2.151

Using the template:

1. Parameter of Interest	Not applicable.	
2. Choice of Test	χ^2	
3. Check of Assumptions	**Statement of Assumptions:** no cell counts < 5	**Verification of Assumptions:** all cell counts > 5.
4. Null Hypothesis	H_0: **(words)** There is no relationship between political philosophy and gender among the seniors at this high school, or, political philosophy and gender are independent in this population. H_0: **(symbols)**	
5. Alternative Hypothesis	H_a: **(words)** There is a relationship between political philosophy and gender among the seniors at this high school, or, political philosophy and gender are dependent in this population. H_a: **(symbols)**	
6. Probability Statement	*P*-value **= probability** (the differences between the observed and expected outcomes for this survey resulted from chance error)	
7. Test Statistic	**Formula:** $$\chi^2 = \sum_{i=1}^{n} \frac{(\text{observed} - \text{expected})^2}{\text{expected}}$$	**Value:** $\chi^2 = 2.15$ $df = (2-1)(3-1) = 2$

<table>
<tr><td>8. Test: Level of Significance
$\alpha = .05$</td><td colspan="2">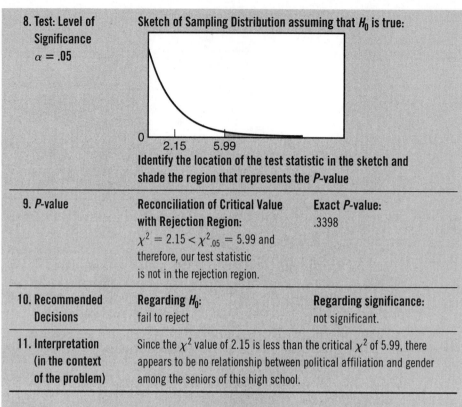
Sketch of Sampling Distribution assuming that H_0 is true:

Identify the location of the test statistic in the sketch and shade the region that represents the P-value</td></tr>
<tr><td>9. P-value</td><td>**Reconciliation of Critical Value with Rejection Region:**
$\chi^2 = 2.15 < \chi^2_{.05} = 5.99$ and therefore, our test statistic is not in the rejection region.</td><td>**Exact P-value:**
.3398</td></tr>
<tr><td>10. Recommended Decisions</td><td>**Regarding H_0:**
fail to reject</td><td>**Regarding significance:**
not significant.</td></tr>
<tr><td>11. Interpretation (in the context of the problem)</td><td colspan="2">Since the χ^2 value of 2.15 is less than the critical χ^2 of 5.99, there appears to be no relationship between political affiliation and gender among the seniors of this high school.</td></tr>
</table>

Note that when the test statistic is such that we reject the null hypothesis, our conclusion would be that we have sufficient evidence to doubt independence between the variables. Therefore, we can conclude that there appears to be a relationship between the variables. In the example, a reasonable conclusion would be that we do not have sufficient evidence to claim that in this population, political affiliation depends on the gender of the respondents.

Summary of Inference Tests for Categorical Data

Test	Assumptions	Null Hypothesis	Test Statistic
One variable	a) no expected counts < 5 or b) no expected counts < 1 and no more than 20% of expected counts < 5	No difference between expected and observed counts	$\chi^2 = \sum \dfrac{(\text{observed} - \text{expected})^2}{\text{expected}}$ $df = $ number of observations $- 1$
Test of Independence of two variables	a) no cell counts < 5 or b) no cell counts < 1 and no more than 20% of cell counts < 5	No relationship between variables	$\chi^2 = \sum \dfrac{(\text{observed} - \text{expected})^2}{\text{expected}}$ $df = (r - 1)(c - 1)$ where $r = $ number of rows, $c = $ number of columns

Note that it is very important that the hypothesis and conclusions be in the *context of the problem.*

Technology Note: The TI-83 can also perform χ^2 tests:

Test	Input	Output
One variable	Enter observed frequencies in L_1, and expected frequencies in L_2.	Let $$L_3 = \frac{(L_1 - L_2)^2}{L_2}$$ The sum of L_3 is the value of χ^2
Two-Way Table	Enter observed frequencies in matrix A. Use the matrix menu for input and display.	**Calculate:** χ^2, p, degrees of freeedom **Draw:** density function with shading, χ^2, p Calculator will return the expected frequencies in matrix B.

Note that the choice of matrices A and B is the default. You can use any matrices in this test as long as you indicate the names of the matrix of observed values and the matrix of the expected values.

Review Exercises

MULTIPLE-CHOICE QUESTIONS

1. Which of the following is not true of the χ^2 probability density function?
   - (A) For small degrees of freedom, the curve displays right-skewness.
   - (B) As the degrees of freedom increase, the curve approaches a normal curve.
   - (C) χ^2 is defined only for positive values of the variable.
   - (D) The area under a χ^2 curve is 1.
   - (E) All of these are true about the χ^2 probability density function.

For questions 2 and 3, use the two-way table specifying favorite ice cream flavors by gender.

	Male	Female
Chocolate	32	16
Vanilla	14	4
Strawberry	3	10

2. What is the expected number of males who prefer chocolate?
   - (A) 27.8
   - (B) 29.2
   - (C) 31.3
   - (D) 36.3
   - (E) None of these.

3. A χ^2 test of significance yields a test statistic of $\chi^2 = 10.71$ and a P-value of .005 with $df = 2$. Which of the following is a valid conclusion from this information?
   - (A) We have sufficient evidence of an association between gender and ice cream flavor preference at the 5% level.
   - (B) There is insufficient evidence of a relationship between gender and ice cream flavor preference.
   - (C) Since we are dealing with the *two* genders, a two-sample *t*-test is more appropriate.
   - (D) No conclusion since a χ^2 test should not have been performed.
   - (E) The information given is not sufficient to draw a conclusion.

4. A genetic model for offspring of two Labrador retrievers states:

   black : yellow : chocolate $= 5:4:1$

   Two Labrador retrievers are bred and a litter consisting of 3 black dogs, 5 yellow dogs, and 2 chocolate dogs is produced. For a goodness of fit test, the χ^2 statistic would be:
   - (A) 1.79
   - (B) 2.05
   - (C) 2.92
   - (D) 4.94
   - (E) 7.08

FREE-RESPONSE QUESTIONS

Open-Ended Question

In each case, complete the list of components we have given as required for full credit:

- statement of parameter of interest,
- statement of null and alternative hypotheses,
- statement and verification of assumptions,
- choice of test and construction and evaluation of a test statistic,
- decisions based on the value of the test statistic, and
- interpretation of test results in the context of the situation.

Use the template provided in the examples as a guide.

1. Genetic research indicates that the following proportions in the color of flowers should occur when cross-pollinating two species of the same flowering shrub:

red : pink : white = 2 : 5 : 1

A random sample of 50 of the flowers contained the following frequencies of colors: red = 7; pink = 33; white = 10. Complete the table below to determine if these results are consistent with the research findings at the 5% level of significance.

Categories	Observed	Expected	$\dfrac{(\text{observed} - \text{expected})^2}{\text{expected}}$
Totals			

2. A television network wanted to study the existence of a relationship between viewer age and viewer preference among the major networks. A simple random sample of 100 adults was taken in which respondents chose their favorite TV network. The data from the sample are summarized in the table:

	ABC	NBC	CBS	PBS	FOX	Totals
35 and under	10	15	8	3	5	41
Between 35 and 55	10	7	7	5	8	37
55 and over	4	3	3	5	7	22
Totals	24	25	18	13	20	100

Do these data dispute the claim that network preference and age are independent at the 5% significance level? Complete the table. Then perform the test.

Categories	Observed	Expected	$\dfrac{(\text{observed} - \text{expected})^2}{\text{expected}}$
Totals			

Chapter 7 Assessment

MULTIPLE-CHOICE QUESTIONS

1. Given $H_0: \mu = 30$, $H_a: \mu < 30$, if you conclude that the mean is less than 30 when it is actually 27:
 (A) You have made a Type II error.
 (B) You have made a Type I error.
 (C) The result of your test was not significant.
 (D) You have drawn a correct conclusion.
 (E) All of the above are true.

2. The local news station reported that the 97% confidence interval for a candidate's support was (43%, 48%). What does the phrase 97% confidence mean?
 (A) 97% of the voters support this candidate.
 (B) 97% of the time, this candidate's level of support will be between 43% and 48%.
 (C) There is a 97% probability that the true level of support is between 43% and 48%.
 (D) There is a 97% probability that any other sample percentage is in the interval (43%, 48%).
 (E) None of these is true.

3. A study of 20 teachers in a school district indicated that the 95% confidence interval for the mean salary of all teachers is ($38,945, $41,245). What assumptions must be true for this confidence interval to be valid?
   (A) No assumptions are necessary. The Central Limit Theorem applies.
   (B) The sample is randomly selected from a population of salaries that is a t-distribution.
   (C) The distribution of the sample means is approximately normal.
   (D) The distribution of all teachers' salaries is approximately normal.
   (E) None of the above.

4. In order to reduce the width of a confidence interval, we can:
   (A) increase sample size only
   (B) increase confidence level only
   (C) increase sample size and increase confidence level
   (D) increase sample size and decrease confidence level
   (E) None of these would reduce the width of the interval.

5. If the 95% confidence interval for μ is (6, 9), what conclusion can we draw if we test H_0: $\mu = 10$ vs. H_a: $\mu \neq 10$ at $\alpha = .05$?
   (A) reject H_0
   (B) fail to reject H_0
   (C) accept H_0
   (D) accept H_a
   (E) There is insufficient information given to draw a conclusion.

6. A bakery determines that it will be profitable if the time the cake decorator takes to decorate each cake does not exceed 45 minutes. The owner documents the time spent on 20 randomly chosen cakes and performs a test of significance. If the P-value of the test is .032, then he should conclude:
   (A) At $\alpha = .05$, fail to reject H_0.
   (B) At $\alpha = .05$, reject H_0.
   (C) At $\alpha = .03$, reject H_0.
   (D) At $\alpha = .025$, reject H_0.
   (E) We cannot draw a conclusion from this information.

7. The rejection region for a test H_0: $p = .4$ vs. H_a: $p < .4$, with $n = 50$ and $\alpha = .05$ is given by
   (A) Reject H_0 if $z > 1.96$ or $z < -1.96$.
   (B) Reject H_0 if $z > 1.645$ or $z < -1.645$.
   (C) Reject H_0 if $z < -1.96$.
   (D) Reject H_0 if $z < -1.645$.
   (E) Reject H_0 if $t > 2.59$.

Use the following information for questions 8–10: Do boys perform better in math than girls? A randomly selected group of each gender were given the same math assessment. The score results were:

	Boys	Girls
n	110	13.5
Mean	71.6	68.3
Standard Deviation	10.4	11.2

8. What design seems to have been employed?
   (A) Matched pairs design
   (B) Simple random design
   (C) Multi-stage cluster design
   (D) Independent samples design
   (E) Randomized block design

9. What would be the null and alternative hypotheses of a test to determine if boys' scores were higher than girls' scores?
   (A) H_0: $\mu_b - \mu_g = 0$; H_a: $\mu_b - \mu_g < 0$
   (B) H_0: $\mu_b - \mu_g = 0$; H_a: $\mu_b - \mu_g \neq 0$
   (C) H_0: $\mu_b - \mu_g = 0$; H_a: $\mu_b - \mu_g > 0$
   (D) H_0: $\mu_b - \mu_g < 0$; H_a: $\mu_b - \mu_g = 0$
   (E) H_0: $\mu_b = \mu_g$; H_a: $\mu_b \neq \mu_g$

10. Suppose the P-value of the test is .0344. We can then conclude:
    (A) At $\alpha = .025$, reject H_0.
    (B) At $\alpha = .02$, reject H_0.
    (C) At $\alpha = .01$, reject H_0.
    (D) At $\alpha = .025$, fail to reject H_0.
    (E) A conclusion cannot be drawn from this information.

11. The power of a test is described by all of the following *except*:
    (A) Power = P(rejecting H_0 when H_a is true)
    (B) Power = $1 - \beta$
    (C) Power = $\alpha + \beta$
    (D) The calculation of power requires knowing the values of μ_0, μ_a, σ, and α.
    (E) All of these are correct descriptions of the concept of power.

12. In a matched pairs test of 75 pairs, which of the following assumptions is necessary?
    (A) The distribution of the paired differences should be approximately normal.
    (B) The population variances should be equal.
    (C) The samples are randomly and independently selected.
    (D) The sets of values for each variable are approximately normal.
    (E) None of these assumptions is necessary.

FREE-RESPONSE QUESTIONS

Open-Ended Questions

Perform an appropriate test of significance. Remember to complete the list of components we have given as required for full credit:

- statement of parameter of interest,
- statement of null and alternative hypotheses,
- statement and verification of assumptions,
- choice of test and construction and evaluation of a test statistic,
- decisions based on the value of the test statistic, and
- interpretation of test results in the context of the situation.

Use the template provided in the examples as a guide.

1. A pharmaceutical company claims that 50% of adult males living in a city in the Midwest get at least two colds per year. A random sample of 100 adult males living in the city of interest reported that only 42% of them experienced two or more colds. Do these data indicate (at the 5% significance level) that the true proportion of people who get more than 2 colds per year is less than 50%?

2. It is known that, for a particular school, math scores are normally distributed. A random sample of the scores of 10 students of each gender yielded the following values:

| Girls | 90 | 80 | 70 | 75 | 87 | 92 | 86 | 61 | 94 | 100 |
| Boys | 70 | 75 | 96 | 92 | 85 | 72 | 63 | 95 | 68 | 98 |

Do these data indicate a difference in the mean performance of all the boys and girls in this school at the 5% level of significance?

3. A simple random sample of 100 families living in rural areas in the state of Indiana indicated that 40% of the families watch a certain TV show regularly. A simple random sample of 50 families living in urban areas in Indiana indicated that 44% of these families watch the same TV show. Do these data support the claim that urban families prefer this show more than rural families at the 5% significance level?

4. Students studying Algebra were given a pretest at the beginning of the unit on linear equations and the same exam as a post-test at the end of the unit. A random sample of the performances of 10 students is listed:

| Pre-test | 75 | 82 | 45 | 91 | 65 | 75 | 85 | 82 | 78 | 64 |
| Post-test | 78 | 81 | 55 | 93 | 65 | 78 | 81 | 86 | 82 | 66 |

Do these data indicate at the 5% level that there was an improvement in the scores once the instruction on the unit was completed?

5. A manufacturer packs a prize in each box of its cereal and claims that the probabilities of getting various prizes are as follows:

| Prize | Ring | Key chain | Puzzle | Pen | Flashlight |
| Probability | .20 | .30 | .15 | .25 | .10 |

To see if the company's claim is accurate, a consumer group randomly selects 1,020 boxes of this product and obtains the following data:

| Prize | Ring | Key chain | Puzzle | Pen | Flashlight |
| Number | 186 | 327 | 168 | 225 | 114 |

Do these data support the company's claim at the 5% level?

Investigative Tasks

1. Your company is studying the effect on performance of an assembly line when two different processes, A and B, are employed in its operation. Assembly line performance is measured on the basis of number of complete units produced in a typical workday. The data from 10 randomly selected days of operation under both processes is:

Day	1	2	3	4	5	6	7	8	9	10
Process A	35	21	45	59	23	76	53	21	37	55
Process B	32	17	46	61	15	74	45	18	35	49

a. You believe that a matched-pairs test is appropriate. Complete the test and state your conclusion.

b. Your colleague believes that a two-sample t-test is appropriate. Complete this test and state a conclusion from it.

c. Since it is important that you and your colleague agree, describe how you would convince your colleague that your choice is the appropriate one. Realize that your colleague is only impressed by statistical evidence and argument.

2. There is a relationship between a confidence and a particular test of significance. Consider this situation:

The battery industry has a standard that AAA batteries should have a shelf life of 274.5 days with a standard deviation of 23.7 days. This standard was determined after a great deal of research conducted by an industry trade organization. A study of 50 randomly selected batteries from the Batteries R Us company showed that these batteries had a mean shelf life of 280.1 days.

a. Verify and explain the relationship between confidence intervals and test of significance for the question, "Do these data indicate that the company's batteries have a shelf life that is different from the industry?" Use a 95% confidence level.
   i. confidence interval
   ii. significance test
   iii. relationship between the interval and the test

b. Verify and explain the relationship between confidence intervals and test of significance for the question, "Do these data indicate that the company's batteries have a shelf life that is greater than the industry average?" Use a 95% confidence level.
   i. confidence interval
   ii. significance test
   iii. relationship between the interval and the test

Chapter 8   Interpreting Computer and Calculator Printouts

8.1   Introduction

8.2   Regression Analysis

8.3   Confidence Interval for a Mean

8.4   Hypothesis Test: One-Sample t-Test

8.5   Hypothesis Test: Two-Sample t-Test of Means

8.6   Contingency Tables: Test of Independence

Chapter 8 Interpreting Computer and Calculator Printouts

8.1 Introduction

One of the skills that is required of AP Statistics students is the ability to interpret computer printouts in statistical reports and analyses. The purpose of this chapter is to provide a resource to students and teachers by displaying the output of the following technological tools:

- **Computer software packages:** Data Desk, Minitab, Fathom, and SAS.
- **Calculators:** TI-83.

This chapter presents a variety of typical statistical problems or tasks and displays the outputs of the five technological tools listed above. Applications are included only when they are supported by most of the technological tools. Instructions for input and execution of the individual programs or commands are not discussed in this review, nor are complete inventories of the capabilities of these tools included. Students are encouraged to refer to the technology manuals for instructions and to learn about additional capabilities of each tool.

8.2 Regression Analysis

A service center for kitchen appliances has hired a large group of new technicians. During the first 20 weeks of their employment, data were collected documenting the number of appliances serviced by a random sample of these technicians.

Week	1	2	3	4	5	6	7	8	9	10	11	12	13	14	15	16	17	18	19	20
Number	12	21	18	13	28	20	29	35	26	20	36	40	28	52	32	32	55	56	49	60

Displayed below are the outputs each tool creates to show the scatterplot, regression and inference, and residual plot.

Data Desk

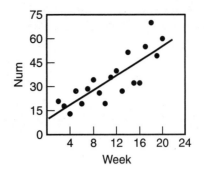

Dependent variable is: **Num**
No Selector
R squared = 71.2%   R squared (adjusted) = 69.6%
s = 8.869 with 20 – 2 = 18 degrees of freedom

Source	Sum of Squares	df	Mean Square	F-ratio
Regression	3497.18	1	3497.18	44.5
Residual	1416.02	18	78.6678	

Variable	Coefficient	s.e. of Coeff	t-ratio	prob
Constant	9.72105	4.12	2.36	0.0298
Week	2.29323	0.3439	6.67	≤ 0.0001

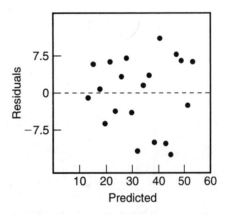

Minitab

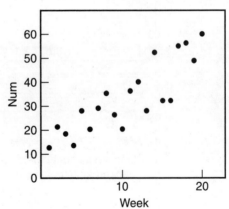

Regression Analysis

The regression equation is
Num = 10.7 + 2.14 Week

Predictor	Coef	StDev	T	P
Constant	10.679	3.554	3.00	0.008
Week	2.1353	0.2967	7.20	0.000

S = 7.651   R-Sq = 74.2%   R-Sq(adj) = 72.8%

Analysis of Variance

Source	DF	SS	MS	F	P
Regression	1	3032.2	3032.2	51.80	0.000
Error	18	1053.6	58.5		
Total	19	4085.8			

Residuals Versus the Fitted Values
(response is Num)

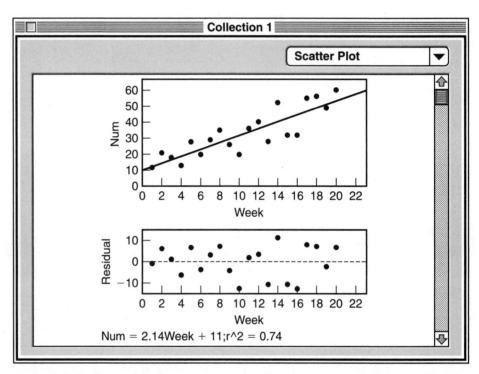

Fathom

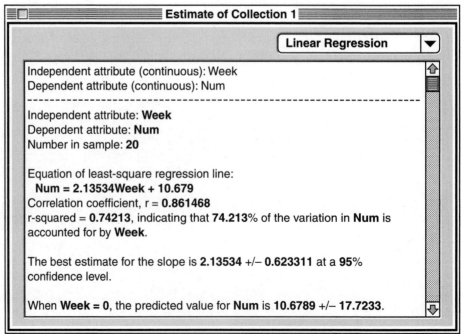

Num = 2.14Week + 11;r^2 = 0.74

Estimate of Collection 1

Linear Regression ▼

Independent attribute (continuous): Week
Dependent attribute (continuous): Num

Independent attribute: **Week**
Dependent attribute: **Num**
Number in sample: **20**

Equation of least-square regression line:
  Num = 2.13534Week + 10.679
Correlation coefficient, r = **0.861468**
r-squared = **0.74213**, indicating that **74.213**% of the variation in **Num** is accounted for by **Week**.

The best estimate for the slope is **2.13534** +/– **0.623311** at a **95**% confidence level.

When **Week = 0**, the predicted value for **Num** is **10.6789** +/– **17.7233**.

SAS

Scatterplot of *y* vs. *x* : *y* = NUM; *x* = Week
Plot of *Y**X. Symbol used is •.

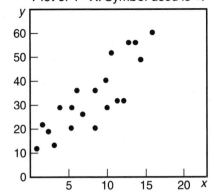

Regression Model

Model: MODEL1
Dependent Variable: Y

Analysis of Variance

Source	DF	Sum of Squares	Mean Square	F Value	Prob>F
Model	1	3032.18045	3032.18045	51.802	0.0001
Error	18	1053.61955	58.53442		
C Total	19	4085.80000			

Root MSE	7.65078	R-square	0.7421
Dep Mean	33.10000	Adj R-sq	0.7278
C.V.	23.11414		

Parameter Estimates

Variable	DF	Parameter Estimate	Standard Error	T for H0: Parameter=0	Prob > |T|
INTERCEP	1	10.678947	3.55402751	3.005	0.0076
X	1	2.135338	0.29668448	7.197	0.0001

Plot of Residuals vs. Predicted Values
Plot of RESID*PREDICT. Symbol used is •.

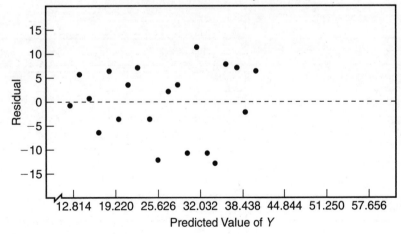

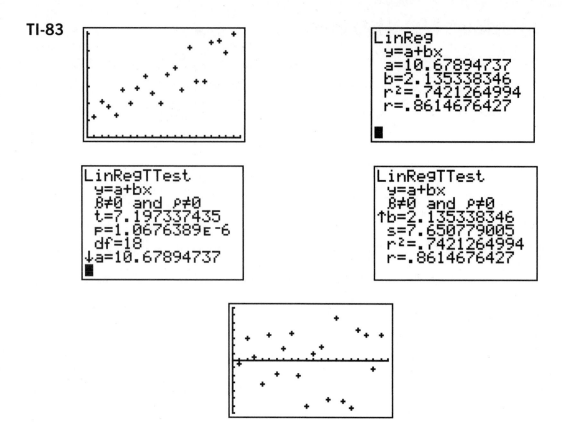

TI-83

Note that not all of the digits of the TI-83 display need to be reported. Also, note that TI displays do not include labels.

Review Exercises

SHORT ANSWER

Complete the chart by entering a "✓" if the tool displays the item or an "X" if it does not.

Item	Data Desk	Minitab	SAS	Fathom	TI-83
1. Regression equation					
2. Value of R^2					
3. Standard error of the estimate					
4. Test statistic					
5. 2-sided *P*-value of the test for H_0: $\beta = 0$					
6. Degrees of freedom of the test					

8.3 Confidence Interval for a Mean

Suppose the heights of eighth grade girls is known to be a normal distribution. A sample of the heights in inches of 23 randomly selected eighth grade girls in a large suburban school district were: 60, 65, 57, 54, 53, 62, 65, 64, 61, 66, 66, 58, 64, 58, 57, 61, 60, 63, 64, 62, 67, 79, 68.
Find the 95% confidence interval of the population mean.

Data Desk

```
t-Interval for Individual μ's

No Selector

Individual Confidence 95.00%

Bounds: Lower Bound < μ < Upper Bound

With 95.00% Confidence, 60.002345 < μ(Heights) < 64.693308
```

Note that Data Desk does not display sample size or standard error.

Minitab

```
Confidence Intervals

Variable    N      Mean    StDev  SE Mean      95.0 % CI
Heights    23     62.35     5.42     1.13    (60.00,   64.69)
```

Fathom

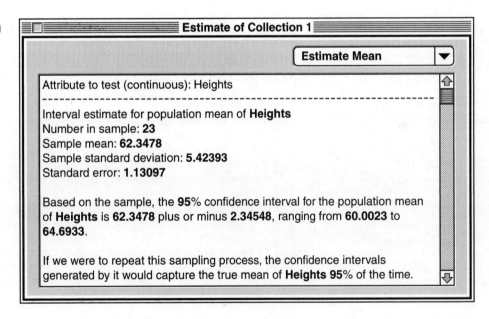

SAS There is no separate SAS procedure that generates confidence intervals.

TI-83

```
TInterval
(60.002,64.693)
x̄=62.34782609
Sx=5.423925915
n=23
```

8.4 Hypothesis Test: One-Sample *t*-Test

Refer to the data for the problem in Section 8.3. Suppose the school district has always believed that the mean height of their eighth grade girls was 60 inches. Do these data cast doubt on this belief at the 5% level of significance?

Data Desk

```
t-Test of the Individual μ's

No Selector

Individual Alpha Level 0.05

Ho: μ = 60 Ha: μ ≠ 60


Heights:
Test Ho: μ(Heights) = 60 vs Ha: μ(Heights) ≠ 60
Sample Mean = 62.347826 t-Statistic = 2.076 w/22 df
Reject Ho at Alpha = 0.05
p = 0.0498
```

Minitab

```
T-Test of the Mean

Test of mu = 60.00 vs mu not = 60.00

Variable      N      Mean     StDev    SE Mean        T          P
Heights      23     62.35      5.42       1.13     2.08      0.050
```

Fathom

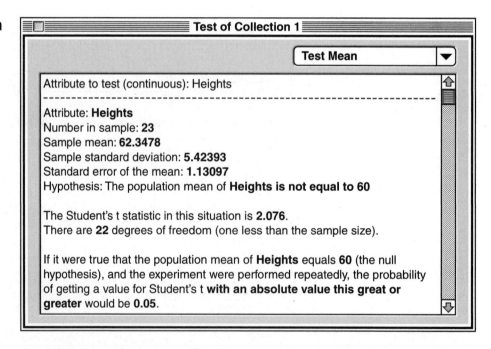

SAS There is no separate SAS procedure that generates tests for one population mean.

TI-83

```
T-Test
μ≠60
t=2.075946194
p=.0497905852
x̄=62.34782609
Sx=5.423925915
n=23
```

or

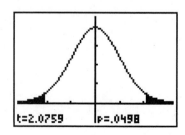

Review Exercises

SHORT ANSWER

Complete the chart by entering a "✓" if the tool displays the item or
an "X" if it does not.

Item	Data Desk	Minitab	SAS	Fathom	TI-83
1. Sample mean					
2. Sample size					
3. Null and alternative hypotheses					
4. Test statistic					
5. Degrees of freedom of the test					
6. *P*-value of the test					
7. What conclusion can you make based on these printouts?					

8.5 Hypothesis Test: Two Sample *t*-Test of Means

Two populations of 300 employees at a large corporation were enrolled in training sessions with the same content but with very different teaching methodologies: activity-based and lecture. In order to compare the effectiveness of each methodology, the Statistical Analysis Department first concluded by their research that performance on the 15-question effectiveness assessment is approximately normally distributed. They gathered an independent random sample from each group and came up with the following results:

The sample of the Activity-Based Group consisted of 15 members whose scores were: 10.6, 15.3, 12.4, 17.5, 9.9, 10.3, 16.4, 12.0, 15.4, 8.9, 8.6, 9.0, 6.0, 10.1, 18.7.

The sample of the Lecture Group consisted of 11 members whose scores were: 9.8, 10.2, 13.4, 15.6, 16.2, 12.8, 13.0, 12.5, 9.0, 17.9, 15.3.

Do these data indicate that there is a difference in the effectiveness scores of the two groups at the 5% level?

Data Desk

```
2-Sample t-Test of μ1-μ2

No Selector

Individual Alpha Level 0.05

Ho: μ1-μ2 = 0  Ha: μ1-μ2 ≠ 0


Lecture - Activity:
Test Ho: μ(Lecture)-μ(Activity) = 0 vs Ha: μ(Lecture)-μ(Activity) ≠ 0
Difference Between Means = 1.1721212  t-Statistic = 0.9091 w/23 df
Fail to reject Ho at Alpha = 0.05
p = 0.3724
```

Minitab

```
Two Sample T-Test and Confidence Interval

Two sample T for Lecture vs Activity
             N     Mean    StDev   SE Mean
Lecture     11    13.25    2.83     0.85
Activity    15    12.07    3.74     0.97

95% CI for mu Lecture - mu Activity: ( -1.50,  3.84)
T-Test mu Lecture = mu Activity (vs not =): T= 0.91  P=0.37  DF= 23
```

Fathom

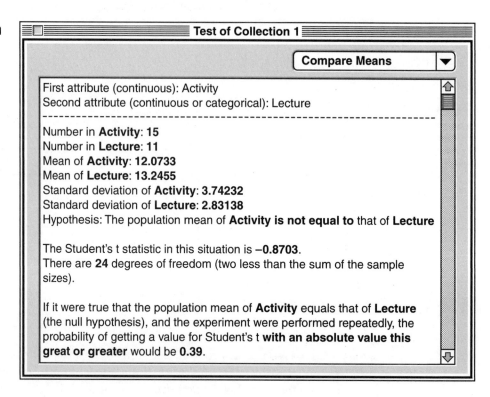

SAS

```
Two-Sample t-test

                TTEST PROCEDURE

Variable: X

GROUP     N      Mean        Std Dev   Std Error   Minimum       Maximum
-----------------------------------------------------------------------
  1      15  12.07333333  3.74231912  0.96626264  6.00000000   18.70000000
  2      11  13.24545455  2.83138257  0.85369397  9.00000000   17.90000000

Variances    T        DF      Prob>|T|
-------------------------------------------
Unequal   -0.9091    24.0      0.3724
Equal     -0.8703    24.0      0.3927

For H0: Variances are equal, F'= 1.75 DF = (14,10) Prob>F' = 0.3785
```

TI-83

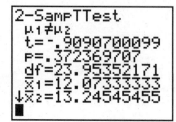

or

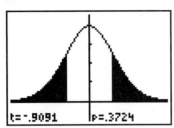

t=-.9091   p=.3724

Review Exercises

SHORT ANSWER

Complete the chart by entering a "✓" if the tool displays the item or
an "X" if it does not.

Item	Data Desk	Minitab	SAS	Fathom	TI-83
1. Two sample means (or the difference of the sample means)					
2. Alternative hypothesis					
3. Test statistic					
4. Degrees of freedom					
5. *P*-value of the test					
6. What conclusion can you make based on these printouts?					

8.6 Contingency Tables: Test of Independence

Forty adults were surveyed regarding their political affiliation. The results are summarized in the following table:

	Female (F)	Male (M)
Democrat (D)	6	8
Republican (R)	4	8
Independent (I)	9	5

Determine (at the 5% level) if the survey indicates that political affiliation is independent of gender classifications.

Data Desk

```
Rows are levels of                              Politics
Columns are levels of                           Gender
No Selector
120 total cases of which 80 are missing

            F        M      total

D           6        8       14
            6.65     7.35    14

I           9        5       14
            6.65     7.35    14

R           4        8       12
            5.7      6.3     12

total       19       21      40
            19       21      40

table contents:
Count
Expected Values

Chi-square =        2.669  with  2  df
p = 0.2633
```

Minitab

Tabulated Statistics

```
Rows: Gender      Columns: Politics

            D        R        I       All

M           8        8        5       21
            7.35     6.30     7.35    21.00

F           6        4        9       19
            6.65     5.70     6.65    19.00

All         14       12       14      40
            14.00    12.00    14.00   40.00

Chi-Square = 2.669, DF = 2, P-Value = 0.263


    Cell Contents --
                       Count
            Exp Freq
```

Fathom

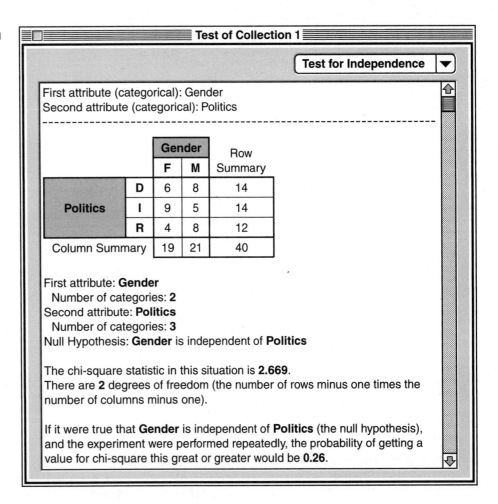

SAS

```
Chi-Square Test for Independence

TABLE OF PARTY BY GENDER

PARTY        GENDER

Frequency   |
Expected    |Female   |Male     |Total
------------+---------+---------+-----
Demo        |   6     |   8     |  14
            | 6.65    | 7.35    |
------------+---------+---------+-----
Indep       |   9     |   5     |  14
            | 6.65    | 7.35    |
------------+---------+---------+-----
Repub       |   4     |   8     |  12
            | 5.7     | 6.3     |
------------+---------+---------+-----
Total          19        21        40


    STATISTICS FOR TABLE OF PARTY BY GENDER

Statistic                      DF   Value   Prob
------------------------------------------------
Chi-Square                      2   2.669   0.263
Likelihood Ratio Chi-Square     2   2.705   0.259
Mantel-Haenszel Chi-Square      1   0.166   0.683
Phi Coefficient                     0.258
Contingency Coefficient             0.250
Cramer's V                          0.258

Sample Size = 40
```

TI-83   X²-Test
          X²=2.668576202
          P=.2633455841
          df=2

or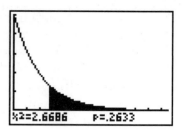

Expected frequencies:

[B]
    [[6.65 7.35]
     [5.7 6.3]
     [6.65 7.35]]

Review Exercises

SHORT ANSWER

Complete the chart by entering an "✓" if the tool displays the item or
a "X" if it does not.

Item	Data Desk	Minitab	SAS	Fathom	TI-83
1. Expected frequencies					
2. Test statistic					
3. Degrees of freedom					
4. *P*-value of the test					
5. What conclusion can you make based on these printouts?					

15. Valid sampling methods include:

(A) a census of the population.
(B) selection of participants using procedures that depend on a probability model.
(C) interviewing a randomly selected person from each household.
(D) designs that guarantee that the demographics of the sample match those of the population.
(E) None of these.

16. Which best describes statistical bias?

(A) Bias is the tendency for a distribution to be skewed.
(B) Bias is not an issue with symmetric mound-shaped distributions.
(C) Bias increases variation in responses.
(D) Bias is a systematic error in the survey results.
(E) None of these describes bias.

17. Which of the following is *not* an important characteristic of a valid experimental design?

(A) random assignments of groups
(B) blocking
(C) comparison of groups
(D) replication
(E) All of these are important.

18. In a study of performance improvement resulting from the completion of an SAT preparation course, the investigator believes that gender may be an influence in the result. Which of the following designs would address her concern?

(A) a completely randomized design, since everyone in the population of interest would have an equal chance of selection
(B) random sample stratified for gender
(C) randomized design blocked for gender
(D) completely randomized design of males only
(E) None of these addresses the concern.

19. Subjects for a study of identical twins, one of whom has died of cancer, were identified by a nationwide search of hospital records. Once identified, individuals were asked to participate in the study dealing with the effects of the loss on the surviving twin. This method of selection is best described as

(A) quota sampling.
(B) an observational study.
(C) a randomized experiment.
(D) a voluntary response sample.
(E) a controlled experiment.

20. A probability distribution of earnings from a $1,000 investment in an Internet company for a term of 3 years is

-1,000	0	1,000	2,000	3,000
.13	.15	.24	.35	.13

How much should you expect to earn from this 3-year investment?

(A) $800
(B) $1,000
(C) $1,200
(D) $2,000
(E) $2,200

21. Which of the following is *not* true about the variance in a binomial distribution $B(n, p)$?

(A) For a fixed p, the variance increases as n increases.
(B) For a fixed n, the variance is maximum when $p = 0.5$.
(C) The variance depends only on n.
(D) The variance is constant for a specific n and p.
(E) None of these.

22. The probability of a success on any one trial is .4 and you have a maximum of 10 trials in which to win. Which of the following expressions will calculate the probability that you will get a success on one of your first four attempts?

(A) $\binom{10}{4}(.4)^4(.6)^4$

(B) $\binom{10}{10}(.4)^{10}(.6)^0$

(C) $.4 + .4(.6) + .4(.6)^2 + .4(.6)^3$
(D) $.6 + .4(.6) + .4(.6)^2 + .4(.6)^3$
(E) $P(.5 \le X \le 4.5)$ where $X \sim Normal(4, \sqrt{10(.4)(.6)}\,)$

SECTION I

Questions 1–40
Spend 90 minutes on this part of the exam.

Directions: The questions or incomplete statements below are each followed by five possible answers or completions. Select the choice that best answers the question or completes the statement.

1. Which of the following is *not* categorical?

   (A) hair color ✓
   (B) eye color ✓
   (C) athletic jersey number
   (D) numbers in a street address
   (E) All of these are categorical.

2. Which of the following plots is least useful in determining the shape of a distribution?

   (A) box plot
   (B) stem plot
   (C) histogram
   (D) dot plot
   (E) All of these are very useful in determining shape.

3. Which of the following statements can be inferred from this histogram?

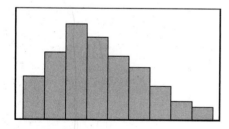

   (A) median = mean
   (B) median < mean
   (C) median > mean
   (D) The data are skewed left.
   (E) None of these statements can be inferred.

4. If 10 is added to every value of a data set, which of the following occurs?

   (A) The mean increases by 10.
   (B) The median remains the same.
   (C) The range increases by 10.
   (D) The mode increases by $\sqrt{10}$.
   (E) The mean increases by 100.

5. Which of the following is false about the standard deviation?

   (A) For mound-shaped, symmetric distributions, approximately 95% of the data are within 2 standard deviations of the mean.
   (B) Standard deviation cannot be computed for skewed distributions.
   (C) Standard deviation is the square root of variance.
   (D) For mound-shaped, symmetric distributions, the interval [−1 standard deviation, + 1 standard deviation] is wider than the interquartile range.
   (E) All of these are true.

6. A girl scores a 23 in math on the ACT and 560 on the SAT. Suppose both distributions are approximately normal and the mean of the ACT was 19 with a standard deviation of 6 while the mean of the SAT was 490 with a standard deviation of 140. Which of the following is *not* true?

   (A) Comparison of z-scores will identify the better score.
   (B) The number of students who took each exam will impact the comparison of scores.
   (C) The z-score of the ACT score is .67 while the z-score of the SAT is .5.
   (D) Comparison of percentiles will identify the better score.
   (E) All of these are true.

7. Which of the following is *not* true of a normal curve?

(A) It is centered at 0 and has a standard deviation of 1.
(B) It is asymptotic to the *x*-axis.
(C) There are points of inflection at $\mu \pm 1$ standard deviation.
(D) The area under the curve equals 1.
(E) All of these are true.

8. Which of the following is *false* about the correlation coefficient?

(A) $-1 \le r \le 1$
(B) If *r* is negative, an inverse relationship is indicated.
(C) A one-to-one relationship will have $r > 1$.
(D) If the data set contains two points, then $r = \pm 1$
(E) All of these are true.

9. A least squares regression line was determined from a study of car performance. The equation was $mpg = 33.06 - 0.05 \, hP$, where *mpg* is miles per gallon and *hP* is horsepower. What is a valid and reasonable conclusion from this regression?

(A) A car with no horsepower will get 33.06 miles per gallon.
(B) Horsepower and miles per gallon are directly related.
(C) If you increase horsepower, you will increase miles per gallon.
(D) High horsepower has a negative impact on miles per gallon.
(E) None of these is valid and reasonable.

10. At a particular value, the residual for a linear regression has a value of 1.2. Which of the following is a true statement?

Actual - estimated

(A) $r^2 = 0.85$ for the regression
(B) The regression line overestimates the actual value at this point.
(C) The regression line underestimates the actual value at this point.
(D) A non-linear regression would provide a better fit.
(E) None of these is true.

11. If a data set is transformed using $(x, y) \to (\ln x, \ln y)$ and least squares regression is performed on the transformed set, then the resulting regression model, relative to the original data, will be

(A) a power model
(B) an exponential model
(C) a quadratic model
(D) a linear model
(E) The type of model cannot be determined.

12. Suppose the bivariate set of data (weight, mpg) for 30 domestic cars has the following statistics: $s_{mpg} = 4.1$ gal and $r = 0.90$. If the least squares regression model is $mpg = 12.7 + .01(weight)$, then s_{weight} is approximately

(A) 310 lbs.
(B) 369 lbs.
(C) 410 lbs.
(D) 560 lbs.
(E) The value cannot be determined.

13. Which of the following is *not* a consideration in determining the goodness of fit of a model?

(A) the value of r^2
(B) the slope of its residual plot
(C) the existence of influential points
(D) the existence of pattern in the residual points
(E) All of these are considerations.

14. The residual plot of a linear regression is shown below. An appropriate next step in the analysis would be to

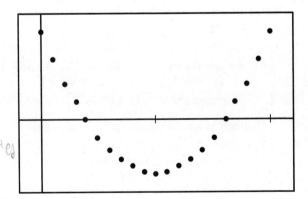

(A) implement a transformation to find an exponential model.
(B) implement a transformation to find a power model.
(C) implement a transformation to find a quadratic model.
(D) stay with the linear regression but eliminate outliers.
(E) None of these.

GO ON TO THE NEXT PAGE

15. Valid sampling methods include:

(A) a census of the population.
(B) selection of participants using procedures that depend on a probability model.
(C) interviewing a randomly selected person from each household.
(D) designs that guarantee that the demographics of the sample match those of the population.
(E) None of these.

16. Which best describes statistical bias?

(A) Bias is the tendency for a distribution to be skewed.
(B) Bias is not an issue with symmetric mound-shaped distributions.
(C) Bias increases variation in responses.
(D) Bias is a systematic error in the survey results.
(E) None of these describes bias.

17. Which of the following is *not* an important characteristic of a valid experimental design?

(A) random assignments of groups
(B) blocking
(C) comparison of groups
(D) replication
(E) All of these are important.

18. In a study of performance improvement resulting from the completion of an SAT preparation course, the investigator believes that gender may be an influence in the result. Which of the following designs would address her concern?

(A) a completely randomized design, since everyone in the population of interest would have an equal chance of selection
(B) random sample stratified for gender
(C) randomized design blocked for gender
(D) completely randomized design of males only
(E) None of these addresses the concern.

19. Subjects for a study of identical twins, one of whom has died of cancer, were identified by a nationwide search of hospital records. Once identified, individuals were asked to participate in the study dealing with the effects of the loss on the surviving twin. This method of selection is best described as

(A) quota sampling.
(B) an observational study.
(C) a randomized experiment.
(D) a voluntary response sample.
(E) a controlled experiment.

20. A probability distribution of earnings from a $1,000 investment in an Internet company for a term of 3 years is

$-1,000$	0	1,000	2,000	3,000
.13	.15	.24	.35	.13

How much should you expect to earn from this 3-year investment?

(A) $800
(B) $1,000
(C) $1,200
(D) $2,000
(E) $2,200

21. Which of the following is *not* true about the variance in a binomial distribution $B(n, p)$?

(A) For a fixed p, the variance decreases as n increases.
(B) For a fixed n, the variance is maximum when $p = 0.5$.
(C) The variance depends only on n.
(D) The variance is constant for a specific n and p.
(E) None of these.

22. The probability of a success on any one trial is .4 and you have a maximum of 10 trials in which to win. Which of the following expressions will calculate the probability that you will get a success on one of your first four attempts?

(A) $\binom{10}{4}(.4)^4(.6)^4$

(B) $\binom{10}{10}(.4)^{10}(.6)^0$

(C) $.4 + .4(.6) + .4(.6)^2 + .4(.6)^3$
(D) $.6 + .4(.6) + .4(.6)^2 + .4(.6)^3$
(E) $P(.5 \le X \le 4.5)$ where $X \sim Normal(4, \sqrt{10(.4)(.6)})$

23. Which of the following is true about the continuity adjustment?

(A) It is only used with binomial distributions.
(B) It should be used on all continuous distributions.
(C) It should be used on all continuous approximations to discrete distributions.
(D) It is used only with normal approximations.
(E) None of these is true.

24. A company claims that no more than 2 apples of a shipment of 24 apples will be rotten upon delivery. A recent shipment of 24 apples contained 3 rotten apples. When confronted, the salesman said that this is not a very unlikely event. You decide to run a simulation to determine how likely it would be to find 3 rotten apples out of a shipment of 24 when the true proportion is $\frac{2}{24}$. Which of the following techniques is *not* an acceptable method for this simulation?

(A) Remove the aces from a standard deck of 52 playing cards. Designate the kings as rotten fruit and all other cards as acceptable fruit. Shuffle and deal 24 cards; count the number of kings. Repeat the simulation.
(B) Assign the digits 01 and 02 to rotten fruit and 03 through 24 to acceptable fruit. Using a random digit table, begin at any place in the digit table and choose two-digit numbers until 24 are selected from the set {01, 02, . . ., 24}. Count the number of 01's and 02's. Repeat the simulation.
(C) Using a random integer generator, designate 1 and 2 as rotten fruit and 3 through 24 as acceptable. Generate sets from the 24 integers from 1 to 24; count the number of 1's and 2's.
(D) Using two 12-sided dice, designate the 1 on each die as a rotten fruit and all other numbers as acceptable fruit. Roll both dice 12 times and count the number of 1's that appear. Repeat the simulation.
(E) This situation does not lend itself to simulation.

25. The following table displays the results of a sample of 99 subjects in which each person indicated his or her favorite sport of three listed. The data are organized by favorite sport and age group.

AGE	FOOTBALL	BASEBALL	SOCCER
Over 40	15	8	7
Between 20 and 40	20	11	15
Under 20	8	7	8

What is the probability that a person chosen at random will be under 20 and favor baseball?

(A) $\frac{7}{26}$
(B) $\frac{7}{99}$
(C) $\frac{26}{99}$
(D) $\frac{7}{23}$
(E) None of these.

26. If the mean of the sampling distribution for a sample proportion is not equal to the value of the parameter that it is estimating, then which of the following is true?

(A) The sample mean is biased.
(B) The sample mean is unbiased.
(C) The sampling technique is invalid.
(D) There was no random selection in the sample.
(E) None of these is true.

27. The amount of time that a certain airline runs behind schedule for arrivals has been shown to follow a uniform distribution on the interval of 38 to 52 minutes. Which of these best approximates the probability that a flight will land between 40 and 45 minutes late?

(A) .071
(B) .284
(C) .357
(D) .643
(E) .929

28. Which of the following statements are true about discrete probability distributions?
   I. The sum of the probabilities must equal 1.
   II. There are a finite number of outcomes.
   III. All the probabilities must be non-negative.

(A) I only
(B) I and II
(C) I, II and III
(D) I and III
(E) II only

GO ON TO THE NEXT PAGE ▶

29. Which of the following is a valid probability density function on the interval [0, 2]?

(A) $f(x) = .5x$
(B) $f(x) = x$
(C) $f(x) = 2x$
(D) $f(x) = 3 - 1.5x$
(E) None of these.

30. A 95% confidence interval of the mean hourly salary of part-time lifeguards at public swimming pools in a particular county during the summer is (5.65, 7.45). Which of the following are correct conclusions of this confidence interval?

I. There is a 95% probability that the mean hourly salary of all lifeguards in the county is in this confidence interval.
II. The mean of the sample is $6.55.
III. 95% of all confidence intervals from samples of the same size will contain the mean hourly salary of all lifeguards in the county.

(A) I only
(B) I and III
(C) II and III
(D) I, II, and III
(E) III only

31. An experimenter plants half of each of six flowerbeds with a new hybrid flower seed and the other half of each with the standard seed. Each bed is given the same amount of water and fertilizer. At the end of one week, the number of sprouts is counted and compared. Which of the following tests would be most appropriate in establishing a difference in the two seeds?

(A) t-test of means
(B) two-sample proportion z-test
(C) matched pairs t-test
(D) two-sample proportion t-test
(E) chi-square test

32. A one-tailed hypothesis test is conducted at the $\alpha = .05$ level of significance resulting in a P-value $=.032$. Which of the following conclusions is *not* valid?

(A) A two-tailed hypothesis test for the same situation would indicate a non-significant result.
(B) The probability of making a correct decision is .032.

(C) If the sample and population values stayed the same and the sample size increased, then the P-value would decrease.
(D) The 95% confidence interval of the sample result would contain the expected population value.
(E) All of these are valid conclusions.

33. By what factor (approximately) will the margin of error for the value of a population proportion increase if we increase the confidence level from 95% to 98%?

(A) .43
(B) .98
(C) 1.19
(D) 1.68
(E) 2.33

34. A CEO of a small corporation wishes to hire your consulting firm to conduct a simple random sample of its customers to determine the proportion that consider her company as their primary source of her product. She tells your staff that she requires that the margin of error in the proportion be no more than 3% with 95% confidence. Earlier studies have indicated that the approximate proportion is 37%. What is the minimum size of the sample that you would recommend to meet the requirements of your client if you use the earlier results?

(A) 697
(B) 748
(C) 999
(D) 1,407
(E) No sample of any size will meet the requirements.

35. Which of the following is *not* necessarily true regarding inference for the slope of a regression line?

(A) The variables are linearly related.
(B) The distribution of the y's associated with each x have the same variance.
(C) The set of x's and the set of y's are normally distributed.
(D) The sum of the residuals equals 0.
(E) All of these statements are true.

36. A random sample of 100 cereal boxes is selected and the frequency of occurrence is counted for each of four game cards contained in the boxes. The table lists the actual and expected frequencies of occurrence for each of the cards. Which of the following are valid conclusions?

Card	A	B	C	D
Actual Frequency	25	40	3	32
Expected Frequency	30	50	2	18

   I. When a chi-square test is performed on the data, the test statistic equals 14.22.
   II. The degrees of freedom for this chi-square test are 3.
   III. For this chi-square test, these data are significant.

(A) I
(B) I and II
(C) I, II, and III
(D) I and III
(E) A chi-square test cannot be performed.

37. Part of a printout of a computer regression analysis of the effect of a change in a manufacturing process is shown. Output-A represents the output of stations before the change and Output-B represents the output of the stations after the change.

```
Predictor    Coef     StDev      T       P
Constant    81.29    88.30    0.92    0.366
Output-A   0.82728  0.05364  15.42    0.000

S = 314.6   R-Sq = 90.8%   R-Sq(adj) = 90.5%
```

Which of the following is the regression equation?

(A) Output-B = 81.29 + .82728(Output-A)
(B) Output-A = 81.29 + .82728(Output-B)
(C) Output-B = .82728 + 81.29(Output-A)
(D) Output-A = .82728 + 81.29(Output-B)
(E) The regression equation cannot be determined from this information.

38. A light bulb manufacturer claims that its bulbs have a mean life of 139.5 hours with a standard deviation of 14.5 hours. You select a simple random sample to test this claim. Your sample of 10 bulbs has a mean life of 137.0 hours with a standard deviation of 12.5 hours. Which of the following would be the most appropriate test for establishing that the manufacturer's claim is high?

(A) z-test for means
(B) t-test for means
(C) chi-square test
(D) z-test for proportions
(E) None of these tests would be appropriate.

39. A newspaper publishes a claim that 80% of students from its city's high schools go on to post-secondary education. A watch-dog group decides to test this hypothesis at the 5% level of confidence. Which of the following is *not* an appropriate interpretation of the 5% level of significance?

(A) 5% is the probability of a Type I error.
(B) 5% is the probability of rejecting the hypothesis that $p_0 = .80$ when the hypothesis is true.
(C) 5% is the probability of accepting the hypothesis that $p_0 = .80$ when the hypothesis is false.
(D) 5% is the criteria for judging whether the sample statistic is sufficiently extreme to cast doubt on the newspaper's claim.
(E) None of these is an appropriate interpretation of the 5%.

40. A two-tailed hypothesis ($\alpha = .05$) of a population mean has a P-value of .072. Which of the following conclusions is valid?

(A) The null hypothesis should be accepted.
(B) The null hypothesis should be rejected.
(C) A one-tailed test of the null hypothesis using the same sample will be significant.
(D) The P-value of .072 indicates the probability that the null hypothesis is false.
(E) None of these is a valid conclusion.

END OF SECTION I

Part A
Questions 1–5
Spend about 60 minutes on this part of the exam.
Percent of Section II grade—75

In order to receive full credit for your free-response questions, you must completely analyze each situation and clearly communicate your analyses and results. In order to earn partial credit when warranted, be sure to show enough work so that your reasoning process can be followed.

1. The graph below displays the cumulative relative frequencies of the outcomes of adding the results of rolling two dice that may or may not be fair.

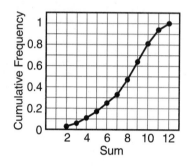

   a. Approximate the median of the distribution. Explain the reason for your answer.

   b. Calculate the theoretical probability distribution of the sum on two fair dice.

   c. Draw and label a cumulative relative frequency plot of the distribution calculated in part b.

   d. Compare the given plot to the plot drawn in part c and make a conclusion as to whether you believe the dice are fair. Justify your opinion.

2. An experiment to determine the effect of a fertilizer on the growth of grass is to be conducted in a controlled environment. Identical soil and seeds are placed in plots that are attached to immovable laboratory tables as the figure below indicates. Once the grass shoots appear, some plots are treated with the fertilizer while the rest receive no fertilizer. All other conditions regarding water, temperature, etc. are identical except for the proximity of the single light source to the plots. In the figure, each rectangular region represents a test plot. The light source is indicated by the shaded circle in the drawing of the test site.

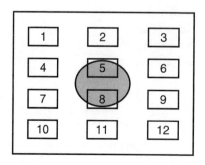

   Describe how the experiment should be designed so that the intensity of the light is not a confounding variable.

3. A manufacturer claims that its quality control is so effective that no more than 2% of the parts in each shipment are defective. A simple random sample of 100 parts from the last shipment contained 3 defectives.

   a. In a test of significance to determine the validity of the company's claim, why is it inappropriate to use the normal approximation to the binomial? Explain your answer.

   b. What is the minimum sample size for which a test of the claim would be appropriate? Show your work.

   c. Suppose your answer in part b were the sample size used. Perform an appropriate test of the manufacturer's claim at the 5% level of significance. Assume that the observed proportion is .03 for this sample size.

4. A study comparing car life (in years) to purchase price of the car (in dollars) was conducted using 11 randomly selected American-made cars. Using a statistical software program, a least squares regression line was fit to the data and yielded the following printout.

```
Dependent variable is:  Life
No Selector
R squared = 50.2%      R squared (adjusted) = 44.6%
s = 1.149  with 11 - 2 = 9 degrees of freedom

Source       Sum of Squares   df    Mean Square    F-ratio
Regression   11.9633          1     11.9633        9.06
Resudual     11.884           9     1.32045

Variable   Coefficient   s.e. of Coeff   t-ratio   prob
Constant   0.935199      1.153           0.811     0.4382
Cost       0.000163839   0.00005443      3.01      0.0147
```

   a. What is the regression equation? Use the variable names listed in the printout.

   b. Interpret the slope of the regression line in the context of the study.

The residual plot for this regression is displayed below:

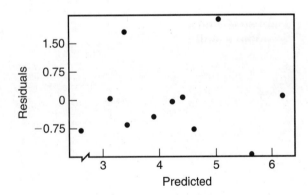

   c. Comment on the goodness of fit of the model to the data. Explain your reasoning.

   d. Estimate the approximate life of a car in the sample whose purchase price is $25,000.

   e. Does this model overestimate or underestimate the actual life of the car in part d? Explain the reasons for your answer.

GO ON TO THE NEXT PAGE

5. The following table displays the viewing preferences among the four major networks by academic department based on a census of teachers at a large urban high school:

	ABC	NBC	CBS	FOX
English	12	7	3	8
Math	6	8	9	7
Science	2	6	3	4
Social Studies	9	4	10	6

a. What is the probability that a teacher selected at random is a math teacher who prefers FOX?

b. What is the probability that a teacher selected at random is a math teacher, given that he or she prefers FOX?

c. What is the probability that a teacher selected at random prefers FOX, given that the person is a math teacher?

Part B
Question 6
Spend about 30 minutes on this part of the exam.
Percent of Section II grade—25

6. The following table consists of 200 responses to a hypothetical question in which answers could range between 1 and 100 inclusive.

62	22	57	48	81	68	53	90	4	36	41	24	14	30	34	7	17	60	10	97
92	21	100	95	75	93	6	64	84	94	8	37	21	60	90	82	84	39	79	70
52	17	6	17	30	84	78	80	86	83	52	5	75	68	61	88	96	81	21	75
91	31	80	76	75	20	19	23	86	78	28	40	63	14	32	34	69	95	24	9
24	31	77	75	19	50	7	15	97	44	4	22	46	73	60	49	78	96	89	10
82	5	10	43	28	62	50	13	45	2	33	91	78	82	82	25	46	26	52	21
5	82	69	78	30	15	19	59	9	37	73	91	98	44	67	87	73	73	20	65
43	33	76	58	65	23	24	45	35	10	20	40	96	27	5	100	100	92	29	91
40	79	60	41	2	47	41	30	77	80	68	3	46	100	71	95	6	13	9	98
18	29	5	90	67	99	85	87	43	5	98	95	28	3	24	68	72	100	18	77

Each row consists of 20 data values and should be coded: Row 1: 1–20; Row 2: 21–40; etc. If we accept these 200 data values as our population, $\mu = 51.78$.

a. Select a simple random sample of size 25 from our population by selecting 25 codes from the random digits table in the Appendix. Record the coding value and the data value for your sample in a table similar to the one shown:

Code	
Data	

b. Calculate the sample statistics $\bar{x}$ and s for your sample.

c. Construct the 95% confidence interval for μ.

d. Interpret your interval in the context of the situation.

e. Is μ in your interval? Is this fact surprising? Explain your answers.

END OF EXAMINATION

MODEL EXAMINATION 2

SECTION I

Questions 1–40

Spend 90 minutes on this part of the exam.

Directions: The questions or incomplete statements below are each followed by five possible answers or completions. Select the choice that best answers the question or completes the statement.

1. In determining ratings of TV shows, a rating company gathers data on many variables. Which of these is categorical?

   (A) age of viewers in years
   (B) family income of viewers
   (C) gender of viewers
   (D) number of TVs in household
   (E) number of hours TV is watched

2. Which of the following is always true of a discrete variable?

   (A) Discrete variables have finite domains.
   (B) Discrete variables cannot have negative values.
   (C) Consecutive values of a discrete variable may or may not differ by a fixed (constant) amount.
   (D) Discrete variables can describe a day of the week, e.g., Monday, Tuesday, . . .
   (E) Discrete variables can be added.

3. Which of the following conclusions is inappropriate based on the plot?

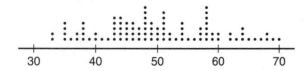

   (A) The data are normal.
   (B) The data are discrete.
   (C) The mean is approximately equal to the median.
   (D) The mean is approximately 50 and the standard deviation is approximately 20.
   (E) All of these are appropriate.

4. The statement "The median of a distribution is approximately equal to the mean of the distribution" can be made true by adding which of the following:

   (A) for all distributions.
   (B) only for symmetric, mound-shaped distributions.
   (C) for skewed distributions.
   (D) for symmetric distributions
   (E) None of these.

5. If 10 is added to the maximum value of a data set, which of the following occurs?

   (A) the mean increases by 10
   (B) the median remains the same
   (C) the range remains the same
   (D) the mode increases by $\sqrt{10}$
   (E) the mean increases by 100

6. A symmetric, mound-shaped distribution has a mean of 42 and a standard deviation of 7. Which of the following is true?

   (A) There are more data values between 42 and 49 than between 28 and 35.
   (B) It is impossible that the distribution contains a data value greater that 70.
   (C) Approximately 95% of the data lie between 35 and 49.
   (D) The interquartile range is approximately 14.
   (E) None of these is true.

7. A distribution of weekly sales has a mean of $1,250 with a standard deviation of 230. Which of the following can be concluded from this information?

(A) The distribution is mound-shaped and symmetric.
(B) A negative z-score would correspond to a value less than $1,250.
(C) Some weekly sales were negative.
(D) A z-score tells the number of standard deviations a value is from the median.
(E) None of these can be concluded.

8. Suppose we graph two normal curves, A and B, on the same axis. If $\mu_A = 50$ and $\sigma_A = 18$, and $\mu_B = 50$ and $\sigma_B = 12$. Which of the following will *not* be true?

(A) Curve B has a larger maximum than curve A.
(B) Both are centered at $x = 50$.
(C) The area under B equals the area under A
(D) The domain of A is greater than the domain of B
(E) All of these are true.

9. A teacher has two sections of AP Statistics. On the last test, out of 100 points, Class A had a mean of 75 with a standard deviation of 10. Class B had a mean of 82 with a standard deviation of 7. Which of the following is necessarily true?

(A) The highest score of all students combined is 78.5.
(B) The highest score in B is greater than the highest score in A.
(C) The range of A is greater than the range of B.
(D) The number in each class must be known in order to compute the mean of the combined classes.
(E) None of these is true.

10. Which of the following scatterplots will have a correlation coefficient near 0?

(A)

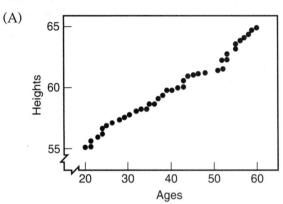

(B)

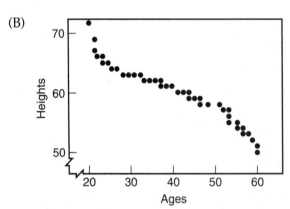

(C)

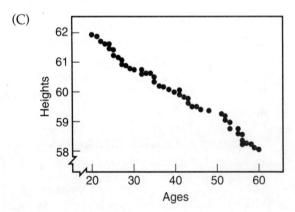

(D)

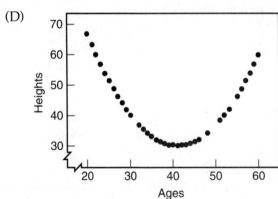

(E) None of these appears to have a correlation near 0.

GO ON TO THE NEXT PAGE

11. A linear regression model from a study of weight loss and daily exercise time was Weight loss = −0.63 + 0.29(Time). This indicates which of the following?

(A) The correlation coefficient is negative.
(B) If you exercise longer, you will lose more weight.
(C) You may gain weight if you don't exercise.
(D) (0, −0.63) is an outlier
(E) None of these is indicated.

12. A residual plot of a linear regression provides evidence of a good fit if which of the following statements are true?
   I. The points are randomly scattered above and below the horizontal axis.
   II. The distances from the horizontal axis to the points are approximately the same.
   III. The values of the deviations from the horizontal are small.

(A) I only
(B) I and II only
(C) I, II, III
(D) II only
(E) II and III only

13. Suppose a data set of (number of hours of study, semester average) has a scatterplot like the one below. Which of the following transformations should we consider as good candidates to linearize the data?

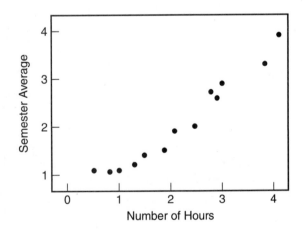

   I. $(x, y) \rightarrow (x, y^2)$
   II. $(x, y) \rightarrow (x, \sqrt{y})$
   III. $(x, y) \rightarrow (x, e^y)$

(A) I only
(B) II only
(C) I and III
(D) II and III
(E) None of the above.

14. Suppose the least squares regression line of the set {(hours of part-time work per week, GPA)} for 1,000 high school seniors was GPA = 3.21 − .04(hours). The average GPA of students who worked 20 hours per week is approximately

(A) 2.41
(B) 2.55
(C) 2.8
(D) None of the above.
(E) The value cannot be determined.

15. A study to determine the existence of a relationship between the number of students and number of teachers in 30 high schools in a particular state yielded the regression equation Teachers = 0.2 + 0.27(Students) with a correlation coefficient of 0.73. Which of the following is a correct conclusion?

(A) This equation predicts the number of teachers accurately 73% of the time.
(B) The student-teacher ratio in the schools studied was 0.27.
(C) An increase of 30 new students would motivate the hiring of one new teacher.
(D) The association between number of students and number of teachers is positive.
(E) None of these is a correct conclusion.

16. Which of the following should be considered when evaluating the goodness of fit?
   I. value of r^2
   II. residual plot
   III. y-intercept of the regression equation

(A) I only
(B) I and II
(C) II only
(D) III
(E) All of these.

17. A simple random sample of 100 adults in a particular suburb is chosen. Suppose that only 60% of those selected responded. Which of the following is correct?

(A) Since the original design was a simple random sample, the results are valid.
(B) This is an example of a multi-stage sample.
(C) The sampling frame does not represent the population.
(D) The results may be affected by the non-response bias.
(E) None of these is correct.

18. Which of the following will *not* be a cause of response bias?

(A) honesty of the respondent
(B) wording of questions
(C) appearance of interviewer
(D) the method of selection of participants
(E) All of these could be a cause of response bias.

19. In an experiment in which there are three factors with three levels each, what is the maximum number of treatments that may be studied?

(A) 3
(B) 6
(C) 9
(D) 27
(E) The number of treatments cannot be determined.

20. Two antifreezes are to be tested for minimum temperature ratings. Sixteen ounces of antifreezes A and B are placed in a freezer and the amount of liquid is measured after 15 minutes of exposure to various temperatures. The data were

	20°F	0°F	−20°F	−40°F	−60°F
A	16 oz	16 oz	14 oz	6 oz	0 oz
B	16 oz	16 oz	4.5 oz	10 oz	4 oz

Which of the following principles of design was not present in the experiment?
  I. comparison
 II. randomization
III. replication

(A) I only
(B) II only
(C) III only
(D) I and II
(E) II and III

21. Customers at a local video store were observed from 8 PM until 10 PM on a particular Friday night and it was found that the mean numbers of videos rented was 2.1 videos with a standard deviation of 1.6. Which of these is a valid conclusion of this study?

(A) The mean number of videos rented on Friday nights at this store is approximately 2.1 videos.
(B) The mean number of videos rented on this Friday night throughout the city is approximately 2.1 videos.
(C) As the number of customers increases, the standard deviation of the sample will approach the mean of the population.
(D) The number of videos rented at this store for this time period has a mean of 2.1 videos with a standard deviation of 1.6 videos.
(E) None of these is a valid conclusion.

22. In the game of roulette, there are 18 red numbers, 18 black numbers, and 2 green numbers. You may bet on red or black, but not green. If you win a $1 bet on the color, the house pays you $1. What is the expected value of each $1 you play at this game?

(A) −.50
(B) −.10
(C) −.05
(D) −.01
(E) None of the above.

23. If the expected value of successes in a binomial experiment of 100 trials is 55, the standard deviation of the number of successes is approximately

(A) 2.23
(B) 2.49
(C) 4.97
(D) 24.75
(E) None of these.

GO ON TO THE NEXT PAGE

24. Consider the experiment of rolling two dice and adding up the outcomes. To find the probability that a 7 will come up before a 4 does, you should use which of the following?

(A) permutations
(B) combinations
(C) conditional probability techniques
(D) geometric probability techniques
(E) binomial probability techniques

25. Consider the normal approximation to the binomial distribution *Binomial*(20, .4). If we wish to calculate $P(x \geq 16)$ for this binomial distribution, we could do which of the following?
   I. calculate the sum of $P(16)$, $P(17)$, ..., $P(20)$ in *Binomial*(20, .4)
   II. calculate $P(x \geq 15.5)$ in *Normal*(8, $\sqrt{4.8}$)
   III. calculate $P(x \geq 16)$ in *Normal*(8, $\sqrt{4.8}$)

(A) I only
(B) I and II
(C) I and III
(D) I, II, and III
(E) II only

26. Which of the following best describes the difference between a standard simulation and a wait-time simulation?

(A) The wait-time simulation takes longer since you must wait for the occurrence of interest.
(B) Random digit charts cannot be used for wait-time simulations.
(C) Technology cannot be used for wait-time simulations.
(D) A wait-time simulation is not as accurate as a standard simulation.
(E) All of these statements about wait-time simulations are false.

27. The following table displays the results of a sample of 99 in which the subjects indicated their favorite sport of three listed. The data are organized by favorite sport and age group.

AGE	FOOTBALL	BASEBALL	SOCCER
Over 40	15	8	7
Between 20 and 40	20	11	15
Under 20	8	7	8

What is the probability that a person chosen at random will be under 20 if he or she favors baseball?

(A) $\frac{7}{24}$

(B) $\frac{30}{99}$

(C) $\frac{24}{99}$

(D) $\frac{7}{26}$

(E) None of these.

28. Which of the following best characterizes the Central Limit Theorem?

(A) For a large n, it says that the population is approximately normal.
(B) For any population, the sampling distribution is approximately normal, regardless of sample size.
(C) For a large n, the distribution of sample means is approximately normal, regardless of the shape of the population.
(D) For any sample size, the distribution of sample means is approximately normal.
(E) None of these accurately characterizes the Central Limit Theorem.

29. The probability density function for a uniform distribution on the interval [0, 4] equals

(A) .004
(B) .04
(C) .4
(D) 4
(E) None of these.

30. A sample space contains only 5 elements. Which of the following could *not* be its probability distribution? Assume that the sets of the probabilities correspond to the elements A, B, C, D, and E.

(A) {.3, 0, .3, 0, .4}
(B) {.1, .2, .3, .4, .1}
(C) {.9, .05, .05, 0, 0}
(D) {0, 0, 0, 0, 1}
(E) All of these are valid sets of probabilities.

31. Which of the following describes a correct effect on the width of a confidence interval?
   I. As sample size increases, the width of the confidence interval decreases.
   II. As the confidence level increases, the width of the confidence interval increases.
   III. As the standard error of the estimate increases, the width of the confidence interval increases.

   (A) I only
   (B) II only
   (C) I and III
   (D) II and III
   (E) I, II, and III

32. A university anticipates that next year it will need to house 47% of its undergraduate students. The student newspaper conducts a random sample of 50 freshmen, sophomores, and juniors who claim to be returning next year and finds that 57% of the students indicate that they would need housing from the university. Which of the following tests would be most appropriate for establishing that the university should increase their estimate?

   (A) *t*-test of means
   (B) one-sample proportion *z*-test
   (C) matched pair *t*-test
   (D) one-sample proportion *t*-test
   (E) chi-square test

33. A test is conducted to determine if a random sample of 100 fish whose mean length is 53 centimeters provides evidence that the expected mean length of 50.5 centimeters is low. The *P*-value of the appropriate test is .072. This *P*-value represents the probability that

   (A) the corresponding confidence interval captures the expected mean of 50.5.
   (B) the sample result causes an error in the expected result.
   (C) a sample of size 100 would have a mean of 53 centimeters when the true mean is 50.5 centimeters.
   (D) a sample of size 100 would provide a more accurate mean than the expected value of the mean.
   (E) None of these is correct.

34. As sample size increases, if all other information stays the same, which of the following effects is reasonable?

   (A) The margin of error increases.
   (B) The margin of error decreases.
   (C) The confidence level increases.
   (D) The confidence level decreases.
   (E) None of these is affected by sample size.

35. A CEO of a small corporation wishes to hire your consulting firm to conduct a simple random sample of its customers to determine the proportion that consider her company as their primary source of her product. She tells your staff that she requires that the margin of error be no more than 3% with 95% confidence. Earlier studies have indicated that the approximate proportion is 37%. Using the CEO's research, your staff calculates that a sample size of 995 or more will meet her requirements. By how many *more* people would you increase the sample size if you use the most conservative estimate of the sample proportion?

   (A) 12
   (B) 52
   (C) 73
   (D) 112
   (E) 1,068

36. Which of the following is the reason that the conditions dealing with np and $n(1 - p)$ are included in assumptions for *z*-tests for proportions and differences of proportions?

   (A) np must be greater than 30 in order for the Central Limit Theorem to apply.
   (B) Small samples cannot be used with *z*-tests.
   (C) *z*-tests should not be used on highly skewed sampling distributions.
   (D) The conditions address the issue of the value of the mean of the sampling distribution.
   (E) None of these is the reason for these conditions.

GO ON TO THE NEXT PAGE

37. The following table displays by gender the number of people in a bridge club who favor a particular political party.

PARTY	FEMALE	MALE
Democratic	20	30
Republican	35	25
Independent	45	50

If we were to do a chi-square test, which expression would calculate correctly the expected frequency of the number of females who favor the Republican party?

(A) $\dfrac{60}{205} \times 100$

(B) $\dfrac{35}{105} \times 60$

(C) $\dfrac{60}{105} \times 100$

(D) $\dfrac{35}{100} \times 205$

(E) $\dfrac{35}{205} \times 100$

38. An advertiser claims that 80% of the adult population chooses their company's product over the product of their closest competitor. A simple random sample of adult consumers is selected. This random sample of 100 adults indicates that only 60% would choose the product in question. Which of the following would be the most appropriate test for establishing that the advertiser's claim is high?

(A) z-test for means
(B) t-test for means
(C) chi-square test
(D) z-test for proportions
(E) None of these tests would be appropriate.

39. A hypothesis test whose null hypothesis is $\mu = 101.5$ is conducted at the $\alpha = .02$ level of significance. Which of the following statements is true? Let β = probability of a Type II error.

(A) Since $\alpha = .02$, $\beta = .98$.
(B) The power of the test is .98.
(C) The power of the test is .02.
(D) The power of the test cannot be calculated from this information.
(E) The value of $\beta = .98$ but the power of the test cannot be calculated from this information.

40. The test statistic from a two-tailed hypothesis test of the mean of the differences of a matched pair study of pre- and post-tests of arithmetic for a class of 3rd graders produces a P-value of .12. Suppose that the level of significance is .02. Which of the following statements is *not* true?

(A) The P-value is the probability of a sample yielding this difference or a larger difference when the null hypothesis is true.
(B) The 98% confidence interval of the mean difference of the population includes the value of 0.
(C) A one-tailed test with the same sample information will generate a P-value of .06.
(D) A two-sample t-test of the data will produce the same P-value as this matched pair t-test.
(E) All of these are true statements.

END OF SECTION I

Part A
Questions 1–5
Spend about 60 minutes on this part of the exam.
Percent of Section II grade—75

In order to receive full credit for your free-response questions, you must completely analyze each situation and clearly communicate your analyses and results. In order to earn partial credit when warranted, be sure to show enough work so that your reasoning process can be followed.

1. A simple random sample of college students were asked to indicate the number of traffic accidents in which they were involved during the previous two years. The table details their responses:

Number of accidents	0	1	2	3	4	5
Frequency	6	10	14	20	18	12

a. Draw a cumulative relative frequency plot of this data.

b. Determine the mean and the median of these data.

c. Which of these measures best describes the typical number of accidents for these college students? Explain.

2. A fast food restaurant chain is conducting an incentive program of including 1 of 6 different characters from a popular cartoon movie in their children's meal at no extra charge.

a. Describe how you would design a simulation using a random digits table to determine the probability that a person will get at least 3 of the 6 characters in a random purchase of 10 children's meals.

b. Conduct your simulation three times using the random digits table. Indicate each simulation in a separate row of the table; begin at the far left of each row.

14378	34198	32178	76032	13054	52306	28905	12956
54920	62179	21098	45082	13067	21784	41826	31451
76931	35093	13495	54679	14283	23085	12984	19683

c. One of the characters is of a new superstar, Bill Dunkle. Describe how you would design a simulation using a random digits table to determine the probability that a person will get Bill's character before getting the character of Bill's arch rival, Joe Teepee.

d. Conduct your simulation three times using the random digits table below. Indicate each simulation in a separate row of the table; begin at the far left of each row.

14378	34198	32178	76032	13054	52306	28905	12956
54920	62179	21098	45082	13067	21784	41826	31451
76931	35093	13495	54679	14283	23085	12984	19683

GO ON TO THE NEXT PAGE

3. The Chamber of Commerce of a small town has published a report that claims the average gross income of households in the town during 1997 was $45,982.50. A simple random sample of 5 households taken during January, 1999 indicated that the mean income was $47,534.74 with a standard deviation of $12,546.70.

   a. Perform a test of significance ($\alpha = .05$) to determine whether the mean income of households in the town has increased during this period of time.

   b. Calculate the 95% confidence interval for the population mean gross income based on these data.

   c. Is the confidence interval in part b consistent with the outcome of the test in part a? Explain your answer.

4. The table below details the growth in the number of users of an Internet company during the period from 1990 through 1998:

Year	1990	1991	1992	1993	1994	1995	1996	1997	1998
Users (1,000's)	10	12	16	24	36	52	78	104	130

   a. Calculate a linear regression line for these data that will predict the number of users in any year. Comment on the goodness of fit of your line using statistical evidence.

   b. Perform the transformation of the data $(x, y) \rightarrow (x, \sqrt{y})$. Calculate a linear regression line for the transformed data. Comment on the goodness of fit of the line for the transformed data using statistical evidence.

   c. Perform the transformation of the data $(x, y) \rightarrow (x, \ln y)$. Calculate a linear regression line for the transformed data. Comment on the goodness of fit of the line for the transformed data using statistical evidence.

   d. Which of these three lines explains more of the variation in the number of users in any year? Justify your answer.

5. It has been determined that the distribution of heights of 9th grade female students is a normal distribution. A sample of 20 9th grade female students indicated a mean height of 63.6 inches with a standard deviation of 4.5 inches.

   a. Would it be surprising if a 21st 9th grade female student was measured and found to have a height of 70 inches? Justify your answer statistically.

   b. Would it be surprising if another sample of 20 9th grade female students had a mean of 70 inches? Justify your answer statistically.

Part B
Question 6
Spend about 30 minutes on this part of the exam.
Percent of Section II grade—25

6. The data listed below document the class grade (Course) and the AP Calculus grade (AP) of 36 students. An asterisk (*) indicates a missing result and should be ignored.

Student	Course	AP	Student	Course	AP
1	88	3	19	79	1
2	85	2	20	88	2
3	97	5	21	83	3
4	95	3	22	88	3
5	87	3	23	77	1
6	88	3	24	87	3
7	90	3	25	83	2
8	93	4	26	95	3
9	101	5	27	89	3
10	*	2	28	82	2
11	*	2	29	80	3
12	81	2	30	91	3
13	95	4	31	77	1
14	78	1	32	87	1
15	80	1	33	81	1
16	84	1	34	89	3
17	90	1	35	79	1
18	*	3	36	91	3

a. Draw a scatter plot of these data

b. Determine the correlation coefficient and the regression line for these data.

c. Draw the residual plot for this fit.

d. Calculate s, the standard error of the estimate.

e. Test the hypothesis that ρ (the population correlation coefficient) equals 0. Show the test statistic and P-value. Interpret your results.

f. Based on your analysis, should you look for a non-linear model for these data? State your reasoning.

END OF EXAMINATION

MODEL EXAMINATION 3

SECTION I

Questions 1–40
Spend 90 minutes on this part of the exam.

Directions: The questions or incomplete statements below are each followed by five possible answers or completions. Select the choice that best answers the question or completes the statement.

1. A new grading program implemented in a high school gathers data on a number of items. Which of the following is categorical?

   (A) number of periods absent
   (B) subject with highest grade
   (C) total number of points in a math course
   (D) GPA
   (E) number of credits earned

2. The length of wait of a drive-up ATM can be best described as

   (A) a categorical variable.
   (B) an infinite discrete variable.
   (C) a finite continuous variable.
   (D) a statistic.
   (E) a parameter.

3. The scatterplot displays the ages and weights of a set of adults in a small manufacturing company. Which of the following best represents the distribution of the ages of the respondents displayed in the scatterplot?

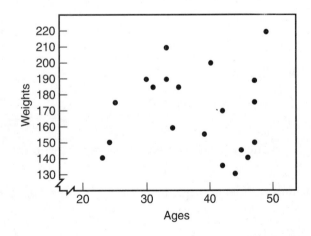

(A)
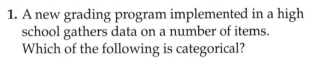

(B)
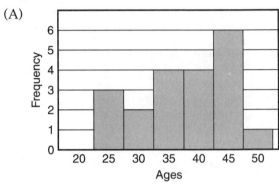

(C)
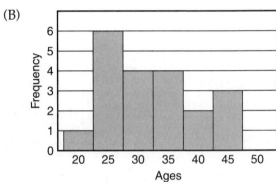
```
2 | 1 3 3 3 4
2 | 5 6 8 8
3 | 0 1
3 | 5 6 7 7 9
4 | 0
4 | 5 6 7
```
Leaf Unit = 1.0, n = 20

(D)
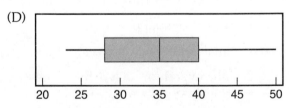

(E) None of these represents the distribution of the ages of the respondents.

4. Which of the following can be inferred from this cumulative frequency histogram of ages of residents in an apartment building in a local suburb?

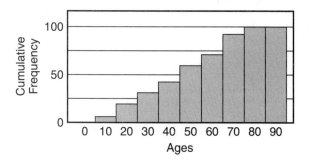

(A) The median age is about 60.
(B) The median age is about 20.
(C) The interquartile range is about 37.
(D) This building tends to appeal to younger tenants.
(E) None of these can be inferred.

5. Which of the following is resistant to extreme values?
   I. mean
   II. median
   III. mode
   IV. range

   (A) II, III
   (B) I, II, IV
   (C) II, III, IV
   (D) II only
   (E) All are resistant to extreme values.

6. Which of the following is *not* possible?

   (A) The standard deviation is greater than the mean.
   (B) The 5-number summary has 3 identical values.
   (C) The mean is negative and the standard deviation is positive.
   (D) The interquartile range is equal to the range.
   (E) All of these are possible.

7. Give the correct order of the following from least to greatest.
   I. 3rd quartile
   II. value at 70th percentile
   III. value with a z-score of 1

   (A) I, II, III
   (B) II, I, III
   (C) III, II, I
   (D) I, III, II
   (E) III, I, II

8. Which of the following graphs represents a normal distribution with a mean of 40 and a standard deviation of 8? Note that the window in each graph is X: [20, 60] by 10's; Y:[− .01,.1].

(A)
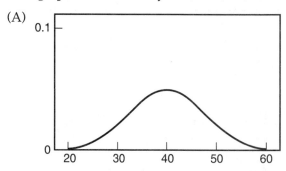

(B)
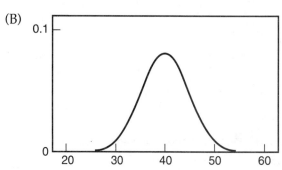

(C)
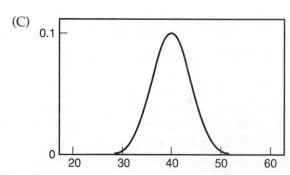

(D)
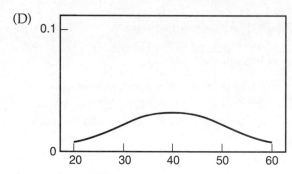

(E) None of the above.

GO ON TO THE NEXT PAGE

9. A pretzel company calculated that there is a mean of 72.5 broken pretzels in each production run with a standard deviation of 7.1. If the distribution is approximately normal, find the probability that there will be fewer than 60 broken pretzels in a run.

(A) 0
(B) .04
(C) .06
(D) .10
(E) None of these.

10. If r is close to 0, which of the following must be true?

(A) There is no association between the variables.
(B) The scatterplot shows no pattern.
(C) There is at least one outlier.
(D) There is a polynomial association between the variables.
(E) None of these must be true.

11. An outlier in a linear regression is identified by which of the following criteria?

(A) Both coordinates are outliers of their respective sets.
(B) The value is also influential.
(C) The deviation of the value from the grand mean is very large.
(D) The corresponding residual is large.
(E) None of these.

12. In the regression equation $y = b_0 + b_1x$, which of the following statements about b_0 is not always true?

(A) b_0 is the y-intercept of the line.
(B) b_0 is the value of the response variable when the explanatory variable has a value of 0.
(C) b_0 provides important contextual information about the relationship between the variables.
(D) b_0 depends on the values of b_1, $\bar{x}$, and $\bar{y}$.
(E) All of these are true.

13. A bivariate data set is transformed using $(x, y) \rightarrow (x, \ln y)$. If the correlation coefficient of $\ln y = b_0 + b_1x$ is 0.6, then the value of r^2 for the exponential model of the original data is approximately

(A) 0.
(B) 0.360
(C) $e^{0.6}$
(D) 1.825
(E) The value of r^2 cannot be determined.

14. Suppose a bivariate set of data {(heights, weights)} of 250 adult women had a correlation coefficient of 0.6. Suppose a woman had a height that was 1 standard deviation above the average height of the women in the set. Her predicted weight will be

(A) 1 standard deviation above the weight of the women in the set.
(B) greater than 1 standard deviation above the weight of the women of the set.
(C) less than 1 standard deviation above the weight of the women of the set.
(D) approximately equal to the average weight of the women of the set.
(E) The value cannot be determined.

15. Which of the following data sets has a correlation coefficient of -1?
   I. $\{(3, 7), (5, 5)\}$
   II. $\{(2, 5), (3, 18), (-6, -19)\}$
   III. $\{(x, y) \mid y = 2 - 4x\}$

(A) I only
(B) II only
(C) I and II
(D) I and III
(E) None of these.

16. If representation of all four classes in a high school sample is of importance, which of the following sampling designs is appropriate?

(A) simple random sample
(B) systematic sample
(C) quota sample
(D) stratified random sample
(E) None of these is appropriate.

17. If the persons in a sample are chosen to meet the demographics of the population, the sample will be

   (A) a quota sample.
   (B) a stratified sample.
   (C) a cluster sample.
   (D) a voluntary response sample.
   (E) None of these.

18. Blocking is a technique used to

   (A) assist with random selection.
   (B) reduce variation within experimental groups.
   (C) create stratified sample groups.
   (D) isolate the effect of the treatment.
   (E) None of these.

19. Randomization

   (A) is necessary in all experimental designs.
   (B) is not required in block design.
   (C) is not required in match pairs designs.
   (D) is for simple random samples.
   (E) reduces the error in the estimate of the mean.

20. Causation *cannot* be inferred for

   (A) valid randomized block designs.
   (B) valid completely randomized designs.
   (C) valid observational studies where n is large.
   (D) valid matched pairs designs.
   (E) any statistical study.

21. In a particular game of solitaire, the object of the game is to reduce the cards into one stack by moving stacks one to the left or three to the left. Stacks of cards are moved to the left if their top card matches either the suit or the number of the top card of a stack in the position listed above. The following outcomes and probabilities are given:

Number of Stacks	1	2	3	4	5 or more
Win/Lose	$1	$.50	$.25	$0	−$.25
Probability	.05	.10	.17	.28	.40

If you play this game 10 times, your net winnings should be approximately

(A) −0.48
(B) −0.12
(C) 0.43
(D) 0.74
(E) None of the above.

22. Let $H = B(100, .3)$ and $K = B(100, .6)$. Which of the following best describes a comparison of H and K?
   I. $\mu_H > \mu_K$
   II. $\mu_H < \mu_K$
   III. $\sigma_H > \sigma_K$
   IV. $\sigma_H < \sigma_K$

   (A) I and III
   (B) II and IV
   (C) II and III
   (D) I and IV
   (E) They are not comparable since they are discrete.

23. The probability that any individual catches a cold during the month of January is estimated to be .15. Assume that each person represents an independent experiment in which the probability of catching a cold is .15. Which of the following can be used to calculate the probability that no more than 3 out of 20 people will catch colds this January?

   (A) $P(0) + P(1) + P(2)$ where $x \sim Binomial(20, .15)$
   (B) $P(x \le 2.5)$ where
      $x \sim Normal(20(.15), \sqrt{20(.15)(.85)})$
   (C) $1 - P(x \ge 3.5)$ where
      $x \sim Normal(20(.15), \sqrt{20(.15)(.85)})$
   (D) $P(x = 3)$ where $x \sim Geometric(.15)$
   (E) None of these will calculate the desired probability.

24. Random digit tables and random number generators follow which of the following distributions?

   (A) uniform
   (B) chi-square
   (C) normal
   (D) t
   (E) binomial

GO ON TO THE NEXT PAGE

25. The following table displays the results of a sample of 99 in which the subjects indicated their favorite sport of three listed. The data are organized by favorite sport and age group.

AGE	FOOTBALL	BASEBALL	SOCCER
Over 40	15	8	7
Between 20 and 40	20	11	15
Under 20	8	7	8

What is the probability that a person chosen at random will be over 40 if he or she favors football?

(A) $\dfrac{15}{43}$

(B) $\dfrac{15}{30}$

(C) $\dfrac{15}{99}$

(D) $\dfrac{43}{99}$

(E) $\dfrac{30}{99}$

26. Which of the following items is not important when applying the Central Limit Theorem of the distribution of sample means?

(A) The mean and standard deviation of the population.
(B) The mean and standard deviation of the sample.
(C) The shape of the sampling distribution.
(D) The shape of the population distribution.
(E) All of these are important when working with the Central Limit Theorem.

27. The weight of a box of crackers labeled "Net Wt. 1 pound" has been found to be uniformly distributed on the interval of [15.1 ounces, 16.4 ounces]. Which of these best approximates the probability that a box chosen at random will weigh more than one pound?

(A) .769
(B) .692
(C) .534
(D) .308
(E) .154

28. What is the expected value of the discrete probability given in the table below?

Outcome	1	2	3	4	5	6
Probability	.1	.2	.3	.3	0	.1

(A) 3.0
(B) 3.2
(C) 3.5
(D) 3.8
(E) This is not a valid probability distribution.

29. Which of the following is a valid probability density function on the interval [0, 1]?

(A) $f(x) = .5x$
(B) $f(x) = x$
(C) $f(x) = 2x$
(D) $f(x) = 3 - 1.5x$
(E) None of these.

30. A sample of 100 engineers in a large consulting firm indicated that the mean amount of time they spend reading for pleasure each week is 1.4 hours. Three interns independently calculate different confidence intervals of the true mean amount of time for all of the engineers in the company. The confidence intervals of the interns were A: (.17, 2.63); B: (.554, 2.446); and C: (1.167, 1.633). Which conclusion is valid?

(A) All are calculated correctly with different levels of confidence.
(B) A and C have reasonable intervals but B does not.
(C) A and B have reasonable intervals but C does not.
(D) B and C have reasonable intervals but A does not.
(E) None of these intervals is reasonable.

31. It has always been thought that of the three major radio stations that service a large metropolitan area, station A had a 30% share of the market while stations B and C each enjoyed a 35% market share. A study of 75 randomly chosen radio listeners indicated that 30 people listen to station A, 25 listen to station B, and the rest listen to station C. Which of the following tests would be most appropriate in establishing that the market shares have changed?

(A) *t*-test of means
(B) two-sample proportion *z*-test
(C) matched pair *t*-test
(D) two-sample proportion *t*-test
(E) chi-square test

32. A test of independence for data organized in a two-way table relating number of siblings and number of family relocations is conducted using the chi-square distribution. The *P*-value of the test is .045. If $\alpha = .05$, then which of the following is a valid conclusion of the test?

(A) The mean is significant.
(B) We reject the hypothesis that the variables are dependent.
(C) We accept the hypothesis that the variables are independent.
(D) We have sufficient evidence to reject the hypothesis that the variables are independent.
(E) The variables are independent.

33. One of the formulas for the margin of error for the estimate of a population mean uses a critical value from the normal distribution corresponding to the level of confidence that we wish in the margin of error. Of those listed, which quantity is automatically required to use this formula?

(A) the appropriate *t*-value
(B) the null hypothesis
(C) the sample standard deviation
(D) an estimate of the population standard deviation
(E) the mean of the sample

34. Two investigators are arguing over what estimate to use to calculate the sample size for a study that they wish to conduct of a population proportion. They have agreed to the same margin of error and the same confidence level. However, investigator A wishes to use .30 for the estimated sample proportion based on his analysis of previous studies while investigator B wishes to use .41 as the estimate based on her analysis of the earlier studies and some evidence regarding trends in their industry. What is the ratio of the sample size of investigator A to the sample size of investigator B?

(A) .5
(B) .686
(C) .868
(D) .945
(E) 1.15

35. Which of the following is the reason that the tests for difference of proportions and difference of means include a requirement of independent samples?

(A) The sample proportions or means could be skewed if the samples were not independent.
(B) The tests do not apply to samples from the same population.
(C) The samples will not be simple random samples unless they are independent.
(D) Variances from independent samples can be combined easily whereas variances from dependent samples are not as easily combined.
(E) None of these is the reason for this requirement.

GO ON TO THE NEXT PAGE

36. The following table displays by gender the number of people in a bridge club who favor a particular political party.

PARTY	FEMALE	MALE
Democratic	20	30
Republican	35	25
Independent	45	50

If we were to do a chi-square test, which expression would calculate correctly the expected count of the number of males who favor the Democratic party?

(A) $\dfrac{30}{105} \times 50$

(B) $\dfrac{30}{205} \times 50$

(C) $\dfrac{50}{105} \times 205$

(D) $\dfrac{50}{205} \times 105$

(E) $\dfrac{30}{100} \times 105$

37. Part of a printout of a computer regression analysis of the effect of a change in a manufacturing process is shown. Output-A represents the output of stations before the change and Output-B represents the output of the stations after the change.

```
Predictor    Coef      StDev       T        P
Constant     81.29     88.30      0.92    0.366
Output-A    0.82728   0.05364    15.42    0.000

S = 314.6   R-Sq = 90.8%   R-Sq(adj) = 90.5%
```

What conclusion can be drawn from this printout?

(A) There is a 90.8% probability that the model contains all of the data points.
(B) The model contains 90.8% of the data points.
(C) The slope of the regression line is significant.
(D) The slope of the regression line is too close to 0 to conduct a test of significance.
(E) None of these is a valid conclusion.

38. One of your peers claims that boys do better in math classes than girls. Together you run two independent simple random samples and calculate the given summary statistics of the boys and the girls for comparable math classes. In Calculus, 15 boys had a mean percentage of 82.3 with standard deviation of 5.6 while 12 girls had a mean percentage of 81.2 with standard deviation of 6.7. Which of the following would be the most appropriate test for establishing whether boys do better in math classes than girls?

(A) two-sample z-test for means
(B) two-sample t-test for means
(C) chi-square test
(D) two-sample z-test for proportions
(E) None of these tests would be appropriate.

39. Which of the following best describes a Type I error for a hypothesis test?

(A) It is the probability of accepting H_0 when H_0 is false.
(B) It is the probability of rejecting H_0 when H_0 is true.
(C) It is the complement of a Type II error.
(D) It is the complement of the power of the test.
(E) None of these describes a Type I error.

40. A two-way table relates the favored country of origin of car and the income of a set of 100 respondents of a survey. If a χ^2 test of independence indicates a significant result, which of the following is *not* a valid fact about the test?

(A) The null hypothesis of the test is that the variables are independent.
(B) The χ^2 test is, by definition, one-tailed.
(C) The degrees of freedom of the test are found by multiplying the rows of the table and the columns of the table.
(D) The calculated value of χ^2 must exceed the critical value of the χ^2 distribution of the appropriate number of degrees of freedom.
(E) All of these statements are valid.

END OF SECTION I

Part A
Questions 1–5
Spend about 60 minutes on this part of the exam.
Percent of Section II grade—75

In order to receive full credit for your free-response questions, you must completely analyze each situation and clearly communicate your analyses and results. In order to earn partial credit when warranted, be sure to show enough work so that your reasoning process can be followed.

1. The following table summarizes the number of instances of each letter grade given in each of the four academic departments listed at the end of the spring semester at a large university:

	A	B	C	D	F
History	17	25	18	13	7
English	23	28	16	12	9
Science	8	20	42	15	8
Math	10	15	34	35	10

a. Complete this chart with the relative frequencies of the grade distributions for each department.

	A	B	C	D	F
History					
English					
Science					
Math					

b. Draw and label a segmented bar graph of the frequencies of the grade distributions for each department.

c. Describe the steps you would perform to verify whether the grade distributions depend on the department that assigns the grades. Do not perform the steps you describe.

2. An investigator is interested in determining the effectiveness of a new medicine for hypertension (high blood pressure). She desires that the focus of the study be the difference between current blood pressure levels and baseline levels for subjects that are differentiated by age.

a. Describe an experimental design by which the effectiveness of the medicine can be determined for the following age groups: 21–35, 36–50, and over 50. Draw a graphic to support your description.

b. Describe how you would analyze the data gathered by your design in part a.

GO ON TO THE NEXT PAGE

The investigator has determined that gender may also influence the outcome of the study.

  c. Describe how your design in part a could be changed to control for gender.

  d. Would your suggestion for analysis of the data for the design in part c be different from the suggestion you included in part b? Explain your answer.

3. In a recent publication, it was reported that the average highway gas mileage of tested models of a new car was 33.5 mpg and approximately normally distributed. A consumer group conducts its own tests on a simple random sample of 12 cars of this model and finds that the mean gas mileage for their vehicles is 31.6 mpg with a standard deviation of 3.4 mpg.

  a. Perform a test to determine if these data support the contention that the true mean gas mileage of this model of car is different from the published value ($\alpha = .05$).

  b. Perform a test to determine if these data support the contention that the true mean gas mileage of this model of car is less than the published value ($\alpha = .05$).

  c. Explain why the answers to part a and part b are different.

4. The following data are for intelligence-test (IT) scores, grade-point averages (GPA), and reading rates (RR) of 20 at-risk students.

IT	295	152	214	171	131	178	225	141	116	173
GPA	2.4	.6	.2	0	1	.6	1	.4	0	2.6
RR	41	18	45	29	28	38	25	26	22	37
IT	230	195	174	177	210	236	198	217	143	186
GPA	2.6	0	1.8	0	.4	1.8	.8	1	.2	2.8
RR	39	38	24	32	26	29	34	38	40	27

  a. Calculate the line of best fit that predicts GPA on the basis of IT scores.

  b. Calculate the line of best fit that predicts GPA on the basis of RR scores.

  c. Which of the two lines calculated in parts a and b best fits the data? Justify your answer citing statistical evidence of goodness of fit.

5. It has been determined that the amount of time that videotapes are returned late to a certain rental store is modeled by a uniform distribution from 0 to 4 days. Answer each question showing a figure and your work.

  a. What is the probability that a randomly selected videotape will be returned between 3 and 4 days late?

  b. What is the probability that a randomly selected videotape will be returned more than 1 day late?

Part B
Question 6
Spend about 30 minutes on this part of the exam.
Percent of Section II grade—25

6. Consider the set of heights {52, 65, 68, 69, 70} as the heights of a population of brothers in a particular family.

   a. Calculate the mean, standard deviation $(n - 1)$, and variance of the heights in the population.

   b. How many samples of two brothers' heights can be drawn from this population?

   c. Make a table similar to the one shown listing all of the possible samples of two brothers' heights.

SAMPLE	ELEMENTS	SAMPLE MEAN	SAMPLE STANDARD DEVIATION	SAMPLE VARIANCE
Means				

   d. Determine whether the sample mean, standard deviation, and/or variance is an *unbiased estimator* of the corresponding population parameter. *Note:* an estimator is unbiased if the mean of the estimates of all possible samples equals the value of the population parameter.

END OF EXAMINATION

MODEL EXAMINATION 4

SECTION I

Questions 1–40
Spend 90 minutes on this part of the exam.

Directions: The questions or incomplete statements below are each followed by five possible answers or completions. Select the choice that best answers the question or completes the statement.

1. In a test of gas mileage of new American cars, some of the variables included the following. Which one is a continuous variable?

    (A) number of cylinders in the engine
    (B) number of speeds in the transmission
    (C) whether the transmission is standard or automatic
    (D) whether the car is front-wheeled or rear-wheeled drive
    (E) None of these is a continuous variable.

2. Given the following box plots of ages of viewers of 3 local TV stations during one primetime slot, which of the following is a valid conclusion?

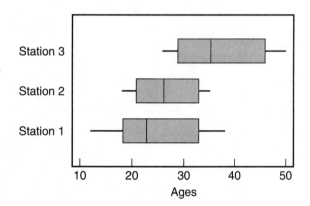

    (A) Station 2 appeals to a wide age group.
    (B) Teenagers watch more TV than any other age group.
    (C) If you owned a skateboard factory, you would be wise to advertise on Station 2.
    (D) A program about events in the 1960s would probably not do well on Station 1.
    (E) None of these is a valid conclusion.

3. Which of the following plots is not appropriate for categorical data?

    (A) dot plot
    (B) bar graph
    (C) pie graph
    (D) segmented bar graph
    (E) All of these are appropriate.

4. If 10 is added to the maximum value and 10 is subtracted from the minimum value of a data set, which of the following is true?

    (A) The mean and median are unchanged.
    (B) The mean changes but the median does not change.
    (C) The median changes but the mean does not change.
    (D) The effect on the mean and median cannot be determined without knowing the other data values.
    (E) None of these is true.

5. If 10 is added to each value of a data set, which of the following is true?

    (A) Standard deviation remains unchanged.
    (B) Standard deviation increases by 10.
    (C) Standard deviation increases by $\sqrt{10}$.
    (D) Standard deviation will exceed the range.
    (E) None of these is true.

6. A distribution with mean 47 has a data value of 32 that corresponds to a z-score of -1.5. The value of the standard deviation is:

    (A) -15
    (B) 1
    (C) 10
    (D) 15
    (E) The value cannot be determined.

7. Which of the following graphs could *not* be a density function?

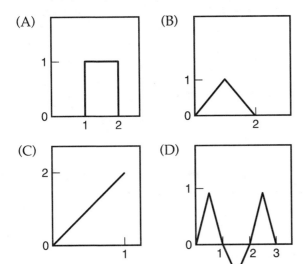

(A)

(B)

(C)

(D)

(E) All could be density functions.

8. For a typical week, a national airline finds that the differences (actual − scheduled) from scheduled arrival times are normally distributed with a mean of approximately 9.2 minutes and a standard deviation of 10.8 minutes. Find the probability that the next flight will arrive early.

(A) 0
(B) 0.1
(C) 0.2
(D) 0.3
(E) 0.5

9. Suppose the bivariate set (age, income) from 50 men has a correlation of 0.7 and a bivariate set with the same variables for 30 women has a correlation coefficient of 0.5, then the correlation coefficient of the combined set

(A) can be found by $\left(\frac{5}{8}\right)(0.7) + \left(\frac{3}{8}\right)(0.5)$

(B) is 0.6
(C) is less than 0.5
(D) lies between 0.5 and 0.7
(E) cannot be determined from this information.

10. If two bivariate sets of data have the same least squares regression line, then which of the following must be true?

(A) They have the same r.
(B) They have the same r^2.
(C) They model the same data.
(D) They will either both be significant or non-significant.
(E) None of these must be true.

11. In the regression equation, $y = b_0 + b_1 x$, what does b_1 represent?

(A) the slope of the regression
(B) the unit change of the response variable with respect to the explanatory variable
(C) information regarding the direction of the relationship
(D) (A), (B), and (C) are all true.
(E) None of these is true.

12. Suppose a bivariate set {(time (days), bacterial count (1,000s))} appears exponential and has a correlation coefficient of 0.4. Suppose also the transformation $(x, y) \to (x, \ln y)$ results in a least squares regression line $\ln(\text{count}) = 2.15(\text{time})$. The value of r^2 for the exponential model is approximately

(A) 0.16
(B) 0.25
(C) 0.51
(D) 0.63
(E) The value of r^2 cannot be determined.

13. Given: $r = -0.47$, $\bar{x} = 19.5$, $\bar{y} = 201.5$, $s_x = 6.1$, $s_y = 15.7$, the least squares regression line has the equation:

(A) $y = 225.07 + 1.209x$
(B) $y = 225.07 - 1.209x$
(C) $y = 177.92 + 1.209x$
(D) $y = 177.92 - 1.209x$
(E) None of these.

GO ON TO THE NEXT PAGE

14. If (12, 60) is an influential point for the regression line $y = 7.908 + 4.098x$, then which of the following must be true?

 (A) removal of (12, 60) will improve r.
 (B) removal of (12, 60) will not affect r.
 (C) removal of (12, 60) will change the value of the slope of the regression line.
 (D) (12, 60) has a large residual.
 (E) None of these.

15. The residual value of $(\bar{x}, \bar{y})$ in a linear regression is

 (A) negative
 (B) 0
 (C) positive
 (D) dependent on the value of r
 (E) The value cannot be determined.

16. There are approximately 8,000 high schools in a particular region. A simple random sample of 100 of the schools is selected. Within each school, a simple random sample of 5 teachers is selected and interviewed. Which best describes this sampling design?

 (A) simple random sample
 (B) systematic sample
 (C) quota sample
 (D) stratified random sample
 (E) None of these is correct.

17. A TV news magazine runs a survey on a controversial issue by asking viewers to call one of two 900 numbers: one signifying yes, the other no. The results of this survey

 (A) may exhibit non-response bias.
 (B) represent a valid sample of the viewing population.
 (C) may exhibit substantial variation.
 (D) represent a valid sample since conflicting biases will cancel out.
 (E) None of these.

18. Three brands of popcorn are to be tested in an experiment to determine the best brand for percent of kernels popped. Two hundred kernels of each are to be placed in three air poppers and heated until there are no pops. The unpopped kernels are then counted and compared. How might the investigator control for the differences due to the three air poppers?

 (A) Use a random number generator to match the brand of popcorn to one of the poppers.
 (B) Run three iterations of the experiment with 200 kernels of each brand popped in each popper and count the number of unpopped from the three trials.
 (C) Randomly mix the three brands and divide the mix evenly into each popper.
 (D) Increase the number of kernels to increase the sample size and thereby reduce variation.
 (E) Block for brand of poppers and randomly assign kernels from each brand to each popper.

19. A study to determine whether right- or left-handed men are more chivalrous to women was conducted in the following way. A simple random sample of all restaurants without doormen in a town was taken. Observers were instructed to identify one right-handed male with a woman and one left-handed male with a woman in their restaurant. The observers were there to notice whether, upon leaving, the men opened the door for their female companion. Data from sites were then compiled and a two-way table was generated. Which of the following sources of error was present in this study?

 (A) Results could be confounded by types of restaurants.
 (B) Response bias was not controlled .
 (C) This was a voluntary response sample.
 (D) This was a convenience sample.
 (E) None of these errors occurred in this study.

20. Suppose that, based on many observations, the probability outcomes of shooting an arrow at a target are as given in the table:

Outcome	Bull's Eye	1st Circle	2nd Circle	3rd Circle	Miss
Probability	.12	.22	.53	.10	.03
Score	4	3	2	1	0

If each outcome gains the archer the number of points listed as Score in the table, we would expect the arrow to hit

(A) bull's eye
(B) 1st circle
(C) 2nd circle
(D) 3rd circle
(E) miss the target

21. Which of the following best describes the effect on a binomial distribution if the number of trials is held constant but the probability of success increases?

(A) The mean and standard deviation both increase.
(B) The mean increases but standard deviation decreases.
(C) The mean decreases but standard deviation increases.
(D) The mean and standard deviation both decrease.
(E) The mean increases but standard deviation can increase or decrease.

22. Suppose a basketball player has a probability of scoring of .79 on each of his free throw attempts. Assuming that this probability does not change, he would like to compute the probability that he will score on 1 or more of his next 4 attempts. He should use:

(A) binomial techniques
(B) geometric techniques
(C) normal curve techniques
(D) normal opposed to binomial
(E) None of these.

23. The probability that any individual catches a cold during the month of January is estimated to be .15. Assume that each person represents an independent experiment in which the probability of catching a cold is .15. Which of the following statements is true about the calculation of the probability that no more than 3 of 20 people will catch a cold this January?

(A) The probability can be calculated using the normal approximation, using $Normal(20(.15), \sqrt{20(.15)(.85)})$.
(B) The probability can be calculated using the normal approximation, using $Normal(0, 1)$.
(C) The probability can be calculated using the normal approximation, using $Normal(20, .15)$.
(D) The probability cannot be calculated using the normal approximation.
(E) The probability can be calculated either by the formula for $Binomial(20, .15)$ or the normal approximation, $Normal(3, \sqrt{2.55})$.

24. Which of the following is *not* a reason to simulate results?

(A) A simulation can give us insight into complex theoretical results.
(B) A simulation can help us investigate situations that we do not wish to happen in reality.
(C) A simulation can be cheaper to conduct than deriving theoretical probability results.
(D) A simulation allows a researcher to investigate a hypothesis before attempting to prove it.
(E) All of these are valid reasons for simulation.

25. A manufacturing company has three suppliers for parts for its assembly line. The proportions of parts from suppliers A, B, and C are .4, .3, and .3 respectively. The proportion of defective parts from suppliers A, B, and C are .03, .05, and .02 respectively. What is the probability that a defective part, chosen at random, came from supplier A?

(A) .182
(B) .364
(C) .456
(D) .818
(E) None of these.

GO ON TO THE NEXT PAGE

26. Which of the following statements is the reason that the Central Limit Theorem is very important in statistics?

(A) It applies for any sample size as long as the population is normal.
(B) It applies for any population distribution as long as the population mean is known.
(C) It applies for any population distribution as long as the sample size is large.
(D) It applies for any sample as long as the population distribution is known.
(E) None of these is the reason for the importance of the Central Limit Theorem.

27. Which of the following is *not* true about uniform distributions?

(A) The interval over which the distribution is defined cannot contain negative values.
(B) The interval over which the distribution is defined must have finite length.
(C) The probability density function must equal a positive constant.
(D) Probability is calculated as the area of an appropriate rectangle.
(E) All of these statements are true.

28. Of those listed, which of the following is the only valid difference between the binomial probability distribution and the geometric probability distribution?

(A) The binomial is discrete while the geometric is continuous.
(B) The binomial has only a finite set of values while the geometric has an infinite set of values.
(C) The binomial is calculated using areas while the geometric is calculated using sums.
(D) The binomial does not have a value at $x = 0$ while the geometric does.
(E) None of these is valid.

29. Consider the function $f(x) = \frac{1}{6}x + \frac{5}{6}$ defined on the interval $[1, 3]$. Which of the following statements is true regarding this function?

(A) $f(x)$ could not be a continuous probability density function.

(B) $P(1 \leq x \leq 2) = \frac{1}{2}$

(C) $P(1 \leq x \leq 2) = \frac{5}{6}$

(D) $P(1 \leq x \leq 2) = \frac{7}{12}$

(E) $P(1 \leq x \leq 2) = \frac{11}{12}$

30. A random sample of 55 senior citizens in a retirement community indicated that 42 felt that there were not enough overnight excursions available through the community. Which of the following is a valid conclusion based on this information?

(A) The 95% confidence interval is approximately (.651, .876).
(B) If 3 more seniors had voted that there were not enough trips, the width of the 95% confidence interval would decrease by approximately .02.
(C) There is sufficient information to calculate a confidence interval.
(D) This situation does not satisfy the assumptions and therefore, a confidence interval should not be calculated.
(E) None of these is a valid conclusion.

31. In 1990, a random sample of 100 households in a particular suburb indicated that 65 of the households sampled had more than one person who was employed on a full-time basis outside of the home. In 1998, another random sample of 100 households was conducted and it found that 73 of the households sampled had more than one person who was employed on a full-time basis outside the home. Which of the following tests would be most appropriate in establishing that there had been an increase in the percentage of households with more than one person employed on a full-time basis outside of the home during the span of those 8 years?

(A) t-test of means
(B) two-sample proportion z-test
(C) matched pair t-test
(D) two-sample proportion t-test
(E) chi-square test

32. In a test of the equality of the proportions of men and women who take prescription drugs every day, the null hypothesis is that the difference is 0. If the P-value indicates that the null hypothesis should be rejected, which of the following statements is *not* justified?

(A) The test was two-tailed.
(B) The test statistic is in the rejection region for the test.
(C) The test statistic is more extreme than the critical value of the sampling distribution for the appropriate level of significance.
(D) The conclusion does not address the truth of the alternative hypothesis.
(E) The P-value indicates that it is unlikely that a sample similar to the one in question would have this difference or a more extreme difference if the actual difference is 0.

33. A news program stated that one of the candidates for mayor of a certain city commissioned a popularity study to ascertain his chances of re-election. The report claimed that 55% of the voters randomly sampled in this study favored the incumbent; it also detailed that there was a margin of error of 3% with 95% confidence. Which of the following best describes the meaning of this margin of error?

(A) 3% of the time, the result of 55% will be wrong.
(B) There is a probability of 3% that the sample is biased in favor of the incumbent.
(C) There is a probability of 97% that 55% is the true value.
(D) It is likely that the true percentage is within $\pm 1.96 \times 3\%$ of the 55%.
(E) It is likely that the true percentage is within 3% of the 55%.

34. The sample size for a proposed study is calculated using the most conservative estimate of the sample proportion and a margin of error of 3% with 95% confidence. Which of the following numbers best approximates the factor by which the original sample size would have to be multiplied in order to reduce the margin of error to 1% with 95% confidence?

(A) 3
(B) 4
(C) 8
(D) 9
(E) 16

35. The decision between a z-test for a population mean or a t-test for a population mean is based on

(A) the sample size.
(B) whether the samples are simple random samples or not.
(C) the shape of the distribution from which the samples are taken.
(D) the size of the standard deviation of the sample.
(E) None of the above.

36. A two-way table consists of 4 rows and 5 columns of data. If the assumptions for a test of independence are satisfied, which of the following best approximates the critical value of the chi-square test at the 5% level of significance?

(A) 21.03
(B) 28.87
(C) 31.41
(D) 34.17
(E) There is not sufficient information to determine the critical value.

37. A computer printout of a regression analysis of two fields is shown below:

```
The regression equation is
Field-B = 140 + 0.793 Field-A

Predictor     Coef      StDev        T         P
Constant     140.0     129.9      1.08     0.292
Field-A     0.7933    0.2110      3.76     0.001

S = 341.5   R-Sq = 37.1%   R-Sq(adj) = 34.4%
```

The value S in the report is

(A) the standard deviation of the explanatory variables.
(B) the standard deviation of the response variables.
(C) related to the sum of the squares of the residuals.
(D) related to the sum of the deviations of the y's from the average y value.
(E) not explained by any of these.

GO ON TO THE NEXT PAGE

38. An experiment is developed to test the effectiveness of a new fertilizer for plant growth. Randomly selected shoots are placed either in a control flat or in a treatment flat. The control flat is supplied with water only, while the treatment flat is given water and the new fertilizer. The percent of growth for each group is computed after three weeks and the mean percentage of growth is reported. Sixteen plants in the control flat had a mean percentage of .78 while 16 plants in the treatment flat had a mean proportion of .83. Which of the following would be the most appropriate test for establishing the effectiveness of the new fertilizer?

(A) two-sample z-test for means
(B) two-sample t-test for means
(C) chi-square test
(D) two-sample z-test for proportions
(E) None of these tests would be appropriate.

39. A hypothesis test on a null hypothesis of $\mu_0 = 50.5$ is conducted at the 5% level of significance. The value of β is calculated and found to be .12 for an alternative hypothesis of $\mu_a = 52.25$. Which of the following statements is *not* true about β?

(A) β is the probability of accepting H_0 when H_0 is false.
(B) The power of the test is .88.
(C) β is the probability of a Type II error.
(D) β is the complement of the probability of a Type I error.
(E) All of these statements are true about β.

40. A company claims that their battery lasts 52.5 hours in continuous use in a flashlight. A simple random sample of batteries yields a sample mean life of 48.9 hours with a standard deviation of 5.2 hours. A computer calculates a test statistic of $t = -1.832$ and a P-value of .1167. If the test utilizes the degrees of freedom of 71, then the best estimate of the sample size is

(A) 71
(B) 72
(C) 73
(D) 74
(E) There is not sufficient information to determine the number of batteries in the sample.

END OF SECTION I

Model Examination 4

CONTINUED

SECTION II

Part A
Questions 1–5

Spend about 60 minutes on this part of the exam.
Percent of Section II grade—75

In order to receive full credit for your free-response questions, you must completely analyze each situation and clearly communicate your analyses and results. In order to earn partial credit when warranted, be sure to show enough work so that your reasoning process can be followed.

1. A simple random sample of 50 adults who live in a large urban area were asked to indicate the number of parking tickets that each had received over the last 5 years. A stem and leaf plot of the data is shown below.

1	0 0 1
1	2 2 3 3 3
1	4 4 4 4 4 4 5 5 5
1	6 7 7 7
1	8 9 9 9
2	0 0 1 1 1
2	2 3
2	4 4 5 5 5
2	6 6 6 7 7
2	8 8 8 8 8 9 9 9

Leaf Unit = 1.0, n = 50

a. Draw and label a sketch of the box plot of these data.

b. Compare the box to the stem-and-leaf plot. Explain your answer.

c. Based on the given stem and leaf plot and the box plot you sketched in part a, describe the relation between the mean and the median of these data.

2. A research department at a local university has decided to study the effect on blood pressure of drinking 4 or more cups of caffeinated coffee per day. Assuming that the researcher wishes to control for gender, suggest a design using the methodology specified:

a. an observational study

b. a controlled experiment

Assume that each methodology is carried out and the results indicate that people who drink 4 or more cups of caffeinated coffee per day have high blood pressure. State a reasonable conclusion for each methodology:

c. an observational study

d. a controlled experiment

GO ON TO THE NEXT PAGE

3. The following table displays the preferences of ice cream flavor of three age groups of young adults based on a large study.

	Chocolate	Vanilla	Strawberry
16–18	130	110	74
19–21	105	135	80
22–24	93	154	78

a. Based on these data, what is the probability that a young adult chosen at random will be in the age group 22–24 and prefer chocolate ice cream?

b. Based on these data, what is the probability that a young adult chosen at random will be in the 22–24 age group given that the person selected prefers chocolate ice cream?

c. Is there a relationship between age group and ice cream flavor preference? Provide statistical evidence to support your answer.

4. A machine which can be run at different speeds produces motor parts of which a certain number are defective. The following table was assembled since some of the engineers feel that the number of defectives produced per hour depends on the speed of the machine.

Speed (rps)	8	12	14	16
Defectives per hour	5	8	9	11

A regression analysis was run using a computer and produced the following partial printout of results:

```
Predictor    Coef      StDev       T        P
Constant   -0.8571    0.6357    -1.35    0.310
Speed       0.72857   0.04949   14.72    0.005

S = 0.2928  R-Sq = 99.1%  R-Sq(adj) = 98.6%
```

a. What is the equation of the regression line that predicts the number of defectives per hour based on the speed of the machine?

b. Determine if the correlation between run speed and number of defectives is significant at the 5% level.

5. An insurance company that specializes in renter's coverage anticipates that it will have to pay benefits to its customers in the amounts listed in the table below. In addition, it estimates the probabilities of each payment:

Benefit ($)	500	1,000	2,000	5,000	10,000
Probability	.10	.35	.40	.10	.05

a. Does this table specify a probability distribution? Explain the reasons for your answer.

b. How much would you estimate that the company can expect to pay for a claim?

c. What is the standard deviation of the estimate in part b?

d. Explain the meaning of the standard deviation in part c.

Model Examination 4
CONTINUED
SECTION II

Part B
Question 6
Spend about 30 minutes on this part of the exam.
Percent of Section II grade—25

6. A small city has two hospitals, A and B. Typically, hospital A attends to 20 emergencies per day while hospital B attends to 50 emergencies per day. Assume that the proportion of emergencies that are life-threatening is approximately .3 at each hospital.

a. At which hospital would you find it more likely that the percentage of life-threatening emergencies on a given day is at least 40%? Explain the reasons for your answer.

b. Use the given random digits table to simulate this event to determine which hospital is more likely to equal or exceed 40% life-threatening emergencies. Show clearly how your simulation operates for each hospital. State the results of your simulation.

Hospital A

9435974025	9083188611	4668782925	1470195054	0580964187
3381121120	4399198753	3936252594	9546634112	0034026187
9807010099	5189983326	2209784733	3694814382	0078387869
9351587791	1080114624	0062633066	5489861799	8555803142
9770842465	2783088265	2752142947	1217901355	0525898067
2237931570	1256556214	2111829173	0763515019	7220777198
2881701368	3781148461	8123118520	5080954298	4662442672

Hospital B

9435974025	9083188611	4668782925	1470195054	0580964187
3381121120	4399198753	3936252594	9546634112	0034026187
9807010099	5189983326	2209784733	3694814382	0078387869
9351587791	1080114624	0062633066	5489861799	8555803142
9770842465	2783088265	2752142947	1217901355	0525898067
2237931570	1256556214	2111829173	0763515019	7220777198
2881701368	3781148461	8123118520	5080954298	4662442672

c. Compare the result of your simulation to the result of your conclusion in part a.

END OF EXAMINATION

MODEL EXAMINATION 5

SECTION I

Questions 1–40
Spend 90 minutes on this part of the exam.

Directions: The questions or incomplete statements below are each followed by five possible answers or completions. Select the choice that best answers the question or completes the statement.

1. In their application to serve a local airport, an airline supplies the following projections. Which of these are categorical?

   (A) projected number of flights per week
   (B) projected number of passengers per flight
   (C) projected cities to be connected
   (D) projected gross weight of aircraft
   (E) projected advertising volume in local media

2. Using the following code, identify which plot would be useful to determine the center of a distribution.

   I. histogram
   II. dot plot
   III. stem plot
   IV. box plot

   (A) I and II only
   (B) I, II, and III only
   (C) I, III, and IV only
   (D) IV only
   (E) All of the plots would be useful.

3. Which description is appropriate for this graph?

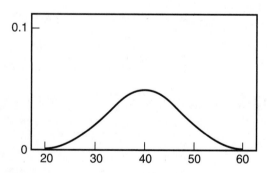

   (A) skewed left and right
   (B) inverse mound-shaped
   (C) bimodal
   (D) symmetric
   (E) granular

4. If each value of a data set is multiplied by 10, which of the following occurs?

   (A) The mean is unchanged.
   (B) The mean is multiplied by 10.
   (C) The mean is multiplied by 100.
   (D) The mean is multiplied by $\sqrt{10}$.
   (E) The mean is multiplied by 0.1.

5. If each value of a data set is increased by 10% then the standard deviation will

   (A) remain unchanged.
   (B) increase by a factor of 0.1.
   (C) increase by 10.
   (D) increase by a factor of 0.01.
   (E) The effect cannot be determined.

6. A distribution had a mean of 29 and a standard deviation of 5. Which of the following statements must be true?

   (A) Percentiles should be calculated using z-scores only if the distribution is mound-shaped and symmetric.
   (B) The z-score of the median is 0.
   (C) The distribution is mound-shaped and symmetric.
   (D) The variable is discrete.
   (E) The box plot has outliers.

7. In order to calculate $P(-1.5 \le z \le 0.5)$ using tables where z is a value from the standard normal distribution, which of the following expressions could be used?

   (A) $P(z \le 0.5) - P(z \le -1.5)$
   (B) $P(z \le -1.5) + P(z \le 0.5)$
   (C) $P(z \ge -1.5) \times P(z \le 0.5)$
   (D) $4 \times P(z \le -1.5)$
   (E) None of these can be used.

8. If the probability is .06 that a student will score 90 or above on a test whose mean is 78, what is the approximate standard deviation of the distribution of scores?

(A) 0.77
(B) 4.74
(C) 7.7
(D) 47.4
(E) None of these.

9. A bivariate set has a value of $r^2 = 0.81$. Which is an appropriate conclusion?

(A) $r = 0.9$
(B) 81% of the data is usable.
(C) There is an 81% chance that the regression line will fit the data.
(D) 81% of the variation between the variables is accounted for by the model.
(E) None of these is appropriate.

10. An influential point in a regression setting must

(A) have an x-coordinate that is an outlier.
(B) be a point whose deletion from the data set would have a substantial impact on the regression.
(C) have a large residual.
(D) have both x- and y-coordinates as outliers in the respective sets.
(E) None of these must be true.

11. If a bivariate set of data has the least squares regression equation $\hat{y} = 10.2 + 4.15x$, which of the following must be true?

(A) The standard deviation of the values of the response variable must be greater than the standard deviation of the explanatory variable.
(B) The grand mean has an approximate value of (11.2, 56.7).
(C) The correlation coefficient is 0.72.
(D) The line contains at least 51% of the data points.
(E) None of these must be true.

12. Suppose a data set is transformed using $(x, y) \rightarrow (x, \ln y)$ and a least squares linear regression procedure is performed on the transformed data. If the residual plot of this regression shows a curved pattern, which of the following is an appropriate conclusion?

(A) A quadratic model should be used with the original data.
(B) A square root transformation should be applied to the transformed data.
(C) The correlation coefficient of the set of transformed data is 0.
(D) The exponential transformation is not appropriate.
(E) None of these is appropriate.

13. After data are collected from an agricultural experiment, suppose a transformation is performed on the bivariate set (inches of water, total plant growth). If the linear regression of the transformed data has the equation $\ln(\text{growth}) = 0.7 + 1.93 \ln(\text{water})$, the regression model of the original data is

(A) growth $= 0.7 + 1.93(\text{water})$
(B) growth $= 2.01 + 1.93(\text{water})$
(C) growth $= (2.01)(1.93)^{\text{water}}$
(D) growth $= 2.01(\text{water})^{1.93}$
(E) None of these.

14. The cost of a long distance phone call depends on many factors. A least squares regression relating cost to time on line determines an equation of cost $= 4.70 + 0.15(\text{time})$. Which is *not* correct?

(A) Long distance service is predicted to cost 15 cents per minute.
(B) The monthly fixed cost of long distance service is, on average, $4.70.
(C) Adding another phone will raise cost 0.15.
(D) r^2 cannot be determined from this information.
(E) All of these are correct.

15. A value in a bivariate set of data is an influential point if

(A) it has a large residual.
(B) it is an outlier with respect to the values of the response variables.
(C) its removal creates a substantial change in r.
(D) its removal changes the sign of r.
(E) None of these.

GO ON TO THE NEXT PAGE

16. A teacher chooses the students in the first row to display homework problems on the chalkboard. This is an example of

(A) a simple random sample
(B) a quota sample
(C) a cluster sample
(D) a voluntary response sample
(E) None of these.

17. A TV commercial states that 4 out of 5 doctors recommend product A for headaches. Your colleague claims that the following three items of information are necessary to evaluate the claim. With which do you agree?
   I. Sample size
   II. Sampling frame
   III. Sample design

(A) I only
(B) I and II only
(C) I, II, and III
(D) II and III
(E) I and III

18. Matched pairs designs can be used in all but which situation?

(A) Two measurements of the same variable are taken on each subject.
(B) On each subject, a measurement is taken before treatment and another measurement is taken after treatment.
(C) There is a natural pairing between units in the two samples.
(D) A difference between means is the quantity of interest.
(E) A relationship between the elements of each sample can be demonstrated.

19. A simple random sample of vegetarians aged 18–20 at a university indicated that 40% exhibited a calcium deficiency in their diets when compared to the recommended levels of daily calcium requirements. Which of the following is a valid conclusion?

(A) Vegetarians aged 18–20 have calcium deficiencies.
(B) Vegetarians aged 18–20 should take calcium supplements.
(C) Vegetarian diets cause calcium deficiencies in 40% of vegetarians.
(D) A non-vegetarian diet provides more calcium.
(E) None of these is a valid conclusion.

20. A company must make a decision between two marketing strategies. The data on each plan are listed in the tables:

PLAN A

Predicted increase	$10,000	$20,000	$50,000	$100,000
Probability	.20	.40	.25	.15

PLAN B

Predicted increase	$10,000	$20,000	$50,000	$100,000
Probability	.18	.40	.28	.14

The company decides to choose the strategy that has the greatest expected return. Which of the following lists the best strategy and the difference between the strategies' expectations?

(A) A, $300
(B) A, $500
(C) B, $300
(D) B, $500
(E) Cannot be determined.

21. Let $M = B(50, .9)$ and $N = B(50, .1)$. Which of the following best describes a comparison of M and N?
   I. $\mu_M > \mu_N$
   II. $\mu_M < \mu_N$
   III. $\sigma_M = \sigma_N$
   IV. $\sigma_M < \sigma_N$

(A) I and III
(B) II and IV
(C) II and III
(D) I and IV
(E) I only

22. A fast food restaurant has a give-away promotion. The restaurant claims that the probability of winning a prize on either the first or second visit is .40. What can we conclude about the probability of winning on the first visit?

(A) The probability is less than .40.
(B) The probability is equal to .40.
(C) The probability is greater than .40.
(D) The probability is equal to $\sqrt{.40}$.
(E) No conclusions can be drawn.

23. To approximate $P(y \geq 10)$ in *Binomial*(50, .4) we could use all of the following expressions *except* which one?

(A) $P(y \geq 9.5)$ where $y \sim Normal(20, \sqrt{12})$
(B) $1 - P(y \leq 9.5)$ where $y \sim Normal(20, \sqrt{12})$
(C) $P(y \geq 9.5)$ where $y \sim Normal(0, 1)$
(D) $P(y \geq -3.03)$ where $y \sim Normal (0, 1)$
(E) All of these can be used.

24. Which of the following statements is *not* true about the relation between simulation and actual probability?

(A) As the number of trials increases, the simulated results will approach the actual probability of interest.
(B) To get an accurate approximation of an actual probability using simulation, one must take care as to whether the selection is made with or without replacement.
(C) The accuracy of a simulation depends on how well the simulation matches the actual phenomenon of interest.
(D) Calculation of the actual probability is always preferable to the running of a simulation.
(E) All of these are true statements about the relation between simulation and probability.

25. A manufacturing company has three suppliers for parts for its assembly line. The proportions of parts from suppliers A, B, and C are .4, .3, and .3 respectively. The proportion of defective parts from suppliers A, B, and C are .03, .05, and .02 respectively. What is the probability that a defective part, chosen at random, came from either supplier A or B?

(A) .182
(B) .364
(C) .456
(D) .818
(E) None of these.

26. A sample of 100 students is taken from a normal population and it is found that the mean of the number of hours they work at part-time jobs during the school year is 12.23 hours with a standard deviation of 4.52 hours. Which of the following is a valid conclusion based on the application of the Central Limit Theorem?

(A) The sampling distribution is normal regardless of the shape of the population distribution.
(B) The sampling distribution is approximately normal.
(C) The mean of the population is exactly 12.23 hours.
(D) The standard deviation of the sampling distribution is 4.52 hours.
(E) The Central Limit Theorem does not tell us any of these.

27. As part of a weight-loss program in a private men's club, all members were weighed at one of their monthly meetings. It was found that their weights were uniformly distributed over the interval (in pounds) [184, 246]. Based on these facts, which of the following best approximates the percent of the members whose weight was over 200 pounds?

(A) 25%
(B) 50%
(C) 65%
(D) 75%
(E) 80%

28. A new game is introduced in a 2nd grade class to encourage the students to practice their addition facts. The game uses a spinner that has three regions, labeled 1, 3, and 5 respectively. The areas of the regions are 40%, 20%, and 40% respectively. In each round, each child is given a turn to spin the needle three times and add the results. The child with the highest correct total wins the round. If you were to advise the teacher as to what sum she should expect to see from each student, your advice would be which of the following?

(A) 3
(B) 6
(C) 9
(D) 12
(E) Since this is a game of chance, there is no way to predict what to expect.

GO ON TO THE NEXT PAGE

29. Consider the function $f(x)$ in the sketch below defined on the interval $[-1, 1]$. Note that the height of the triangle is 1. Which of the following statements is true regarding this function?

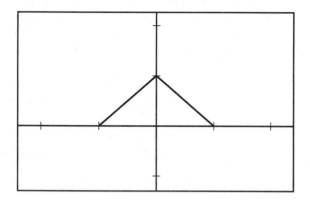

(A) $f(x)$ could not be a continuous probability density function.

(B) $P(-1 \leq x \leq .5) = \dfrac{2}{3}$

(C) $P(-1 \leq x \leq .5) = \dfrac{3}{4}$

(D) $P(-1 \leq x \leq .5) = \dfrac{7}{8}$

(E) $P(-1 \leq x \leq .5) = \dfrac{11}{12}$

30. An AP Statistics class performs a simulation in which each of the students rolls a die 10 times and calculates the mean and standard deviation of the values that occur. Based on these values, each student computes the 99% confidence interval of the mean. Which of the following statements is a valid conclusion from this simulation?

(A) There is a 99% probability that any one of the confidence intervals will contain the true mean of the values.

(B) There is a 99% probability that all of the confidence intervals will contain the true mean of the values.

(C) Approximately 99% of the confidence intervals calculated by the students will contain the true mean of the values.

(D) Confidence comes from the 99% probability that the true mean will be in any of the intervals.

(E) None of these statements is to be expected.

31. A random sample of 45 sophomore girls at an urban high school indicated that they worked an average of 33.5 hours per week out of school. The standard deviation of their responses was 4.5 hours. The school claims that their students work an average of no more than 25 hours per week with a standard deviation of no more than 2 hours. Which of the following tests would be most appropriate in establishing that the school's estimate is low?

(A) one-sample z-test of means
(B) one-sample proportion z-test
(C) one-sample t-test of means
(D) one-sample proportion t-test
(E) chi-square test

32. The P-value of a two-tailed t-test for a population mean is .064 when the level of significance is .05. Which of the following statements are true?
   I. A one-sided t-test using the same data would indicate a significant result.
   II. The mean in the null hypothesis is true.
   III. Even if the test indicates a significant result, it may not indicate an important result in the context of the problem.

(A) I only
(B) I and II
(C) I, II, and III
(D) I and III
(E) III only

33. Which of the following is true about the margin of error in a sample?
   I. The margin of error depends on the level of confidence desired in the sample results.
   II. The margin of error depends on the sample mean that is found in the sample data.
   III. The margin of error decreases as sample size increases.

(A) I only
(B) I and II
(C) I and III
(D) III only
(E) I, II, and III

34. The sample size for a proposed study is calculated using the most conservative estimate of the sample proportion and a margin of error of 3% with 95% confidence. Which of the following numbers best approximates the factor by which the original sample size would have to be multiplied in order to maintain the margin of error at 3% but with 99% confidence?

(A) 1.7
(B) 2.5
(C) 3.4
(D) 5.2
(E) 8.3

35. A high school principal includes the following statement in a parent newsletter: "Our students continue to excel as evidenced by the fact that the average grade given on the first semester report cards was 83.4, which is a solid B!" The Student Council conducts a simple random sample of 20 students and determines that their average grade was 80.6 with a standard deviation of 11.7. A z-test for the population mean using H_0: $\mu = 83.4$ concluded that this sample did not provide sufficient evidence to doubt the principal's claim at the 5% level. Why was the Student Council's conclusion invalid?

(A) They needed to do a stratified sample so that all classes in the high school were equally represented.
(B) The number of students did not meet the minimum sample size requirement for a z-test.
(C) The sample standard deviation was too large for the population to be normal.
(D) The standard deviation of the population was not known.
(E) The conclusion is valid.

36. A set of 150 data values from a breeding experiment is tested against a genetic model using a chi-square test at the 2% level of significance. If there are 5 categories of offspring listed and the chi-square value is 11.58, which of the following conclusions are valid?
   I. The data are significant and the hypothesis that the data fits the model should be rejected.
   II. The data are not significant and we fail to reject the hypothesis that the data fits the model.
   III. The data would not be significant if the test were conducted at the 1% level of significance.

(A) I only
(B) II only
(C) I and III
(D) II and III
(E) There is insufficient data to make any conclusion.

37. Which of the following is *not* true regarding inference for regression?

(A) The distribution of the response values at a particular explanatory value is normal.
(B) The variance of all of the distributions of the response values at a particular explanatory value is constant for all explanatory values.
(C) The sum of the residuals equals 0.
(D) 95% of the data points are within two standard deviations of the grand mean $(\bar{x}, \bar{y})$.
(E) All of these are true.

GO ON TO THE NEXT PAGE

38. It is known that student performance on each portion of the SAT follows a normal distribution. At a particular school, a principal decides to study whether her students perform better on the Math section or the Verbal section of the test. She chooses a simple random sample of students whose scores are known. She subtracts the Math score from the Verbal score and finds that the mean difference in the scores is 23.3 with a standard deviation of 10.1. Which of the following would be the most appropriate test for determining whether her students perform better on the Math or on the Verbal sections of the test?

(A) two-sample z-test for means
(B) two-sample t-test for means
(C) t-test for matched pairs
(D) two-sample z-test for proportions
(E) None of these tests would be appropriate.

39. Which of the following statements is *not* true regarding Type II error for a specific alternative hypothesis?

(A) The probability of a Type II error is the probability of accepting H_0 when H_0 is false.
(B) The probability of a Type II error is the probability that the alternative hypothesis is true.
(C) The probability of a Type II error is related to the power of the test.
(D) The probability of a Type II error is used in the calculation of the sensitivity of a hypothesis test.
(E) None of these statements is false regarding Type II error.

40. A marketing study determined that 55% of randomly selected adults preferred their company's new type of crackers. Earlier it was anticipated that adults would be evenly split on their preference for the company's new product. If a hypothesis test for the population proportion is conducted, what is the standard error that will be used in the test?

(A) .012
(B) .025
(C) .051
(D) .076
(E) There is insufficient information to calculate the standard error for the test.

END OF SECTION I

Part A
Questions 1–5
Spend about 60 minutes on this part of the exam.
Percent of Section II grade—75

In order to receive full credit for your free-response questions, you must completely analyze each situation and clearly communicate your analyses and results. In order to earn partial credit when warranted, be sure to show enough work so that your reasoning process can be followed.

1. The table below lists the attendance of seniors at a large suburban high school on the last Friday of the listed months of the school year.

	Absent	Present
March	4	251
April	110	145
May	251	3

   a. Draw a segmented bar graph to explore whether there is a relationship between the month of the school year and attendance on the last Friday of the month.

   b. Based on your graph, state a reasonable conclusion for the study.

   c. Can you use a chi-square test to establish a relationship? If so, execute the test and provide the details. If not, explain why you cannot use the test.

2. A high school Guidance Department wants to study whether students at its school who take a particular SAT preparation course perform better on the Math section of the exam than those who do not. The department chooses two simple random samples of their students: Group A consists of those who have taken the course and Group B consists of those who have not taken the course. Scores from the students' first attempt at the SAT were compiled. All of the subjects in Group A had taken the preparation course prior to the first sitting of the test.

   a. Is this design an observational study or an experiment? Explain your answer.

   b. Does the random selection of each group address the issue of confounding? Explain your answer including some examples of potential compounding factors.

   c. Suggest how the data gathered by this design might be appropriately analyzed and interpreted.

3. A simple random sample of students in a large suburban high school is to be taken to determine the proportion of students who favor a change in the Student Council constitution.

   a. Determine the sample size so that there will be at least 95% confidence that the sample proportion will differ from the true proportion by no more than .1.

   b. The Student Council Officers believe that the proportion of students favoring the change is approximately .7. If this proportion is correct, what is the minimum sample size that will be necessary to guarantee that there will be 95% confidence that the sample proportion will be within .1 of the true value?

GO ON TO THE NEXT PAGE

4. A manufacturer of precision lenses for telescopes has the following data concerning the number of lenses produced and the cost per unit of production:

Number	1	3	5	10	12
Cost/Unit	$58	$55	$40	$37	$22

These data were processed on computer software that produced the following printout:

```
Dependent variable is: Cost per Unit
No Selector
R squared = 89.5%   R squared (adjusted) = 86.0%
s =   5.474  with   5 - 2 = 3   degrees of freedom

Source        Sum of Squares   df   Mean Square   F-ratio
Regression          763.304     1      763.304      25.5
Residual             89.8963    3       29.9654

Variable   Coefficient   s.e. of Coeff   t-ratio   prob
Constant       60.7857         4.389       13.8     0.0008
Number         -2.96544        0.5876      -5.05    0.0150
```

a. What is the equation of the regression line that predicts the cost per unit based on the number of lenses produced?

b. Which of the following two hypotheses is more reasonable?

   (1) The population correlation coefficient is 0.

   (2) The population correlation coefficient is −.9.

Provide statistical evidence to justify your answer.

5. The AP Statistics Final Exam at a large high school last year was graded holistically with all the grades listed in the table below.

Grades	60	70	80	90	100
Frequencies	9	15	28	35	21

a. State the summary statistics of this distribution.

b. If a random sample of 30 students is selected from this population 100 times, what would you expect the mean and standard deviation of the distribution of the 100 sample means? Explain the reasons for your answers.

c. Describe what you would expect about the shape of the distribution of the 100 sample means to be. Explain the reasons for your answer.

Part B
Question 6
Spend about 30 minutes on this part of the exam.
Percent of Section II grade—25

6. A candy maker coats her candy with one of three colors: red, yellow, or blue, in published proportions of .3, .3, and .4 respectively. A simple random sample of 50 pieces of candy contained 8 red, 20 yellow, and 22 blue pieces.

   a. Does the number of red candies in the sample cast doubt on the published proportion of red? Give appropriate statistical evidence to justify your answer.

   b. Is the distribution of colors consistent with the published proportions? Give appropriate statistical evidence to justify your answer.

   c. Compare the results of part a and part b. What conclusion can you draw from these analyses? Explain your answer.

END OF EXAMINATION

Appendix

Formulas and Tables
Technology Resources
AP Statistics Resources
Recommended Reading and References

Formulas and Tables

Formulas

I. Descriptive Statistics

$$\bar{x} = \frac{\sum x_i}{n}$$

$$s_x = \sqrt{\frac{1}{n-1}\sum(x_i - \bar{x})^2}$$

$$s_p = \frac{(n_1 - 1)s_1^2 + (n_2 - 1)s_2^2}{(n_1 - 1) + (n_2 - 1)}$$

$$y = b_0 + b_1 x$$

$$b_1 = \frac{\sum(x_i - \bar{x})(y_i - \bar{y})}{\sum(x_i - \bar{x})^2}$$

$$b_0 = \bar{y} - b_1\bar{x}$$

$$r = \frac{1}{n-1}\sum\left(\frac{x_i - \bar{x}}{s_x}\right)\left(\frac{y_i - \bar{y}}{s_y}\right)$$

$$b_1 = r\frac{s_y}{s_x}$$

$$s_{b_1} = \frac{\sqrt{\sum\frac{(y_i - y_i)^2}{n-2}}}{\sqrt{\sum(x_i - \bar{x})^2}}$$

II. Probability

$$P(A\cup B) = P(A) + P(B) - P(A\cap B)$$

$$P(A\,|\,B) = \frac{P(A\cap B)}{P(B)}$$

$$E(X) = \mu_x = \sum x_i p_i$$

$$Var(X) = \sigma_x^2 = \sum(x_i - \mu_x)^2 p_i$$

If X has a binonial distribution with parameters n and p, then:

$$P(X = k) = \binom{n}{k}p^k(1 - p)^{n-k}$$

$$\mu_x = np$$

$$\sigma_x = \sqrt{np(1 - p)}$$

$$\mu_p = p$$

$$\sigma_p = \sqrt{\frac{p(1 - p)}{n}}$$

If $\bar{x}$ is the mean of a random sample of size n from an infinite population with mean μ and standard deviation σ, then:

$$\mu_{\bar{x}} = \mu$$

$$\sigma_{\bar{x}} = \frac{\sigma}{\sqrt{n}}$$

III. Inferential Statistics

Standardized test statistic: $\dfrac{\text{estimate} - \text{parameter}}{\text{standard deviation of the estimate}}$

Confidence interval: estimate $\pm$ (critical value) • (standard deviation of the estimate)

SINGLE SAMPLE

Statistic	Standard deviation
mean	$\dfrac{\sigma}{\sqrt{n}}$
proportion	$\sqrt{\dfrac{p(1-p)}{n}}$

TWO SAMPLE

Statistic	Standard deviation
difference of means (unequal variances)	$\sqrt{\dfrac{\sigma_1^{\,2}}{n_1} + \dfrac{\sigma_2^{\,2}}{n_2}}$
difference of means (equal variances)	$\sigma\sqrt{\dfrac{1}{n_1} + \dfrac{1}{n_2}}$
difference of proportions (unequal variances)	$\sqrt{\dfrac{p_1(1-p_1)}{n_1} + \dfrac{p_2(1-p_2)}{n_2}}$
difference of proportions (equal variances)	$\sqrt{p(1-p)}\ \sqrt{\dfrac{1}{n_1} + \dfrac{1}{n_2}}$

Chi-square test statistic $= \displaystyle\sum \dfrac{(\text{observed} - \text{expected})^2}{\text{expected}}$

Areas Under the Normal Curve

Table entry for z is the probability lying below z.

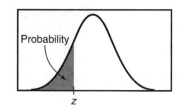

STANDARD NORMAL PROBABILITIES

z	.00	.01	.02	.03	.04	.05	.06	.07	.08	.09
−3.4	.0003	.0003	.0003	.0003	.0003	.0003	.0003	.0003	.0003	.0002
−3.3	.0005	.0005	.0005	.0004	.0004	.0004	.0004	.0004	.0004	.0003
−3.2	.0007	.0007	.0006	.0006	.0006	.0006	.0006	.0005	.0005	.0005
−3.1	.0010	.0009	.0009	.0009	.0008	.0008	.0008	.0008	.0007	.0007
−3.0	.0013	.0013	.0013	.0012	.0012	.0011	.0011	.0011	.0010	.0010
−2.9	.0019	.0018	.0018	.0017	.0016	.0016	.0015	.0015	.0014	.0014
−2.8	.0026	.0025	.0024	.0023	.0023	.0022	.0021	.0021	.0020	.0019
−2.7	.0035	.0034	.0033	.0032	.0031	.0030	.0029	.0028	.0027	.0026
−2.6	.0047	.0045	.0044	.0043	.0041	.0040	.0039	.0038	.0037	.0036
−2.5	.0062	.0060	.0059	.0057	.0055	.0054	.0052	.0051	.0049	.0048
−2.4	.0082	.0080	.0078	.0075	.0073	.0071	.0069	.0068	.0066	.0064
−2.3	.0107	.0104	.0102	.0099	.0096	.0094	.0091	.0089	.0087	.0084
−2.2	.0139	.0136	.0132	.0129	.0125	.0122	.0119	.0116	.0113	.0110
−2.1	.0179	.0174	.0170	.0166	.0162	.0158	.0154	.0150	.0146	.0143
−2.0	.0228	.0222	.0217	.0212	.0207	.0202	.0197	.0192	.0188	.0183
−1.9	.0287	.0281	.0274	.0268	.0262	.0256	.0250	.0244	.0239	.0233
−1.8	.0359	.0351	.0344	.0336	.0329	.0322	.0314	.0307	.0301	.0294
−1.7	.0446	.0436	.0427	.0418	.0409	.0401	.0392	.0384	.0375	.0367
−1.6	.0548	.0537	.0526	.0516	.0505	.0495	.0485	.0475	.0465	.0455
−1.5	.0668	.0655	.0643	.0630	.0618	.0606	.0594	.0582	.0571	.0559
−1.4	.0808	.0793	.0778	.0764	.0749	.0735	.0721	.0708	.0694	.0681
−1.3	.0968	.0951	.0934	.0918	.0901	.0885	.0869	.0853	.0838	.0823
−1.2	.1151	.1131	.1112	.1093	.1075	.1056	.1038	.1020	.1003	.0985
−1.1	.1357	.1335	.1314	.1292	.1271	.1251	.1230	.1210	.1190	.1170
−1.0	.1587	.1562	.1539	.1515	.1492	.1469	.1446	.1423	.1401	.1379
−0.9	.1841	.1814	.1788	.1762	.1736	.1711	.1685	.1660	.1635	.1611
−0.8	.2119	.2090	.2061	.2033	.2005	.1977	.1949	.1922	.1894	.1867
−0.7	.2420	.2389	.2358	.2327	.2296	.2266	.2236	.2206	.2177	.2148
−0.6	.2743	.2709	.2676	.2643	.2611	.2578	.2546	.2514	.2483	.2451
−0.5	.3085	.3050	.3015	.2981	.2946	.2912	.2877	.2843	.2810	.2776
−0.4	.3446	.3409	.3372	.3336	.3300	.3264	.3228	.3192	.3156	.3121
−0.3	.3821	.3783	.3745	.3707	.3669	.3632	.3594	.3557	.3520	.3483
−0.2	.4207	.4168	.4129	.4090	.4052	.4013	.3974	.3936	.3897	.3859
−0.1	.4602	.4562	.4522	.4483	.4443	.4404	.4364	.4325	.4286	.4247
−0.0	.5000	.4960	.4920	.4880	.4840	.4801	.4761	.4721	.4681	.4641

Table entry for z is the
probability lying below z.

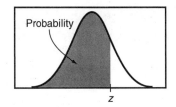

Probability

z

z	.00	.01	.02	.03	.04	.05	.06	.07	.08	.09
0.0	.5000	.5040	.5080	.5120	.5160	.5199	.5239	.5279	.5319	.5359
0.1	.5398	.5438	.5478	.5517	.5557	.5596	.5636	.5675	.5714	.5753
0.2	.5793	.5832	.5871	.5910	.5948	.5987	.6026	.6064	.6103	.6141
0.3	.6179	.6217	.6255	.6293	.6331	.6368	.6406	.6443	.6480	.6517
0.4	.6554	.6591	.6628	.6664	.6700	.6736	.6772	.6808	.6844	.6879
0.5	.6915	.6950	.6985	.7019	.7054	.7088	.7123	.7157	.7190	.7224
0.6	.7257	.7291	.7324	.7357	.7389	.7422	.7454	.7486	.7517	.7549
0.7	.7580	.7611	.7642	.7673	.7704	.7734	.7764	.7794	.7823	.7852
0.8	.7881	.7910	.7939	.7967	.7995	.8023	.8051	.8078	.8106	.8133
0.9	.8159	.8186	.8212	.8238	.8264	.8289	.8315	.8340	.8365	.8389
1.0	.8413	.8438	.8461	.8485	.8508	.8531	.8554	.8577	.8599	.8621
1.1	.8643	.8665	.8686	.8708	.8729	.8749	.8770	.8790	.8810	.8830
1.2	.8849	.8869	.8888	.8907	.8925	.8944	.8962	.8980	.8997	.9015
1.3	.9032	.9049	.9066	.9082	.9099	.9115	.9131	.9147	.9162	.9177
1.4	.9192	.9207	.9222	.9236	.9251	.9265	.9279	.9292	.9306	.9319
1.5	.9332	.9345	.9357	.9370	.9382	.9394	.9406	.9418	.9429	.9441
1.6	.9452	.9463	.9474	.9484	.9495	.9505	.9515	.9525	.9535	.9545
1.7	.9554	.9564	.9573	.9582	.9591	.9599	.9608	.9616	.9625	.9633
1.8	.9641	.9649	.9656	.9664	.9671	.9678	.9686	.9693	.9699	.9706
1.9	.9713	.9719	.9726	.9732	.9738	.9744	.9750	.9756	.9761	.9767
2.0	.9772	.9778	.9783	.9788	.9793	.9798	.9803	.9808	.9812	.9817
2.1	.9821	.9826	.9830	.9834	.9838	.9842	.9846	.9850	.9854	.9857
2.2	.9861	.9864	.9868	.9871	.9875	.9878	.9881	.9884	.9887	.9890
2.3	.9893	.9896	.9898	.9901	.9904	.9906	.9909	.9911	.9913	.9916
2.4	.9918	.9920	.9922	.9925	.9927	.9929	.9931	.9932	.9934	.9936
2.5	.9938	.9940	.9941	.9943	.9945	.9946	.9948	.9949	.9951	.9952
2.6	.9953	.9955	.9956	.9957	.9959	.9960	.9961	.9962	.9963	.9964
2.7	.9965	.9966	.9967	.9968	.9969	.9970	.9971	.9972	.9973	.9974
2.8	.9974	.9975	.9976	.9977	.9977	.9978	.9979	.9979	.9980	.9981
2.9	.9981	.9982	.9982	.9983	.9984	.9984	.9985	.9985	.9986	.9986
3.0	.9987	.9987	.9987	.9988	.9988	.9989	.9989	.9989	.9990	.9990
3.1	.9990	.9991	.9991	.9991	.9992	.9992	.9992	.9992	.9993	.9993
3.2	.9993	.9993	.9994	.9994	.9994	.9994	.9994	.9995	.9995	.9995
3.3	.9995	.9995	.9995	.9996	.9996	.9996	.9996	.9996	.9996	.9997
3.4	.9997	.9997	.9997	.9997	.9997	.9997	.9997	.9997	.9997	.9998

Critical Values from the *t*-Distribution

Table entry for *p* and *C* is the point *t** with probability *p* lying above it and probability *C* lying between − *t** and *t**.

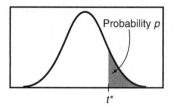

Probability *p*

*t**

t DISTRIBUTION CRITICAL VALUES

						Tail probability *p*						
df	.25	.20	.15	.10	.05	.025	.02	.01	.005	.0025	.001	.0005
1	1.000	1.376	1.963	3.078	6.314	12.71	15.89	31.82	63.66	127.3	318.3	636.6
2	.816	1.061	1.386	1.886	2.920	4.303	4.849	6.965	9.925	14.09	22.33	31.60
3	.765	.978	1.250	1.638	2.353	3.182	3.482	4.541	5.841	7.453	10.21	12.92
4	.741	.941	1.190	1.533	2.132	2.776	2.999	3.747	4.604	5.598	7.173	8.610
5	.727	.920	1.156	1.476	2.015	2.571	2.757	3.365	4.032	4.773	5.893	6.869
6	.718	.906	1.134	1.440	1.943	2.447	2.612	3.143	3.707	4.317	5.208	5.959
7	.711	.896	1.119	1.415	1.895	2.365	2.517	2.998	3.499	4.029	4.785	5.408
8	.706	.889	1.108	1.397	1.860	2.306	2.449	2.896	3.355	3.833	4.501	5.041
9	.703	.883	1.100	1.383	1.833	2.262	2.398	2.821	3.250	3.690	4.297	4.781
10	.700	.879	1.093	1.372	1.812	2.228	2.359	2.764	3.169	3.581	4.144	4.587
11	.697	.876	1.088	1.363	1.796	2.201	2.328	2.718	3.106	3.497	4.025	4.437
12	.695	.873	1.083	1.356	1.782	2.179	2.303	2.681	3.055	3.428	3.930	4.318
13	.694	.870	1.079	1.350	1.771	2.160	2.282	2.650	3.012	3.372	3.852	4.221
14	.692	.868	1.076	1.345	1.761	2.145	2.264	2.624	2.977	3.326	3.787	4.140
15	.691	.866	1.074	1.341	1.753	2.131	2.249	2.602	2.947	3.286	3.733	4.073
16	.690	.865	1.071	1.337	1.746	2.120	2.235	2.583	2.921	3.252	3.686	4.015
17	.689	.863	1.069	1.333	1.740	2.110	2.224	2.567	2.898	3.222	3.646	3.965
18	.688	.862	1.067	1.330	1.734	2.101	2.214	2.552	2.878	3.197	3.611	3.922
19	.688	.861	1.066	1.328	1.729	2.093	2.205	2.539	2.861	3.174	3.579	3.883
20	.687	.860	1.064	1.325	1.725	2.086	2.197	2.528	2.845	3.153	3.552	3.850
21	.686	.859	1.063	1.323	1.721	2.080	2.189	2.518	2.831	3.135	3.527	3.819
22	.686	.858	1.061	1.321	1.717	2.074	2.183	2.508	2.819	3.119	3.505	3.792
23	.685	.858	1.060	1.319	1.714	2.069	2.177	2.500	2.807	3.104	3.485	3.768
24	.685	.857	1.059	1.318	1.711	2.064	2.172	2.492	2.797	3.091	3.467	3.745
25	.684	.856	1.058	1.316	1.708	2.060	2.167	2.485	2.787	3.078	3.450	3.725
26	.684	.856	1.058	1.315	1.706	2.056	2.162	2.479	2.779	3.067	3.435	3.707
27	.684	.855	1.057	1.314	1.703	2.052	2.158	2.473	2.771	3.057	3.421	3.690
28	.683	.855	1.056	1.313	1.701	2.048	2.154	2.467	2.763	3.047	3.408	3.674
29	.683	.854	1.055	1.311	1.699	2.045	2.150	2.462	2.756	3.038	3.396	3.659
30	.683	.854	1.055	1.310	1.697	2.042	2.147	2.457	2.750	3.030	3.385	3.646
40	.681	.851	1.050	1.303	1.684	2.021	2.123	2.423	2.704	2.971	3.307	3.551
50	.679	.849	1.047	1.299	1.676	2.009	2.109	2.403	2.678	2.937	3.261	3.496
60	.679	.848	1.045	1.296	1.671	2.000	2.099	2.390	2.660	2.915	3.232	3.460
80	.678	.846	1.043	1.292	1.664	1.990	2.088	2.374	2.639	2.887	3.195	3.416
100	.677	.845	1.042	1.290	1.660	1.984	2.081	2.364	2.626	2.871	3.174	3.390
1000	.675	.842	1.037	1.282	1.646	1.962	2.056	2.330	2.581	2.813	3.098	3.300
∞	.674	.841	1.036	1.282	1.645	1.960	2.054	2.326	2.576	2.807	3.091	3.291
	50%	60%	70%	80%	90%	95%	96%	98%	99%	99.5%	99.8%	99.9%

Confidence level *C*

Table entry for p is the
point (χ^2) with probability p
lying above it.

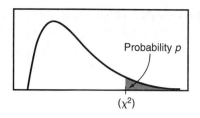

Probability p

(χ^2)

χ^2 CRITICAL VALUES

df	.25	.20	.15	.10	.05	.025	.02	.01	.005	.0025	.001
					Tail probability p						
1	1.32	1.64	2.07	2.71	3.84	5.02	5.41	6.63	7.88	9.14	10.83
2	2.77	3.22	3.79	4.61	5.99	7.38	7.82	9.21	10.60	11.98	13.82
3	4.11	4.64	5.32	6.25	7.81	9.35	9.84	11.34	12.84	14.32	16.27
4	5.39	5.99	6.74	7.78	9.49	11.14	11.67	13.28	14.86	16.42	18.47
5	6.63	7.29	8.12	9.24	11.07	12.83	13.39	15.09	16.75	18.39	20.51
6	7.84	8.56	9.45	10.64	12.59	14.45	15.03	16.81	18.55	20.25	22.46
7	9.04	9.80	10.75	12.02	14.07	16.01	16.62	18.48	20.28	22.04	24.32
8	10.22	11.03	12.03	13.36	15.51	17.53	18.17	20.09	21.95	23.77	26.12
9	11.39	12.24	13.29	14.68	16.92	19.02	19.68	21.67	23.59	25.46	27.88
10	12.55	13.44	14.53	15.99	18.31	20.48	21.16	23.21	25.19	27.11	29.59
11	13.70	14.63	15.77	17.28	19.68	21.92	22.62	24.72	26.76	28.73	31.26
12	14.85	15.81	16.99	18.55	21.03	23.34	24.05	26.22	28.30	30.32	32.91
13	15.98	16.98	18.20	19.81	22.36	24.74	25.47	27.69	29.82	31.88	34.53
14	17.12	18.15	19.41	21.06	23.68	26.12	26.87	29.14	31.32	33.43	36.12
15	18.25	19.31	20.60	22.31	25.00	27.49	28.26	30.58	32.80	34.95	37.70
16	19.37	20.47	21.79	23.54	26.30	28.85	29.63	32.00	34.27	36.46	39.25
17	20.49	21.61	22.98	24.77	27.59	30.19	31.00	33.41	35.72	37.95	40.79
18	21.60	22.76	24.16	25.99	28.87	31.53	32.35	34.81	37.16	39.42	42.31
19	22.72	23.90	25.33	27.20	30.14	32.85	33.69	36.19	38.58	40.88	43.82
20	23.83	25.04	26.50	28.41	31.41	34.17	35.02	37.57	40.00	42.34	45.31
21	24.93	26.17	27.66	29.62	32.67	35.48	36.34	38.93	41.40	43.78	46.80
22	26.04	27.30	28.82	30.81	33.92	36.78	37.66	40.29	42.80	45.20	48.27
23	27.14	28.43	29.98	32.01	35.17	38.08	38.97	41.64	44.18	46.62	49.73
24	28.24	29.55	31.13	33.20	36.42	39.36	40.27	42.98	45.56	48.03	51.18
25	29.34	30.68	32.28	34.38	37.65	40.65	41.57	44.31	46.93	49.44	52.62
26	30.43	31.79	33.43	35.56	38.89	41.92	42.86	45.64	48.29	50.83	54.05
27	31.53	32.91	34.57	36.74	40.11	43.19	44.14	46.96	49.64	52.22	55.48
28	32.62	34.03	35.71	37.92	41.34	44.46	45.42	48.28	50.99	53.59	56.89
29	33.71	35.14	36.85	39.09	42.56	45.72	46.69	49.59	52.34	54.97	58.30
30	34.80	36.25	37.99	40.26	43.77	46.98	47.96	50.89	53.67	56.33	59.70
40	45.62	47.27	49.24	51.81	55.76	59.34	60.44	63.69	66.77	69.70	73.40
50	56.33	58.16	60.35	63.17	67.50	71.42	72.61	76.15	79.49	82.66	86.66
60	66.98	68.97	71.34	74.40	79.08	83.30	84.58	88.38	91.95	95.34	99.61
80	88.13	90.41	93.11	96.58	101.9	106.6	108.1	112.3	116.3	120.1	124.8
100	109.1	111.7	114.7	118.5	124.3	129.6	131.1	135.8	140.2	144.3	149.4

Random Digit Table	7766893650	1788494747	3356441243	3732801634	9075697424
	8721402456	6120102198	3292853424	3100809402	9946377115
	9465603411	8094059374	1515565358	3368789559	8995665289
	5615196475	7155225594	6830167756	3749998169	0657354701
	4745207851	8471668760	4015903625	8025278305	2629345285
	3909778925	7021700995	0512283638	4421843279	4558672744
	5626388151	204079865	6938059459	2708292612	9741756855
	9666876041	8440095037	3179797888	4521436505	4584259844
	0867467089	1248480134	4929656476	2174062877	5296566790
	9856793322	8599006450	0063709789	4106309451	2267958159
	8963053942	084430340	7222968997	7245457784	1381073582
	3168853914	1890313205	5124340881	4384709300	7751836252
	9781052367	9223094872	4371631466	3276864623	3974698862
	1629880791	0876812772	8653044474	1741306917	1985369844
	0101158212	6850142723	5105893573	6451774858	2905040718
	1921056996	7618930168	3154673150	3998604819	5338047435
	5607150623	4145197081	9772400521	8139230981	5133059750
	4715669440	0208933748	8333166742	7065396256	6379727126
	6848275920	9095970753	3562500116	8136951109	4042206220
	5588238465	0963022934	5983486274	7513791312	2873928882

Technology Resources

Data Desk®
Data Description, Inc.
840 Hanshaw Road, Suite 9
Ithaca, NY 14850
www.datadesk.com

Minitab®
Minitab, Inc.
3081 Enterprise Drive
State College, PA 16801-3008
www.minitab.com

Fathom Dynamic Statistics Software
KCP Technologies
Key Curriculum Press
P.O. Box 2304-ASCK
Berkeley, CA 94702-0304
www.keypress.com

SAS®
SAS Institute, Inc.
SAS Campus Drive
Cary, NC 27513-2414
www.sas.com

TI-83
Texas Instruments Inc.
7800 Banner Drive
Dallas, TX 75251
www.ti.com/calc

AP Statistics Resources

AP Statistics Discussion Group

AP Statistics Mailing List and List Serve
Instructions for subscribing:
Email message to majordomo@etc.bc.ca
Leave topic line blank.
Enter this message:
subscribe apstat-l <your email address>
(Note that it is a lowercase L after the hyphen, not the number 1.)

AP Statistics List Serve Archive
http://forum.swarthmore.edu/epigone/apstat-l

College Board Online
http://www.collegeboard.org

Private sites
These sites contain a great deal of information and resources including links to other sites as listed below:

Buckingham Browne & Nichols School
http://www.bbns.org/us/math/ap_stat/internet_resource.html

- Course information and projects
- Links to data sources
- Link to College Board Online
- Link to the American Statistical Association

New Bedford High School
http://www.newbedford.k12.ma.us/srhigh/apstats/apstats.htm

- Course information
- Links to other schools
- Links to data sources
- Link to AP Statistics online

Recommended Reading and References

Activity-Based Statistics
Richard Scheaffer, Mrudulla Gnanadesikan, Ann Watkins, and Jeffrey Witmer. New York: Springer-Verlag, 1996.

Exploring Data
James Landwehr and Ann Watkins. Palo Alto, CA: Dale Seymour Publications, 1987.

How to Lie With Statistics
Darrell Huff. New York: W. W. Norton & Company, 1993.

Introduction to the Practice of Statistics, 3rd Edition
David S. Moore and George P. McCabe. New York: W. H. Freeman & Co., 1999.

Statistics, 3rd Edition
David Freedman, Robert Pisani, Roger Purves. New York: W. W. Norton & Company, Inc., 1997.

Statistics: The Exploration and Analysis of Data, 3rd Edition
Jay Devore and Roxy Peck. Belmont, CA: Duxbury Press, 1997.

Statistics: Learning in the Presence of Variation
Robert L. Wardrop. Dubuque, IA: William C. Brown, 1995.

The Art and Techniques of Simulation
Mrudulla Gnanadesikan, Richard Scheaffer, and Jim Swift. Palo Alto, CA: Dale Seymour Publications, 1987.

The Basic Practice of Statistics, 2nd Edition
David S. Moore. New York: W. H. Freeman & Co., 2000.

The Practice of Statistics
Daniel S. Yates, David S. Moore, George P. McCabe. New York: W. H. Freeman & Co., 1999.

Workshop Statistics
Allan J. Rossman. New York: Springer-Verlag, 1995.

Answer Key

Chapter 2   Exploring Univariate Data
Chapter 3   Exploring Bivariate Data
Chapter 4   Planning a Study: Deciding What and How to Measure
Chapter 5   Anticipating Patterns: Producing Models Using
             Probability and Simulation
Chapter 6   Sampling Distributions
Chapter 7   Statistical Inference
Chapter 8   Interpreting Computer and Calculator Printouts
             Five Model Examinations
             Calculating Your AP Score

Chapter 2 Exploring Univariate Data

Section 2.1 Basic Definitions

CHECKLIST (page 9)

1. **Categorical** since the data values are the names of cars.

2. **Quantitative – continuous:** the data are measurements and are continuous since height can take on any value within an appropriate interval.

3. **Quantitative – continuous:** the data are measurements and are continuous since age in years can take on any value in an appropriate interval.

4. **Categorical:** the data refer to age categories.

5. **Quantitative – continuous:** the data are in percents.

6. **Quantitative – continuous:** the data are measurements and are continuous since height can take on any value within an appropriate interval.

7. **Quantitative – discrete:** the data are scores that can only take on integer values.

8. Answers will vary.

9. Answers will vary.

Section 2.2 Constructing Graphical Displays of Univariate Data

MULTIPLE-CHOICE QUESTIONS (page 15)

1. **C** A histogram and a bar graph are inherently different since the bar graph displays categories whose bars should not be touching. The histogram's "bars" display continuous data and therefore should touch and can be specified either by cut-points (boundaries of intervals) or midpoints of the intervals.

2. **D** Dot plots are used to display the shape of a distribution of discrete data values.

3. **C** Since the data are sorted in a stem and leaf plot, it is easy to count the data values and divide them into quartiles.

4. **D** Since a histogram does not display the data values, a stem and leaf plot could not be constructed.

5. **B** For example, construct a box plot for the set {5, 5, 5, 5, 5, 5, 5, 5, 5, 5}.

SHORT ANSWER (page 15)

1 – 4. Answers will vary.

5. a. Dot plot, histogram, and stem and leaf are all acceptable.
   b. Dot plot, histogram, and stem and leaf are all acceptable.
   c. Dot plot, histogram, and stem and leaf are all acceptable.
   d. Dot plot, histogram, and stem and leaf are all acceptable.
   e. Dot plot, histogram, and stem and leaf are all acceptable.
   f. Dot plot, histogram, and stem and leaf are all acceptable.

6. a. 67.6
   b. 69.7
   c. Between 67 and 69 inclusive.

7. Answers will vary. It is not appropriate to have only 3 stem elements using the tens digit. It is appropriate to split the stems into two or five substems.

Section 2.3 Interpreting Graphical Displays of Univariate Data

FREE-RESPONSE QUESTIONS

Open-Ended Questions (page 17)

1. Center: approximately 35 or 36
   Spread: approximately 27 to 45
   Clusters: one major mound
   Gaps: none
   Outliers: none
   Shape: approximately symmetric

2. Center: approximately 5
   Spread: from 0 to 15
   Clusters: one major mound
   Gaps: none
   Outliers: none
   Shape: skewed right

3. Center: approximately 4
   Spread: from 0 to approximately 16
   Clusters: cannot be determined
   Gaps: cannot be determined
   Outliers: appears to have 3 outliers
   Shape: since the right whisker is longer than the left whisker, there is probably some skewness to the shape.

4. Center: center of the largest cluster is approximately 5
   Spread: main cluster ranges from 0 to 20 but there are extreme outliers in the 50–60 range
   Clusters: one major cluster
   Gaps: gap between 20 and 50
   Outliers: several in the 50–60 range
   Shape: skewed right

5. Center: approximately 10
   Spread: from 2 to 22
   Clusters: one large cluster
   Gaps: none
   Outliers: none
   Shape: skewed right

Section 2.4 Summarizing Distributions Numerically: Center and Spread

MULTIPLE-CHOICE QUESTIONS (page 25)

1. **B** Due to the long right tail and the larger distance between the median and Q3, the distribution appears to be skewed right. Caution needs to be exercised when making this interpretation from a box plot.

2. **D** If the distribution is symmetric and mound-shaped, the empirical rule should be approximately accurate. However, since values cannot be less than 0, there is an inconsistency in the given information. The choice of the standard deviation being too large does address this inconsistency.

3. **C** The interquartile range is unaffected by extreme data values.

4. **E** Remember to list the data in ascending order before determining the five-number summary.

5. **B** Remember to do a weighted average based on the number of students with each mean. Note that the combined mean is closer to the mean with the greater number of students since the larger number "weights" its mean in the calculation.
   $$\frac{30(75.6) + 24(68.4)}{30 + 24} = 72.4.$$

6. **A** Assuming the data are mound-shaped and symmetric, approximately 99.7% falls within 3 standard deviations of the mean. Therefore, 99.7% of the data is spanned by approximately 6 standard deviations.

FREE-RESPONSE QUESTIONS

Open-Ended Questions (page 25)

1. Answers will vary.

2. min = 54; Q1 = 68; median = 76; Q3 = 82; max = 99; mean = 75.575; standard deviation = 10.772

3. It appears from both the graphical displays and the summary statistics indicated that the data are slightly skewed right.

4. a. Since 195 is 2 standard deviations above the mean, the interval between the mean and 195 should contain approximately 47.5% of the data or 475 scores.

   b. 155 is 2 standard deviations below the mean and 165 is 1 standard deviation below the mean. Therefore, approximately 13.5% of the data (that is, 47.5% − 34%), or 135 scores should be in this interval.

   c. 170 is one-half of a standard deviation below the mean. The best that we can say is that the percentage of data in this interval is *less* than 34%. At this point, we have not reviewed techniques for partitioning the area sufficiently to determine a more exact answer.

5. $\frac{1,360}{2,000}$ is 68% of the data. Therefore, using the empirical rule, an interval within one standard deviation of the mean should have approximately 68% of the data: an approximate interval is
   $(5.3 − .7, 5.3 + .7) = (4.6, 6.0)$

6. If a graph is skewed severely in either direction, the five-number summary would be appropriate since the quartiles and the median are not affected by extreme values in the way that the mean and standard deviation are.

7. 68.168 inches. A weighted average should be calculated: $\frac{24(68.3) + 1(65)}{25} = 68.168.$

8. The graphs will be centered in approximately the same place but the graph from school B will be flatter and more spread out than the graph from school A.

Section 2.5 Summarizing Distributions: Relative Location and Position

MULTIPLE-CHOICE QUESTIONS (page 29)

1. **B** The z-score for I is 3.38; the z-score for II is 3.73.

2. **B** When the values are listed in order there are 3 values below 10. This places 10 in the 37.5 percentile as well as in the second quartile.

3. **E** Without a context or more information regarding the distribution of data, there is no way to determine other percentiles.

4. **B** The student's present z-score is .67. With the changes in the mean and standard deviation, the student must increase his score by 9 points in order to achieve the same level on the second test.

5. C The percentile of a z-score of 1 is approximately 84%, and the percentile of Q3 is 75%.

6. C Both the mean and standard deviation will increase by 10%.

7. C Since the data in C represent a uniform decrease of 2 from the original set, the standard deviations of the two sets must be the same.

8. B A uniform shift of all data maintains the percentages of data in shifted intervals.

9. B Conversions to z-scores shift the mean and standard deviation to 0 and 1 respectively for *any* distribution, not just symmetric and mound-shaped ones.

FREE-RESPONSE QUESTIONS

Open-Ended Questions (page 30)

1. 65 is in the third quartile.

2. 65 is in the 59th percentile since 38 of the 64 values are below it.

3. .442467. First calculate the mean and standard deviation of the data: mean = 54.828125; standard deviation = 22.98899301. Therefore, z-score = .442467.

4. Answers will vary.

5. a. 81 is the smallest number in the 4th quartile; therefore we would have to add 16 to 65 to move from the 3rd to the 4th quartile. Note that if we considered the 4th quartile to be the 75th percentile then we would need to add to 65 an amount that would make its new z-score equal to .68. The addition of 3.4 points would accomplish this.
   b. To move 65 to the 64th percentile we would have to add a sufficient number so that there would be approximately 41 values below it. Since there are 5 values of 65, we do not need to add any amount.
   c. A z-score of .58 corresponds to a data value of 66.14. Therefore, it would be necessary to add 1.14 points.

6. a. Multiply each summary statistic by 100: {900, 489.8, 200, 500, 900, 1300, 1600}
   b. Divide each summary statistic by 1,000: (.009, .004898, .002, .005, .009, .013, .016}

7. min: 0 percentile; Q1: 25th percentile (25% of data below Q1); median: 50th percentile (50% of data below the median); Q3: 75th percentile (75% of data below Q3); max: $\frac{n-1}{n}$ percentile ($n - 1$ data values are below the maximum if there are n data values in total).

Section 2.6 Comparing Distributions

FREE-RESPONSE QUESTIONS

Open-Ended Questions (page 32)

1. Graphs will vary.

	Men	Women
mean	67.2	66.1
standard deviation	3.52	2.03
min	62	64
Q1	64	64.5
median	67	65
Q3	70.5	67.5
max	72	70

Responses should include the fact that the distribution of men's heights is slightly higher and more wide-spread than the women's distribution.

2. Graphs will vary.

	Vega	Datsun
mean	33.7	32.7
standard deviation	5.30	2.74
min	24	30
Q1	29.5	31
median	35	32
Q3	37	33.5
max	41	40

Responses should include that the distribution of the Vega's gas mileages is slightly higher and more wide-spread with a cluster in the 20–24 range. It should be pointed out that the mileages of the Datsun were very consistent (small spread) but that there was an outlier value of 40.

3. Graphs will vary.

	A	B
mean	80.8	77.5
standard deviation	3.81	8.86
min	76	62
Q1	77	73.5
median	82	77
Q3	84.5	82
max	86	94

Responses should include the fact that class A's center is greater than class B's and its distribution exhibits considerably less spread than class B. A histogram (interval size 2) of class A's data appears skewed right whereas a histogram (interval size 2) of class B appears more symmetric and mound-shaped. *Note:* By adjusting the interval size, you can make both distributions appear uniform.

Chapter 2 Assessment

MULTIPLE-CHOICE QUESTIONS (page 33)

1. B One out of the 25 values, or 4%.

2. C 51 is the 13th value.

3. C Most likely the mean is greater than the median since the distribution is skewed right and there is an outlier on the high end.

4. B

5. B This box plot shows a minimum at 32, Q1 at 47.5, median at 51, Q3 at 63.5, and maximum at 71 with an outlier at 92.

6. D Since the standard deviation is 19.49, the variance is approximately 381.94.

7. C $\dfrac{72 - 40}{19} \approx 1.68$

8. D Pie charts should be used only for categorical data.

9. A The long tail to the right suggests that the mean is greater than the median, which is greater than the mode.

10. D The z-score for this value is -1.

11. D $\dfrac{150 - 125}{10} = 2.5$

12. C Approximately 15% of the data falls below a score of 70.

FREE-RESPONSE QUESTIONS

Open-Ended Questions (page 34)

1. $\dfrac{75(52.6) + 25(48.4)}{100} = 51.55$ pounds

2. $\dfrac{500(67.8) - 150(63.0)}{350} \approx 69.86$ inches

3. Answers will vary. A bimodal "camel-back" graph is one correct possibility.

4. Answers will vary. However, Q1 must equal the minimum value and Q3 must equal the maximum value.

5. Comparison of z-scores is an appropriate method:

z-score for 78: $\dfrac{78 - 72}{6.5} \approx .9231$

z-score for 83: $\dfrac{83 - 77}{8.4} \approx .7143$

Therefore, 78 is a better grade since it is further above its mean (in standard units) than 83 is above its mean.

Investigative Tasks (page 34)

1. a. Histogram

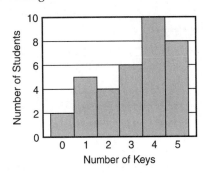

The histogram indicates a distribution that is skewed left.

b. Box Plot

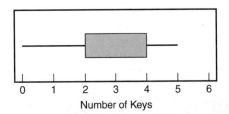

The box plot indicates that the median is either Q1 or Q3 (it is Q3) and the longer left whisker indicates some skewness to the left.

c. The histogram displays the overall shape of the data, but the box plot details the 5-number summary. Answers will vary as to the choice of the "best" plot.

d. mean = 3.17
standard deviation = 1.56
minimum = 0
Q1 = 2
median = 4
Q3 = 4
maximum = 5
Answers to the "best" summary will vary. However, since the data is provided in a frequency table, the five-number summary really does not add a great deal of information that is not immediately discernable from the graph.

2. a. Back-to-back stem and leaf plots

Class A		Class B
5	4	
5 2	6	5 5
5 4	7	4 5 5 8
6 2 1	8	2 3
7 5 1	9	8 8
	10	0

Leaf = 1 point

Parallel box plots

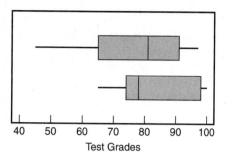

Test Grades

b. Answers will vary.

c.

	Class A	Class B
mean	77.55	81.18
standard deviation	15.64	12.59
min	45	65
Q1	65	74
median	81	78
Q3	91	98
max	97	100

d. Answers will vary. However, since the distribution of grades in class A is skewed to the left, the mean and standard deviation is of less value for class A than the five-number summary.

e. Answers will vary.

Chapter 3 Exploring Bivariate Data

Section 3.1 Patterns in Scatterplots

FREE-RESPONSE QUESTIONS

Open-Ended Questions (page 40)

1. Scatterplot

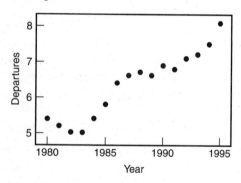

Description: fairly linear indicating a positive relationship.

2. Scatterplot

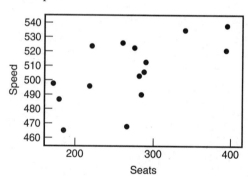

Description: fairly scattered indicating a slight positive relationship.

3. Scatterplot

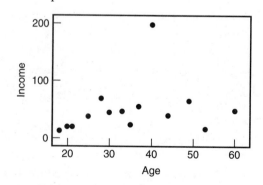

Description: fairly linear except for one point indicating a slight positive relationship.

Section 3.2 Means and Standard Deviations

FREE-RESPONSE QUESTIONS

Open-Ended Questions (page 42)

1. Scatterplot

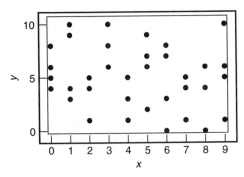

2. 1st value: mean: 4.5; standard deviation: 2.9089
   2nd value: mean: 5.1; standard deviation: 2.8537

3. 1st value: mean ± 2 standard deviations →
   (−1.32, 10.32)
   2nd value: mean ± 2 standard deviations →
   (−.61, 10.81)
   100% of the data is within the rectangle.

4. We would expect only about 95.25% of the data to lie within the rectangle.

5.

x	0	1	2	3	4	5	6	7	8	9
y-means	5.75	6.50	3.75	8.50	3.00	6.00	4.50	3.50	4.00	5.50

6. There is no apparent pattern.

Section 3.3 Correlation and Linearity

MULTIPLE-CHOICE QUESTIONS (page 46)

1. **C** The quantity r^2 relates the percentage of the variation explained by the model. The value of r only quantifies the strength and direction of a linear relationship.

2. **B** Changing the order of the coordinates does not change the correlation coefficient. A change in scale by multiplying by a constant does not change the correlation coefficient.

3. **A** Correlation quantifies the strength and direction of a linear relationship. The steepness of the line of best fit depends on other quantities as well as the correlation coefficient.

4. **C** We do not have sufficient information to determine whether the sign on the correlation coefficient is plus or minus. Note that A is incorrect since r^2 measures the variation in the dependent variable accounted for by the model, not between the variables.

FREE-RESPONSE QUESTIONS

Open-Ended Questions (page 47)

1. The correlation coefficient is close to +1.

2. The correlation coefficient is between 0 and +1 but closer to 0 than +1.

3. The correlation coefficient is negative and moderately large.

4. The correlation coefficient is close to −1.

5. x-values: mean: 12; standard deviation: 9.74
   y-values: mean: 25.375; standard deviation: 17.28

   The table is completed (rounded to two decimal places) as:

$\dfrac{x_i - \bar{x}_i}{s_x}$	$\dfrac{y_i - \bar{y}_i}{s_y}$	$\left(\dfrac{x_i - \bar{x}_i}{s_x}\right)\left(\dfrac{y_i - \bar{y}_i}{s_y}\right)$
−1.23	−1.22	1.51
−1.03	−1.05	1.08
−0.72	−0.59	0.43
−0.31	−.25	0.08
0.10	0.15	0.02
0.61	0.26	0.16
1.03	1.01	1.04
1.54	1.70	2.61
Sum		6.92

Therefore, since $n - 1 = 8 - 1 = 7$, $r = \dfrac{6.92}{7} = .9879$

6. A correlation coefficient of .63 indicates a moderate positive relationship between weight and height. Therefore, men with above average heights tend to have weights that are above average as well. Since r equals the sum of the products of the z-scores of the height and weight data and since the man in question is one standard deviation taller than the average man, we would expect that he weighs .63 standard deviations pounds above the mean of the weights for men of the same height.

7. One example is a curved relationship with half of the points above zero and the other half below zero.

Section 3.4 Least Squares Regression Line

MULTIPLE-CHOICE QUESTIONS (page 52)

1. **A** slope $= .75\left(\dfrac{10{,}540}{1.4}\right) \approx 5{,}646.4$;
   intercept $= 34{,}250 - 5{,}646.4(2.1) \approx 22{,}392$

2. **E** Choice A shows a correct interpretation of the y-intercept; Choice B shows a correct interpretation of the slope; Choice C shows a correct substitution; Choice D is correct because the correlation coefficient and the slope of the regression have the same sign.

3. D There is a relationship between the value of a correlation coefficient and the steepness of a regression line.

4. D This is the only choice with a positive slope and positive y-intercept.

FREE-RESPONSE QUESTIONS

Open-Ended Questions (page 53)

1. Scatterplot

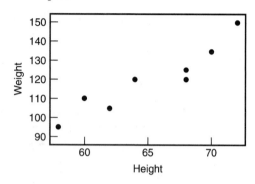

Description: fairly strong positive relationship.

2. $r = .938$

3. $b = r\left(\dfrac{s_y}{s_x}\right) = .938\left(\dfrac{17.32}{5.01}\right) = 3.24 \text{ lbs/in.}$

$a = \bar{y} - b\bar{x} = 120 - 3.24(65.25) = -91.41$ pounds

Answers may vary due to rounding.

4.

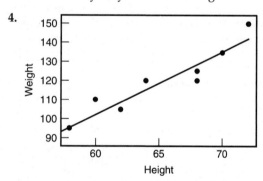

5. The slope indicates that for each additional inch of height, a person will be 3.24 pounds heavier. The y-intercept indicates that a person with no height will have a weight of -58 pounds.

6. Predicted weight $= -58 + 3.24(65) = 152.6$ pounds

7. a. For each additional centimeter in length, weight increases approximately 15.9 grams.
  b. For each additional degree in temperature, length decreases by approximately 3.2 cm.
  c. For each additional year of service, income increases approximately $650.
  d. For each additional mile, cost increases by approximately 35 cents.
  e. For each additional attempt, the score increases by approximately 3.24%.

8. a. When length = 0, weight = 0.
  b. The length of the object is 90 cm when the temperature is 0°F.
  c. Starting pay is $22,300.
  d. The cost is $5.85 before traveling any distance.
  e. The scoring percentage is 40% before any attempts are made.

9. a. $y = -3.40 + 4.20x$. Slope: For each increase in x, y will increase approximately 4.20 units. y-intercept: When $x = 0$, $y = -3.40$.

  b.

x	y	$\hat{y}$	residual
1	3	.8	2.2
2	4	5	−1
3	7	9.2	−2.2
4	12	13.4	−1.4
5	20	17.6	2.4

  c. Sum = 0. The sum of the errors in the prediction should always equal 0.

Section 3.5 Residual Plots, Outliers, and Influential Points

MULTIPLE-CHOICE QUESTIONS (page 58)

1. D This is the only option that is not a correct conclusion.

2. D This is the only graph to display random scatter and have all points falling in a constant horizontal band.

3. B Since most residuals are positive, we can infer that most of the predicted values are less than their actual counterparts.

4. E None of these lines of fit would produce a residual plot similar to the given residual plot.

FREE-RESPONSE QUESTIONS

Open-Ended Questions (page 59)

1. Scatterplot

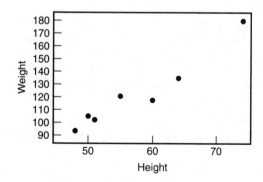

Description: Very linear with a positive relationship.

2. Weight = −52.50 + 3.04(Height); for each additional inch in height, weight should increase by 3.04 pounds.

3. The set of residuals is {−.42, 5.5, −.54, 6.3, –11.9, −7.06, 7.54}.

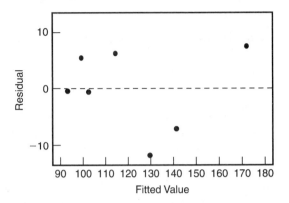

4. The residual of the value (74, 180) does not meet the criterion of being more than 1.5 · IQR greater than the third quartile of the residuals. Therefore, the value (74, 180) is not an outlier.

5. There does not appear to be an obvious curvature in the residual plot and the value of R^2 is high (93.7%). Therefore, we can conclude that this is a reasonable fit.

6. If the value (74, 180) is removed and the regression is recalculated, the resulting equation is Weight = −12.4 + 2.28(Height). This line is much less steep, indicating that (74, 180) is influential since it did "pull" the regression line up closer to it.

7. The regression line tells us that there is a positive relationship between weight and height.

8. An outlier is not necessarily influential, especially if it occurs at an x-value near $\bar{x}$. An influential value is probably not an outlier since it pulls the regression line towards it.

Section 3.6 Transformations to Achieve Linearity

MULTIPLE-CHOICE QUESTIONS (page 65)

1. **B** Substitution into the linear regression must be followed by reversing the logarithmic transformation. Therefore, substituting 12 for time in the linear equation, we have ln y = 5.876, or $y = e^{5.876} = 356.38$. Notice the slight discrepancy due to round-off error.

2. **E** All of the techniques shown could be used to try to achieve linearity from the scatterplot shown.

Open-Ended Questions (page 65)

1. Scatterplot

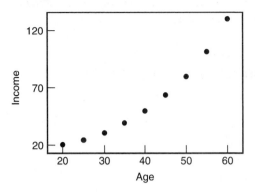

2. Income = −48.23 + 2.69(Age)

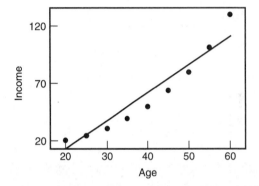

3. r = .96 indicating a strong positive linear relationship. However, the residual plot indicates a very curved pattern. Therefore, this model cannot be considered accurate.

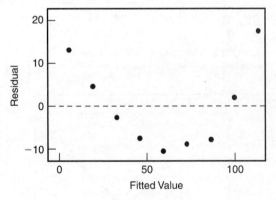

4. Exponential: $(x, y) \rightarrow (x, \ln y)$; Power: $(x, y) \rightarrow (\ln x, \ln y)$

Age	Income	ln(Age)	ln(Income)
20	18.5	2.9957	2.9178
25	23.6	3.2189	3.1612
30	29.8	3.4012	3.3945
35	38.5	3.5553	3.6507
40	49.0	3.6889	3.8918
45	64.1	3.8067	4.1604
50	78.5	3.9120	4.3631
55	102.0	4.0073	4.6250
60	130.8	4.0943	4.8737

5. Exponential: ln(Income) = 1.94 + 0.0489(Age)
Power: ln(Income) = −2.58 + 1.78 ln(Age)

6. The correlation for the exponential fit is .9999 and the residual plot indicates a somewhat scattered pattern; the correlation for the power fit is .9880 but there is a substantial curved pattern in its residual plot.

Exponential

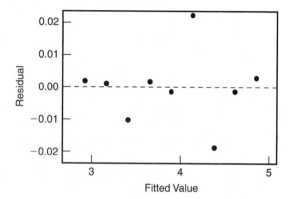

Power

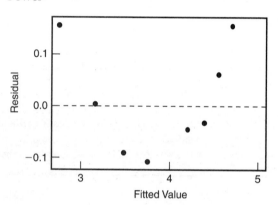

7. Exponential: Income = 6.95 × 1.05^{Age}
Power: Income = .08 × Age$^{1.78}$

Exponential

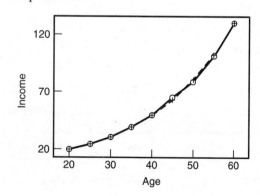

Power

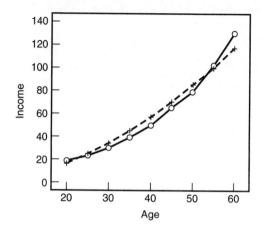

Residual Plots:

Exponential

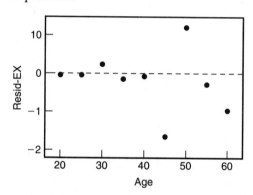

Power

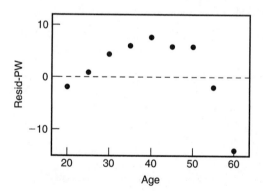

8. It appears that the exponential transformation is best since it has higher r and R^2 values and its residual plot shows the least pattern.

Section 3.7 Exploring Categorical Data

FREE-RESPONSE QUESTIONS

Open-Ended Questions (page 69)

1. Bar Graph

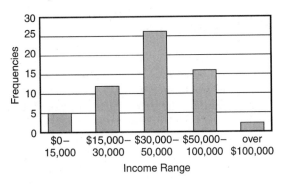

The bar graph appears relatively symmetric and mound-shaped.

Pie Graph

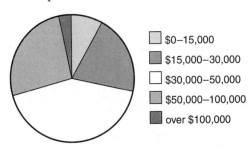

- $0–15,000
- $15,000–30,000
- $30,000–50,000
- $50,000–100,000
- over $100,000

The largest sector is the $30,000–$50,000 range. The smallest sector is the over $100,000 category.

2. There are 38 persons in this income range and 61 persons in the sample. $\frac{38}{61} = 62\%$ of the data.

3. These ranges are data categories and therefore width of the interval is not important.

4. No. Since these are data categories and we don't know the distribution of the values within the categories, it is impossible to calculate any summary statistic other than identifying the modal class (i.e., the class with the greatest frequency). Further, since the last range is "over $100,000", there is no way to quantify that category as a number.

5. Urban: 403; Suburban: 482; Rural: 198

Under 25: 325; 25–50: 535; over 50: 223

6. Segmented Bar Graph

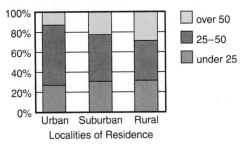

- over 50
- 25–50
- under 25

7. $\frac{53}{403} \approx 13\%$ of the urban dwellers are over 50.

8. $\frac{58}{223} \approx 26\%$ of residents over 50 live in rural areas.

9. Inspection of the segmented bar graph and calculation of the conditional distributions of proportions in each category seem to indicate that older residents prefer non-urban areas and that the 25–50 group prefers urban living.

10. First two years, batting average: Player A = .400; Player B = .300
Second two years, batting average: Player A = .200; Player B = .100
All four years, batting average: Player A = .240; Player B = .260
The paradox arises since Player B has most of his or her at bats during the first two years when both players hit a higher average, while Player A had most of his or her hits during the second two years, when both averages were less. Therefore, Player B's overall batting average was weighted towards the higher average.

Chapter 3 Assessment

MULTIPLE-CHOICE QUESTIONS (page 70)

1. B In a bar graph, each column is separate, displaying the value for a distinct category of data.

2. E All of the statements given are accurate.

3. D This value is the y-intercept of the regression line. Therefore, its interpretation is that a person would have an income of $-\$92,040$ if the person has no education.

4. B R^2 does not give an indication of the direction of the relationship. Statements A, C, and D are true.

5. C The term "least squares" refers to the minimization of the sum of the squares of the residual values.

6. C Since each distinct value is a different distance from the mean, each value has a distinct z-score.

FREE-RESPONSE QUESTIONS

Open-Ended Questions (page 70)

1. Box plot

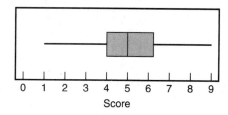

Main features: Very symmetric with no outliers.

2. mean = 5.158; standard deviation = 1.827

3. Since the variable is quantitative, all plots other than the bar graph and pie graph would be appropriate. Since the data are integral, the dot plot or stem plot may be appropriate. However, because of the size of the frequencies, a histogram with the scores at the center of each bar may be the best choice.

4. a. 84th percentile, since approximately 68% of the data is within one standard deviation of the mean.
   b. 2.5 percentile, since approximately 95% of the data is within two standard deviations of the mean.

5. Since the distribution is symmetric and mound-shaped, it is reasonable to use standard scores: The 16th percentile corresponds to a z-score of -1.
$$\frac{x - 70}{10} = -1; x = 60.$$
The 95th percentile corresponds to a z-score of 1.645.
$$\frac{x - 70}{10} = 1.645; x = 86.45$$

6. 23 students. Solving $\dfrac{57.30 \cdot 27 + 65.30n}{27 + n} = 60.98$, we get $n = 23$.

7. Since there are 5 data values, the median must be the 3rd value. However, Q1 must be the average of the first two values and Q3 must be the average of the last two values. Therefore, the data values are not unique. For example, both of these sets satisfy the conditions: {10, 14, 15, 16, 20} and {12, 12, 15, 18, 18}. However, while the data set is not unique, the mean will be!

8. Cents/dozen = 1.0 + 0.678(year)

9. No — the relationship is not very linear. In addition, the residual plot displays a diamond-shaped pattern.

10. The year 1995 corresponds to year 95 from our coding. Therefore, cents/dozen = 65.37. The residual value is -1.37 cents/dozen. While this is a relatively small residual, we would expect the line to overestimate the price per dozen because of the negative value of the residual.

11. With the addition of the 1995 point, the new regression equation is cents/dozen = 6.5 + 0.615(year). Neither the equation, the value of R^2, nor the residual plot changes substantially with the addition of this new data point.

12. Mean = 62.1 and standard deviation = $\sqrt{6.76}$ = 2.6. Therefore, from the z-score formula, $1.5 = \dfrac{x - 62.1}{2.6}; x = 66$.

13. a. The regression equation is cost = 306 − .244(units).
    b. cost = 306 − .244(450) = \$192.20
    c. cost = 306 − .244(800) = \$110.80
    d. Since interpolation is generally more trustworthy than extrapolation, one should have more faith in the prediction in part a than the prediction in part b.

14. a. Scatterplot

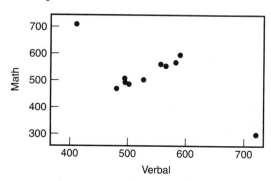

   b. Math = 926.40 − 0.752(Verbal)
   c. Math = 926.40 − 0.752(602) = 473.7
   d. A box plot of the residual values indicates no outliers in the data. The issue of influential points is another matter. The regression equation with (720, 303) deleted is Math = 630 − 0.166(Verbal). Similarly, when the value (410, 714) is deleted, the new regression equation is Math = 770 − 0.482(Verbal). The deletion of either point significantly impacts the original regression equation and therefore each qualifies as an influential point.
   e. While the residual plot displays some degree of scatter, the value of R^2 = .3637 indicates that only 36.37% of the variation in math scores is accounted for in this model. Therefore, we conclude that this model is not a very good predictor.

Investigative Tasks (page 72)

1. a. Scatterplot

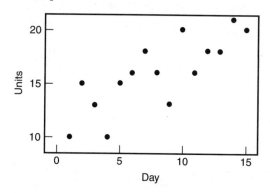

b. Histogram

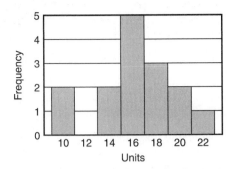

c. Since the question asks for the number of units on a given day, the scatterplot is the best choice.

d. Units = 11.1 + 0.604(Day)

e. Residual Plot

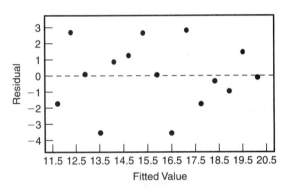

$R^2 = 63.4\%$

f. The residual plot does not display any obvious pattern. Even though R^2 is a bit low, the answers to part e indicate a fairly good fit.

2. a. Scatterplot

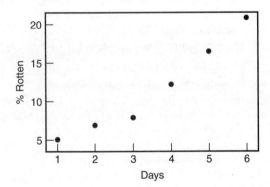

Description: The scatterplot shows a positive relationship that appears fairly linear.

b. Regression line: % Rotten = 0.35 + 3.22(Days)

c. While the value of R^2 is high (95.1%), the residual plot indicates a distinct pattern. Therefore this is not a good fit.

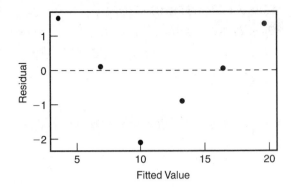

d. Several transformations may be appropriate. We include a logarithmic one as an example.

Row	Days	% Rotten	ln(% Rotten)
1	1	5.1	1.62924
2	2	6.9	1.93152
3	3	7.9	2.06686
4	4	12.3	2.50960
5	5	16.5	2.80336
6	6	21.0	3.04452

e. Regression equation on transformed data:
ln(% Rotten) = 1.32 + 0.290(Days)

f. Since the value of R^2 has increased to 98.5% and the residual plot for the regression of the transformed data displays more scatter, we conclude that this transformation did provide a better model. Comparisons of models should focus on the values of R^2 and on the residual plots.

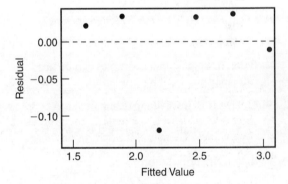

Chapter 4 Planning a Study:
Deciding What and How to Measure

Section 4.1 Basic Terminology and Census

MULTIPLE-CHOICE QUESTIONS (page 75)

1. **B** This is the only choice that includes all members of the population.

2. **C** Note that due to practical difficulties, the US Census does not include 100% of the population.

3. **B** Since the survey only included engineers from a single company, the population cannot be considered all engineers in the industry.

4. **B** Since this is a census, 35% is a parameter, not a statistic.

FREE-RESPONSE QUESTION

Open-Ended Question (page 75)

Answers will vary. It is important for the procedure to include all of the students. Problems involved with the process should focus on the reasonableness and efficiency of the process.

Section 4.2 Sampling

MULTIPLE-CHOICE QUESTIONS (page 82)

1. **C** People may choose whether or not to participate.

2. **B** Multi-stage cluster samples can be used to infer information about a population.

3. **C** This is a multi-stage design.

4. **D** Since not all of the selected lawyers responded, we do not know if those who did are still representative of the population.

5. **C** We can only consider the 63 respondents as our sample. We do not know anything about the lawyers who did not respond.

6. **B** This is the correct method for using a random digit table to select a sample.

7. **B** Note that the 0 is ignored in the progression of digits in the table.

8. **C** In a simple random sample, every subset should have an equal chance of being selected.

FREE-RESPONSE QUESTIONS

Open-Ended Questions (page 83)

1. a, b. Answers will vary depending on the choice of selection.
   c. The mean of the population is 65.89
   d, e. Answers will vary depending on the choice of selection.

2. a. Yes
   b. No

3. a. Yes
   b. No

4. a. No
   b. Perhaps

5. a. No
   b. Yes

6. a. No
   b. Yes

7. a. No
   b. Yes

8. a. No
   b. Yes

9. a. Population: All fast food restaurants that advertise in the yellow pages.
   b. Sampling Method: Simple random sample
   c. Sampling Valid? Yes
   d. Reason: Simple random samples are valid.

10. a. Population: All viewers of the broadcast.
    b. Sampling Method: Voluntary response
    c. Sampling Valid? No
    d. Reason: Only viewers with strong opinions will call.

11. a. Population: Student body of the school.
    b. Sampling Method: Systematic
    c. Sampling Valid? Yes
    d. Reason: All subsets have the same chance of selection.

12. a. Population: All students in the high school.
    b. Sampling Method: Quota
    c. Sampling Valid? No
    d. Reason: Not all subsets have the same chance of selection.

13. Answers may vary. One possible set of descriptions is:
  a. Voluntary response sampling: Teacher asks for 5 volunteers.
  b. Convenience sampling: Teacher chooses the last 5 students to enter the room.
  c. Quota sampling: Teacher chooses students in proportion to gender distribution in class.
  d. Simple random sampling: Teacher assigns numbers to each student and randomly selects 5 numbers.
  e. Stratified random sampling: Teacher performs a random selection of one student from each of 5 rows of seats.
  f. Multi-stage cluster sampling: Teacher randomly chooses 2 rows. Teacher randomly selects 3 from one and 2 from the other.
  g. Systematic sampling: Teacher uses numbers on the class list. Teacher selects a starting point randomly and uses an appropriate interval so that 5 students will be selected.

14. Answers will vary. A set of possible answers is:
  a. Voluntary response sampling: Only the well-prepared students will volunteer.
  b. Convenience sampling: Only the less motivated might enter the room last.
  c. Quota sampling: A significant difference in the number of boys and girls could skew the probability of an individual being selected.

Section 4.3 Controlled Experiments

MULTIPLE-CHOICE QUESTIONS (page 91)

1. B

2. B

3. D

4. B

5. C

6. C

FREE-RESPONSE QUESTIONS

Open-Ended Questions (page 91)

1. a. No. Subjects choose whether they are in the treatment or control groups.
   b. Explanatory: location; Response: voting preference. Levels of the explanatory variable: rural, suburban, urban.
   c. Answers will vary. Be careful to make sure that all teachers in all settings have a chance to be included in the sample.
   d. Run a simple random sample within rural schools, suburban schools, and urban schools.

2. Answers will vary. An example of a correct answer is

a.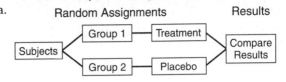

b.

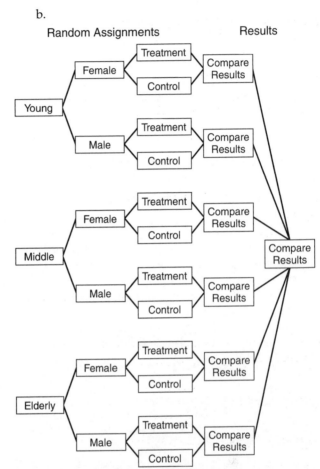

3. a. The investigator can randomly place individuals interested in the surgery into groups for procedure A and for procedure B. Perform the surgeries and monitor the degree of improvement for each group. Compare the mean degree of improvement for each group.
  b. Perform procedure A on one eye, randomly selected, and procedure B on the other eye and compare the difference in the degrees of improvements of each eye (the A eye – the B eye) for each participant.
  c. Answers will vary.
  d. Answers will vary but should focus on the recruitment of subjects for each group.

Section 4.4 Observational Studies

MULTIPLE-CHOICE QUESTIONS (page 92)

1. C

2. B

3. C

FREE-RESPONSE QUESTIONS

Open-Ended Questions (page 93)

1. There could be many lurking variables such as pace of life, levels of stress, diet, lack of exercise, etc.

2. Comparisons of rates are suspicious.

3. In a temperate climate, there are fewer very hot days each year during which a riot could occur.

4. Answers will vary. One possible design for the observational study might be: Randomly select 200 kernels of each brand and pop them in the same popper. Count the number of unpopped kernels when finished. Make sure that the popper is cool before starting each popping session. An experiment is not possible since the investigator cannot impose the brands on the kernels.

Chapter 4 Assessment

MULTIPLE-CHOICE QUESTIONS (page 93)

1. C

2. C

3. **B** The director is investigating whether gender affects lunchtime activities.

4. E

5. C

6. E

7. D

8. E

9. E

10. E

11. **A** We do not necessarily have to code all of the members, but we must be able to calculate the probability that any particular one is selected.

12. E

13. D

14. E

15. C or **B** C is preferable but B is also valid.

FREE-RESPONSE QUESTIONS

Open-Ended Questions (page 95)

1. a. Select a simple random sample of 10 from each class.
   b. Select a simple random sample of 20 males and a simple random sample of 20 females.
   c. Select a simple random sample of size 40.

2. Answers may vary. One possible correct answer would be to block beds (1, 4), (2, 5), and (3, 6). *Within each pair,* assignment of beds to the new fertilizer or the traditional fertilizer should be accomplished randomly. A coin could be flipped; random digit tables could be used; or a random number generator could be employed as well. With the block arrangement, data from each pairing should be compared and analyzed separately.

Investigative Tasks (page 95)

1. The five tables of the random samples will vary. Coding should be consistent with the instructions for coding the given population.
   b. Means and standard deviations will depend on samples selected.
   c. Plots will vary but the five means should be relatively close to the mean of the population (64.275) and the standard deviations should be relatively close to the population standard deviation (4.49).
   d. The data analysis and plots should show that there is a consistency in the sample means and sample standard deviations.

2. Answers may vary. Possible correct graphics are shown below.

a.

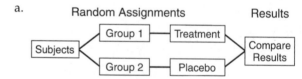

b.

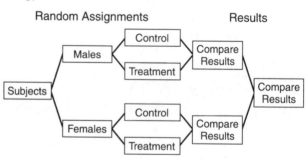

c.

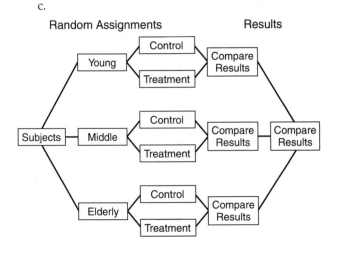

Random Assignments   Results

d.

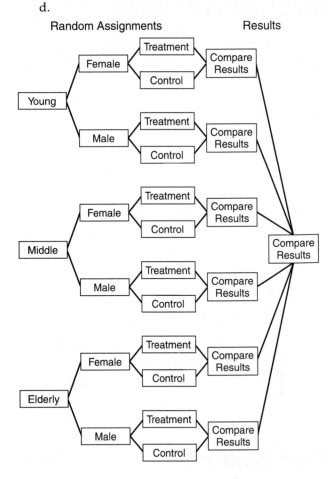

Random Assignments   Results

Chapter 5 Anticipating Patterns:
Producing Models Using Probability and Simulation

Section 5.1 Basic Concepts

MULTIPLE-CHOICE QUESTIONS (page 102)

1. D We observe twelve 3s in the 60 rolls. $\frac{12}{60} = \frac{1}{5}$.

2. D The sums can range from 2 to 12.

3. C These are complementary probabilities: $1 - \frac{1}{3} = \frac{2}{3}$

4. A Choice II is geometric; Choice III has more than 2 outcomes.

5. D Calculate accidents/year as a percent of daily traffic flow. *W*: .16; *X*: .20; *Y*: .14; *Z*: .23.

FREE-RESPONSE QUESTIONS

Open-Ended Questions (page 103)

1. a. The cards are: {1, 1, 2, 3, 3, 4, 5, 5, 6, 7, 7, 8, 9, 9, 10}
The sample space is: {1, 2, 3, 4, 5, 6, 7, 8, 9, 10}

b.

X	1	2	3	4	5	6	7	8	9	10
P(X)	$\frac{2}{15}$	$\frac{1}{15}$	$\frac{2}{15}$	$\frac{1}{15}$	$\frac{2}{15}$	$\frac{1}{15}$	$\frac{2}{15}$	$\frac{1}{15}$	$\frac{2}{15}$	$\frac{1}{15}$

c. All probabilities are greater than or equal to 0; the sum of the probabilities is 1.

d.

Event	Subset	Probability
Number is even	{2, 4, 6, 8, 10}	$\frac{5}{15}$
Number > 7	{8, 9, 10}	$\frac{4}{15}$
Number is prime	{2, 3, 5, 7}	$\frac{7}{15}$
Number is a multiple of 3	{3, 6, 9}	$\frac{5}{15}$

2. a. {2, 3, 4, 5, 6, 7, 8, 9, 10, 11, 12}

b.

X	2	3	4	5	6	7	8	9	10	11	12
P(X)	$\frac{1}{36}$	$\frac{2}{36}$	$\frac{3}{36}$	$\frac{4}{36}$	$\frac{5}{36}$	$\frac{6}{36}$	$\frac{5}{36}$	$\frac{4}{36}$	$\frac{3}{36}$	$\frac{2}{36}$	$\frac{1}{36}$

c. All probabilities are greater than or equal to 0; the sum of the probabilities is 1.

d.

Event	Subset	Probability
Sum = 7	{7}	$\frac{6}{36} = \frac{1}{6}$
Sum is even.	{2, 4, 6, 8, 10, 12}	$\frac{18}{36} = \frac{1}{2}$
Sum is between 4 and 9, inclusive.	{4, 5, 6, 7, 8, 9}	$\frac{27}{36} = \frac{2}{3}$
Sum is less than 5.	{2, 3, 4}	$\frac{6}{36} = \frac{1}{6}$

3. a. Neither. The probability is not the same for each trial.

   b. Geometric. The probabilities are the same on each trial and we are looking for the number of trials before a success occurs. In addition, each trial is independent.

   c. Binomial. The probability is the same for each trial, independence is given, and we are looking for the probability that a certain number of successes occurs in a fixed number of trials.

   d. Neither. The probability is a function of the distance traveled.

Section 5.2 Calculating Probabilities for Combinations of Events

MULTIPLE-CHOICE QUESTIONS (page 108)

1. D P(good then defective or defective then good)

2. E $P(A \mid B) = 0$ if A and B are disjoint; $P(A \mid B) = A$ if A and B are independent; $P(A \mid B) = B$ if $P(A$ and $B)$ $= [P(B)]^2$; $P(A \mid B) = 1$ if A is a subset of B.

3. D The probability of the event of both A and B occurring cannot be greater than either the probability of event A occurring or the probability of event B occurring.

4. C A and C cannot happen at the same time.

5. E P(on committee and chair) $= P$(chair $\mid$ on committee) $\cdot P$(on committee) $= .06$.

6. D This is the complement of the result in question 5.

FREE-RESPONSE QUESTIONS

Open-Ended Questions (page 108)

1. P(flipping a head and rolling a sum of 8) $=$

P(flipping a head) $\times P$(rolling a sum of 8) $= \frac{1}{2} \times \frac{5}{36}$

$= \frac{5}{72}$.

2. P(nickel, dime, nickel) $= \frac{11}{20} \times \frac{4}{19} \times \frac{10}{18} = \frac{11}{171}$.

3. P(sum of 8 or both even) $= P$(sum of 8) $+$

P(both even) $- P$(sum of 8 and both even)

$= \frac{5}{36} + \frac{9}{36} - \frac{3}{36} = \frac{11}{36}$.

4. P(saw the commercial and bought) $=$
P(bought $\mid$ saw) $\cdot P$(saw) $= .6(.15) = .09$

5. A tree is helpful for this problem.

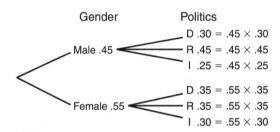

   a. P(Women) $= .55$

   b. P(Male and Republican) $= (.45)(.45) = .2025$

   c. P(Male $\mid$ Democrat) $= \dfrac{(.45)(.30)}{(.45)(.30) + (.55)(.35)} = .4122$

6. P(5 heads in 5 tosses) $= \left(\dfrac{1}{2}\right)^5 = \dfrac{1}{32}$

7. P(ace then king) $= P$(ace) $\cdot P$(king $\mid$ ace) $= \dfrac{4}{52} \cdot \dfrac{4}{51} = .06$

8. A tree may be helpful for this problem.

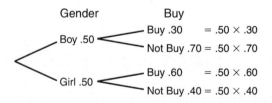

P(buy on the Internet) $= (.5)(.3) + (.5)(.6) = .45$

P(girl $\mid$ buy on the Internet) $= \dfrac{(.5)(.6)}{(.5)(.6) + (.5)(.3)} = \dfrac{2}{3}$

9. P(desk and computer) $= P$(desk) $+ P$(computer) $-$
P(desk or computer) $= .6 + .8 - .9 = .5$

Section 5.3 Counting Techniques (Optional)

FREE-RESPONSE QUESTIONS
Open-Ended Questions (page 112)

1. $5 \cdot 7 \cdot 4 = 140$

2. $26 \cdot 26 \cdot 26 \cdot 10 \cdot 10 \cdot 10 = 17{,}576{,}000$

3. $41 \cdot 41 \cdot 41 = 68{,}921$

4. $9 \cdot 5 \cdot 10 \cdot 5 = 2{,}250$. *Note:* Only 9 numbers are possible for the 1st digit.

5. $4 \cdot 3 \cdot 2 \cdot 1 \cdot 4 \cdot 3 \cdot 2 \cdot 1 = 576$

6. a. 10
   b. 10
   c. 210
   d. 210
   e. 2,598,960
   f. 2,598,960

7. a. $\binom{100}{96} = \binom{100}{4} = 3{,}921{,}225$

   b. $\binom{250}{247} = \binom{250}{3} = 2{,}573{,}000$

   c. $\binom{n}{r} = \binom{n}{n-r}$

8. a. $\binom{10}{4} = 210$

   b. Order matters since each order will give a different set of officers. Therefore, we have $_{10}P_4 = 5{,}040$.

9. $\binom{10}{3}\binom{8}{2}\binom{5}{1} = 16{,}800$

10. $\dfrac{\binom{150}{0}\binom{40+35+20}{12}}{\binom{245}{12}} = 7.36 \times 10^{-6}$, very unlikely.

11. $\dfrac{\binom{4}{3}\binom{4}{2}\binom{44}{0}}{\binom{52}{5}} = 9.23 \times 10^{-6}$

Section 5.4 Binomial and Geometric Probability

MULTIPLE-CHOICE QUESTIONS (page 118)

1. **D** For 8 games, this situation follows *Binomial*(8, .4).

2. **A or C** We are counting the number of arrangements for a specific order.

3. **B** This is a geometric situation.

4. **C** This is only a characteristic of a binomial.

5. **C** $nPr = r! \cdot nCr$

FREE-RESPONSE QUESTIONS
Open-Ended Questions (page 118)

1. a. Binomial: probability is the same on each trial; each trial is independent; fixed number of trials.
   b. Let X = the number of homeruns in the 50 at-bats.
   c. $P(X) = \dfrac{2}{11}$; number of trials = 50
   d. {0, 1, 2, ..., 50}

2. a. Let X = number of boxes until you get a picture of Babe Ruth
   b. Probability on each trial is the same; independent trials; X = number of trials.
   c. {1, 2, ...}

It is recommended that these probabilities be calculated directly as indicated and checked using the functions on the *DISTR* menu of the TI-83.

3. $\binom{10}{7}(.6^7)(.4^3) = .2150$

4. $\binom{30}{15}(.79^{15})(.21^{15}) = .00031$

5. No, because p may not be the same on all trials; each trial may not be independent as well.

6. $\binom{5}{3}(.5^3)(.5^2) = .3125$

7. $\binom{6}{0}(.75^0)(.25^6) + \binom{6}{1}(.75^1)(.25^5) + \ldots + \binom{6}{5}(.75^5)(.25^1)$
   $= binomcdf(6, .75, 5)$
   $= 1 - \binom{6}{6}(.75^6)(.25^0)$
   $= .8220$

8. $\binom{10}{8}(.7^8)(.3^2) + \binom{10}{9}(.7^9)(.3^1) + \binom{10}{10}(.7^{10})(.3^0)$
   $= binomcdf(10, .7, 10) - binomcdf(10, .7, 6) = .6496$

9. a. Geometric; $.8(.2) = .16$
   b. Geometric; $(.8^9)(.2) = .0268$
   c. P(getting Babe Ruth) = .2; P(getting Mickey Mantle) = .2. Therefore, P(getting neither Babe nor Mickey) = .6
   Therefore, $p = .2 + (.6)(.2) + (.6^2)(.2) + \ldots$
   $= \sum_{i=1}^{\infty} .2(.6)^{i-1}$ that is, an infinite geometric series
   $= \dfrac{.2}{1-.6} = .5$
   Or note that since the probability of getting either star is the same, there is a probability of 50% that one will occur before the other assuming that there are equal numbers of pictures available.

Section 5.5 Probability Distributions of Discrete Random Variables

MULTIPLE-CHOICE QUESTIONS (page 122)

1. **B** I: sum of the probabilities is greater than 1; IV: one of the probabilities is negative.

2. **B** Only II and III are probability distributions, and the values of III are negative.

3. **C** Only II and III are probability distributions and the range is smaller in III.

4. **B** For example, the graph of a geometric distribution is not symmetric.

5. **C** $\binom{100}{0}(.04^0)(.96^{100}) = binompdf(100, .04, 0) = .0169$

6. **D**

FREE-RESPONSE QUESTIONS

Open-Ended Questions (page 123)

1. a.

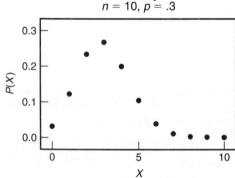

Binomial Probability Distribution
$n = 10, p = .3$

b.

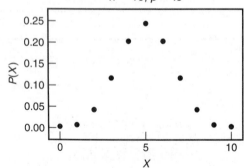

Binomial Probability Distribution
$n = 10, p = .5$

c.

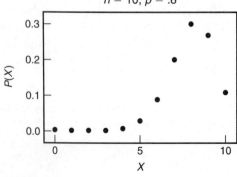

Binomial Probability Distribution
$n = 10, p = .8$

2. a. mean = 3; standard deviation = 1.45
   b. mean = 5; standard deviation = 1.58
   c. mean = 8; standard deviation = 1.26

3. a. Expected value = $(+1)\left(\dfrac{18}{38}\right) + (-1)\left(\dfrac{20}{38}\right) = -.0526$

   b. Expect to *lose* 5.26 cents for each dollar bet.

4. Expected value using the strategy = $(.50)(.6) + (1.25)(.4) = .80$; On average, using the strategy will cost 80 cents. Therefore it is better to use Machine A each time.

5. a. Expected value = $162.7(.7) = 113.4$
   b. Standard error = $\sqrt{162.7(.7)(.3)} = 5.83$ assuming the probability (.7) is the same for each game and that each game is independent.

6. Expected value = $(+35)\left(\dfrac{1}{38}\right) + (-1)\left(\dfrac{37}{38}\right) = -.0526$

Section 5.6 Probability Distributions of Continuous Random Variables

MULTIPLE-CHOICE QUESTIONS (page 128)

1. **E**

2. **B** $z = -1.28 = \dfrac{38 - 50}{\sigma}$ or $z = 1.28 = \dfrac{62 - 50}{\sigma}$

3. **E** I is true only for mound-shaped symmetric; II is not necessarily true; III: z-scores should only be used with normal distributions.

FREE-RESPONSE QUESTIONS

Open-Ended Questions (page 128)

1. X = height of a randomly chosen man;
   $X \sim Normal(69.1, 3.5)$: so
   a. .02125
   b. .5802
   c. .3985
   d. 1, since they span the entire sample space.

2. a. 10.6 or 11
   b. 290.1 or 290
   c. 199.25 or 199

3. X = length of ride; $X \sim Normal\,(25, 12.3)$: $P(X > 60$ when mean = 25, st. dev. = 12.3) = .0022
   Taking 60 minutes when the mean is 25 and the standard deviation is 12.3 is very unlikely.

4. 736.95 or 737 — 95th percentile corresponds to a z-score of 1.645. $\dfrac{x - 556}{110} = 1.645$

5. X = household income, $X \sim Normal\,(52137, 19452)$: .4677

6. It would seem that the distribution is skewed right since if it were symmetric there would have to be negative distances to satisfy the Empirical Rule (64–95–99.7). However, just knowing the mean and standard deviation does not guarantee anything about the shape of the distribution.

7. $P(X > 12$ when $\bar{x} = 9.4$, s unknown$) = .05$

   $1.645 = \dfrac{12 - 9.4}{s}$

   $s = 1.58$ miles

Section 5.7 Normal Approximation of the Binomial Distribution

MULTIPLE-CHOICE QUESTIONS (page 133)

1. **D** These conditions monitor skewness. If the distribution is severely skewed, the approximation will be inaccurate.

2. **E**

FREE-RESPONSE QUESTIONS

Open-Ended Questions (page 134)

1. X = number of games bowler scored 200 or more; $X \sim Binomial(5, .4)$.

   Formula: $\binom{5}{3}(.4^3)(.6^2) + \binom{5}{4}(.4^4)(.6^1) + \binom{5}{5}(.4^4)(.6^0) = .3174$

   TI-83: $1 - binomcdf(5, .4, 2) = .3174$

   Normal Approximation: Not valid since $np = 5(.6) = 3$ is not greater than 10.

2. X = number of days with a gross over \$1000; $X \sim Binomial(6, .8)$.

   Formula: $\binom{6}{5}(.8^5)(.2^1) + \binom{6}{6}(.8^6)(.2^0) = .6554$

   TI-83: $1 - binomcdf(6, .8, 4) = .6554$

   Normal Approximation: Not valid since $np = 6(.8) = 4.8$ is not greater than 10.

3. X = number of doctors with correct diagnosis; $X \sim Binomial(10, .95)$

   Formula: $\binom{10}{10}(.95^{10})(.05^0) = .5987$

   TI-83: $1 - binomcdf(10, .95, 9) = .5987$

   Normal Approximation: Not valid since $np = 10(.05) = .5$ is not greater than 10.

4. P(diagnosis correct when pathological) $= \dfrac{4}{5}$

   P(diagnosis correct when normal) $= \dfrac{3}{5}$

   X = number of correct diagnoses
   a. $X \sim Binomial(3, .8)$

   Formula: $\binom{3}{1}(.8^1)(.2^2) = .0960$

   TI-83: $binomcdf(3, .8, 2) - binomcdf(3, .8, 0) = .0960$

   Normal Approximation: Not valid since $np = 8(.3) = 2.4$ is not greater than 10.

b. $X \sim Binomial(3, .6)$

   Formula: $\binom{3}{1}(.6^1)(.4^2) = .2880$

   TI-83: $binomcdf(3, .6, 2) - binomcdf(3, .6, 0) = .2880$

   Normal Approximation: Not valid since $np = 3(.6) = 1.8$ is not greater than 10.

Section 5.8 The Sum and Difference of Random Variables

MULTIPLE-CHOICE QUESTIONS (page 138)

1. B	2. B
3. C	4. D

5. **B**

6. **D** B would be the correct answer if we assume that the regions are independent; however it is more reasonable that the regions are not independent.

FREE-RESPONSE QUESTIONS

Open-Ended Questions (page 138)

1. Combined mean: $\mu_1 + \mu_2 = 42 + 38 = 80$. Combined standard deviation is not possible because the scores are not independent.

2. Mean difference $= 72.5 - 65 = 7.5$. Combined standard deviation is not possible because the heights are not independent.

3. Mean score $= 113.3 + 10(6.2) = 175.3$. Combined standard deviation is not possible because the scores are not independent.

4. a.

$2L + M$	5	6	7	8	9	10	11	12	13	14
P	.01	.01	.04	.08	.07	.15	.10	.22	.08	.24

   b. Mean $= 11.3$; standard deviation $= \sqrt{4 + 1.01} = \sqrt{5.01} \approx 2.24$

Section 5.9 Overview of Theoretical Probability Functions

MULTIPLE-CHOICE QUESTIONS (page 143)

1. **D** $P(success) = .7$

2. **A** The area does not equal 1.

3. **A**

4. **C**

5. **D** X = number of visits until he receives his first \$100 credit; $X \sim Geometric(.01)$

Open-Ended Questions (page 143)

1.

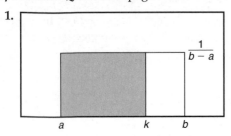

$P(a < X < b)$ = area of rectangle under the function over the interval from a to b.

2. The Binomial focuses on the probability of a number of successes in a given, fixed number of trials. The Geometric focuses on the probability of the first success on a specific trial.

3. X = number of games until 1st win;
$X \sim Geometric(.6)$: $P = .4^2 + .4^3(.6) = .1344$

4. X = number of tests passed; $X \sim Binomial(10, .4)$; so
   a. $\binom{10}{4}(.4^4)(.6^6) = .2508$
   b. $(.6^3)(.4) = .0864$

5. a.

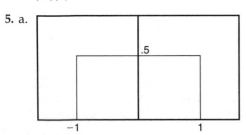

   b. $f(x) = \begin{cases} .5 & -1 \le x \le 1 \\ 0 & \text{otherwise} \end{cases}$

   c. all probabilities = areas; therefore, all probabilities ≥ 0; area of rectangle = 1.

   d.

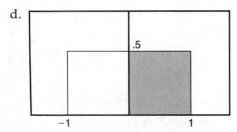

   $P(0 < x < 1) = .5$

Section 5.10 Simulating Events With Random Digits Tables and the TI-83

FREE-RESPONSE QUESTIONS

Open-Ended Questions (page 145)

1. Answers may vary. Examples of possible solutions: Using a random digit table, assign 0 and 1 to a success (getting a special prize) and 2 to 9 a failure.

   a. Randomly choose 10 blocks of 10 digits each and record how many of them have only one 0 or 1. Calculate the proportion. Repeat.
   b. Begin at any location in the table and record how many digits occur before the first 0 or 1 occurs. Repeat.

2. Answers may vary. Examples of possible solutions: Using a random digit table, assign 0 to a success (finding gold) and 1 to 9 a failure.
   a. Randomly choose blocks of 20 digits and record the number of the blocks that contain two 0's. Calculate the proportion.
   b. Begin at any location in the table and record how many digits occur before the second 0 occurs. Repeat.

3. a. Standard, because there is a fixed sample size (250).
   b. Assign 0 to 2 to female managers; 3 to 9 to male managers.
   c. Use blocks of 10 digits. Proportions of female managers are .2, .4, .2, .4, .3, .7, .1, .2, .3, .5, .5, .2, .3, .2, .2, .2, .6, .4, .1, .3. Show the blocks using vertical bars: | |, and circle the successes.
   d. $\frac{7}{20}$. Out of the 20 blocks, there were 7 with 20% female managers.

4. a. Wait-time, because we continue the simulation until the desired situation occurs.
   b. Assign 2-digit blocks from 00 to 14 to failure, and 15 to 99 to success.
   c. Record the number of pairs of digits until 2 pairs from 00 to 14 occur. Results: 8, 25, 22, 24, 11. Show blocking of pairs using | | and circle the failures.
   d. Mean number of events before the 2 failures occur is 18. Therefore, we expect about 18 trials.

Chapter 5 Assessment

MULTIPLE-CHOICE QUESTIONS (page 146)

1. **B** Assuming only one winner; probabilities must total 1.

2. **E** P(two teens) + P(teen and adult)

3. **C** Product of the four probabilities since the events are independent.

4. **D** Complementary probability:
   P(at least one works) = $1 - P$(none works)

5. **B** There are 96 republicans of whom 32 are over the age of 50.

6. **A** Total number of adults = 238; 17 are democrats between 41 and 50.

7. **B** There are 63 people between 31 and 40 of whom 10 are independent.

8. C $\frac{61}{238} + \frac{54}{238} - \frac{15}{238}$ (15 adults in both categories.)

9. B Since $P(A \text{ and } B)$ is non-zero, A and B are not mutually exclusive; Since $P(A \text{ and } B)$ does not equal $P(A)P(B)$, the events are not independent.

10. A The probability is .5 for each trial; we are looking for 3 successes in 6 trials, assuming one of the genders is a success.

11. D In any large group, height is likely to follow a normal curve. Note that the mean and standard deviation are given.

12. A The probability is .04 for each fruit. We are looking for no more than 6 successes in 100 trials, assuming that a rotten fruit is considered a success.

13. B The probability is .27 for each trial. We are looking for the first success that occurs in a variable number of trials.

FREE-RESPONSE QUESTIONS

Open-Ended Questions (page 148)

1. X = number of free throws made;
$X \sim Binomial\,(5, .7)$: $\binom{5}{3}(.7^3)(.3^2) = .3087$

2. X = shot number of first score; $X \sim Geometric\,(.7)$:
$(.3^2)(.7) = .063$

3. a. $(.07)(.98) + (.93)(.01) = .0779$
  b. $\dfrac{.07(.98)}{.07(.98) + .93(.01)} = .8806$
  c. The test is not reliable: 12% of the time, a patient who is free of the disease tests positive. A reliable test should show positive results for a patient who is free of the disease a much smaller percentage of the time.

4. a. X = number of boxes with 3 or more rotten oranges; $X \sim Binomial(20, .05)$: $\binom{20}{2}(.05^2)(.95^{18}) = .1887$
  b. $np = 1$: does not satisfy the skewness criterion.

5. Density or mass functions for discrete variables provide probabilities as the values of the dependent variable of the function. Density functions for continuous variables use areas under the curve over specified intervals to determine probabilities.

Investigative Tasks (page 148)

1. a. X = number of bull's eyes; $X \sim Binomial\,(70, .6)$:
  $\binom{70}{40}(.6^{40})(.4^{30}) = .0853$
  b. $binompdf(70, .6, 40) = .0853$
  c. $np = 70(.6) = 42$; $n(1-p) = 70(.4) = 28$; therefore, normal approximation is justified.
  d. $normalcdf(39.5, 40.5, 70(.6), \sqrt{70(.6)(.4)}\,) = .0862$
  e. The answer in d is a good approximation of a and b.
  f. Assign the digits 0 through 5 to bull's eye and 6 through 9 to misses. Choosing blocks of 70 digits repeated, record how many blocks contain 40 bull's eyes (0 to 5). Calculate the proportion of successes.
  g. New question: Determine the probability that she will hit her 40th bull's eye on the 70th shot.

2. a. (1).

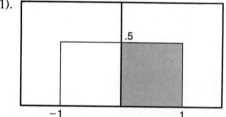

$p = 3\left(\dfrac{1}{8.75}\right) = .3429$
  (2) $normalcdf(12, 15, 13.65, 3.75) = .3106$
  (3) $\chi^2 cdf(12, 15, 14) = .2281$
  b. Based on these investigations, a good response would be that there is approximately a 30% chance that the package can be delivered within 12 to 15 hours of its pickup.

Chapter 6 Sampling Distributions

Section 6.1 Introduction

MULTIPLE-CHOICE QUESTION (page 151)

C I: The mean of the population is constant no matter what sample is taken from this population. II: Sample standard deviations may vary from sample to sample.

Section 6.2 The Concept of a Sampling Distribution

MULTIPLE-CHOICE QUESTIONS (page 154)

1. **C** The sampling distribution is the distribution of all of the statistics calculated from all possible samples of size n that can be selected from the population — not data values.

2. **E** Note that the variance of the sampling distribution will not be close to the variance of the population since it decreases as sample size increases.

3. **B**

4. **B**

5. **E** The histograms will become more mound-shaped and symmetric as the sample size increases, not the number of simulations.

6. **C** Since both populations are greater than 10 times their samples, sample size determines whether the sample statistics obtained are unbiased estimators.

FREE-RESPONSE QUESTION

Open-Ended Question (page 155)

There are $\frac{3}{5}$ = .6 red cards in the population. Thus, the center of the sampling distribution should be close to .6. Since $np = 10(.6) = 6$, we can't expect a normal symmetric shape. Changing the number of samples does not change the variability.

Section 6.3 The Sampling Distribution of a Sample Proportion

MULTIPLE-CHOICE QUESTIONS (page 159)

1. **D** Assuming that the size of the population is much bigger than the sample size, the sampling distribution variance depends only on the sample size. The formula for the variance of the sampling distribution of a proportion attains a maximum when $p = .5$.

2. **C**

3. **C** Since the standard deviation of the sampling distribution of the sampling proportion is .04 (using $p = .2$), a difference of 5% is not extreme.

4. **A** Remember to use the population parameter, p, in this calculation. Since $p = .15$ and $n = 50$,

$$\sigma = \sqrt{\frac{.15(.85)}{50}} = .0505.$$

FREE-RESPONSE QUESTIONS

Open-Ended Questions (page 160)

1. SRS? Stated ✓
   Population large? All adults ✓
   $np = 200(.6) = 120 \geq 10$ ✓

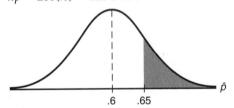

   $n(1 - p) = 200(.4) = 80 \geq 10$ ✓
   Want $P(\hat{p} \geq .65)$ assuming $n = 200$ and $p = .6$.

   $\sigma\hat{p} = \sqrt{\frac{.6(.4)}{200}} = .035$

   $z = \frac{\hat{p} - p}{\sigma\hat{p}} = \frac{.65 - .6}{.035} = 1.44$

   Therefore, $P(\hat{p} > .65) = .075$
   This indicates that such a sample result ($\hat{p} > .65$) would happen only about 7.5% of the time in a sample of size 200 (large) when $p = .6$.

2. $\hat{p} = \frac{5}{50} = .10$. What is the probability that a sample of size 50 would result in a sample proportion of 5 or fewer defectives?
   SRS? Stated ✓
   Population large? Manufacturing process ✓
   $np = 50(.05) = 2.5$ Calculation of the probability cannot be completed since 2.5 is less than 10.

3. SRS? Stated ✓

Population large? Yes, assuming that the sample is drawn from students enrolled in math classes over a period of time.

$np = 50(.70) = 35$ ✓

$n(1 - p) = 50(.30) = 15$ ✓

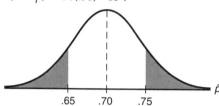

Want $P(\hat{p} \le .65$ or $\hat{p} \ge .75$ when $p = .7)$

$\sigma\hat{p} = \sqrt{\dfrac{.7(.3)}{50}} = .0648$

$z = \dfrac{.65 - .7}{.0648} = -.772 \qquad P(\hat{p} \le .65) = .2206$

$z = \dfrac{.7 - .75}{.0648} = .772 \qquad P(\hat{p} \ge .75) = .2206$

So the probability of obtaining a sample proportion more than .05 away from $p = .7$ is $.2206 + .2206 = .4412$. So such a result would happen in 44% of samples of size 50 drawn from this population and would not be surprising.

4. SRS? Stated ✓

Population large? $200(10) = 2,000 > 1,000$. Since the population size of 1,000 is only 5 times, not 10 times the size of the sample we cannot consider this assumption met.

5. Assuming a large population, what we want to find is the sample size needed to produce a proportion less than .61 5% of the time and more than .65 5% of the time. Since the z-value that corresponds to this situation is 1.645, we substitute in the formula for a z-score to find n, the sample size.

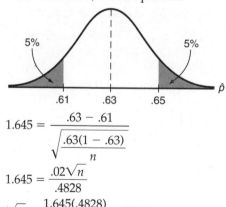

$1.645 = \dfrac{.63 - .61}{\sqrt{\dfrac{.63(1 - .63)}{n}}}$

$1.645 = \dfrac{.02\sqrt{n}}{.4828}$

$\sqrt{n} = \dfrac{1.645(.4828)}{.02} = 39.71$

$n = 1,576.93$

So we need an n of at least 1,577 (always round up).

Section 6.4 The Sampling Distribution of a Difference of Two Proportions

MULTIPLE-CHOICE QUESTIONS (page 164)

1. C

2. B Remember that the formula for adding variances requires the two sample proportions, $\hat{p}_1$ and $\hat{p}_2$, to be independent.

3. C

4. A $\sigma_{\hat{p}1 - \hat{p}2} = \sqrt{\dfrac{.44(.56)}{10} + \dfrac{.44(.56)}{25}} = .1857$

The small sample size indicates that we cannot assume normality, but the formula for the standard deviation is true regardless of the shape of the distribution.

Note: Even though the data come from a single sample, the performances of males and females can be considered independent. Therefore, the assumption of independent samples is not violated.

FREE-RESPONSE QUESTIONS

Open-Ended Questions (page 164)

1. Independent SRSs? Stated ✓
Large populations? High school students ✓
Large enough sample sizes?
$.9(100) = 90 \ge 10$ ✓
$.1(100) = 10 \ge 10$ ✓
$.14(75) = 10.5 \ge 10$ ✓
$.86(75) = 64.5 \ge 10$ ✓
Independent? Males and females ✓
$P(\hat{p}_F - \hat{p}_M \le .71$ when $p_F - p_M = .76)$

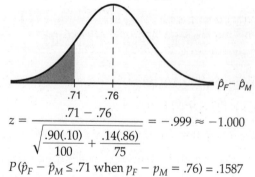

$z = \dfrac{.71 - .76}{\sqrt{\dfrac{.90(.10)}{100} + \dfrac{.14(.86)}{75}}} = -.999 \approx -1.000$

$P(\hat{p}_F - \hat{p}_M \le .71$ when $p_F - p_M = .76) = .1587$

2. Independent SRSs? Stated ✓
Large populations? Large university ✓
Large enough sample sizes?
$.3(56) = 16.8 \ge 10$ ✓
$.7(56) = 39.2 \ge 10$ ✓
$.22(44) = 9.68 \approx 10$ ✓
$.78(44) = 34.32 \ge 10$ ✓
Independent? Males and females ✓
Claim: $p_F - p_M = .08$

$\hat{p}_M = \dfrac{15}{56} = .268$

$$\hat{p}_F = \frac{17}{44} = .386$$

$P(\hat{p}_M - \hat{p}_F < -.118 \text{ when } p_M - p_F = .08)$

$$z = \frac{-.118 - .08}{\sqrt{\dfrac{.30(.70)}{56} + \dfrac{.22(.78)}{44}}} = -2.26$$

$P(\hat{p}_M - \hat{p}_F < -.118 \text{ when } p_M - p_F = .08) = .0119$

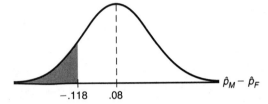

3. $50(.04) = 2$, which is not greater than or equal to 10. The large enough sample size assumption is violated.

4. We want a probability of .2, in both tails. This corresponds to a z-value of ± 1.28. So we want

$$1.28 = \frac{.03}{\sqrt{\dfrac{.05(.95)}{n} + \dfrac{.05(.95)}{n}}}$$

$$1.28 = \frac{.03}{\sqrt{\dfrac{2(.05)(.95)}{n}}}$$

$$1.28 = \frac{.03\sqrt{n}}{.308}$$

$$\frac{1.28(.308)}{.03} = \sqrt{n}$$

$$13.15 = \sqrt{n}$$

$$172.92 \approx n$$

Each sample should contain 173 plants (always round up).

Section 6.5 The Sampling Distribution of a Sample Mean (σ known)

MULTIPLE-CHOICE QUESTIONS (page 167)

1. **C**

2. **D** $\sigma_{\bar{x}} = \dfrac{\sigma}{\sqrt{25}} = 3.5$; so $\sigma = 3.5(5) = 17.5$

3. **B** Since the sample size is large ($n = 100 > 30$) it is reasonable to assume that the sampling distribution of the sample mean is approximately normal with a mean of 625 and standard deviation $\dfrac{\sigma}{\sqrt{n}} = \dfrac{44.5}{\sqrt{100}} = 4.45$.

4. **C** The standard deviation of the sampling distribution can't equal the population standard deviation since it will decrease as the sample size is increased (making the $\bar{x}$ values lie closer to μ).

5. **A** Since the sample size is large ($n = 100 > 30$) we will assume that the sampling distribution is approximately normal, with mean 3.5 and standard deviation $\dfrac{\sigma}{\sqrt{n}} = \dfrac{1.9}{\sqrt{100}} = .19$ minutes. We want to

find $P(\bar{x} > 4)$.

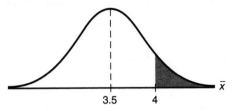

Standardizing, $z = \dfrac{4 - 3.5}{.19} = 2.63$

Using a table or the TI-83, we find $P(\bar{x} > 4) = .0042$

FREE-RESPONSE QUESTIONS

Open-Ended Questions (page 167)

1. "Provide appropriate statistical evidence" means to talk in terms of probability and the data. According to the problem $\mu = \$251.92$ and $\sigma = \$58.21$. Then $P(\bar{x} > 285.16)$ can be calculated assuming the sampling distribution of $\bar{x}$ is approximately normal (reasonable here since $n = 40 > 30$).

$z = \dfrac{285.16 - 251.92}{\dfrac{58.21}{\sqrt{40}}} = 3.62$. Using the table or

TI-83, $P(\bar{x} > 285.16)$ is around .0001. Thus, a result as extreme (or more extreme) as \$285.16 is very unlikely if $\mu = \$251.92$. Since the sample did indicate \$285.16, we were either very unlucky, or the average amount spent (for the population) has changed.

2. We want $P(\bar{x} > 55) = .6$

This means that the proportion below 55 is .4, which corresponds to a z-value of -2.53.

$-2.53 = z = \dfrac{55 - 57}{\dfrac{5.6}{\sqrt{n}}}$. Therefore, $n = 50.18$.

Answer = 51 (always round up).

3. a. $P(X > 49)$ where X is $Normal(45.5, 3.4)$

$z = \dfrac{49 - 45.5}{3.4} = 1.03$

Using a table or the TI-83, $P(x > 49) = .1515$

b. $P(\bar{x} > 49)$ where $\bar{x}$ is $Normal\left(45.5, \dfrac{3.4}{\sqrt{50}}\right) = .481$

$z = \dfrac{49 - 45.5}{.481} = 7.28$

Using a table or the TI-83, $P(\bar{x} > 49) < .0001$

Note that this probability is much smaller. While finding one protozoan alive after 49 days isn't all that unusual, it would be quite surprising to find a sample of 50 protozoa whose mean lifetime exceeds 49 days. This would require several of the protozoa to live longer to keep the average that high.

4. We want to calculate $P(\bar{x} > \$1,650)$

where $\bar{x} \sim Normal\left(1637.52, \dfrac{623.16}{\sqrt{400}} = 31.16\right)$

$z = \dfrac{1650 - 1637.52}{31.16} = .40$

Using a table or the TI-83, $P(\bar{x} > \$1,650) = .345$

Thus, there is about a 35% chance that a random sample of 400 accounts at this bank will have a mean balance that exceeds $1,650.

5. We want $P(\bar{x} < 15.75)$

where $\bar{x} \sim Normal\left(16.5, \dfrac{1.5}{\sqrt{25}} = .3\right)$

$z = \dfrac{15.75 - 16.5}{.3} = -2.50$

Using a table or the TI-83, $P(\bar{x} < 15.75) = .0062$

Thus, the probability that a random sample of 24 workers will have a mean hourly wage less than $15.75 is .0062.

6. a. We want $P(490 < \bar{x} < 510)$

where $\bar{x} \sim Normal\left(500, \dfrac{100}{\sqrt{100}} = 10\right)$

$z_1 = \dfrac{490 - 500}{10} = -1 \qquad P(\bar{x} < 490) = .1587$

$z_2 = \dfrac{510 - 500}{10} = 1 \qquad P(\bar{x} < 510) = .8413$

Probability between $= .8413 - .1587 = .6826$
(This corresponds to the 68% of scores we would expect to find within one standard deviation of the mean.)

b. The probability that the mean score of 100 randomly chosen students would exceed 525 is:

$z = \dfrac{525 - 500}{10} = 2.5$

$P(\bar{x} > 525) = .0062$

Thus, it would be unlikely to find a sample of 100 students whose mean score was above 525 points. Such a result would be in the 99th percentile of sample means for samples of this size drawn from this population.

Section 6.6 The Sampling Distribution of a Sample Mean (σ unknown)

MULTIPLE-CHOICE QUESTIONS (page 172)

1. C

2. E The larger the degrees of freedom, the less spreading the distribution. This also means that the tails are "lighter," so that fewer observations fall out into the tails.

3. B

4. B

5. D

6. B $\dfrac{s}{\sqrt{n}} = \dfrac{.305}{\sqrt{64}} = .038$

7. B $t = \dfrac{2.987 - 3.125}{.038} = -3.63$

FREE-RESPONSE QUESTIONS

Open-Ended Questions (page 173)

1. SRS? Stated ✓
   Normal population? Stated ✓
   We want $P(\bar{x} \le 14.3 \text{ hours})$,
   $t = \dfrac{14.3 - 15.6}{\dfrac{2.5}{\sqrt{15}}} = -2.01$

   Follows a $t(15 - 1 = 14)$ distribution.
   $P(\bar{x} \le 14.3 \text{ hours}) = tcdf(-1E99, -2.01, 14) = .032$
   Thus, the probability that a sample of size 15 would indicate that the mean number of hours of TV watched by these students would be less than 14.3 hours is .032.

2. SRS? Stated ✓
   Normal population? No, but $n = 50 > 40$ ✓
   We want $P(\bar{x} > 11.56 \text{ cm})$
   $t = \dfrac{\bar{x} - \mu}{\dfrac{s}{\sqrt{n}}} = \dfrac{11.56 - 11.25}{\dfrac{.54}{\sqrt{50}}} = 4.06$

   Follows a $t(50 - 1 = 49)$ distribution.
   $P(\bar{x} > 11.56 \text{ cm}) = tcdf(4.06, 1E99, 49) = 8.81 \times 10^{-5}$
   which is very close to 0.
   Thus, it would be very unlikely to find a sample of 50 parts with a mean length in excess of 11.56 cm.

3. a. $P(\bar{x} > 57.5) = P\left(t_{24} > \dfrac{57.5 - 56}{\dfrac{4.5}{\sqrt{25}}} = 1.67\right) = .054$

   b. $P(\bar{x} > 57) = P\left(t_{59} > \dfrac{57 - 56}{\dfrac{2.5}{\sqrt{60}}} = 3.10\right) = .0015$

   By comparing the two probabilities, it can be seen that the second outcome is more unlikely.

4. a. $\bar{x} = 20$ hours, $s = 3.16$ hours
   b. SRS? Stated ✓
      Normal population? Stated ✓
      We want $P(\bar{x} < 20 \text{ hours})$ for $\mu = 21.5$ hours and $n = 6$.
      $t = \dfrac{20 - 21.5}{\dfrac{3.16}{\sqrt{6}}} = -1.16$

      follows a $t(6 - 1 = 5)$ distribution
      $P(\bar{x} < 20 \text{ hours}) = tcdf(-1E99, -1.16, 5) = .1492$
      Thus, there is about a 15% chance that data on battery life from a sample of size 6 will indicate a mean battery life of 20 or fewer hours when $\mu = 21.5$.
   c. Based on the above analysis, an outcome of 20 hours doesn't seem so unusual and doesn't give us any reason to doubt the company's claim.

5. SRS? Stated ✓
   Normal population? Stated ✓
   $\bar{x} = 7910$ lbs, $s = 90$ lbs
   We want $P(\bar{x} < 7910 \text{ lbs})$ when $n = 10$ and $\mu = 8000$
   $t = \dfrac{7910 - 8000}{90/\sqrt{10}} = -3.16 \text{ follows a } t(10 - 1 = 9) \text{ distribution}$

   $P(\bar{x} < 7910 \text{ lbs}) = tcdf(-1E99, -3.16, 9) - .00575$

Section 6.7 The Distributions Associated With a Difference of Sample Means

MULTIPLE-CHOICE QUESTIONS (page 177)

1. B

2. C $\sigma_{\bar{x}_1 - \bar{x}_2} = \sqrt{\dfrac{10.7^2}{25} + \dfrac{9.8^2}{20}} = 3.06$ points

3. E $t = \dfrac{(72.5 - 75.3) - 0}{3.06} = -.915$

4. C $P(\bar{x}_1 - \bar{x}_2) \geq 2.8, t \approx -.92$ for $t(20 - 1 = 19) = .1846$

FREE-RESPONSE QUESTIONS

Open-Ended Questions (page 177)

1. $P(\bar{x}_F - \bar{x}_M > 3.2)$ when $\mu_1 - \mu_2 = 2.9$
$n_M = 10; \bar{x}_M = 43.5; s_M = 8.9$
$n_F = 10; \bar{x}_F = 46.7; s_F = 12.1$

SRSs? Stated ✓
Independent samples? Males and females ✓
Normal populations? Stated ✓
$t = \dfrac{(46.7 - 43.5) - 2.9}{\sqrt{\dfrac{12.1^2}{10} + \dfrac{8.9^2}{10}}} = .063$

Follows approximately a $t(10 - 1)$ distribution.
$P(\bar{x}_F - \bar{x}_M > 3.2) = tcdf(.063, 1E99, 9) = .4756$
Thus, the probability is .4756 that in samples of this size, the women's sample mean will exceed the men's sample mean by more than 3.2 years.

2. SRS? Stated ✓
Independent Samples? Two separate companies ✓
Normal populations? No, but $n_1 + n_2 = 100 + 50 = 150 > 40$ ✓
$P(|\bar{x}_1 - \bar{x}_2| > .15)$
$t = \dfrac{.15 - 0}{\sqrt{\dfrac{.3^2}{100} + \dfrac{.2^2}{50}}} = 3.64$

Follows a t distribution with $50 - 1 = 49\ df$
$P(\bar{x}_1 - \bar{x}_2 > .15) = tcdf(3.64, 1E99, 49) = .000328$
$P(\bar{x}_1 - \bar{x}_2 < -.15) = tcdf(-1E99, -3.64, 9) = .000328$
Probability in both tails = $2(.000328) = .00066$
So the probability of a difference of at least .15 between the amounts in the cans of these two soda companies is .00066. That is, if both companies claim to fill their cans to 12 ounces, we'd be very surprised to find the mean amount of soda in each group of to differ by more than .15 ounces.

3. We want to find $P(\bar{x}_{Math} - \bar{x}_{LA} > 2.9)$ when $\mu_1 - \mu_2 = 0$
SRSs? Stated ✓
Independent samples? No. Performance in math may not be independent of performance in language arts. In addition, since the problem considers math and language arts scores for the same sample of 5th graders, we should not consider this assumption met.

4. a. $\bar{x}_A = 2.5, s_A = .8165, n = 4$
$\bar{x}_B = 3, s_B = .7071, n = 6$
$\bar{x}_A - \bar{x}_B = -.5$
b. $P(\bar{x}_B - \bar{x}_A > .5)$ when $\mu_1 - \mu_2 = 0$
SRSs? Not stated, but assume that the items being manufactured were randomly chosen, since most quality control tests are designed to insure random selection of items to be tested.
Independent? Stated ✓
Normal populations? Stated ✓
$t = \dfrac{.5 - 0}{\sqrt{\dfrac{.8165^2}{4} + \dfrac{.7071^2}{6}}} = 1$

Follows approximately a $t(4 - 1 = 3)$ distribution.
$P(\bar{x}_B - \bar{x}_A > .5) = tcdf(1, 1E99, 3) = .196$
So the probability that $\bar{x}_B - \bar{x}_A > .5$ assuming that the processes are equally effective is .196.

Chapter 6 Assessment

MULTIPLE-CHOICE QUESTIONS (page 180)

1. D

2. C Since $n = 64$, we can apply the central limit theorem to tell us that $\bar{x}$ is approximately normal with mean 9.2 and standard deviation $\dfrac{5.3}{\sqrt{64}} = .6625$, even though the population distribution is skewed left. Then, $P(\bar{x} > 10)$:
$z = \dfrac{10 - 9.2}{.6625} = 1.21$
Therefore, from a table or the TI-83 *normalcdf* command, $P(\bar{x} > 10) = .113$

3. A We want $P(\hat{p} \geq .7)$ when $p = .64$ and $n = 400$
$np = 400(.64) = 256$ and $n(1 - p) = 400(.36) = 144$. Since both exceed 10, we can apply the normal approximation to the binomial. So $\hat{p}$ is approximately normal with mean .64 and standard deviation $\sqrt{\dfrac{.64(1 - .64)}{400}} = .024$.
So $z = \dfrac{.7 - .64}{.024} = 2.5$
Therefore, from a table or the TI-83 *normalcdf* command, $P(\hat{p} \geq .7) = .0062$
The chance that 70% or more of the applicants in this random sample of 400 will pass the math entrance exam is 0.6%.

4. A We want $P(\bar{x} \leq 64.82)$ when $\mu = 65.42$ and $\sigma = 2.32$. Since σ is given and n is greater than 30, we can assume that the sample follows an approximately normal distribution.
$z = \dfrac{64.82 - 65.42}{\dfrac{2.32}{\sqrt{144}}} = -3.10$

Therefore, $P(\bar{x} \leq 64.82) = .00096$

5. B The sample size is large enough for us to apply the central limit theorem which says that for sample sizes larger than 30, the sampling distribution will be approximately normal with mean $\mu = 31.3$ and standard deviation $\frac{6.4}{\sqrt{100}} = .64$

6. C We want $P(\hat{p} > \frac{216}{400} = .54)$ when $p = .5$ and $n = 400$.

Since np and $n(1 - p)$ both exceed 10, we can apply the normal approximation to the binomial to state that $\hat{p}$ follows an approximately normal distribution with mean .5 and standard deviation $\sqrt{\frac{.5(.5)}{400}} = .025$

$z = \frac{.54 - .5}{.025} = 1.6$

Therefore, from a table or the TI-83 *normalcdf* command, $P(\hat{p} > .54) = .055$

7. C We want $P(\hat{p} > .045)$ when $p = .03$ and $n = 400$
Since np and $n(1 - p)$ both exceed 10, we can apply the normal approximation to the binomial to state that $\hat{p}$ follows an approximately normal distribution with mean .03 and standard deviation $.\sqrt{\frac{03(1 - .03)}{400}} = .0085$

$z = \frac{.045 - .03}{.0085} = 1.76$

Therefore, from a table or the TI-83 *normalcdf* command, $P(\hat{p} > .045) = .039$

8. C

9. D We want $P(|\hat{p}_M - \hat{p}_F| > .03)$ when $p_M - p_F = .02$
Since $n_F(p_F) = 100(.12) = 12$ and $n_F(1 - p_F) = 100(.88) = 88$; and $n_M(p_M) = 75(.14) = 10.5$ and $n_M(1 - p_M) = 75(.86) = 64.5$ all exceed 5, we can apply the Central Limit Theorem.

$z = \dfrac{.03 - .02}{\sqrt{\dfrac{.14(.86)}{75} + \dfrac{.12(.88)}{100}}} = .1938$

Therefore, using a table or the TI-83 *normalcdf* command, $P(|\hat{p}_M - \hat{p}_F| > .03) = .423$.
The probability that independent random samples of 100 female and 75 male teens will produce results that differ by more than 3% in either direction $= .423(2) = .846$.

FREE-RESPONSE QUESTIONS

Open-Ended Questions (page 181)

1. a. Let x = number of correct answers. Then $100 - x$ is the number of incorrect answers, so the student's point total is
$x - .25(100 - x) = 1.25x - 25$

The probability of a correct guess is $\frac{1}{4}$ or .25.

If $1.25x - 25 > 60$, then, solving for x, we get
$x > \frac{60 + 25}{1.25}$ or 68.

$P(1.25x - 25 > 60) = P(x > 68)$

The student would need to get 68 right (and 32 wrong) to score 60 points.
x follows a *Binomial*(100, .25) distribution.
Since $np = 100(.25)$ and $n(1 - p) = 100(1 - .25)$ both exceed 10, then $\hat{p} = \frac{x}{100}$ follows a normal distribution with mean $100(.25) = 25$ and standard deviation $\sqrt{\frac{.25(1 - .25)}{100}} = .0433$.
Then we can find $P\left(\hat{p} > \frac{68}{100}\right)$ using this normal approximation to the binomial.
$z = \frac{.68 - .25}{.0433} = 9.93$
This has virtually no chance of happening. The student has very little chance of passing the exam (getting 68 points) if she guesses on all 100 questions.

b. If the student leaves 5 questions blank, then she would have to get 67 of the remaining 95 questions correct to score 60 points.
$x - .25(95 - x) = 1.25x - 23.75$
So $x = \frac{60 + 23.65}{1.25} = 66.92$ or 67
Now x follows a *Binomial* (95, .25) distribution.
$P\left(\hat{p} > \frac{67}{95} = .705\right) = P\left(z > \dfrac{.705 - .25}{\sqrt{\dfrac{.25(.75)}{95}}}\right) = P(z > 10.24)$

Since the z-value is larger, the probability of this occurring is lower. The student does not improve her chances by leaving 5 questions blank.

2. We want $P\left(\hat{p} > \frac{21}{100}\right)$ when $p = \frac{1}{6}$.

Since $100\left(\frac{1}{6}\right) = 16.67$ and $100\left(\frac{5}{6}\right) = 83.33$ and both exceed 10, we can apply the Central Limit Theorem.
So $\hat{p}$ is approximately normal with mean $\frac{1}{6}$ and

standard deviation $\sqrt{\dfrac{\frac{1}{6}\left(\frac{5}{6}\right)}{100}} = .037$

$z = \dfrac{.21 - \frac{1}{6}}{.037} = 1.16$

Therefore, using a table or the TI-83 *normalcdf* command, $P\left(\hat{p} > \frac{21}{100}\right) = .123$

Thus, the chance that a 6 will come up 21 times is not all that unusual in a sample of size 100. It should happen about 12 – 13% of the time. This gives us no reason to doubt the results came from a fair die.

3. We have two samples: small fabric stores ($n_1 = 42$) and pizza take-out stores ($n_2 = 75$).
$\bar{x}_1 = 725.6$, $s_1 = 63.5$, $\bar{x}_2 = 764.5$, $s_2 = 74.5$
$|\bar{x}_1 - \bar{x}_2| = |725.6 - 764.5| = 38.9$
The US Small Business Administration expects
$\mu_1 - \mu_2 = 0$
We want $P(|\bar{x}_1 - \bar{x}_2| \geq 38.9)$

SRSs? Stated ✓
Independent samples? Yes, separate businesses ✓
Normal populations? Not stated, but sample sizes sum to more than 30 ✓
Population standard deviations known? No: use t-procedure.

$$t = \frac{38.9 - 0}{\sqrt{\frac{63.5^2}{42} + \frac{74.5^2}{75}}} = 2.98$$

follows approximately $t(42 - 1 = 41)$ distribution
Therefore, $P(\bar{x}_1 - \bar{x}_2 \leq -38.9) = tcdf(-1E99, -2.98, 41) = .0024$
and $P(\bar{x}_1 - \bar{x}_2 \geq 38.9) = tcdf(2.98, 1E99, 41) = .0024$
The probability that samples of these sizes would differ by $38.90 or more if the Small Business Administration was correct is $.0024(2) = .0048$.

4. $\mu = 5.6$ times, $n = 50$ students, $\bar{x} = 6.2$ times, $s = 2.3$ times
We want $P(\bar{x} \geq 6.2)$ for $\mu = 5.6$ and $n = 50$

a. $z = \dfrac{6.2 - 5.6}{\dfrac{2.3}{\sqrt{50}}} = 1.844$

$P(\bar{x} \geq 6.2) = .0325$

b. $t = \dfrac{6.2 - 5.6}{\dfrac{2.3}{\sqrt{50}}} = 1.855$, with $50 - 1 = 49\ df$

$P(\bar{x} \geq 6.2) = .0356$

c. Since the sample size is large, the $t(49)$ distribution is not that different in shape or spread from the standard normal distribution. The discrepancy would be much larger with a smaller sample size.

d. The calculation in part a is incorrect since the standard deviation used was the sample standard deviation. σ is unknown.

Investigative Tasks (page 182)

1. a. A t-distribution with 9 degrees of freedom. Since the population standard deviation is not known, we have no choice. It is worth noting that with a sample size of 10, the approximation of $t(df = 9)$ to the sampling distribution will not be very good since we do not know about the nature of the population.

b. $P(\bar{x} \geq 3,235,678$ when $\mu = 3,165,567)$

$$= P\left(t \geq \frac{3,235,678 - 3,165,567}{\frac{125,645}{\sqrt{10}}}\right)$$

$= P(t \geq 1.765) \approx .056$

c. If we assume that the population standard deviation equals the sample standard deviation, we may choose to use the normal distribution,

$Normal\left(3165567, \dfrac{125,645}{\sqrt{10}}\right)$. However, the normal approximation to the sampling distribution may not be very close due to the small sample size.

d. $P(\bar{x} \geq 3,235,678$ when $\mu = 3,165,567)$

$$= P\left(z \geq \frac{3,235,678 - 3,165,567}{\frac{125,645}{\sqrt{10}}}\right)$$

$= P(z \geq 1.765) \approx .039$

e. Both techniques indicate an unlikely result, but neither fits the sampling distribution assumptions.

f. One should report that it is unlikely that the published mean of $3,165,567 is correct.

2. a.

Sample Sizes	Theoretical Standard Deviations
10	$\dfrac{5.65}{\sqrt{10}} = 1.79$
20	$\dfrac{5.65}{\sqrt{20}} = 1.26$
25	$\dfrac{5.65}{\sqrt{25}} = 1.13$
50	$\dfrac{5.65}{\sqrt{50}} = 0.80$
75	$\dfrac{5.65}{\sqrt{75}} = 0.65$
100	$\dfrac{5.65}{\sqrt{100}} = 0.57$

b. (1). Since these are clearly quantitative data, an appropriate choice of sampling distribution of the differences between the observed and theoretical standard deviations is the t-distribution with 5 degrees of freedom. We will work with the differences from the pairs for each sample size.

(2)

Sample Size	10	20	25	50	75	100
Sample Standard Deviations	2.02	1.16	1.23	0.83	0.54	0.49
Theoretical Standard Deviations	1.79	1.26	1.13	0.80	0.65	0.57
Differences	0.23	−0.10	0.10	0.03	−0.11	−0.08

$\bar{d} = 0.0117$; $s_d = 0.135$
$P(\bar{d} \geq 0.0117$ when the true mean difference $= 0)$

$$= P\left(t \geq \frac{0.0117 - 0}{\frac{.135}{\sqrt{6}}}\right)$$

$= P(t \geq .212) \approx 0.42$
$df = 5$

(3) The probability indicates that a mean difference of this magnitude is quite likely. Consequently, the observed standard deviations appear consistent with the theoretical ones.

Chapter 7 Statistical Inference

Section 7.1 The Concept of Confidence

MULTIPLE-CHOICE QUESTIONS (page 187)

1. C

2. C By definition, a confidence interval is constructed in order to estimate the parameter from the information in a sample. If we conduct a census, we know the parameter exactly, and there is no reason to construct an interval.

   Note: If we increase the sample size, the sampling distribution will have less variability, meaning the $\hat{p}$ values will tend to lie even closer to p. Thus, the interval within two standard deviations of p is smaller, or if we want the same interval length, we can increase our confidence that the parameter is captured in that interval. Generally, a wider interval, since it specifies more values, allows you to be more confident that the interval captures the parameter.

3. E

4. B Since a confidence interval is constructed around the sample statistic, the sample statistic is at the center. We don't know where the parameter is inside the interval, or even whether it is truly inside the interval at all.

5. C

FREE-RESPONSE QUESTIONS

Open-Ended Questions (page 187)

1. Since the confidence level and the sample proportions are the same, the width of the confidence interval is inversely proportional to the sample size. The larger the sample the narrower the confidence interval.

2. Let p = proportion of students at the high school who bike to school. We must assume there are more than 10(64), or 640, students at the school for the population to be enough larger than the sample, but this seems reasonable since the problem states that the sample was drawn from the student population of a large high school. We want to check np and $n(1 - p)$ but we don't know p. Instead, we will substitute $\hat{p}$: 60(.2) = 12 and 60(.9) = 48. Since both exceed 10 we can apply the Central Limit Theorem to find the confidence interval.
   Formula
   90% confidence level—Critical $z = 1.645$

   $.2 \pm 1.645 \sqrt{\dfrac{.2(.8)}{64}} = (.1178, .2823)$

   We are 90% confident that between 11.8% and 28.2% of the high school students bike to school.

3. Group D since $\hat{p} = .45$ is not in the center of the interval.

4. Since p is not a random variable, p is either in the interval or it is not, with a probability of 1 or 0.

Section 7.2 Calculation of Confidence Intervals

FREE-RESPONSE QUESTIONS

Open-Ended Questions (page 191)

1. a. Let p = proportion of high school seniors in the city that favor the ban on prayer in public schools.
   b. Assumptions:
   SRS? Stated ✓
   Large population? Assume that there are more than 1,000 high school seniors in this particular city.
   $n\hat{p} > 10$, $n(1 - \hat{p}) > 10$? $n\hat{p} = 100(.15) = 15 > 10$
   $n(1 - \hat{p}) = 100(.85) = 85 > 10$ ✓
   Formula:

   $.15 \pm 1.96 \sqrt{\dfrac{.15(.85)}{100}} = .15 \pm .07 = (.08, .22)$

   c. We are 95% confident that between 8% and 22% of the high school seniors in this town favor the ban on prayer in public schools. By "95% confident" we mean that if we constructed all possible confidence intervals from samples of size 100 from this population, 95% of these intervals would capture p, the actual population proportion. So we are 95% confident that this is one of those intervals.

2. a. Let μ = mean number of defective bulbs per package for this brand.
   b. Assumptions:
   SRS? Stated ✓
   Normal population or n is large ($n \geq 30$)? $n = 40 > 30$ so we can use the Central Limit Theorem to describe the distribution of $\bar{x}$. ✓
   σ known? No, use a t-procedure with $df = 40 - 1 = 39$. Since 39 degrees of freedom is not in the table, we will approximate the critical value using 40 degrees of freedom.
   Formula:

   $.79 \pm 1.684 \dfrac{.2}{\sqrt{40}} = .79 \pm .053 = (.737, .843)$

   We are 90% confident that the average number of defectives per package is between .737 and .843 bulbs. Thus, we expect fewer than 1 defective bulb per package.
   c. By "90% confidence" we mean that if all possible samples of size 40 were taken from the population of packages manufactured by this company and a 90% confidence interval were constructed for each sample, then 90% of those intervals would include μ, the mean number of defectives per package.

3. a. Let μ = mean radius of the new food cans made by this company.

b. Assumptions:

SRS? Stated ✓

Normal population or n is large ($n \geq 30$)? Not stated and our sample size is on the small side (< 30). It is not too unreasonable to assume the population of food can radii measurements follows a normal distribution, but we should proceed with caution. σ known? No, use a t-procedure with $df = 25 - 1 = 24$.

Formula:

$$3.13 \pm 2.064 \frac{.04}{\sqrt{25}} = 3.13 \pm .0165 = (3.11, 3.15)$$

c. We are 95% confident that the mean radius of this new food can is between 3.11 and 3.15 inches (as long as the population of radius measurements is approximately normal). Even if μ were 3.15 inches, a sample mean of 3.32 would be

$$\frac{3.32 - 3.15}{\frac{.04}{\sqrt{25}}} = 21.25,$$ more than 21 standard

deviations away from this population mean, (assuming the same sample standard deviation). This would be extremely surprising.

4. a. Let p = proportion of the CEOs in all 30,000 companies that hold at least a master's degree.

Assumptions:

SRS? Stated. ✓

Large population? $30,000 > 10(250)$ ✓

$n\hat{p} > 10, n(1 - \hat{p}) > 10?$ $n\hat{p} = 250\left(\frac{210}{250}\right) = 210 > 10$

$n(1 - \hat{p}) = 250\left(\frac{40}{250}\right) = 40 > 10$ ✓

Formula:

$$.84 \pm 1.96\sqrt{\frac{.84(.16)}{250}} = .84 \pm .045 = (.795, .885)$$

b. We are 95% confident that between 79.5% and 88.5% of CEOs in these 30,000 companies hold at least a master's degree.

By 95% confident, we mean that if we construct all possible intervals for samples of size 250 from this population of 30,000 companies, 95% of these intervals would include the true population proportion, so we are 95% confident that this interval does.

c. Assumptions:

SRS? This is a "cluster sample," not an SRS. We chose 250 companies, and then found the number of junior executives who had a master's degree out of all junior executives in these companies. Therefore, a confidence interval *cannot* be constructed around this proportion using the methods in this course.

5. $n_1 = 75, \hat{p}_1 = .63; n_2 = 45, \hat{p}_2 = .68$

SRS? Stated. ✓

Independent samples? Stated (separate high schools). ✓

$n_1\hat{p}_1 > 5, n_1(1 - \hat{p}_1) > 5?$

$n_1\hat{p}_1 = 75(.60) = 45, n_1(1 - \hat{p}_1) = 75(.40) = 30$ ✓

$n_2\hat{p}_2 > 5, n_2(1 - \hat{p}_2) > 5?$

$n_2\hat{p}_2 = 50(.68) = 34, n_2(1 - \hat{p}_2) = 50(.32) = 16$ ✓

Formula:

$$(.60 - .68) \pm 1.96\sqrt{\frac{.60(.40)}{75} + \frac{.68(.32)}{50}} = -.08 \pm .17 =$$

$(-.25, .09)$

We're 95% confident that $p_1 - p_2$ is between $-.25$ and $.09$. This means it is plausible for North High school to have up to 25% more students with jobs outside of school or for South High School to have up to 9% more students with jobs outside of school. Thus, we can't conclude that one school tends to have more students working outside of school.

6. SRS? Stated. ✓

Independent samples? Stated and separate clubs. ✓

Normal populations or $n_1 + n_2 > 40$? Not stated and sample sizes are relatively small, $15 + 12 = 27 < 40$. However, if the skewness is not extreme and the shapes of both populations and the sample sizes are similar, we can apply the t-procedure (with $\min(15, 11) = 11$ df) with extreme caution.

Formula:

$$(17.25 - 16.45) \pm 1.796\sqrt{\frac{2.4^2}{15} + \frac{3.6^2}{12}} = .8 \pm 2.17 =$$

$(-1.37, 2.97)$

b. We're 90% confident that the difference in mean time spent in volunteer community service is between -1.37 and 2.97 days.

Section 7.3 Properties of Confidence Intervals

MULTIPLE-CHOICE QUESTIONS (page 198)

1. E Since $\hat{p} = .85$, by substituting in the formula we get

$$\left(\frac{z_{(\alpha/2)}}{ME}\right)^2 [\hat{p}(1 - \hat{p})] = \left(\frac{1.645}{.02}\right)^2 (.85)(.15) = 862.55$$

Therefore, $n = 863$ is the smallest sample size that would result in a margin of error of $\pm 2\%$ for 90% confidence and $\hat{p} = .85$.

2. E

3. B

$$ME = z_{(\alpha/2)} \times \frac{\sigma}{\sqrt{n}}$$

$$2.1 = 1.96\frac{\sigma}{\sqrt{30}}$$

$$\sigma = 2.1\frac{\sqrt{30}}{1.96} = 5.868$$

4. C

5. A

6. D

$$\frac{ME_{newspaper}}{ME_{humane}} = z_{(\alpha/2)} \times \sqrt{\frac{\hat{p}(1-\hat{p})}{n}} \Big/ z_{(\alpha/2)} \times \sqrt{\frac{\hat{p}(1-\hat{p})}{n}}$$

$$= \frac{\sqrt{n_{humane}}}{\sqrt{n_{newspaper}}} = \frac{.025}{.037} \text{ since Critical } z \text{ and Critical } \hat{p}$$

are the same.

$$= \frac{\sqrt{n_{humane}}}{\sqrt{n_{newspaper}}} = \frac{.025}{.037} = .676$$

Squaring both sides and inverting, $\dfrac{n_{newspaper}}{n_{humane}} = \left(\dfrac{1}{.676}\right)^2$

$$= 2.19 \approx \frac{13}{6}.$$

FREE-RESPONSE QUESTIONS

Open-Ended Questions (page 199)

1. a. $\bar{x} = 51.5, s = 4.25$

(1) Critical $t(99) \approx$ Critical $t(100) = 1.984$

95% confidence interval $= 51.5 \pm 1.984\dfrac{4.25}{\sqrt{100}} =$

(50.66, 52.34)

(2) Critical $t(399) \approx z$

95% confidence interval $= 51.5 \pm 1.96\dfrac{4.25}{\sqrt{400}} =$

(51.08, 51.92)

b. The width of the confidence interval = 2(critical value)(standard error) or 2(Critical t) $\dfrac{\sigma}{\sqrt{n}}$. Thus, if everything else stays the same, the width decreases by a factor of $\sqrt{a}$ when the sample size increases by a factor of a. However, with the t-distribution, we have to remember that the critical value will change as well since the degrees of freedom change as sample size increases. Thus, the change in the width is not only a simple factor of a. (Though with such large sample sizes it's pretty close.) For example, if $n = 1,000$, Critical $t = 1.962$.

$$51.5 \pm 1.962\dfrac{4.25}{\sqrt{1,000}} = (51.24, 51.76)$$

$$\text{width} = 2(1.962)\left(\dfrac{4.25}{\sqrt{1,000}}\right) = .5274$$

If $n = 100$, width $= 2(1.984)\left(\dfrac{4.25}{\sqrt{100}}\right) = 1.686$

A ratio of $\dfrac{1.962\sqrt{100}}{1.984\sqrt{1,000}} = 3.127$

$\sqrt{10} = 3.16$ (difference due to rounding)

2. Take $\sigma = 7.85$ hours.

$$ME = z_{(\alpha/2)} \times \dfrac{\sigma}{\sqrt{n}}$$

$$2 = (1.96)\dfrac{7.85}{\sqrt{n}}$$

So $n = \left(\dfrac{1.96(7.85)}{2}\right)^2 = 59.18$

So the smallest sample size needed for the estimate of the population mean to have a margin of error of less than 2 hours at the 95% confidence level is 60 (remembering always to round up).

3. $ME = z_{(\alpha/2)} \times \sqrt{\dfrac{\hat{p}(1-\hat{p})}{n}}$

Using the conservative approach, let $\hat{p} = .5$.

$$.02 = 2.576\sqrt{\dfrac{.5(.5)}{n}}$$

$$n = \left(\dfrac{2.576}{.02}\right)^2(.5)(.5) = 4,147.36$$

The smallest sample size that would guarantee that the results of the survey would have a margin of error of no more than 2% at the 99% confidence level is 4,148 voters.

4. a. $n = \left(\dfrac{1.96}{.03}\right)^2(.5)(.5) = 1,067.11$ so 1,068 must be the sample size that Company A is planning to use.

b. 98% confidence corresponds to a critical value of 2.33

$$n = \left(\dfrac{2.33}{.02}\right)^2(.5)(.5) = 3,393.06 \text{ so } 3,394 \text{ is the}$$

sample size that Company B should use to meet their projected margin of error.

It takes a much larger sample size to be more precise *and* more confident.

Section 7.4 The Concept of Significance

MULTIPLE-CHOICE QUESTIONS (page 201)

1. B

2. C

3. C

FREE-RESPONSE QUESTIONS

Open-Ended Questions (page 201)

1. P(random sample of 50 of this year's freshmen would indicate that 41% or fewer were placed on probation when the true percentage is 45%) $= P(\hat{p} < .41 \mid p = .45)$

2. P(random sample of size 100 would indicate that the number of children under 12 per household is 2.8 or more when the true mean is 2.4 children under 12 per household) $= P(\bar{x} > 2.8 \mid \mu = 2.4)$

3. P(the percentage of boys who would choose Phys. Ed. as their favorite subject would be at least 3% greater than the percentage of girls who would do so if the two population proportions were equal $= P(\hat{p}_B - \hat{p}_G > .03 \mid p_B = p_G)$ (for samples of the same size)

4. P(boys' sample times would be at least 4.9 seconds faster than girls' times if the difference in the population means was still 4.3 seconds) $= P(\bar{x}_G - \bar{x}_B > 4.9 \mid m_G - m_B = 4.3)$ (for samples of the same size)

Section 7.5 Tests of Significance

MULTIPLE-CHOICE QUESTIONS (page 220)

1. **B** We examine the research hypothesis put forth by the investigator to determine whether the results should be in a specific direction.

2. **D**

3. **D**

4. **E** The *P*-value is the probability of observing a sample result as extreme or more extreme when the null hypothesis is true. It does not tell us anything about the probability of either hypothesis being true—one of them just is, but we'll never know for sure that we made the correct decision.

5. **E** If the *P*-value of a significance test is greater than the significance level, we "fail to reject H_0." This is distinct from "accepting H_0" or believing H_0 is definitely true. All we can say is that we don't have enough evidence to say that H_0 is *not* true.

6. **A** If the *p*-value is less than α then we have a "statistically significant" result. We reject H_0. This corresponds to the test statistic falling in the rejection region.

7. **B** For a one-tailed one-sample proportion *z*-test to be significant at the 5% level, the test statistic must exceed 1.645.

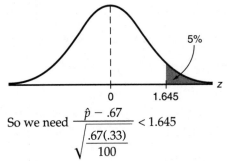

So we need $\dfrac{\hat{p} - .67}{\sqrt{\dfrac{.67(.33)}{100}}} < 1.645$

which implies that $\hat{p} < .7473$
This means that if their sample result is anything less than 74.7%, they will conclude that their customers are significantly less satisfied than the industry standard. Therefore, the approximate minimum difference is $.747 - .67 = .077 = 7.7\%$

8. **D**

FREE-RESPONSE QUESTIONS

Open-Ended Questions (page 221)

1. Let μ_1 = mean lifetime of the company's new halogen bulbs and μ_2 = mean lifetime of the incandescent bulbs.
   Parameter of interest: $\mu_1 - \mu_2$, the difference in the lives of the new and the old light bulbs
   Choice of test: 2-sample *t*-test
   Null hypothesis: H_0: The new halogen bulb lasts at least 25 hours longer than the incandescent bulb. $(\mu_1 - \mu_2 \geq 25)$

2. **Parameter of interest:** p = proportion of middle school children who prefer their bag
   Choice of test: 1-sample *z*-test
   Null Hypothesis: H_0: 55% of middle school children prefer this bag. $(p = .55)$

3. Let μ_1 = mean performance of urban districts
   Let μ_2 = mean performance of suburban districts
   Parameter of interest: $\mu_1 - \mu_2$, difference in means of tests from urban and suburban districts
   Choice of test: 2-sample *t*-test
   Null hypothesis: H_0: There is no difference in performance between urban and suburban districts. $(\mu_1 - \mu_2 = 0)$

4. Let p_1 = proportion of males who go on to post-secondary education.
   Let p_2 = proportion of females who go on to post-secondary education
   Parameter of interest: $p_1 - p_2$, difference in the proportion of males and females who go on to post-secondary education
   Choice of test: 2-sample *z*-test
   Null hypothesis: H_0: There is no difference in the proportion of males and females who go on to post-secondary education. $(p_1 - p_2 = 0)$

5. Since we have retested the same group of students, this is a matched pairs design. Let Δ_0 = average difference in reading scores for third graders.
   Parameter of interest: Δ_0, the mean difference between the pre- and post-test scores
   Choice of test: 1-sample *t*-test
   Null hypothesis: H_0: There is no improvement in reading level over the course of the third grade for this population of students. $(\Delta_0 = 0)$

6.

Probability Statement	**P-value** = P(of 50 randomly chosen adults, at most 66% prefer a certain toothpaste if the marketing company's claim is true that 75% of the population prefers this toothpaste)
Test Statistic	**Formula:** $z = \dfrac{.66 - .75}{\sqrt{\dfrac{.75(.25)}{50}}}$ **Value:** -1.47

7.

Probability Statement	**P-value** = P(a random sample of 75 students will indicate an average difference in their bill of at least \$12.82 if the true mean amount spent on textbooks for the Fall 1999 semester is \$325.16)
Test Statistic	**Formula:** $z = \dfrac{312.34 - 325.16}{\dfrac{76.42}{\sqrt{75}}}$ **Value:** -1.45

8.

Probability Statement	**P-value** = P(random samples of these sizes will indicate a difference in the proportion of defectives of at least .004 if there is no difference in the proportion of defectives produced by each process)
Test Statistic	**Formula:** $z = \dfrac{0.29 - .025}{\sqrt{\dfrac{.029(.971)}{100} + \dfrac{.025(.975)}{75}}}$ **Value:** .1624

But remember we won't be able to accurately calculate this *p*-value since $n\,\hat{p}_2 = 75(.025)$ = 1.875, which is less than 5.

9.

Probability Statement	**P-value** = P(samples of these sizes will indicate a difference in the final exam scores of these Statistics students of at least 2 points if performance of all of these instructors' students is actually the same)
Test Statistic	**Formula:** $t = \dfrac{79 - 81}{\sqrt{\dfrac{12.7^2}{35} + \dfrac{11.4^2}{45}}}$ **Value:** $-.73$

Before we calculate this *P*-value, we would have to determine whether or not it is reasonable to view these two classes as independent simple random samples drawn from the larger population of students of these two professors.

10. Since we aren't given any information about how we think this die might be biased, we'll assume a two-sided hypothesis.

Probability Statement	**P-value** = P(a fair die yields at least 20 sixes in 100 rolls)
Test Statistic	**Formula:** $z = \dfrac{.2 - \dfrac{1}{6}}{\sqrt{\dfrac{\dfrac{1}{6}\left(\dfrac{5}{6}\right)}{100}}}$ **Value:** .89

11.

1. Parameter of Interest	p = percentage of complaints not addressed within 2 weeks by the current administration	
2. Choice of Test	1-proportion z-test	
3. Check of Assumptions	**Statement of Assumptions:** SRS? Large population? Sample size?	**Verification of Assumptions:** Stated ✓ Need more than $50(10) = 500$ complaints. Seems believable. ✓ $np = 50(.45). = 22.5$ and $n(1 - p) = 50(.55) = 27.5$ ✓
4. Null Hypothesis	H_0: **(words)** The percentage of complaints that go unaddressed for at least 2 weeks is 45% H_0: **(symbols)** $p = .45$ as the candidate claims	
5. Alternative Hypothesis	H_a: **(words)** The percentage of complaints that go unaddressed for at least 2 weeks is less than 45%. H_a: **(symbols)** $p < .45$	
6. Probability Statement	**P-value = probability** ($\hat{p} \leq .40$ if $p = .45$)	
7. Test Statistic	**Formula:** $$z = \frac{.40 - .45}{\sqrt{\dfrac{.45(1 - .45)}{50}}}$$	**Value:** $-.71$
8. Test: Level of Significance $\alpha = .05$	**Sketch of Sampling Distribution assuming that H_0 is true:** **Identify the location of the test statistic in the sketch and shade the region that represents the P-value.**	
9. P-value	**Reconciliation of Critical Value with Rejection Region:** Since $z = -.71 >$ Critical $z = -1.645$, our test statistic is not in the rejection region.	**Exact P-value:** $P(z < -.71) = .239$
10. Recommended Decisions	**Regarding H_0:** Since P-value is large (more than .05, and the test statistic does not fall in the rejection region), we fail to reject the null hypothesis.	**Regarding significance:** Not significant.
11. Interpretation (in the context of the problem)	There is not sufficient evidence to reject the candidate's claim that the true percentage of complaints not addressed within two weeks of submission is 45%.	

[Verification on TI-83: 1-PropZTest with $p_0 = .45$, $x = .4(50) = 20$, $n = 50$
We find $z = -.7107$ and $p = .2386$]

12. Let μ_1 = mean science exam score for men in 1998
μ_2 = mean science exam score for women in 1998

1. Parameter of Interest	$\mu_1 - \mu_2$, the difference in average science placement scores by gender	
2. Choice of Test	Two-sample t-test	
3. Check of Assumptions	**Statement of Assumptions:** SRSs? Independent Samples? Normal populations? Assume unequal variances. Use an unpooled test.	**Verification of Assumptions:** Stated ✓ Yes, split into gender categories. ✓ Exam scores tend to follow normal distributions, but even if they didn't, $24 + 35 > 40$. ✓
4. Null Hypothesis	H_0: (words) There is no difference by gender in science placement exam performance in 1998. H_0: (symbols) $\mu_1 - \mu_2 = 0$	
5. Alternative Hypothesis	H_a: (words) There is a difference by gender in science placement exam performance in 1998. H_a: (symbols) $\mu_1 - \mu_2 \neq 0$	
6. Probability Statement	**P-value = probability** (samples this size will show a difference of .3 or more in science placement exam scores by gender when there is no difference in scores by gender for the population.)	
7. Test Statistic	**Formula:** $$t = \frac{71.5 - 71.2}{\sqrt{\dfrac{10.3^2}{25} + \dfrac{11.4^2}{35}}}$$ $df = \min(25, 35) - 1 = 24$	**Value:** .1064
8. Test: Level of Significance $\alpha = .05$	**Sketch of Sampling Distribution assuming that H_0 is true:** −.1063　　0　　.1063 **Identify the location of the test statistic in the sketch and shade the region that represents the P-value.**	
9. P-value	**Reconciliation of Critical Value with Rejection Region:** Our test statistic is not in the rejection region.	**Exact P-value:** $2P(T_{24} > .1064) =$ $2(.4581) = .9162$
10. Recommended Decisions	**Regarding H_0:** Since this p-value is large (> .05), and the test statistic does not fall in the rejection region, we fail to reject H_0	**Regarding significance:** Not significant.
11. Interpretation (in the context of the problem)	There is not sufficient evidence to conclude that there is a significant difference by gender in the mean science placement exam scores in the 1998 class.	

[Verification with TI-83: 2-SampTTest gives $t = .1063$ and $p = .9157$]

13. To be significant at the 5% level, the z-statistic for a two-sided one-sample proportion test would have to exceed 1.645.

$$z = \frac{.03}{\sqrt{\frac{.5(.5)}{n}}} > 1.645$$

$$\sqrt{n} > 1.645\sqrt{\frac{.25}{.03}} = 27.42$$

$$n > 751.7$$

We need a sample size of at least 752 to detect a difference of .03 at the 5% level.

14. We will use the value of $\sigma = 4.2$ inches given for the population. We are also told that this is a simple random sample and we know that heights tend to follow a normal distribution, though our sample size is large enough to counteract moderate deviations from normality in the population and still give us a reasonably normal sampling distribution for $\bar{x}$).
Let μ = mean height of eighth graders in this state.
   a. The 95% confidence interval for μ:

   Formula $= 65 \pm 1.96\dfrac{4.2}{\sqrt{40}} = (63.7, 66.3)$

   Since the published result, 62, does not fall in the 95% confidence interval, it does not appear to be a plausible value for μ.
   b. H_0: $\mu = 62$ (mean height of eighth graders in this state is the same as the published report)
   H_a: $\mu \neq 62$ (mean height of eighth graders in this state differs from the published report)
   p-value $= P(\bar{x} \geq 65 \text{ or } \bar{x} \leq 59 \text{ when } \mu = 62)$
   Using a one-sample z-test:

   $$z = \frac{65 - 62}{\frac{4.2}{\sqrt{40}}} = 4.52$$

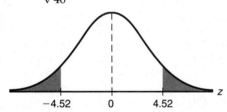

   p-value $= 2P(z > 4.52) \approx 0$ (6.26×10^{-6} on the TI-83)
   With such a small p-value (and the test statistic falls in the rejection region), we reject H_0. We conclude that μ differs significantly from 62, the same conclusion as above.
   Note: The endpoints of the confidence interval are the boundaries of the rejection region in the significance test.

15. Want to find the largest $\bar{x}$ value that leads us to reject H_0: $\mu = 50$. To reject at the 5% level, the two-sided critical value of the $t(50 - 1 = 49)$ distribution is approximately 2.009 ($df = 50$). So we need

$$\frac{\bar{x} - 50}{\frac{12}{\sqrt{50}}} < -2.009$$

$$\bar{x} < -2.009\frac{12}{\sqrt{50}} + 50 = 46.59.$$

Thus, 46.59 would be the largest sample mean less than μ that would produce a significant result.

Section 7.6 Type I and Type II Errors and the Concept of Power

MULTIPLE-CHOICE QUESTIONS (page 229)

1. **E** Power $+ \beta = 1$, but α and β can be set separately from each other. Also, $\alpha = P$(reject H_0 when H_0 is true)

2. **D**

3. **C** Note that $\mu_a < \mu_0$ in this sketch

4. **C**

FREE-RESPONSE QUESTIONS

Open-Ended Questions (page 230)

1. This means that 87% of the samples will yield a mean that will lead the investigator to reject H_0 if H_0 is false. Remember, however, that the power was calculated for a specific value of the alternative.

2. Answers may vary. An example of each is displayed.
   a.

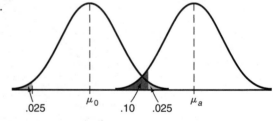

   b.

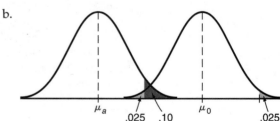

3. a. decreases
   b. increases
   c. both decrease

Section 7.7 Inference for the Slope of a Regression Line

MULTIPLE-CHOICE QUESTIONS (page 236)

1. A

2. C

3. A With a p-value of .006, we reject H_0: $\beta_1 = 0$ and conclude that there is a relationship between the two variables involved.

4. A With 200 observations (in problem statement), $df = 200 - 2 = 198$. Using $df = 100$ in the table, we get Critical $t = 1.984$ formula $= .001699 \pm 1.984(.0006098) = (.0005, .0029)$

5. D

FREE-RESPONSE QUESTIONS

Open-Ended Questions (page 236)

1. a. predicted temp 2 = .2074 + 1.05651(temp 1)

   b. The slope indicates that the predicted temp 2 increases by an average of 1.05651 degrees for each additional degree of temp 1.

   c. R^2 indicates that 96.2% of the variation in temp 2 values can be explained by the variation in temp 1 values.

   d. $t = \dfrac{1.05651 - 0}{.02221} = 47.57$

   We want to compare the t-value found above to a t-critical with $90 - 2 = 88\ df$. Using a table with $df = 100$, we find that 47.57 is off the chart, so the two-sided p-value is less than $2(.0005) = .001$ (and probably much less than that!)

2. a. Predicted total score = 12.96 + 4.0162(ProbSolv)

   b. The total score increases by about 4 points on average for each additional point of the problem-solving subscore.

   c. R^2 indicates that 62% of the variation in total scores can be explained by the variation in ProbSolv scores.

   d. S is an estimate of the standard deviation in total scores with respect to each ProbSolv score.

   e. 95% CI for β:

   $n = 36$, so $df = 34$. Using technology or interpolation, Critical $t = 2.032$

   Formula $= 4.0162 \pm 2.032(.5393) = (2.92, 5.11)$

   f.

1. Parameter of Interest	β_0 = true regression slope between the ProbSolv scores and the Total scores.	
2. Choice of Test	t-test for regression slope	
3. Check of Assumptions	**Statement of Assumptions:** • Linearity of ProbSolv Scores and Total scores. • Constant variance of each score distribution at each ProbSolv score. • Normality of each total score with respect to each ProbSolv score.	**Verification of Assumptions:** ✓ ✓ ✓

Note: Without residual plots, we cannot truly "verify" the assumptions for this problem.

4. Null Hypothesis	H_0: (words) There is no relationship between ProbSolv scores and Total scores on the midterm. H_0: (symbols) $\beta_0 = 0$

5. Alternative Hypothesis	H_a: (words) There is a relationship between ProbSolv scores and Total scores on the midterm H_a: (symbols) $\beta_0 \neq 0$	
6. Probability Statement	P-value = probability (we find a slope as large as 4.0162 or larger if there is no relationship)	
7. Test Statistic	Formula: $$t = \frac{4.0162}{.5393}$$	Value: 7.45 (from printout)
8. Test: Level of Significance $\alpha = .05$	Sketch of Sampling Distribution assuming that H_0 is true: -7.45 0 7.45 Identify the location of the test statistic in the sketch and shade the region that represents the P-value.	
9. P-value	Reconciliation of Critical Value with Rejection Region: Our test statistic is in the rejection region	Exact P-value: value = .000 (from printout)
10. Recommended Decisions	Regarding H_0: With such a small p-value (<.05) and a test statistic that falls in the rejection region, we reject H_0.	Regarding significance: Significant.
11. Interpretation (in the context of the problem).	We conclude that there is a significant relationship between ProbSolv scores and Total scores on this midterm.	

g. Since the confidence interval did not contain 0, we would expect that the result of a two-sided hypothesis test would be to reject H_0: $\beta_0 = 0$. Both procedures indicate that 0 is not a plausible value for this parameter.

Section 7.8 Inference for Categorical Data

MULTIPLE-CHOICE QUESTIONS (page 243)

1. E

2. E 48 of 79 people prefer chocolate (60.76%), so 60.76% of the 49 males should. .6076(49) = 29.77

3. A Since the p-value is small, we reject H_0: there is no relationship between gender and flavor preference.

4. B Comparing observed to expected,
$$\text{formula} = \frac{(3-5)^2}{5} + \frac{(5-4)^2}{4} + \frac{(2-1)^2}{1} = 2.05$$

FREE-RESPONSE QUESTIONS

Open-Ended Questions (page 244)

1.

Categories	Observed	Expected	$\dfrac{(\text{observed} - \text{expected})^2}{\text{expected}}$
Red	7	$\frac{2}{8}(50) = 12.5$	2.42
Pink	33	$\frac{5}{8}(50) = 31.25$	.098
White	10	$\frac{1}{8}(50) = 6.25$	2.25
Totals	50	50	4.77

1. Parameter of Interest	$p_{red}, p_{pink}, p_{white}$	
2. Choice of Test	Chi-square goodness of fit test	
3. Check of Assumptions	**Statement of Assumptions:** All expected counts are at least 5	**Verification of Assumptions:** Yes, according to the table.
4. Null Hypothesis	H_0: **(words)** The proportions of red, pink, and white flowering shrubs were as expected H_0: **(symbols)** $p_{red} = \frac{2}{8}$, $p_{pink} = \frac{5}{8}$, $p_{white} = \frac{1}{8}$	
5. Alternative Hypothesis	H_a: **(words)** At least one of these proportions of red, pink, and white flowering shrubs differs from what was expected. H_a: **(symbols)** $p_{red} \neq \frac{2}{8}$, or $p_{pink} \neq \frac{5}{8}$, or $p_{white} \neq \frac{1}{8}$	
6. Probability Statement	**P-value = probability** (observed counts this extreme or more extreme will happen by chance alone)	
7. Test Statistic	**Formula:** chi-square = 4.768 with $df = 3 - 1 = 2$	**Value:** 4.768
8. Test: Level of Significance $\alpha = .05$	**Sketch of Sampling Distribution assuming that H_0 is true:** 4.77 $\chi^2(df = 2)$ **Identify the location of the test statistic in the sketch and shade the region that represents the P-value.**	
9. P-value	**Reconciliation of Critical Value with Rejection Region:** From table 4.768 is between 4.61 and 5.99 so .05 < p-value < .10 The critical value of χ^2 at the 5% level is 5.99.	**Exact P-value:** From TI-83 $\chi^2 cdf$ command: p-value = $\chi^2 cdf$ (4.768, 1E99,2) = .092
10. Recommended Decisions	**Regarding H_0:** With this p-value (>.05) and since the test statistic does not fall in the rejection region, we fail to reject H_0.	**Regarding significance:** Not significant.
11. Interpretation (in the context of the problem)	We conclude there is insufficient evidence to indicate that the proportion of red, pink, and white flowering shrubs in the random sample of 50 is different from what would be expected.	

2.

	ABC	NBC	CBS	PBS	CNN	Totals
Young (35 and under)	10	15	8	3	5	41
Middle (between 35 and 55)	10	7	7	5	8	37
Older (55 and over)	4	3	3	5	7	22
Totals	24	25	18	13	20	100

Categories	Observed	Expected	$\dfrac{(\text{observed} - \text{expected})^2}{\text{expected}}$
Young ABC	10	$\dfrac{41(24)}{100} = 9.84$	.003
Middle ABC	10	$\dfrac{37(24)}{100} = 8.88$	.141
Older ABC	4	$\dfrac{22(24)}{100} = 5.28$	.310
Young NBC	15	$\dfrac{41(25)}{100} = 10.25$	2.201
Middle NBC	7	$\dfrac{37(25)}{100} = 9.25$	.547
Older NBC	3	$\dfrac{22(25)}{100} = 5.50$	1.136
Young CBS	8	$\dfrac{41(18)}{100} = 7.38$	.052
Middle CBS	7	$\dfrac{37(18)}{100} = 6.66$	.017
Older CBS	3	$\dfrac{22(18)}{100} = 3.96$	.233
Young PBS	3	$\dfrac{41(13)}{100} = 5.33$	1.019
Middle PBS	5	$\dfrac{37(13)}{100} = 4.81$	.008
Older PBS	5	$\dfrac{22(13)}{100} = 2.86$	1.601
Young CNN	5	$\dfrac{41(20)}{100} = 8.20$	1.249
Middle CNN	8	$\dfrac{37(20)}{100} = 7.40$	.049
Older CNN	7	$\dfrac{22(20)}{100} = 4.4$	1.536
Totals	100	100	10.102

No real parameters to define in this problem. Chi-square test of independence

Since $\dfrac{4}{15}$ or 27% of the expected cell counts are less than 5, we cannot proceed with a χ^2 test of independence because of the assumption that only 20% of the expected cell counts can be less than 5.

Chapter 7 Assessment

MULTIPLE-CHOICE QUESTIONS (page 244)

1. **D**

2. **B**

3. **D** You must have either a normal population or a large sample to satisfy the assumptions.

4. **A**

5. **A**

6. **B**

7. **D**

8. **D** We have two independent samples here, boys and girls.

9. **B**

10. **D**

11. **C**

12. **A**

1.

1. Parameter of Interest	p = proportion of adult males in the midwestern city who get at least 2 colds per year	
2. Choice of Test	One-proportion z-test	
3. Check of Assumptions	**Statement of Assumptions:** SRS? Large population? Sample size?	**Verification of Assumptions:** Stated ✓ More than 10(100) adult males in the city. ✓ $np = 100(.50) = 50 > 10$ so we can apply the Central Limit Theorem. ✓
4. Null Hypothesis	H_0: **(words)** 50% of adult males in the midwestern city get at least 2 colds per year. H_0: **(symbols)** $p = .5$	
5. Alternative Hypothesis	H_a: **(words)** The proportion of adult males in the midwestern city who get at least 2 colds per year is less than 50%. H_a: **(symbols)** $p < .5$	
6. Probability Statement	**P-value = probability** (A sample of size 100 results in a $\hat{p}$ of .42 or less when $p = .5$)	
7. Test Statistic	**Formula:** $z = \dfrac{.42 - .5}{\sqrt{\dfrac{.5(.5)}{100}}}$	**Value:** -1.6
8. Test: Level of Significance $\alpha = .05$	**Sketch of Sampling Distribution assuming that H_0 is true:** Identify the location of the test statistic in the sketch and shade the region that represents the P-value.	
9. P-value	**Reconciliation of Critical Value with Rejection Region:** Critical value for one-sided z-test at 5% level: -1.645	**Exact P-value:** P-value = $P(z < -1.645) = .0548$
10. Recommended Decisions	**Regarding H_0:** With this p-value and a z-statistic outside the rejection region, we fail to reject H_0.	**Regarding significance:** Not significant.
11. Interpretation: (in the context of the problem)	There is not sufficient evidence to convince us that the true proportion of adult men in this city who get at least 2 colds a year is significantly less than the 50% claimed by the pharmaceutical company.	

2.

1. Parameter of Interest	μ_G = mean math score for all girls at this school μ_B = mean math score for all boys at this school	
2. Choice of Test	Two-sample t-test	
3. Check of Assumptions	**Statement of Assumptions:** Simple Random Samples? Independent Samples? Normal populations?	**Verification of Assumptions:** Stated. ✓ Not stated but samples of boys and girls are independent. ✓ Stated. ✓
4. Null Hypothesis	H_0: **(words)** There is no difference in average math scores of girls and boys at this school. H_0: **(symbols)** $\mu_G - \mu_B = 0$	
5. Alternative Hypothesis	H_a: **(words)** There is a difference in average math scores of girls and boys at this school. H_a: **(symbols)** $\mu_G - \mu_B \neq 0$	
6. Probability Statement	**P-value = probability** (sample means from samples of size 10 drawn from this population differ by this much if there is no difference in mean math scores between boys and girls at this school)	
7. Test Statistic	**Formula:** $\bar{x}_G = 83.5, s_G = 11.965, n_G = 10$ $\bar{x}_B = 81.4, s_B = 13.235, n_B = 10$ $t = \dfrac{83.5 - 81.4}{\sqrt{\dfrac{11.965^2}{10} + \dfrac{13.235^2}{10}}}$ $df = \min(10, 10) - 1 = 9$ [Verification with TI-83 2-SampTTest: $t = .3722, p = .714$]	**Value:** .3722
8. Test: Level of Significance $\alpha = .05$	**Sketch of Sampling Distribution assuming that H_0 is true:** Identify the location of the test statistic in the sketch and shade the region that represents the P-value.	
9. P-value	**Reconciliation of Critical Value with Rejection Region:** Critical value for two-sided t-test at 5% level: 2.262	**Exact P-value:** P-value $= 2P(t > .3722) = 2(.3592) = .718$ with TI-83 $tcdf$ command. Or, since $.3277 < .706$ with $df = 8$, we know P-value $> 2(.25) = .5$
10. Recommended Decisions	**Regarding H_0:** With such a large P-value (and test statistic outside the rejection region) we fail to reject H_0.	**Regarding significance:** Not significant.
11. Interpretation (in the context of the problem)	We conclude that there is no significant evidence of a difference in the mean math performance of the boys and girls at this school.	

$-.3722 \quad 0 \quad .3722$

3.

1. Parameter of Interest	p_1 = percent of families in rural areas of Indiana who watch this television show. p_2 = percent of families in urban areas of Indiana who watch this television show.	

2. Choice of Test	Two-sample-proportions z-test

3. Check of Assumptions

Statement of Assumptions:	**Verification of Assumptions:**
SRSs?	Yes, stated that these were randomly selected from the population of families in Indiana. ✓
Independent samples?	Yes, rural families and urban families. ✓
Sample sizes?	Smallest $= 50(.43) = 21.5 > 5$ so we can apply the Central Limit theorem. ✓
Large populations?	Yes, assuming there are more than $50(10)$ and $100(10)$ families in these regions. ✓

4. Null Hypothesis

H_0: **(words)** There is no difference in the percentage of rural and urban families in Indiana who watch this show.

H_0: **(symbols)** $p_1 - p_2 = 0$

5. Alternative Hypothesis

H_a: **(words)** There is a higher percentage of urban families who watch this show.

H_a: **(symbols)** $p_1 - p_2 < 0$

6. Probability Statement

P-value = probability (at least 3% more urban families watch the show if there is no difference between the percentage of urban and rural viewers in Indiana)

7. Test Statistic

Formula:

$$\hat{p} = \frac{.4(100) + .43(50)}{150} = .41$$

$$z = \frac{.4 - .43}{\sqrt{(.41)(1 - .41)\left(\frac{1}{100} + \frac{1}{50}\right)}}$$

Value:

$-.352$

8. Test: Level of Significance $\alpha = .05$

Sketch of Sampling Distribution assuming that H_0 is true:

$-.352$

Identify the location of the test statistic in the sketch and shade the region that represents the P-value.

9. P-value

Reconciliation of Critical Value with Rejection Region:
critical value for a one-sided test with $\alpha = .05$ is $z = 1.645$

Exact P-value:
.3624

10. Recommended Decisions

Regarding H_0:
With such a large P-value and a test statistic outside the rejection region, we fail to reject H_0.

Regarding significance:
Not significant.

11. Interpretation: (in the context of the problem).	We conclude that there is not sufficient evidence to support the claim that there is a higher percentage of watchers in the urban areas in Indiana.

4.

1. Parameter of Interest	Let d_0 = mean difference in test scores for students after the instructional unit is completed.
2. Choice of Test	One-sample t-test (matched pairs design) Since we have tested the same students twice, this is a matched pairs design and we want to analyze the before/after difference.
3. Check of Assumptions	**Statement of Assumptions:** SRS? Normality of differences? 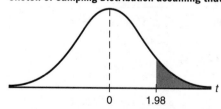 Score Differences	**Verification of Assumptions:** Yes, not stated but a graph of the differences is reasonably symmetric. ✓ A sample size of 10 is probably sufficient to use the Central Limit Theorem.
4. Null Hypothesis	H_0: (words) There is no significant improvement in student performance after completion of the unit on linear equations. H_0: (symbols) $d_0 = 0$
5. Alternative Hypothesis	H_a: (words) There is a significant improvement in student performance after completion of the unit on linear equations. H_a: (symbols) $d_0 > 0$
6. Probability Statement	**P-value = probability** (there will be at least a 2.3-point improvement after instruction when there really is no difference in the before/after scores)
7. Test Statistic	**Formula:** $$t = \dfrac{2.3 - 0}{\dfrac{3.69}{\sqrt{10}}}$$ $df = 10 - 1 = 9$	**Value:** 1.97
8. Test: Level of Significance $\alpha = .05$	**Sketch of Sampling Distribution assuming that H_0 is true:** 0 1.98 t **Identify the location of the test statistic in the sketch and shade the region that represents the P-value.**

9. *P*-value	**Reconciliation of Critical Value with Rejection Region:** Critical value for one-sided *t*-test at 5% level: 1.833 Verification on TI-83 with T-Test: $t = 1.975$	**Exact *P*-value:** *P*-value from table is between .025 and .05 (since test statistic is between 1.860 and 2.306). *P*-value from *tcdf* command: $tcdf(1.98, 1E99, 9) = .0395$
10. Recommended Decisions	**Regarding H_0:** With *P*-value $= .0395 < \alpha = .05$, we reject H_0.	**Regarding significance:** Significant.
11. Interpretation (in the context of the problem)	We conclude that there is evidence at the 5% level of a significant improvement in exam scores for this population of students after the unit on linear equations is completed.	

5. Expected cell counts
   Ring: .2(1020) = 204
   Key chain = .3(1020) = 306
   Puzzle = .15(1020) = 153
   Pen = .25(1020) = 255
   Flashlight = .1(1020) = 102

1. Parameter of Interest	$p_{ring} =$ probability of drawing a ring, etc.	
2. Choice of Test	Chi-square goodness of fit test	
3. Check of Assumptions	**Statement of Assumptions:** All expected cell counts are at least 5?	**Verification of Assumptions:** Yes. ✓
4. Null Hypothesis	H_0: **(words)** The probabilities of getting the various prizes are as expected. H_0: **(symbols)** $p_{ring} = .2$, $p_{key\ chain} = .3$, $p_{puzzle} = .15$, $p_{pen} = .25$, $p_{flashlight} = .10$	
5. Alternative Hypothesis	H_a: **(words)** At least one of these probabilities is different. H_a: **(symbols)** $p_{ring} \neq .2$, or $p_{key\ chain} \neq .3$, or $p_{puzzle} \neq .15$, or $p_{pen} \neq .25$, or $p_{flashlight} \neq .10$	
6. Probability Statement	***P*-value = probability** (observed cell counts will be different from the expected counts by chance alone)	
7. Test Statistic	**Formula:** The sample size is $186 + 327 + 168 + 225 + 114 = 1,020$ Chi-square $= \dfrac{(186 - 204)^2}{204} + \dfrac{(327 - 306)^2}{306} + \dfrac{(168 - 153)^2}{153} + \dfrac{(225 - 255)^2}{255} + \dfrac{(114 - 102)^2}{102}$ $df = (5 - 1) = 4$	**Value:** 9.44

8. Test: Level of Significance $\alpha = .05$	**Sketch of Sampling Distribution assuming that H_0 is true:** 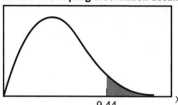 9.44 χ^2 **Identify the location of the test statistic in the sketch and shade the region that represents the P-value.**	
9. *P*-value	**Reconciliation of Critical Value with Rejection Region:** Critical value for χ^2 distribution at 5% level: 9.49	**Exact P-value:** P-value from $\chi^2 cdf$ command: $\chi^2 cdf\,(9.44, 1E99, 4) = .051$
10. Recommended Decisions	**Regarding H_0:** At the 5% level, we would *barely* fail to reject this null hypothesis (P-value > .05).	**Regarding significance:** Not significant.
11. Interpretation: (in the context of the problem)	Thus, we conclude that there is insufficient evidence at the 5% level in support of a significant difference between the probabilities of obtaining the various prizes and the manufacturer's claim. Normally we would say with a result this close that we might want a larger sample size, though 1,020 is pretty large.	

Investigative Tasks (page 246)

1. a. Matched pairs test yields: $t = 3.098$ and p-value = .0063. Therefore, we would conclude that there is a significant difference in the processes.

   b. The 2-sample t-test yields: $t = .3877$ and p-value = .3514. Therefore, we would conclude that there is not sufficient evidence to doubt the claim that there is no difference.

   c. The question of which test is appropriate can be resolved by examining the data for relationships. If the samples are independent, then the 2-sample t-test is the appropriate choice. Similarly, if we can show that the variables in the samples are related (statistically), then matched-pairs is appropriate. If we do a regression analysis of the pairs in the data, we find that $b = 1.0488$ with an r^2 of .9726. We can show the strength of the relationship by performing a test on the slope of the regression line. The results of the test ($H_0: \beta_0 = 0$, $H_a: \beta_0 \neq 0$) yield: $t = 16.851$ and p-value = 1.558×10^{-7}. Therefore, we can conclude that there is a significant relationship between the stations and a matched-pairs t-test is the appropriate choice.

2. The relationship between confidence intervals and significance tests for means can be summarized as follows: If the null value of the parameter is in the confidence interval, then the test will indicate that the result is not significant. If the null value of the parameter is outside the confidence interval, then the result of the test is significant. The relationship is not necessarily true for proportions.

a. This is a two-tailed situation.
   i. 95% confidence interval = (273.53, 286.67)
   ii. z-test (5% level) yields $z = 1.671$ and p-value = .0946. This implies that the test is significant and that there is not sufficient evidence to doubt that the industry standard applies to these batteries.
   iii. Note that the null value of the mean 274.5 is in the confidence interval. This fact indicates that there is not sufficient evidence to doubt that the mean is 274.5

b. This is a one-sided situation since the research question explores whether the shelf life for the tested batteries is longer than the industry standard.
   i. In order to do a "one-sided" confidence interval, we wish to have all of the 5% area outside of the confidence interval at one side. Consequently, we can calculate a "two-sided" 90% confidence interval:
   "one-sided" 95% confidence interval = (274.59, 286.67)
   ii. z-test (5%; one-sided) yields $z = 1.671$ and p-value = .0478.
   iii. Since the null value of the mean 274.5 is not in the confidence interval, we must reject it. We must also reject it as a result of the z-test. Note that these data provide barely enough evidence to reject the null hypothesis (p-value of $\alpha = .0478$ vs. .05). Note also how close the value of the mean 274.5 is to the lower endpoint of the confidence interval.

Chapter 8 Interpreting Computer and Calculator Printouts

Section 8.2 Regression Analysis

SHORT ANSWER (page 254)

Item	Data Desk	Minitab	SAS	Fathom	TI-83
1. Regression equation	✓	✓	✓	✓	✓
2. Value of R^2	✓	✓	✓	✓	✓
3. Standard error of the estimate	✓	✓	✓	X	✓
4. Test statistic	✓	✓	✓	X	✓
5. 2-sided P-value of the test for H_0: $\beta = 0$	✓	✓	✓	X	✓
6. Degrees of freedom of the test	✓	✓	✓	X	✓

Section 8.4 Hypothesis Test: One-Sample *t*-Test

SHORT ANSWER (page 257)

Item	Data Desk	Minitab	SAS	Fathom	TI-83
1. Sample mean	✓	✓	N/A	✓	✓
2. Sample size	X	✓	N/A	✓	✓
3. Null and alternative hypotheses	✓	✓	N/A	✓	✓
4. Test statistic	✓	✓	N/A	✓	✓
5. Degrees of freedom of the test	✓	X	N/A	✓	X
6. P-value of the test	✓	✓	N/A	✓	✓

7. Reject H_0 — These data provide evidence that the true mean of the heights is not 60 inches. Note that the P-value is right at the critical value of .05 on several of the printouts due to rounding.

Section 8.5 Hypothesis Test: Two-Sample *t*-Test of Means

SHORT ANSWER (page 259)

Item	Data Desk	Minitab	SAS	Fathom	TI-83
1. Two sample means (or the difference of the sample means)	✓	✓	✓	✓	✓
2. Alternative hypothesis	✓	✓	X	✓	✓
3. Test statistic	✓	✓	✓	✓	✓
4. Degrees of freedom	✓	✓	✓	✓	✓
5. *P*-value of the test	✓	✓	✓	✓	✓

6. Fail to reject H_0 — These data do not provide sufficient evidence to doubt the claim that the effectiveness of each approach is equal.

Section 8.6 Contingency Tables: Test of Independence

SHORT ANSWER (page 262)

Item	Data Desk	Minitab	SAS	Fathom	TI-83
1. Expected frequencies	✓	✓	✓	X	✓
2. Test statistic	✓	✓	✓	✓	✓
3. Degrees of freedom	✓	✓	✓	✓	✓
4. *P*-value of the test	✓	✓	✓	✓	✓

5. Fail to reject H_0 — These data do not provide sufficient evidence to doubt the claim that political affiliation is independent of gender.

Model Examination 1

Section I (page 264)

1. **E** Jersey numbers and address numbers in street addresses are labels and therefore categorical.

2. **A** A box plot is a great plot to display spread of data but not necessarily to show the shape of the distribution since it does not display gaps.

3. **B** The long tail to the right indicates that the data are skewed toward the higher values, which "pulls" the mean to the right of the median.

4. **A** Addition of a constant to a data set shifts the center of the distribution by that constant since all of the data are affected.

5. **B** The standard deviation can be computed for any distribution. It may not have the same meaning for skewed distributions as for mound-shaped and symmetric distributions.

6. **B** The number of students does not impact the position of the scores in their respective distributions.

7. **A**

8. **C** A correlation coefficient is never greater than 1.

9. **D** The conclusions must be reasonable; answer C implies causation and therefore is not valid.

10. C A residual is equal to the actual value minus the predicted value; therefore, a positive residual indicates that the actual value is greater than the predicted value.

11. A The transformation $(x, y) \rightarrow (\ln x, \ln y)$ produces a power model.

12. B Since the slope of a regression line $= r \cdot \dfrac{s_y}{s_x}$, $.01 = .9\left(\dfrac{4.1}{s_{\text{weight}}}\right)$. So $s_{\text{weight}} = 369$ pounds.

13. B A residual plot is a scatterplot and therefore there is no line or slope.

14. C A quadratic residual plot indicates that a quadratic model might be appropriate.

15. B This is one of the two essential requirements of valid sampling.

16. D Bias and shape of a distribution are unrelated.

17. B Blocking is an optional technique and is not an important characteristic of valid experimental design.

18. B Blocking would be an appropriate design in an experiment. This is not an experiment.

19. D Participants had the option to respond.

20. C Expected value is equal to $\sum x \cdot P(x) = .13(-1,000) + .15(0) + .24(1,000) + .35(2,000) + .13(3,000) = \$1,200$.

21. C Variance depends on the values of p and n since $\sigma^2 = np(1 - p)$

22. C This situation is an example of a *Geometric* (.4).

23. C The adjustment is sometimes used with the normal approximation to the binomial since it is a continuous approximation of a discrete variable.

24. A Since there is no replacement of the kings in the deck, the maximum number of rotten fruit would be 4 for every shipment of 24 fruit.

25. B There are 7 people who are in the relevant age group and favor baseball out of the entire population of 99.

26. A The sample proportion, $\mu_{\hat{p}}$, is an unbiased estimator of the population proportion. Therefore, since $\mu_{\hat{p}} \neq p$, there is bias in the sampling method.

27. C Probability(flight will land between 40 and 45 minutes late) = the area of a rectangle with length of 5 (from $45 - 40$) and height $\dfrac{1}{14}$ $\left(\text{from } \dfrac{1}{52 - 38}\right) = \dfrac{5}{14} = .357$.

28. D Discrete variables may have an infinite number of values.

29. A The area under any density function must equal 1.

30. C Option I must be excluded since the probability that the true value is in the interval is 0 or 1.

31. C The differences within each flowerbed should be compared.

32. D A one-tailed test at the $\alpha = .05$ level corresponds to a 90% confidence interval.

33. C Since the critical z-value changes from 1.96 to 2.33, the margin of error increases by a factor of $\dfrac{2.33}{1.96} = 1.19$.

34. C 999 produces a margin of error of $\pm .0299$ using the earlier results.

35. C The sets of x's and y's need not be normal.

36. E The expected count is less than 5 and therefore does not meet the requirements for the chi-square test.

37. A

38. B Even though the population standard deviation is known, sample size is sufficiently small so that a t-test should be performed.

39. C α is the probability of a Type I error.

40. C The P-value of a one-tailed test would be .036, which is less than .05.

Section II

PART A (page 270)

1. a. median $= 8 -$ value for which the cumulative relative frequency is approximately .5

b. Theoretical probability distribution:

Sum	Probability	Sum	Probability
2	$\dfrac{1}{36}$	8	$\dfrac{5}{36}$
3	$\dfrac{2}{36}$	9	$\dfrac{4}{36}$
4	$\dfrac{3}{36}$	10	$\dfrac{3}{36}$
5	$\dfrac{4}{36}$	11	$\dfrac{2}{36}$
6	$\dfrac{5}{36}$	12	$\dfrac{1}{36}$
7	$\dfrac{6}{36}$		

c. Cumulative relative frequency plot.

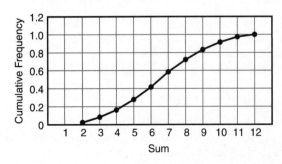

d. Comparison and conclusion: it appears that the cumulative relative frequencies for the sums of 5, 6, 7, 8, and 9 are lower than what the theoretical distribution produces. Therefore, there is reason to doubt the honesty of the dice.

SCORING GUIDE

4 Complete	All four parts essentially correct
3 Substantial	Part a incorrect or correct answer with inadequate reason. Parts b, c, and d essentially correct.
2 Developing	Part a correct. Part b incorrect. Part c correct for the distribution listed in b. Part d reasonable for the graph in c.
1 Minimal	Part a is essentially correct. No other parts are correct.
0	No parts correct.

2. Answers may vary. A good design would be to block 1–3–10–12; 4–6–7–9; 2–11; 5–8; and randomly assign the fertilizers within each block. Correct answers should clearly indicate blocking in such a way that the lighting effect is the same for all flowerbeds within each block.

SCORING GUIDE

4 Complete	Block 1–3–10–12; 4–6–7–9; 2-11; 5–8 Explanation of why this blocking is advisable and the need for random assignment of treatment and control.
3 Substantial	Block 1–3–10–12; 4–6–7–9; 2–11; 5–8 Reasonable explanation of why this blocking is advisable but no reference to random assignment of treatment and control.
2 Developing	Block 1–4–7–10–3–6–9–12; 2–11; 5–8 Missing or inadequate explanation — no reference to random assignment of treatment and control.
1 Minimal	Some attempt at blocking. Missing or inadequate explanation — no reference to random assignment of treatment and control.
0	No blocking indicated.

3. a. The condition $np > 10$ would not be satisfied since $np = 2$.
   b. The sample size would have to be such that $np > 10$. Therefore, the minimum size would be 501 by solving $n(.02) > 10$.
   c. H_0: $p = .02$
      H_a: $p \neq .02$
      Test: z-test for a proportion
      Assumptions: $np > 10$; $np = 501(.02) = 10.02$, $n(1 - p) > 10$; $np = 501(.98) = 489.8$.
      $$z = \frac{.03 - .02}{\sqrt{\frac{(.02)(.98)}{501}}} = 1.5988 \rightarrow P\text{-value} = .1120$$

Therefore, since $.1120 > .05$, we fail to reject the null hypothesis; these data do not provide sufficient evidence to doubt the manufacturer's claim of 2% defective.

SCORING GUIDE

4 Complete	Parts a, b, and c essentially correct.
3 Substantial	Part a correct; part b incorrect; part c correct for the sample size of part b.
2 Developing	Part a correct; part b incorrect; part c contains substantial errors (choice of test, assumptions, test statistic, P-value or rejection region and conclusion).
1 Minimal	Part a correct; part b incorrect; no attempt in part c.
0	No parts correct.

4. a. Life $= 0.935199 + 0.000163839$ (cost)
   b. For each dollar of purchase price, the car life is expected to increase by 0.000163839 years.
   c. Since there are more points below residual $= 0$ than above it, the residual plot does not display a great deal of random scatter. In addition, we can conclude that the regression line tends to overestimate the car life for the majority of initial cost values.
   d. Life $= 0.935199 + 0.000163839$ (25000) $= 5.031174$ years
   e. The value of the residual for a car with purchase price $25,000 and a predicted life of 5 years is positive. Therefore, we can conclude that the regression line underestimates the car life for this purchase price.

SCORING GUIDE

4 Complete	All five parts essentially correct.
3 Substantial	Parts a – d essentially correct; part e incorrect or inadequately explained.
2 Developing	Parts a, b, d essentially correct; parts c and e incorrect or inadequately explained.
1 Minimal	Parts a and b essentially correct; parts c, d, and e incorrect or inadequately explained.
0	No parts correct.

5. The complete table with the marginal totals is

	ABC	NBC	CBS	FOX	Totals
English	12	7	3	8	30
Math	6	8	9	7	30
Science	2	6	3	4	15
Social Science	9	4	10	6	29
Totals	29	25	25	25	104

a. Probability(math teacher who prefers FOX) $= \dfrac{7}{104}$

b. Probability(math teacher | prefers FOX) $= \dfrac{7}{25}$

c. Probability(prefers FOX | math teacher) $= \dfrac{7}{30}$

SCORING GUIDE

4 Complete	All three parts are correct.
3 Substantial	Parts b and c are correct. Part a is incorrect.
2 Developing	Part a is correct. Parts b and c are incorrect — no conditional probability.
1 Minimal	Any one part displays some understanding of probability.
0	No part has merit.

Section II

PART B (page 273)

6. a. Answers will vary. The correct answer will display 25 codes ranging from 1 to 200 with the corresponding values.

   b. The mean and standard deviation stated are correct for the sample data.

   c. The confidence interval uses a critical t-value $= 2.064$ with $df = 24$ in the calculation using the statistics in part b.

   d. Answers may vary. Reasons should include a correct interpretation of the confidence interval in the context of the problem.

SCORING GUIDE

4 Complete	All four parts essentially correct.
3 Substantial	Parts a, b, and c are essentially correct. Explanation in part d is incorrect or inadequate.
2 Developing	Parts a and b are essentially correct. Part c is calculated using $z = 1.96$. Explanation in part d is incorrect or inadequate.
1 Minimal	Part a and b are essentially correct. Parts c and d are missing or incorrect.
0	No part is correct.

Model Examination 2

Section I (page 274)

Section I (page 274)

1. **C** The gender variable has values of male or female.

2. **E** In (A) through (C) a counterexample can be found. (A) A variable of a geometric distribution is infinite. (B) The amount of loss in dollars is negative. (C) A discrete set {1, 2, 4, 8, ...} where consecutive values do not differ by the same amount. (D) Days of the week are categorical.

3. **A** Discrete data are never normal — a variable must be continuous to be a candidate for following the normal distribution.

4. **D** Symmetry is the key condition for the mean to be approximately equal to the median.

5. **B** The median is resistant to changes at the extremes of any data set.

6. **A** A one-standard deviation interval near the mean contains more data than a similar interval farther from the mean. Using the empirical rule, there should be approximately 34% of the data between 42 and 49 and approximately 15% of the data between 28 and 35.

7. **B** The z-score of the mean is 0; values less than the mean would have negative z-scores.

8. **D** The domain of all normal distributions is the set of all real numbers.

9. **D** A weighted mean depends on the numbers of subjects in each group in addition to the values.

10. **D** There is no linear association in a quadratic pattern.

11. **E** Note that (B) and (C) are incorrect since they imply that there is a causal relationship between the variables.

12. **A** While not sufficient, it is productive to have a residual plot that exhibits random scatter with balance around the horizontal.

13. **B** This transformation is the only one listed that will "bend" the tendency more towards a linear relationship.

14. **A** GPA = $3.21 - .04(20) = 2.41$

15. **D** A positive slope indicates a positive correlation coefficient.

16. **B** The y-intercept is considered when determining the meaningfulness of the equation, not the fit.

17. **D** 40% of the sample chose not to respond; there is a real possibility of non-response bias.

18. **D** Response bias deals with the responses of the selected subjects, not the selection process.

19. **C** $3 \times 3 = 9$

20. **E** It is assumed that the results of the trial will be compared. There is no randomization apparent nor any discussion of replication.

21. **D** Inference to any of the populations referenced would not be appropriate based on this sample.

22. **C** Expected value = sum of prob(values) = $\left(\frac{18}{38}\right)(1) + \left(\frac{20}{38}\right)(-1) = -.05$. Therefore, in the long run you will lose a nickel for each dollar you bet.

23. **C** Expected value = 55 so $p = .55$ and standard deviation = $\sqrt{\frac{.55(.45)}{100}} = .0497$. Expected standard deviation = $100(.0497) = 4.97$.

24. **D** Geometric probability deals with the probability of getting a success after n trials.

25. **B** I is the exact binomial; II is the normal approximation using the continuity adjustment. III is an inappropriate estimation since it will not include the value 16.

26. **E** They are all false.

27. **D** There are 7 subjects under 20 who prefer baseball out of 26 total who prefer baseball.

28. **C** This is exactly one of the components the Central Limit tells us.

29. **E** The density function would be $f(x) = \begin{cases} \frac{1}{4} & \text{if } x \in [0, 4] \\ 0 & \text{otherwise} \end{cases}$

30. **B** The sum of the probabilities does not equal 1.

31. **E** All three statements are true.

32. **B** We are testing the proportion from one sample against an expected proportion.

33. **C** This statement is exactly an example of the meaning of the P-value in a test of significance.

34. **B** Confidence level is independent of sample size. Further, as sample size increases, error or variation decreases.

35. **C** The most conservative value of p is .5.

36. C z-tests assume a relatively normal distribution. A highly skewed distribution will make the approximation inaccurate.

37. A We expect that the female Republicans will be in the same ratio as the Republicans are to the entire population.

38. D We are testing a sample proportion against an expected proportion.

39. D Power can be calculated only when an alternative mean is considered. Note that $\alpha + \beta$ does not equal 1.

40. D A two-sample *t*-test will produce a *P*-value different from this one.

Section II

PART A (page 281)

1. a.
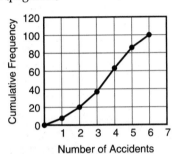
b. Mean = 2.875; median = 3
c. Either answer can be justified.

2. a. Answers will vary. One possible correct design would be to select random digits until 10 digits between 1 and 6 inclusive are selected. Determine whether 3 or more of different digits from 1 to 6 are included in the set. Repeat the simulation.
b. The 10 visits in which a prize is received are underlined.
14378 34198 32178 76032 13054 52306 28905 12956
54920 62179 21098 45082 13067 21784 41826 31451
76931 35093 13495 54679 14283 23085 12984 19683
In trial one, the prizes received were 1, 2, 3, 4, and 6.
In trial two, the prizes received were 1, 2, 4, 5, and 6. In trial three, the prizes received were 1, 3, 4, 5, 6. Therefore, on all three simulations we received 3 or more of the prizes.
c. Again there are 6 possible prizes so the numbers 1 to 6 can be utilized. For this task, assign 1 to Bill and 2 to Joe. Beginning with the first digit of each row, determine whether a 1 occurs before a 2.
d. Underline the first 1 or 2 that occurs in each row.
14378 34198 32178 76032 13054 52306 28905 12956
54920 62179 21098 45082 13067 21784 41826 31451
76931 35093 13495 54679 14283 23085 12984 19683
In our 3 simulations, Bill's character was received 2 out of 3 times.

3. a. $H_0: \mu = 45{,}982.50$
$H_a: \mu > 45{,}982.50$
Choice of test: One sample *t*-test
Assumptions:
Simple random sample? Given.
Normal population? Reasonable from the context.
σ is unknown.
test statistic:
$$t = \frac{47534.74 - 45982.50}{\frac{12546.70}{\sqrt{5}}} = .2766 \text{ and } df = 4$$
P-value = .3979
Conclusion: fail to reject; these data provide insufficient evidence to doubt that the true mean of the gross income of households is $45,982.50.
b. 95% Confidence Interval
$$= 47534.74 \pm (2.776)\frac{12546.70}{\sqrt{5}} = 47534.74 \pm 15576.29$$
$$= (31958.45, 63111.03)$$

Note: The TI-83 will give the interval as (31956, 63114).

c. This confidence interval is not equivalent to the test in part a. Since the test of significance is one-sided at the $\alpha = .05$ level, a 90% confidence interval would be equivalent.

4. a. The regression line is:
   Users $= -30124.5 + 15.1$(Year)
   The value of R^2 is .906 which indicates that 90.6% of the variation in the User total is explained by the model.
   The residual plot indicates a clear pattern.

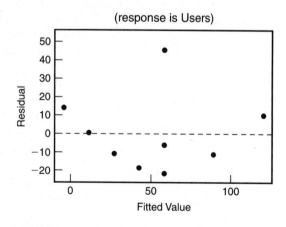

(response is Users)

Therefore, we would conclude that this is not a good fit.

b. The regression line is:
   $\sqrt{\text{Users}} = -2158.1 + 1.09$(Year).
   The value of R^2 is .968 but the residual plot still exhibits a great deal of pattern.

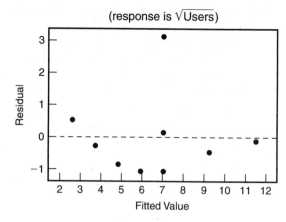

(response is $\sqrt{\text{Users}}$)

Therefore, even though the value of R^2 has improved, we still conclude that this transformation did not improve the fit.

c. The regression line is:
   ln(Users) $= -683.7 + .347$(Year)
   The value of R^2 is .993.
   The residual plot has less pattern than the others but does not display random scatter.

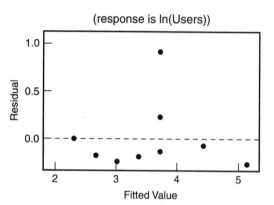

(response is ln(Users))

Consequently, we would conclude that this is the best fit of the three models.
Note: In all three models the number of users (original and transformed) for the year 1994 may be an outlier due to its large residual value.

d. The logarithmic model explains more based on a comparison of the values of R^2 of the three models.

5. a. Answers may vary. An example of a correct answer could be:

No, it would not be surprising to find a 9th grade girl who is 70 inches tall since, using the mean and standard deviation of the sample as estimators of the population parameters, a measurement of 70 inches is between one and two standard deviations above the mean.

b. The standard deviation of the sampling distribution is $s_{\bar{x}} = \dfrac{s}{\sqrt{n}} = \dfrac{4.5}{\sqrt{20}} = 1.006$. Therefore, a sample mean of 70 would be approximately 6.5 standard deviations above the mean. This would be a very surprising result.

SCORING GUIDE

4 Complete	Both parts essentially correct.
3 Substantial	Answers to both parts correct but justification is inadequate.
2 Developing	Answers to both parts are correct but justifications are missing or incorrect.
1 Minimal	Answer to one part is correct with justification.
0	No part is correct.

Section II

PART B (page 283)

6. a.

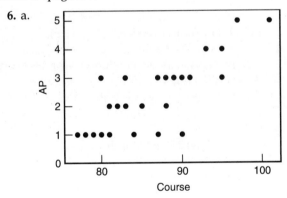

b. Correlation Coefficient = .801; regression equation is AP = −10.7 + 0.152(Course)

c.

(response is AP)

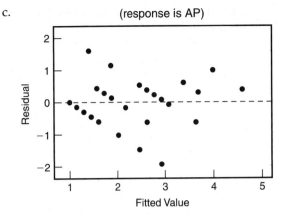

d. $s = .7134$

e. The test of the significance of the correlation coefficient is equivalent to the test for the significance of the slope (β) of the regression line.

Assumptions:
Variables are linearly related (from graph) ✓
Constant variation (apparently) ✓
Normality of responses (too few points to verify)
H_0: $\beta = 0$
H_a: $\beta \neq 0$
Test: Test of slope of linear regression
Test statistic: $t = \dfrac{b - \beta}{s_\beta} = \dfrac{.15165 - 0}{.02034} = 7.46$ with $df = 31$.
→ P-value of approximately 0.
Conclusion: Reject the null hypothesis. The slope of the regression is significant, therefore the correlation coefficient is also significant.

f. Answers may vary. Correct answers should focus on the value of R^2 and the residual plot. One answer that should be given full credit is:
The value of R^2 is 64.2. The residual plot does display some randomness and balance between positives and negatives in its scatter and appears to display relatively constant variance in the residuals.

SCORING GUIDE

4 Complete	All parts essentially correct.
3 Substantial	All parts essentially correct but test of significance has substantial errors or omissions.
2 Developing	Parts a, b, and c correct. Parts d and/or f missing or incomplete. Part e has substantial errors.
1 Minimal	Only parts a, b, and c correct.
0	Parts a, b, and c are not sufficient to merit a 1.

Model Examination 3

1. **B** Only choice that has a descriptor as a value.

2. **C** Even though it may not feel like it sometimes, the length of time in a line is finite. Time in this context is always a continuous variable.

3. **A**

4. **C** The Interquartile Range is the length of the interval between Q1 and Q3, the 25th and 75th percentiles.

5. **A** The median and the mode are not affected by making an extreme value more extreme.

6. **E** All are possible.

7. **B** The 3rd quartile is the 75th percentile; the value whose z-score is 1 is approximately in the 84th percentile.

8. **A** There should be approximately 5% of the data outside the interval (24, 56) using the Empirical Rule.

9. **B** $P(x \leq 60) = P(z \leq -1.76) = 0.039$

10. **E** A correlation coefficient close to 0 indicates that there is no *linear* association and that the scatterplot does not display any *linear* pattern. Other types of associations or patterns may be present.

11. **D** Outliers in linear regression are indicated by inspecting the residuals.

12. **C** Sometimes the value of the y-intercept makes no sense in the context of the problems. For example, if the regression equation were Length $= -4.35 +$ 1.02(Time), the y-intercept indicates that there was a length of -4.35 at time $= 0$.

13. **B** We merely square the r value from the linear regression.

14. **C** We would expect that her weight would be .6(1 standard deviation of the weight) above the weight of the women in the set.

15. **D** I and III have a correlation of -1; II is not collinear.

16. **D** A stratified random sample with the classes as the strata will guarantee representation from all four classes.

17. **A**

18. **B** Blocking is used to make the treatment and control groups more similar.

19. **A** Randomization is one of the critical components in valid design.

20. **C** Causation cannot be inferred for any observational study.

21. **C** The expected value on any one play is 0.043. Therefore, we expect to win approximately $0.43 in 10 games.

22. **B** $\mu_H = 30$; $\mu_K = 60$; $\sigma_H = 4.583$; $\sigma_K = 4.899$.

23. **E** Answer C is in the correct form but np is small; therefore the normal approximation is not appropriate.

24. **A** Every number generated should have the same probability of occurring.

25. **A** 43 favored football and 15 of them were over 40.

26. **D** The Central Limit deals with the nature of the sampling distribution and its relationship to the parameters of the population distribution. The shape of the population distribution is of no consequence.

27. **D** Probability $= \dfrac{16.4 - 16.0}{16.4 - 15.1} \approx .308$

28. **B**

29. **C** The area under the probability density function over its domain must equal 1.

30. **B** Interval B is not centered on the mean of 1.4 hours.

31. **E** This is a categorical variable problem with Stations A, B, and C being the values of the variable.

32. **D** The null hypothesis in a test of independence is that the variables are independent. Since the P-value is less than α, we have sufficient evidence to reject this hypothesis.

33. **D**

34. **C** The sample sizes will be in the same ratio as the products of p and $1 - p$ for each value of p.

35. **D**

36. **D** The 105 males should be split in proportion to the number of people in the population who favor the Democratic Party.

37. **C** The P-value of the slope of the regression line is close to 0 and therefore, highly significant.

38. **B** We have two independent samples of different populations whose standard deviations are not known.

39. **B**

40. **C** Subtract 1 before multiplying the number of rows by the number of columns.

Section II

PART A (page 291)

1. a. Relative Frequencies

	A	B	C	D	F
History	.213	.313	.225	.163	.088
English	.261	.318	.182	.136	.102
Science	.086	.215	.452	.161	.086
Math	.096	.144	.327	.337	.096

b.

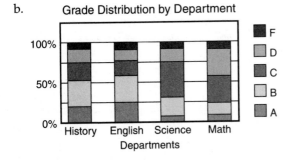

c. Steps:
    (1) State a null and alternative hypothesis.
    (2) Check assumptions for a chi-square test of independence.
    (3) Determine expected frequencies.
    (4) Calculate the chi-square statistic.
    (5) Calculate a *P*-value or compare to a critical value.
    (6) State a conclusion.

SCORING GUIDE

4 Complete	All parts essentially correct.
3 Substantial	Parts a and b essentially correct; part c references a chi-square test but is incomplete.
2 Developing	Parts a and b essentially correct; part c does not reference a chi-square test of independence.
1 Minimal	Only part a is correct.
0	No part is correct.

2. a. A randomized block design is appropriate. Assignment into treatment and control groups within each block is made randomly.

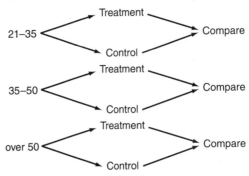

b. The means of the differences between the current reading and the baseline reading of those in the treatment group would be compared to the mean difference of those persons in the control group *within each age block.*

c. Each age block listed above should be split into sub-blocks of gender. Within each of the gender blocks, treatment and control groups would be created using random assignment.

d. Comparison of the means of differences should be made within each gender sub-block.

SCORING GUIDE

4 Complete	All parts essentially correct.
3 Substantial	All parts essentially correct but without statement of random assignment into groups within each block.
2 Developing	Part a is essentially correct; part b is missing or inadequate; part c is essentially correct.
1 Minimal	Part a is the only correct part.
0	No part is correct.

3. a. $H_0: \mu = 33.5$
    $H_a: \mu \neq 33.5$
Choice of test: one-sample *t*-test
Assumptions:
Normal population? The population of new car gas mileage is given as normal.
σ is not known.
Test Statistic: $t = \dfrac{31.6 - 33.5}{\dfrac{3.4}{\sqrt{12}}} = -1.93$

Since this test is two-sided, the *P*-value = .079. Therefore, we do not have sufficient evidence to reject the null hypothesis. We conclude that these data do not cast significant doubt on the publication's claim.

b. H_0: $\mu = 33.5$
H_a: $\mu < 33.5$
Choice of test: one-sample t-test
Assumptions:
Normal population? The population of new car gas mileage is given as normal.
σ is not known.
Test Statistic: $t = \dfrac{31.6 - 33.5}{\dfrac{3.4}{\sqrt{12}}} = -1.93$

Since this test is one-sided, the P-value $= .039$. Therefore, we have sufficient evidence to reject the null hypothesis. We conclude that there is sufficient evidence to doubt the publication's claim that the average gas mileage of this model is 33.5 mpg.

c. Testing a hypothesis whose alternative is a "not equal to" statement is two-tailed; therefore, the P-value of a two-sided test is twice that of a one-sided test whose alternative hypothesis involves an inequality.

SCORING GUIDE

4 Complete	All parts essentially correct.
3 Substantial	Parts a and b correct with at most two omissions of essential components; part c is reasonable.
2 Developing	Parts a and b exhibit one or more significant errors; part c is reasonable.
1 Minimal	Parts a and b exhibit one or more significant errors; part c is unreasonable or missing.
0	No part is correct.

4. a. GPA $= -0.964 + 0.0105$(IT)
b. GPA $= 0.57 + 0.0137$(RR)
c. The regression line for part a has an $R^2 = 20.8\%$ and a relatively randomly scattered residual plot. The regression line in part b has an $R^2 = 1.1\%$ with a similar and somewhat more scattered residual plot. Answers may vary: part a has a better R^2 but a less scattered residual plot; part b has a very low R^2 but a more scattered residual plot.
d.

(response is GPA)

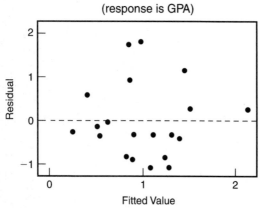

Fitted Value

(response is GPA)

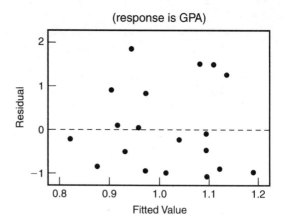

Fitted Value

SCORING GUIDE

4 Complete	All three parts are essentially correct. Part c is correct only if the answer addresses both the value of R^2 and the residual plot.
3 Substantial	Part a and b are essentially correct; part c references either the value of R^2 or the residual plot but not both.
2 Developing	Parts a and b are essentially correct; part c is incorrect or missing.
1 Minimal	Parts a and b have minor errors; part c is incorrect or missing.
0	No part is correct.

5. a. P(randomly selected videotape will be returned between 3 and 4 days late) $= \dfrac{4 - 3}{4 - 0} = .25$

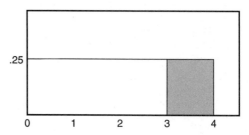

b. P(randomly selected videotape will be returned more than one day late) $= \dfrac{4 - 1}{4 - 0} = .75$

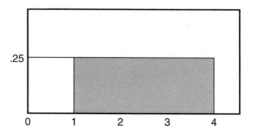

SCORING GUIDE

4 Complete	Both computations and graphs are accurate.
3 Substantial	Both computations are accurate but the graphs are incorrect or missing.
2 Developing	Only one of the computations is accurate and its corresponding graph is correct. The other computation and/or graph has substantial errors.
1 Minimal	The calculations in a and b are correct but the graphs are incorrect or missing.
0	No part is correct.

d. This simulation indicates that the sample mean and variance are unbiased estimators of the population mean and variance respectively while the standard deviation is not an unbiased estimator.

SCORING GUIDE

4 Complete	All parts are essentially correct.
3 Substantial	Part a is correct; part b and the number of rows in part c are incorrect. Part d is answered appropriately for the data provided.
2 Developing	Parts a, b, and c are essentially correct; part d is missing or incorrect.
1 Minimal	Parts a and c are essentially correct; part b is incorrect and therefore, so is the number of rows in the table in part c. Part d is incorrect or missing
0	No part is correct.

Section II

PART B (page 293)

6. a. Mean = 64.8; standard deviation $(n - 1) = 7.396$; variance = 54.7

b. $\binom{5}{2} = 10$

c.

Sample	Elements	Sample Means	Sample Standard Deviation	Sample Variance
1	{52, 65}	58.5	9.192	84.5
2	{52, 68}	60	11.314	128.0
3	{52, 69}	60.5	12.021	144.5
4	{52, 70}	61	12.728	162.0
5	{65, 68}	66.5	2.121	4.5
6	{65, 69}	67	2.828	8.0
7	{65, 70}	67.5	3.536	12.5
8	{68, 69}	68.5	.707	0.5
9	{68, 70}	69	1.414	2.0
10	{69, 70}	69.5	0.707	.5
Means		64.8	5.657	54.7

Model Examination 4

Section I (page 294)

1. **E** A and B are discrete; C and D are categorical.

2. **D** None of the data represented for Station 1 is over 40. Consequently, the 60's would undoubtedly be considered as "ancient history" to the viewers of Station 1.

3. **A** Dot plots should be used for quantitative data only.

4. **A** These changes to the data offset each other in the sum that calculates the mean; the middle value continues to be the middle value.

5. **A** The spread of data is unchanged.

6. **C**

7. **D** The sum of the areas is greater than 1.

8. **C** P(next flight is early) $= P(x \le 0) = P(z \le -.851)$ $\approx .197$

9. **E** The correlation coefficient of the combined set depends on the orientation of the data values of the combined set.

10. **E**

11. **D**

12. **E** R^2 is calculated for the linearized model of $(x, \ln y)$. Therefore, the correlation coefficient of the original data is irrelevant.

13. **B** $b_1 = (-0.47)\dfrac{15.7}{6.1} = -1.209;$

    $b_0 = 201.5 - (-1.209)19.5 = 225.07.$

14. **C** A point is influential if its removal causes a substantial change in the regression equation.

15. **B** The regression line always contains the grand mean.

16. **E** This is a multi-stage cluster sample.

17. **E** This is a voluntary response survey with only two outcomes; non-response is not an issue in a voluntary response survey.

18. **B** Since each type of popcorn is popped in each popper and the results combined, the effect of the different poppers is the same for all three brands.

19. **D** There was no random selection of the couples in the restaurants.

20. **C** The expected value is 2.3 which places the arrow in the 2nd circle.

21. **E** The mean will always increase since it is given by np; the standard deviation attains its maximum for $p = .5$. Therefore, the change in the standard deviation depends on the original value of p and the amount of increase in p.

22. **A** The probability of a success on each trial is fixed and he is interested in a specific set of successes out of 4 trials.

23. **D** The value of np is too small to justify the use of the normal approximation to the binomial.

24. **E**

25. **B** The conditional probability is calculated by $\dfrac{.4(.03)}{.4(.03) + .3(.05) + .3(.02)} = .363636\ldots$

26. **C** As the sample size increases, the Central Limit Theorem states the shape and parameters of the sampling distribution regardless of the nature of the data distribution.

27. **A** The domain of a uniform distribution can be any interval of finite length.

28. **B** The number of trials is fixed for the binomial; the number of trials until the first success occurs is the focus of the geometric.

29. **A** The area under the function over its domain does not equal 1.

30. **B** The width of the original confidence interval is .225 while the width of the new confidence interval is .204.

31. **B**

32. **A** The decision regarding rejection of the null hypothesis gives no insight to the form of the alternative hypothesis.

33. **E** Margin of error = the value of the critical z times the standard error.

34. **D** A factor of 9 times the sample size will decrease the margin of error by a factor of $\dfrac{1}{3}$.

35. **E** The decision depends on whether the standard deviation of the population is known.

36. **A** The area greater than 21.03 for a chi-square distribution with 12 degrees of freedom is .04994.

37. C $S = \dfrac{\sum\limits_{i=1}^{n}(y - \hat{y})^2}{n - 1}$

38. E The means are given but not the standard deviations which would be necessary for the use of a two-sample t-test.

39. D β is not related to the complement of α, the amount of a Type I error.

40. B For a one-sample t-test, the degrees of freedom is $n - 1$.

Section II

PART A (page 301)

1. a.

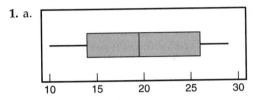

10   15   20   25   30

Min = 10; Q1 = 14; Median = 19.5; Q3 = 26; Max = 29

b. Answers may vary. One correct comment is that the stem and leaf plot appears relatively symmetric but not mound-shaped while the box plot appears quite symmetric.

c. We would anticipate that the mean is greater than the median because of the large cluster at the high end of the stem and leaf plot and since the distance between Q3 and the median exceeds the distance between the median and Q1. The actual value of the mean is 19.9 which is slightly greater than the median.

SCORING GUIDE

4 Complete	All three parts essentially correct.
3 Substantial	Part a is essentially correct; the answer in part b does not include important features of the plots (shape, symmetry); part c is reasonable for the plots displayed and clearly references the plots in the explanation.
2 Developing	Part a is essentially correct; the answer in part b does not include important features of the plots (shape, symmetry); part c is reasonable for the plots displayed but does not clearly reference the plots in the explanation.
1 Minimal	Part a is the only correct part.
0	No part is correct.

2. a. Answers may vary. The research could survey adults regarding their coffee habits, take the participants' blood pressures, and calculate mean blood pressures of the groups: women over 4 cups, women 4 cups and under, men over 4 cups, men 4 cups and under.

b. Answers may vary. The researcher could select a set of women and a second set of men and then assign the genders into "4 cups or under" and "over 4 cups" groups in which each member of each group would drink the prescribed amount of caffeinated coffee per day. After a period of time, blood pressures would be taken of all participants. Analysis would be first within the groups and then between the groups.

c. The best conclusion possible in an observational study is that there appears to be an association between the explanatory and response variables. Therefore, the most that could be concluded is that there is an association between the amount of caffeinated coffee and blood pressure.

d. Since this is an experiment, the results may indicate that there is a causal relationship between the variables.

SCORING GUIDE

4 Complete	All four parts essentially correct.
3 Substantial	Part a indicates the self-selection of groups; part b indicates the imposition of treatment and control on the subjects by the experimenter; one of parts c and d does not adequately address the issue of causation/no causation.
2 Developing	Part a indicates the self-selection of groups; part b indicates the imposition of treatment and control on the subjects by the experimenter; neither of parts c and d adequately addresses the issue of causation/no causation.
1 Minimal	Parts a and b do not clearly address the issue of selection; parts c and d do not clearly address the issue of causation or are missing.
0	No part is correct.

3. a. $\dfrac{93}{959}$

b. $\dfrac{93}{328}$

c. A chi-square test for independence is appropriate.
H_0: Age and preference of ice cream flavor are independent.
H_a: Age and preference of ice cream flavor are not independent.
Assumptions:

The expected frequencies are:

107.4	130.6	76.0
109.5	133.1	77.4
111.2	135.2	78.6

Since all expected frequencies are greater than 5, the test is appropriate.

Test Statistic: Chi-square = $13.9 \rightarrow P$-value = .0075

Conclusion: reject the null hypothesis. Therefore, age group and preference of ice cream flavor are not independent.

SCORING GUIDE

4 Complete	All three parts are essentially correct.
3 Substantial	Parts a and b are essentially correct; part c is a chi-square test but does not show the essential ingredients of a test.
2 Developing	Parts a and b are essentially correct; part c is argued from a segmented bar graph.
1 Minimal	Part a and/or b is essentially correct; part c is argued from the percentages of each group.
0	No part is correct.

4. a. Defectives = $-0.8571 + 0.72857(\text{Speed})$

   b. A test of significance of a correlation coefficient is equivalent to a test of significance of the slope of the regression line. Therefore,

   $H_0: \beta_1 = 0$

   $H_a: \beta_1 \neq 0$

   Choice of Test: Slope of a regression line

   Assumptions: the sample gives no evidence to believe that the relationship is not linear.

   Test statistic: $t = \dfrac{b_1 - \beta_1}{s_{\beta_1}} = \dfrac{0.72857 - 0}{0.04949} =$

   $14.72 \rightarrow P$-value = 0.005

   Conclusion: Reject the null hypothesis. Therefore, the slope of the regression line is not 0. Consequently, we conclude that the relationship between the speed of the machine and the number of defectives is significant.

SCORING GUIDE

4 Complete	Both parts are essentially correct.
3 Substantial	Part a reverses the y-intercept and slope of the regression line; part b is essentially correct for this regression line.
2 Developing	Part a has either the correct or reversed equation; part b displays a test of the slope but does not address all of the requirements of a test of significance.
1 Minimal	Part a has either the correct or reversed equation; part b does not have a statistical test of the slope of the regression line.
0	No part is correct.

5. a. Yes, this is a valid probability distribution since each probability is greater than or equal to 0 and the sum of the probabilities is 1.

   b. The expected value of a benefit = sum of (Benefit)(Probability) = $2200

   c. Standard deviation of a probability distribution

   is given by $\sqrt{\sum_{i=1}^{n}(x - \mu)^2 p_i}$

   = square root of $[(500 - 2200)^2.1 + (1000 - 2200)^2.35 + (2000 - 2200)^2.4 + (5000 - 2200)^2.1 + (10000 - 2200)^2.05] = \sqrt{4635000} = 2152.9$

   d. Answers may vary but should include the fact that 95% of the claims should be in the interval $2200 \pm 1.96(2152.9) = (-2019.68, 6419.68)$. Since these are discrete data, the problem could also be interpreted in terms of the "average deviation from expected payment." This would help in comparing these results to another benefit plan. The data are somewhat symmetric, so applying the empirical rule is fairly acceptable.

SCORING GUIDE

4 Complete	All four parts essentially correct.
3 Substantial	Parts a and b are essentially correct; part c is incorrect; part d is reasonable for the answers in parts b and c.
2 Developing	Parts a and b are correct; parts c and d are incorrect.
1 Minimal	Only one part is correct.
0	No part is correct.

Section II

PART B (page 303)

6. a. Hospital A. Reasons may vary. Credit should be given for each of the following:

   (1) Comment that deviation from the expected decreases as sample size increases.

   (2) The standard error at Hospital A is .1025 while the standard error at Hospital B is .0648. Therefore, an occurrence of $\hat{p} = .4$ is more likely for Hospital A.

   (3) z-score for Hospital A = $.9765 \rightarrow p = .164$; z-score for Hospital B = $1.543 \rightarrow p = .061$.

   b. For both simulations, assign the digits 0, 1, and 2 to be life-threatening while the rest are not life-threatening. To simulate Hospital A, we consider blocks of 20 digits and determine the proportion of 0's, 1's, and 2's. For Hospital B, we do the same with blocks of 50 digits. We will underline and block the digits in the displays to represent 5 trials of each simulation:

Hospital A

|9435974025 9083188611 |4668782925 1470195054 |0580964187
3381121120 |4399198753 3936252594 |9546634112 0034026187|
9807010099 5189983326 |2209784733 3694814382 0078387869
9351587791 1080114624 0062633066 5489861799 8555803142
9770842465 2783088265 2752142947 1217901355 0525898067
2237931570 1256556214 2111829173 0763515019 7220777198
2881701368 3781148461 8123118520 5080954298 4662442672

Trial 1: 5; Trial 2: 6; Trial 3: 10; Trial 4: 3; Trial 5: 8.
40% or more of the 20 would be 8 or more. Therefore,
40% was equaled or exceeded in 2 of the 5 trials.

Hospital B

|9435974025 9083188611 4668782925 1470195054 0580964187|
|3381121120 4399198753 393625259 9546634112 0034026187|
|9807010099 5189983326 2209784733 3694814382 0078387869|
|9351587791 1080114624 0062633066 5489861799 8555803142|
|9770842465 2783088265 2752142947 1217901355 0525898067|
2237931570 1256556214 2111829173 0763515019 7220777198
2881701368 3781148461 8123118520 5080954298 4662442672

Trial 1: 15; Trial 2: 18; Trial 3: 14; Trial 4: 16; Trial 5: 16.
40% or more of the 50 would be 20 or more. Therefore,
40% was equaled or exceeded in 0 of the 5 trials.

c. The results of the simulation confirm the answer in part a.

SCORING GUIDE

4 Complete	All three parts essentially correct.
3 Substantial	Part a is incorrect or has an inadequate explanation; part b is acceptable; part c is reasonable based on the answers in a and b.
2 Developing	Part a is incorrect; part b is acceptable; part c is inadequate or missing.
1 Minimal	Part a is correct; part b is not acceptable; part c is missing or does not reflect the results in parts a and b.
0	No part is correct.

Model Examination 5

Section I (page 304)

1. **C** Cities are identified by names.

2. **E** In I, II, and III, the mean is identifiable as the balance point of the display; in IV, the median is identified.

3. **D** The graph is symmetric about its center line.

4. **B** Multiplying each value of the set by 10 increases the sum and therefore the mean by a factor of 10 also.

5. **B** The variance increases by a factor of $(.10)^2$. Therefore, the standard deviation increases by a factor of .10.

6. **A** Using z-scores and normal distribution techniques provide reasonable estimates only for mound-shaped and symmetric distributions.

7. **A** The tables provide the area to the left of the z-value.

8. **C** Probability of .06 for 90 and above has a critical z-score of 1.55. Solving for σ yields 7.7.

9. **D** This is the definition of r^2. Note we cannot conclude $r = 0.9$ since r could also be negative as well.

10. **B** The reason the point is called influential is that it exerts a great influence on the regression.

11. **A** Since $|r|$ is never greater than 1, a slope that is greater than 1 indicates that the standard deviations must be as described in choice A.

12. **D** This transformation produces an exponential fit to the original data. Since the residual plot of the fit to the transformed data still exhibits a pattern, we can conclude that the transformation, and therefore, the exponential fit, are not appropriate.

13. **D** A transformation $(x, y) \rightarrow (\ln x, \ln y)$ produces a power model.

14. **C** The explanatory variable is time, not number of phones.

15. **C** Its presence or removal influences the regression and the correlation.

16. **E** This is an example of a convenience sample.

17. **C** All need to be considered when evaluating a statistical claim.

18. **D** The desire to have a difference of means is not sufficient to mandate a matched-pairs approach.

19. **E** This was at best a study of these students only.

20. **C** The expected return from A is $37,500 while the expected return from B is $37,800.

21. **A** These distributions are inverses of each other. The mean of *Binomial*(50, .9) is 45 while the mean of *Binomial*(50, .1) is 5. The standard deviations are the same because of the use of complementary probabilities in the formula.

22. **A** The probability of .40 is for a success on the first or second try. The probability on more than one try will exceed the probability on any one try.

23. **C** *Normal*(0, 1) is the standard normal distribution. There is no indication of a conversion to z-scores.

24. **D** At times, the calculation of a probability may not be prudent.

25. **D** Conditional probability: $\dfrac{.4(.03) + .3(.05)}{.4(.03) + .3(.05) + .3(.02)}$

26. **A** The sampling distribution will be exactly normal when the population is normal.

27. **D** Probability $= \dfrac{246 - 200}{246 - 184} = .742$

28. **C** Expected value $= 1(.40) + 3(.20) + 5(.40) = 3$; therefore, we expect a sum of 9 for three spins.

29. **D** The area under the triangle to the left of $x = .5$ is $\dfrac{7}{8}$.

30. **C** This is the meaning of the 99% Confidence Interval.

31. **C** The population standard deviation is not known.

32. **D** A one-tailed test has a P-value that is half of the two-tailed value; importance and significance of a test are not synonymous. A test never establishes the truth of the null hypothesis.

33. **C** The sample mean is not an issue for margin of error.

34. **A** A sample of size of 1068 will produce a 3% margin of error with 95% confidence. One would need a sample size of 1849 to achieve a 3% margin of error with 99% confidence. The ratio of these sample sizes is 1.7.

35. **D** The Student Council should have used a t-test since the population standard deviation is not known.

36. **D** The P-value of the test is .0208, which is slightly more than α. Therefore, we fail to reject and would also fail to reject for any smaller value of α.

37. **D** The Empirical Rule extended to a bivariate case indicates that there would be approximately (.95)(.95) of the points within two standard deviations of the grand mean.

38. **C** Since the performance on the Math and Verbal parts of the SAT cannot be considered as independent, the matched pairs is the best choice.

39. **B** Type II error refers to a decision regarding H_0, not the truth or falsity of the alternative hypothesis.

40. **E** There is no sample size indicated.

Section II

PART A (page 311)

1. a.

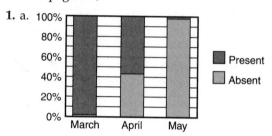

b. It appears that attendance goes down substantially as the school year ends.

c. The expected frequencies can be summarized:

	Absent	Present
March	121.8	133.2
April	121.8	133.2
May	121.4	132.7

Therefore we can conduct the chi-square test:
H_0: There is no relationship between attendance and these months.
H_a: There is a relationship between attendance and these months.
Test statistic: $\chi^2 = \dfrac{(o - e)^2}{e} = 485.645 \rightarrow P$-value ≈ 0.
Therefore, reject the null hypothesis and conclude that there is a significant relationship between months and level of attendance.

SCORING GUIDE

4 Complete	All three parts are correct.
3 Substantial	Parts a and c are correct; part b includes a weak interpretation.
2 Developing	Part c is correct; parts a and b contain substantial errors or are missing.
1 Minimal	Either part a or c is correct exclusively.
0	No part is correct.

2. a. Observational study — the subjects had chosen whether they took the course or not. The course was not imposed by the researcher.

b. The random selection is intended to minimize the effects of confounding factors. There are some sources of potential confounding that should be considered: The level of performance of the students in each group could be a factor: did weaker students take the prep course? Did more motivated students take the course? Random selection within each group may not sufficiently protect the study.

c. Because there is no evidence that baseline data was gathered, analysis and interpretation of these data will be quite problematic. A two-sample *t*-test can be employed to determine if there is a significant difference in the means of the two groups. However, generalizing to the entire population may be inappropriate.

SCORING GUIDE

4 Complete	All three parts are correct.
3 Substantial	Part a is correct; part b contains weak or missing examples; part c references a 2-sample *t*-test.
2 Developing	Part a is correct; part b is incorrect; part c is weak.
1 Minimal	Only part a is correct.
0	No part is correct.

3. a. Margin of error $= \pm z \sqrt{\dfrac{p(1-p)}{n}}$

$.1 = \pm 1.96 \sqrt{\dfrac{.5(.5)}{n}}$

$n = 96.04 \approx 97$

b. Margin of error $= \pm z \sqrt{\dfrac{p(1-p)}{n}}$

$.1 = \pm 1.96 \sqrt{\dfrac{.7(.3)}{n}}$

$n = 80.67 \approx 81$

SCORING GUIDE

4 Complete	Both parts are correct.
3 Substantial	Calculations for both parts are correct but errors in rounding or choice of *z* have occurred.
2 Developing	Calculations for both parts are correct but part a does not use *p* = .5. Answers may include errors in rounding or choice of *z*.
1 Minimal	Part a is incorrect but part b is correct with errors only in rounding or choice of *z*.
0	Neither part is correct.

4. a. Cost per unit $= 60.7857 - 2.96544$(number)

b. Choice 2: A test of the significance of the slope of the regression line has a test statistic of $t = -5.05$ and a *P*-value of 0.0150. Therefore, we reject the hypothesis that the slope is 0. This implies that the value of *r* is not zero.

SCORING GUIDE

4 Complete	Both parts are correct.
3 Substantial	Part a is correct; part b identifies choice 2 but includes a weak argument based on a test of slope.
2 Developing	Part a is correct; part b identifies choice 2 but does not cite test of slope results.
1 Minimal	Part a is correct; part b is incorrect.
0	Neither part is correct.

5. a. $n = 108$; mean $= 84.07$; standard deviation $= 11.92$; min $= 60$; Q1 $= 80$; median $= 90$; Q3 $= 90$; max $= 100$.

b. We would expected that the mean of the sampling distribution would be approximately 84.07 with a standard deviation of $\dfrac{11.92}{\sqrt{30}} = 2.18$.

Central Limit Theorem states that for large sample sizes, the mean and standard deviation of the sampling distribution approach μ and $\dfrac{\sigma}{\sqrt{n}}$ respectively.

c. Even though the data distribution is not normal (skewed left slightly), we would expect that the sampling distribution would be approximately normal by the Central Limit Theorem.

SCORING GUIDE

4 Complete	All three parts are correct.
3 Substantial	Part a is correct; parts b and c are correct but one or both contains a weak explanation.
2 Developing	Part a is correct; parts b and c are correct but one or both parts have an incorrect or missing explanation.
1 Minimal	Only part a is correct.
0	No part is correct.

Section II

PART B (page 313)

6. a. Proportion of reds $= \dfrac{8}{50} = .16$. We will do a one-proportion z-test:

Assumptions:

$np > 10$? $50(.3) = 15$ ✓

$n(1 - p) > 10$? $50(.7) = 35$ ✓

H_0: $p = .3$

H_a: $p \neq .3$

Test statistic: $z = \dfrac{.16 - .3}{\sqrt{\dfrac{.3(.7)}{50}}} = 2.160 \to P\text{-value} = .0308$

Therefore, we reject the null hypothesis and conclude that the proportion of reds in this sample is significantly different than the proportion we expected.

b. We will do a chi-square test:

Assumptions:

All expected cell counts > 5 ✓

H_0: The observed is consistent with the expectation.

H_a: The observed is not consistent.

	Observed	Expected	$\dfrac{(o - e)^2}{e}$
Red	8	15	3.267
Yellow	20	15	1.667
Blue	22	20	0.200
Total	50	50	5.134

Chi-square $= 5.134$ with $df = 3 - 1 = 2 \to P\text{-value} = .077$.

Therefore, we fail to reject the null hypothesis and conclude that we do not have sufficient evidence to establish that these data deviate from the published proportions.

c. While the proportion of the red is significantly different from the expected proportion, the overall distribution of colors is consistent with the expected proportions. We can conclude that just because one of the components of a distribution may be significant, the overall distribution may not be.

SCORING GUIDE

4 Complete	All parts are correct.
3 Substantial	Part a contains a correct 1-proportion z-test; part b contains a significance test but not a correct chi-square test; part c is reasonable for answers in parts a and b.
2 Developing	Part a contains a correct 1-proportion z-test; part b does not contain a significance test; part c is reasonable for answers in parts a and b.
1 Minimal	Only part a is correct.
0	No part is correct.

Calculating your AP Score

The following guide is based on the published guide from the calculation of AP Statistics Scores from the released 1997 exam. Adjustments are made due to the fact that in 1997, only 35 multiple-choice questions were included, rather than the current 40 multiple-choice questions. Important facts about the scoring:

1. There is a penalty for guessing on the multiple-choice questions. One-fourth of the number of wrong answers is subtracted from the number of correct answers to calculate the multiple-choice component of the test.

2. The five open-ended questions contribute 75% of the Free-Response component of the test while the Investigative Task contributes 25% of the Free-Response component.

3. It has been determined that the Multiple-Choice and Free-Response components will be weighted equally in the calculation of the Composite Score. Each component is scaled so that there are 50 possible points for each component.

You may use the following template to determine the Composite Score for each of the five Model Examinations.

Section I Multiple-Choice Questions

$$(\underline{\hspace{2cm}} - \left(\frac{1}{4}\right) \times \underline{\hspace{2cm}}) \times (1.25) = \underline{\hspace{2cm}}$$
$\qquad$ # of correct $\qquad$ # of incorrect $\qquad\qquad$ MC score

Multiple-Choice Component (round your result) = _____

Section II Free-Response Questions

Do not round your scores for the Free-Response questions.

Question 1 = _____ × 1.875 = _____
$\qquad\quad$ out of 4

Question 2 = _____ × 1.875 = _____
$\qquad\quad$ out of 4

Question 3 = _____ × 1.875 = _____
$\qquad\quad$ out of 4

Question 4 = _____ × 1.875 = _____
$\qquad\quad$ out of 4

Question 5 = _____ × 1.875 = _____
$\qquad\quad$ out of 4

Question 6 = _____ × 3.125 = _____
$\qquad\quad$ out of 4

Free-Response Component = _____

Composite Score = _____ + _____ = _____
$\qquad\qquad\qquad$ MC Component FR Component

Round the Composite Score to nearest whole number.

AP Conversion Chart

While the calculation of the Composite Score is uniform from year to year, the setting of cutoff scores and ranges for the AP scores is decided based on a thorough statistical analysis of the difficulty of the specific test and student performance on it. Consequently, it is very difficult to project the ranges for any given test. Included here are the scoring ranges that were used on the 1997 test to give you some indication of an approximate AP score on the Model Examinations.

Composite Score (Rounded)	AP Score
68 – 100	5
54 – 67	4
41 – 53	3
29 – 40	2
0 – 28	1

Index

A

Advanced Placement Statistics, *see* AP Statistics
alpha (α), 200
and notation, 107
Anticipating patterns, 98–148
AP Statistics, 2
    about the exam, 3–4
    Examinations, 2
    important features, 4–5
    structure of the exam, 3–4
    website, 4
Arrangement, 110
Association, 92
Average, weighted sample, 19
Axes
    horizontal and vertical, 11
    titled and scaled, 10

B

Bar graphs, 66
    histograms versus, 66
    segmented, 67–68
    stacked, 67
Best fit, 48
    intuitive curve of, 60–63
Bias, 77, 199
    hidden, 88
    household, 81
    non-response, 81
    response, 80–81
Binomial distribution, 130
    normal approximation of, 129–133
Binomial probability, 113–116
Binomial probability distribution, mean and standard deviation of, 120
Binomial probability mass functions, 139–140
Binomial random variables, 113
Binomial variables, 101, 102
    probability distributions of, 119–120
Bivariate data
    defined, 9
    exploring, 38–72
Block, 89
Block design, 89–90

C

Calculators, 4, *see also* Technology
Capital letters, 101
Categorical data, 8
    exploring, 66–68
    inference for, 237–243
Causation, 88, 92
cdf (cumulative density function), 124, 139
Census, 74–75
Center, 16
    measure of, 18–20
    measuring, 18–20
Central Limit Theorem
    for the difference of two proportions, 160–163
    for a proportion, 156–159
Central tendency, measure of, 18
Chance error, 100, 200
Change, effects of, 28–29
Chapter Assessment, 2
Chi (χ), 142
Chi-square analysis, 237
Chi-square probability density function, 142
Chi-square statistic, 237
Chi-square test
    for goodness of fit, 238–240
    of independence, 240–242
Circle graphs, 66
Cluster sample, multi-stage, 79
Clusters, 16, 79
Collinear pairs, 44
Column variable, 67
Combinations, 110–112
Comparative experiments, 84
Comparison in experiments, 86–87
Complement, 100
Complementary probability, 114
Completely randomized design, 87
Computer software packages, 250, *see also* Technology
Conditional percentages, 67
Conditional probability, 105–106
Confidence, concept of, 184–187
Confidence interval for a mean,

technology and, 255
Confidence intervals, 185
    calculation of, 188–191
    half-width of, 193
    properties of, 192–197
    significance tests and, 215–216
    for the slope of a regression line, 231–233
Confidence level, interval width in relation to, 193
Confounded variables, 85
Confounding influence, 68
Continuity correction, 131, 159
Continuous probability density functions, 140–142
Continuous quantitative data, 8
Continuous random variables, 101
    probability distributions of, 124–127
Control, 88
Control group, 85
Controlled experiments, 84–90
Controlled placement, 85, 88
Convenience sampling, 76
Coordinates, 45
Correlation, linearity and, 42–46
Correlation coefficient, 43
Counting Principle, Fundamental, 109–110
Counting techniques, 109–112
Course Description booklet, 4
Cumulative density function (*cdf*), 124, 139
Cumulative frequency graph, 13
Cumulative relative frequencies, 13
Cutpoints, 11

D

Data, 8
    bivariate, *see* Bivariate data
    categorical, *see* Categorical data
    many-variable, 9
    one-variable, 9
    qualitative, 8
    quantitative, 8
    two-variable, 9
    univariate, *see* Univariate data
Data collection procedures, 74

B (Box plots)

Box plots, 13–14
    comparing, 31–32

Data Desk, 250, *see also* Technology
    confidence interval for a mean output from, 255
    one-sample t-test output from, 256
    regression analysis output from, 251
    test of independence output from, 260
    two sample t-test of means output from, 257
Degrees of freedom (*df*), 142
Dependent events, 104
Dependent random variables, 135
Difference
    of random variables, 134–137
    of sample means, sampling distributions associated with a, 174–176
Discrete probability mass functions, 139–140
Discrete quantitative data, 8
Discrete random variables, 101
    general, mean and standard deviation of, 121–122
    probability distributions of, 119–122
Disjoint events, 106
Dispersion, measure of, 20, 22–24
Distribution(s)
    binomial, *see* Binomial distribution
    comparing, 31–32
    mound-shaped, 23–24
    normal, 124
    probability, *see* Probability distributions
    sampling, *see* Sampling distributions
    shape of, 16, 20
    summarizing, 26–29
    symmetric, 23–24
Dot plots, 11
    comparing, 32
Double-blind experiments, 88

E
Effects of change, 28–29
Empirical probabilities, 100
Empirical rule, 23–24
Endpoints, 11
English letters, 22, 74, 150
Equally likely outcomes, 99, 100
Error(s)
    chance, 100, 200
    margin of, 193–195
    sampling, 81
    Type I and Type II, 223–228

Estimated population parameters, 76
Event *A*, 99
    probability of, 99
Events
    calculating probabilities for combinations of, 104–107
    dependent, 104
    disjoint, 106
    independent, 104
    mutually exclusive, 106–107
    simulating, with random digits tables, 144–145
Expected result, 199
Expected value, 121–122
Experimental probabilities, 100
Experiments, 84, 98
    comparative, 84
    comparison in, 86–87
    controlled, 84–90
    double-blind, 88
Explanatory variables, 48, 84
Exponential model, 60–62
Extrapolation, 52

F
Factors, 85
Failure, 102, 113, 116
Fathom, 250, *see also* Technology
    confidence interval for a mean output from, 255
    one-sample t-test output from, 256
    regression analysis output from, 252
    test of independence output from, 261
    two sample t-test of means output from, 258
First quartile, 24
Five-number summary, 24
Formulas, 5
Free-Response items, 3
Frequency
    marginal, 67
    relative, 100
        cumulative, 13
Frequency graph, cumulative, 13
Frequency tables, 10, 66–67
    two-way, 66–67
Fundamental Counting Principle, 109–110

G
Gaps, 16
General discrete random variables, mean and standard deviation of, 121–122

General Multiplication Rule, 105
Geometric probability, 116–117
Geometric probability mass functions, 140
Geometric random variables, 116
Geometric variable, 102
Goodness of fit, chi-square test for, 238–240
Grand mean, 41
Graphical displays
    back-to-back, 31
    parallel, 31–32
    of univariate data
        constructing, 10–14
        interpreting, 16–17
Greek letters, 22, 74, 150

H
Half-width of confidence interval, 193
Hidden bias, 88
Histograms, 11
    bar graphs versus, 66
    comparing, 31–32
Historical controls, 88
Horizontal axis, 11
Household bias, 81

I
Independence
    chi-square test of, 240–242
    test of, technology and, 259–262
Independent events, 104
Independent random variables, 135
Inference
    for categorical data, 237–243
    for the slope of a regression line, 230–136
    statistical, *see* Statistical inference
Inferred population parameters, 76
Influential points, 57–58
Information, missing, solving for, to achieve a significant result, 217
Interpolation, 52
Interquartile range, 20, 21
Interval estimate, 184
Interval width
    in relation to confidence level, 193
    in relation to sample size, 192–193
Intuitive curve of best fit, 60–63
Investigative Task, 3

L

Lacks realism, term, 88
Law of Large Numbers, 100
Least squares regression line,
    48–52
Leaves in stem and leaf plots, 12
Level of significance, 200
Levels, 85
Line of best fit, 48
Linear association, 43
Linear regression, 48
    simple, 54
Linearity
    correlation and, 42–46
    transformations to achieve,
        60–64
Lowercase letters, 101
Lurking variables, 85, 92

M

Many-variable data, 9
Margin of error, 193–195
Marginal frequencies, 67
Matched pairs design, 89–90
Matching process, 86
Maximum, 24
Mean(s), 18–19
    of binomial probability
        distribution, 120
    confidence interval for a,
        technology and, 255
    of general discrete random
        variables, 121–122
    grand, 41
    sample
        difference of, sampling
            distributions associated
            with a, 174–176
        when σ is known, sampling
            distributions of a,
            165–166
        when σ is unknown,
            sampling distributions
            of a, 168–172
    two sample t-test of,
        technology and, 257–259
Measure
    of center, 18–20
    of central tendency, 18
    of dispersion, 20, 22–24
    of spread, 20, 22–24
Median, 18, 19, 24
Midpoint, 11
Minimum, 24
Minitab, 250, see also Technology
    confidence interval for a mean
        output from, 255
    one-sample t-test output from,
        256

regression analysis output
    from, 251–252
test of independence output
    from, 260
two sample t-test of means
    output from, 258
Missing information, solving for,
    to achieve a significant
    result, 217
Missing values, finding, in
    normal curve problems,
    126–127
Mode, 18
Modified box plot, 13
Mound-shaped distributions,
    23–24
Mu (μ), 121
Multi-stage cluster sample, 79
Multiple-Choice items, 3
Multiplication Rule
    for dependent events, 105
    General, 105
    for independent events, 104
Mutually exclusive events,
    106–107

N

Non-outlier values, 13
Non-response bias, 81
Non-sampling method error, 81
Normal approximation of binomi-
    al distribution, 129–133
Normal curve problems, finding
    missing values in, 126–127
Normal density function, 141
Normal distribution, 124
Normal probabilities, calculation of
    using tables, 124–126
    using technology, 126
Normal random variables, 102
not A notation, 100
Null hypothesis, 203
Number of successes, 102
Number of trials, 102

O

Observational studies, 92
Observed result, 190
One-sample t-test, 208
    technology and, 256
One-sample z-test, 208
One-variable data, 9
Open-Ended Questions, 3
or notation, 107
Outcomes, 98
    equally likely, 99, 100
    probability of, 98
Outliers, 13, 16, 21, 56–57

P

P-value, 206
Paired t-test, 208
Parameters, 74, 150
Patterns
    anticipating, 98–148
    in scatterplots, 38–40
pdf, see Probability density func-
    tions
Percentages, conditional, 67
Percentiles, 26
Permutations, 110
Pie graphs, 66
Placebo, 86
Placebo effect, 86
Planning studies, 74–96
Point estimators, 184
Polynomial regression, 64
Pooled two-sample t-test, 208, 209
Population, 74, 150
Population mean, 19
Population standard deviation
    known, 165–166
    unknown, 168–172
Power, concept of, 228–229
Power model, 60–62
Predictions, using the regression
    line to make, 52
Probability(ies), 98–100
    basic rules of, 99–100
    binomial, 113–116
    calculating, for combinations
        of events, 104–107
    complementary, 114
    conditional, 105–106
    empirical, 100
    of event A, 99
    experimental, 100
    geometric, 116–117
    normal, see Normal
        probabilities
    of outcomes, 98
    theoretical, 100
Probability density functions (pdf),
    124, 140
    continuous, 140–142
Probability distributions, 101, 119
    of binomial variables, 119–120
    of continuous random
        variables, 124–127
    of discrete random variables,
        119–122
Probability functions, theoretical,
    139–142
Probability mass functions
    binomial, 139–140
    discrete, 139–140
    geometric, 140

Probability sampling methods, alternative, 78–81
Process, 150
Proportion(s)
    Central Limit Theorem for a, 156–159
    sample, sampling distributions of a, 156–159
    two
        Central Limit Theorem for the difference of, 160–163
        sampling distributions of a difference of, 160–163

Q
Quadrants, 45
Qualitative data, 8
Quantitative data, 8
Quartile values, 21
Quartiles, 26
Quota sampling, 76

R
Random digits tables, simulating events with, 144–145
Random sample
    simple (SRS), 77–78
    stratified, 78
Random sampling error, 81
Random variables, 101–102, 151
    binomial, 113
    continuous, *see* Continuous random variables
    dependent, 135
    difference of, 134–137
    discrete, *see* Discrete random variables
    geometric, 116
    independent, 135
    normal, 102
    sum of, 134–137
Randomization, 87, 88
Randomized design, completely, 87
Range, 20–21
    interquartile, 20, 21
Regression
    linear, *see* Linear regression
    polynomial, 64
Regression analysis, technology and, 250–254
Regression coefficients, 50
Regression equation, 48
Regression line, 48
    determining the, 48–51
    interpreting the coefficients of a, 51
    least squares, 48–52

slope of a, *see* Slope of a regression line
using the, to make predictions, 52
Relative frequency(ies), 100
    cumulative, 13
Replacement in sample
    with, 104
    without, 77
Replication, 87, 88
Residual, 48
Residual plots, 54–56
Response, voluntary, 76
Response bias, 80–81
Response variable, 48, 84
Review Exercises, 2
Row variable, 67

S
Sample, 150
    systematic, 79–80
Sample average, weighted, 19
Sample design, 76–78
Sample size
    determining, 195–197
    interval width in relation to, 192–193
Sample space, 98
Sample survey, 75
Sampling, 76–78
    convenience, 76
    quota, 76
Sampling distributions, 150–182
    associated with a difference of sample means, 174–176
    concept of, 151–154
    of a difference of two proportions, 160–163
    of a sample mean
        when σ is known, 165–166
        when σ is unknown, 168–172
    of a sample proportion, 156–159
    summary of, 176–177
Sampling errors, 81
Sampling frame, 80
Sampling method error, 81
Sampling methods, probability, alternative, 78–81
Sampling variability, 151
SAS, 250, *see also* Technology
    confidence interval for a mean output from, 255
    one-sample t-test output from, 256
    regression analysis output from, 253

test of independence output from, 261
two sample t-test of means output from, 258
Scaled axes, 10
Scatterplots, 38
    patterns in, 38–40
Segmented bar graphs, 67–68
Sensitivity, 19–20
Sigma (σ), 121
Significance, concept of, 199–200
Significance test(s), 202–207
    confidence intervals and, 215–216
    for the slope of a regression line, 234–235
    summary of, 207–215
    template for, 202–207
Significant result, solving for missing information to achieve a, 217
Significant statistic, 200
Simple linear regression, 54
Simple random sample (SRS), 77–78
Simpson's paradox, 68
Simulating events with random digits tables, 144–145
Simulation, 144
    standard, 144
    wait-time, 145
Slope, 48, 51
"Slope-intercept" form, 48
Slope of a regression line
    confidence intervals for the, 231–233
    inference for the, 230–136
    significance test for the, 234–235
    test for the, technology and, 236
Something significant, term, 200
Splitting techniques, 64
Spread, 16
    measure of, 20, 22–24
    measuring, 20–23
SRS (simple random sample), 77–78
Stacked bar graphs, 67
Standard deviation, 20, 22, 23–24
    of binomial probability distribution, 120
    of general discrete random variables, 121–122
Standard error, 121, 169, 185
Standard simulation, 144
Standard z-histogram, 27
Standardized scores, 26–28

Statistical inference, 76, 184–247
  technology and, 218–219
Statistics, 74, 150
  AP, *see* AP Statistics
  purpose of, 8
Stem and leaf plots, 12
  comparing, 31–32
Strata, 77–78
Stratified random sample, 78
Student's *t*-distribution, 168–172
Studies
  observational, 92
  planning, 74–96
Subjects, 84
Success, 102, 113, 116
Sum of random variables, 134–137
Summary statistics, comparing, 32
Symmetric distributions, 23–24
Systematic sample, 79–80

T
t-distribution, 168–172
t probability density function, 141
t-test
  one-sample, *see* One-sample
    t-test
  paired, 208
  two-sample, *see* Two-sample
    t-test
Tables, 5
  calculation of normal
    probabilities using, 124–126
  random digits, simulating
    events with, 144–145
Technology, 4
  calculation of normal
    probabilities using, 126
  confidence interval for a mean
    and, 255
  one-sample *t*-test and, 256
  regression analysis and,
    250–254
  statistical inference and,
    218–219
  test for the slope of a
    regression line and, 236

test of independence and,
    259–262
  two sample *t*-test of means
    and, 257–259
Theoretical probability, 100
Theoretical probability functions,
    139–142
Third quartile, 24
TI-83, 250, *see also* Technology
  confidence interval for a mean
    output from, 255
  one-sample *t*-test output
    from, 256
  regression analysis output
    from, 254
  test of independence output
    from, 262
  two sample *t*-test of means
    output from, 258–259
Titled axes, 10
Transformations to achieve lineari-
    ty, 60–64
Treatment, 85
Treatment group, 85
Tree diagrams, 106–107
Two-proportion *z*-test, 208
Two-sample *t*-test, 208
  of means, technology and,
    257–259
  pooled, 208, 209
  unpooled, 208, 209
Two-sample *z*-test, 208
Two-tailed hypothesis test, 215
Two-tailed situation, 189
Two-variable data, 9
Two-way frequency tables, 66–67
Type I and Type II errors, 223–228

U
Unbiased estimators, 153
Uniform density function, 141
Units, 84
Univariate data
  constructing graphical
    displays of, 10–14
  defined, 9

exploring, 8–35
  interpreting graphical
    displays of, 16–17
Unpooled two-sample *t*-test, 208,
    209

V
Variable(s), 8
  binomial, *see* Binomial
    variables
  column, 67
  confounded, 85
  explanatory, 48, 84
  geometric, 102
  lurking, 85, 92
  random, *see* Random variables
  response, 48, 84
  row, 67
Variance, 20, 22
Venn Diagrams, 107
Vertical axis, 11
Voluntary response, 76

W
Wait-time simulation, 145
Weighted sample average, 19
Whiskers, 13, 21

X
x-coordinate, 45

Y
y-coordinate, 45
y-intercept, 48, 51
  calculating, 49

Z
z-score, 26–28, 125
z-test
  one-sample, 208
  two-proportion, 208
  two-sample, 208

Acknowledgements

Data Desk is a registered trademark of Data Description, Inc.
Minitab is a registered trademark of Minitab, Inc.
Fathom is a registered trademark of Key Curriculum Press
SAS is a registered trademark of SAS Institute, Inc.
TI is a registered trademark of Texas Instruments, Inc.
For additional information, see the Appendix.

Amsco gratefully acknowledges Texas Instruments' generosity and assistance in the preparation of this book.